Maine

AN EXPLORER'S GUIDE

Yachts in Camden Harbor

Maine

AN EXPLORER'S GUIDE

CHRISTINA TREE &
ELIZABETH ROUNDY

PRINCIPAL PHOTOGRAPHY
BY KIM GRANT

Ninth Edition

The Countryman Press
Woodstock, Vermont

Dedications

To Timothy Alfred Davis—C. T.
To the memory of Nancy Gilles—E. R.

Library of Congress Cataloging-in-Publication Data
Tree, Christina.
Maine : an explorer's guide / Christina Tree & Elizabeth Roundy. — 9th ed.
          p.   cm.
Includes index.
ISBN 0-88150-460-2 (pbk. : alk. paper)
1. Maine—Guidebooks. I. Roundy, Elizabeth. II. Title.
F17.3.T73 1999
917.4104'43—dc21   98-56010
CIP

Maps by Mapping Specialists, © 1999 The
    Countryman Press
Book design by Glenn Suokko
Page composition by Cristen Brooks
Cover painting by William B. Hoyt
Back cover photographs of lighthouse and
    souvenirs by Kim Grant
Published by The Countryman Press
    P.O. Box 748, Woodstock, Vermont 05091
Distributed by W. W. Norton & Company,
    Inc., 500 Fifth Avenue, New York, New
    York 10110
Printed in the United States of America
10 9 8 7 6 5 4 3

Explore With Us!

We have been fine-tuning *Maine: An Explorer's Guide* for the past 17 years, a period in which lodging, dining, and shopping opportunities have more than quadrupled in the state. As we have expanded our guide, we have also been increasingly selective, making recommendations based on years of conscientious research and personal experience. What makes us unique is that we describe the state by locally defined regions, giving you Maine's communities, not simply her most popular destinations. With this guide you'll feel confident to venture beyond the tourist towns, along roads less traveled, to places of special hospitality and charm.

WHAT'S WHERE

In the beginning of the book you'll find an alphabetical listing of special highlights and important information that you may want to reference quickly. You'll find advice on everything from where to buy the best local lobster to where to write or call for camping reservations and park information.

LODGING

We've selected lodging places for mention in this book based on their merit alone; **we do not charge innkeepers for inclusion.** We're the only travel guide that tries personally to check every bed & breakfast, farm, sporting lodge, and inn in Maine, and one of the few that do not charge for inclusion.

Prices: Please don't hold us or the respective innkeepers responsible for the rates listed as of press time in 1999. Some changes are inevitable. The 7 percent state rooms and meals tax should be added to all prices unless we specifically state that it's included in a price. We've tried to note when a gratuity is added but it's always wise to check before booking.

Smoking: Many B&Bs are now smoke-free, and many inns and restaurants feature smoke-free rooms. If this is important to you, be sure to ask when making reservations.

RESTAURANTS

In most sections, please note a distinction between *Dining Out* and *Eating Out*. By their nature, restaurants included in the *Eating Out* group are generally inexpensive.

KEY TO SYMBOLS

☙ The special-value symbol appears next to selected lodging and restaurants that combine quality and moderate prices.

✐ The kids-alert symbol appears next to lodging, restaurants, activities, and shops of special interest or appeal to youngsters.

♿ The wheelchair symbol appears next to lodgings, restaurants, and attractions that are partially or completely handicapped-accessible.

🐾 The dog-paw symbol appears next to lodgings that accept pets (with prior notification) as of press time in 1999, as well as other places where pets are allowed.

We would appreciate any comments or corrections. Please address your correspondence to Explorer's Guide Editor, The Countryman Press, P.O. Box 748, Woodstock, Vermont 05091.

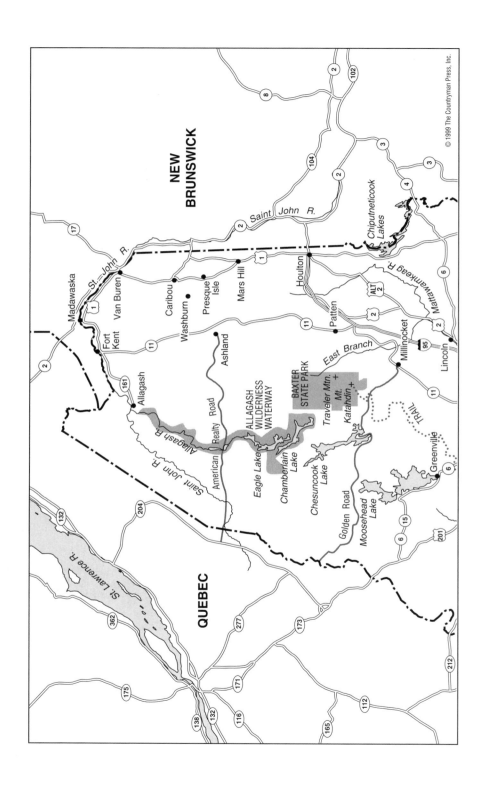

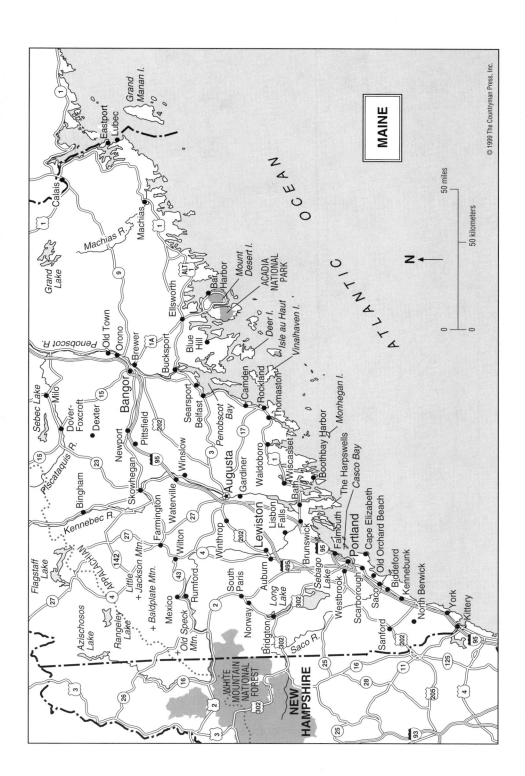

MAINE

© 1999 The Countryman Press, Inc.

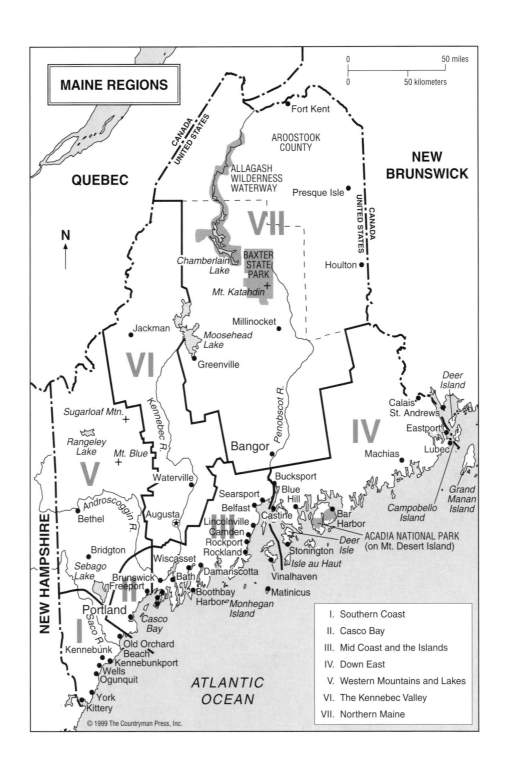

Contents

Introduction

He who rides and keeps the beaten track studies the fences chiefly.
—*Henry David Thoreau,* The Maine Woods, *1853*

Back in the 1920s, "motor touring" was hailed as a big improvement over train and steamer travel because it meant you no longer had to go where everyone else did—over routes prescribed by railroad tracks and steamboat schedules.

Ironically, though, in Maine cars have had precisely the opposite effect. Now 90 percent of the state's visitors follow the coastal tourist route as faithfully as though their wheels were grooved to Route 1.

Worse still, it's as though many tourists are on a train making only express stops—at rush hour. At least half of those who follow Route 1 stop, stay, and eat in all the same places (such as Kennebunkport, Boothbay or Camden, and Bar Harbor)—in August. Although this book should help visitors and Maine residents alike enjoy the state's resort towns, it is particularly useful for those who explore less frequented places.

When *Maine: An Explorer's Guide* first appeared in 1982, it was the first 20th-century guidebook to describe New England's largest state region by region rather than by tourist towns listed alphabetically. From the start, we critiqued places to stay and to eat as well as everything to see and to do—based on merit rather than money (we don't charge anyone to be included).

In the beginning it didn't seem like a tall order, but over the years—which coincided with a proliferation of inns, B&Bs, and other lodging options—we've been including more and more of Maine, from Matinicus to Madawaska and from the White Mountains to Campobello, not to mention all of Route 1 from Kittery to Fort Kent.

In all, we now describe more than 500 places to stay, ranging from campgrounds to grand old resorts and including farms as well as B&Bs and inns—in all corners of the state and in all price ranges. We have also checked out many hundreds of places to dine and to eat (we make a distinction between dining and eating), and, since shopping is an important part of everyone's travels, we include exceptional stores we encounter. We have opinions about everything we've found, and we don't hesitate to share them. In every category, we record exactly what we see, again because we charge no business to be included in the book.

Guidebooks either atrophy and die after an edition or two, or they take on a life of their own. We are relieved to report that by now *Maine: An Explorer's Guide* has introduced so many people to so many parts of Maine that it has become a phenomenon in its own right.

Chris was born in Hawaii and bred in Manhattan, and she has been living in Massachusetts since she came there to work for the *Boston Globe* in 1968. She is addicted to many Maines. As a toddler she learned to swim in the Ogunquit River and later watched her three sons do the same in Monhegan's icy waters—and then learn to sail at summer camp in Raymond and paddle canoes on the Saco River and down the St. John. Before beginning this book, she thought she "knew" Maine, having already spent a dozen years exploring it for the *Boston Globe,* describing the charm of coastal villages and the quiet of inland mountains and lakes. For the *Globe,* she continues to write about a variety of things to do, from skiing at Sugarloaf and Sunday River and llama trekking and horseback riding in Bethel to sea kayaking off Portland and wind-jamming on Penobscot Bay. But after 18 years, some 90,000 miles, and nine editions of the book, Chris no longer claims to "know" Maine. What she does know are the state's lodging places (she also coauthors *Best Places to Stay in New England*), restaurants, and shops, from Kittery to Calais and from Monhegan to Kokadjo and Grand Lake Stream.

Elizabeth was born and raised in the Bangor area, and she took Maine for granted, never appreciating its beauty and uniqueness until she returned after moving out of state for a few years. She has lived in the Bangor area, Augusta, Bar Harbor, and the Portland area and has spent time in "camps" on lakes with her family as a child; one of her favorite spots remains a large lodge overlooking the ocean on Sandy Point, where she spent many special summers. She, too, thought she knew Maine, but in the course of this research realized that she was wrong, that there are many less-traveled areas that even a native can overlook, places she had avoided with misconceived notions of how they would be, only to be pleasantly surprised. She also discovered some amazing history she had been missing but won't soon forget.

Maine's history continues to fascinate both of us. We are intrigued by the traces of ancient Native American habitations and pre-Pilgrim settlements, by colorful tales of 17th-century heroes like Baron de St. Castin (scion of a noble French family who married a Penobscot Indian princess), and by the state's legendary seafaring history, well told in the Maine Maritime Museum in Bath (where a total of 5,000 vessels have been launched over the years) and at the Penobscot Marine Museum (in Searsport, a small village that once boasted of being home to a full 10 percent of all American sea captains). And, of course, there is the heady saga of the lumbering era (dramatized in the Lumberman's Museums in Patten and Rangeley), which finally ensured Maine's admission to the Union in 1820, but not until Massachusetts had sold off all unsettled land, the privately owned "unorganized townships" that add up to nearly half of inland Maine.

We are also fascinated by the ways in which 150 years of tourism, as much as any industry, have helped shape Maine's current landscape. Guidebooks, incidentally, have played a prominent role in this process.

Tourism has always been driven by images. In the 1840s Thomas Cole, Frederick Church (both of whom sketched and painted scenes of Mount Desert), and many lesser known artists began projecting Maine as a romantic, remote destination in the many papers, magazines, and children's books of the decade. While Henry Davied Thoreau's *The Maine Woods* was not published until 1864, many of its chapters appeared as magazine articles years before (Thoreau first climbed Katahdin in 1846), and in 1853 *Atlantic Monthly* editor James Russell Lowell visited and wrote about Moosehead Lake.

After the Civil War, Maine tourism boomed. Via railroad and steamboat, residents of cities throughout the East and Midwest streamed into the Pine Tree State, most toting guidebooks, many published by rail and steamboat lines to boost business.

Male "sports" in search of big game and big fish patronized "sporting camps" throughout the North Woods. Thanks to the rise in popularity of fly-fishing and easily maneuverable canoes, women were able to share in North Woods soft adventure. Splendid lakeside hotels were built on the Rangeley lakes and Moosehead, and farms took in boarders throughout the Western Lakes region. Along the coast and on dozens of islands hotels of every size were built, most by Maine natives. Blue-collar workers came by trolley to summer religious camp meetings, and the wealthy built themselves elaborate summer "cottages" on islands and around Bar Harbor, Camden, and Boothbay Harbor. Developments and sophisticated landscaping transformed much of the previously ignored sandy Southern Coast.

Although it's difficult to document, it's safe to say that Maine attracted the same number of visitors in the summer of 1899 that it does in 1999. This picture altered little for another decade. Then came World War I, coinciding with the proliferation of the Model A.

The 1922 founding of the Maine Publicity Bureau (renamed the Maine Tourism Association in 1999), we suspect, reflects the panic of hoteliers (founder Hiram Ricker himself owned three of the state's grandest hotels: the Mount Kineo House, the Poland Spring House, and Samoset). Over the next few years these hotels went the way of passenger service, and "motorists" stuck to motor courts and motels along Route 1 and a limited number of inland routes.

By 1968, when Chris began writing about Maine for the *Boston*

Globe, much of the state had dropped off the tourist map, and in the decades since she has chronicled the reawakening of most of the old resort areas. Whale-watching and white-water rafting, skiing and snowmobiling, windjamming and kayaking, outlet shopping, and the renewed popularity of country inns and the spread of B&Bs have all contributed to this reawakening. Maine is, after all, magnificent. It was just a matter of time.

Between the eighth and ninth editions of this book, the extent of waterside (both coastal and inland) walks open to the public has increased dramatically. It's interesting to note that this phenomenon of preserving and maintaining outstanding landscapes—from Oqunquit's Marginal Way to the core of what's now Acadia National Park—was also an offshoot of Maine's first tourism boom.

While the number of Maine guidebooks has proliferated too, we remain proud of the depth and scope of ours. We strive not only to update details but also to simplify the format and to sharpen the word pictures that describe each area.

This book's introductory section, "What's Where in Maine," is a quick reference directory to a vast variety of information about the state. The remainder of the book describes Maine region by region. The basic criterion for including an area is the availability of lodging.

Note that "off-season" prices are often substantially less than those in July and August. September is dependably sparkling and frequently warm. Early October in Maine is just as spectacular as it is in New Hampshire and Vermont, with magnificent mountains rising from inland lakes as well as the golds and reds set against coastal blue. It's also well worth noting that the inland resorts of Bethel and the Sugarloaf area are "off-season" all summer as well as fall.

Maine is almost as big as the other five New England states combined, but her residents add up to fewer than half the population of greater Boston. That means there is plenty of room for all who look to her for renewal—both residents and out-of-staters.

We would like to thank Ann Kraybill in particular at The Countryman Press for shepherding this monster manuscript through the many stages of production. We would both also like to thank Nancy Marshall for her unfailing help with gathering information throughout Maine and Greg Burke for his help with the Southern Maine Coast.

Chris owes thanks, as always, to Virginia Fieldman in Jonesboro, also to John Willard and Toni Blake of the Moosehead area, to Victor Block and Evelyn McAllister of the Rangeley Lakes Region, and to Robin Zinchuk and Wende Gray of Bethel. Along the coast, thanks are due to Sue Antal in York, Pat and Jerry Houlihan in Ogunquit, Karen Arel in Kennebunkport, Steve and Marcie Normand in Brunswick, Mary and Frank Shorey of Bailey's Island, Jamie Kleinstiver and Kim Peckham in Boothbay Harbor, Bobby Whear of Damariscotta Mills,

Beth and Warren Busteed of Pemaquid Point, John Murdock of Monhegan, Lynn Smith of South Thomaston, John Foss of Rockland, Gail Reinertsen and Fred and Bena Pillsbury on Vinalhaven, Jim and Sally Littlefield and Bette Noble of Brooksville, Ann and Bob Hamilton of Brooklin, Toby Strong and Dick Homer of Southwest Harbor, Cynthia and Dan Leif of Islesford, and to her ever-helpful and long-suffering husband, William Davis.

Elizabeth owes thanks to Marjorie Wright at the Maine Office of Tourism, Cathy Latham of Camden, Jessica Turner of Portland's Convention and Visitor's Bureau, Rick Webb of Lewiston, and the whole gang (Ken, Lynn, Mike, Kevin, Karen, Staci, and Craig) who spent three days helping her canoe the Allagash with a sprained ankle. She also owes her family thanks for their continuing support.

We would also like to thank all the people who have taken the time to write about their experiences in Maine. We can't tell you how much your input—or simply your reactions to how we have described things—means to us. We welcome your comments and appreciate all your thoughtful suggestions for the next edition of *Maine: An Explorer's Guide.* Note the postcard in this book for that purpose. You can also contact us directly by e-mail: ctree@traveltree.net or emroundy@aol.com.

What's Where in Maine

AREA CODE
The area code for Maine is **207.**

ABENAKI
Abenaki (also spelled "Wabanaki") means "people of the dawn." It's the name of Native American tribes who have lived in Maine and eastern Canada for several thousand years, judging from shell heaps and artifacts found in the Damariscotta/Boothbay area, local artifacts displayed in the **Robert Abbe Museum** in Acadia National Park, and pictographs on the Kennebec River and in Machiasport. An excellent exhibit, "12,000 Years in Maine," in the **Maine State Museum** in Augusta dramatizes their history. Two North Woods sites were sacred to these people: the Katahadin Iron Works, in Brownville Junction, source of the yellow ocher found sprinkled on the burial sites of Maine's so-called Red Paint People, and Mount Kineo on Moosehead Lake, source of the flintlike volcanic stone widely used for arrowheads. Early French missions at Mount Desert and Castine proved battlegrounds between the French and English and by the end of the 17th century thousands of Abenakis had retreated either to Canada or to the Penobscot community of Old Town and to Norridgewock, where Father Sebastian Rale insisted that the Indian lands "were given them of God, to them and their children forever, according to the Christian oracles." The mission was obliterated (it's now a pleasant roadside rest area) and by the end of the French and Indian wars only four tribes remained. Of these the Micmacs and Malecites made the unlucky choice of siding with the crown and were subsequently forced to flee (but communities remain near the Aroostook County–Canadian border in Presque Isle and Littleton respectively). That left only the Penobscots and Passamaquoddies.

In 1794 the Penobscots technically deeded most of Maine to Massachusetts in exchange for the 140 small islands in the Penobscot River, and in 1818 Massachusetts agreed to pay them an assortment of trinkets for the land. In 1820, when Maine became a state, a trust fund was set aside but ended up in the general treasury. "Indians" loomed large in Maine lore and greeted 19th-century tourists as fishing and hunting guides in the woods and as snowshoe- and canoe-makers and guides, while Native American women sold their distinctive sweetgrass and ash-splint baskets and beadwork at the many coastal and inland summer hotels and boardinghouses.

Thanks to a 10-year suit for reparations both for money and land, in 1980 the tribes received $80.6 million and today the Penobscot reservation at Old Town and the Passamaquoddy reservations at Pleasant Point (near Eastport) and Indian Township are far more pleasant places to live than they were previously. Check out the **Waponahki Museum and Resource Center** at Pleasant Point, the **Penobscot Nation Museum** on Indian Island in Old Town, and the nearby **Hudson Museum** at the University of Maine, Orono, which hosts an annual early-December **Maine Indian Basketmakers Sale and Demonstration,** featuring the work of all four tribes.

Annual mid-August **Indian Ceremonial Days** are held at the Pleasant Point Reservation to celebrate Passamaquoddy culture, climaxing in dances in full regalia. **Nowetah's American Indian Museum** in New Portland (see "Sugarloaf Area") and the **L. C. Bates Museum** in Hinckley (see "Upper Kennebec Area") both also have major Maine Native American collections.

ACADIANS

Acadians trace their lineage to French settlers who came to farm and fish in Nova Scotia in the early 1600s and who, in 1755, were forcibly deported by an English governor. This "Great Disturbance," dispersing a population of some 10,000 Acadians, brutally divided families. In a meadow overlooking the St. John River in Madawaska's **Tante Blanche Museum,** a large marble cross marks the spot on which several hundred displaced Acadians landed in 1787. **Village Acadien,** a dozen buildings forming a mini–museum village just west of Van Buren, only begins to tell the story. Acadian scholarship is centered at the University of Maine, Fort Kent. While the sizable Franco-American communities in Biddeford, Lewiston, and Brunswick have a different history (their forebears were recruited from Quebec to work in 19th-century mills), they have shared a long repression of their culture and recent resurgence of pride in a shared French heritage. **La Kermesse,** held in late June in Biddeford, is a major Franco-American festival, as is the **Festival de Joie** in Lewiston.

AGRICULTURAL FAIRS

The season opens with the small, family-geared **Pittston Fair** in late June (pig scrambles, antique tractor show) and culminates with the big, colorful **Fryeburg Fair** during the first week of October. Among the best traditional fairs are the **Union Fair** (late August) and the **Blue Hill Fair** (Labor Day weekend). The **Common Ground Country Fair** (late September, at the fairgrounds in Unity) draws Maine's back-to-the-earth and organic gardeners from all corners of the state, and the **Full Circle Summer Fair** at the Union Fairgrounds (mid-July) is a smaller, even less "commercial" gathering. Request a pamphlet listing all the fairs from the Maine Department of Agriculture (287-3871), State House Station 28, Augusta 04333.

AIRPORTS AND AIRLINES

Portland International Jetport (774-7301), with connections to most American and Canadian cities, is served by Business Express (1-800-345-3400), Continental Airlines (1-800-525-0280), Delta Air Lines (1-800-221-1212), United Airlines (1-800-241-6522), and US Airways (1-800-428-4322). **Bangor International Airport** (947-0384), serving northern and Down East Maine, also offers connections to all parts of the US via Business Express, Continental Airlines, Delta Air Lines, and US Airways, as well as being served by American Airlines (1-800-345-3400), Northwest Airlines (1-800-345-3400), and Delta Connections (1-800-345-3400). Continental Connection's Colgan Air (1-800-272-5488) serves **Bar Harbor/Hancock County Regional** airport and **Rockland/Knox County Regional** airports. **Presque Isle/Northern Maine Regional** is served by Business Express (1-800-345-3400) and US Airways (1-800-428-4322).

AIR SERVICES
Also called flying services, these are useful links with wilderness camps and coastal islands. Greenville, prime jumping-off point for the North Woods, claims to be New England's largest seaplane base. In this book, flying services are also listed in the "Rangeley," "Moosehead," and "Katahdin" chapters. Check the "Rockland/Thomaston" chapter for air taxis to several islands, including Vinalhaven, North Haven, and Matinicus.

AMTRAK
Passenger service has been promised for Maine's Southern Coast towns and Portland for some years, but this time it looks like the service is actually on track, due to reach Wells by fall of 1999. Stay tuned. Phone 1-800-USA-RAIL.

AMUSEMENT PARKS
Funtown/Splashtown USA in Saco is Maine's biggest, with rides, water slides, and pools, and **Aquaboggan** (pools and slides) is also on Route 1 in Saco. **Palace Playland** in Old Orchard Beach is a classic, with a 1906 carousel, a Ferris wheel, rides, and a 60-foot water slide. **York's Wild Kingdom** at York Beach and **Funland** in Caribou are small areas offering kiddie rides and arcades.

ANTIQUARIAN BOOKS
Maine is well known among book buffs as a browsing mecca. Within this book we have noted antiquarian bookstores where they cluster along Route 1 in Wells and in Portland. **Maine Antiquarian Booksellers** publishes a directory; download it at their web site: http://antiquarian.com/maba.

ANTIQUES
A member directory listing more than 100 dealers is produced by the **Maine Antiques Dealers' Association, Inc.,** and available for $3 by mail from Edward Welch, RR 3, Box 1290, Augusta Road, Winslow 04901 (872-5849; edwelch@metiques.com); the association maintains an active web site listing auctions: www.metiques.com. Another useful resource is the monthly *Maine Antiques Digest,* available in many bookstores.

APPALACHIAN TRAIL
The 275 Maine miles of this 2,144-mile Georgia-to-Maine footpath enters the state in the Mahoosuc range (see the "Bethel Area" map), accessible there from Grafton Notch State Park (the Mahoosuc Notch section is extremely difficult) and continues north into the Rangeley and Sugarloaf areas, on up through the Upper Kennebec Valley to Monson. West of Moosehead Lake it runs through Gulf Hagas and on around Nahmakanta Lake, through Abol Bridge to Baxter State Park, ending at the summit of 5,627-foot Mount Katahdin. Hikes along the trail are noted within specific chapters; lodging places catering to AT through-hikers include Mrs. G's and Harrison's Pierce Pond Camps in Bingham, Shaw's Boarding Home in Monson, and Little Lyford Camps near Gulf Hagas. For a list of publications write to: Appalachian Trail Conference, P.O. Box 807, Harpers Ferry, WV 25425-0807.

APPLES

Fall brings plenty of pick-your-own opportunities across the state, and many orchards also sell apples and cider. For a list of orchards, contact the Department of Agriculture (287-3491). In York, the **Parsons Family Winery** is putting an old orchard to new uses.

AQUARIUMS

The Department of Maine Resources Aquarium in Boothbay Harbor displays regional fish and sea creatures, many of them surprisingly colorful. The stars of the show are the sharks and skates in a large touch tank. The **Mount Desert Oceanarium** has several locations in the Bar Harbor area.

ART MUSEUMS

Portland Museum of Art has an outstanding collection of American paintings, but it is the **Farnsworth Museum** in Rockland, with its permanent collection and special exhibits of specifically Maine art, as well as its new **Farnsworth Center for the**

© ERIC HOPKINS

Wyeth Family in Maine, that is drawing art lovers from around the country. The **Ogunquit Museum of American Art,** the **Bowdoin College Museum of Art** in Brunswick, and the **Colby College Museum of Art** in Waterville (see "Augusta and Mid Maine") are all described within their respective chapters.

ARTISTS AND ART GALLERIES

Maine's dramatic coastal and island scenery, its lakes and mountains, have drawn major artists since the mid–19th century, and the experience of art as a major part of the Maine visitor's experience has dramatically increased in recent years. Within each chapter we describe a good percentage of the commercial galleries that have proliferated throughout the state but especially in Rockland, Northeast Harbor, Stonington, Blue Hill, and Eastport. Several recent art books are also popularizing the work of dozens of significant artists; a standout is *Art of the Maine Islands* by Carl Little and Arnold Skolnick (Down East Books). Artist-owned galleries, which have become destinations in their own right, are found in Sullivan and Stonington and on the islands of Monhegan, North Haven, and Little Cranberry. For weeklong summer art workshops see our *To Do* listings in Stonington (see "Deer Isle") and Port Clyde (see "Rockland/Thomaston"). For summer art programs, see *Camps, for Adults.*

BALLOONING

Hot-air rides are available across the state from **Balloons over New England** (499-7575; 1-800-788-5562) in Kennebunk; **Hot Fun** (799-0193) in South Portland; **Balloon Rides** (761-8373) in Portland; **Freeport Balloon Company** (865-1712) in Pownal; and **Sails Aloft** (623-1136) in Augusta.

BEACHES

Just 2 percent of the Maine coast is public, and not all of that is beach. Given the summer temperature of the water (from 59 degrees in Ogunquit to 54 degrees at Bar Harbor), swimming isn't the primary reason you come to Maine. But Maine beaches (for instance at York, Wells, the Kennebunks, Portland, Popham, and Pemaquid) can be splendid walking, sunning, and kite-flying places. At **Ogunquit** and in **Reid State Park,** there are also warmer backwater areas in which small children can paddle. Families tend to take advantage of the reasonably priced cottages available on lakes, many of them just a few miles from the seashore (see *Lakes*). Other outstanding beaches include 7-mile-long **Old Orchard Beach** and, nearby, state-maintained **Crescent Beach** on Cape Elizabeth; **Scarborough Beach** in Scarborough; and **Ferry Beach** in Saco. The big, state-maintained freshwater beaches are on **Lakes Damariscotta, St. George, Sebec, Rangeley, Sebago,** and **Moosehead;** also on **Pleasant Pond** in Richmond. All state beaches include changing facilities, rest rooms, and showers; many have snack bars. The town of Bridgton has several fine little lakeside beaches.

BED & BREAKFASTS

We have visited hundreds of B&Bs and been impressed by what we have seen. They range from elegant town houses and country mansions to farms and fisherman's homes. Prices vary from $45 to $450 (on the coast in August) for a double and average $85 in high season on the coast. With few exceptions, they offer a friendly entrée to their communities. Hosts are usually delighted to advise guests on places to explore, dine, and shop. The *Maine Guide to Inns and Bed & Breakfasts,* published by the Maine Tourism Association, is free from

the Maine Office of Tourism (1-800-533-9595).

BICYCLING

Mountain biking is particularly popular on the carriage roads in Acadia National Park. Four ski areas also specialize in summer mountain biking: Sunday River in the Bethel area and Shawnee Peak in Bridgton offer lift-assisted, high-altitude trails; Lost Valley in Auburn opens its trails to mountain bikers, and Sugarloaf/USA offers rentals and trail maps to trails on and off the mountain. Bicycle touring is, however, limited. Route 1 is too heavily trafficked and rural roads are generally unsuitable to bicycling. Dedicated recreation paths are beginning to appear, notably in Portland and Brunswick/Bath. Bicycling also makes sense in heavily touristed resorts in which a car can be a nuisance; rentals are available in Ogunquit, Kennebunkport, Portland, Camden, Southwest Harbor, Northeast Harbor and Bar Harbor; also in Bethel and Rangeley. Hosteling International maintains nominally priced, bicyclist-geared hostels descrbed in "Portland" and "Bar Harbor." Also check out *25 Bicycle Tours in Maine* by Howard Stone (Backcountry Publications).

The *Maine Bicycle Map* published by the Maine DOT in 1999 represents a massive effort to identify roads throughout the state that are scenic, wide-shouldered, and relatively little trafficked; for a copy, phone 287-6600. The **Maine Bicycle Coalition** (288-3028) serves as a conduit for information about both off- and on-road bicycling throughout the state; request an info packet from MBC, P.O. Box 5275, Augusta 04332.

BIRDING

The **Maine Audubon Society** (781-2330), based at Gilsland Farm in Falmouth, maintains a number of birding sites and sponsors nature programs and field trips, which include cruises to Matinicus Rock and to Eagle Island. (For details about the **National Audubon Ecology Camp** on Hog Island, see "Damariscotta.") **Laudholm Farm** in Wells, **Biddeford Pool, Scarborough Marsh, Merrymeeting Bay,** and **Mount Desert** are also popular birding sites. **Monhegan** is the island to visit. The **Moosehorn National Wildlife Refuge** (454-3521) in Washington County represents the northeastern terminus of the East Coast chain of wildlife refuges and is particularly rich in bird life. We recommend *A Birder's Guide to the Coast of Maine* by Elizabeth Cary Pierson and Jan Erik Pierson (Down East Books). (Also see *Puffin-Watching* and *Nature Preserves.*) The official state bird is the chickadee.

BLUEBERRYING

Maine grows 98 percent of America's low-bush blueberries. More than 40 million pounds are harvested annually from an estimated 25,000 acres. Because of pruning practices, only half the acreage produces berries in a given year, and there are absolutely no human-planted wild blueberry fields. Low-bush blueberry plants spread naturally in the present commercial fields after the forests are cleared or by natural establishment in abandoned pastures. Unfortunately, very few berries are sold fresh (most are quick-frozen), and few growers

allow U-pick, at least not until the commercial harvest is over. (One exception is **Staples-Homestead Blueberries** in Stockton Springs.) Then the public is invited to go "stumping" for leftovers. On the other hand, berrying along roads and hiking paths, under power lines, and on hilltops is a rite of summer for all who happen to be in southern Maine in late July or farther Down East in early August. For a look at the **blueberry barrens**—thousands of blueberry-covered acres—you must drive up to Cherryfield, Columbia, and Machias (site of the state's most colorful blueberry festival in August) in Washington County. For more about Maine's most famous fruit, write: Wild Blueberry Association of North America, 142 Kelley Road, Orono 04473.

BOATBUILDING

Wooden Boat School (359-4651) in Brooklin (see "Blue Hill") offers more than 75 warm-weather courses, including more than 24 on various aspects of boatbuilding. The **Maine Maritime Museum** in Bath offers an apprenticeship program; the **Landing School of Boatbuilding & Design** in Kennebunk offers summer courses in building sailboats; and the **Washington County Technical College, Marine Trades Center** at Eastport attracts many out-of-staters.

BOAT EXCURSIONS

You don't need to own your own yacht to enjoy the salt spray and views, and you really won't know what Maine is about until you stand off at sea to appreciate the beauty of the cliffs and island-dotted bays. For the greatest concentrations of boat excursions, see "Boothbay Harbor," "Rockland," and "Bar Harbor and Ellsworth"; there are also excursions from Ogunquit, Kennebunkport, Portland, Belfast, Camden, Castine, and Stonington. (Also see *Coastal Cruises,*

Ferries, Sailing, and *Windjammers.* See "Sebago and Long Lakes," "Rangeley," and "Augusta and Mid Maine" for lake excursions.) A partial list of more than 100 cruises, ferries, and deep-sea fishing options is published in Maine Tourism Association's annual free magazine, "Maine Invites You" (see *Information*).

BOAT RENTALS
Readily available in the Belgrade Lakes, the Sebago Lake area, in Rangeley, Jackman, Rockwood, and all other inland lake areas. (Also see *Sea Kayaking.*)

BOOKS
Anyone who seriously sets out to explore Maine should read the following mix of Maine classics and guidebooks: *The Maine Woods* by Henry David Thoreau, first published posthumously in 1864, remains very readable and gives an excellent description of Maine's mountains (we recommend the Penguin edition). Our favorite relatively recent Maine author is Ruth Moore, who writes about Maine islands in *The Weir, Spoon Handle,* and *Speak to the Wind* (originally published in the 1940s, reissued by Blackberry Books, Nobleboro); happily the 1940s books by Louise Dickinson Rich, among which our favorites are *The Coast of Maine: An Informal History* and *We Took to the Woods,* are now published by Down East Books in Camden, along with Henry Beston's 1940s classic *Northern Farm: A Chronicle of Maine.* Sarah Orne Jewett's classic, *The Country of the Pointed Firs and Other Stories* (W. W. Norton), first published in 1896, is still an excellent read, set on the coast around Tenants Harbor. The children's classics by Robert McCloskey, *Blueberries for Sal* (1948), *Time of Wonder* (1957), and *One Morning in Maine* (1952), are as fresh as the day they were written. John Gould, an essayist

who wrote a regular column for the *Christian Science Monitor* for more than 50 years, has published several books, including *Dispatches from Maine,* a collection of those columns, and *Maine Lingo* (with Lillian Ross), a humorous look at Maine phrases and expressions. E. B. White has some wonderful essay collections as well, along

KIM GRANT

with his ever-popular children's novels, *Charlotte's Web* and *Stuart Little.*

Recent classics set in Maine include Carolyn Chute's *The Beans of Egypt, Maine* (1985), *Letourneau's Used Auto Parts* (1988), and *Merry Men* (1994), and Cathie Pelletier's *The Funeral Makers* (1987) and *The Weight of Winter* (1991). *Maine Speaks,* an anthology of Maine literature published by the Maine Writers and Publishers Alliance (see "Brunswick"), contains all the obvious poems and essays and many pleasant surprises; *The Maine Reader,* edited by Charles and Samuella Shain, is an anthology of writing from the 1600s to the present.

Guides to exploring Maine include the indispensable *Maine Atlas and Gazetteer* (DeLorme) and, from Down East Books, *A Birder's Guide to the Coast of Maine* by Elizabeth Cary Pierson and Jan Erik Pierson, *Walking the Maine Coast* by John Gibson, and *Islands in Time: A Natural and Human History of the Islands of Maine* by Philip W. Conkling. Serious hikers should secure the *AMC Maine Mountain Guide*

(AMC Books); also *50 Hikes in the Maine Mountains* by Cloe Chunn and *50 Hikes in Southern and Coastal Maine* by John Gibson (both Backcountry Publications). Also worth noting: *The Wildest Country: A Guide to Thoreau's Maine* by J. Parker Huber (AMC Books). *Maine,* by Charles C. Calhoun (Compass American Guides), complements this guide with its superb illustrations and well-written background text.

BUS SERVICE

Concord Trailways (1-800-639-3317) serves Portland, Brunswick, Bath, Wiscasset, Damariscotta, Waldoboro, Rockland, Camden, Belfast, Searsport, and Bangor; **Greyhound Bus Lines** (1-800-221-2222) serves Bangor and Portland; and **Vermont Transit** (772-6587; 1-800-451-3292) serves Augusta, Lewiston, and Waterville as well as Portland and Bangor.

CAMPING

Almost half of Maine lies within "unorganized townships": wooded, privately owned lands, most of which are open to the public on the condition that basic rules be observed. These rules vary with the owners. See the "Northern Maine" chapters for details about camping within these vast fiefdoms, also for camping in **Baxter State Park** and along the **Allagash Wilderness Waterway.** For camping within **Acadia National Park,** see the chapter under "Mount Desert Island." For the same within the **White Mountain National Forest,** see the "Bethel" chapter. For private campgrounds, the booklet "Maine Camping Guide," published by the Maine Campground Owners Association (782-5874), lists most privately operated camping and tenting areas. Request a copy from MCOA, 655 Main Street, Lewiston 04240 (fax, 782-497; e-mail, info@campmaine.com; web site, www.campmaine.com). Reservations are advised for the state's 13 parks that

KIM GRANT

offer camping (see *Parks, State*). We have attempted to describe the state parks in detail wherever they appear in this book (see Damariscotta, Camden, Cobscook Bay, Sebago, Rangeley, and Greenville). Note that though campsites can accommodate average-sized campers and trailers, there are no trailer hook-ups. Warren Island (just off Islesboro) and Swan Island (just off Richmond) offer organized camping, and primitive camping is permitted on a number of islands through the Island Institute (see *Islands*). Within this book we occasionally describe oustanding campgrounds.

CAMPS, FOR ADULTS

The **Appalachian Mountain Club** maintains a number of summer lodges and campsites for adults and families seeking a hiking and/or canoeing vacation. Intended primarily for members, they are technically open to all who reserve space, available only after April 1. The full-service camps in Maine (offering three daily meals, organized hikes, evening programs) are at **Echo Lake** on

Mount Desert and **Cold River Camp** in Evans Notch (near the New Hampshire border within the White Mountain National Forest). For details about all facilities and membership, contact the AMC (617-523-0636). The Rockland-based **Hurricane Island Outward Bound School** offers a variety of adult-geared outdoors adventures on Hurricane Island (off Vinalhaven), in Newry (near Bethel), and in Greenville, as well as throughout the country. **National Audubon Ecology Camp** on Hog Island off Bremen offers a series of weeklong courses (see "Damariscotta/Newcastle and Pemaquid").The **University of Maine at Machias** offers summer ornithology workshops. Photographers should check out the **Maine Photographic Workshop** in Camden; also check *Boatbuilding* (**Wooden Boat** offers much more than boatbuilding) and **Elderhostel** (617-426-7788), which offers a variety of programs throughout Maine for everyone over age 60. Art courses include **Merle Donovan's Maine Coast Workshops** in Port Clyde and the **Stonington Painter's Workshop** in Stonington. (Also see *Crafts*.) The most prestigious summer arts workshop in Maine is the **Skowhegan School of Painting and Sculpture** (474-9345).

KIM GRANT

CAMPS, FOR CHILDREN
More than 200 summer camps are listed in the exceptional booklet published annually by the Maine Youth Camping Association (581-1350), P.O. Box 455, Orono 04473.

CAMPS, RENTAL
In Maine, "camp" is the word for a second home or cottage. See *Cottage Rentals* for inexpensive vacation rentals.

CANOEING, GUIDED TRIPS
The slow-moving, shallow **Saco River** is great for beginners and offers a number of well-maintained camping sites. Several outfitters in the Fryeburg area (see *To Do* in "Sebago and Long Lakes Region") offer rentals and shuttle service, and **Saco Bound,** just over the New Hampshire line, offers guided tours. The **Moose River** near Jackman (see *To Do* in "Upper Kennebec Valley") offers a similar camping/canoeing trip, and **Sunrise Canoe Expeditions** based on Cathance Lake (see *To Do* in "Calais and the St. Croix Valley") offers guided trips down the Grand Lake chain of lakes and the St. Croix River. Also see www.maineoutdoors.com.

CANOEING THE ALLAGASH
The ultimate canoe trip in Maine (and on the entire East Coast, for that matter) is the 7- to 10-day expedition up the Allagash Wilderness Waterway, a 92-mile ribbon of lakes, ponds, rivers, and streams through the heart of northern Maine's vast commercial forests. Since 1966 the land flanking the waterway has been owned (500 feet back on either side of the waterway) by the state of Maine. The general information numbers for the Allagash Wilderness Waterway are 941-4014 or 435-7963. A map pinpointing the 65 authorized campsites within the zone (and supplying other crucial information) is available free from the Bureau of Parks and Lands (287-4984), State House Station 22, Augusta 04333. A more detailed map, backed with historical and a variety of other handy information, is DeLorme's "Map and Guide to the Allagash

and St. John." Anybody contemplating the trip should be aware of blackflies in June and the "no-see-ums" when warm weather finally comes. For further information, check *Camping* and *Guide Services,* and check out www.maineoutdoors.com. Also see *To Do—Canoeing* in the "Aroostook County" chapter.

CLAMMING

Maine state law permits the harvesting of shellfish for personal use only, unless you have a commercial license. Individuals can take up to ½ bushel of shellfish or 3 bushels of hen or surf clams (the big ones out in the flats) in 1 day, unless municipal ordinances further limit "the taking of shellfish." Be sure to check locally at the town clerk's office (source of licenses) before you dig, and make sure there's no red tide. Some towns do prohibit clamming, and in certain places there is a temporary stay on harvesting while the beds are being seeded. In a few places clamming has been banned because of pollution.

COASTAL CRUISES

"Cruise" is a much used (and abused) term along the Maine coast, used chiefly to mean a boat ride. "Maine Invites You" has a list of over 100 cruises, ferries, and deep-sea fishing choices, most of them described in the appropriate chapters of this book. We have also tried to list the charter sailing yachts that will take passengers on multiday cruises and have described each of the windjammers that sail for 3 and 6 days at a time (see *Windjammers*).

COTTAGE RENTALS

Cottage rentals are the only reasonably priced way to go for families who wish to stay in one Maine spot for a week or more (unless you go for camping). Request the booklet "Maine Guide to Camp & Cottage Rentals" from the Maine Office of Tourism (1-800-533-9595), or contact the Maine Tourism Association (623-0363). The current booklet's weekly rates for coastal cottages in July and August begin at $350. If you have your heart set on one particular area and cannot get satisfaction through the booklet, we recommend obtaining a printout of real estate agencies just for that county, then sending notes off to agents in the precise area in which you are interested. The printouts are available for a small fee by writing to the Maine Department of Business Regulation, Central Licensing Division, State House Station 35, Augusta 04333 (287-2217).

COVERED BRIDGES

Of the 120 covered bridges that once spanned Maine rivers, just 9 survive. A leaflet guide is available from the Maine Tourism Association (623-0363). The most famous, and certainly as picturesque as a covered bridge can be, is the **Artist's Covered Bridge** (1872) over the Sunday River in Newry, northwest of Bethel. The others are: **Porter Bridge** (1876), over the Ossipee River, 0.5 mile south of Porter; **Babb's Bridge,** recently rebuilt, over the Presumpscot River between Gorham and Windham; **Hemlock Bridge** (1857), 3 miles northwest of East Fryeburg; **Lovejoy Bridge** (1883), in South Andover; **Bennett Bridge** (1901), over the Magalloway River, 1.5 miles south of the Wilson's Mills post office; **Robyville Bridge** (1876), Maine's only completely shingled covered bridge, in the town of Corinth; and the **Watson Settlement Bridge** (1911), between Woodstock and Littleton. Carefully reconstructed **Low's Bridge** (1857), across the Piscataquis River between Guilford and Sangerville, was added in 1990.

CRAFTS

"Maine Cultural Guide," available free from the **Maine Crafts Association** (780-

1807), 15 Walton Street, Portland 04103 is a geographical listing of studios, galleries, and museums throughout Maine. "Directions," published by the **Maine Crafts Guild** (P.O. Box 10832, Portland 04104), lists members by category and the annual schedule of shows. **United Maine Craftsmen, Inc.** (621-2818), also sponsors several large shows each year. **Haystack Mountain School of Crafts** (see "Deer Isle") is a summer school nationally respected in a variety of crafts, offering 3-week courses beginning mid-June and continuing through mid-September. Applicants must be more than 18 years old; enrollment is limited to 65. Work by students is displayed in the visitors center, which also serves as a forum for frequent evening presentations. The surrounding area (Blue Hill to Stonington) contains the largest concentration of Maine craftspeople, many of whom invite visitors to their studios.

DOGSLEDDING
Although racing is a long-established winter spectator sport, the chance actually to ride on a dogsled is relatively recent and growing in popularity. Tim Diehl at **Sugarloaf/USA** offers half-hour rides throughout the day during ski season (you ride behind a team of friendly, frisky Samoyeds). In Newry, Polly Mahoney and Kevin Slater **(Mahoosuc Mountain Adventures)** offer multiday treks with their huskies. Diehl also offers summer rides. In

the Mooosehead Lake region, Stephen Medera's **Song of the Woods** offers full day trips on which you actually do the driving; we were surprised at how smoothly the dogs responded to our commands on a 10-mile woods road.

EVENTS
We have listed outstanding annual events within each chapter of this book, and leaflet guides to events are published by the state four times a year. Events are listed on the Web: **www.visitmaine.com.**

FACTORY OUTLETS
See the "Kittery" and "Freeport" chapters.

FALL FOLIAGE
Autumn is extremely pleasant along the coast; days tend to be clear, and the changing leaves against the blue sea can be spectacular. Many inns remain open through foliage season, and the resort towns of Ogunquit, Kennebunkport, Boothbay Harbor, Bar Harbor, and Camden all offer excellent dining, shopping, and lodging through Columbus Day weekend. Off-season prices prevail, in contrast with the rest of New England, at this time of year. Check the Maine web site, www.visitmaine.com, for frequently updated foliage reports and suggested routes.

FARM B&BS
In 1998, 15 farms are described in a brochure available from the Maine Farm Vacation B&B Association, RR 3, 377 Gray Road, Route 26, West Falmouth 04105 (797-5540; fax, 797-7599; quakerbb@aol.com). Note that this is a promotional association, not an officially approved and inspected group. Properties vary widely. Some are just what you might expect: plenty of space, animals, big breakfasts, friendly, informal atmosphere, and reasonable prices. Others are

MAINE OFFICE OF TOURISM

more formal. Some are not farms. The properties are scattered across Maine. Though we haven't made it to all of those listed yet, the ones we have seen are recommended in their regions. We wish there were some in Aroostook County.

FARMER'S MARKETS
The **Maine Department of Agriculture** (Division of Market and Production Development, 28 State House Station, Augusta 04330; 549-7448; maine.grown@state.me.us) publishes a pamphlet listing over 25 farmer's markets statewide.

FERRIES, TO CANADA
Portland to Yarmouth, Nova Scotia: **Prince of Fundy Cruises** offers nightly sailings (departing 9:30 PM) late April through the Columbus Day weekend. The ferry itself is a car-carrying cruise ship with gambling, restaurants, and cabins aboard (1-800-482-0955 in Maine; 1-800-341-7540 from elsewhere in the United States). **Northumberland/Bay Ferries** (1-888-249-7245 operates a high-speed catamaran between Bar Harbor and Yarmouth (spring through fall). Note that it's very possible to use these ferries as part of a loop: going on one and returning on the other. Mid-June to mid-September **East Coast Ferries Ltd.** (506-747-2159), a small car ferry based on Deer Island, serves Eastport (30 minutes) and Campobello (45 minutes), and the small provincial (free) **Deer Island–L'Etete Ferry** (506-453-2600) connects Deer Island with the New Brunswick mainland. The 65-car **Coastal Transport Ltd. Ferry** (506-662-3724) runs year-round from Blacks Harbour, not far east of L'Etete, to the island of Grand Manan.

FERRIES, IN MAINE
Maine State Ferry Service (1-800-521-3939 in-state; 207-596-2202 outside of Maine), Rockland 04841, operates year-round service from Rockland to Vinalhaven and North Haven, from Lincolnville to Islesboro, and from Bass Harbor to Swan's Island and Frenchboro. For private ferry services to Monhegan, see "Boothbay Harbor" and "Mid-Coast Islands"; for the Casco Bay islands, see "Portland"; for Matinicus, see "Mid-Coast Islands"; and for Isle au Haut, see "East Penobscot Bay Region."

FILM
Northeast Historic Film (1-800-639-1636; fax, 469-7875) is based at "The Alamo," a vintage 1916 movie house (P.O. Box 900, Bucksport 04416) that they have restored. This admirable group has created a regional moving-image archive of films based on or made in New England that were shown in every small town during the first part of the century. Films also record life in the lumbering and fishing industries. Request the catalog "Videotapes of Life in New England."

FIRE PERMITS
Maine law dictates that no person shall kindle or use outdoor fires without a permit, except at authorized campsites or picnic grounds. Fire permits in the organized towns are obtained from the local town warden; in the unorganized towns, from the nearest forest ranger. Portable stoves fueled by propane gas, gasoline, or sterno are exempt from the rule.

FISHING
"The Maine Guide to Hunting and Fishing," published by the Maine Tourism Association (623-0363) and available by phoning 1-800-533-9595, is a handy overview of rules, license fees, and other matters of interest to fishermen. Detailed descriptions of camps and rustic resorts catering to fishermen can be found in chapters under "Western Mountains and Lakes," "The Kennebec Valley," and "Northern Maine." A 1-day fishing li-

cense cost nonresidents $10 in 1999; 3-, 7-, and 15-day licenses are also available at most general stores and sporting-goods outlets or by writing to the Maine Department of Inland Fisheries and Wildlife (287-2571), 284 State Street, Augusta 04333.

FORTS

To be married to a fort freak is to realize that there are people in this world who will detour 50 miles to see an 18th-century earthworks. Maine's forts are actually a fascinating lot, monuments to the state's unique and largely forgotten history. Examples: **Fort William Henry** at Pemaquid, **Fort Edgecomb** in Edgecomb, **Fort George** in Castine, **Fort Kent** and **Fort Knox** near Bucksport, **Fort McClary** in Kittery, **Fort O'Brien** near Machias, **Fort Popham** near Bath, and **Fort Pownall** at Stockton Springs.

GOLDEN ROAD

This legendary 96-mile road (almost entirely gravel) is the privately owned high road of the North Woods, linking Millinocket's paper mills on the east with commercial woodlands that extend to the Quebec border. Its name derives from its multimillion-dollar cost in 1975, but its value has proven great to visitors heading up from Moosehead Lake, as well as from Millinocket to Baxter State Park. It's also used by the white-water rafting companies on the Penobscot and the Allagash Wilderness Waterway, and for remote lakes like Chesuncook. Expect to pay a user fee for your vehicle and to pull to the side to permit lumber trucks to pass. The road is exceptionally maintained, even (especially) in winter.

GOLF

"Maine Invites You" (see *Information*) lists golf courses across the state. We list them under *To Do* within each chapter. The major resorts catering to golfers are the

Samoset in Rockport, the **Bethel Inn** in Bethel, **Sebasco Harbor Resort** near Bath, the **Country Club Inn** in Rangeley, and **Sugarloaf/USA** in the Carrabassett Valley.

GORGES

Maine has the lion's share of the Northeast's gorges. There are four biggies. The widest is the **Upper Sebois River Gorge** north of Patten, and the most dramatic, "Maine's Miniature Grand Canyon," is **Gulf Hagas** near the Katahdin Iron Works (see "Katahdin Region"). Both **Kennebec Gorge** and **Ripogenus Gorge** are now popular white-water-rafting routes.

GUIDE SERVICES

In 1897 the Maine legislature passed a bill requiring hunting guides to register with the state; the first to register was Cornelia

KIM GRANT

Thurza Crosby (better known as "Fly Rod" Crosby), whose syndicated column appeared in New York, Boston, and Chicago newspapers at the turn of the century. The Maine Guide Association (785-2061) publishes a directory; write to MGA, P.O. Box 847, Augusta 04332. Becoming a Registered Maine Guide entails passing one of several specialized tests—in hunting, fishing, or one of a growing number of recreational categories including white-water rafting, canoeing, or kayaking—administered by the Maine Department of Inland Fisheries and Wildlife.

There are currently some 3,000 Registered Maine Guides, but many of these do not use their skills professionally, and of those who do, just a few hundred are full-time professional guides. A useful commercial web site listing a wide variety of outfitters is www.maineguides.com; www.midcoast.com/guides is the site of the 500-member Maine Professional Guides Association, the core group who make all or part of their living by guiding, and who pride themselves on a strong code of ethics.

Also see *Hunting* and *Fishing*.

HANDICAPPED ACCESS
Within this book, handicapped-accesible lodging, restaurants, and attractions are marked with a wheelchair symbol &. Maine, by the way, offers an outstanding handicapped skiing program, both cross-country and alpine; phone 1-800-639-7770.

HIKING
For organized trips, contact the Appalachian Mountain Club's Boston office (617-523-0636). In addition to the *AMC Maine Mountain Guide* (available from AMC Books Division, Dept. B, 5 Joy Street, Boston, MA 02108) and the AMC map guide to trails on Mount Desert, we recommend investing in *50 Hikes in Southern and Coastal Maine* by John Gibson and *50 Hikes in the Maine Mountains* by Cloe Chunn (both from Backcountry Publications), which offer clear, inviting treks up hills of every size throughout the state. The *Maine Atlas and Gazetteer* (DeLorme) also outlines a number of rewarding hikes. Also see *Appalachian Trail.*

HISTORY
Within this book Maine's rich history is told through the places that still recall or dramatize it. See *Abenaki* in this section for sites that tell of the long presettlement history.

For traces of early-17th-century settlement see our descriptions of **Phippsburg, Pemaquid,** and **Augusta.** The French and Indian Wars (1675-1760), in which Maine was more involved than most of New England, are recalled in the reconstructed English Fort Henry at **Pemaquid** and in historical markers scattered around **Castine** (Baron de Saint Castine, a young French nobleman married to a Penobscot Indian princess, controlled the coastal area we now call "Down East." A striking house built in 1760 on **Kittery Point** (see "Kittery and the Yorks," *Scenic Drives*) evokes Sir William Pepperell, credited with having captured the fortress at Louisburg from the French, and restored buildings in **York Village** (same chapter) suggests Maine's brief, peaceful colonial period.

In the Burnham Tavern at **Machias** you learn that townspeople captured a British man-of-war on June 1, 1775, the first naval engagement of the Revolution. Other reminders of the Revolution are less triumphant: At the Cathedral Pines in **Eustis** and spotted along Route 202 in the **Upper Kennebec Valley,** historical markers tell the poignant saga of Col. Benedict Arnold's ill-fated 1775 attempt to capture Quebec. Worse: markers at Fort George in Castine detail the ways in which a substantial patriot fleet utterly disgraced itself there. Maine's brush with the British didn't end with the Revolution: The Barracks Museum in **Eastport** tells of British occupation again in 1814.

Climb the six steep floors of the **Portland Observatory** (built 1807) and hear how Portland ranked second among New England ports, its tonnage based on lumber, the resource that fueled fortunes like those evidenced by the amazingly opulent **Black Mansion in Ellsworth** and the elegant **Ruggles House** way Downeast in Columbia Falls. In 1820 Maine finally became a state (the 23rd) but, as we note in our introduction to "The North Woods," not without a price. The mother state, her coffers at their usual low, stipulated an even division of all previously undeeded wilderness and some 10.5 million acres were quickly sold off, vast privately owned tracts that survive today as the Unorganized Townships.

Plagued in 1839 by boundary disputes that were ignored in Washington, the new, timber-rich state built its own northern forts (the **Fort Kent Blockhouse** survives). This "Aroostook War" was terminated by the Webster/Ashburton treaty of 1842, a deal which we note in our introduction to Washington County because it gave Campobello and Grand Manan to Canada (the story goes that it was a foggy night and Webster couldn't see how much nearer the islands are to Maine than to New Brunswick). In 1844 the state built massive **Fort Knox** at the mouth of the Penobscot River (see "Bucksport"), just in case. Never entirely completed, it makes an interesting state park. This era was, however, one of great prosperity and expansion within the new state.

We note in the introduction to "Brunswick" that it can be argued that the Civil War began and ended there. Unfortunately the state suffered heavy losses: some 18,000 young soldiers from Maine died, as Civil War monuments in every village remind us. The end of the war, however, ushered in a boom decade. Granite from Maine islands (see "The Fox Islands: Vinalhaven and North Haven") fed the demand for monumental public buildings throughout the country and both schooners and Down Easters (graceful, square-rigged vessels) were in great demand (see the **Penobscot Marine Museum** in Searsport and the **Marine Maritime Museum** in "Bath Area").

In the late 19th century many Maine industries boomed, tourism included. We de-

scribe Maine's tourism history in our introduction because it is so colorful, little recognized, and so much a part of what you see today.

Maine, the Pine Tree State from Prehistory to the Present by Judd, Churchill, and Eastman (University of Maine) is a good, recent, readable history (paperback).

HORSE RACING

Harness racing can be found at **Scarborough Downs** (883-4331), US 1, or exit 6 off the Maine Turnpike, April through November. The **Bangor Raceway** is open late May through late July. **County Raceways** has several scheduled dates in June, July, and August. The leaflet guide "Maine Agricultural Fairs" also lists harness-racing dates for the current season. Contact the Maine Harness Racing Commission (287-3221) for more information.

HORSEBACK RIDING

Northern Maine Adventures (see "Moosehead Lake") offers entire days and overnights as well as shorter stints in the saddle. For trail riding, our favorite place is **Speckled Mountain Ranch,** catering both to beginners and experienced riders, offering trail rides and riding camps both for adults and youngsters ages 12–15. Also check "Old Orchard Beach," "Boothbay Harbor," "Sebago and Long Lakes," and "Moosehead Lake."

HUNTING

Hunters should obtain a summary of Maine hunting and trapping laws from the Maine Department of Inland Fisheries and Wildlife (287-3371), 284 State Street, Augusta 04333. For leads on Registered Maine Guides who specialize in organized expeditions (complete with meals and lodging), contact the sources we list under *Fishing, Guide Services, Canoeing,* and *Camping.* You might also try the **Moosehead Region**

Chamber of Commerce (695-2702). "The Maine Guide to Hunting and Fishing," published annually by the Maine Tourism Association (623-0363, available by phoning 1-800-533-9595), is filled with information and ads for hunting lodges, guides, and the like.

INFORMATION

The Maine Office of Tourism maintains an excellent web site: www.visitmaine.com. Unfortunately, however, there's no staff person to answer specific questions. The information line—1-800-533-9595—connects with a fulfillment clerk at L. L. Bean who will send you the thick, four-season guide, "Maine Invites You." They will also send—if you request them—the specialized guides to "Hunting and Fishing," "Camp & Cottage Rentals" and "Bed & Breakfasts," all published by the Maine Tourism Association

NEAL PARENT

(formerly the Maine Publicity Bureau; 623-0363), which maintains its own web site: www.mainetourism.com. Maine also offers unusually well-stocked and -staffed welcome centers at its southern gateway at Kittery (439-1319) on I-95 northbound (also accessible from Route 1); just off coastal Route 1 and I-95 in Yarmouth (846-0833); both northbound and southbound on I-95 in Hampden near Bangor (862-6628/6638); in Calais (454-2211); and in Houlton (532-6346). There is also an information center on the New Hampshire line on Route 302 in Fryeburg (935-3639) and on Route 2 in Bethel (shared quarters with the White Mountain National Forest information staff: 824-4582. Also see *Web Sites.*

INNS

In this book, we have been more selective than in earlier editions because there are simply so many more new places to stay out there. While researching this book, we personally inspected hundreds of inns and B&Bs. Realizing that "inn books" tend to focus on the higher end of the price spectrum, we have tried to include more reasonably priced, equally appealing options in the same area. *Best Places to Stay in New England* by Christina Tree and Kimberly Grant (Houghton Mifflin) also includes a wide range of places to stay in Maine.

ISLANDS

In all there are reportedly 3,250 offshore Maine islands, most uninhabited. We describe each of the islands that offer overnight lodging—Chebeague and Peaks Islands in Casco Bay, Monhegan, Vinalhaven, Islesboro, and Matinicus along the Mid-Coast, and Isle au Haut, Islesford, and Swan's Island in the Down East section—in varying detail. In Casco Bay the ferry also serves Long and Cliff Islands (summer rentals are available), and Eagle Island, former home of Admiral Perry, is served by daily excursion boats from Portland. For information on public or private islands on which low-impact visitors are welcome contact the **Maine Island Trail Association** (596-6456; web site: www.mita.org); the address is P.O. Box C, Rockland 04841. MITA maintains 80 islands and charges $40 for membership, which brings with it a detailed guidebook and the right to land on these islands. **The Island Institute** (594-9202; web site: www.islandinstitute.org), which spawned MITA, now serves as an umbrella organization for the island communities; with $40 membership come its publications: *Island Journal, Working Waterfront,* and *Inter Island News.*

LAKES

Maine boasts some 6,000 lakes and ponds, and every natural body of water over 10 acres—which accounts for most of them—is, theoretically at least, available to the public for "fishing and fowling." Access is, of course, limited by the property owners around the lakes. Because so much acreage in Maine is owned by paper companies and other land-management concerns that permit public use, provided the public obey their rules (see *Camping*), there is ample opportunity to canoe or fish in solitary waters. Powerboat owners should note that most states have reciprocal license privileges with Maine; the big exception is New Hampshire. For more about the most popular resort lakes in the state, see Bridgton, Rangeley, Greenville, and the Belgrade Lakes. The state parks on lakes are **Aroostook** (camping, fishing, swimming; Route 1 south of Presque Isle), **Damariscotta Lake State Park** (Route 32; Jefferson), **Lake St. George State Park** (swimming, picnicking, fishing; Route 3 in Liberty), **Lily Bay State Park** (8 miles north of Greenville), **Peacock Beach State Park** (swimming, picnicking; Richmond), **Peaks-Kenny State Park** (Sebec Lake in Dover-Foxcroft), **Rangeley Lake State Park** (swimming, camping; Rangeley), **Range Ponds State Park** (Poland), **Sebago Lake State Park** (swimming, picnicking, camping; near Bridgton), **Mount Blue Lake State Park** (Weld), and **Swan Lake State Park** (Swanville). Families with small children should be aware of the many coastal lakes surrounded by reasonably priced cottages (see *Cottages, Rental*).

LIGHTHOUSES

Maine takes pride in its 63 lighthouses. The most popular to visit are **Portland Head Light** (completed in 1790, automated in 1990, now a delightful museum featuring the history of lighthouses) on Cape Elizabeth; **Cape Neddick Light** in York; **Marshall Point Light** at Port Clyde; **Fort Point Light** at Stockton Springs; **Pemaquid Point** (the lighthouse keeper's house is now a museum, there's an art gallery, and the rocks below are peerless for scrambling); **Owl's Head** near Rockland (built 1826); **Bass Harbor Head Light** at Bass Harbor; and Lubec's **West Quoddy Head,** the start of a beautiful shore path. On **Monhegan,** the lighthouse keeper's house is a seasonal museum, and at **Grindle Point** on Islesboro there is also an adjacent seasonal museum. True lighthouse buffs also make the pilgrimage to **Matinicus Rock,** the setting for

34

children's books. Lighthouse aficionados tell us that getting to **East Quoddy Head Lighthouse** on the island of Campobello, accessible at low tide, is the ultimate adventure; it is also a prime whale-watching post. Captain Barna Norton (497-5933) runs charters from Jonesport to lighthouses on Libby Island, Moose Peak, Nash Island, and Petit Manan, as well as to Machias Seal (see *Puffin-Watching*).

LITTER

Littering in Maine is punishable by a $100 fine; this applies to dumping from boats as well as other vehicles. Most cans and bottles are redeemable.

LLAMA TREKKING

The principle is appealingly simple: The llama carries your gear; you lead the llama. From the **Telemark Inn** (836-2703), surrounded by semiwilderness west of Bethel, Steve Crone offers day and multiday treks. At **Pleasant Bay Bed & Breakfast** (483-4490) in Addison, guests can walk the property's waterside trails with the llamas, and at **Maine-lly Llamas Farm** (929-3057) in Hollis, guests can also take a nature trek with llamas.

LOBSTER POUNDS

A lobster pound is usually a no-frills seaside restaurant that specializes in serving lobsters and clams steamed in seawater. The most

basic and reasonably priced pounds are frequently fishermen's co-ops. The Pemaquid Peninsula (see "Damariscotta") is especially blessed: Check out both the **New Harbor Co-op** and neighboring **Shaw's**, the **Pemaquid Fisherman's Co-op,** and, in nearby Round Pond, both **Muscongus Bay Lobster** and **Round Pond Lobster. Cod End** in Tenants Harbor, **Miller's Lobster Company** on Spruce Head, and **Waterman's Beach Lobsters** in South Thomaston are also the real thing. Expect good value but no china plates or salads at **Chauncey Creek** in Kittery, **Harraseeket Lunch & Lobster Company** in South Freeport, and the **Fisherman's Landing** in Bar Harbor; other lobster-eating landmarks include **Nunan's Lobster Hut** in Cape Porpoise, **Eaton's** on Deer Isle, **Robinson's Wharf** at Townsend Gut near Boothbay, the **Lobster Shack** in Cape Elizabeth, **Young's Lobster Pound** in Belfast, the **Lobster Pound** in Lincolnville Beach, the **Lobster Shack** in Searsport, **Trenton Bridge** on Route 3 at the entrance to Mount Desert, and **Thurston's** on the island. The **Ogunquit Lobster Pound** in Ogunquit and **Beal's** in Southwest Harbor tend to be the state's priciest pounds.

THE MAINE FESTIVAL

Maine's biggest, splashiest cultural happening of the year, the festival is held for 4 days around the second weekend in August at Thomas Point Beach in Brunswick. Performing artists are from everywhere, but the Maine folk artists are definitely local, as are the craftspeople; children's entertainment, a food garden, and plenty of outdoor sculpture are also part of the scene. Sponsored by Maine Arts (772-9012; 1-800-639-4212).

MAINE GROWN

There is a multitude of locally grown and locally produced food items, including fresh meats, blueberries and blueberry products, smoked seafood, teas, ployes, beer, maple syrup, and lobster stew, to name just a few. Deanne Herman at the Maine Department of Agriculture (287-7561) is a helpful source of information on many of these specialty items, or ask at local chambers. The Department of Agriculture also produces a number of helpful brochures on topics such as picking your own berries, vegetables and flowers, apples, and more. Another great place to pick up locally grown produce and food items are farmer's markets. A number of these are held weekly in the summer season; a brochure is available from the Department of Agriculture (287-3491; maine.grown@state.me.us).

MAINE MADE
Maine also offers a large variety of locally made products (many carefully crafted by hand rather than on machines), including Indian baskets, woolen products, shoes, Shaker furniture, and more. The Department of Agriculture (287-3491) can offer helpful information on such products, and local chambers can steer you to local craftspeople and businesses producing hand-crafted items. Request a "Maine Made" catalog (1-800-541-5872; www.mainemade.com).

MAINE PUBLIC BROADCASTING
Public broadcasting is represented statewide with both television and radio. Programs and services can be found on the Maine Public Broadcasting web site at www.mpbc.org. The five stations of Maine Public Television are: Channel 10 in Augusta, Channel 12 in Orono, Channel 13 in Calais, Channel 10 in Presque Isle, and Channel 26 in Biddeford. In addition to many national public broadcasting programs, local programming includes *Made in Maine*, a profile of business in Maine; *Maine Watch*, highlighting important issues

in Maine each week; and the *Maine State Concert Series*, featuring concerts by some of Maine's best performing artists. Maine's six public radio stations can be found on the dial at 89.7 in Calais, 90.1 in Portland, 90.9 in Bangor, 91.3 in Waterville, 106.1 in Presque Isle, and 106.5 in Fort Kent. In addition to popular National Public Radio programs, MPR also offers the radio version of *Maine Watch; Maine Things Considered,* a news program highlighting state news; and *Maine Stage,* a classical music series.

MAINE TURNPIKE
For travel conditions and construction updates, phone 1-800-675-PIKE. Tolls are now a flat rate (no more tickets), paid when getting on the turnpike. Heading north, the first booth is in Kittery. If you remain on the turnpike all the way to Augusta, you will pass through two other booths requiring a toll (New Gloucester and just outside of Augusta). Unless you need to exit at Gray or Lewiston Auburn, it's cheaper and quicker to follow I-95 (exit 9) rather than the Maine Turnpike (I-495) north to Augusta and Bangor.

MAPLE SUGARING
Maine produces roughly 8,000 gallons of syrup a year, and the Maine Department of Agriculture publishes a list of producers who welcome visitors on **Maine Maple Sunday** (also known as Sap Sunday) in late March.

MOOSE-WATCHING
The moose, the state animal, has made a comeback from its near-extinct status in the 1930s and now numbers more than 20,000. Your chances of spotting one are best in early morning or at dusk on a wooded pond or lake or along logging roads. If you are driving through moose country at night, go slowly because moose typically freeze rather than retreat from oncoming headlights. For

KIM GRANT

details about commercial moose-watching expeditions, check the "Rangeley" and "Moosehead Lake" chapters. The Moosehead Lake Region Chamber of Commerce sponsors **"Moosemainea"** mid-May through mid-June, with special events and a huge moose locator map. Suspicious that this promotion coincided with Moosehead's low tourist season, we queried the state's moose expert, who assures us that moose are indeed most visible in late spring.

MUSEUM VILLAGES
What variety! Open seasonally as a commercial attraction, **Willowbrook** at Newfield is a 19th-century village center consisting of 31 buildings that have been restored on the inspiration of one man. Other attractions include the old village center of **Searsport,** restored as a fine maritime museum; **Sabbathday Lake Shaker Museum,** still a functioning religious community; **York Village,** with its Old Gaol, school, tavern,

church, and scattering of historic houses open to the public, all adding up to a picture of late-18th-century life in coastal Maine; **Norlands,** a former estate with a neo-Gothic library, school, and farm buildings, as well as a mansion that invites you to come and live for a weekend as if you were in this particular place (Livermore) in the 1870s. Also see *Acadians.*

MUSEUMS
Also see *Abenaki* and *Art Museums.* Easily the most undervisited in the state, the **Maine State Museum** in Augusta has outstanding displays on the varied Maine landscape and historical exhibits ranging from traces of the area's earliest people to rifles used by State of Mainers in Korea; you can also see exhibits on fishing, agriculture, lumbering, quarrying, and shipbuilding. Our favorites also include the **Peary-MacMillan Arctic Museum** at Bowdoin College in Brunswick, the **Seashore Trolley Museum** in Kennebunkport, the **Owl's Head Transportation Museum** near Rockland, the **Robert Abbe Museum** in Acadia National Park (outstanding for its regional Native American artifacts), the **Wilson Museum** in Castine, the **L. C. Bates Museum** in Hinckley, the **Patten Lumberman's Museum,** the **Rangeley Lakes Region Logging Museum,** and the **Colonial Pemaquid Restoration** in Pemaquid (which presents fascinating archaeological finds from the adjacent, early-17th-century settlement). The **Maine Maritime Museum** in Bath stands in a class by itself and should not be missed.

MUSIC CONCERT SERIES
The best-known summer concert series are the **Bar Harbor Festival** (288-5744) and **Bowdoin College Summer Concerts** in Brunswick (725-8731, ext. 321), also the **Mount Desert Festival of Chamber**

Music (276-5039). Other summer series include the **Arcady Music Festival** (288-3151), the **Sebago/Long Lakes Region Chamber Music Festival** in North Bridgton (627-4939); the **Bay Chamber Concerts,** presented in the Rockport Opera House (236-2823); a series of outdoor picnic concerts at the **Round Top Center for the Arts** (563-1507) in Damariscotta; **Kneisel Hall** (374-2811) chamber concerts in Blue Hill; and **Machias Bay Chamber Concerts** in Machias (255-8685). There is, of course, the **Portland Symphony Orchestra** (773-8191), which also has a summertime pops series, and the **Bangor Symphony Orchestra** (945-6408). Music lovers should also take note of the **Annual Rockport Folk Festival** in mid-July, the **Downeast Jazz Festival in Rockland** every August, the **Lincoln Arts Festival** of classical and choral music held throughout the Boothbay Harbor Region in summer months, and the **Bluegrass Festival** at Thomas Point Beach in September.

MUSIC SCHOOLS

Notable are **Bowdoin Summer Music Festival** (see *Music Concert Series*); **Kneisel Hall** in Blue Hill (call 725-8731 only after June 24; prior inquiries should be addressed to Kneisel Hall, Blue Hill 04614); the **Pierre Monteux Memorial Domaine School** in Hancock (442-6251); **Salzedo Summer Harp Colony** in Camden (236-2289); **New England Music Camp** in Oakland (465-3025); **Maine Summer Youth Music** at the University of Maine, Orono (581-1960); and **Maine Music Camp** at the University of Maine, Farmington (778-3501).

NATURE PRESERVES, COASTAL

From **Kittery's Brave Boat Harbor Trail** to the **Bold Coast Trail** way down in Wash-

ington County not far from Quoddy Light, oceanside walking trails have multiplied in the last few years. Within each chapter we describe these under *Green Space* or *To Do—Hiking*. On the Southern Coast the **Wells National Estuarine Research Reserve** at Laudholm Farm includes two barrier beaches. On Casco Bay the Maine Audubon Society headquarters at **Gisland Farm** in Falmouth include 70 acres of nature trails; Maine Audubon also offers canoe tours and many summer programs at their **Scarborough Marsh** nature center and maintains picnic and tenting sites at **Mast Landing Sanctuary** in Freeport. Along the Mid-Coast both the **Boothbay Region Land Trust** and the **Damariscotta River Association** now maintain a number of exceptional preserves and **Camden Hills State Park** includes miles of little-trafficked trails with magnificent views. Down East in the Blue Hill area the 1,350-acre **Holbrook Island Sanctuary** in West Brooksville is a beauty, and in Ellsworth, 40-acre **Birdsacre** includes nature trails and a museum honoring ornithologist Cordelia Stanwood. **Acadia National Park,** the state's busiest preserve, offers 120 miles of hiking paths on Mount Desert, also trails on **Isle au Haut** and at **Schoodic Point. Schoodic Mountain** north of Sullivan is one of the area's most

spectacular hikes. Right across the line in Washington County the 6,000-acre **Petit Manan National Wildlife Refuge**, based in Steuben, includes two coastal peninsulas and 24 offshore islands. Near Jonesport **Great Wass Island** (accessible by land) is maintained by the Maine chapter of The Nature Conservancy, a beautiful preserve with a 2-mile shore trail. **Western Head,** near Machias, is now maintained by Maine Coast Heritage Trust; Maine's Bureau of Parks and Lands maintains a 5.4-mile **Bold Coast Trail** along the high bluffs west of Cutler; **West Quoddy Light State Park** includes a splendid 2-mile shore trail. **Roosevelt Campobello International Park** also includes many miles of shore paths, and **Cobscook Bay State Park** (see "Eastport and Cobscook Bay") and **Moosehorn National Wildlife Refuge** ("Calais and the St. Croix Valley") also offers hiking trails. Two islands that maintain magnificent hiking trails are **Monhegan** and **Vinalhaven.** The Maine chapter of The Nature Conservancy (729-5181) has published *Maine Forever,* a "Guide to Nature Conservancy Preserves in Maine." The Maine Coast Heritage Trust (729-7366) also makes available several useful brochures about its holdings.

NATURE PRESERVES, INLAND

In the Rangeley area the **Rangeley Lakes Heritage Trust** has, in recent years, preserved more than 10,000 acres, including 20 miles of lake and river frontage and 10 islands; the **Stephen Phillips Memorial Preserve Trust** maintains a number of campsites on its land along Lake Mooselookmeguntic. In the Sugarloaf area the Maine Bureau of Parks and Lands now offers detailed maps to trails within the 35,000-acre **Bigelow Preserve.** Within each chapter we describe nature preserves along with state parks under *Green Space* or *Hiking.* Among our favorites are Vaughan Woods ("Kittery and the Yorks"), a 250-acre state preserve with wooded hiking trails along the Salmon River and trails to the top of **Mount Kineo** overlooking Moosehead Lake. **Baxter State Park** (see "Katahdin") is, of course, the greatest inland preserve.

PARKS AND FORESTS, NATIONAL

Acadia National Park (288-3338; www.nps.gov/acad/), which occupies roughly half of Mount Desert, plus scattered areas on Isle au Haut, Little Cranberry Island, Baker Island, Little Moose Island, and Schoodic Point, adds up to more than 40,000 acres offering hiking, ski touring, swimming, horseback riding, canoeing, and a variety of guided nature tours and programs, as well as a scenic 27-mile driving tour. Note that an entry fee is charged to drive the Park Loop Road. Camping is by reservation only at Blackwoods, and first-come, first-served at Seawall. See "Acadia National Park" for details. The **White Mountain National Forest** encompasses 41,943 acres in Maine, including five campgrounds under the jurisdiction of the Evans Notch Ranger District (824-2134), Bridge Street, Bethel 04217. For details see "Bethel Area."

PARKS, STATE

The Bureau of Parks and Lands (287-3821; www.state.me.us/doc/prkslnds/prkslnds.htm), State House Station 22, Augusta 04333, can send a packet of information describing each of the parks and camping facilities. In the text, we have described parks as they appear geographically. In 1998 day-use fees were between $1 and $2.50 per adult; children 5–11, $.50; free for children under 5 and for seniors over 65. The camping fee was $9–13 for residents, $11–17 for nonresidents. There is also a $2 per night reservation fee for camping. Call the reservations hotline (1-800-332-1562 within Maine; 207-287-3824 from outside the state) at least 7 days in advance to make a campground reservation, or use the online registration form. (Also see *Lakes*.)

PLOYES
This traditional Acadian pancake/flatbread, as delicate as a crêpe, is a specialty throughout the St. John Valley. The Bouchard Family Farm produces a line of French-Canadian food products: 1-800-239-3237.

POPULATION
Approximately 1.2 million.

PUFFIN-WATCHING
Atlantic puffins are smaller than you might expect. They lay just one egg a year and were heading for extinction around the turn of the century, when the only surviving birds nested either on Matinicus Rock or Machias Seal Island. Since 1973 the Audubon Society has helped create nesting areas on Eastern Egg Rock in Muscongus Bay, 6 miles off Pemaquid Point. Since 1984, there has been a similar puffin-restoration project on Seal Island in outer Penobscot Bay, 6 miles from Matinicus Rock. The best months for viewing puffins are June and July or the first few days of August. The only place from which you are allowed to view the birds on land is at Machias Seal Island, where visitors are permitted in limited numbers. Contact **Barna and John Norton** in Jonesport, **Bold Coast Charter** in Cutler, and **Atlantic Expeditions** in Rockland. With the help of binoculars (a must), you can also view the birds from the water via tours offered by **Lively Lady Enterprises** based on Vinalhaven, **Offshore Passenger & Freight** in Rockland, **Cap'n Fish Boat Trips** in Boothbay Harbor, **Sea Bird**

KIM GRANT

Watcher in Bar Harbor, **Hardy Boat Cruises** out of New Harbor, and the **Maine Audubon Society.**

RAILROAD RIDES & MUSEUMS
Boothbay Railway Village delights small children and offers railroad exhibits in its depot. For rail fans there are other sites to see and excursions to take: the **Sandy River Railroad** in Phillips, the **Belfast & Moosehead Lake Railroad Company** in Belfast, the **Maine Coast Railroad** in Wiscasset, the **Bangor & Aroostook Railroad Company** in Bangor and the **Maine Narrow Gauge Railroad Company & Museum,** Portland.

RATES
Please do not regard any prices listed for *Lodging, Dining Out,* and *Eating Out,* as well as for museums and attractions, as set in stone. Call ahead to confirm them. MAP stands for Modified American Plan: breakfast and dinner included in rate. AP stands for American Plan: three meals included in rate. EP stands for European Plan: breakfast included in rate. B&B stands for bed and breakfast: continental breakfast included in rate.

ROCKHOUNDING
Perham's Maine Mineral Store at Trap Corner in West Paris, which claims to at-

tract an annual 90,000 visitors, displays Maine minerals and offers access to its four quarries. The store also offers information about other quarries and sells its own guide-books to gem hunting in Oxford County and throughout the state. Open year-round 9–5 daily except Thanksgiving and Christmas. For other rockhounding meccas, check the "Bethel" chapter. Thanks to the high price of gold, prospectors are back-panning Maine streambeds; a list of likely spots is available from the Maine Geological Survey (287-2801), Department of Conservation, State House Station 22, Augusta 04333.

SAILING

Windjammers and yacht charter brokers aside, there are a limited number of places that will rent small sailing craft, fewer that will offer lessons to adults and children alike. **Blue Seas Adventure Co.** in Camden rents sailboats by the day or longer, as does **Mansell Boat Company,** Southwest Harbor. Learn-to-sail programs are offered by **Wooden Boat School** in Brooklin and in Camden by both the **Camden Yacht Club** and **Bay Island Sailing School.** Sailboat rentals and daysails are listed throughout the book. (Also see *Windjammers.*)

SEA KAYAKING

Sea kayaking is the fastest-growing sport along the coast of Maine, and outfitters are

responding to the demand, offering guided half-day and full-day trips, also overnight and multiday expeditions with camping on Maine islands. Paddling a kayak is comfort-able—you're not crouching, as in a canoe, or arched over, as in a rowboat. You're also low, so low that you can stare down a duck or a cormorant, or study the surface of the water and its kaleidoscopic patterns. Maneu-verable in as little as 6 inches of water, kay-aks are ideal craft for "gunkholing" (poking in and out of coves) around the rocky edges of Maine islands. The leading outfitters are **Maine Island Kayak Company** (766-2373) on Peaks Island off Portland, and **Maine Sport Outfitters** (236-8797) in Rockport, both of which specialize in multiday camping trips and offer intro-ductory lessons. Others include **Kayak Adventures** (967-5243) in Kennebunkport, **H2Outfitters** (833-5257) on Orrs Island near Brunswick, **Tidal Transit** (633-7140) in Boothbay Harbor, **Outward Bound School** (1-800-341-1744), **The Phoenix Center** (374-2113) in Blue Hill Falls, **Coastal Kayaking Tours** (288-9605) in Bar Harbor, **Schoodic Kayak Tours** (963-7958) in Corea, **Norumbega Outfitters** (773-0910) in Portland, **Saco River Canoe & Kayak** (935-2369) in Fryeburg, and the **Chewonki Foundation** (882-7323) outside of Wiscasset. **L. L. Bean Sea Kayak Symposium,** held in early July at the Maine Maritime Academy in Castine (by reserva-tion only), is New England's oldest and still its biggest annual kayaking event: a 2-day program geared to neophytes and all levels of ability, with lessons and equipment demonstrations. **L. L. Bean's Coastal Kayaking Workshop,** held the beginning of August at the University of New England, Biddeford, is a smaller, more skills-oriented event. For details and reservations call 1-800-341-4341, ext. 2509. *Sea Kayaking Along the New England Coast* by Tamsin

Venn (Appalachian Mountain Club, 1991) includes detailed guidance to kayaking routes from Portland to Cobscook Bay; it also offers tips on local lodging and dining as well as an overall introduction to the sport.

SKIING, CROSS-COUNTRY
The Maine Nordic Ski Council (1-800-SKI-XCME; www.mnsc.com), P.O. Box 645, Bethel 04217 is a great source of information about conditions, ski centers, and outfitters. **Carrabassett Valley Touring Center** at Sugarloaf is the largest commercial Nordic network in the state. Bethel, with four trail networks (**Sunday River Inn**, the **Bethel Inn, Carter's X-C Ski Center,** and **Telemark Inn & Llama Treks**), offers varied terrain. The trails at **Saddleback Mountain** in Rangeley are the highest in Maine and may, in fact, be snow-covered when no place else is. The most adventurous touring is found in the Katahdin/Moosehead area in Maine's North Woods. **The Birches** in Rockwood and **Little Lyford Camps** near Brownville Junction offer guided wilderness tours. **Mahoosuc Mountain Adventures** in the Bethel area also offers guided trips with dogsleds toting gear for overnight camping.

SKIING, DOWNHILL
Ski Maine Association (761-3774; www.skimaine.com) lists information about mountains in Maine, snow conditions, and more on their web site. **Sugarloaf/USA** in the Carrabassett Valley and **Sunday River** in the Bethel area, both owned by the Bethel-based American Skiing Company, vie for the title of Maine's number-one ski resort. The two are very different and actually complement each other well. Sugarloaf is a high, relatively remote mountain with New England's only lift-serviced snowfields on its summit and a classy, self-contained condo-village at its base. Sunday River, just

MAINE OFFICE OF TOURISM

1 hour north of Portland, consists of eight adjoining (relatively low-altitude) mountains; snowmaking is a big point of pride, and facilities include a variety of slope-side condo lodging. **Saddleback Mountain** (in the Rangeley area) is a big, relatively undeveloped mountain with a small, enthusiastic following. **Mount Abram** (also in the Bethel area) is a true family area with a strong ski school and some fine runs. **Shawnee Peak** in Bridgton is a medium-sized, family-geared area that offers night as well as day skiing. **Squaw Mountain** in Greenville and the **Camden Snow Bowl** in Camden are also medium-sized but satisfying. Locally geared ski hills include **Lost Valley** in Auburn, **Mount Jefferson** in Lee, **Titcomb Mountain** in Farmington, and **Eaton Mountain** in Skowhegan.

SNOWMOBILING
Maine has reciprocal agreements with nearly all states and provinces; for licensing and rules, contact the Department of Inland Fisheries and Wildlife (287-2043), 41 State House Station, Augusta 04330. The **Maine**

Snowmobile Association (MSA) (622-6983; www.mesnow.com), P.O. Box 77, Augusta 04332) represents over 280 clubs and maintains some 12,500 miles of an ever-expanding cross-state trail network. Aroostook County, given its reliable snow conditions, is a particularly popular destination, geared to handling visitors. In the Upper Kennebec Valley many white-water rafting companies now operate year-round (phone Sled Maine: 1-877-2SLED-ME). Jackman and the entire Moosehead and Rangeley Lake areas are snowmobiling meccas; for details contact the MSA. For maps and further information, write to the Snowmobile Program, Bureau of Parks and Lands, State House Station 22, Augusta 04333; MSA maintains a trail condition hotline: 626-5717.

SPA
Northern Pines in Raymond is the only fully developed spa program of which we are aware in Maine (see *Lodging—Rustic Resorts* in the "Sebago and Long Lakes Region").

SPORTING CAMPS
The Maine sporting camp is a distinctly Maine phenomenon that began appearing in the 1860s—a gathering of log cabins around a log lodge by a lake, frequently many miles from the nearest road. In the 19th century, access was usually via Rangeley or Greenville, where "sports" (urbanites who wanted to hunt wild game) would be met by a guide and paddled up lakes and rivers to a camp. With the advent of floatplanes, many of these camps became more accessible (see *Air Services*), and the proliferation of private logging roads has put most within reach of sturdy vehicles. True sporting camps still cater primarily to fishermen in spring and hunters in fall, but since August is neither hunting nor a prime fishing season, they are increasingly hosting families who just want to be in the woods by a lake in summer. True sporting camps (as opposed to "rental camps") include a central lodge in which guests are served all three meals; boats and guide service are available. The Maine Sporting Camp Association (P.O. Box 89, Jay 04239) publishes a truly fabulous map/guide to its more than 50 members. For every edition we do our best to get to as many sporting camps as possible but cannot do as thorough a job as the guide *In The Maine Woods: An Insider's Guide to Traditional Maine Sporting Camps* by Alice Arlen (The Countryman Press).

THEATER, SUMMER
The **Ogunquit Playhouse** (646-5511) is among the oldest and most prestigious summer theaters in the country, and the **Arundel Barn Playhouse** (985-5552) in Kennebunk is the newest. The **Hackmatack Playhouse** in Berwick (698-1807) and **Biddeford City Theater** (282-0849) are other Southern Coast options. In Portland note the **Portland Stage Company** (774-0465), and in Brunswick, the **Maine State Music Theater** and **Children's Theatre Program** on the Bowdoin campus (725-8769), and the **Theater Project** (729-8584). Farther along the coast, look for the **Camden Civic Theatre** based in the refurbished Opera House in Camden (236-4866), **The Belfast Maskers** in Belfast (338-4427), **Cold Comfort Summer Theatre** (326-8830) in Castine, the **Surry Opera Company** in Surry (667-2629), the **Acadia Repertory Theatre** (244-7260) in Somesville, **Down River Theater Company** (255-4997) in Machias, and the **Eastport Arts Center** (853-4133) in Eastport. Inland look for the **Theater at Monmouth** (933-2952), **Lakewood Theater** (474-7176) in Madison, **DeerTrees Theater** (583-6747) in Harrison, and **Celebration Barn Theater** (743-8452) in South Paris.

THEATER, YEAR-ROUND

Penobscot Theatre in Bangor offers a variety of winter productions (942-3333). Other companies are the **Performing Arts Center** in Bath (442-8455), the **Camden Civic Theatre** in Camden (236-4885), and the **Kennebec Performing Arts Center** in Gardiner (582-1325). **The Portland Stage Company** (774-1043) presents a series of productions at 25A Forest Avenue, Portland. The **Portland Players** (799-7337) present a winter season of productions, as does the **Maine Acting Company** (784-1616) in Lewiston. Most universities and colleges also offer performances throughout the school year.

WATERFALLS

The following are all easily accessible to families with small children: **Snow Falls Gorge** off Route 26 in West Paris offers a beautiful cascade (ask for directions at Perham's Gem Store); **Smalls Falls** on the Sandy River, off Route 4 between Rangeley and Phillips, has a picnic spot with a trail beside the falls; **Jewell Falls** is located in the Fore River Sanctuary in the heart of Portland; **Step Falls** is on Wight Brook in Newry off Route 26; and just up the road in Grafton Notch State Park is **Screw Auger Falls,** with its natural gorge. Another Screw Auger Falls is in Gulf Hagas (see *Gorges*), off the Appalachian Trail near the Katahdin Iron Works Road, north of Brownville Junction. **Kezar Falls,** on the Kezar River, is best reached via Lovell Road from Route 35 at North Waterford. An extensive list of "scenic waterfalls" is detailed in the *Maine Atlas and Gazetteer* (DeLorme). Check out 90-foot **Moxie Falls** at The Forks.

WEB SITES

The Internet is quickly becoming a prime source of information for many travelers. Some of the best sites we've found, with links to many attractions, activities, and information sites are: **www.maineguides.com** and **www.maineoutdoors.com,** great sources of information about outdoor recreation in Maine; **www.visitmaine.com,** the Maine Office of Tourism site; **www.mainetourism.com,** the Maine Tourism Association site; and **www.state.me.us,** the Maine State government site, with general information about the state, as well as information on the legislature and state agencies.

Within each chapter we limit our listings of web sites to regional and local chamber of commerce information sources and nonprofit organizations. These sites in turn provide links to dozens of lodgings and attractions.

WEDDINGS

At this writing no one conduit exists for information about the ever-increasing number of services (photographers, musicians, carriage operators, caterers, and florists, as well as inns and venues) geared to helping couples wed by Maine water. Several chambers of commerce, notably York, Kennebunkport, Boothbay, and Camden, are particularly helpful. Within the book we note properties that specialize in weddings. A Maine marriage license currently costs just $20.

WHALE-WATCHING

Each spring humpback, finback, and minke whales migrate to New England waters, where they remain until fall, cavorting, it sometimes seems, for the pleasure of excursion boats. One prime gathering spot is **Jeffrey's Ledge,** about 20 miles off Kennebunkport, and another is the **Bay of Fundy.** For listings of whale-watch cruises, see "The Kennebunks," "Portland Area," "Bar Harbor and Ellsworth," and "Washington County." The East Quoddy (Campobello) and West Quoddy (Lubec) lighthouses are also prime viewing spots.

WHITE-WATER RAFTING

White-water rafting is such a spring-through-fall phenomenon in Maine today that it's difficult to believe it only began in 1976, coincidentally the year of the last log drive on the Kennebec River. Logs were actually still hurtling through Kennebec Gorge on that day in the spring of 1976 when fishing guide Wayne Hockmeyer (and eight bear hunters from New Jersey he had talked into coming along) plunged through it in a rubber raft. At the time, Hockmeyer's rafting know-how stemmed solely from having seen *River of No Return,* in which Robert Mitchum steered Marilyn Monroe down the Salmon River. Needless to say, Hockmeyer's **Northern Outdoors** and the more than a dozen other major outfitters now positioned around the tiny village of The Forks, near the confluence of the Kennebec and Dead Rivers, are all well skilled in negotiating the rapids through nearby 12-mile-long Kennebec Gorge. Numbers on the river are now strictly limited, and rafts line up to take their turns riding the releases—which gush up to 8,000 cubic feet of water per second—from the Harris Hydroelectric Station above the gorge. Several rafting companies—notably **Northern Outdoors, New England Whitewater Center, Crab Apple White Water,** and **Unicorn Rafting Expeditions**—have fairly elaborate base facilities in and around The Forks, while **Wilderness Expeditions** offers facilities both there and at The Birches, a family-geared resort on nearby Moosehead Lake. Several outfitters—including **Northern Outdoors, Wilderness Expeditions, New England Whitewater Center,** and **Unicorn**—have established food and lodging facilities for patrons who want to raft the Penobscot near Baxter State Park. **Downeast Whitewater,** based on the Maine–New Hampshire border, rafts five different rivers. **Windfall Outdoor Center** is based at the luxurious Sky Lodge in Jackman. **Moxie Outdoor Adventures** is located at one of Maine's oldest sporting camps on pristine Lake Moxie. Some 80,000 rafters of all ages and abilities now raft in Maine each year. For information about most outfitters, contact Raft Maine: 1-800-723-8633; www.raftmaine.com.

WINDJAMMERS

In 1935 a young artist named Frank Swift fitted a few former fishing and cargo schooners to carry passengers around the islands of Penobscot Bay. At the time, there were plenty of these old vessels moored in every harbor and cove, casualties of progress. Swift called his business **Maine Windjammer Cruises,** and during the next two decades it grew to include more than a dozen vessels. Competitors also prospered through the 1950s, but the entire windjammer fleet almost faded away with the advent of rigorous Coast Guard licensing requirements in the '60s and the increased cost of building and rebuilding schooners. The '70s and '80s saw the rise of a new breed of windjammer captain. Almost every one of those now sailing has built or restored the vessel he or she commands. Members of the current Maine windjammer fleet range from the *Stephen Taber* and the *Lewis French,* both originally launched in 1871, to the *Heritage,* launched in 1983, to the *Kathryn B* (a luxury version of the others), launched in 1996.

Taber co-captain Ellen Barnes recalls her own joy upon first discovering the windjammers as a passenger: "No museums had gobbled up these vessels; no cities had purchased them to sit at piers as public-relations gimmicks. These vessels were the real thing, plying their trade as they had in the past with one exception: The present-day cargo was people instead of pulpwood, bricks, coal, limestone, and granite."

Windjammers offer a sense of what the Maine coast and islands are all about. Most sail with the tide on Monday mornings with no set itinerary; where they go depends on the wind and the tide. Clad in old jeans and sneakers, passengers help haul a line and then lounge around the decks, gradually succumbing to the luxury of steeping in life on the face of Penobscot Bay. As the wind and sun drop, the schooner eases into a harbor. Supper is hearty Yankee fare, maybe fish chowder and beef stew with plenty of fresh corn bread. Before or after supper, passengers can board the vessel's yawl for a foray into the nearest village or onto the nearest road (most landlubbers feel the need to walk a bit each day). By Wednesday, the days begin to blur. Cradled in a favorite corner of the deck, you sun and find yourself seeing more: flocks of cormorants and an occasional seal or minke whale, eagles circling over island nests. The sky itself seems closer, and you are mesmerized by the ever-changing surface of the sea.

© VANDERWHACKER

Choosing which vessel to sail on, in retrospect, turns out to be the most difficult part of a windjammer vacation. All have ship-to-shore radios and sophisticated radar, and some offer more in the way of creature comforts; some are known for their food or a captain with great jokes or songs. Within the "Rockport, Camden, and Lincolnville" chapter, we have described each vessel in the kind of detail we devote to individual inns. Windjammers accommodate between 12 and 44 passengers, and the cost of 3- to 6-day cruises ranges $300–700 (the *Kathryn B* charges $496–1,295). Excessive drinking is discouraged on all the vessels, and guests are invited to bring their musical instruments. Children under 14 are permitted only on some vessels. See the "Rockland" and "Rockport" chapters for details and toll-free numbers for the various vessels. Questions you might like to ask in making your reservation include the following: (1) What's the bunk arrangement? Double bunks and cabins for a family or group do exist. (2) What's the cabin ventilation? Some vessels offer cabins with portholes or windows that open. (3) What's the rule about children? On some vessels passengers must be at least 16, on others 10, but several schooners schedule special family cruises with activities geared to kids. (4) What's the extent of weatherproof common space? It varies widely. (5) Is smoking allowed? (6) Is there evening entertainment of any kind?

The **Maine Windjammers Association** (1-800-807-WIND; www.sailmainecoast.com) represents all the major windjammers, which claim to be "the largest fleet of merchant ships operating under sail in America."

WORKSHOPS
See *Camps, for Adults.*

I. SOUTHERN COAST

KIM GRANT

Nubble Light

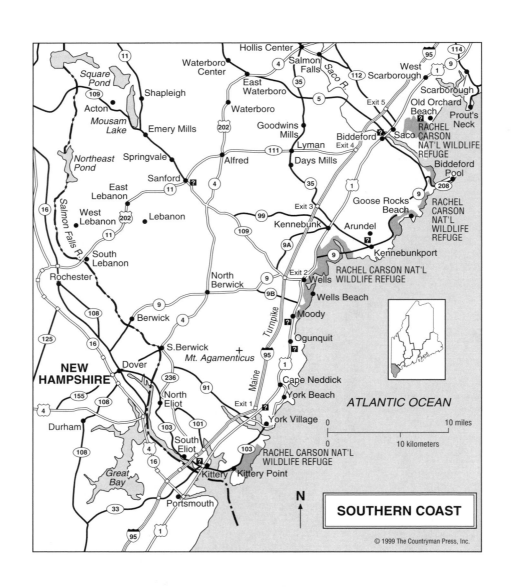

Square Pond

Mousam Lake

Northeast Pond

Salmon Falls R.

Shapleigh
Acton
Emery Mills
Springvale
Sanford
East Lebanon
West Lebanon
Lebanon
South Lebanon
Rochester
Berwick
S.Berwick
Mt. Agamenticus
Dover
North Eliot
Durham
South Eliot
Great Bay
Kittery
Kittery Point
Portsmouth

NEW HAMPSHIRE

Waterboro Center
East Waterboro
Waterboro
Goodwins Mills
Lyman
Alfred
Days Mills
North Berwick

Hollis Center
Salmon Falls
Saco R.
West Scarborough
Scarborough
Old Orchard Beach
Prout's Neck
RACHEL CARSON NAT'L WILDLIFE REFUGE
Biddeford
Saco
Exit 4
Exit 5
Biddeford Pool
Goose Rocks Beach
RACHEL CARSON NAT'L WILDLIFE REFUGE
Arundel
Exit 3
Kennebunk
Kennebunkport
RACHEL CARSON NAT'L WILDLIFE REFUGE
Wells
Wells Beach
Moody
Ogunquit
Cape Neddick
York Beach
York Village
Exit 1
RACHEL CARSON NAT'L WILDLIFE REFUGE
Exit 2
Turnpike
Maine

ATLANTIC OCEAN

0   10 miles
0   10 kilometers

N

SOUTHERN COAST

© 1999 The Countryman Press, Inc.

Southern Coast

The smell of pine needles and salt air, the taste of lobster and saltwater taffy, the shock of cold green waves, and, most of all, the promise of endless beach—this is the Maine that draws upward of half the state's visitors, those who never get beyond its Southern Coast. The southern Maine coast comprises just 35 miles of the state's 35,000 coastal miles but contains 90 percent of its sand.

Beyond their sand these resort towns—and the villages within them—differ deeply. York Village and Kittery are recognized as the oldest communities in Maine, Wells dates from the 1640s, and Kennebunkport was a shipbuilding center by the 1790s. All were transformed in the second half of the 19th century, an era when most Americans—not just the rich—began to take summer vacations, each in his or her own way.

Maine's Southern Coast was one of the country's first beach resort areas, and it catered—as it does today—to the full spectrum of vacationers, from blue-collar workers to millionaires. Before the Civil War, Old Orchard Beach rivaled Newport, Rhode Island, as the place to be seen; when the Grand Trunk Railroad to Montreal opened in 1854, it became the first American resort to attract a sizable number of Canadians.

While ocean tides are most extreme way Down East, the ebb and flow of tourist tides wash most dramatically over this stretch of Maine. Nowhere are the 1930s-era motor courts thicker along Route 1, now sandwiched between elaborate '90s condo-style complexes with indoor pools and elevators. Most of the big old summer hotels vanished by the 1950s, the era of the motor inns that now occupy their sites. But in the past few decades hundreds of former sea captains' homes and summer mansions have been transformed into small inns and bed & breakfasts, rounding out the lodging options. Luckily, the lay of the land—salt marsh, estuarine reserves, and other wetlands—largely limits commercial clutter.

GUIDANCE

The **Coalition of Southern Maine Chambers of Commerce** maintains a toll-free number that connects with each of the six chambers: 1-800-639-2442. Request the free booklet guide. Check the web site: www.southernmainecoast.com.

Kittery and the Yorks

The moment you cross the Piscataqua River you know you are in Maine. You have to go a long way Down East to find any deeper coves, finer lobster pounds, rockier ocean paths, or sandier beaches than those in Kittery and York.

Both towns claim to be Maine's oldest community. Technically Kittery wins, but York looks older . . . depending, of course, on which Kittery and which York you are talking about.

Kittery Point, an 18th-century settlement overlooking Portsmouth Harbor, boasts Maine's oldest church and some of the state's finest mansions. The village of Kittery itself, however, has been shattered by so many bridges and rotaries that it seems to exist only as a gateway, on one hand for workers at the Portsmouth Naval Shipyard and on the other for patrons of the outlet malls on Route 1. The Kittery Historical and Naval Museum is worth searching out, as are the dining, strolling, and swimming spots along coastal Route 103.

In the late 19th century, artists and literati gathered at Kittery Point. Novelist William Dean Howells, who summered here, became keenly interested in preserving the area's colonial-era buildings. He, his friend Sam Clemens (otherwise known as Mark Twain), and wealthy summer people began buying up the splendid old buildings in York, where the school, church, burial ground, and abundance of 1740s homes made up Maine's oldest surviving community.

In 1900 Howells suggested turning the "old gaol" in York Village into a museum. At the time, you could count the country's historic house museums on your fingers. In the Old Gaol of today, you learn about the village's bizarre history, including its origins as a Native American settlement called Agamenticus, one of many settlements wiped out by a plague in 1616. In 1630 it was settled by English colonists, and in 1642 it became Gorgeana, America's first chartered city. It was then demoted to the town of York, part of Massachusetts, in 1670. Fierce Native American raids followed, but by the middle of the 18th century the present colonial village was established, a crucial way station between Portsmouth and points east.

York is divided into so many distinct villages that Clemens once observed, "It is difficult to throw a brick . . . in any one direction without

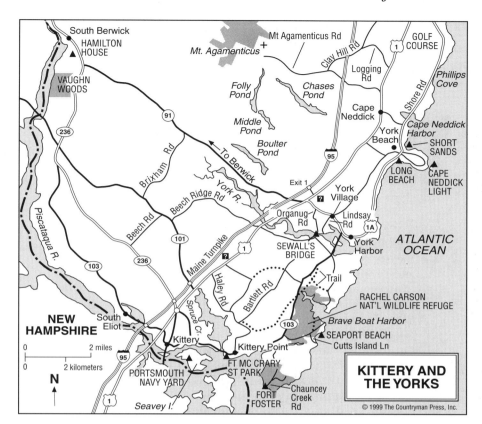

danger of disabling a postmaster." Not counting Scotland and York Corners, York includes York Village, York Harbor, York Beach, and Cape Neddick—such varied communities that locals can't bring themselves to speak of them as one town; they refer instead to "the Yorks."

The rocky shore beyond York Village was Lower Town until the Marshall House was opened near the small, gray sand beach in 1871 and its address was changed to York Harbor. Soon the hotel had 300 rooms, and other mammoth frame hotels appeared at intervals along the shore. All the old hotels are gone. All, that is, except the 162-room Cliff House, which, although physically in York, has long since changed its address and phone to Ogunquit, better known now as a resort town.

Still, York Harbor remains a delightful, low-key retreat. The Marshall House has been replaced by the modern Stage Neck Inn, and several dignified old summer "cottages" are now inns and B&Bs. A narrow, mile-or-so path along the shore was first traced by fishermen and later smoothed and graced with small touches such as the Wiggly Bridge, a graceful little suspension bridge across the river and through Steedman Woods.

Landscaping and public spaces were among the consuming interests of the 19th-century summer residents, who around the turn of the century also became interested in zoning. In *Trending into Maine* (1935), Kenneth Roberts noted York Harbor's "determination to be free of billboards, tourist camps, dance halls and other cheapening manifestations of the herd instinct and Vacationland civilization."

A York Harbor corporation was formed to impose its own taxes and keep out unwanted development. The corporation's biggest fight, wrote Roberts, was against the Libby Camps, a tent-and-trailer campground on the eastern edge of York Harbor that "had spread with such funguslike rapidity that York Harbor was in danger of being almost completely swamped by young ladies in shorts, young men in soiled undershirts, and fat ladies in knickerbockers."

Libby's Oceanside Camp still sits on Roaring Rock Point, its trailers neatly angled along the shore. Across from it is matching Camp Eaton, established in 1923. No other village boundary within a New England town remains more clearly defined than this one between York Harbor and York Beach.

Beyond the campgrounds stretches 2-mile Long Sands Beach, lined with a simpler breed of summer cottage than anything in York Village or York Harbor. There is a real charm to the strip and to the village of York Beach, with its Victorian-style shops, boardwalk amusements, and the Goldenrod—known for its taffy Goldenrod Kisses. This restaurant is still owned by the same family that opened it in 1896, about the time the electric streetcar put York Beach within reach of the "working class."

During this "trolley era," a half-dozen big hotels accommodated 3,000 summer visitors, and 2,000 more patronized boardinghouses in York Beach. Today's lodgings are a mix of motels, cottages, and B&Bs. There are beaches (with free or metered parking), Fun-O-Rama games and bowling, and York's Wild Kingdom, with exotic animals and carnival rides. York Beach, too, has now gained "historic" status, and the Old York Historical Society, keeper of the half-dozen colonial-era buildings open to the public in York Village, now sponsors York Beach walking tours.

GUIDANCE

The **Kittery Information Center** (439-1319), Maine's gatehouse in a real sense, is on I-95 northbound in Kittery, with exhibits on Maine regions and products and a desk staffed by Maine Tourism Association employees, who dispense advice on local as well as statewide lodging, dining, and attractions. You can also check out regional web sites and lodging by computer. Open daily except Christmas and Thanksgiving, 8–6 in summer months, otherwise 9–5 (bathrooms open 24 hours daily). We usually stop by the center for information and a weather update (press a button outside the men's room to get a full report). The rest area also includes vending machines and picnic tables under the pines. The **Kittery-Eliot Chamber of Commerce** (439-7545; 1-800-639-9645), upstairs over the Weathervane Restaurant, Route 1. Phone queries answered 10–2 weekdays, year-round. Office open 9–5 weekdays; stocked with local brochures.

York Chamber of Commerce (363-4422; via the Southern Maine link, 1-800-639-2442; www.yorkme.org), P.O. Box 417, York 03909. On Route 1 just off exit 4 (York), a handsome information center modeled on a Victorian summer "cottage" is open daily year-round, 9–5 (later on Friday and Saturday) in summer, shorter hours off-season.

GETTING THERE

Trailways (1-800-639-3317) serves Portsmouth, New Hampshire, some 12 miles south. **Little Brook Airport** in Eliot serves private and charter planes. **York Taxi** (363-7007) picks up everywhere.

GETTING AROUND

From late June through Labor Day, 10 AM–8 PM, an **open-sided trolley** links York Village, Harbor, and Beach with Cape Neddick and Route 1. Narrated tours are offered every hour. For details, check with the chambers of commerce (see *Guidance*). A trolley also serves the Kittery outlets during peak periods and York Taxi (see above) operates 24 hours.

MEDICAL EMERGENCY

York Hospital 24-Hour Emergency Services (363-4321), Lindsay Road, York Village.

TO SEE

In Kittery

Kittery Historical and Naval Museum (439-3080), Route 1, just north of the Route 236 rotary. Open weekdays June through October, 10–4. $3 adults, $1.50 ages 7–15; senior, family, and group rates. A fine little museum filled with ship models, naval relics from the Portsmouth Naval Shipyard, and exhibits about the early history of this stretch of the Southern Coast. Displays include archaeological finds, ship models, early shipbuilding tools, navigational instruments, trade documents, and mariner's folk art, including samples of work by Kittery master ship's carver John Haley Bellamy (1836–1914).

Portsmouth Naval Shipyard (open 1 day a week and by appointment: 439-7140), sited on several islands and a lot of landfill in the Piscaqataqua River, which divides Maine and New Hampshire, was, until the advent of the outlets, what Kittery (from which it is accessed) was all about. Established in 1806, it was the site of the treaty ending the Russo-Japanese War in 1905 and was responsible for building half of all American submarines during World War II. Today the navy yard remains an important submarine maintenance point. The PNS Command Museum has exhibits from the yard's past.

Fort McClary, Route 103. A state park open seasonally (grounds accessible year-round). A hexagonal, 1846 blockhouse on a granite base, it was the site of fortifications in 1715, 1776, and 1808. The site was first

The Wiggly Bridge suspension bridge in York.

fortified in the early 18th century to protect Massachusetts's vessels from being taxed by the New Hampshire colony. This is a good place to picnic, overlooking Portsmouth Harbor, but the formal picnicking area is across the road.

For **Fort Foster,** see *Green Space.*

For **Hamilton House,** the **Sarah Orne Jewett Birthplace,** and **Kittery Point,** see *Scenic Drives.*

In York

Old York (363-4974; www.historicalsocietyoldyork.org). The nonprofit Old York Historical Society maintains seven historic buildings, open to the public from mid-June through mid-October, Tuesday through Saturday 10–5, Sunday 1–5; $6 adults, $2.50 children includes admission to all buildings. The society also sponsors walking tours and special events and offers a local historical research library and archives in its headquarters, a former bank building at 207 York Street in the middle of York Village. Begin your tour at the **Jefferds Tavern Visitors Center,** Route 1A, a 1759 building moved from Wells in 1939. Watch the orientation video for Old York and purchase tickets to other museum buildings and tours. Exhibits change, and food is frequently cooking on the hearth at the tavern kitchen. The **Old School House** next door, an original, mid-18th-century York school, contains an exhibit on education of the period. **Old Gaol** (Jail), York Village center. Dating from 1719 and billed as the oldest remaining public building of the English colonies, it once served the whole province of Maine and continued to house York County prisoners until 1860. You can inspect the cells and jailer's quarters and learn about York's early miscreants. **Emerson-Wilcox House,** Route 1A. Dating in part from 1742 and expanded over the years, period rooms and gallery space trace the development of domestic interiors and decorative arts in York from the Revolutionary period to the 1930s. Exhibits include furniture, ceramics, glass, and a complete set of bed hangings embroidered by Mary Bulman in 1745. **Elizabeth Perkins House,** Lindsay Road (at Sewall Bridge—a replica of the first pile bridge in America, built on this spot in 1761). Our favorite building, this 1730 farmhouse is down by the York River. It is still filled with colonial-era antiques and with the spirit of the real powerhouse behind York's original Historic Landmarks Society. It was Miss Perkins who saved the Jefferds Tavern. She's buried under the simple plaque that's in a boulder at the edge of the lawn overlooking the river. **John Hancock Warehouse and Wharf,** Lindsay Road. An 18th-century warehouse with exhibits of 18th-century life and industry on and around the York River. **George Marshall Store** (a former chandlery at which large schooners once docked), 140 Lindsay Road, houses changing exhibits. **First Parish Church,** York Village. An outstanding, mid-18th-century meetinghouse with a fine old cemetery full of old stones with death's heads and Old English spelling. **Civil War Monument,** York Village. Look closely at the monument in the middle of the village—the soldier is wearing a rebel uniform. The statue commissioned for York stands in a South Carolina town because the sculptor made a mistake. At the time, both towns agreed that freight rates were too high to make the switch, a consensus that continues to prevail every time a swap is seriously considered.

In York Harbor and York Beach

Sayward-Wheeler House (603-436-3205), 79 Barrell Lane, York Harbor. Open June through October 15, weekends 11–4; tours on the hour. $4 adults, $3.50 seniors, $2 children 12 and under. Maintained by the Society for the Preservation of New England Antiquities (SPNEA). A fine, early-18th-century house built by Jonathan Sayward—merchant, ship owner, judge, and representative to the Massachusetts General Court—who earned the respect of the community despite his Tory leanings. It remained in the same family for 200 years and retains its Queen Anne and Chippendale furnishings, family portraits, and china brought back as booty from the expedition against the French at Louisburg in 1745. It overlooks the river and is accessible from York's Shore Path, near the Wiggly Bridge (see *Green Space—Walks*).

Nubble Light, York Beach. From Shore Road, take Nubble Road out through the Nubble (a cottage-covered peninsula) to Sohier Park at the tip of the peninsula. It includes a parking area, rest rooms, and a seasonal information center and overlooks an 1879 lighthouse perched on a small island of its own.

& **York's Wild Kingdom** (363-4911; 1-800-456-4911), York Beach. Rides open daily at noon, Memorial Day weekend through Labor Day weekend (weekends only in June and September); zoo is open 10–5. This is a combination amusement area and zoo with paddleboats, midway rides,

and over 200 animals including some real exotica. There are also miniature golf and both pony and elephant rides. It's $13 adults, $9.75 children 4–10, and $3.50 for 3 and under for zoo/ride admission. Zoo only: $10 adults, $7.75 children; $1 ages 3 and under.

SCENIC DRIVES

Kittery Point, Pepperrell Cove, and Gerrish Island. From Route 1, find your way to Route 103 (see map) and follow its twists and turns along the harbor until you come to the white First Congregational Church and a small green across from a striking, privately owned Georgian-style house. An old graveyard overlooking the harbor completes the scene. Park at the church (built in 1730, Maine's oldest), notice the parsonage (1729), and walk across the road to the old graveyard. The neighboring, magnificent house was built in 1760 for the widow of Sir William Pepperrell, the French and Indian War hero who captured the fortress at Louisburg from the French. Knighted for his feat, Pepperrell went on to become the richest man in New England. For a splendid view of the harbor, continue along Route 103 to Fort McClary, and for the same view combined with good food, stop up the road at Cap'n Simeon's Galley (see *Dining Out*) in Pepperrell Cove, where everyone seems to be named Frisbee. It's hidden behind **Frisbees Market,** in business since 1828, claiming to be America's oldest family-run grocery store (also known for its handmade corned beef). Four large hotels once clustered in this corner of Kittery, but today it's one of the quietest along the Southern Coast. You sense layerings of history here. At the back of the parking lot across from Frisbee's a seemingly forgotten tomb is inscribed with a plaque commemorating Colonel William Pepperrell, born in Devonshire in 1646, died in Kittery in 1754 (did he really live to be 108?), and Sir William Pepperrell (1696–1759). Just beyond you can still see the foundations of one of the former summer hotels. Turn right beyond Pepperrell Cove and follow Gerrish Island Lane to a T; then take Pocahantas (the name of another vanished hotel) to World War I–era **Fort Foster**, now a park (see *Green Space*). Also see **Chauncey Creek Lobster Pound** (under *Lobster*) and **Seapoint Beach** (under *Green Space*). Route 103 winds on by the mouth of the York River and into York Harbor.

South Berwick. A short ride north of the Route 1 outlets and clutter transports you to a bend in the Salmon Falls River that is capped by a splendid, 1780s Georgian mansion, restored through the efforts of local author Sarah Orne Jewett; a formal garden and riverside trails through the woods add to the unusual appeal of this place. From Kittery, take either Route 236 north from the I-95 Eliot exit or Route 101 north from Route 1 (through high farmland to join Route 236). From York, take Route 91 north. Hamilton House and **Vaughan Woods** are the first left after the junction of Routes 236 and 91 (Brattle Street); follow signs. **Hamilton House** (384-5269) is open June through October 15,

Wednesday through Sunday 11–4, with tours on the hour ($4 adults, $3.50 seniors, $2 children 12 and under); grounds open every day dawn to dusk, Sunday-afternoon garden concerts in-season. The foursquare Georgian mansion built in 1785 on a promontory above the river had fallen into disrepair by the time Sarah Orne Jewett was growing up in nearby South Berwick; she used it as the setting for her novel *The Tory Lover,* and persuaded wealthy friends to restore it in 1898 (the same period that William Dean Howells was involved in restoring nearby York Village). The SPNEA also maintains the **Sarah Orne Jewett House** (384-5269) farther up Route 236, smack in the middle of the village of South Berwick at the junction with Route 4. This is another fine 1774 Georgian house that has been preserved to look much as the author knew it. She actually grew up in the house next door, now the town library. Joint ticket to the two houses is $6.

TO DO

BOAT EXCURSIONS

Lobstering trips (call between 5 and 6 PM: 363-3234), Town Dock #2, York Harbor. When he's not teaching science at the local school, Tom Farnum offers 1-hour lobstering trips around York Harbor in his 22-foot, wooden lobster skiff. $6.50 per person.

Isles of Shoals Steamship Co. (603-431-5000) in Portsmouth, New Hampshire, offers daily cruises in-season to the Isles of Shoals, stopping at Star Island, site of a vast old white summer hotel that's now a Unitarian conference center. Visitors are welcome to this barren but fascinating place, webbed with walking trials. The ride on the 90-foot replica of an old steamboat takes 1 hour each way.

Also see "Ogunquit and Wells" for excursions from Perkins Cove.

FISHING

Check with the **York Chamber of Commerce** (see *Guidance*) about the half-dozen deep-sea-fishing boats operating from York Harbor. Surf casting is also popular along Long Sands and Short Sands beaches and from Sohier Park in York. The **York Parks & Recreation Department** (363-1040) offers a 4-week introduction to fly-fishing. **Elredge Bros. Fly Shop** (363-2004), Meadowbrook Mall, Route 1, York (just north of the Turnpike exit 1), open Monday through Saturday. Billed as Maine's largest supplier of fly-fishing equipment, the shop offers casting classes, guided trips.

FRIGHTS

Ghostly Tours (363-000), 250 York Street (Route 1A) next to Rick's Restaurant. Late June through Halloween, Monday through Saturday, candlelight tours through Old York Village guided by a hooded ghost-tale teller. $5 per person.

York Beach

KIM GRANT

GOLF
York Corner Golf (363-5439), Route 1, York. Nine holes, par 3.

Highland Farm Golf Club (351-2727), Route 91. Driving range, putting green, 9-hole course.

The Ledges Golf Club (351-3000), off Route 91, York. Opened with 9 holes in 1998, 18 holes promised for 1999. Carts, pro shop, favored by local residents.

HORSEBACK RIDING
Mount Agamenticus Riding Stables (361-2840), summit of Mount Agamenticus (turn off Route 1 at Flo's Hot Dogs). Open daily late June through Labor Day, 8–8: 1-hour trail rides, extended rides, corral rides, private lessons.

KAYAKING
Harbor Adventures (363-8466) in York Harbor offers guided tours.

York Recreation Department (363-1040) offers rentals, guided tours, and a 6-week-long summer program.

MOUNTAIN BIKING
The **Mount Agamenticus base lodge** is a source of rental bikes to use on the mountain's trails. For details, call 363-1040.

SCUBA DIVING
York Beach Scuba (363-3330), Railroad Avenue, York Beach. Guided dives around Nubble Light, boat dives, rental equipment, and instruction are all offered.

SUMMER YOUTH PROGRAM
York Parks & Recreation Department (363-1040) offers summer baseball, basketball, mountain biking, and dance programs for younger children and teens. The office is in Recreation Hall, Church Street, York Beach.

GREEN SPACE

BEACHES
In Kittery

Seapoint Beach, Kittery, is long with silky soft sand. Parking is residents-only right at the sand, but there's limited public parking 0.5 mile back up Curtis Island Lane (off Route 103).

✎ **Fort Foster**, Gerrish Island (see *Parks*) is shallow a long way out, and also has low-tide tidal pools with crabs and snails.

Long Sands is a 2-mile expanse of coarse, gray sand stretching from York Harbor to the Nubble, backed by Route 1A and summer cottages, great for walking. Metered parking the length of the beach and a bathhouse midway. Lifeguard in high season.

✎ **Short Sands** is a shorter stretch of coarse, gray sand with a parking lot (meters), toilets, and a fenced-in playground. At low tide look for starfish, snails, and crabs. The Victorian-era village of York Beach is just behind it.

York Harbor Beach is small and pebbly, but pleasant. Very limited parking.

✎ **Cape Neddick Beach,** Shore Road just east of Route 1A, is smallest of all, at the river's mouth, sheltered, and a good choice for children.

PARKS

Fort Foster Park. Beyond Pepperrell Cove, look for Gerrish Island Lane and turn right at the T onto Pocahontas Road, which leads, eventually, to this 92-acre town park. The World War I fortifications are ugly, but there is a choice of small beaches with different exposures, one very popular with windsurfers, also extensive walking trails and picnic facilities. Fee.

Piscataqua River Boat Basin (439-1813), Main Street, Eliot. Open May to October. Boat launch, picnic area, beach, rest rooms.

Mount Agamenticus (363-1040), open weekdays 8:30–4:30. Just 580 feet high but billed as the highest hill on the Atlantic seaboard between York and Florida. A defunct ski area now owned by the town of York, it can be reached by an access road from Mountain Road off Route 1 (turn at Flo's Hot Dogs; see *Eating Out*). The summit is cluttered by radio and TV towers, but the view is sweeping. Rocks mark the grave of St. Aspinquid, a Native American medicine man who died at age 94 in 1682; according to the plaque, 6,723 wild animals were sacrificed here at the wise man's funeral. See *To Do* for details about mountain biking and horseback riding. Inquire about the pleasant trail to the summit.

Vaughan Woods, South Berwick. A 250-acre preserve on the banks of the Salmon Falls River; picnic facilities and nature trails. The first cows in Maine are said to have been landed here at Cow Cove in 1634. See directions under *Scenic Drives.*

Sohier Park, Route 1A, York. See Nubble Light under *To See.* A popular picnic and scuba diving spot.

Goodrich Park. A good picnic spot on the banks of the York River, accessible from Route 1 South; look for the entrance just before the bridge.

Mason Park. Route 1A, York Harbor. adjoining Harbor Beach. Created in 1998 when several classic York Harbor cottages were destroyed in accordance with the wills of their former owners. Another possible picnic spot.

WALKS

Shore Path, York Harbor. For more than a mile you can pick your way along the town's most pleasant piece of shorefront. Begin at the George Marshall Store (see *To See*) and walk east along the river and through the shady Steedman Woods. Go across the Wiggly Bridge (a mini-suspension bridge), then continue across Route 103, past the Sayward House, along the harbor, down the beach, and along the top of the rocks. Route 103 cuts through the middle of this walk, offering convenient access in either direction.

Brave Boat Harbor Trail. One of the few walkable segments in the 10-part Rachel Carson National Wildlife Refuge: a 2-mile trail begins at the pullout on Brave Boat Harbor Road off Route 103. It offers a little history and a lot of birds.

LODGING

Note: York Beach offers many **summer cottage rentals,** and rentals can also be found elsewhere in town. Check with the **York Chamber of Commerce** (see *Guidance*) for individual rentals as well as reliable realtors.

In Kittery, Eliot, and South Berwick

The Inn at Portsmouth Harbor (439-4040), 6 Water Street, Kittery 03904. Open year-round. Terry and Kim O'Mahoney bought what was called, until fall of 1998, Gundalow Inn. The 1890s brick village house just off the Kittery green is across the road from the Piscataqua River, within walking distance (across the bridge) from downtown Portsmouth, New Hampshire. Common rooms now feature English antiques and Victorian watercolors and the six guest rooms are carefully, imaginatively furnished; all have private baths (some with claw-foot tubs), phones with data ports, and cable TV. $85–135 includes a full breakfast. No smoking.

High Meadows Bed & Breakfast (439-0590), Route 101, Eliot 03903. Technically in Eliot, this pleasant retreat is really just a few miles off Route 1. Open April through October. A 1736 house with four nicely furnished rooms, all with private bath. Our favorite is what we call the sea chest room. Common space includes a comfortable common room with a woodstove and a formal living room with a fireplace; a wicker-furnished porch overlooks landscaped grounds. Walking trails lead through the surrounding 30 acres. No children under 12. Rooms are $80–90, less off-season, a full breakfast and afternoon snack included.

The Moses Paul Inn (439-1861; 1-800-552-6058), 270 Goodwin Road (Route 101), Eliot 03903. Open year-round. Just 5.5 miles from Kittery's outlets, this red 1780 house has an away-from-it-all feel. Your hosts are Joanne Weiss, an interpreter for the deaf, and her husband, Larry James, a merchant marine. Larry goes to sea for three-month stints and when he comes home not only helps make beds and breakfast but routinely adds a bathroom, maybe a room or two. Interestingly, this is one of only two Maine B&Bs we know of that preserve the old tradition of a wife taking in guests while her husband is away at sea, and both houses have ghosts (ask about Henri). There are presently two attractive downstairs guest rooms with private baths, and three upstairs, one (the Admiral's Room) with a private bath and two that share. A new suite, the product of Larry's last shore time, has an open-faced woodstove, a sitting room, and a full bath with claw-foot tub. The low-beamed original living room with its fireplace is complemented by the sunny new dining/relaxing space in a new addition off the open kitchen, overlooking a mowed meadow. $90 for private, $80 for shared bath; $120 for the suite, less off-season.

The Academy Street Inn (384-5633), 15 Academy Street, South Berwick 03908. A 1903 mansion just off the main drag in an attractive village, handy to the Piscataqua River, the Sarah Orne Jewett Birthplace, and Hamilton House (see *Scenic Drives*). Paul and Lee Fopeano offer five spacious guest rooms (private baths); a full breakfast is served at the dining room table. There's plenty of space for relaxing—a large porch as well as parlor. $60–75.

INNS

In York Village and York Harbor

Dockside Guest Quarters (363-2868; 1-800-270-1977), P.O. Box 205, Harris Island Road, York 03909. Open daily May through October, weekends the rest of the year. Two generations of the Lusty family imbue this fine little hideaway with a warmth that few inns this size possess. Situated on a peninsula in York Harbor, it offers splendid views, especially from the porch of the gracious, 19th-century Maine House, which is the centerpiece of a 7-acre compound that includes four newer, multi-unit cottages, and the **Dockside Restaurant** (see *Dining Out*). In all there are 26 guest rooms—including several with gas fireplaces and six apartment/suites with kitchenettes—all with private decks and water views. Breakfast is served buffet-style in the Maine House. It's a nominally priced, "continental plus" (fruit compote, baked goods, etc.), muffins-and-juice breakfast, laid out on the dining room table—a morning gathering place for guests who check the blackboard weather forecast and plan their day. Guests can use the house fishing equipment and bicycles, rowing skiff or Boston whaler, or take advantage of regularly scheduled harbor and river cruises. Special lodging and cruise packages are offered June through October. Two-night minimum stay during July and August. $69–174 in high season, $65–125 off-season.

Stage Neck Inn (363-3850; 1-800-222-3238), York Harbor 03911. Open year-round. An attractive 1970s complex of 58 rooms built on the site of the 19th-century Marshall House. Located on its own peninsula, the inn offers water views (by request), a formal dining room (see *Dining Out*), a less formal **Sandpiper Grille,** tennis courts, an outdoor pool, a small indoor pool, and a Jacuzzi. The lobby, sitting room, and main dining room are formal; a frequent conference site. $110–245 per room in-season; no meals included.

    York Harbor Inn (363-5119; 1-800-343-3869), P.O. Box 573, York Street Route 1A), York Harbor 03911. Open year-round. The inn's water views were enhanced in 1998 when the fine old cottages across the road were demolished (through no fault of the Dominquez family who own the inn) to form a park. The beamed lobby is said to have been built in 1637 on the Isles of Shoals. An exclusive men's club in the 19th century, this is now a popular dining spot (see *Dining Out*), and the **Wine Cellar Pub Grill**, with an elaborately carved bar, is a local gathering place. The 33 rooms all have private baths and air-conditioning, several in the old house have working fireplaces, some in the newer, neighboring Yorkshire House have Jacuzzis and sitting areas, and most have water views. $99–195 double, continental breakfast included; the neighboring **Harbor Cliffs Inn,** a private residence until 1997, is now another adjunct to the inn proper but one with its own elegant common rooms and several suites, the most luxurious accessed by a spiral staircase and walled-in windows overlooking the harbor (there's also a balcony) as well as a gas fireplace and whirlpool bath. $159–229 including continental breakfast. Inquire about the many special packages.

BED & BREAKFASTS
In York Harbor 03911

    Inn at Harmon Park (363-2031), P.O. Box 495. Open year-round. A shingled 1899 Victorian in the middle of the village of York Harbor, within walking distance of the beach and Shore Path, this B&B has been Sue Antal's home for more than 25 years. It's attractive and airy, with a comfortable living room with a fireplace and front porch with rockers, but guests tend to gather in the kitchen (you discover it on your way in from the parking lot), where Sue can usually be found, happy to dispense suggestions for exploring the immediate area. The four guest rooms vary, from the small Celia Thaxter in the back with its water view (nice if you are alone) to the suite with working fireplace (nice if you aren't). All are bright and thoughtfully furnished in wicker, antiques, and beds dressed with antique quilts. All have private baths, also radios, small TVs and VCRs (for Sue's library of Maine videos). Room diaries are filled with thanks to the innkeeper for her unusual hospitality. She is, incidentally, a justice of the peace and knows all the most beautiful spots (indoors and out) to arrange weddings in the area. $79–109 includes a full, healthy breakfast, maybe baked eggs with lemon cream scones or mushroom crustless quiche, served at small tables on the sunporch. Less off-season.

Edwards' Harborside Inn (363-3037), P.O. Box 866. Open year-round. Nicely sited across from York Harbor Beach with a long wharf of its own, this solidly built summer mansion is owned by Jay Edwards, a third-generation innkeeper. Breakfast is served in one of the most pleasant rooms in the area: a sunporch with an unbeatable view of the harbor. You can enjoy the vista all day from a lawn chair. Many of the 10 guest rooms (8 with private baths) also have water views and all are air-conditioned and have TVs; the York Suite is a lulu, with water views on three sides and a Jacuzzi overlooking the water, too. Rooms $90–120 and suites from $210 in July and August, $70–190 in shoulder months, $50–160 in winter.

Tanglewood Hall (363-7577), 611 York Street, P.O. Box 12. Open June through mid-October. This shingled 1880s summer mansion was a summer home of bandleader Tommy Dorsey and his brother Jimmy. Set in gardens and woods, it was professionally decorated in 1994 as a show house to benefit the local historical society. The York Harbor Suite ($130) has a fireplace and conservatory, but we liked the Winslow Homer Room best (Homer is said to have been a guest; $95); all three rooms have private baths; the octagonal game/music room and many-windowed dining room are also special.

🏵 **Bell Buoy** (363-7264), 570 York Street (Route 1A). Open year-round. Wes and Kathie Cook have restored a spacious 19th-century summer "cottage," offering plenty of common space, rooms with private baths, and a two-room suite. $70–85 in-season includes a full breakfast in the dining room or, weather permitting, on the large porch. No view but within walking distance of Long Sands Beach (a real plus, given the challenge of parking). Off-season: $60–75.

In York Beach 03910

🏵 **The Katahdin Inn** (363-1824; in winter, 617-938-0335), 11 Ocean Avenue Extension. Open mid-May through October. "Bed and beach" is the way innkeeper Rae LeBlanc describes her pumpkin-colored 1890s guesthouse overlooking Short Sands Beach and the ocean. Eight of the 11 guest rooms have water views. Number 9 on the third floor is small and white with a window and a skylight that seem to suspend it above the water. All rooms have a small fridge. More water views from the living room and two porches (one enclosed), which are equipped with games for poor weather. From $75 (shared bath) to $95 for a large room, private bath; less off-season. No breakfast but morning tea and coffee.

♿ **View Point** (363-2661), 229 Nubble Road, P.O. Box 1980. Office open daily in summer, selected days off-season. A nicely designed, oceanfront, condominium-style complex overlooking the Nubble Lighthouse. All 9 suites have a living room, kitchen, porch or patio, gas fireplace, phone, cable TV, CD stereo, VCR, washer/dryer. $200 for one-bedroom to $320 for three-bedroom units in-season; less in winter. Weekly rates available.

✔ **The Anchorage Inn** (363-5112), Route 1A, Long Beach Avenue. A total of 178 motel-style rooms, most with water views across from Long Sands Beach. For families, this is a good choice; facilities include indoor and outdoor pools, rooms that sleep four, TV, small fridge. $109–154 per room in high season, $195–240 for spa suites; much less off-season; inquire about packages.

Cape Neddick 03902

Cape Neddick House (363-2500), 1300 Route 1, Box 70. Open year-round. Although it is right on Route 1, this Victorian house (in the Goodwin family for more than 100 years) offers an away-from-it-all feel and genuine hospitality. There are five guest rooms with private baths, one suite with a working fireplace, all furnished with antiques. Breakfast is an event—maybe strawberry scones and ham with apple biscuits—served on the back deck (overlooking garden and woods), in the dining room, or in the homey kitchen. A six-course dinner—from stuffed mushrooms to raspberry cheesecake, all cooked on the 80-year-old Glenwood woodstove—can be reserved in advance. $70–120 double, depending on room and season.

CAMPGROUND

✔ **Dixon's Campground** (363-2131), 1740 Route 1. A long-established campground with 100 sites on 40 acres, many wooded tent sites as well as more open sites for small RVs. Playground, camp store, and shuttle bus. No pets.

WHERE TO EAT

DINING OUT

Cape Neddick Inn and Gallery (363-2899), Route 1, Cape Neddick. Open year-round for dinner and Sunday brunch; closed Monday and Tuesday from Columbus Day to mid-June. A combination art gallery and restaurant that's been York's leading restaurant since it opened in 1979 and was totally revamped by owner Glenn Gobeille and chef Michele Duval in 1998. White linen tablecloths and napkins set the tone and a pianist plays 5 nights a week. The menu is large and varied. Entrées might include wasabi and sesame-crusted halibut ($14) and ginger- and juniper-marinated duck braised in a sweet and tart gooseberry sauce with a summer melon and Bermuda onion salad ($17). The desserts are spectacular. Reservations suggested.

The York Harbor Inn (363-5119), Route 1A, York Harbor. Open year-round for lunch and dinner, also Sunday brunch. Four pleasant dining rooms, most with views of water. The menu is large. The seafood chowder is studded with shrimp, scallops, crabmeat, and haddock ($4.95 a cup); milk-fed veal and fresh seafood are the specialties. Dinner entrées might include Yorkshire lobster supreme (lobster stuffed with scallop and shrimp filling, $25.95), veal Swiss (sautéed with shallots, mushrooms, and a demi-glace with Swiss cheese, $19.95), and pesto-baked scallops ($19.95). Sunday brunch is big. The wine selection is large. There is also an inviting **Wine Cellar Pub Grill** with a menu running to burgers, soups, sandwiches, and salads.

* **Dockside Restaurant** (363-2722), off Route 103, York Harbor. Open for lunch and dinner late May through Columbus Day except Monday. Reservations suggested for dinner. Docking as well as parking. The view of York Harbor from Phil and Anne Lusty's glass-walled dining room and screened porch is hard to beat. Understandably the decor is nautical and the menu features seafood: at lunch, fish-and-chips, also chicken potpie or a smoked turkey BLT; at dinner, bouillabaisse (including half a lobster), lobster, scrod, and more; roast stuffed duckling is also a house specialty. Children get a "Dockside Vacation" coloring book to use while waiting. Dinner entrées $12.95–19.95.

Harbor Porches (363-3850), Stage Neck Road, York Harbor. Open year-round for breakfast, lunch, and dinner. The gilded-era decor harkens back to the glory days of the Marshall House, a grand hotel that occupied this site for many decades, and the glass walls overlook the open ocean. This isn't the place to eat lobster (see *Lobster*) but it's always on the menu, along with a choice of seafood and standbys like grilled New York sirloin. Entrées begin at $18.95.

Cap'n Simeon's Galley (439-3655), Route 103, Pepperrell Cove. Open year-round for lunch and dinner and Sunday brunch; closed Tuesdays mid-October to Memorial Day. A special place with a fabulous water view. You enter through the original Frisbee Store (the building is said to date back to 1680; the store opened in 1828) to a spacious dining area with picture windows overlooking the cove and beyond to Portsmouth Harbor. Seafood is the specialty, but you can get anything from a grilled cheese sandwich ($2.75) to a New York choice sirloin steak ($13.50). Try the broiled scallops or fisherman's seafood platter (all seafood is fried in 100 percent vegetable oil).

Fazio's (363-7019), 38 Woodbridge Road, York Village. Open daily for dinner from 4 PM. This popular trattoria is decorated with original murals and photos of Annette Fazio's mother. The menu is traditional— fettuccine carbonara (pancetta, cheese, cream, cracked pepper, and egg) and chicken Francese (white wine and lemon sauce served with cheese pasta); also interesting daily specials. The pasta is made daily. Patrons would not complain at twice the price. Entrées $10.50–15.95. Children's menu. **La Stalla Pizzeria**, part of the family, is a source of good pizzas, also subs and salads, from 11 AM.

Mimmo's (363-3807), Route 1A, Long Sands, York Beach. Open for breakfast and dinner June through September and for dinner only the rest of the year, closed on Christmas and Thanksgiving. Named for its colorful chef Mimmo Basileo, this trattoria is a hot spot in summer (reservations necessary). Tables are closely packed, the water view is limited to the front dining room, and the menu ranges from eggplant parmigiana through a variety of pastas to seafood "coastazurro" (mussels, shrimp, haddock, and calamari sautéed with garlic). Entrées $15.95–17.95; BYOB.

Note: Also see **Clay Hill Farm** under *Dining Out* in "Ogunquit and Wells." One of the region's finest restaurants, it's accessed from Route 1 in York.

LOBSTER

The Lobster Barn (363-4721), Route 1, York. Open year-round for lunch and dinner. A pubby, informal, popular dining room with wooden booths and a full menu. Specialties such as scallop and shrimp pie earn this place top marks from locals. In summer, lobster dinners (in the rough) are served under a tent out back. Lobster is priced daily.

Chauncey Creek Lobster Pound (439-1030), Chauncey Creek Road, Kittery Point. Open during summer only. Lobster in rolls and in the rough; steamed clams and mussels are the specialty. There is also a raw bar. An average lobster dinner with steamers is exceptionally reasonably priced, but don't expect any extras. The locals bring their own salad, bread, and wine. The setting is great, but service can be slow.

Cape Neddick Lobster Pound (363-5471), Route 1A (Shore Road), Cape Neddick. Open March through November for lunch and dinner. Situated at the mouth of a tidal river, this attractive modern building with dining inside and out (on a deck) has the look of having always been there. Besides lobster and clams, the menu offers a wide choice of everything from pasta and sandwiches, soups and salads, to filet mignon and bouillabaisse. Dinner entrées from $12.95. Fully licensed.

Warren's Lobster House (439-1630), 1 Water Street, Kittery. Open year-round; lunch, dinner, and Sunday brunch; docking facilities. A rambling, low-ceilinged, knotty-pine dining room overlooking the Piscataqua River and Portsmouth, New Hampshire, beyond. An old dining landmark with 1940s decor. The salad bar features over 50 selections (a meal in itself), and the specialty is "Lobster, Lobster, and More Lobster" (priced daily). The menu is, however, large and varied with several beef dishes and plenty of seafood; baked stuffed sole is just $10.50.

Fox's Lobster House (363-2643), Nubble Point, York Beach. Open daily in-season 11:45–9. A large, tourist-geared place with a water view and a menu ranging from hot dogs ($3.50) to lobster any number of ways from plain old boiled ($12.95) to deep-fried lobster tails ($18.95).

York Beach Fish Market (363-2763), Route 1A, York Beach. Billed and generally agreed to be the best lobster rolls in York Beach. Eat in the new booths or walk to the beach to enjoy. Crab rolls, chowder, hot dogs and more also served.

EATING OUT

The Goldenrod (363-2621), York Beach. Open Memorial Day through Columbus Day for breakfast, lunch, and dinner. In business since 1896, one of the best family restaurants in New England; same menu all day

8 AM–10:30 PM, but lunch and dinner specials, served up at time-polished, wooden tables in the big dining room with a fieldstone fireplace as well as at the old-style soda fountain. Famous Goldenrod Kisses (saltwater taffy) are cooked and pulled in the windows. A wide selection of homemade ice creams and yogurts, good sandwiches (cream cheese and olive or nuts is still $1.95).

Frankie & Johnny's (363-1909), 15494 Route 1, Cape Neddick. Open at 5 PM July and August, Wednesday through Monday; open Thursday through Sunday in spring and fall. Weekend reservations recommended. Behind the pre-fab exterior is one of the best vegetarian restaurants (even vegans will be happy) along the Maine coast. But it's also more. You can start with tofu sushi ($6.25) or Asian vegetable soup ($3.75) and move on to a vegetable tostada Napoleon ($12.75) or a "crustoli" (a house original, like French-bread-crust pizzas with endless combinations of toppings and in two sizes). Or you might begin with Cajun crab cakes ($5.75) and dine on Mama Thea's lemon chicken and dill pasta ($16.75) or ostrich du jour ($18.75). The pasta, spaetzle, breads, soups, and sauces are all made from scratch. Tables are lit with small candles and walls are hung with owner Frank Rostad's sister's bold, bright paintings ranging from abstract to ostrich (or are they camel?) faces. Obviously this is the kind of place you really have to experience for yourself. BYOB.

Lunch Break (363-6039), Route 1 South, York. Open Monday through Saturday year-round, 7 AM–3:30 PM. No credit cards. Easy to miss because it's in a house set back from the road, this pleasant little restaurant offers good taste in both senses. We lunched well on chowder and half a BLT (with provolone), listened to patrons chatting with chef-owner Cathy Cole, and eyed the delectable-looking tortilla salad at the next table. In summer, dining includes tables on the deck.

Cap'n Simeon's Galley (see *Dining Out*) is also the best bet in Kittery for a fried scallop roll or burger at lunch.

Flo's Hot Dogs, Route 1. Open only 11–3 and not a minute later. The steamers are just $1.50 but that doesn't explain the long lines, and it's not Flo that draws the crowds because Flo sold it to Gail. This is just a great place. It's even fun to stand in line here. Request the special sauce.

Bob's Clam Hut (439-4233), Route 1, Kittery. Open year-round. The best fried clams on the strip. Here since 1956 and now, finally, with indoor seating.

Rick's All Seasons Restaurant (363-5584), 240 R York Street, York Village. Open daily from 4 AM for breakfast until 2:30 PM weekdays, closing earlier on weekends, for dinner only Wednesday and Thursday until 8 PM. Prices are unbeatable and specialties include omelets, quiche, and a range of side orders like corned beef hash and hot apple pie with cheese. Rick Ciampa has been operating this town gossip center since 1980.

Village Cafe (363-7801), 226 York Street, middle of York Village. Open year-round for breakfast and lunch, weekends for dinner. Across the street and brighter, smoke-free, and more of a restaurant, this is a pleasant alternative to Rick's. We wish current owner Lee Kouskoutis the best of luck. Try the Greek omelet or Greek-style chicken.

Sun of a Beach Outdoor Cafe and Take-out (363-8345) is a good bet for Mexican.

SNACKS

Brown's Ice Cream (363-4077), Nubble Road, a quarter-mile beyond the lighthouse, York Beach. Seasonal. All ice cream is made on the premises. Exotic flavors, generous portions.

Pie in the Sky Bakery (363-2656), Route 1, Cape Neddick, York Beach. Open Monday through Saturday except January; hours vary off-season. The purple house at the corner of River Road is filled with delicious smells and irresistible muffins, pies, tortes, and breads, all baked here by John and Nancy Stern.

Also see the **Goldenrod** under *Eating Out* for Goldenrod Kisses (saltwater taffy) and ice cream.

ENTERTAINMENT

Ogunquit Playhouse (see *To See* in "Ogunquit and Wells") is the nearest and most famous summer theater.

Hackmatack Playhouse (698-1807), in Berwick, presents summer-stock performances most evenings; Thursday matinees.

Seacoast Repertory Theatre (603-433-4472; 1-800-639-7650), 125 Bow Street, Portsmouth, New Hampshire. Professional theater productions.

York Beach Cinema (363-2074), 6 Beach Street, York. First-run movies.

SELECTIVE SHOPPING

ANTIQUES

A half dozen antiques dealers are spotted along Route 1 between the **Olde Stuff Shop** (early country furniture, garden accessories, and glass) in York and **Columbary Antiques** (group shop) in Cape Neddick. Stop in one and pick up the leaflet guide to the couple of dozen member shops between York and Arundel.

At the Sign of the Goose (363-5627), Route 1, Cape Neddick, is in a class of its own, a mix of fine antiques and new furniture, fine arts, and fabrics, operated by Jerry Rippletoe and Tony Sienicki, who established their reputation as interior decorators during years of operating the adjacent Wooden Goose Inn.

ART GALLERIES

York Art Association Gallery (363-4049/2918), Route 1A, York Harbor. Annual July art show, films, and workshops.

Shooting Star Gallery (439-6397), 74 Wallkinfrod Square, downtown Kittery. Just off Route 103. This contemporary gallery, featuring fine art but also handcrafted jewelry, glass, wearable art, and more, is a good excuse to pause in Kittery's elusive old downtown.

CRAFTS AND ANTIQUES

York Village Crafts (363-4830), 211 York Street, York Village. Open daily 9–5. Housed in the vintage 1834 church in the center of York Village, more than 100 displays of crafts, art, books, and antiques.

River Place (351-3266), 250 York Street, York Village, features fine crafted pottery, prints, ceramics, and jewelry, also books, cards, and games.

SPECIAL STORES

Stonewall Kitchen (352-2713; 1-800-207-JAMS), York Corners, Route 1. What began as a display of offbeat vinegars at a local farmer's market in 1991 is now a more than $48 million business with a big wholesale and mail-order component. Owners Jonathan King and Jim Stott are quick to claim, however, that all their products—from roasted garlic and onion red pepper jelly or raspberry peach champagne jam through sun-dried tomato mustard to fresh lemon curd and dozens of vinegars, chutneys, barbecue sauces, and specially packaged children's jelly—are still made with homemade care and concern. You can see—and sample—them all in the shop attached to this roadside corporate headquarters; a more elaborate "Farmhouse Corporate Headquarters" is due to open beside the York Chamber of Commerce late in 1999.

Whiffletree Furniture (363-8624), 244 York Street, York Village. Open Tuesday through Saturday, 3–5. Father and son Ron and Jeff Fortin make and sell a full line of traditional and contemporary-style furniture and furnishings.

Gravestone Artwear (1-800-564-4310), 250 York Street, York Village. This departure point for Ghostly Tours (see *To Do*) is a trove of ghostly and graveyard-related products, from carvings to cards, T-shirts, and more.

Rocky Mountain Quilts (363-6800; 1-800-762-5940), 130 York Street (Route 1A), York Village. Open May through October daily 10–5, call off-season. Betsey Telford not only makes and restores quilts but sells antique quilts, blocks, and fabrics from the late 1700s to the 1940s (more than 300 in stock, "from doll to king"); also decorating accessories.

The Museum Shop, 196 York Street (Route 1A), York Village. Open May to December, Tuesday through Saturday 10–5, Sunday 1–5. The museum shop for the **Old York Historical Society**.

YORK OUTLET MALLS

Note: For the Kittery shopping strip, take I-95, exit 3. At this writing, the 120 discount stores within a 1.3-mile strip of Route 1 in Kittery represent a mix of clothing, household furnishings, gifts, and basics. All purport to offer savings of at least 20 percent on retail prices, many up to 70 percent. Open daily, year-round; hours vary; call 439-7545. The **Kittery Trading Post** (439-2700) is the original anchor store of this strip. A local institution since 1926, the sprawling store is always jammed with shoppers in search of sportswear, shoes, children's clothing, firearms, outdoors books, and fishing or camping gear. The summer-end sales are legendary, and many items are routinely discounted. The strip is divided into a series of malls, among them the **Maine Outlet Mall**, with more than 32 shops, including Banister Shoe, the Children's Outlet, and Dress Barn. **Tidewater Outlet Mall** is a small but quality shopping center, worth the stop for Lenox China and Boston Traders. In the **Kittery Outlet Center** you'll find Royal Doulton, Van Heusen, and Le Sportsac. Eddie Bauer, Benetton, Brooks Brothers, Corning Revere, Polo/Ralph Lauren, Gap, Dexter Shoe, and Bass Shoe are also here.

WINERY

The Parsons Family Winery (363-3332), Brixham Road, York. Open Monday through Saturday 10–5; Sunday noon–5. From Route 1 in York take Route 91; go 4.8 miles, turn left onto Brixham Road, and look for the big white farmhouse that's now an apple winery. The winery also sells locally crafted products, but this place is all about the orchards that once covered this landscape for miles around and the wine that one family (farming in this spot for 280 years), began producing in 1996. Tours and tastings are offered. Four apple varietals are made at this writing, along with blueberry, peach, pear, and raspberry wines, not to mention old-fashioned hard cider ("like what Grandad made, only smoother"). Visitors are welcome and will learn about local history; you need not buy wine.

SPECIAL EVENTS

Note: Be sure to pick up the area's unusually lively "Summer Social Calendar" at the York Chamber of Commerce (see *Guidance*).

June: **Strawberry Festival,** South Berwick.

July: **Independence Day celebrations,** in York—parades, cannon salutes, militia encampment, crafts and food fair, picnic, and dinner; Kittery—**Seaside Festival** at Fort Foster's Park. **Band concerts,** Wednesday evenings at Short Sands Pavilion, York Beach. **Old York Designers' Show House** sponsored by the Old York Historical Society. **York Days Celebration** (*last days of month, see August*)—raffle, puppet shows, skits.

August: **York Days Celebration** (*beginning of the month*)—flower show, church supper, concerts, square dances, parade, and sand castle contest. **Seacoast Crafts Fair** (*late in the month*).

September: **House Tours. Eliot Festival Days** (*late September*).

October: **Harvest Fest,** York Village (*third weekend*)—an ox roast, ox-cart races, hay- and horse rides, militia encampment, music, and live entertainment.

December: **Christmas Open House Tours. Kittery Christmas Parade and Tree Lighting** and **York Festival of Lights Parade,** first weekend in December.

Ogunquit and Wells

Ogunquit and Wells share many miles of uninterrupted sand, and the line between the two towns also blurs along Route 1, a stretch of restaurants, family attractions, and family-geared lodging places. The two beach resorts are, however, very different.

Named for the English cathedral town, Wells was incorporated in 1653 and remains a year-round community with summer cottages, condo complexes, and campgrounds strung along the beach and Route 1—parallel strips separated by a mile-wide swatch of salt marsh. Wells is a resort for families, the place to find a reasonably priced weekly rental.

Ogunquit was part of Wells until 1980 but seceded in spirit long before that, establishing itself as summer resort in the 1880s and a magnet for artists in the 1890s. It remains a compact, walk-around resort village clustered between its magnificent beach and picturesque Perkins Cove; these two venues are connected by the mile-long Marginal Way, an exceptional shore path. The village offers a vintage movie house and the Ogunquit Playhouse, one of New England's most famous summer theaters. Most of Ogunquit's big old wooden hotels were razed during the 1960s and replaced by luxury motels. With the 1980s came condos, B&Bs, more restaurants, and boutiques. Luckily, it also brought trolleys-on-wheels to ease the traffic crunch at Perkins Cove and the beach.

Natural beauty remains surprisingly accessible in both Ogunquit and Wells. Given the vast expanse of sand, you can always find an uncrowded spot, and Wells harbors more than 4,000 acres of conservation land, much of it webbed with trails (see *Nature Preserves*).

On weekends a tidal wave of day-tripping Bostonians spreads over the beach and eddies through Perkins Cove, but it recedes on Sunday evenings. Both Ogunquit and Wells are relatively peaceful midweek in summer and especially delightful in September and October.

GUIDANCE

Ogunquit Chamber of Commerce (646-2939; 1-800-639-2442), Route 1, just south of Ogunquit Village. Open weekdays 9–5 year-round with offices in the town information center (646-5533); May through October, volunteers supplement chamber staff and keep the center

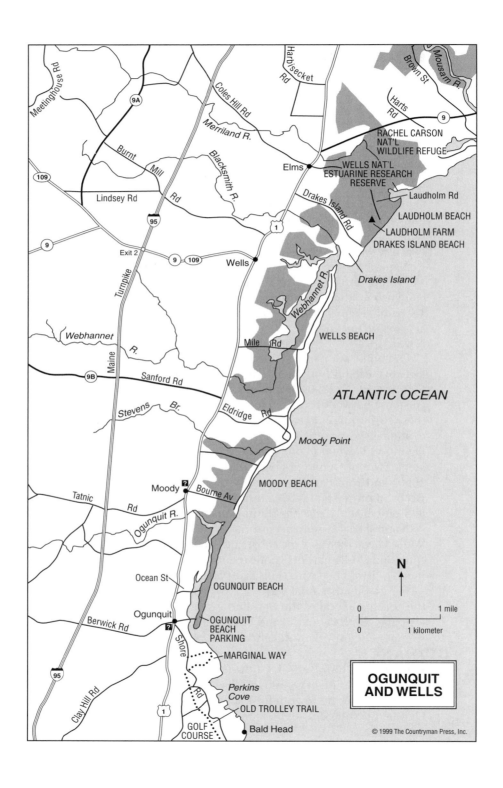

Meetinghouse Rd

9A

Coles Hill Rd

Harb'secket Rd

Brown St

Mousam R.

Merriland R.

Burnt

Mill

Harts Rd

9

RACHEL CARSON NAT'L WILDLIFE REFUGE

109

Blacksmith R.

Elms

WELLS NAT'L ESTUARINE RESEARCH RESERVE

Lindsey Rd

Rd

Drakes Island Rd

Laudholm Rd

LAUDHOLM BEACH

95

LAUDHOLM FARM

9

Exit 2

9   109

Wells

DRAKES ISLAND BEACH

1

Drakes Island

Webhannet

R.

Webhannet R.

WELLS BEACH

Maine

Mile   Rd

9B

Sanford Rd

ATLANTIC OCEAN

Turnpike

Stevens   Br.

Eldridge   Rd

Moody Point

Tatnic

Rd

Moody

Bourne Av

MOODY BEACH

Ogunquit R.

N

Ocean St

OGUNQUIT BEACH

0   1 mile

Berwick Rd

Ogunquit

OGUNQUIT BEACH PARKING

0   1 kilometer

95

Shore

MARGINAL WAY

Clay Hill Rd

Rd

Perkins Cove

1

OLD TROLLEY TRAIL

OGUNQUIT AND WELLS

GOLF COURSE

Bald Head

© 1999 The Countryman Press, Inc.

open weekends and until 8 PM Friday and Saturday. It's stocked with pamphlets and offers rest rooms.

Wells Chamber of Commerce (646-2451; 1-800-639-2442), 136 Post Road (Route 1, northbound side) in Moody. Open daily Memorial Day through Columbus Day, 9–5, weekdays the rest of the year.

GETTING THERE

By car: Coming north on I-95, take exit 1 (York) and drive up Route 1 to the village of Ogunquit. Coming south on I-95, take exit 2 (Wells).

By train: **AMTRAK** service from Boston was promised for 1996, then '97, then '98; now it's fall of 1999. Stay tuned.

Brewster's Taxi (646-2141), billed as serving Ogunquit since 1898, offers local and long-distance service.

GETTING AROUND

Seasonal **open-sided trolleys** make frequent stops throughout the village of Ogunquit, Perkins Cove, at the beach, and along Route 1. They connect with the trolleys that circulate up and down Route 1 and through the beach and lodging areas in Wells. Fare is nominal. Trolley maps are available from the chambers of commerce.

PARKING

Park and walk or take the trolley. In summer this is no place to drive. There are at least seven public lots; rates are $4–6 per day. There is also free parking (2-hour limit) on Route 1 across from the Leavitt Theatre just north of Ogunquit Square or adjacent to Cumberland Farms. Parking at the main entrance to Ogunquit Beach itself is pricey. (For more on beach parking, see *Beaches.*) In Wells, parking at the five public lots is $7 per day; monthly permits are available from the town office.

MEDICAL EMERGENCY

Ambulance/Rescue Squad (646-5111), town of Ogunquit.

York Hospital (363-4321), 24-hour emergency, 15 Hospital Drive, York Village. For ambulance service in Ogunquit phone the fire department: 646-5111.

Wells Ambulance (646-9911). In Wells, you may be nearer to **Southern Maine Medical Center** (283-3663), 1 Mountain Road, Biddeford.

TO SEE

Perkins Cove. This is probably Maine's most painted fishing cove, with some 40 restaurants and shops now housed in weathered fish shacks. It is the departure point for the area's excursion and fishing boats, based beside the famous draw-footbridge. Parking is nearly impossible in summer, but public lots are nearby, and the trolley stops here regularly. The cove can also be reached on foot via the Marginal Way (see *Walks*).

Ogunquit Museum of American Art (646-4909), Shore Road, Ogunquit (0.4 mile west of Perkins Cove). Open July through September (closed

Labor Day), 10:30–5 daily, Sunday 2–5; $4 adults, $3 seniors, free under 12. Built superbly of local stone and wood with enough glass to let
in the beauty of the cove it faces, the museum displays selected paintings from its permanent collection, which includes the strong, bright
oils of Henry Strater and other one-time locals such as Reginald Marsh;
also Thomas Hart Benton, Marsden Hartley, Edward Hopper, Rockwell
Kent, and William and Marguerite Zorach. Special exhibitions feature
nationally recognized artists.

Museum at Historic First Meeting House (646-4755), Route 1, Wells
(opposite Wells Plaza). Open for tours June through October, Tuesday,
Wednesday and Thursday (varying hours), otherwise Wednesday and
Thursday 1–4 and by appointment. The Wells-Ogunquit Historical society displays old photos, memorabilia, ship's models, and such. Nominal admission.

✐ **Wells Auto Museum** (646-9064), Wells. Open daily mid-June to mid-
September, 10–5. More than 70 cars dating from 1900 to 1963, including
a 1919 Stutz Bearcat and a 1941 Packard convertible, plus nickelodeons,
toys, and bicycles. Rides in antique cars are offered.

TO DO

BICYCLING
Wheels & Waves (646-5775), 578 Post Road (Route 1), Wells, offers rentals.
BOAT EXCURSIONS
From Perkins Cove
Finestkind (646-5227). Scenic cruises to Nubble Light, cocktail cruises, and
"lobstering trips" (watch lobster traps hauled, hear about lobstering).
Ugly Anne (646-7202). Half- and full-day, deep-sea-fishing trips with
Captain Ken Young Sr. ***The Bunny Clark*** (646-2214). Half- and full-
day, deep-sea-fishing trips with Captain Tim Tower. ***Deborah Ann*** (361-
9501), Perkins Cove, offers whale-watching cruises.

FISHING FROM SHORE
Tackle and bait can be rented at Wells Harbor. The obvious fishing spots
are the municipal dock and harbor jetties. There is surf casting near
the mouth of the Mousam River. Also see "Kittery and the Yorks" and
"The Kennebunks."
GOLF
Merriland Farm (464-5008), 545 Coles Hill Road off Route 1. Nine-hole,
par-3 course on a working farm. Also a café serving Memorial Day week-
end to early fall, 8–4 (see *Special Shops*).
MINI-GOLF
✐ **Wells Beach Mini-Golf,** next to Big Daddy's Ice Cream, Route 1, Wells.
Open daily in-season 10–10.
✐ **Wonder Mountain,** Route 1, Wells. A mini-golf mountain, complete with
waterfalls; adjoins **Outdoor World.**
Sea-Vu Mini Golf is another Route 1 option in Wells.

Marginal Way in Ogunquit

TENNIS

Three public courts in Ogunquit. Inquire at **Dunaway Center** (646-9361).
Wells Recreation Area, Route 9A, Wells. Four courts.

THEATER

Ogunquit Playhouse (646-5511), Route 1 (just south of Ogunquit Village). Open late June through August. Billing itself as "America's Foremost Summer Theater," this grand old summer-stock theater (now air-conditioned) opened for its first season in 1933 and continues to feature top stars in productions staged Monday through Saturday at 8 PM; matinees are Wednesday and Thursday at 2:30. Usually we describe summer stock under *Entertainment* near the end of a chapter, but in this case a visit to the Playhouse is a must-do.

GREEN SPACE

BEACHES

Three-mile-long **Ogunquit Beach** offers surf, soft sand, and space for kite flying, as well as a sheltered strip along the mouth of the Ogunquit River for toddlers. It can be approached three ways: (1) The most popular way is from the foot of Beach Street. There are boardwalk snacks, changing facilities, and toilets, and it is here that the beach forms a tongue between the ocean and the Ogunquit River (parking in the lot here is $2 per hour in-season). (2) The Footbridge Beach access (take Ocean Street off Route 1 north of the village) offers rest rooms and is less crowded. (3) Eldridge Street, Wells. Be sure to park in the lot provided. Walk west onto Ogunquit Beach, not to Moody Beach, now private above the high-water mark.

Wells Beach. Limited free parking right in the middle of the village of Wells Beach, also parking at the east end by the jetty. Wooden casino and boardwalk, clam shacks, clean public toilets, a cluster of motels, concrete benches—a gathering point for older people who sit while enjoying the view of the wide, smooth beach.

Drakes Island. Take Drakes Island Road off Route 1. There are three small parking areas on this spit of land lined with private cottages.

NATURE PRESERVES

Wells National Estuarine Research Reserve at Laudholm Farm (646-1555), Laudholm Road (off Route 1, just south of junction with Route 9; look for the sign between the Lighthouse Depot and the Maine Diner), managed by the Laudholm Trust. The reserve consists of 1,600 acres of estuarine habitat for the area's wildlife. "Estuarine," by the way, describes an area formed where ocean tides meet freshwater currents (an estuary). The reserve is divided into two parts, each with its own access point. Grounds include meadows and two barrier beaches at the mouth of the Little River and Laudholm Farm, a former estate that began as a saltwater farm in the 1620s. Owned by the Lord family from 1881 until 1986 (George C. Lord was president of the Boston & Maine Railroad), it was farmed until the 1950s. The farm itself now includes a visitors center (open Monday through Saturday 10–4, Sunday noon–4) with a slide show, exhibits, rest rooms, and parking ($2 in July and August). Seven miles of trails meander through fields, woods, and wetlands (bring a bathing suit if you want to swim at the beach). The Laudholm Trust grounds are open year-round (gates open daily 8–5), and guided trail walks are offered daily (10:30 AM) in summer, weekends in spring and fall. This is a birder's mecca. Inquire about Laudholm Farm Day (last Saturday in July) and Laudholm Nature Crafts Festival on the weekend after Labor Day.

Rachel Carson National Wildlife Refuge (operated by the US Fish and Wildlife Service), off Route 9 on the Wells-Kennebunk line. See description under *Green Space* in "The Kennebunks."

WALKS

Marginal Way. In 1923 Josiah Chase gave Ogunquit this windy path along the ocean. A farmer from the town of York just south of here, Chase had driven his cattle around rocky Israel's Head each summer to pasture on the marsh grass in Wells, just to the north. Over the years, he bought land here and there until, eventually, he owned the whole promontory. He then sold off sea-view lots at a tidy profit and donated the actual ocean frontage to the town, thus preserving his own right-of-way. There is very limited parking at the mini-lighthouse on Israel's Head.

✎ **Wells Harbor.** Here is a pleasant walk along a granite jetty and a good fishing spot. There is also a playground and gazebo where concerts are held.

Old Trolley Trail. An interesting nature walk and cross-country ski trail; begins on Pine Hill Road North, Ogunquit.

Mount Agamenticus is a defunct ski area and the highest hill on the Atlantic between Florida and Bar Harbor. Take the Big A access road off Agamenticus Road, Ogunquit. See "Kittery and the Yorks" for details and information about horseback riding and mountain bike rentals there.

LODGING

Note: Room rates drop more precipitously here the day after Labor Day than any other place we know in Maine, a factor to consider because September is such a pleasant month here, usually still warm enough for beaching and far less crowded than August.

All listings are for Ogunquit 03907 unless otherwise indicated.

RESORT

&. **The Cliff House** (361-1000), P.O. Box 2274. Open late March to mid-December. The tower-topped, mansard-roofed Cliffscape Building, opened in 1990, is now the centerpiece of this 162-room, 70-acre resort. The new building's multitiered lobby and dining rooms make the most of the oceanside roost atop Bald Head Cliff, and the atmosphere is a blend of new amenities (including an indoor lap pool) and family antiques. Innkeeper Kathryn Weare is a great-granddaughter of Elsie Jane Weare, the indomitable lady who opened The Cliff House in 1872.

The family-run resort continued to maintain its status through the Roaring Twenties and shaky 1930s, but World War II about did it in. The resort was literally drafted—as a radar station, keeping a 24-hour vigil for Nazi submarines. When the Weares were finally permitted back on their property, they found it a shambles. Discouraged, Charles Weare placed an ad in a 1946 edition of the *Wall Street Journal:* "For sale. 144 rooms. 90 acres, over 2,500 feet ocean frontage for just $50,000."

There were no takers. Charles turned the property over to his son Maurice, who went with the times, shaving off the top two floors and transforming it into a "resort motel"—which is what it was until 1990. High-season summer rates range from $160 for a motel-like unit with a limited view to $230 for a one-bedroom suite; off-season rates run $125–195. These prices do not include meals, but a variety of packages bring the rack rate way down. Facilities include outdoor and indoor pools, a sauna and Jacuzzi, an exercise room, a game room, tennis courts, and a summertime trolley into the village and to the beach.

RESORT MOTOR INNS

Our usual format places inns before motels, but in the 1960s, some of Ogunquit's leading resorts replaced their old hotel buildings with luxury "motor inns."

&. **Sparhawk** (646-5562), Shore Road, Box 936. Open mid-April to late October. The 50 prime units in this complex, each with a balcony, overlook the entrance to the Ogunquit River and the length of Ogunquit

Beach. The 20 units in neighboring Ireland House (with balconies canted toward the beach) are combination living room/bedroom suites, and the Barbara Dean, a spacious old village house, has seven suites and three apartments. The Sparhawk Apartment, a three-room house with fireplace and private deck overlooking the ocean, is rented by the week. Guests register and gather in Sparhawk Hall; a continental breakfast is served here, and there are books and comfortable spaces to read and to study local menus. Recreation options include a pool, shuffleboard, croquet, and tennis. One-week minimum stay, June 30 to mid-August; $150–175 in high summer, $75–90 in spring and fall.

✒️&. **Aspinquid** (646-7072), Box 2408, Beach Street. Open mid-March through mid-October. A picture of the old Aspinquid hangs above the check-in counter of this condo-style complex just across the bridge from Ogunquit Beach. Built in 1971 by the owners of the old hotel, the two-story clusters still look modern. They are nicely designed and range in size from motel units to two-room apartments; all have two double beds, phones, and TVs; most have kitchenettes. Facilities include a pool, a lighted tennis court, a sauna, a spa, and a fish pond with waterfall ideal for peaceful reading and relaxation. Rates vary with the season: $60–130 for a motel room, $55–140 for an efficiency unit, $80–205 for an apartment.

INNS AND HOTELS

✒️ **Beachmere** (646-2021; 1-800-336-3983), Box 2340. Open late March to mid-December. Sited on the Marginal Way with water views, this complex consists of an expansive mansion and a two-story motel-style annex angled in such a way as not to detract from the main house and so that almost all units have water views; there are also rooms in Mayfair and Bullfrog cottages a half-mile away on Israel's Head Road. All rooms have kitchenettes and cable TV and most have private balconies, decks, or terraces; many are large enough to accommodate families. In the mansion no two rooms are alike and three have working fireplaces. Common space is limited to one small room but the large, inviting grounds overlook Ogunquit Beach, and smaller beaches are a few minutes' walk. High-season rates: $120–295, drop in shoulder seasons to $80–190 and after Columbus Day and before May 15 to $60–125.

🏵 **The Grand Hotel** (646-1231), 102 Shore Drive. Open mid-April through November. An attractive three-floor, 28-suite hotel across the road from the shore but with water views from upper floors. Outfall from the 1980s real estate boom, this was built as a condominium complex, but it makes a great small hotel. All suites are two rooms, with wet bar, fridge, color cable TV, and private sun deck or balcony; fireplaces on the top floor. There's an elevator, an interior atrium, and an indoor pool. $150–200 in high season, much less in winter.

&. **The Colonial** (646-5191; 1-800-233-5191), 61 Shore Road, P.O. Box 895. Open April 16 through October 18. This 80-room complex, owned for many years by Chet and Sheila Sawtelle, includes a four-story 1887 summer hotel, the last of more than a dozen similar hotels that once lined this mile of shore (the last that's still operating as a hotel). It's an inviting, informal place with a large old-fashioned lobby filled with flower-patterned sofas and armchairs (too bad the breakfast room features a soda machine). The guest rooms we checked are pleasant, some with ocean views, ranging $79–99 in July and August, $42–55 right after Labor Day. Also depending on the season, a studio apartment is $45–125, and two-room family suites (with efficiency unit) run $50–149. Four separate two-room apartments in the Guesthouse are $90–150. All rooms have private baths, air-conditioning, and direct-dial phones. Only some upstairs rooms in the hotel have sea views but the location is good, steps from the Marginal Way and midway between the village and Perkins Cove.

BED & BREAKFASTS

The Trellis House (646-7909; 1-800-681-7909), 2 Beachmere Place, P.O. Box 2229. Open year-round. This is a find. Pat and Jerry Houlihan's shingled, turn-of-the-century summer cottage offers appealing common areas, including a wraparound screened porch (where breakfast is served in nice weather) and comfortable seating around the hearth. Upstairs are three guest rooms, all with full private baths, one with a water view. The most romantic room is a cottage in the garden but the four rooms in the carriage house also have a squirreled-away feel; we prefer the upstairs to the downstairs rooms there; all rooms have air-conditioning. This is one of those places that guests—whether they come alone or in couples—mingle without stiffness. The Houlihans are genuine hosts. $100–210 in-season, from $75 off-season, includes a breakfast (served anytime between 8:30 and 10) that might include a fruit compote and zucchini pie, or maybe apple-cinnamon French toast and sausage. The inn is handy both to the village and to Perkins Cove via the Marginal Way.

Marginal Way House and Motel (646-8801; 363-6566 in winter), Box 697, 8 Wharf Lane. Open late April through October. Ed and Brenda Blake have owned this delightful complex since 1968. Just a short walk from the beach and really in the middle of the village, it is hidden down a back, waterside lane. There are old-fashioned guest rooms with private baths in the inn itself, and six standard motel rooms in a small, shingled, waterside building, as well as seven efficiency apartments (one or two bedrooms). The landscaped grounds have an ocean view. $42–110 per room off-season; $86–175; apartments are rented only by the week in high season.

Morning Dove (646-3891), P.O. Box 1940, 30 Bourne Lane. Open year-round. On a quiet side street off Shore Road, within walking distance of everything, is this carefully restored 1860s farmhouse. We like the feel of the living room with its white marble fireplace, and of the seven nicely decorated guest rooms (five with private bath); the innkeepers are Jane and Fred Garland. $60–125 (depending on season) per room includes breakfast.

Ye Olde Perkins Place (361-1119), 749 Shore Road (south of Perkins Cove), Cape Neddick 03902. Open late June through Labor Day. Overlooking the ocean, this 1717 homestead has six rooms, three in a more modern annex. Away from the village but within walking distance of Perkins Cove and right above a pebble beach in a pretty cove. $60–70 per room; coffee, juice, and muffins included. No credit cards.

Above Tide Inn (646-7454), 26 Beach Street. Open May 15 through October 15. Location! Location! Sited right at the start of the Marginal Way and steps from the footbridge leading over to Ogunquit Beach, also steps from village shops and jutting right out into the water. The nine rooms are all shaped differently, totally filling the small house. All but one room have water views and everyone shares access to the big deck, where a continental breakfast is served. Rooms are brightly, simply, tastefully furnished and all have a small fridge, TV, and shower or bath. Mid-July thorough Labor Day rates begin at $115, at $85 in mid-September and at $65 before and after that.

The Pine Hill Inn (361-1004), P.O. Box 2336. Open mid-May to mid-October. A Victorian summer house set in a rock garden, high above a quiet residential road but within walking distance of Perkins Cove. Walls throughout the house are all tongue-and-groove paneling, the five guest rooms have private baths, and the large living room and screened-in porch offer plenty of inviting common space. Frank and Lou-Ann Agnelli are your hosts. Children over age 12, please; younger children allowed in the neighboring two-bedroom cottage. $85–95 per room includes breakfast. Cottage, $800 for a week.

The Hayes Guesthouse (646-2277), 127 Shore Road. Open June through October. Elinor Hayes has been renting rooms in her country home at the entrance to Perkins Cove since 1950. The house is furnished with antiques, and Mrs. Hayes's collections of 500 dolls (many of which she made) and 1,000 salt dishes and spoons are displayed. There is a small outdoor pool. Guest rooms have air conditioners and private baths ($90 per night); a small "semi-efficiency" is $90 per day, $550 per week; a two-bedroom apartment with a sunporch is $135 per day, $800 per week.

Rockmere Lodge (646-2985), 40 Stearns Road. Open year-round. One of the 1890s summer mansions along the most private stretch of the Marginal Way. Andy Antoniuk and Bob Brown offer eight rooms, each different; our favorite is the Anna-Marie, a corner room on the second floor with an ocean view from the queen-sized wrought-iron bed (there's also a twin) and from the window seat. $100–155 in-season; from $75 off-season.

Beach Farm Inn (646-8493), Eldredge Road, Wells 04090. Open year-round. A 19th-century farmhouse, in the process of total renovation when we visited it in September of 1998. We assume that under new ownership the character of this old farmhouse will be preserved. It's back from the road in a peaceful setting with a country feel and a pool, handy to the beach and on the trolley line. There are also three efficiency cottages, two with heat. $80–90 per couple, including breakfast; less off-season and for long stays.

COTTAGES

We have noted just a few of the dozens of cottage, condominium, and motel complexes that line Route 1. The helpful Wells Chamber of Commerce (see *Guidance*) keeps track of vacancies in these and in many private cottages.

The Dunes (646-2612), Box 917, Route 1. Open mid-May to mid-October. Set way back from the highway on 12 acres of landscaped grounds and fronting on the Ogunquit River, the complex offers direct access to Ogunquit Beach by rowboat at high tide and on foot at low tide. Owned by the Perkins family for more than 60 years, this is really a historic property, the best of the coast's surviving "cottage colonies," as well as a great family find: The 36 units include 19 old-style Maine classics—white cottages with green trim—scattered over spacious, well-kept grounds. Most have fireplaces. Refrigerators and color TVs in all rooms. One- and two-bedroom cottages are $85–100 off-season, $125–145 in-season (June 19 through Labor Day). Two-week minimum stay in July and August in the larger cottages. Cottage suites (part of a larger building typically with one or two attached units, with living room/bedroom with fireplace and a kitchen) are $110–125. Motel rooms are $65–85 double off-season, $84–135 in-season.

Cottage in the Lane Motor Lodge (646-7903), 84 Drakes Island Road, Wells 04090. There are 11 housekeeping cottages all facing landscaped grounds under the pines (an artistic play structure and a pool form the centerpiece); salt marsh beyond. It's a ¾-mile walk or bike ride to the beach. The quiet setting borders the Rachel Carson Wildlife Refuge and Laudholm Farm (see *Nature Preserves*). $465–490 per week for a three-room cottage accommodating four, and $545–625 for a four-room cottage good for five people; less off-season, the only time that pets are accepted.

The Seagull Motor Inn and Cottages (646-5164), Route 1, Wells 04090. Open late April to late October. Facilities include 24 motel units, 24 one- and two-bedroom cottages with screened porches, a pool, a playground, and lawn games on 23 acres. Having spent four summer vacations here as a child (more than 40 years ago), Chris Tree is happy to report that the place is still essentially the same family value, with plenty of common space, a water view, and a loyal following. Rentals are nightly or by the week, $360–720 for housekeeping cottages. Motel units are $44–84.

MOTELS

Riverside Motel (646-2741), P.O. Box 2244, Shore Road. Open late April through late October. Just across the draw-footbridge and overlooking Perkins Cove is this trim, friendly place with 41 units; also four rooms in the 1874 house. The property has been in Harold Staples's family for more than 100 years. All rooms have color TVs and full baths, and all overlook the cove; continental breakfast is included and served in the lobby around the fireplace or on the sun deck. $50–145, depending on season and location of room. Three-day minimum July 28 through August 17.

Studio East (646-7297), Main Street, Ogunquit Square. Open early April to mid-November. Lorraine and Denis Latulippe's tidy motel is tucked behind the attractive restaurant (see *Eating Out*) on the northern fringe of Ogunquit Village. No view but quiet and handy to the beach, village, and Marginal Way, with nicely decorated units that are $94–119 mid-July to mid-August ($124–134 for a suite with kitchenette accommodating four), from $84 in early July and late September, and $49–59 in early June and right after Labor Day. Off-season $39–49.

WHERE TO EAT

DINING OUT

Arrow's (361-1100), Berwick Road, Ogunquit. Dinner 6–9, late April through October. Considered one of the best—and most expensive—restaurants in Maine, with an emphasis on fresh local ingredients. A 1765 farmhouse is the setting for nouvelle-inspired dishes. Appetizers might include leek and asparagus soup, or a sautéed crabmeat pillow with a rice wrapper; entrées could be braised rabbit with herb puff pastry, *haricots verts*, and chive–crème fraîche pearl onions. The chef-owners are Mark Gaier and Clark Frasier. Entrées $25.95–31.95.

Hurricane Restaurant (646-6348), Perkins Cove. Year-round, 11:30–10:30 daily. "Our view will blow you away—our menu will bring you back" is the boast of the most popular place to dine in Perkins Cove. Reserve. Dining rooms maximize the ocean view. The same menu all day ranges from soups and salads and small plates like grilled wild boar sausage pizza ($9) or deviled Maine lobster cakes with salsa ($13) to roasted zucchini with hazelnut and wild rice stuffing ($15) to fire-roasted, pistachio-encrusted veal chop with wild mushroom and truffled potato cake ($26). Save room for desserts like mile-high cheesecake or warm fruit and berry cheesecake. Lunch entrées are around $10.

98 Provence (646-9898), Shore Road, Ogunquit. Open April through December 1 for dinner (5:30–9:30) except Tuesday. Provençale cuisine that's outstanding. You might begin with *soupe de pecheur* studded with mussels, shrimp, clams, and scallops ($7.25) and dine on pan-seared Maine venison ($27.99).

Gypsy Sweethearts (646-7021), 18 Shore Road, Ogunquit Village. Open May to October. Dinner nightly in-season and breakfast weekends; closed Monday off-season. Fine dining in a charming old house. A place that all Ogunquit regulars hit at least once in their stay. Chef-owner

Judy Clayton's specialties include light seafood dishes like shrimp Margarite ($15.95) and chicken breast in citrus sauce ($15.95); early-bird (5:30–6) specials at $14.95. Award-winning wine list.

Clay Hill Farm (361-2272), Agamenticus Road (north of Ogunquit Village). Open year-round for dinner but closed Monday and Tuesday in winter. A gracious old farmhouse set in landscaped gardens halfway up Mount Agamenticus, with valet parking and an elegant decor; geared to functions but with a reliable menu that might include veal Piccata with prosciutto or linguine with artichokes, sun-dried tomatoes, and mushrooms in roasted garlic sauce. Entrées $13.95–22.95.

Cliff House (361-1000), Bald Hill Cliff, Shore Road, Ogunquit. Open for breakfast and dinner most of the year, for lunch in July and August. The dining room is in the Cliffscape Building, with dramatic ocean views. Unique creations like lobster tails lightly breaded in hazelnuts and sautéed in lemon-wine butter and bourbon marinated lamb rib. Entrées $12.95–28.50. Sunday breakfast buffet (7:30 AM–1 PM) is a deal: $10.95 adult, $8.95 child.

Dianne's Fine Food & Spirits (646-9703), 211 Main Street (Route 1), Ogunquit. Open for dinner early May through Columbus Day, also weekends in spring and fall. Chef-owner Scott Walker, ably assisted by wife Dianne, has created a very pleasant setting for dining from a menu that includes chicken béarnaise ($15.95), lobster Newburg in puff pastry ($18.50), and steak *au poivre* ($19.95). Entrées from $9.95.

The Old Village Inn (646-7088), 30 Main Street, Ogunquit. Open all year but not all nights off-season. Check. This village landmark includes various Victorian-style dining rooms and an English pub-style bar with an equally varied menu, ranging from pastas and stir fries to roast rack of lamb, filet mignon, and the lobster of the evening. Entrées $13.95–21.95.

Jonathan's Restaurant (646-4777), 2 Bourne Lane, Ogunquit. There are two entirely distinct parts to this place, both hugely popular. The downstairs restaurant consists of a series of dimly lit, nicely decorated rooms (one with a 600-gallon tropical aquarium) hung with work by local artists and surrounded by landscaped gardens. The food is reliably good. Entrées range from vegetarian pasta or jaeger schnitzel (pork, pan-fried with mushrooms in a bordelaise sauce, $14.75) to seafood sauté provençal with lobster and salmon ($22.50). For more about what happens upstairs see *Entertainment*.

Poor Richard's Tavern (646-4722), Shore Road and Pine Hill, Ogunquit. This local dining landmark is back where it began 30 years ago, in a charming old house near Perkins Cove. Chef-owner Richard Perkins prides himself on his lobster stew and Infamous Lobster Pie and offers a large menu ranging from meat loaf to charbroiled fillet of salmon. Entrées $12.95–24.95.

Blue Water Inn (646-5559), Beach Street, Ogunquit. The water view is hard to beat, and the specialty is fish—mako shark as well as mackerel and haddock. Entrées $10.95–17.95.

Shore Cafe (646-6365), 22 Shore Road. Open May to mid-October for breakfast (7–12) and dinner (from 5), specializing in Mediterranean and California-inspired dishes. This is a pleasant place to dine—in the dimly lit lounge side as well as in the more formal part of the restaurant, where entrées might include braised duck breast with eggplant and mushrooms in a fresh sage sauce over grilled Parmesan polenta ($16.95) or broiled haddock in white wine served with a tomato-chive lemon butter ($15.95).

Grey Gull Inn (646-7501), 475 Webhannet Drive, Moody Point (Wells). Open year-round for dinner. Across the road from the ocean, a dependable dining room with minimal atmosphere. Entrées might include coquilles St. Jacques ($17.95).

LOBSTER

Note: Maine's southernmost beach resorts are the first place many visitors sample real "Mane Lobsta" the way it should be eaten: messily, with bib, broth, butter, and a water view.

Barnacle Billy's, Etc. (646-5575), Perkins Cove. Open April through October for lunch and dinner. What began as a no-frills lobster place (the one that's still next door) has expanded to fill a luxurious dining space created for a more upscale restaurant. Lobster and seafood dishes remain the specialty and it's difficult to beat the view combined with comfort, which frequently includes the glow from two great stone fireplaces. Full bar; entrées from $12.95 for grilled chicken to $18.95 for a boiled lobster. You can also order lobster at the counter and wait for your number, dine on the outdoor deck, order burgers.

Lobster Shack (646-2941), end of Perkins Cove. Open April through mid-October, 11–9 in-season. A genuine old-style, serious lobster-eating place since the 1940s (when it was known as Maxwell and Perkins); oilcloth-covered tables, lobster by the pound, steamer clams, good chowder, house cole slaw, also reasonably priced burgers, apple pie à la mode, wine, beer.

Ogunquit Lobster Pound (646-2516), Route 1 (north of Ogunquit Village). Open Mother's Day through Columbus Day weekend for dinner. After more than 40 years of ownership by the Hancock family, this is still notoriously expensive, and service is frequently slow, but patrons return year after year. Dine either in the rustic log building or outside on swinging, wood-canopied tables. Beer and wine are available along with cheeseburgers and steak, but lobsters and clams are what the place is about. Don't pass up the deep-dish blueberry pie.

Fisherman's Catch (646-8780), Wells Harbor. Open Mother's Day through Columbus Day, 9–8 daily. Set in a salt marsh, with rustic tables; a traditional seafood place with unbeatable prices. Our kind of place.

Good chowder ($3.95 a bowl, not cup) and really good lobster stew ($4.75 a cup), homemade crab cakes ($4.95), baked haddock with rice or french fries ($8.95). Lobster dinners, children's menu, beer on tap.

EATING OUT

Studio East Restaurant (464-7297), 47 Maine Street (Route 1), Ogunquit Village. Open for breakfast and lunch in-season (mid-April through mid-November), possibly dinner (on again, off again). Lorraine and Denis Latulippe have created a bright, pleasant dining room with a European feel. Salads and a reasonably priced large lobster roll are the specialties at lunch, and Denise's pies are well known locally. Beer is served.

Cafe Amore (646-6661), 4 Perkins Cove, Ogunquit. Open mid-March to mid-December. In-season 7 AM–10 PM, off-season 7–3, closed selected days. A thoroughly cheerful place, good for a leisurely breakfast or an afternoon cappuccino. Specialty omelets (try the "In Your Teeth": spinach, mushrooms, onions, and cheese) and specialty sandwiches (maybe "Capri": lettuce, provolone, and veggies in a tortilla roll-up).

Lord's Harborside Restaurant (646-2651), Wells Harbor. Open April through November for lunch and dinner, closed Tuesday in spring and fall. A big, ungarnished dining room with a harbor view and a reputation for fresh fish and seafood. Lobster (fried, boiled, and baked).

Jake's Seafood (646-6771), Route 1, Bourne Avenue, Moody. Open for all three meals year-round. Specializes in good American cooking, fresh seafood, homemade ice cream.

Congdon's Donuts Family Restaurant, Route 1, Wells. Open 6:30–2 year-round. Fresh muffins, breads, pastries, and doughnuts; also ice cream made on premises.

Maine Diner (656-4441), Route 1, Wells. Open year-round 7 AM–9 PM, near the junction of Routes 1 and 9. A classic diner with a large menu for all three meals, plus beer, wine, takeout; breakfast all day, great corned beef hash, and outstanding clam chowder. The homemade chicken potpie takes a few minutes longer, but it's worth the wait.

  ☞ **Gourmet Express** (646-2989), Ogunquit. Sue Pollard's service—pizzas, roll-ups, stuffed baguettes, eggplant parmigiana, pastas, and a children's menu to match—is a real service for everyone whose accommodations include a small table, let alone all those people with cooking facilities who are too tired to go out or cook. Good, reasonably priced food, free delivery. Ask about the dessert of the day.

SNACKS

Bread & Roses Bakery (646-4227), 28A Main Street (up an alley), Ogunquit. A pleasant source of muffins, coffee, and delectable pastries.

Scoop Deck (646-5150), Eldridge Road just off Route 1, Wells. Memorial Day through Columbus Day. Mocha almond fudge and dinosaur crunch (blue vanilla) are among the more than 40 flavors; the ice cream is from Thibodeau Farms in Saco. Also yogurt, cookies, brownies, and hot dogs.

ENTERTAINMENT

THEATER
Hackmatack Playhouse (698-1807), Route 9, Berwick. Stages live performances throughout the year. **Hope Hobbs Gazebo** at Wells Harbor Park offers summer Saturday-night concerts. **Jonathan's** (646-4777; 1-800-464-9934), 2 Bourne Lane, Ogunquit. Open April to October. Upstairs over this popular restaurant is a performance space featuring nationally known performers most nights in-season. Pick up a schedule and reserve tickets ahead. **Leavitt Fine Arts Theatre** (646-3123), 40 Main Street, Ogunquit Village. Open early spring through fall. An old-time theater with new screen and sound; showing first-run films since 1923. **Ogunquit Playhouse**. Such a must-do part of Ogunquit we describe it under *To Do*. **Ogunquit Square Theatre** (646-5151), Shore Road, Ogunquit Village. Another old-time theater with all the latest movies.

SELECTIVE SHOPPING

ANTIQUARIAN BOOKS
Boston book lovers drive to Wells to browse in this cluster of exceptional bookstores along Route 1. They include **Douglas N. Harding Map & Print Gallery** (646-8785), huge and excellent: 4,500 square feet of old and rare books, maps, and prints, plus some 100,000 general titles. **The Book Barn** (646-4926) specializes in old paperbacks, comic books, baseball cards, and collectors' supplies. **East Coast Books** (646-3584), Depot Street at Route 109, has a large general collection, autographs, prints, drawings, paintings, and historical paperbacks.

ANTIQUES SHOPS
Route 1 from York through Wells and the Kennebunks is studded with antiques shops, among them: **MacDougall-Gionet** (646-3531), open 9–5 Tuesday through Sunday; a particularly rich trove of country furniture in a barn; 60 dealers are represented. **R. Jorgensen Antiques** (646-9444) has nine rooms filled with antique furniture, including fine formal pieces from a number of countries.

ART GALLERIES
In addition to the Ogunquit Museum of Art (under *To See*), there is the **Ogunquit Art Association** (646-8400), Shore Road and Bourne Lane, Ogunquit. Open Memorial Day through September, Monday through Saturday 11–5 and Sunday 1–5. The gallery showcases work by members; also stages frequent workshops, lectures, films, and concerts. Ogunquit's galleries (all seasonal) also include: **June Weare Fine Arts** (646-8200), Shore Road; open mid-May to mid-October, 10–4. Original prints, paintings, and sculpture. In Perkins Cove look for the **George Carpenter Gallery** (646-5106). A longtime area resident, Carpenter paints outdoors in the tradition and style of New England's

1920s marine and landscape artists. **Hearthstone at Stonecrop Gallery** (361-1678), Shore Road at Juniper Lane, three doors south of the Ogunquit Museum; landscape paintings and handsome stoneware by a husband and wife, displayed in their unusual gallery/home. **Shore Road Gallery** (646-5046), 112 Shore Road; open Memorial Day through Columbus Day weekend, daily. Fine arts, jewelry, and fine crafts by nationally known artists. **Bartok Studio/Gallery** (646-7815), 104 Shore Road. Watercolors by John Bartok.

SPECIAL SHOPS

Perkins Cove, the cluster of former fish shacks by Ogunquit's famous draw-footbridge, harbors more than a dozen shops and galleries. Our favorites are the **Carpenter Gallery** (see *Art Galleries*); **Dock Square Clothiers** (646-8548), featuring natural-fiber clothing; and **Books Ink.** (646-8393), a collection of toys, games, cards, wine, books, and other things owner Barbara Lee Chertok finds interesting or educational. Sit on the terrace and look over the cove.

Ogunquit Camera (646-2261), at the corner of Shore Road and Wharf Lane in Ogunquit Village. Open year-round, and features 1-hour film developing. A great little shop that's been here since 1952. It's also a trove of toys, towels, windsocks, beach supplies, and sunglasses.

Harbor Candy Shop, 26 Main Street, Ogunquit. Seasonal. Chocolates and specialty candies are made on the spot; there's also a selection of imported candies.

Merriland Farm (646-5040), 545 Coles Hill Road, off Route 1, Wells. This 200-year-old farm offers a view of the Wells that was here for centuries before its sandy shore was developed. In addition to operating a café specializing in pies and berry shortcake and a 9-hole golf course (see *Golf*), this is a place to pick cultivated high-bush blueberries in July and August and to buy jams, raspberry vinegar, and gift baskets.

Lighthouse Depot (646-0608), Route 1 North, Wells. Look for the lighthouses outside (just before turnoff for Laudholm Farm). Open year-round, closed Sundays off-season. Billed as "the largest selection of lighthouse gift items in the world," this is two floors filled with lawn lighthouses, lighthouse books, ornaments, jewelry, paintings, replicas, etc., etc. Inquire about the monthly *Lighthouse Digest.*

Ogunquit Round Table (646-2332), 117 Shore Road. New in 1998 and easy to miss because it's set back (plenty of parking), this is the only full-service bookstore serving Kittery, the Yorks, and Ogunquit. Well stocked, it offers plenty of space for browsing.

SPECIAL EVENTS

April: Big **Patriot's Day celebration** at Ogunquit Beach.

June: **Ogunquit Chamber Music Festival** *(first week);* **Laudholm Farm Day** *(midmonth).* **Wells Week** *(end of the month)*—a weeklong celebration centering on Harbor Park Day; boat launchings, a chicken barbecue, a sand-sculpture contest, and a crafts fair.

July: **Independence Day fireworks** at Ogunquit Beach. **Sand-castle-building contest** *(midmonth).*

August: **Sidewalk art show, Great Inner Tube Race, Kite Day,** all in Ogunquit.

September: **Open Homes Day** sponsored by the Wells Historical Society. **Nature Crafts Festival** at Laudholm Farm *(second weekend).* **Capriccio,** a celebration of the performing arts, Ogunquit.

December: **Christmas parade** in Wells; **Christmas by the Sea** in Ogunquit.

The Kennebunks

The Kennebunks have been around under one name or another since the 1620s. They began as a fishing stage near Cape Porpoise, which was repeatedly destroyed by Native American raids. In 1719 the present "port" was incorporated as Arundel, a name that stuck through its peak shipbuilding and seafaring years until 1821, when the name was changed to Kennebunkport. Later, when the novel *Arundel* by Kenneth Roberts (born in Kennebunk) had run through 32 printings, residents attempted to reclaim the old name. They succeeded in doing so in 1957, at least for North Kennebunkport.

In the 1870s, this entire spectacular 5-mile stretch of coast—from Lord's Point at the western end of Kennebunk Beach all the way to Cape Porpoise on the east—was acquired by a Massachusetts group, the Boston and Kennebunkport Sea Shore Company. No fewer than 30 grand hotels and dozens of summer mansions evolved to accommodate the wave of visitors that train service brought. The Kennebunks, however, shared the 1940s to 1960s decline suffered by all Maine coastal resorts, losing all but a scattering of old hotels. Then the tourist tide again turned and over the past few decades surviving hotels have been condoed, inns have been rehabbed, and dozens of B&Bs and inns have opened.

You can bed down a few steps from Dock Square's lively shops and restaurants, 2 miles away in the quiet village of Cape Porpoise, or out at Goose Rocks, where the only sound is the lapping of waves on endless sand. Most B&Bs are, however, the former sea captains' homes grouped within a few stately streets of each other, within walking distance of both Dock Square and the open ocean.

This is the least seasonal resort town on the Southern Coast. Most inns and shops remain open through Christmas Prelude in early December (see *Special Events*), and many never close.

GUIDANCE

Kennebunk/Kennebunkport Chamber of Commerce (967-0857; 1-800-982-4421; www.kkcc.maine.org), P.O. Box 740, Kennebunk 04043. Open daily in summer, weekdays year-round plus Saturdays during special events like Christmas Prelude. The information center is in a yellow building on Route 9 just east of its junction with Route 35 (at

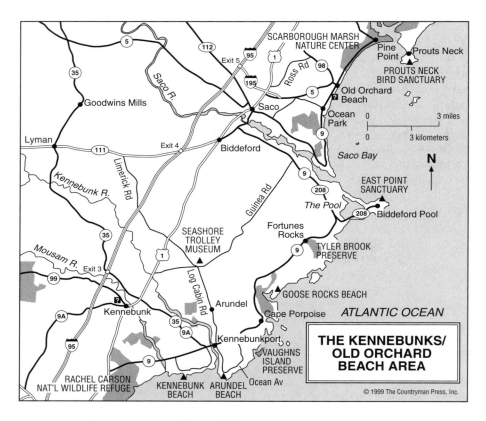

MAP labels:
- SCARBOROUGH MARSH NATURE CENTER
- Pine Point
- Prouts Neck
- PROUTS NECK BIRD SANCTUARY
- Old Orchard Beach
- Ocean Park
- Saco Bay
- Goodwins Mills
- Saco
- Saco R.
- EAST POINT SANCTUARY
- Lyman
- Biddeford
- The Pool
- Biddeford Pool
- Kennebunk R.
- Limerick Rd.
- Guinea Rd.
- Fortunes Rocks
- SEASHORE TROLLEY MUSEUM
- TYLER BROOK PRESERVE
- Mousam R.
- Log Cabin Rd.
- GOOSE ROCKS BEACH
- Arundel
- Cape Porpoise
- ATLANTIC OCEAN
- Kennebunk
- Kennebunkport
- VAUGHNS ISLAND PRESERVE
- RACHEL CARSON NAT'L WILDLIFE REFUGE
- KENNEBUNK BEACH
- ARUNDEL BEACH
- Ocean Av

THE KENNEBUNKS/ OLD ORCHARD BEACH AREA

© 1999 The Countryman Press, Inc.

the light in Lower Village). There's plenty of parking in the rear of the building. Staff are unusually helpful and the chamber publishes an excellent free guide.

Kennebunkport Information and Hospitality Center (967-8600). Open May through mid-December. Rest rooms and information in Dock Square.

GETTING THERE

By air: You can fly your own plane into **Sanford Airport;** otherwise Portland International Jetport (see "Portland Area") is served by **Lilley's Limo** (773-5765); also **Mermaid Transportation** (1-800-696-2463), which also serves Boston and Manchester, New Hampshire.

By car: Drive up I-95 to exit 3 and take Route 35 into Kennebunk, on to Kennebunkport and Kennebunk Beach. Coming up Route 1, take Route 9 east from Wells.

By train: See "Ogunquit and Wells" for possible AMTRAK service in 1999. Stay tuned.

GETTING AROUND

Kennebunk is a busy commercial center straddling the strip of Route 1 between the Mousam and Kennebunk Rivers. A 10-minute ride down

Summer Street (Route 35) brings you to Kennebunkport. Then there are Kennebunk Beach, Cape Porpoise, Goose Rocks Beach, Cape Arundel, and Kennebunk Lower Village. Luckily, free, detailed maps are readily available.

Intown Trolley Co. (967-3686) offers narrated sightseeing tours with $6 tickets good for the day, so you can also use them to shuttle between Dock Square and Kennebunk Beach.

Bicycles work well here, and are a good way to handle the mile between Dock Square and the ocean or Kennebunk Beach (see *Bicycling*).

PARKING

A municipal parking lot is hidden behind the commercial block in Dock Square. There are also two free nearby lots: one at St. Martha's Catholic Church, 30 North Street, the other at the Consolidated School, Route 9.

MEDICAL EMERGENCY

Southern Maine Medical Center (283-7000), Medical Center Drive (off Route 111), Biddeford. **Kennebunk Walk-in Clinic** (985-6027), Route 1 North, Kennebunk.

TO SEE

MUSEUMS

The Brick Store Museum (985-4802), 117 Main Street, Kennebunk. Open year-round, Tuesday through Saturday 10–4:30. $5 per adult, $4.50 senior, $2 per student and child, no charge 8 and under. A block of early-19th-century commercial buildings, including William Lord's **Brick Store** (1825), a space used for changing exhibits of fine and decorative arts and marine collections. You enter through the gift store. The permanent collection upstairs includes some striking portraits, seascapes, furniture, ship's models, and decorative arts primarily from the community's Federal era. **The Taylor-Barry House,** a vintage 1803 shipmaster's home, 24 Summer Street, is open June through September, Tuesday through Friday, for guided tours ($4). Combination tickets available. Also see *To Do—Walks*.

Seashore Trolley Museum (967-2800), Log Cabin Road, located 3.2 miles up North Street from Kennebunkport or 2.8 miles north on Route 1 from Kennebunk, then right at the yellow blinker. Open daily May through October, otherwise varying hours; call to check on special events. Admission is $7 for adults, $4.50 children, and family rates. This nonprofit museum has preserved the history of the trolley era, displaying more than 200 vehicles from the world over. The impressive collection began in 1939, when the last open-sided Biddeford–Old Orchard Beach trolley was retired to an open field straddling the old Atlantic Shore Line railbed. The museum now owns 300 acres as well as cars shipped here from London, Budapest, Rome, and Nagasaki, among other cities. A 4-mile, round-trip excursion on a trolley takes visitors out

Dock Square in Kennebunkport

through woods and fields, along a route once traveled by summer guests en route to Old Orchard Beach.

Kennebunkport Historical Society (967-2751). Based in the Town House School on North Street. Open year-round Wednesday through Friday 1–4. Displays local memorabilia; also maritime exhibits housed in the adjoining office of the Clark Shipyard. The society maintains the **Nott House,** open mid-June through Columbus Day, Tuesday through Friday 1–4. A Greek Revival mansion with Doric columns, original wallpapers, carpets, and furnishings. $3 per adult. Also see *To Do—Walks.*

HISTORIC SIGHTS

Wedding Cake House, Summer Street (Route 35), Kennebunk. This 1826 house is laced up and down with white wooden latticework. The tale is that a local sea captain had to rush off to sea before a proper wedding cake could be baked, but he more than made up for it later.

South Congregational Church, Temple Street, Kennebunkport. Just off Dock Square, built in 1824 with a Christopher Wren–style cupola and belfry; Doric columns added in 1912.

Louis T. Graves Memorial Library (967-2778), Main Street, Kennebunkport. Built in 1813 as a bank, which went bust, it later served as a customs house. It was subsequently donated to the library association by artist Abbott Graves, whose pictures alone make it worth a visit. You can still see the bank vault and the sign from the customs collector's office. Upstairs, the book sale room is full of bargains.

First Parish Unitarian Church, Main Street, Kennebunk. Built in 1772–1773 with an Asher Benjamin–style steeple added in 1803–1804, along with a Paul Revere bell. In 1838 the interior was divided into two levels, with the church proper elevated to the second floor.

Kennebunkport Maritime Museum & Shop (967-3218). Open May 15 through October 15, 10–4. Admission. This "museum" occupies the former boathouse in which Booth Tarkington wrote. The last remnants of the schooner *Regina* and a collection of early-19th-century scrimshaw and other nautical memorabilia are displayed. There is a museum shop.

SCENIC DRIVE

Ocean Avenue follows the Kennebunk River a mile to Cape Arundel and the open ocean, then winds past many magnificent summer homes, including **Walker's Point,** former president Bush's summer estate (it fills a private, 11-acre peninsula). Built by his grandfather in 1903, its position was uncannily ideal for use as a president's summer home, moated by water on three sides, yet clearly visible from the pull-out places along the avenue. Continue along the ocean (you don't have to worry about driving too slowly, because everyone else is, too). Follow the road to Cape Porpoise, site of the area's original 1600s settlement. The cove is still a base for lobster and commercial fishing boats and the village is a good place to lunch or dine. Continue along Route 9 to Clock Farm Corner (you'll know it when you see it) and turn right on Dyke Road to Goose Rocks Beach; park and walk. Return to Route 9 and cross it, continuing via Goose Rocks Road to the Seashore Trolley Museum (see *Museums*) and then Log Cabin Road to Kennebunkport.

TO DO

BALLOONING

Balloons over New England (499-7575; 1-800-788-5562), based in Kennebunkport, offers champagne flights year-round. $200 per person.

BICYCLING

Cape-Able Bike Shop (967-4382), Townhouse Corners (off Log Cabin Road), Kennebunkport, billed as Maine's biggest bike shop, rents a variety of bikes, including tandems and trail-a-bikes, and owner Peter Sargent is the local biking guru, source of maps and advice. Open most of the year; in summer months Monday through Saturday 9–6, closed Mondays off-season. The lay of this land lends itself to exploration by bike, a far more satisfying way to go in summer than by car since you can stop and park wherever the view and urge hit you. Inquire about the **Bridle Path** (an old trolley-line route) and **Wonderbrook Parkland.**

BOATBUILDING SCHOOL

The Landing School of Boat Building and Design (985-7976), River Road, Kennebunk, offers a September-to-June program in building sailing craft. Visitors welcome if you call ahead.

BOAT EXCURSIONS
See *Fishing, Sailing,* and *Whale-Watching,* and check with the chamber of commerce (see *Guidance*).

CARRIAGE RIDES
Rockin Horse Stables (967-4288), 245 Arundel Road, Kennebunkport. $10 per adult. Tours of Kennebunkport's historic district (25 minutes) in a spiffy white vis-à-vis carriage with burgundy-colored velvet seats and antique lanterns are offered by Vincent Thelin.

DAY CAMP
Kennebunk Beach Improvement Association (967-2180; September through May, 967-4075) offers weekly sessions for 3- to 18-year-olds featuring swimming, sailing, rowing, fishing, golf, tennis, arts and crafts, photography, and sand-castle building.

FISHING
Deep Sea Fishing is available on charter boat **Lady J** (985-7304) and on party boat **Venture Inn** (967-0005).

Guided fly- and spin-fishing is offered through **Northeast Angler** (967-5889), an Orvis distributor in Lower Village, Kennebunk.

GOLF
Cape Arundel Golf Club (967-3494), Kennebunkport, 18 holes. These are the local links former president Bush frequents. Open to the public except 11–2:30. **Webhannet Golf Club** (967-2061), Kennebunk Beach, 18 holes. Open to the public except 11:30–1. **Dutch Elm Golf Course** (282-9850), Arundel, 18 holes; cart and club rental, lessons, pro shop, snack bar, putting greens.

Hillcrest Pitch & Putt and Driving Range (967-4661), Kennebunk. Open daily 9–dusk; balls and clubs furnished.

KAYAKING
Kayak Adventures (468-3472), Kennebunkport. Guided ocean and river trips in open-cockpit-design kayaks.

SAILING
Several schooners and yachts offer daysails; check with the chamber of commerce.

TROLLEY RIDE
See **Seashore Trolley Museum** under *To See.*

WALKS
Volkswalk, an officially sanctioned, do-it-yourself 11-km (6.8-mile) walk through Lower Village and Kennebunkport. Pick up a map from the "walk box" at the Village Take-out in Kennebunkport's Village Market Place. Also see *Green Space.*

WHALE-WATCHING
This is a popular departure point for whale-watching on Jeffrey's Ledge, about 20 miles offshore. If you have any tendency toward seasickness, be sure to choose a calm day. Chances are you'll see more than a dozen whales. Frequently sighted species include finbacks, minkes, rights, and

humpbacks. The *Nautilus* (967-0707), a 65-foot boat carrying up to 100 passengers, offers narrated trips daily from May to October. *Indian Whale Watch* (967-5912), a 75-foot boat holding 72 passengers, is slower and takes longer to reach the whales than some but features narration by a mammalogist (July through October). *First Chance* (967-5507) also offers whale-watching and sunset cruises.

WINTER PASTIMES

CROSS-COUNTRY SKIING
Harris Farm (499-2678), Buzzell Road, Dayton. A 500-acre dairy farm with more than 20 miles of trails. Equipment rentals available. Located 1.5 miles from the Route 5 and Route 35 intersection.

SLEIGH RIDES
Vincent and Susan Thelin of **Rockin Horse Stables** (967-4288), 245 Arundel Road, Kennebunkport, offer half-hour to 40-minute sleigh rides on their 100-acre farm; $10 per adult, $6 per child; group rates.

GREEN SPACE

BEACHES
The Kennebunks discourage weekend day-trippers by requiring a permit to park at major beaches. Day and seasonal passes must be secured from the chamber of commerce, town hall, police department, or local lodging places. You can also park in one of the town lots and walk, bike, or take a trolley to the beach.

Goose Rocks Beach, a few miles north of Kennebunkport Village on Route 9, is the area's most beautiful beach: a magnificent, wide, smooth stretch of silver-white sand backed by the road.

Kennebunk and **Gooch's Beaches** in Kennebunk are both long, wide strips of firm sand backed by Beach Avenue, divided by Oak's Neck. Beyond Gooch's Beach, take Great Hill Road along the water to **Strawberry Island,** a great place to walk and examine tidal pools. Please don't picnic. Keep going and you come to **Mother's Beach,** small and very sandy.

Arundel Beach, near the Colony Hotel at the mouth of the Kennebunk River, offers nice rocks for climbing.

Parsons Beach, south of Kennebunk Beach on Route 9, requires no permit, but it's impossible to park nearby in-season; off-season it's a splendid place for a walk.

NATURE PRESERVES
   ♿ **Rachel Carson National Wildlife Refuge** (646-9226). Headquarters for this approximately 50-mile, nearly 5,000-acre preserve are just south of the Kennebunkport line at 321 Port Road (Route 9) in Wells. Office open weekdays, 8–4:30. The preserve is divided among 10 sites along Maine's Southern Coast. Pick up a leaflet guide to the mile-long, wheelchair-

accessible nature trail here. (Also see **Laudholm Farm** described under *Nature Preserves* in "Ogunquit and Wells.")

Kennebunkport Conservation Trust, P.O. Box 7028, Cape Porpoise 04014, maintains several properties. These include the **Tyler Brook Preserve** near Goose Rocks, the 148-acre **Emmons Preserve** along the Batson River (access from unpaved Gravelly Road, off Beachwood Road), and the **Vaughns Island Preserve,** which offers nature trails on a wooded island separated from the mainland by two tidal creeks. Cellar holes of historic houses are accessible by foot from 3 hours after to 3 hours before high tide.

The Nature Conservancy (729-5181) maintains 14-acre **Butler Preserve** on the Kennebunk River, including Picnic Rock, and the **Kennebunk Plains Preserve** (1,500 acres of blueberry plains in West Kennebunk; take Route 99 toward Sanford).

East Point Sanctuary, off Route 9 (east of Goose Rocks Beach) in Biddeford Pool. A 30-acre Maine Audubon Society preserve, well known to birders, who flock here during migrating seasons. Beautiful any time of year. From Route 9 turn right just beyond Goose Rocks Beach onto Fortune Rocks Beach Road to Lester B. Orcutt Boulevard; turn right, drive almost to the end and look for a chain-link fence and Audubon sign. The trail continues along the golf course and sea.

WALKS

Henry Parsons Park, Ocean Avenue, is a path along the rocks leading to Spouting Rock and Blowing Cave, both sights to see at midtide. A great way to view the beautiful homes along Ocean Avenue.

St. Anthony Monastery and Shrine (967-2011), Kennebunkport. Some 20 acres of peaceful, riverside fields and forests on Beach Road, now maintained by Lithuanian Franciscans as a shrine and retreat. Visitors are welcome; gift shop. Ask about summer lodging in the Guesthouse.

LODGING

The Kennebunks represent one of the Maine coast's largest concentrations of inns and B&Bs; some 80 lodging places belong to the chamber. These, however, add up to just 1,400 rooms, all of which are filled on August weekends. For this reason we list a number of options in different price ranges ($65–399 in-season); this is still just a fraction of what's available. These lodging places tend to stay open at least through the first two weekends in December, when the town celebrates "Christmas Prelude," and many are year-round.

All listings are for Kennebunkport 04046 unless otherwise indicated.

RESORT HOTEL

The Colony Hotel (967-3331; 1-800-552-2363), Ocean Avenue and King's Highway. Open May through October. With 125 rooms (all private baths) in four buildings, this is one of the last of New England's coastal resorts that are still maintained in the grand style. It's set on a rise, overlooking the point at which the Kennebunk River meets the Atlantic. It's been owned by the Boughton family since 1948; many guests have been coming for generations. Amenities include a saltwater pool, a private beach, an 18-hole putting green, a social program, nightly entertainment, and dancing. A 2-night minimum is required for weekend reservations for July and August. $164–314 double per day includes two meals; $40 per extra person (children, from $16) plus $12 for service. Worth it. Handicapped-accessible rooms. Pets are $22 per day.

TOP DOLLAR INNS AND B&BS

Captain Lord Mansion (967-3141), P.O. Box 800. Open year-round at the corner of Pleasant and Green Streets. This splendid mansion, built in 1814, is one of the most romantic inns around. The three-story, Federal-era home is topped with a widow's walk from which guests can contemplate the town and sea beyond. Other architectural features include a three-story, suspended elliptical staircase, and pine doors that have been painted trompe l'oeil–style to simulate inlaid mahogany. There are 16 meticulously decorated rooms, 15 with gas fireplaces, some with high four-posters and canopy beds—and all with antiques and private baths. One (Merchant Captain's Suite; $349 per night) boasts what's probably the largest, most elaborate bathroom in Maine. The gathering room is also very elegant, but the full breakfast is an informal affair, served in the large country kitchen. Since 1978 hosts Bev Davis and Rick Litchfield have devoted their considerable energies to making this one of Maine's outstanding inns. Phebe's Fantasy, a separate building, has four more rooms with fireplaces. $179–399 per room in high season, breakfast and tea included; $99–299 off-season.

White Barn Inn (967-2321), P.O. Box 560C, Beach Street. Open year-round. The "barn" is now an elegant dining room (see *Dining Out*) attached to the inn. Built in 1820 as a farmhouse, later enlarged as the Forest Hills Hotel, this complex midway between Dock Square and Kennebunk Beach has no view, and the least expensive rooms are small, but it represents the height of Southern Coast luxury and formality. Choose an antiques-furnished room in the original farmhouse, a suite in the carriage house (four-poster king beds, fireplaces, and marble baths with whirlpool tubs), a cottage suite with its specially crafted furnishings, a double-sided fireplace, Jacuzzi, and steam shower, or the former loft suite of owner Laurie Bongiorno. Guests breakfast in the inn's original, old-fashioned dining room, and common space consists of a sitting room and the landscaped pool area. The 25 rooms vary in size, decor, plumbing, and niceties like fireplaces, as prices—$140–395 per couple (including breakfast, afternoon tea, and use of touring bikes)—suggest. Inquire about special packages.

MODERATELY EXPENSIVE INNS AND B&BS
On the Water

Cape Arundel Inn (967-2125), Ocean Avenue, Box 530A. Open mid-April through December. The most dramatic location in town, facing the open ocean with just Walker Point (the islandlike estate of former president Bush) interrupting the water view. One of the area's 19th-century mansion "cottages," this has been an inn for some time but has become one of the coast's best places to stay only in the past couple of years, since Jack Nahil, former owner of the White Barn Inn and present owner of Salt Marsh Tavern (see *Dining Out*) began transforming it room by room. Nahil has added windows (as if there weren't already enough) to maximize the views and has obviously enjoyed painting and decorating each of the seven rooms in the main house and six in the adjacent motel (a 1950s addition but weathering nicely with picture windows facing the water, parking in back, TVs). He also added phones in all rooms, brightened the living room with Oriental rugs, comfortably elegant furnishings, and good art (some of it his own), and totally transformed the dining room, which is open for dinner to the public (see *Dining Out*). Rates are $125–180; includes a light breakfast.

✎ **Tides Inn By-the-Sea** (967-3757), RR 2, Box 252, Goose Rocks Beach. Open May to October. Away from Dock Square but right across from the area's best beach: wide, firm enough for running, long and silvery. This is one of the area's best-kept secrets—a small, very Victorian inn built by Maine's foremost shingle-style architect, John Calvin Stevens, in 1899. Guests have included Teddy Roosevelt and Sir Arthur Conan Doyle. Owned since 1972 by Marie Henriksen and now run jointly with her daughter Kristin Blomberg, it is one of the area's most popular places to eat (see *Dining Out*), but guests also have plenty of comfortable sitting space around the fireplace downstairs. Rooms in the main building are furnished with antiques, and we recommend going for the high-end rooms with both private bath and view. We were lulled to sleep by the sound of the waves in Room 24, a third-floor aerie with an ocean view from the bed. $105–225. This is one place that manages to be both romantic and a family find. Next door, **Tides Too** offers one- and two-bedroom apartments ($2,000–2,500 per week in-season; from $125 per night off-season). Inquire about Emma Foss (the ghost).

The Ocean View (967-2750), 171 Beach Avenue, Kennebunk Beach 04043. Open April through mid-December. Bob and Carole Arena's painted lady is right across from Kennebunk Beach. The main house has four guest rooms and one suite, a comfortable TV room, and a living room with fireplace and a sunny breakfast room with a view of the ocean across the street. A separate building houses four pretty suites with sitting areas, color TVs, and private terraces. All rooms offer bathrobes, a CD player, ceiling fans, a mini-fridge, and phone. Breakfasts are consciously healthy as well as full. "Breakfast in bed" is served to guests in suites. High-season rates run $180–250; low, $100–180.

KIM GRANT

View from the front porch of the Cape Arundel Inn

Seaside Inn & Cottages (967-4461), P.O. Box 631, Gooch's Beach. Rooms in the 1756 inn are rented just from July through Labor Day; cottages are rented May through October; the motor inn is year-round. An attractive complex formed by a 1720s homestead, a 1756 inn, a modern 22-room motor inn, and 10 housekeeping cottages—all on a private beach next to one of Maine's best public strands. This property has been in the Severance family for 13 generations. The old homestead is rented as a cottage, and there are still four antiques-furnished guest rooms in the old inn. A buffet breakfast is included in the rates. Cottages are per month in July and August, per week the rest of the season. One-week minimum in oceanfront rooms and 2-day minimum in terrace-side rooms in high season. $158–178 per night for motel rooms, $109–149 for rooms in the 1756 inn; less off-season. Rates include breakfast. Pets are accepted in the cottages.

Bufflehead Cove (967-3879), Box 499, off Route 35. Open April through December. This is a hidden gem, sequestered on 6 acres at the end of a dirt road, overlooking an 8-foot tidal cove, but less than a mile from the village of Kennebunkport. It's a Dutch Colonial–style home in which Harriet and Jim Gott raised their children. Harriet is a native of nearby Cape Porpoise, and Jim is a commercial fisherman. There are five pretty guest rooms and a suite, some with hand-painted or stenciled wall designs. The Hideaway features a fireplace that opens into the bedroom on one side and into the sitting area on the other. The living room has a hearth and deep window seats; you'll also find an inviting veranda, and woods and orchard to explore. $95–250 includes a full breakfast and afternoon wine and cheese.

The Inn at Harbor Head (967-5564), 41 Pier Road, Cape Porpoise. Open year-round. Dick and Eve Roesler offer two rooms and two suites (both with fireplaces) in their rambling, shingled home overlooking Cape Porpoise harbor. The Summer Suite has a view of the picturesque harbor from the bath as well as from the bed. Most rooms have water views and hand-painted seascapes on the walls; all are decorated with florals and antiques. Guests share the dock, terrace, and sitting rooms, with an inviting fireplace in the library. Fresh-baked goods top off large breakfasts; afternoon tea or wine and cheese are served. Beach passes and towels provided for nearby Goose Rocks Beach. No smoking, no TV. $190–295 per room in-season, $130–215 in winter.

In Kennebunkport

Kennebunkport Inn (967-2621; 1-800-248-2621), Dock Square. Open year-round; dining room closed November to April. Originally an 1890s mansion, but an inn since 1926. Although just a skip from Dock Square, it's set back from the hubbub. The feel here is of a small, personable European hotel, the kind with one innkeeper (Rick Griffin) behind the check-in desk and the other (Martha Griffin) supervising the well-respected kitchen. There are 34 rooms, one with a fireplace. The inn has three sections—the main house; a 1980s Federal-style addition; and a 1930s river house, with smaller rooms and stenciled walls. Each room is individually decorated with antiques, and all have TVs, private baths, and air-conditioning; many have water views. In summer, a small pool on the terrace is available to guests. The cocktail lounge is dark and friendly with a huge old bar and green-hooded lights, evening piano music. Special packages include meals and a lobster cruise. High-season rates $85–289 per room, off-season $69.50–209.

Inn on South Street (967-5151; 1-800-963-5151), South Street, P.O. Box 478A. Open year-round. A Greek Revival home on a quiet street preserves a sense of the era in which it was built. Innkeeper Jack Downs is a retired professor with a keen interest in the China trade, and the living room decor includes the kind of Chinese furniture and furnishings a Kennebunkport sea captain might well have brought back. There are three guest rooms and a suite. Our favorite room, named for "Mrs. Perkins," has a fireplace, a pine four-poster bed with a canopy, Oriental rugs, a new bath, and a portrait of its namesake tucked in the closet. The first-floor suite has its own sitting room, a four-poster bed and wood-burning stove, a bath with Jacuzzi, a kitchen, and a porch overlooking the herb garden. Breakfast is either in the dining room or on the terrace by the landscaped garden in the back; afternoon tea is also served, and is included in rates that run $105–149 for a double room, $149–155 for fireplace room, $155–225 for the suite.

   ♿ **The Captain Fairfield Inn** (967-4454; 1-800-322-1928), corner of Pleasant and Green Streets. Open year-round. Bonnie and Dennis Tallagnon are born-again innkeepers: They ably ran a Vermont inn, retired from it, missed innkeeping, and now greet you at the door of this Federal-era captain's home on the River Green. There are nine bedrooms, all decorated with antiques and wicker, four-poster and canopy beds. Each has a private bath; one is handicapped accessible. Four have wood-burning fireplaces, and the library suite—with its canopy bed, hearth, ample sitting space, and own porch—seems to have everything. There is a sense of light and space both inside and out—plenty of comfortable, gracious common spaces and a lawn that stretches back across the width of the block into that of the neighboring Inn on South Street (see above). Dennis is an accomplished chef and offers a choice for breakfast, maybe crêpes, blueberry pancakes, or eggs Benedict. $89–225; $25 per extra person.

Old Fort Inn (967-5353; 1-800-828-FORT), P.O. Box M. Open mid-April to mid-December. An unusual combination of things, but it works. The reception area is in an antiques store in the former barn. This is also where you'll find a spacious sitting room in which guests enjoy a morning buffet breakfast and are otherwise drawn to relax. Grounds and buildings represent the remnants of an 1880s resort, nicely converted to serve 1990s guests, with a pool, tennis court, horseshoes, and shuffleboard. The sturdy stone and brick carriage house now offers 16 guest rooms with private baths, antiques, color TV, phones, air-conditioning, and wet bars. Two suites available. A path leads down to the ocean. Unsuitable for children under 12. Two-night minimum during high season. $135–285 in high season, $95–210 off-season; breakfast included.

  ♨ **The Captain Jefferds Inn** (967-2311; 1-800-839-6844), 5 Pearl Street, Box 691. This strikingly handsome, Federal-era mansion has received a thorough makeover thanks to Dick and Pat Bartholomew and their daughter Jane. Each of the 16 guest rooms is now named for one of their favorite places in the world and vary in feel from Bilbo's Hideaway in the carriage house (a double bed under a skylight, a small bath and private entrance ($105) to Assisi, a suite with a king-sized iron bed, a gas fireplace, large Italian tiled bathroom, and an indoor garden with a fountain ($240). Our favorite is actually "Florida," a bright contemporary room with a skylight over the bed and two trapezoidal doors overlooking the garden ($155). The four rooms in the carriage house are less formal than the main house, which offers several elegant common rooms. A three-course breakfast is served either by candlelight in the dining room or on the terrace, and tea is served in the afternoon. Dick is a veterinarian who genuinely loves dogs. Kate, a golden retriever, is in residence, and guest dogs are accepted by reservation; $20 extra.

Maine Stay Inn and Cottages (967-2117; 1-800-950-2117), Box 500A, 34 Maine Street. Open year-round. The 1860 house is big, white, and distinctive, with a large cupola. It offers four guest rooms—each with private bath, one with a fireplace and deck—and two suites, both with fireplaces. What sets this place apart from the other gracious B&Bs in Kennebunkport are the 11 cottages of varying sizes sequestered in nicely landscaped grounds, six with fireplaces, all but three with efficiency kitchens. This is one of the few attractive places for families to stay within walking distance of Dock Square. A full breakfast is served and might include blueberry blintzes or apricot scones (cottage guests have the option of breakfast delivered in a basket). All guests can enjoy a full afternoon tea in the attractive living room or on the wraparound porch. Carol and Lindsay Copeland are warm hosts, eager to help you make the most of your stay. $145–225 per night; winter, $85–175.

The 1802 House (967-5632; 1-800-932-5632), P.O. Box 646-A, 15 Locke Street. Open year-round. Ron and Carol Perry offer six guest rooms furnished with antiques, also a three-room suite with fireplace, fridge, and double shower, and a Roman garden room with a double whirlpool tub overlooking a private deck. Most rooms have queen-sized four-posters and fireplaces, and many have whirlpool tubs. The house is away from town on the edge of the Cape Arundel Golf Club, with an out-in-the-country feel, shaded by large pines. A ship's bell calls guests to a very full breakfast. Common rooms are airy and comfortable; cozy corners for winter. $119–299.

MODERATELY PRICED INNS AND B&BS

The Green Heron (967-3315), P.O. Box 2578, 126 Ocean Avenue. Open daily mid-May to late October and mid-December through January 1, Wednesday through Sunday during the rest of the year, closed in January. Within walking distance of both village and shore, this old house has 10 guest rooms that are attractive, clean, and bright, individually decorated and filled with the spirit of a friendlier, simpler day. There is also a coveside cottage. The famous breakfast is included in the guest rates; it's also available to the public. Ownership has remained in the Reid family for many decades. The front porch is an inviting evening gathering place, and the paved path overlooking the creek leads to steps to a tiny gravel beach. $90–145; children's rates. Both children and pets are welcome.

Chetwynd House Inn (967-2235), P.O. Box 130TN, Chestnut Street. Open year-round. In 1978 Susan Chetwynd opened Kennebunkport's first B&B, a gracious 1840s home near Dock Square. The four antiques-furnished guest rooms have private baths and TVs; a top-floor two-room suite has skylights and a river view. Generous breakfasts—maybe ham and cheese omelets and a quarter of a melon with peaches, blueberries, and bananas—are served family-style at the dining room table; after-noon refreshments are offered in the sitting room/library. $90–169.

Charrid House (967-5695), 2 Arlington Avenue. Open year-round. Maine native Ann Dubay's cedar-shingled house, squirreled away in the heart of the Port's 19th-century neighborhood of "cottages," was built in 1887 as the "casino" that went with the elite Kennebunk River Club (subse-quently moved from next door to its present site on Ocean Avenue. A short block from Henry Parsons Park (see *Green Space*). The two up-stairs guest rooms (one with twin maple beds and the second with a queen) share a bath, sitting room, and sunroom. The house is charm-ing, furnished with antiques and nicely landscaped. Breakfast is served on the front sunporch. A studio apartment is also available in summer. $65 per room includes a full breakfast.

Kilburn House (967-4762), Chestnut Street, P.O. Box 424. Open year-round. A pleasant, turn-of-the-century home with four guest rooms on the second floor: two with double beds and private baths. A third-floor suite has a skylight and two bedrooms, a sitting room, and bath. New owners Arthur and Rose Mary Wyman are enthusiastic hosts and this is a good value, steps from Dock Square: $65–95 per room, $195 for the suite; full breakfast included.

Cove House Bed & Breakfast (967-3704), RR 3, 11 South Main Street. Kathy Jones has lived in Kennebunkport most of her life and offers a warm welcome to guests. The 18th-century Colonial house is down by Chick's Cove on the Kennebunk River, within walking distance of a beach and easy bicycling distance of Dock Square. The three pleasant guest rooms have private baths; there's a book-lined living room with a woodstove. $75–85, $20 per extra person, includes breakfast. A nearby cottage is $395–575 per week.

OTHER

Yachtsman Lodge and Marina (967-2511; 1-800-9-YACHTS), P.O. Box 2609, Ocean Avenue. Open late April through late October. This is a beautifully positioned property, right on the Kennebunk River, a short walk from Dock Square. Rooms are tastefully decorated with private riverside patios. Slip space for boats available at the marina. $99–179.

Schooners Inn (967-5333), P.O. Box 709, Ocean Avenue. Open seasonally. Every room has a water view, some with balconies and skylights, each named after a schooner and furnished with Thomas Moser furniture.

Amenities include an elevator, cable TV, phones; the master suite has a raised sitting area, whirlpool bath, and private deck. $135–250 high season, less off-season.

🐾✒ **Cabot Cove Cottages** (1-800-962-5424), P.O. Box 1082, 7 South Main Street. Open mid-May to mid-October. Fifteen old-style, knotty-pine-walled, freshly furnished cottages on 2 acres bordering a tidal cove (good for swimming). One- and two-bedroom units, all with new kitchen facilities. Within walking distance of Dock Square and a sandy beach. $95–150 per day, $740–950 per week in high season, $535–740 off-season. Pets accepted.

🐾✒🐾♿**Idlease Guest Resort** (985-4460; 1-800-99-BEACH), P.O. Box 3086, Route 9. Open April through October. A family-owned, family-geared motel and cottage complex within walking distance of Parsons Beach. Facilities include outdoor pool, indoor hot tub, yard games, horseshoes, basketball, and grills. $59–125 in-season, $39–89 off-season, with many off-season packages.

WHERE TO EAT

DINING OUT

White Barn Inn (967-2321), Kennebunk Beach. Open for dinner year-round except January. Rated among New England's top restaurants, the setting in an open-beamed 19th-century barn with a three-story glassed rear wall, overlooking extravagant seasonal floral displays. Walls are hung with original art, tables are set with silver and fine linens, and the fare is characterized as contemporary and regional. The five-course menu changes frequently, but you might begin with a lobster spring roll or boneless quail breast on a potato tart with beans, leeks, mushrooms, and roasted garlic vinaigrette, and dine on roasted rack of lamb and medallions of venison on a flaky pastry of sweet potato and Granny Smith apple puree with celery and red port sauce. Palate cleansers are served throughout the meal to prepare you for the next course. The service is formal and attentive. $62 prix fixe plus tax, beverage, and gratuity.

Kennebunkport Inn (967-2621), Dock Square, Kennebunkport. Open April through December. Breakfast and dinner daily May through October. Elegant fare in two lacy dining rooms. This is a widely respected favorite, with entrées ranging from vegetarian paella ($17) to the inn's signature bouillabaisse: lobster, shrimp, scallops, swordfish, mussels, and clams in a tomato-fennel broth, served with hot pepper sauce on the side ($24). Lighter fare is served in **Martha's Vineyard** (Martha Griffin is the owner-chef), a pleasant garden just off Dock Square, a good place for a glass of wine with grilled bruschetta, mussels, a grilled marinated chicken sandwich, or roasted vegetable Napoleon.

Salt Marsh Tavern (967-4500), Route 9, Lower Village, Kennebunk. Open daily for dinner; closed January to mid-March. Offering gracious dining overlooking a salt marsh, this widely respected restaurant is the work of artist Jack Nahil, former owner of the White Barn Inn. You might dine on an oven-braised rope of mussels in a tasso ham–spiked tomato sauce with whole-wheat couscous ($7.95), followed by applewood-smoked and braised veal osso buco with lemon-infused gravy and garlic mashed potatoes ($21) Save room for a profiterole. Entrées $18.95–26.95.

The Belvidere Room at the Tides Inn By-the-Sea (967-3757), Goose Rocks Beach, 6 miles northeast of Dock Square. Open mid-May to mid-October for breakfast and dinner. The preferred tables are on the sunporch with ocean views. Executive Chef Pamela White Glynn is making culinary waves. The chowder, for starters, is great (oysters and shrimp as well as fish in a light, buttery broth) and the menu might include turbans of sole (stuffed with scallops, crabmeat, and shrimp, finished with a fresh lemon and white wine cream sauce, served on a grilled polenta cake ($21) or homemade and hand-cut ravioli filled with red swiss chard, spinach, and a variety of cheeses ($16.96). Come early enough to walk the neighboring beach before or after.

Cape Arundel Inn (967-2125), Ocean Avenue, Kennebunkport. Open mid-April through December for dinner (closed Sunday evenings). This dining room should be called "Windows on the Ocean" because that's the view, with just one piece of land in view: former president Bush's estate, Walker's Point. Jack Nahil, who also owns the Salt Marsh Tavern, acquired this inn in 1997 and transformed both the dining room (maximizing the water view; tables are clothed in white, dressed with cobalt-blue glass) and the menu. The à la carte menu might include "first plates" like applewood-smoked and bacon-wrapped sea scallops with maple Dijon sauce and shredded radicchio ($9) and entrées like sautéed medallions of veal and portobello mushrooms with angelhair pasta and intense white clam sauce ($23.95).

Windows on the Water (967-3313), Chase Hill, Kennebunkport. Open year-round for lunch, dinner, and Sunday brunch (noon–2:30). A dining room with views of the port through arched windows, screened terrace or al fresco dining, and live entertainment on Friday and Saturday. Seafood is the specialty. Lobster-stuffed potato is popular at lunch. Light-fare selection for smaller appetites. Reservations are a must for dinner. Dinner entrées $18.95–24.95. Brunch is a good value.

𝒮 **The Colony** (967-3331), Ocean Avenue, Kennebunkport. The elegant dining room at this resort is open to the public for all three meals. Menu selections change each night and might include citrus shrimp and scallops on herbed fettuccine, and baked, maple-cured ham with cider sauce. Sunday brunch is served 11–2, with a different theme (such as "Christmas in July") each week The Friday-night buffet is popular at $26 (reserve) and Saturday night is a dinner dance. Sunday brunch (reserve) is good value at $16 per person. Evening pub and children's menus are also available.

Seascapes (967-8500), Pier Road, Cape Porpoise. Open for lunch and dinner daily May through October, closed some days in shoulder seasons. Seascapes combines a great location (on a working fishing pier) with well-known local management (Angela LeBlanc). Specialties include roasted lobster and "Christina's Shrimp." Entrées $17.95–27.50.

Mabel's Lobster Claw (967-2562), Ocean Avenue, Kennebunkport. April to mid-October, open for lunch and dinner. A favorite with locals, including George Bush. The specialty is lobster, pure or richly dressed with scallops, shrimp, and fresh mushrooms in a creamy Newburg sauce, topped with Parmesan cheese. The lunch special is a lobster roll with Russian dressing and lettuce in a buttery, grilled hot-dog roll. Entrées $11.95–16.95.

Arundel Wharf Restaurant (967-3444), 43 Ocean Avenue, Kennebunkport. Open 11:30–9, mid-April through October. A riverside restaurant and deck with a widely ranging menu, everything from a burger to bouillabaisse or prime rib. Desserts are above average. Entrées $7.25–18.95.

Grissini (967-2211), 27 Western Avenue, Kennebunk. Open year-round, except January, for dinner. A northern Italian trattoria opened in 1996 by the owner of the White Barn Inn, this is a 120-seat, informal, and trendy restaurant with seasonal outdoor terrace dining and an à la carte menu. You might dine on fresh Maine trout steamed in foil with extra-virgin oil, tomato, lemon, white wine, and herbs ($12.50) with a house salad ($4.50).

Kennebunk Inn (985-3351), 45 Main Street, Kennebunk 04043. Open daily for dinner. The inn itself is an 1820s building expanded in the later 19th century into the middle-of-Maine-Street (Route 1) inn that's revived its old reputation for fine dining under ownership by John and Kristen Martin and chef Dave Ruitenberg. The dining room is low-beamed and formal and the menu is ambitious. You might begin with crispy potato *galette* roped with a chive crème fraîche and smoked salmon ($6) and dine on herb-roasted breast of duck over a shiitake mushroom and port wine sauce or marinated and grilled loin of lamb set with balsamic-roasted shallots (both $18). The wine list is a point of pride.

Samuel Hill Tavern (985-4018), Route 1, Arundel. New ownership has put this restaurant high on local dining-out lists. The à la carte menu is large and moderately priced. Start with lobster and crab bisque ($4.25) and choose from more than a dozen entrées ranging from penne pasta with roasted eggplant, spicy sausage, and fresh oregano ($8.95) to roasted prime rib and Yorkshire pudding ($17.95 for 16 ounces). House wines by the glass and beer on tap as well as a respectable wine list.

LOBSTER AND CLAMS

Nunan's Lobster Hut (967-4362), Route 9, Cape Porpoise. Open for dinner May through October. This low, shedlike landmark packs them in and charges, too. This is the place for a classic lobster feed—there are sinks with paper towels to wipe off the melted butter. Lobster, clams, and pies are the fare. No credit cards.

The Lobster Pot (967-4607), 62 Mills Road, Cape Porpoise. A full-service restaurant open for lunch and dinner, good for a cheeseburger and fried seafood, steak, or pasta primavera, but it's lobster most people come for. Beer and wine served.

The Clam Shack (967-3321, 967-2560), Kennebunkport (at the bridge). Clams, lobsters, and fresh fish. A year-round seafood market and seasonal take-out stand that's worth the wait. Other seafood markets include **Preble Fish** (967-4620) and **Cape Porpoise Lobster Co.** (967-4268), both in Cape Porpoise, where the locals get their fish and steamed lobster to go. **Port Lobster** (967-2081), Ocean Avenue, Kennebunkport. Live or cooked lobsters packed to travel or ship, and lobster, shrimp, and crab rolls to go (several obvious waterside picnic spots are within walking distance).

EATING OUT

The Wayfarer (967-8961), One Pier Road, Cape Porpoise. Open from 6:30 AM for breakfast, lunch, and dinner. Closed Monday off-season. The atmosphere is upscale coffee shop with a counter and booths, and the food is superb: haddock chowder, spicy pan-blackened swordfish steak, or the night's roast (maybe turkey or Yankee pot roast). Smaller portions on some meals are available for kids. All meals include salad, starch, and hot rolls. BYOB from the general store across the road.

Alisson's (967-4841), 5 Dock Square, Kennebunkport. Open at 6:30 for breakfast; also serves lunch and dinner. A pub and grill "where the nicest people meet the nicest people," the true heart of Dock Square. Our lunch favorite is the salad in a monster tortilla shell with chili, salsa, and sour cream, topped with Monterey Jack. Dinner entrées run $12.95–17.95. **The Market Pub** (smoking permitted) is Dock Square's meeting place.

Boatyard (967-5221), 15 Christiansen Lane, Kennebunk. Just north of the Route 35/Route 9 junction in Lower Village, on the Kennebunk River. Open year-round for lunch and dinner. Hand-cut steaks and fresh pasta are specialties. The lounge and dining room overlook the river. Children's menu. Entrées average $10.

The Green Heron (967-3315), Ocean Avenue, Kennebunkport. *The* place for breakfast, a long-standing tradition, served on a glassed-in, waterside porch. The menu is vast and varied.

The Riverview Restaurant (967-3507), 29 Dock Square, Kennebunkport. Open for breakfast, lunch, and dinner. Pat and Bob Lyna preserve the vintage 1906 marble soda fountain and candy cases installed in the days when this was the Port's premier ice cream parlor (accessible by water as well as road). It's been the Riverview since 1940, and while the porch has been closed in, enlarging the dining rooms, this remains a low-key, good value place for all three meals.

Federal Jack's Restaurant & Brew Pub (967-4322), 8 Western Avenue, Kennebunk Lower Village. Open for lunch and dinner, offering a variety of handcrafted ales. The original Shipyard Ale brewery, located by the bridge into Kennebunkport. Complementing the English-style ales, the menu features chowders, seafood, and pub fare. Live acoustic music on weekends.

Leedy's Restaurant (324-5856), Alfred Square, Alfred. Open 7 AM–8 PM except Sundays, when it opens at noon. This is the kind of place you walk into and know immediately that everything is going to taste good. Straight-shooting, all-American cooking specializing in seafood and prime rib. $3.95–15.95.

Chase Hill Bakery (967-2283), Chase Hill, Kennebunkport. Open year-round. Delectable cookies, brownies, and cakes such as "Lemon Cloud." Everything is made from scratch. Soups and sandwiches. A few tables and fresh-ground Green Mountain Coffee if you like to linger.

ENTERTAINMENT

Arundel Barn Playhouse (985-5552), 53 Old Post Road, just off Route 1 by the Blue Moon Diner. Opened in 1998 in a totally revamped barn, this is a thoroughly professional classic summer theater with performances late every evening (with the exception of days between productions), June through late August, matinees Wednesdays and Fridays; tickets $16–20.

Hackmatack Playhouse (698-1807), Route 9, Beaver Dam, Berwick. Local actors, rave reviews.

Maritime Productions (967-0005; 1-800-853-5002), otherwise known as Kennebunk Theater Cruise, departing nightly June 5 through October 18 from Performance Marine by the bridge in Dock Square. Premiered in 1998 using the *Venture Inn* (see *Fishing*), this 2-hour cruise features dramatic renditions of "Seafaring Legends, Haunts, and Folklore"; beer, wine, and light fare served. $29 per adult, $27 seniors, $25 children.

River Tree Arts (985-4343) stages local productions and happenings.

Thursday-night summer concerts are performed at 7 PM on the lawn of the South Congregational Church in July and August (rain location: Community House; 985-4343).

Also see **Federal Jack's** and the **Colony** under *Where to Eat;* also see *Entertainment* in "Ogunquit and Wells."

SELECTIVE SHOPPING

ANTIQUES SHOPS
The Kennebunks are known as an antiques center with a half-dozen shops, representing a number of dealers, most on Route 1.

ART GALLERIES
You'll find some 50 galleries, most of them seasonal; **Mast Cove Galleries** (967-3453) on Maine Street is touted as the "largest group gallery in the area." Pick up a free copy of the annual "Guide to Fine Art, Studios, and Galleries" published by the **Art Guild of the Kennebunks,** available at the chamber of commerce and most galleries.

FARMS

❧ **Russel Acres Farm and Produce/Orchard Dell Deer Farm** (985-2435), 1797 Alewife Road. A red-deer breeding farm with a 1754 farmhouse. Visitors welcome; venison, quail, pheasant, rabbit, free-range chicken, and ice cream sold. Route 35, 2 miles west of I-95, exit 3.

❧ **Harris Farm** (499-2678), Bizzel Road, Dayton. July to October visitors are welcome to tour the dairy barn; fresh milk, eggs, and produce sold. The last Sunday in September and first in October is pick-your-own pumpkins; a short, pleasant ride up Route 35; call for directions.

SPECIAL SHOPS

Kennebunk Book Port, 10 Dock Square, Kennebunkport. Open year-round. The oldest commercial building in the port (1775) is one of the most pleasant bookstores in New England. Climb an outside staircase into this inviting mecca, which is dedicated to reading as well as to buying. Helpful, handwritten notes with recommendations from staff make browsing even easier. Books about Maine and the sea are specialties.

Tom's of Maine Natural Living Store (985-294), in the Lafayette Center, Storer and Main Streets, Kennebunk. Open daily year-round. This is the outlet for a variety of Tom's of Maine products made in town. Inquire about factory tours.

Brick Store Museum Shop (985-4802) 117 Main Street. A selection of books, handmade quilts, pottery, Indian baskets, painted boxes, and the like.

Port Canvas (967-2717), Dock Square, Kennebunkport. Open year-round. Canvas totes, suitcases, and hats, all made in Kennebunkport.

The Good Earth, Dock Square, Kennebunkport. Open daily May through October, varying hours; closed January to March. Stoneware in unusual designs—mugs, vases, and bowls. Great browsing in the loft showroom.

Clay Art (967-1177), 127 Ocean Avenue, Kennebunkport. A studio/gallery featuring Monique Bousquet's hand-built porcelain.

SPECIAL EVENTS

February: **Winter Carnival Weekend** *(first weekend);* **hay- and sleigh rides** on Saturday all month. Weekend **February Is for Lovers** events (967-0857).

March: **Kennebunkport tours and food show. Annual Kennebunk Fun Run.**

June: **Bed & Breakfast Inn and Garden Tour. Blessing of the Fleet.**

July: Old-fashioned **picnic, fireworks, and band concert.**

August: **Riverfest** *(first Saturday).* **Kennebearport Teddy Bear Show** *(second Saturday).*

September: **Old-Time Fiddlers Contest** *(second Saturday).*

December: **Christmas Prelude** *(first and second weekends);* Dock Square is decked out for Yuletide, and there are champagne receptions, church suppers, concerts, and carols; holiday fairs and open houses.

Old Orchard Beach, Saco, and Biddeford

When Thomas Rogers was granted 12 acres of land in 1657 and planted a fruit orchard, he undoubtedly had no idea his holding would one day become a resort area so popular that its year-round population would multiply by 10 in the summer.

In 1837, E. C. Staples first recognized the region's potential as a summer playground. From taking in boarders on his farm for $1.50 a week, he moved to building the first Old Orchard House. His instincts proved right, for rail travel brought a wave of tourists to the beach from both the rest of the United States and Canada.

The Grand Trunk Railroad did away with the long carriage ride from Montreal, and Canadians discovered that the Maine shore was a great place to vacation. The area is still a popular destination for French Canadian visitors, and you are likely to hear French spoken almost anywhere you go.

When the first pier at Old Orchard Beach was built in 1898, it stood 20 feet above and 1,800 feet out over the water and was constructed entirely of steel. The pavilions housed animals, a casino, and a restaurant. In the decades that followed, the original pier was rebuilt many times after being damaged by fire and storms, until a wider and shorter pier of wood was built in 1980. The pier continues to be a focal point in the community and a hub of activity.

An amusement area appeared in 1902 and grew after World War I. The 1920s brought big-name bands such as those led by Guy Lombardo and Duke Ellington to the Pier Casino, and thousands danced under a revolving crystal ball.

Fire, hard economic times, the decline of the railroad and steamboat industries—all took their toll on Old Orchard Beach over the years. Though the 7 miles of sandy beach and the amusement park near the pier endured, the 1980s saw the area deteriorate and succumb to a younger, wilder crowd.

In the early 1990s, the citizens decided to reclaim their town. A major revitalization plan widened sidewalks, added benches and streetlights, and passed and enforced ordinances that prevent "cruising" (repeatedly driving the same stretch of road). The result is a cleaner, more appealing, yet still lively and fun vacation spot.

Historically diverse, the area is also well known for the camp meetings held beginning in the late 1800s, first by Methodists, then by the Salvation Army. These meetings continue in the Ocean Park community today.

Biddeford and Saco are often called the twin cities, and no two Maine towns are more different or more closely linked. Saco is a classic Yankee town with white-clapboard mansions lining its main street. Biddeford is a classic mill town with a strong French Canadian heritage and mammoth, 19th-century brick textile mills that have stood idle since the 1950s. A few years back, the largest mills were renamed Saco Island and slated for redevelopment as a combination hotel, office, shop, and condo complex, a project that is seeing increasing development, but there is still a lot of unused space. Still, Biddeford is worth visiting, especially for *La Kermesse,* the colorful Franco-American festival in late June. Saco's Route 1 strip of family-oriented amusement parks is a big draw for those with children.

Parts of Scarborough's 49 square miles belong more in Casco Bay descriptions, but Pine Point and its surrounding area is the easternmost tip of Old Orchard Beach, and is often a less crowded, quieter spot to visit. A large saltwater marsh in Scarborough is also good for quiet relaxation and exploring by canoe.

GUIDANCE
Old Orchard Beach Chamber of Commerce (934-2500; fmly_fun@oldorchardbeachmaine.com; http://www.oldorchardbeach maine.com), P.O. Box 600 (First Street), Old Orchard Beach 04064, maintains a seasonal walk-in information center and offers help with reservations.

Biddeford-Saco Chamber of Commerce (282-1567; chamber@ biddefordsacomaine.com; http://www.biddefordsaco maine.com), 110 Main Street, Saco Island, Suite #1202, Saco 04072. Stocks many local brochures; helpful, friendly staff.

GETTING THERE
By air: **Portland International Jetport** is 13 miles north, and rental cars are available at the airport. You can also fly your own plane into **Sanford Airport.**

By car: Exits 5 and 6 off the Maine Turnpike (I-95) take you easily to the center of Old Orchard Beach. You can also find the town from Route 1 (turn by the large flea market).

GETTING AROUND
From many accommodations in Old Orchard Beach, you are close enough to walk to the pier, the town's center of activity. The **Biddeford-Saco-OOB Transit** also takes you right to the center of town. Call 282-5408 for schedules. **Mainely Tours** (774-0808) offers excursions to Portland, and will pick up and drop off at all area motels and campgrounds.

PARKING

An abundance of privately operated lots can be found in the center of Old Orchard Beach. Most charge $2–4 for any length of time—10 minutes or all day. There are meters on the street if you don't mind circling a few times to catch an available one, but at 15 minutes for a quarter, you're better off in lots if you plan to stay long.

MEDICAL EMERGENCY

Southern Maine Medical Center (283-7000), Biddeford.

VILLAGES

Ocean Park is a historic community founded in 1881 by Free Will Baptists and well known for its outstanding religious, educational, and cultural programs. The Ocean Park Association sponsors lectures, concerts, and other events throughout the summer. Within the community, there is a recreation hall, shuffleboard, and tennis courts, as well as an old-fashioned ice cream parlor and a smattering of gift shops. The entire community is a state game preserve.

Pine Point. This quiet and less crowded end of the beach offers a selection of gift shops, restaurants, lobster pounds, and places to stay.

Camp Ellis. At the end of a quiet peninsula where the Saco River blends with the ocean. Residents fight a constant battle with beach erosion, and some of the homes are frighteningly close to the shore. Fishing trips, whale-watching, a long breakwater great for walking, interesting shops, and a couple of good restaurants.

TO SEE AND DO

FOR FAMILIES

The Route 1 strip in Saco and nearby Orchard Beach makes up Maine's biggest concentration of kid-geared "attractions." Be prepared to pay.

* **Funtown/Splashtown USA** (284-5139), Route 1, Saco. Open daily (depending on the weather) mid-June through Labor Day, weekends in spring and fall. Water activities and a large amusement park. In addition to the new 100-foot wooden roller coaster "Excalibur," the park has bumper cars, New England's largest log flume, canoe ride down "Adventure River," hydrofighter, kiddie rides, antique cars.

* **Aquaboggan Water Park** (282-3112), Route 1, Saco. Open June through Labor Day. Several water slides, some with mats or tubes, "aquasaucer," swimming pool, bumper boats, mini-golf, arcade, shuffleboard, toddler area, wave pool.

* **Pirate's Cove Adventure Golf** (934-5086), 70 First Street, Old Orchard Beach. Thirty-six up-and-down miniature golf holes, waterfalls, ponds.

* **Palace Playland** (934-2001), Old Orchard Street, Old Orchard Beach. Open June through Labor Day. For more than 60 years, fun seekers have been wheeled, lifted, shaken, spun, and bumped in Palace Playland

rides. There's a 1906 carousel with hand-painted horses and sleighs, a Ferris wheel, a 60-foot-high (Maine's largest) water slide, and a new roller coaster in 1998. Charge is by the ride or $16.50 for an afternoon pass. An $11 kiddie pass is good for all two-ticket rides.

Village Park (934-7666), Old Orchard Beach. On the other side of the pier, across the road from Palace Playland. Arcade, games, kiddie rides. $6 for an all-day pass.

GOLF

Dunegrass (934-4513), 49 Ross Road, Old Orchard Beach, 27 holes.

Biddeford-Saco Country Club (282-5883), 101 Old Orchard Road, Saco, 18 holes.

Willowdale Golf Club (883-9351), off Route 1, Scarborough, 18 holes.

HORSEBACK RIDING

Horseback Riding Plus (883-6400), 338 Broadturn Street, Scarborough. Guided trail rides and beach rides for adults; kiddie and pony rides.

MUSEUMS

York Institute Museum (283-0958/0684), 371 Main Street, Saco. Open Tuesday, Wednesday, and Friday 1–4, Thursday noon–8. Also open Saturday and Sunday noon–4 June through August. Admission is $2 per adult, $1 under 16 and over 60 (free under 6). Original paintings, furniture, decorative arts, and tools; also natural history specimens. Trace the history of southern Maine; inquire about frequent lectures, tours, and special exhibits. The institute's **Dyer Library** next door has an outstanding Maine history collection.

Harmon Historical Museum, 4 Portland Avenue, Old Orchard Beach, is open Tuesday through Saturday 1–4, June through September, and by appointment. Home of the Old Orchard Beach Historical Society, the building is full of exhibits from the town's past. Each year, in addition to the regular school, fire, and aviation exhibits, there is a special exhibit on display. Pick up the timeline of the area's history and the walking map of historic sites.

RACING

Scarborough Downs (883-4331), off I-95, exit 6 in Scarborough. The largest harness-racing facility in New England. Live harness racing, as well as thoroughbred and harness racing via simulcast. Downs Club Restaurant (883-3022) is open for dinner and Sunday brunch.

Beech Ridge Motor Speedway (883-5227), Holmes Road, Scarborough. Summer stock-car racing every Saturday night.

CROSS-COUNTRY SKIING

Beech Ridge Farm Cross Country Ski Center (839-4098), 193 Beech Ridge Road, Scarborough. One hundred and fifty acres of fields and woods with 15 km of groomed tracks. Warming hut, rentals, lessons.

TENNIS

The Ocean Park Association (934-9325) maintains public tennis courts, open in July and August.

GREEN SPACE

BEACHES

Obviously, **Old Orchard Beach** is the big draw in this area, with 7 miles of sand and plenty of space for sunbathing, swimming, volleyball, and other recreation.

Ferry Beach State Park is marked from Route 9 between Old Orchard Beach and Camp Ellis, in Saco. The 100-plus-acre preserve includes 70 yards of sand, a boardwalk through the dunes, bike paths, nature trails, a picnic area with grills, lifeguards, changing rooms. $1 per person, free under age 12.

Bay View Beach, at the end of Bay View Road near Ferry Beach, is 200 yards of mostly sandy beach; lifeguards, free parking.

Camp Ellis Beach, Route 9, Saco. Some 2,000 feet of beach backed by cottages; also a long fishing pier. The commercial parking lots fill quickly on sunny days.

Pine Point, Route 9 (at the very end) is small and uncrowded, with a lobster pound and restaurant. The larger beach area just a bit closer to Old Orchard, with snack bar, changing room, and bathrooms, charges $5 for parking in the adjacent lot.

HIKING

Saco Trails, P.O. Box 852, Saco 04072, publishes a booklet called "Take a Hike in Saco" which lists several trails that are maintained for hiking.

NATURE PRESERVES

Scarborough Marsh Nature Center (883-5100), Pine Point Road (Route 9). Open daily mid-June through Labor Day, 9:30–5:30. The largest salt marsh (3,000 acres) in Maine is great for quiet canoe exploration. This Maine Audubon Nature Center offers canoe rentals, exhibits, a nature store, guided walking and canoe tours throughout the summer.

East Point Sanctuary (781-2330), Lester B. Orcutt Boulevard, Biddeford Pool. Open sunrise to sunset year-round. A 30-acre Maine Audubon Society preserve with trails, a view of Wood Island Light, and terrific birding in spring and fall.

LODGING

INNS AND BED & BREAKFASTS

The Carriage House (934-2141), 24 Portland Avenue, Old Orchard Beach 04064. Open year-round. Just off the main drag, this Victorian home with carriage house offers a welcome alternative to the abundance of motels and condominiums lining the beach. Eight pretty rooms furnished in period antiques in the main house, all with shared bath. We particularly like the downstairs room with a beautiful antique brass bed. The carriage-house suite is large and private, with a kitchen and TV. Also available is a five-room apartment with a deck. Common areas include a sauna, Jacuzzi, and a few exercise machines. $50–100 in-season.

The Atlantic Birches Inn (934-5295; cbolduc@gwi.net), 20 Portland Avenue, Old Orchard Beach 04064. Just around the corner from the center of activity is this lovely Victorian, shingle-style home, built in the area's heyday. Guest rooms are named after grand hotels from the era when the inn was built. The rooms are bright and cheerful with a mix of old and new furnishings. There is space for relaxing in the living room and on the large front porch shaded by white birches. The "cottage" next door also offers three rooms and two kitchenette suites with separate entrances. The in-ground pool is perfect on a hot day. $55–69 off-season, $75–120 in high season, includes a breakfast of muffins or coffee cake, fruit salad, cereal, coffee, and juice (cottage breakfast is muffins, coffee, and juice).

Crown 'n' Anchor Inn (282-3829; 1-800-561-8865), P.O. Box 228, Saco 04072-0228. This is a rare find: a Greek Revival, pillared mansion built in 1827 by a local lawyer, sold in 1841 to Stephen Goodale, in whose family it remained until 1925. Obviously, these were all well-to-do folk, and Stephen's son George became a Harvard professor of botany, involved with the planning and execution of the university's botanical museum (he was the man who commissioned those famous glass flowers). Hosts John Barclay and Martha Forester (along with Martha's late husband) ran an inn in Newcastle previously, and their experience shows. They continually strive to improve and update their property, and in 1998 the project was a new guest room in the former barn (it's hard to believe it was once a horse stable) as well as a library upstairs in the barn. Other common space, lovely for weddings and receptions (they host several each season) includes a double living room, the front room returned to its traditional look as a "receiving parlor." All rooms are painstakingly restored, each with an elegant bathroom. The Normandy Suite with its two working fireplaces and Jacuzzi bath is particularly nice, as is the new room. Throughout the inn is a large, intriguing collection of British royal family memorabilia. The inn is just up the street from the York Institute and a 10-minute drive from Saco's relatively uncrowded sands (see *Beaches*). A candlelight breakfast is served on fine china in the small but formal dining room. Pets accepted. $60–110 in high season, $60–90 off-season.

Country Farm (282-0208), 139 Louden Road, Saco 04072. Open year-round. Nothing fancy, just a 150-acre working farm (cattle, goats, several kittens, and a horse) that's been in the same family for several generations with two clean, comfortable guest rooms (shared bath) and plenty of space to wander—down to the shore of the Saco River. Arlene and Norman Gonneville seem to enjoy their guests, children included. $45 for a double includes a big breakfast; $10 per additional guest.

🐾 **Maine-lly Llamas Farm** (929-3057), Route 35, Hollis. May to November. A small working farm in a historic area. John and Gale Yohe offer comfortable guest rooms and a chance to learn about the farm or take a nature trek with their gentle llamas. Other animals include turkeys and Angora rabbits. Organically grown vegetable and flower gardens. Rooms are in the carriage house, with a separate staircase, part of an apartment that can be rented with kitchen for $110, including breakfast for up to five guests; otherwise $55 single, $65 double with breakfast. Guided llama treks are $20 per hour for two llamas, $10 for each additional llama.

OTHER LODGING

Old Orchard Beach offers an overwhelming number of motel, cottage, and condominium complexes both along the beach and on main roads. The chamber of commerce publishes a helpful "Old Orchard Beach Vacation Planner" that lists many of your choices (see *Guidance*). A word of caution—some of these establishments have been around for years, with no renovations and poor upkeep. We strongly recommend looking at a room before making reservations. Generally, condominiums on the beach are better kept, and many have reasonable rates.

Aquarius Motel (934-2626; aquarius.@gwi.net), 5 Brown Street, Old Orchard Beach 04064. A small, family-owned and -operated motel that's exceptionally clean, and right on the beach. The patio is a great place to relax after a day of sightseeing. Wes and Barb Carter are friendly and eager to help travelers plan their stay. Rates are $83–140 (for a two-room unit with three double beds and kitchenette) in-season. Many special rates in early spring and late fall. Three-night minimum on holiday weekends.

Ocean Walk Hotel (934-1716; 1-800-992-3779), 195 East Grand Avenue, Old Orchard Beach 04064. Forty-three well-kept rooms, from studios to oceanfront suites. The top-floor rooms in one building have very high ceilings, giving them a light, airy, spacious feel. $110–200 in-season.

Sea View (934-4180; 1-800-541-8439), 65 West Grand Avenue, Old Orchard Beach 04064. Forty-nine rooms, nine of which are oceanfront. Pretty landscaping, with an outdoor pool and a beautiful fountain in front. New rooms are modern and bright, and all the rooms are clean and well kept. The older building was slated for renovation in winter of 1998. $70–150.

The Gull Motel & Inn (934-4321), 89 West Grand Avenue, Old Orchard Beach 04064. An attractive motel, clean and family-oriented. The inn is right on the beach, with a great porch. Cottages also available by the week. $65–115 in high season; cottages $750 per week.

🐾 **Billowhouse** (934-2333), One Temple Avenue, Ocean Park 04063-7543. This 1880 Victorian guesthouse is Mary and Bill Kerrigan's retirement project. Completely renovated, yet retaining some of the old-fashioned charm, like original sinks in guest rooms. There are three ground-level efficiency apartments, and six more kitchenette units in the adjoining motel. The five

B&B rooms include a large fourth-floor room with a play loft for
All accommodations have private baths. Rooms in the guesthouse
deck overlooking the ocean; the beach is just steps away. $70–115 for B
rooms, $100–130 for kitchenette units in-season.

CAMPGROUNDS

Camping is a budget-minded family's best bet in this area. There are at least
a dozen campgrounds here (more than 4,000 sites in the area), many
geared to families and offering games, recreational activities, and trolley service to the beach in-season. Following are a couple of recommendations; check with the chamber (see *Guidance*) for a full listing.

✒️♿ **Bayley's Camping Resort** (883-6043; info@bayleys-camping.com), 27
Ross Road, West Scarborough 04074. Just down the road from Pine
Point, you hardly have to leave the grounds to have a terrific vacation.
Paddleboats, swimming pool, Jacuzzi, horseback riding, fishing, game
room, special programs for children and adults—the list goes on and on.
Four hundred sites and four rental trailers. $31.50–42 depending on
hook-ups; lower rates in spring and fall.

✒️♿ **Powder Horn** (934-4733; 1-800-934-7038; phorn36504@aol.com), P.O.
Box 366, Old Orchard Beach 04064. A 450-site campground with plenty
of recreation options—playgrounds, shuffleboard, horseshoes, volleyball, rec hall and game room, miniature golf, trolley service to the beach
in-season. $24–33 per night.

WHERE TO EAT

DINING OUT

Cornforth House (284-2006), 893 Route 1, Saco. Open for Sunday breakfast and dinner Tuesday through Sunday year-round. A restored brick
Federal farmhouse with a series of small dining rooms. The atmosphere
is casual, yet intimate. Meals are prepared with an emphasis on fresh,
local ingredients. Specialties include French-cut rack of lamb and pecan chicken with raspberry sauce. Save room for the delicious homemade desserts. $11.95–18.95.

✒️ **Village Inn** (934-7370), 213 Saco Avenue, Old Orchard Beach. Open for
lunch and dinner, with a large and varied menu. Also offers a seasonal
breakfast buffet. Lunch specials include fried seafood, pastas, and
chicken cordon bleu. At dinner, choices range from seafood specialties
and lobster to surf-and-turf or pasta. Children's menu. $6.95–17.95.

✒️ **Joseph's by the Sea** (934-5044), 55 West Grand Avenue, Old Orchard
Beach. Open April through December. Serving breakfast and dinner
daily in-season; hours vary the rest of the year, so call ahead. A fine family-
dining tradition in the area since 1968. The dining rooms overlook the
water, or you can dine on the garden patio. Dinner entrées include
grilled Tuscan swordfish and pepper-crusted filet mignon. Children's
menu $3.50–5.95. Entrées $13.95–23.95.

(934-0156), 28 East Grand Avenue, Old Orchard Beach.
ner at 5 PM. Fine dining in a historic house. The menu
'room ravioli primavera and roast duckling. Large wine
's whim" special. $10.95–17.95.

Restaurant (934-7701), Old Orchard Beach Street. Easy
the main road amid all the souvenir shops and take-out
stands, but don't. Established in 1946, this little place is still a great
alternative to the pier snacks. Home-cooked meals for breakfast, lunch,
and dinner at very reasonable prices. Daily lunch specials might include
macaroni and cheese, fish-and-chips. Try the homemade pies.

Chowderheads (883-8333), Oak Hill Plaza, Route 114, Scarborough. A few
minutes away from the center of activity, but just off Route 1. A small
place with a loyal following, now with two other locations in Portsmouth
and Yarmouth. The seafood chowder is thick, hearty, and delicious.
Specialties include swordfish steak, salmon pie, and fried seafood dinners. Portions are quite generous.

Hattie's (282-3435), Biddeford Pool. The local gathering spot for breakfast
and lunch. *The* place (the only place) to eat in Biddeford Pool, and it's a
find. Former president Bush knows it well.

Bufflehead's (284-6000), 122 Hills Beach Road, Biddeford Pool. Open
year-round daily for all three meals. Indoor and outdoor seating with a
great view. The menu includes seafood, pasta, burgers, and pizza.

Wormwoods (282-9679), Camp Ellis Beach, Saco. Open year-round, daily
for lunch and dinner. A large, friendly, old-fashioned place at the beginning of the breakwater. They go all out decorating for the seasons, and
can be counted on for good food, including lobster pie and fried clams.

TAKEOUT

Near the pier and on the main drag of Old Orchard Beach are an abundance of take-out stands and informal restaurants serving pizza, burgers,
hot dogs, fried seafood, fried dough, pier fries, ice cream, and almost
anything else you could want. Our favorites are **Bill's** for pizza, **Lisa's**
for pier fries.

Rapid Ray's (282-1847), 179 Main Street, Saco. A local icon for more than
40 years. Quick and friendly service from people who seem to know
almost everyone who walks through the door. Burgers, hot dogs, lobster
rolls, french fries, onion rings, and the like at great prices.

LOBSTER POUNDS

Bayley's Lobster Pound (883-4571), Pine Point, Scarborough. A popular
place for lobster and seafood.

Lobster Claw (282-0040), Route 5, Ocean Park Road, Saco. Lobsters
cooked outside in giant kettles, stews and chowders, cozy dining room,
and takeout available. Twin lobster specials, also steamers, fried seafood. Lobster packed to travel.

SELECTIVE SHOPPING

✍ **Way-Way General Store** (283-1682), 93 Buxton Road (Route 112). Worth a short drive out of your way to see this little piece of history in a small red and white, stone and tile building. Open since 1929, with family members of the original owner still running it. Small and chock-full of things, including an amazing array of penny candy.

Cascade Flea Market, Route 1, Saco. One of Maine's largest outdoor flea markets open daily in summer.

Stone Soup Artisans, (283-4715), 228 Main Street, Saco. Quality crafts from more than 60 artisans.

ENTERTAINMENT

The Ballpark (934-1124), Old Orchard Beach. Once a professional baseball stadium, the park now features a mix of entertainment throughout the summer including sporting events, concerts, fairs, festivals, and family shows.

City Theater (282-0849), Main Street, Biddeford. This 660-seat, 1890s theater offers a series of live performances.

SPECIAL EVENTS

Late June: **La Kermesse Franco-American Festival,** Biddeford—parade, public suppers, dancing, entertainment highlighting culture and traditions. **Beachfest**—major sand-sculpture exhibit and competitions, entertainment, male and female physique contests, Frisbee tournament, more.

June through Labor Day: Fireworks near the pier every Thursday at 9:30 PM.

August: Ocean Park **Festival of Lights** and **Salvation Army camp meetings** under the new pavilion in Ocean Park. **Beach Olympics,** featuring competitions, music, displays, and presentations to benefit the Maine Special Olympics.

September: **Classic car weekend,** Old Orchard Beach.

December: **Tree-lighting ceremony** with sleigh rides, refreshments, holiday bazaar, caroling, and a bonfire on the beach.

II. CASCO BAY

Casco Bay

KIM GRANT

Portland Area

In Portland, seagulls perch on skyscrapers and a smell and sense of the sea prevails. Northern New England's most sophisticated and one of its most important cities since the 1820s, it is blessed with distinguished buildings from every era. Portland provides a showcase for resident painters, musicians, actors, dancers, and craftspeople.

Portland is Maine's largest city, yet it still has a small-town feel. The total population still hovers around 64,000, and downtown is invitingly walkable. Hundreds of shops and galleries and dozens of restaurants are packed into ornate Victorian buildings in one, five-block waterfront neighborhood. Known as the Old Port Exchange, this area was a canker at the city's heart until the 1970s, when it was first slated for urban renewal.

Portland's motto, *Resurgam* ("I shall rise again"), could not be more appropriate. The 17th-century settlement was wiped out twice by Native Americans, then once by the British. It was not until after the American Revolution that the community really began to prosper—as witnessed by the Federal-era mansions and commercial buildings like the granite and glass Mariner's Church, built in 1820 to be the largest building in the capital of a brand-new state.

This port is the one that was loved by a small boy named Henry Wadsworth Longfellow, who later wrote:

> *I remember the black wharves and the ships*
> *And the sea-tides tossing free*
> *And the Spanish sailors with bearded lips*
> *And the beauty and mystery of the ships*
> *And the magic of the sea.*

Portland continued to thrive as a lumbering port and railroad terminus through the Civil War and until the Independence Day at that war's end. Then disaster struck again. On July 4, 1866, a firecracker flamed up in a Commercial Street boatyard and quickly destroyed most of downtown Portland. The city rose like the legendary phoenix, rebuilding yet again, this time in sturdy brick. The buildings were replete with the kind of flourishes you would expect of the Gilded Age, years during

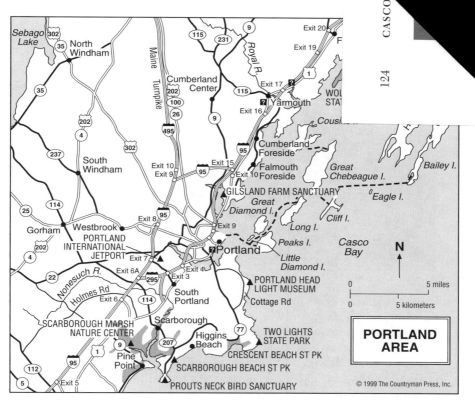

Map labels:
Sebago Lake, North Windham, 302, 35, 115, 231, 9, Exit 20, Exit 19, Maine Turnpike, Royal R., 1, Exit 17, Cumberland Center, 202, 100, 115, Yarmouth, WOL STA, 35, 26, 9, Exit 16, Cousi, 202, 4, 495, 95, Cumberland Foreside, 237, South Windham, 302, Exit 10, Exit 9, Exit 15, 95, Falmouth Foreside, Great Chebeague I., Bailey I., 25, 114, Exit 10, GILSLAND FARM SANCTUARY, Eagle I., Exit 8, 95, Great Diamond I., Cliff I., Gorham, Westbrook, PORTLAND INTERNATIONAL JETPORT, Exit 9, Long I., Casco Bay, N, 0 5 miles, 0 5 kilometers, Peaks I., Portland, 202, 4, Exit 7, Exit 4, Little Diamond I., 22, Nonesuch R., Exit 6A, Exit 3, PORTLAND HEAD LIGHT MUSEUM, Holmes Rd, 295, Exit 6, 114, South Portland, Cottage Rd, SCARBOROUGH MARSH NATURE CENTER, Scarborough, 77, TWO LIGHTS STATE PARK, PORTLAND AREA, 1, 9, 207, Higgins Beach, CRESCENT BEACH ST PK, 112, 95, Pine Point, SCARBOROUGH BEACH ST PK, 5, Exit 5, PROUTS NECK BIRD SANCTUARY, © 1999 The Countryman Press, Inc.

which these city blocks were the core of northern New England's shipping, rail, and manufacturing businesses.

These very buildings, a century later, were "going for peanuts," in the words of a real estate agent who began buying them up in the late 1960s. The city's prominence as a port had been eclipsed by the opening of the St. Lawrence Seaway in 1959, and its handsome Grand Trunk Station was torn down in 1966. Decent folk did their shopping at the department and chain stores up on Congress Street, itself threatened by the Maine Mall out by the interstate highway.

Down by the harbor, artists and craftspeople were renting shop fronts for $50 per month. They formed the Old Port Association, hoping to entice people to stroll through the no-man's-land that separated the shops on Congress Street from the few famous fish restaurants and the ferry dock on Commercial Street. That first winter they strung lights through upper floors to convey a sense of security, and they shoveled their own streets, a service the city had long ago ceased to provide to that area. At the end of the winter, they celebrated their survival by holding the first Old Port Festival, an exuberant street fair that is still held each June.

MAINE CONVENTION & VISITORS BUREAU

Portland Head Light

Portland's Old Port Exchange continues to thrive, and on its fringes, new semi-high-rise, red brick buildings blend with the old and link the Old Port with Congress Street.

Condominiums now line a wharf or two, but Portland remains a working port. It's also a departure point for the ferry to Yarmouth (Nova Scotia) and for the fleet of Casco Bay Liners that regularly transport people, mail, and supplies among Casco Bay's Calendar Islands. These range from Peaks Island—accessible in just 20 minutes by commuter ferry, and offering rental bikes, guided sea kayaking, lodging, and dining—to Cliff Island, more than an hour's ride, offering sandy roads and the feel of islands usually found farther Down East. In summer, these ferries bill their longer runs as Casco Bay Cruises and add Music Cruises and a lazy circuit to Bailey Island. Two excursion lines (one from South Freeport) also service Eagle Island, preserved as a memorial to Arctic explorer Admiral Peary. The waterfront is, moreover, the departure point for deep-sea fishing, harbor cruises, and daysailing.

In recent years, Portland has celebrated a renewed commitment to Congress Street and the surrounding area. This section of the city has been developed as the Arts District, and the arrival of several notable galleries, theater performances, the renovation of Merrill Auditorium, and the summer concert series held in a number of locations have contributed to the thriving arts scene. The old Porteous building is now home to the Maine College of Art, and a number of funky secondhand shops, as well as an L. L. Bean outlet store, have popped up nearby. Guides in purple shirts have been added to the streets in summer months, so finding your way around the area has become increasingly simple and fun.

In 1998, a brand-new public market modeled after Seattle's Pike Place opened, bringing with it the opportunity to purchase fresh fruits, vegetables, breads, baked goods, meat, fish, and much more from a variety of local vendors. The open market, enclosed in glass, houses close to 30 vendors offering their wares year-round. The market is built just a block away from where a market hall stood from 1825 through 1882, in the center of town, what is now Monument Square. Since 1900 an outdoor farmer's market has operated in this location seasonally, and will continue to do so, with an additional farmer's market setting up along Preble Street outside the market building.

Portland was also the boyhood home of the director John Ford, a fact that was little recognized until the summer of 1998, when a John Ford Celebration showcased many of his greatest works. A statue was erected at the corner of Center and Fore Streets in the Gorham's Corner neighborhood where Ford's father operated a pub. The area surrounding this neighborhood offers several artist's studios, galleries, restaurants, and shops.

Art lovers can easily spend a day among Portland's museums and galleries. The Portland Museum of Art quintupled in the 1980s and exhibits American painters like John Singer Sargent, Winslow Homer, George Bellows, and Jamie Wyeth. Next door, the Children's Museum of Maine is sure to please both adults and children with its interactive, educational displays.

The range of ethnic foods available in the city is extensive, from Thai to Japanese to Tex-Mex. Portland boasts more than 40 restaurants, most of which are independently owned rather than large franchises, though there are plenty of those by the mall as well. Downtown harbors some appealing bed & breakfasts, as well as a few good hotels. Cape Elizabeth, just south of Portland, offers beaches and birding, and both Falmouth and Yarmouth, just east of the city, are worth exploring.

GUIDANCE

The Convention and Visitors Bureau of Greater Portland (772-5800; www.visitportland.com), 305 Commercial Street, Portland 04101, publishes *Greater Portland Visitors Guide,* listing restaurants, sights, museums, and accommodations. Its walk-in information center is well stocked with menus and pamphlets, and courtesy phones connect with lodging places and services. There is also a small kiosk in Congress Square, with brochures and maps.

Portland's Downtown District (772-6828; www.portlandmaine.com), 400 Congress Street, Portland 04101, offers information about performances, festivals, and special events. They publish a great little guide to services, attractions, dining, and lodging.

The **Maine Tourism Association** (846-0833) staffs a major state information center on Route 1 in Yarmouth, just off I-95, exit 17.

For details about guided walking tours of the city, contact **Greater**

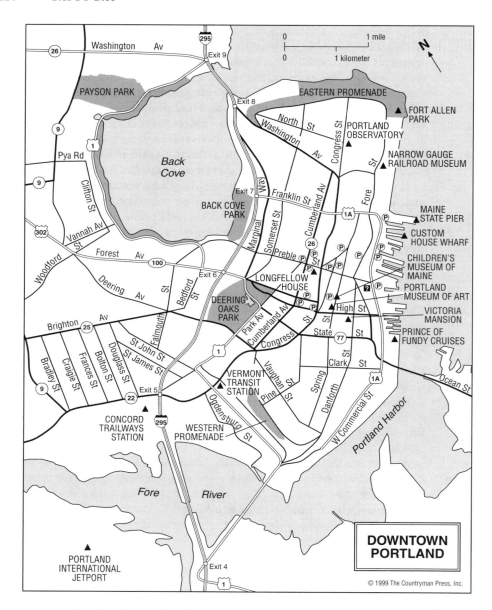

DOWNTOWN PORTLAND

© 1999 The Countryman Press, Inc.

Portland Landmarks (774-5561), 165 State Street, Portland 04101. Be sure to request the self-guided walking tour leaflets (also available from the visitors bureau) that outline walking tours of Congress Street, the Old Port Exchange, State Street, and the Western Promenade.

GETTING THERE

By air: **Portland International Jetport** (774-7301) is served by Delta Air Lines (1-800-221-1212), Continental Airlines (1-800-525-0280),

United (1-800-241-6522), USAir (1-800-428-4322), Northwest Airlink (1-800-225-2525), Pine State Airlines (1-800-353-6334), and Downeast Express (1-800-983-3247). Car rentals at the airport include National, Avis, Hertz, and Budget.

By bus: **Vermont Transit** (772-6587) stops in Portland daily en route from Boston to points farther up the coast and to inland points north. The terminal is dingy, inconvenient to the Old Port and ferries, and it closes early, forcing passengers to stand out in the cold and rain. **Concord Trailways** (828-1151) stops in Portland daily en route from Boston to Bangor or coastal points. Their station is also quite a distance from the Old Port and ferries, but it is bright and clean and remains open for late arrivals. Concord offers movies and music on the way.

By ferry: Canadians may cruise to Portland aboard the **Prince of Fundy Cruises Limited** ferry, *Scotia Prince,* out of Yarmouth, Nova Scotia (775-5616; seasonally, 1-800-482-0955 in Maine; 1-800-341-7540 outside Maine). Overnight cruises are offered early May through October. Prices vary, depending on the season, cabin, or special package. Restaurants, shops, live entertainment, and a casino are some of the features passengers enjoy aboard. The luxury cruise vessel accommodates 1,500 passengers in 800 cabins, plus 250 cars.

GETTING AROUND

The **Metro** (774-0351) bus transfer system serves Greater Portland. The Metro city buses connect airport and city, as well as offering many convenient routes around the city.

PARKING

Portland meters are 25¢ per half hour, limited to 2 hours, hard to come by, and checked often. The city urges visitors to use its many parking garages. The **Fore Street Garage** (439 Fore Street) puts you at one end of the Old Port, and the **Custom House Square Garage** (25 Pearl Street), at the other. The **Casco Bay Garage** (Maine State Pier) and **Free Street Parking** (130 Free Street, just up from the art museum) are also handy. **The Gateway Garage** next to the Radisson Eastland Hotel is close to the arts district.

MEDICAL EMERGENCY

Portland Ambulance Service (dial 911). **Maine Medical Center** (871-0111), 22 Bramhall Street, Portland. **Mercy Hospital** (879-3000).

VILLAGES

Cape Elizabeth is a peaceful residential area. The main village of **Pond Cove** is a refuge for many Portland commuters, who live in homes overlooking the Atlantic Ocean. Two Lights State Park and a large, popular beach are also part of this community.

Falmouth is a suburb of Portland. The village, known as **Falmouth Foreside,** has tremendous old houses in the original section of town. A popular marina and restaurant offer terrific views and water access.

Yarmouth has carried the charm of a Colonial village into the 19th century with style. Commercial and tourist-aimed businesses are relegated to Route 1, leaving the inner village lined with 18th- and 19th-century homes mixed with quaint stores and antiques shops. North Yarmouth Academy's original Greek Revival brick buildings, the 18th-century meetinghouse, and many fine old churches are must-sees for architecture buffs. Several parks are open to the public, including the village green with its historic, round railroad station and Royal River Park, offering recreation in all seasons. In July, Yarmouth really comes alive with the clam festival.

ISLANDS

No one seems sure how many islands there are in Casco Bay. Printed descriptions range from 136 to 222. Seventeenth-century explorer John Smith dubbed them the Calendar Islands, saying there was one for every day of the year. Regular year-round ferry service runs to six of the islands, five of which invite exploration (see *Boat Excursions* under *To Do*).

The best way to experience an island vacation is to rent a cottage and stay for a week. For listings on summer cottages in the Casco Bay Islands, contact Casco Bay Development Association, Peaks Island 04108. Two local realtors also offer rental listings: **Port Island Realty** (766-5966 or 775-7253) and **Ashmore Realty** (772-6992).

Peaks Island. Just 3 miles from Portland (a 20-minute ferry ride), Peaks is one of the most accessible islands for exploring. Ferry service runs regularly, even off-season, as many of the island's approximately 1,000 year-round residents commute to the mainland for work and school. In summer, the population swells to between 5,000 and 6,000, and day-trippers are common. A good way to find out what is happening on the island is to check out the bulletin boards, one at the top of Welch Street, another at Hannigan's IGA. The shore road around the island is about a 5-mile stretch, great for walking or bicycling. When we were poking around, we veered off the beaten path and ended up on a trail that led through the woods, by the remains of the fortifications of Battery Steele, a World War II naval artillery emplacement. Bicycle rentals are available on the island at **Brad's Re-Cycled Bike Shop** (766-5631), next to the **Peaks Island Mercantile,** an interesting shop to browse in. Brad goes by the honor system when he isn't there, depending on folks to fill out the form he leaves, place payment in the box, and return the bikes when they are through. **The Fifth Maine Regiment** is an interesting historical museum that focuses on military paraphernalia from the Civil War to World War II. **Maine Island Kayak** (766-2373; also see *To Do—Sea Kayaking*) offers trips from half a day to several days, along with kayak instruction. If you get hungry while on the island, there are several seasonal choices, including sandwiches at the Peaks Island Mercantile in summer and from Hannigan's IGA year-round. **Jones Landing** (766-5542), just off the ferry, serves lunch and dinner in-season, and offers live entertainment some evenings, as well as reggae music every Sunday. **Peaks Island House** (766-4400) serves all three meals, and has outside deck seating in nice weather. This is also the only place on the island that provides overnight lodging (766-4406 for reservations), unless you rent a cottage. Four rooms, recently renovated, with private baths and water views. The **Peaks Café** (766-2479) offers a complete range of coffee choices, as well as pastries, fruit, and juices. **Bakery on the Bay** (766-2079) is open year-round, selling breads and other bakery goods, sandwiches, and coffee.

Great Chebeague is accessible by both **Casco Bay Lines** and **Chebeague Transportation Company** (846-3700), a community-owned company with far more frequent service. This boat departs from the Cousin's Island Wharf almost every hour in the summer, less often fall through spring. Parking at the wharf is limited much of the time. Your best bet is to call for directions to the Drowne Road Parking Area in Cumberland. A bus picks up passengers and cargo, transporting them to the boat and back. Locals simply call this island Chebeague, since no one lives on Little Chebeague, and access to the smaller island is limited to those with boats, or waders at low tide. Little Chebeague was once a thriving resort until the hotel burned down, cottages were abandoned, and the remains were left to deteriorate. The military used the island for a time during World War II, and in the 1970s it was sold to the state, and is still an undeveloped state park. Camping and swimming are allowed on Little Chebeague, but there are no facilities on the island, and visitors should be aware that ticks and poison ivy abound.

Chebeague is the largest island in Casco Bay, at 4½ miles long and approximately 2 miles wide. The year-round population is around 325, but the summer population grows to around eight times that. A bike is the best way to explore this island. Rentals are available in the basement of the **Sunset House** (846-6568; sunsethse@aol.com) a comfortable place with five guest rooms, each with private bath. Two have water views, and the entire inn is decorated with furniture and objects from the voyages of a sea captain as well as the Komlosy's travels. Breakfast is included and the Sunset House is open year-round. $85–115 depending on room.

Other places to stay on the island include the **Chebeague Orchard Inn** (846-9488), which offers five rooms, all with shared bath, furnished in antiques, some with water views; open year-round. Hosts Vickie and Neil Taliento also have a fireplace in the common room, bikes for guests, and helpful information for visitors. **The Chebeague Island Inn** (846-5155) is a classic summer hotel open Memorial Day through September. The rooms aren't fancy, but the 21-room hotel is the largest accomodations on the island, and some rooms offer private baths and water views. We like the large, open-beamed living room with its massive stone fireplace, brightly upholstered chairs, and rainy-day board games. Rates are $85–125 for a double in-season, including breakfast. The dining room serves all three meals in summer, but it is sometimes closed for private functions.

The **Nellie G. Café** (846-3882), on South Road about a mile from the Stone Pier, serves lunch and dinner year-round (closed Mondays after Columbus Day). One of their specialties is the island crabmeat pie. Take-out options include pizza, burgers, and hot dogs. You can also pick up takeout at Doughty's Island Market.

To relax and enjoy the scenery, head to **Chandler's Cove,** a white sand beach, or the beach near **Coleman's Cove**. Golfers will want to try the **Great Chebeague Golf Club** (846-9478), a beautiful nine-hole course founded in 1923, where nonmembers can play anytime except Monday or Thursday mornings. If you don't have a bike and need help getting around on the island, call **Veteran's Taxi** (846-4878).

Long Island is 3 miles long and approximately a mile wide. There is one general store and a popular restaurant, **The Spar** (766-3310), which serves lunch and dinner featuring fresh local seafood, lobster, steaks, and pasta. Full bar, moorings for boats, picnic lunches available. Bike rentals are also available here. The beaches, tidal pools, and remains of old schooners are fun to explore.

Great Diamond Island. In 1891, construction was begun on an army post on this island. **Fort McKinley** was one of five forts in the harbor, left to deteriorate after the two world wars, until developers began restoration in the early 1980s. **Diamond Cove** (772-2992; 766-5804 for reservations), P.O. Box 3572, Portland 04104, is the result, a resort area offering townhouse rentals and sales. Amenities include a health club, beaches, a restaurant, tennis courts, a heated pool, and a walking path and woodland area for hiking, biking, and cross-country skiing. Expensive and rather exclusive, but it may be worth the splurge. We've received conflicting reports about the restaurant, **Diamond's Edge,** but it is the only place to eat on the island (aside from the beach bar). Open for lunch and dinner from mid-May through October. Popular Sunday brunch.

Cliff Island is the most remote island from the ferry terminal, a full 1½-hour ride. It is also the most rustic of the populated islands, with dirt roads and no overnight accomodations, but a peaceful feel and nice sandy beaches.

TO SEE

MUSEUMS
Portland Museum of Art (775-6148; for a weekly schedule of events and information, 773-ARTS; 1-800-639-4067), 7 Congress Square, Portland.

Tuesday, Wednesday, and Saturday 10–5, Thursday and Friday 10–9, and Sunday noon–5; closed New Year's Day, July 4, Thanksgiving, and Christmas. $6 per adult, $5 per student (with ID) or senior citizen, and $1 per child 6–12. Maine's largest art museum houses an extensive collection of American artists, featuring Maine-based masters such as Winslow Homer, Edward Hopper, and Andrew Wyeth. The adjoining museum buildings include the splendid, Federal-style **McLellan-Sweat** mansion, built for Portland's biggest ship owner in 1800. The museum itself was founded in 1882. In 1991, Joan Whitney Payson's collection was also absorbed into the museum. It includes works by Renoir, Degas, Prendergast, and Picasso, as well as Homer and Wyeth. Changing exhibits also.

𝒮 **Children's Museum of Maine** (828-1234), 142 Free Street, Portland. Next door to the Museum of Art, this elaborate museum offers three levels of interactive, hands-on exhibits, designed to help the young and old learn together. Permanent exhibits include Main Street USA (with cave, farm, supermarket, bank, and fire department), a space shuttle, a news center, and a computer room with games and learning activities. In 1998, the second floor was renovated to become a science center, and a new toddler area was also developed. Enough to keep kids and their parents entertained for an entire afternoon.

𝒮 **The Museum at Portland Head Light** (799-2661), 1000 Shore Road in Fort Williams Park. Open June through October, 10–4, and November, December, April, and May, weekends 10–4. $2 per adult, $1 children 6–18. This is the oldest lighthouse in Maine, first illuminated in 1791 per order of George Washington. It is now automated, and the former keeper's house has been transformed into an exceptional lighthouse museum. This is a great spot to come just for the view. Bring a picnic; there are tables with water views as well as the ruins of an old fort in the surrounding **Fort Williams Park,** just 4 miles from downtown Portland: Take State Street (Route 77) south across the bridge to South Portland, then left on Broadway and right on Cottage Street, which turns into Shore Road. On the way back, you might want to check out the **Spring Point Museum** (799-6337) on Fort Road, marked from Route 77 in South Portland. Open Memorial Day weekend through October, Thursday to Sunday 1–4; $2 per adult, $1 children. Sited in a brick repair shop that was part of Fort Preble and is now part of Southern Maine Technical College, it mounts changing exhibits on local maritime history and features an ongoing restoration of the pieces of the *Snow Squall,* an 1850s Portland clipper ship wrecked in the Falkland Islands. The **Spring Point Lighthouse,** at the end of a breakwater, is another good vantage point on the harbor.

Portland Fire Museum (772-2040), 157 Spring Street. Open mid-June to mid-September, Monday and Thursday 7–9 PM. Donations requested. Given Portland's unusual fire-fighting history, this collection of artifacts and photos is something to see. Housed in a granite Greek Revival firehouse.

✐ **Maine Narrow Gauge Railroad Co. & Museum** (828-0814), 58 Fore Street, Portland. Open daily 10–4. Hard to spot if you aren't looking for it—but you should. From the 1870s to the 1940s, Maine had a unique, smaller-than-standard railroad system, with rails spaced just 2 feet apart. The "2-footers" were more economically viable, and five lines carried visitors to the more remote parts of the state. After the lines went out of business, a millionaire cranberry grower who loved the 2-footers bought as much of the equipment and rail cars as he could. His collection evolved into Edaville, a major tourist attraction until its closing in 1991 due to lease disputes. Phineas Sprague Jr. and a group of railroad enthusiasts brought the cars and equipment back to Portland and set up this great little museum. Displays include the world's only 2-foot parlor car, the "Rangeley," locomotives, a railbus, a model-T inspection car, and a caboose. There is also a short video on 2-footer history, and well-informed, enthusiastic guides show you around. Track has been laid running alongside the new Eastern Prom trail, and train rides are available daily May through October and other times by special arrangement. A "Santa Train" runs in the holiday season.
Also see *Selective Shopping—Galleries*.

HISTORIC SITES

Wadsworth-Longfellow House, 485 Congress Street. Maintained by the Maine Historical Society (879-0427), which also offers the Maine History Gallery and an extensive research library next door. Open June through October, Tuesday through Sunday 10–4 (closed July 4 and Labor Day; gallery and library open in winter, Wednesday through Saturday noon–4). $3 per adult, $1 per child under 18. Allow 45 minutes for a guided tour. Built by the poet's grandfather, this was the home of an important Portland family. Peleg Wadsworth was a Revolutionary War hero, and the entire clan of Wadsworths and Longfellows was prominent in the city. The house, in which Henry spent his childhood, is a good example of how such families lived in the 19th century. The garden behind the house has been adapted from gardens of the era, and most furnishings are original. At Christmastime, the Wadsworth-Longfellow House has a popular open house, with decorations and festivities of the season.

✐ **Portland Observatory** (772-5561), 138 Congress Street. Built in 1807, this octagonal, shingled landmark is the last surviving 19th-century signal tower on the Atlantic. The 102 steps to the top are currently closed to visitors due to the deteriorated state, but Greater Portland Landmarks is working with the city on restoration plans to save the historic building.

Victoria Mansion, the Morse-Libby House (772-4841), 109 Danforth Street (at the corner of Park Street). Open May through October, Tuesday through Saturday 10–4, Sunday 1–5 (closed July 4 and Labor Day). $4 per adult, $2 per child 6–18. About as Victorian as can be, this brownstone Italianate home was built in 1859 for a Maine native who had made his fortune in the New Orleans hotel business. The interior is

extremely ornate: frescoed walls and ceilings, a flying s‍
hand-carved balusters of Santo Domingo mahogany
mirrors, marble mantels, ornate chandeliers, stained
more. The Victoria Mansion reopens during the Chri‍
special programs.

First Parish Church (773-5747), 425 Congress Street. O‍ by appointment. A vintage 1826 meetinghouse in which the pews are tipped forward—so that dozing parishioners would fall onto the floor. This is the site of the drafting of the Maine Constitution, and it now houses artifacts from the 17th century.

Neal Dow Memorial (773-7773), 714 Congress Street. Open year-round, Monday through Friday 11–4. Currently the headquarters of the Maine Women's Christian Temperance Union, this handsome Greek Revival mansion was built in 1829 by Neal Dow, the man responsible for an 1851 law that made Maine the first state to prohibit the manufacture and sale of alcoholic beverages, and it is maintained as a memorial to him.

Tate House (774-9781), 1270 Westbrook Street (follow Congress Street west across the Fore River to Westbrook). Open July and August, Tuesday through Saturday 10–3, Sunday 1–4. $4 per adult, $1 per child under 12. George Tate, mast agent for the Royal Navy, built this Georgian house in 1755 to reflect his important position. Both inside and outside are unusual, distinguished by fine windows, a gambrel roof, wood paneling, and elegant furniture. An 18th-century herb garden is part of the historic landscape.

GUIDED TOURS

Mainely Tours and Gifts, Inc. (774-0808), 5½ Moulton Street. Kathy and John Jenkins have operated this tour company, the only one of its kind, in Portland since 1995, offering narrated tours highlighting the history, architecture, and culture of the city. Held aboard a mini-coach bus, the 90-minute tour leaves five times a day from mid-May through mid-October. Other tours available include a combination bus tour/cruise package, and a tour of Kennebunkport. They will pick up at area hotels with prior reservations.

TO DO

BICYCLING

Hundreds of acres of undeveloped land offer some great bicycling. Call **Portland Trails** (775-2411) for designated trails. Three new maps, available for $1 each, have been put out by the **Bicycle Transportation Alliance of Portland (BTAP)**, P.O. Box 4506, Portland 04112. These detail routes through historic Portland, the islands, and the lighthouse trail. Rentals and service are available at several locations around the city. A couple of good bets are **Back Bay Bicycle** (773-6906), 333 Forest Avenue, and **Cycle Mania** (774-2933), 59 Federal Street. Both shops sponsor group rides and can be great sources of bicycling information. (Also see *Islands*.)

BOAT EXCURSIONS

For ferry information to Chebeague Island, see also *Islands*.

Casco Bay Lines (774-7871), Casco Bay Ferry Terminal, 56 Commercial Street at Franklin. Founded in 1845, this business was said to be the oldest continuously operating ferry company in the country when it went bankrupt in 1980. The present, quasi-municipal Casco Bay Island Transit District looks and functions much the way the old line did. Its brightly painted ferries are still lifelines to six islands, carrying groceries and lumber as well as mail.

Casco Bay excursions include the year-round, daily mail-boat run (3 hours), putting into all the islands in the morning and again in the afternoon, and a variety of seasonal, special excursions including a 5½-hour Bailey Island Cruise (see "Brunswick and the Harpswells"). Also year-round, frequent, daily car-ferry service to Peaks Island.

Coast Watch & Guiding Light Navigation Co. Inc. (774-6498), Long Wharf, Portland. Runs Memorial Day through Columbus Day. The *Kristy K* takes you out to Eagle Island, the former home of Admiral Peary, now maintained by the state as a historic site and nature preserve (see the "Brunswick" and "Freeport" chapters); the 49-passenger *Fish Hawk* is used for a harbor and island cruise and for seal-watching. Group charters available.

Bay View Cruises (761-0496), Fisherman's Wharf, Portland. Daily June through October, weekends from April. Narrated harbor cruises aboard the *Bay View Lady;* harbor lunch cruise (bring your own sandwich) 12:10–12:50, just $3. Otherwise $8 adult, $5 child for a 1½-hour cruise.

Olde Port Mariner Fleet (775-0727), Long Wharf, Portland. Offers whale-watches daily in summer, weekends in early June and after Labor Day. Also summer sunset trips, and a variety of other shorter excursions.

The ultimate cruise out of Portland is the overnight run (early May to late October) to Yarmouth, Nova Scotia (see *Getting There*).

BREWERY TOURS

Microbreweries have popped up all over Portland, many with restaurants alongside them. Most give tours, either on a regular basis or by appointment. For information, contact individual breweries: **Allagash Brewing** (878-5385), 100 Industrial Way; **Casco Bay Brewing** (797-2020), 57 Industrial Way; **D. L. Geary Brewing** (878-2337), 38 Evergreen Drive; **Gritty McDuff's Brew Pub** (772-2739), 396 Fore Street; **Shipyard Brewing** (761-0807), 86 Newbury Street; and **Stone Coast Brewing** (799-4280), 14 York Street.

CANOEING

See Scarborough Marsh Nature Center under *Green Space* in "Old Orchard Beach, Saco, and Biddeford."

DEEP-SEA FISHING AND SAILING

Several deep-sea-fishing boats and sailing yachts are based in Portland every summer. Check with the Convention and Visitors Bureau (772-

5800) for current listings. Also see *Sea Kayaking* for details about self-propelled cruising through Casco Bay.

FOR FAMILIES

🖉 **Smiling Hill Farm** (775-4814), 781 County Road, Westbrook. Kids love this farm with a petting zoo and popular ice cream stand.

🖉 **Southworth Planetarium** (780-4249), University of Southern Maine, Falmouth Street, Portland. Astronomy and laser light shows throughout the year. Special shows for young children in the summer and holidays.

🖉 **Jokers Family Fun 'n' Games** (878-5800) 510 Warren Avenue, Portland. A wonderful rainy-day diversion if you can stand the noise: pizza, huge plastic tunnels and ball pits, an indoor Ferris wheel, loads of video games. Outdoors, they also have an extensive mini-golf course.

GOLF

There are several popular 9- and 18-hole courses in the area, including **Sable Oaks Golf Club**, considered by many one of the most challenging and best courses in Maine (18 holes). **Riverside North** (18 holes) and **Riverside South** (9 holes) in Portland; **Valhalla** (18 holes) in Cumberland; and **Twin Falls** (9 holes) in Westbrook.

HOT-AIR BALLOONING

Hot Fun (799-0193), Box 2825, South Portland. Hot-air balloons carry up to six passengers.

Balloon Rides (761-8373; 1-800-952-2076), 17 Freeman Street, Portland.

ROCK CLIMBING

Maine Rock Gym (780-6370). Hours vary by season. Year-round indoor climbing facility, as well as a 40-foot outdoor climbing wall. Clinics for beginners as well as more experienced climbers.

SEA KAYAKING

Maine Island Kayak Co. (766-2373; 1-800-796-2373), 70 Luther Street, Peaks Island. Late May through October. One of the state's leading kayaking outfitters, offering 1- to 10-day (camping) tours as far Down East as Machias; also weekend overnights on Jewell Island—on the outer fringe of Casco Bay—and 7-day expeditions through the islands of the bay. Introductory paddling sessions available. Casco Bay is a great place to learn to sea kayak, given its easy access both to a wide variety of islands and to open ocean.

Norumbega Outfitters (773-0910; 1-800-529-2548) 58 Fore Street, Portland. Kayak rentals, guided excursions, instruction, and advice.

TENNIS

There are several public, first-come first-served courts across the city. The most popular (and best maintained) courts are at Deering Oaks, Payson Park, and on the Eastern Promenade.

ICE SKATING

There are several outdoor rinks in the area, including the pond at Deering Oaks Park. For indoor skating, the **Portland Ice Arena** (774-8553) has public skating times, pro shop.

GREEN SPACE

BEACHES

Crescent Beach State Park (8 miles from Portland on Route 77) is a mile of sand complete with changing facilities, playground, picnic tables, and snack bar. $2.50 adults, $.50 ages 5–11.

Kettle Cove, just down the road from Crescent (follow the road behind the ice cream shop), is small, with a grassy lawn and rocky beach. There is no admission fee, but limited parking.

Higgins Beach, farther down Route 77 in Scarborough, is an extensive strand within walking distance of lodging—but there is no parking on the street. Private lots charge $4.

Scarborough Beach State Park (Route 207, 3 miles south of Route 1 on Prouts Neck) is a superb beach, but only a 65-foot stretch is technically public. Thanks to limited parking, however, the crowd is rarely excessive. $2.50 per person.

PARKS

Deering Oaks, a 51-acre city park designed by Frederick Law Olmsted, has a pond, ducks and swans, paddleboats, fountains, a restaurant that sometimes offers live evening entertainment, a playground, and a fine grove of oak trees. A farmer's market is held here every Saturday morning throughout the summer and into November. Ice skating on the pond in winter.

Two Lights State Park is open April 15 through November. No swimming, but 40 acres of shore for picnicking and fishing. $2.50 per person. Also see Fort Williams Park and Spring Point Lighthouse in *To See.*

NATURE PRESERVES

Gilsland Farm Sanctuary (781-2330), 118 Route 1, Falmouth Foreside (3 miles east of Portland). The headquarters of the **Maine Audubon Society** is located here. The sanctuary is open sunrise to sunset, year-round. The nature-oriented shop is open Monday through Saturday 9–5, Sunday 2–5. Sixty acres of trails, rolling fields, river frontage, and salt marsh. There is also a solar-heated education center with exhibits; special programs and field trips are year-round.

Prouts Neck Cliff Path and Wildlife Sanctuary. Winslow Homer painted many of his seascapes in the small studio attached to the summer home, which was—and still is—part of the exclusive community on Prouts Neck, beyond the Black Point Inn. It's not far from the inn to Winslow Homer Road, where the Cliff Walk (unmarked) begins. It's a beautiful stroll along the rocks, around Eastern Point, and back almost to the inn. You can also walk through the sanctuary between Winslow Homer Road (just east of St. James Episcopal Church) and Library Lane, donated by Winslow's brother Charles. The studio itself is open July and August 10–4, marked only by a STUDIO sign on the shedlike room attached to a private house.

Fore River Sanctuary (781-2330), near Maine Turnpike exit 8, off Brighton Avenue. This 76-acre preserve owned by the Maine Audubon Society is not what you expect to find in the heart of the city, but it is definitely worth seeking out. Hidden behind a suburban neighborhood where explorers may not think to look, the 2½ miles of hiking trails offer access to Portland's only waterfall, **Jewell Falls.** A set of railroad tracks (be careful—they are active) marks the beginning of a trail that leads you through woods and marshland.

WALKS

Portland Trails (775-2411) is an organization committed to developing hiking and biking trails in the city. They have, in conjunction with the Kids and Transportation program, published a free map describing several city parks, and close to a dozen trails as well as bus routes to take you there. Pick up a copy at the visitor's information center (see *Guidance*).

Eastern Cemetery, Congress Street and Washington Avenue (near the Portland Observatory on Munjoy Hill). More than 4,000 souls are interred in these 9 acres, and the headstones, dating back to the mid–17th century, are embellished with angels and death's heads. Despite its derelict state, this is an utterly fascinating place.

Fort Allen Park dates from 1814 and is on a blustery point on Casco Bay, a sure bet for a fresh breeze on the hottest day, as is the adjacent 68-acre **Eastern Promenade,** part of the turn-of-the-century park system designed by the famous, Boston-based landscape architects the Olmsteds. (The Olmsteds also designed Boston's Emerald Necklace and New York's Central Park.) The new, paved **Eastern Promenade Trail** runs for a little over 2 miles along the base of Munjoy Hill. It is great for biking, walking, and rollerblading. The railroad museum's train runs alongside it, and the smoke from the engine is one of the only drawbacks to this trail.

The **Western Promenade,** first laid out in 1836, is another part of this grand plan. Sited on the edge of a 175-foot-high plateau, it commands a long view to the west (theoretically you can see Mount Washington on a clear day) and serves as the front porch for Portland's poshest and most architecturally interesting residential neighborhood. Pick up a copy of the Portland landmarks leaflet, "Guide to the Western Promenade" ($1), from the visitors bureau (see *Guidance*).

Portland Women's History Trail, a project sponsored by the Women's Studies Program at the University of Southern Maine and the Maine Humanities Council, offers four routes, with over a dozen stops on each, highlighting important sites in women's history, including City Hall, where the first women's suffrage meeting was held in 1870.

Mackworth Island, off Route 1 north of Portland; follow signs to Governer Baxter School for the Deaf. A walking path circles the island, with views across the bay. Small beach for strolling.

❧ **Baxter Boulevard.** A popular 3½-mile path around a cove just off I-295, popular for dog-walking, jogging, biking. Fields also provide a good kite-flying spot.

LODGING

HOTELS
There are more than 2,000 hotel and motel rooms in and around Portland. Right downtown, within walking distance of the Portland Museum of Art and the Old Port, you can choose from the following hotels, all in Portland 04101.

♿ **Radisson Eastland Hotel Portland** (775-5411; 1-800-333-3333), 157 High Street. A 12-story landmark built in 1927. In the mid-1980s it fell into bankruptcy, and the bank owned the property for 10 years. Since then, a number of ownership changes have occurred, and the quality seems to fluctuate depending on the purchaser. In 1998, total renovations of rooms and common spaces were in process. A convenient, friendly in-town hotel that still has elevator operators, a rooftop lounge with great city views, and two restaurants. $79–139 for a double, depending on season.

♿ **Portland Regency** (774-4200; 1-800-727-3436), 20 Milk Street. An interesting 95-room hotel (including 8 suites), housed in a century-old armory in the middle of the Old Port Exchange. Rooms are decorated with reproduction antiques and equipped with amenities such as TV, phones, and an honor bar. The formal dining room serves all three meals and the attractive lounge offers cocktails and lighter fare. The health spa on premises has a cardiovascular center, aerobics classes, a Jacuzzi, and massage therapy available. Complimentary coffee with your wake-up call. $99–199, depending on season.

♿ **Holiday Inn by the Bay** (775-2311; 1-800-HOLIDAY), 88 Spring Street. With 246 rooms, this is Maine's largest hotel. Rooms on the bay side have a fabulous harbor view. Each year, close to a third of the rooms are completely refurbished, keeping all of them looking fresh and new. The hotel has 30,000 square feet of meeting space, making it popular for conventions and business meetings. Indoor pool, small fitness center, cable TV and video-game hook-ups, free parking, laundry facility, nice restaurant and lounge.

✍♿ **Oak Leaf Hotel** (773-7882; everett@maine.rr.com), 51A Oak Street. Describing itself as an "informal, European-style hotel with a homelike atmosphere," this is an inexpensive option tucked onto a side street. Recently renovated, not in any way fancy, but clean and friendly. $42–65.

❧✍♿ **Inn at St. John** (773-6481; 1-800-636-9127) 939 Congress Street. A rather unexpected, comfortable place built in 1897 to accommodate railroad passengers arriving at Union Station, a block from the hotel. The neighborhood leaves a bit to be desired, but the price is right and pets are welcome here. Innkeeper Paul Hood has worked to create an inviting, tasteful turn-of-the-century feel. $40–135 depending on season.

🐾 **Portland Hall** (874-3281), 645 Congress Street, is a summer (June through August) AYH hostel with comfortable dormitory lodging right across from the Portland Museum of Art. Under $20 per person.

Note: Portland does have the major chains, but they are mainly located by I-95 at exit 8 in Westbrook or in South Portland by the mall.

INNS AND BED & BREAKFASTS

Pomegranate Inn (772-1006; 1-800-356-0408), 49 Neal Street, Portland 04102. An extraordinary place to stay. Isabel Smiles, an interior designer and former antiques dealer, has turned this 1880s Western Promenade house into a work of art. Nothing stiff, just one surprise for the eye after another. Eight amazing rooms furnished in a mix of antiques and *objets*, most with hand-painted walls in bold, original designs. Downstairs, the walls of the wide entryway are a hand-mottled tangerine, and the mantel and four columns in the living room are marbleized. Guest rooms have phones, discreet TVs, and private baths; five have gas fireplaces. The living room is well stocked with art books. Breakfast is exquisite. Frankly, we're glad we stayed here before its fame spread, because what has since been described as the Pomegranate's "high style" came as a complete surprise. Still, repeat visits have been as good as the first. $135–175 per room in-season, $95–135 off-season, includes breakfast.

The Inn on Carleton Street (775-1910; 1-800-639-1779), Portland 04102. An attractive town house in the Western Promenade area offers seven rooms furnished with marble-topped sinks and Victorian-era antiques. We like the feel of this place. Proprietor Sue Cox makes guests feel welcome, and they tend to form a congenial group around the breakfast table. No smoking. $65–155 in-season, includes breakfast.

The Danforth (879-8755; 1-800-991-6557; danforth@maine.rr.com), 163 Danforth Street, Portland 04102. An elegant, gracious house in a historic district, offering nine guest rooms with fireplaces, private bath, cable TV, phones, and dataports. Common areas include a library and a wood-paneled billiards room, and the cupola at the top is a wonderful place to relax and watch the sky while the sun rises or sets. $115–225 in-season.

Beyond Portland

♿ **Black Point Inn Resort** (883-2500; 1-800-258-0003), Prouts Neck 04074. Open early May to late October. Easily one of the most elegant inns in the state; a vintage 1878 summer hotel that is so much a part of its exclusive community that guests are permitted to use the Prouts Neck Country Club's 18-hole golf course and 14 tennis courts. Guests may also rent boats or moor their own at the local yacht club. Public rooms are extensive and elegant with views of the Southern Coast on one side and of the open ocean on the other. Facilities include two sandy beaches, indoor and outdoor pools, two Jacuzzis, a sauna, and a manned elevator. There are 80 rooms, poolside buffets, afternoon tea with a pianist, evening cocktails, and dancing. No children under age 8 mid-July to late August. A London taxi serves as a shuttle to the airport and into Portland.

$280–450 for double MAP per night plus 15 percent gratuity. A $15 noon buffet is offered. (See Prouts Neck under *Green Space*.)

  ♧ **Inn by the Sea** (799-3134; innmaine@aol.com), 40 Bowery Beach Road, Cape Elizabeth 04107. Location is the number-one advantage of this pricey, elegant hotel, which offers 43 one- and two-bedroom suites and cottages, all with porch or deck and some kind of water view. Other amenities include TV/VCR, multiple phones in each suite, kitchens, an outdoor pool, tennis courts, and bicycles. A boardwalk leads to the tip of Crescent Beach State Park. $229–449 in summer season. Inquire about special packages.

Higgins Beach Inn (883-6684), 34 Ocean Avenue, Scarborough 04074 (7 miles south of Portland). Open mid-May to mid-November. An 1890s, three-story, wooden summer hotel near sandy Higgins Beach. The pleasant dining room, open July and August, features seafood with an Italian flair. There is also a cocktail lounge, a homey TV room, and a sunporch. Upstairs, the 24 guest rooms are basic but clean and airy, 14 with private bath. Continental breakfast is available after Labor Day. New owners in 1997, but they continue the long-standing tradition, with rates much the same as under the previous owners (who kept them as low as possible). $55–80 double. MAP packages available.

Peter A. McKernan Hospitality Center (767-9672), Fort Road, South Portland 04106. On the campus of Southern Maine Technical College, a training ground for students eager to please. Eight rooms, and they fill up quickly. Walking and biking trails nearby. $80–155.

COTTAGES

South of Portland, cottages in the Higgins Beach and Pine Point areas can be found through the Chamber of Commerce of the Greater Portland Region (772-2811), 145 Middle Street, Portland 04101. Seasonal rentals are also listed in the *Maine Sunday Telegram*.

Also check the "Maine Guide to Camp & Cottage Rentals," available from the Maine Tourism Association (623-0363).

For lodging options on Casco Bay Islands, see *Islands*.

WHERE TO EAT

The claim is that Portland has more restaurants per capita than any other city in America. Take a look at the following partial list, and you will begin to believe it. The quality of the dining is as exceptional as the quantity, making it hard to select our favorites. People from all over Maine look forward to dining in Portland. Enjoy!

DINING OUT

In and around the Old Port Exchange

  ♧ **Cafe Uffa** (775-3380), 190 State Street (in Longfellow Square near the Portland Museum of Art). Open for breakfast and dinner Wednesday through Saturday, Sunday 9 AM–2 PM. Hugely popular for Sunday brunch (get there early); highly rated for its creative and reasonably priced entrées like applewood-grilled salmon with Korean barbecue sauce, and desserts like bourbon pecan tart. Bistro atmosphere, good wine list, sangria made in-house. Occasionally closed for vacation, so call ahead. Sidewalk tables in the summer. Entrées $7.95–14.95.

Fore Street (775-2717), 288 Fore Street. Open for dinner daily. Reservations strongly recommended. You have to know where to look, since the sign is tiny, but once you find it, you won't forget it. Dana Street, owner of Street and Company, has joined forces with well-known chef Sam Hayward to create an upscale place offering wood-grilled entrées prepared in an open kitchen.

Walter's Cafe (871-9258), 15 Exchange Street. Open for lunch and dinner daily. A very popular storefront space that's been deftly transformed into a bistro. Lunch includes unusual soups and salads. At dinner, look for creative offerings like Crazy Chicken, sautéed with prosciutto, scallions, sweet peas, and garlic in a red wine cream sauce over capellini; flash-grilled pork tenderloin; and artichoke, portobello mushroom, and roasted pepper sauté. $11.95–16.95.

Mozon Middle (774-9399), 47 Middle Street. Dinner Tuesday through Sunday. Maureen Terry has turned the former Café Always into an interesting, European-style café. Just off the beaten path, it is worth finding. She still does all of the cooking, so the food is the same wonderful style as before, with the menu changing daily. New, creative cocktails have been added to the repertoire. Prices have been lowered some, now $9.95–18.95 for entrées.

  ♻ **Street & Company** (775-0887), 33 Wharf Street. Open for dinner Sunday through Thursday 5:30–9:30, Friday and Saturday until 10. Year-round. A small, informal, incredibly popular seafood place with an open kitchen and outdoor seating in warm weather. It is always a good idea to make reservations. The 22 seats they leave open for walk-ins go quickly. Seafood grilled, broiled, pan-blackened, and steamed, much of it served right in the pan it's been cooked in. Specialties include lobster diavolo, mussels provençale, and grilled lobster on butter garlic linguine. Homemade desserts. Entrées $11.95–17.95.

  ✿ **The Pepperclub** (772-0531), 78 Middle Street. Open for dinner nightly. A funky, fun spot. Creative menu options, which change frequently, are written on two large blackboards (as well as smaller table versions if you need one). Several vegetarian choices, perhaps portobello pie or lasagna with fresh basil and feta cheese, as well as some beef, chicken, and seafood. Entrées are $11.95 or less.

Hugo's Portland Bistro (774-8538), 88 Middle Street. Dinner Tuesday through Saturday. Eclectic, mismatched antiques decor and live piano music. The varied menu changes monthly. Well known for their crab cakes; other entrées include seared duck breast and Tunisian couscous. Check out the imported beer list. $11.95–17.95.

DiMillo's Floating Restaurant (772-2216), Long Wharf. Open for lunch and dinner. Maine's only floating restaurant, this converted car ferry serves seafood, steaks, and Italian cuisine to customers (mainly tourists) who come as much for the old nautical atmosphere and the views of the waterfront as they do for the food. Entrées run $8.95–24.95.

Boone's Restaurant (774-5725), 6 Custom House Wharf. Open for lunch and dinner year-round. Still going strong in the same location on the wharf that it has occupied since 1898. Specialties include Mediterranean pasta dishes, lobster, and other fresh seafood. Seasonal patio dining overlooking the water. A real slice of the waterfront's long history. Lunch $4.95–7.95, dinner $10.95–17.95.

Beyond the Old Port

Katahdin (774-1740), 106 High Street. Dinner Monday through Saturday 5–10 PM. No reservations and it is often very busy, so you might want to call for the wait time before you go. Inventive New England entrées include wild mushroom ravioli, and specials might include grilled monkfish coated in Moroccan spices with ginger sauce.

Aubergine (874-0680), 555 Congress Street. Open Tuesday through Saturday 5:30–10 PM, and 11–2 for Sunday brunch. David Grant, a former restaurant owner in Camden, has resurfaced in Portland with this attractive, cozy spot. French cuisine, with a menu that changes nightly and might include crispy salmon with spinach Pernod or yellowfin tuna grilled with lemon and capers. Extensive wine list, all available by the glass. Very popular Sunday brunch. $14–16 for entrées.

The Roma Cafe (773-9873), 769 Congress Street. Open for lunch and dinner on weekdays, dinner only on weekends. Elegant dining rooms in the Rines Mansion, a great place for a romantic dinner or a special group gathering. Begin with appetizers like chicken-stuffed artichokes, salads. Entrées include a delicious seafood linguine, roast pork tenderloin, and filet mignon. Special requests (like leaving off the shrimp to create a good vegetarian pasta dish) are cheerfully accommodated when possible. $11.95–17.95.

Madd Apple Café (774-9698), 23 Forest Avenue. Open for dinner Tuesday through Saturday at 5:30. Summer hours vary; call ahead for details. Reservations recommended. The dinner menu changes frequently, with an emphasis on seasonal and local ingredients. Smoked salmon and sweet potato cakes, swordfish au poivre, and steak New Orleans are a few specialties. Special desserts might include bananas Foster. $13.95–19.95.

Back Bay Grill (772-8833), 65 Portland Street. Open for dinner Monday through Saturday. Brightly painted murals add a lively feel to this place. The menu changes about eight times a year as the seasons change. Summer and early fall offer a unique five-course lobster-tasting menu. Their crème brûlée is always a hit. The wine lists are a full page each for reds, whites, dessert wines, and ports. $15.95–24.95.

South of Portland

  ♿ **Black Point Inn** (883-4126), Prouts Neck. Dinner by reservation in a formal dining room with water views. The menu changes nightly; varies from basics like Yankee pot roast and boiled lobster to Cajun-style sautéed shrimp on angelhair pasta; extravagant desserts. $30 prix fixe plus tax and gratuity.

North of Portland

The Cannery Restaurant at Lower Falls Landing (846-1226), Yarmouth. Open daily for lunch and dinner, Sunday brunch. Built in 1913 as a herring factory; then served as a sardine-packing plant from the 1920s right up until 1980. The building, now part of a complex that includes a marina and some interesting shops, makes an attractive restaurant space with a waterside terrace. $7.95–15.95.

EATING OUT

In and around the Old Port Exchange

Note: Most of the restaurants described under *Dining Out* also serve a reasonably priced lunch.

Norm's Bar-B-Q (774-6711), 43 Middle Street. Open Tuesday through Thursday noon–10, Friday and Saturday noon–11, Sunday 3–9. For a memorable pork sandwich or spareribs, or maybe the rib sampler with onion rings, this is the place. Entrées average $9; beer and wine served.

The Porthole (774-3448), 32 Customs Wharf. Open early for breakfast, also serves lunch and dinner. Great chowder; breakfast dishes at unbeatable prices. Cheerful service at both counter and tables. Great all-you-can-eat fish fry ($3.95 at lunch, $5.95 at dinner). If you stick your head in and don't like what you see, this isn't for you; what you see is what you get. This is the last holdout on the funky former Casco Bay wharf.

Becky's (773-7070), 390 Commercial Street. The best late-night breakfast spot around (it is very crowded in the early-morning hours on weekends, when they open at 12:01 AM). Also very reasonable at lunch and dinner.

Gilbert's Chowder House (871-5636), 92 Commercial Street. Open for lunch and dinner. Delicious and filling chowders served in a bread bowl are the best choices here, but they also have a range of fried seafood and other reasonably priced specials. Outside dining in-season.

Dock Fore (772-8619), 336 Fore Street. Open for lunch and dinner. A sunny, casual pub (most seating is at the bar or side bar) serving hearty fare and homelike specialties. Large portions at good prices.

  ♿ **Village Café** (772-5320), 112 Newbury Street. Open for lunch and dinner daily. This is an old family favorite that predates the Old Port renaissance (it's just east of the Old Port). The third generation of the Reali family is now welcoming patrons to the same comfortable place. A large, often crowded space with specialties like fried Maine clams, lobster, veal parmigiana, and steaks.

✿ **Anthony's Italian Kitchen** (774-8668), 151 Middle Street. This great little place is always crowded at lunch time. It smells like a real Italian kitchen, and the aromas are not misleading. Terrific pizza and pasta specialties, homemade meatballs, service that makes you feel like an old friend.

Gritty McDuff's (772-2739), 396 Fore Street. A brew pub specializing in its own ales, stouts, and bitters. Pub fare includes fish-and-chips and shepherd's pie, and the menu also offers pizza, roll-ups, and sandwiches. Gritty's chips (thinly sliced potatoes deep-fried) are a popular snack, and are great with malt vinegar. Long, common tables in two rooms.

Beyond the Old Port

✿ **The Kitchen** (775-0833), 593 Congress Street. A friendly staff, terrific food, and very reasonable prices add up to a great choice for breakfast and lunch. Located conveniently near the PMA and the Children's Musuem. Breakfast served until closing on weekends. The delicious wraps include tofu teriyaki and Jamaican jerk chicken, and are and enough to satisfy almost any appetite. Other choices include soups, salads, and subs.

Sala Thai (797-0871), 1363 Washington Avenue. Not on the tourist route, but worth seeking out if you like Thai food. The menu is large and varied, with the usual choices, but the quality is a cut above many such places. Great sauces, generous portions.

Beyond Portland

The Lobster Shack (799-1677), Cape Elizabeth (off Route 77 at the tip of the cape, near Two Lights State Park). Open for lunch and dinner April to mid-October. A local landmark since the 1920s, set below the lighthouse and next to the foghorn. Dine inside or out. This is the place to pick a lobster out of the tank and watch it being boiled—then eat it "in the rough." Herb and Martha Porch are also known for their chowder and lobster stew, fried Maine shrimp, scallops and clams, lobster, and crabmeat rolls.

Spurwink Country Kitchen (799-1177), 150 Spurwink Road (near Scarborough Beach), Scarborough. Open mid-April to mid-October, 11:30–9. Part of this place's beauty is that it's here at all, right where you wouldn't expect to find a place to eat. Then you discover it's a special place, looking much the same and serving much the same food as when Hope Sargent opened it in 1955. Specials vary with the day and include soup, potato, vegetable or rolls, tea or coffee. Great homemade pies.

The Good Table (799-4663), 526 Ocean House Road, Cape Elizabeth. Open Monday through Friday 11 AM–9 PM, Saturday 8 AM–9 PM, and Sundays 8 AM–3 PM. A bit of a drive from intown Portland, but near Two Lights State Park, and worth every mile. A cozy place offering hearty homestyle meals. Weekend brunch menu might include eggs Benedict and a variety of interesting quiches.

COFFEE BARS

An abundance of cozy cafés serving coffee and espresso drinks have sprung up in Portland. We especially like: **Java Joe's** (761-5637), 13 Exchange Street—a good place to go for late-night coffee and conversation; games, entertainment, and always great people-watching. **Java Net** (1-800-528-2638)—in this age of technology, this is a great spot for travelers who need to check their e-mail or conduct business via the Internet while vacationing. Hourly access rates; you can either bring your own laptop or use their computers. Bright and lively, with comfortable couches and chairs, and plenty of technical assistance if needed. **Coffee by Design** (772-5533), 620 Congress Street, is a friendly, cheerful spot with plenty of tables (sidewalk tables in summer), local art on display (and for sale), and all the usual coffee and espresso choices.

ENTERTAINMENT

Cumberland County Civic Center (775-3481, ext. 2 for 24-hour hotline), 1 Civic Center Square, Portland. A modern arena with close to 9,000 seats, the site of year-round concerts, special presentations, ice-skating spectaculars, winter hockey games, and other events. Pick up a free monthly calendar of events.

State Theatre (879-1112). Since its initial renovation, the theater has closed more than once due to financial and structural difficulties, but it is again open and hosting a variety of performances, from rock to classical. Call for a current schedule of events.

Center for Cultural Exchange (774-0465), One Longfellow Square. Recently renovated, this building is the new center for cultural events in the city, including an Irish festival, an annual Greek festival, Cambodian New Year's celebration, and many varied events from theater and dance performances to concerts and workshops.

MUSIC

Portland Symphony Orchestra (773-8191), City Hall Auditorium, 389 Congress Street, Portland. The winter series runs October through April, Tuesdays at 7:45 PM. In summertime, the symphony delights audiences throughout the state at outdoor pops concerts in some of the most beautiful settings, such as overlooking Casco Bay or by Camden Harbor. Fall and winter performances are held at Merrill Auditorium.

LARK Society for Chamber Music/Portland String Quartet (761-1522). This distinguished chamber group grows in stature every year; performances are in a variety of Portland locations as well as around the state.

PCA Great Performances (772-8630). A series of orchestra, jazz, opera, and musical theater in various locations throughout Maine in summer. In fall and winter, performances are held at the beautifully restored Merrill Auditorium.

PROFESSIONAL SPORTS

The **Portland Pirates** (828-4665), a professional hockey team, play their home games at the Cumberland County Civic Center. The **Portland Sea Dogs,** a double-A baseball team, play in Hadlock Stadium on Park Avenue (next to the Expo).

Exchange Street in the Old Port Historic District

THEATER

Portland Stage Company (774-1043) and the **Ram Island Dance Company** (773-2562), are both based in the city's old Odd Fellows Hall, now an elegant, intimate, 290-seat theater. Both stage a variety of performances throughout the year.

Portland Players (799-7337), Thaxter Theater, 420 Cottage Road, South Portland, stages productions September through June.

Portland Lyric Theater (799-1421), Cedric Thomas Playhouse, 176 Sawyer Street, South Portland. This community theater presents four musicals each winter.

Oak Street Theatre (775-5103), 92 Oak Street. A cozy little theater with 90 seats. Performances vary widely, from comedy to jazz and classic drama.

SELECTIVE SHOPPING

ANTIQUES

There are a plethora of small shops, especially in the Old Port and along Congress Street, where antiques lovers can browse to their hearts' content.

GALLERIES

Baxter Gallery of Portland School of Art (775-5152), 619 Congress Street. Art lovers shouldn't miss the photo and primary gallery in this beautiful old building, just south up Congress Street from the Portland Museum of Art.

Frost Gully Gallery (773-2555), 411 Congress Street. Since 1966, this gallery has shown many fine paintings and sculptures by Maine artists.

Bayview Gallery (773-3007), 75 Market Street. A spacious gallery with fine paintings, as well as an extensive collection of prints from well-known Maine artists.

Gallery 7 (761-7007), 49 Exchange Street. Wide variety of beautifully crafted items, from miniature stone fountains to furniture, glass, and jewelry.

Edgecomb Potters Gallery (780-6727), 35 Exchange Street. One of four in the state, a fine collection of some reasonably priced, interesting pottery. Other merchandise includes glass designs, wind chimes, and jewelery.

Nancy Margolis Gallery (775-3822), 367 Fore Street. We love the papier-mâché mobiles, and the collection of glass, jewelry, and sculptures is just as interesting.

Stein Gallery of Contemporary Glass (772-9072), 195 Middle Street. In its new, larger space, the exquisite glass creations are nicely displayed, from perfume bottles and paper weights to elaborate sculptures.

There are many other fine galleries in the Old Port and the Arts District. Reserve an afternoon to wander, and inquire at the visitors center for other suggestions.

BOOKSTORES

Portland has become a mecca for book lovers. **Books Etc.** (38 Exchange Street) is a very inviting store. **Bookland's** in-town store at One Monument Way stocks a full range of titles and has a great children's section and bargain table. **Harbour Books** (846-6306), at Lower Falls Landing, Yarmouth, is part of the same rehabbed sardine-cannery complex that includes the Cannery Restaurant. This is a very special independent bookstore, the kind book lovers will feel completely comfortable in and probably walk out of with something they never intended to buy. Soft music, views of the harbor, and bargain tables. Open daily 9–6, Friday until 8, Sunday noon–5. Visible from I-95; take exit 17. **Borders Books and Music** by the mall has a huge selection and you can grab a book and read in its café for hours if you want. Antiquarian-book lovers should check out **Carlson-Turner Books** (241 Congress Street); **Emerson Booksellers** (420 Fore Street); and **Allen Scott Books** (89 Exchange Street).

SPECIAL SHOPS

Portland Public Market (772-8140). Located on Cumberland Avenue between Preble and Elm Streets, this 37,000-square-foot indoor market offers fresh foods including meat, poultry, seafood, cheeses, and baked goods, as well as flowers.

Northern Sky Toyz (828-0911), 388 Fore Street. An amazing kite shop, with a variety of other novelties and toys, including windsocks, banners, and games.

Whip and Spoon (774-4020), 161 Commercial Street. Every kitchen gadget you can possible imagine, as well as specialty foods, wines, coffee, chocolate, and more.

Maine Potters Market (774-1633), 376 Fore Street. Beautiful pottery made by Maine artisans.

Zygot Bookworks and Café (775-4121), 61 Pleasant Street. A unique little spot with book-binding materials, journals, handmade paper, pens, photo albums, and workshops offered regularly.

Angel's Arrowhead Gallery (772-7322), 7 Moulton Street. An interesting store with a variety of unusual old beads, jewelry, and collectible glass.

Siempre Mas (879-1676), 377 Fore Street. Our favorite place to find unique printed cotton dresses, shirts, and more, as well as large wool sweaters. Don't miss the sale rack in the back.

The Old Port is full of special shops, from clothing to music, candles to gifts and souvenirs. If you are an avid shopper, allot at least a couple of hours to browse leisurely in this section of the city.

Beyond Portland proper is the **Maine Mall** (exit 7 off I-95), whose immediate complex of more than 100 stores is supplemented by large shopping centers and chain stores that ring it for several miles.

SPECIAL EVENTS

April: **Aucociso,** a 10-day celebration of Casco Bay, centered on the Maine Boatbuilder's show.

First Sunday in June: **Old Port Festival**, a celebration that began in the 1970s with the revival of the Old Port; includes a parade, various performances, street vendors, and special sales.

Mid-July: **Yarmouth Clam Festival,** arts and crafts, plenty of clams, performances, more.

August: **Cumberland Crafts Fair,** Cumberland Fairgrounds. **Sidewalk Art Festival,** Congress Street.

First Weekend in November: **Maine Brewer's Festival.** Each year, this event grows in size, due to the increasing number of Maine microbreweries.

November and December: **Victorian Holiday Portland** with tree lighting, arrival of Father Christmas, costumed carolers, special events through Christmas.

December 31: **Portland New Year's Celebration**—modeled after Boston's First Night, with performances and events throughout the city from afternoon through midnight.

Freeport

Although many think of Freeport as synonymous with shopping, there is much more to this town. Hidden behind the discounts and bargain stores is a history dating back more than 200 years. The area was granted a charter separating itself from North Yarmouth in 1789. With the War of 1812, shipbuilding became an important industry, with one famous ship inspiring Whittier's poem "The Dead Ship of Harpswell." The town is particularly proud of the fact that in 1820 the papers separating Maine from Massachusetts were signed in the historical Jameson Tavern (see *Dining Out*).

These days, shopping is high on visitors' lists. Each year as many as 15,000 cars per day squeeze up and down the mile of Main Street (Route 1) that is lined on both sides with upscale, off-price shops. L. L. Bean, ranked not only as Maine's number-one emporium but also as its number-one man-made attraction, has been a shopping landmark for over 85 years. The establishment of more than 100 neighboring outlet stores, however, didn't begin until the early 1980s.

Although the shops are the major draw for most travelers, the village has retained the appearance of older days—even McDonald's has been confined to a gracious old Colonial house, with no golden arches in sight. Some come to the area simply to stroll wooded paths in Wolfe's Neck Woods State Park and the Maine Audubon's Mast Landing Sanctuary. The Desert of Maine is also an interesting sight. The quiet countryside and waterside retreats away from crowds are enjoyed by many.

GUIDANCE

The Freeport Merchants Association (865-1212; 1-800-865-1994; http://www.freeportusa.com), P.O. Box 452, Freeport 04032, operates a visitors center in a replica of a historic hose tower on Mill Street. Brochures and information, rest rooms, and an ATM can be found here, and the association's office is upstairs. They also gladly respond to telephone and mail requests for information. Among their materials is an excellent, free, visitor's walking map, with a list of stores, restaurants, accommodations, and other services. Be sure to get one in advance or pick one up as soon as you arrive in town—almost all the merchants have them. Also ask for the fun brochure "101 Things to do in Freeport."

The Maine Tourism Association's welcome center in Kittery stocks some Freeport brochures, and there is a state information center on Route 1 just south of Freeport, in Yarmouth, at exit 17 off I-95.

GETTING THERE

Bus service to Freeport from Boston and Portland is available via **Greyhound.** A number of **bus tour companies** also offer shopping trips to Freeport from Boston and beyond. Most people drive, which means there's often a shortage of parking spaces, especially in peak season. The best solution to this problem is to stay at an inn or B&B within walking distance and leave your car there.

MEDICAL EMERGENCY

Mid Coast Hospital (729-0181), 58 Baribeau Drive, Brunswick.

VILLAGES

South Freeport has been a fishing center from its beginning. Between 1825 and 1830, up to 12,000 barrels of mackerel were packed and shipped from here each year. Later, the area specialty became crabmeat packing. A very different feel from the chaotic shopping frenzy of downtown Freeport, the harbor is still bustling with activity and offers some great seafood. From here you can take a cruise to explore Eagle Island in summer.

Porter's Landing. Once the center of commercial activity, this is now a quiet residential neighborhood, amid rolling hills, woods, and streams. The village is part of the Harraseeket Historic District on the National Register of Historic Places.

TO SEE AND DO

✍ **Desert of Maine** (865-6962), Desert Road, Freeport. Open daily, early May to mid-October, 9 AM to dusk. Admission fee. Narrated tram tours and self-guided walks through 40 acres of sand that was once the Tuttle Farm. Heavily farmed, then extensively logged to feed the railroad, the topsoil eventually gave way to the glacial sand deposit beneath it, which spread . . . and spread until entire trees sank below the surface. It is an unusual sand, rich in mineral deposits that make it unsuitable for commercial use but interesting to rock hounds. Children love it, especially the gem hunt (stones have been scattered in a section of the desert for children to find). There's a sand art demonstration and museum in the 1783 barn, plus gift and souvenir shops; 2.5 miles from downtown Freeport. Overnight camping available.

Freeport Balloon Company (865-1712; 1-800-808-1712), 41 Tuttle Road, Pownal 04069. Year-round hot-air-balloon flights for groups of 2-4 passengers, weather permitting, just after sunrise and a couple of hours before sunset. Rates begin at $150 per person.

L. L. Bean, the nerve center of Freeport's shopping district.

The Maine Bear Factory (846-1570), 294 Route 1 South, Freeport 04032. Kids and adults both love this place. When you visit you will learn how teddy bears are designed, cut, and sewn. Then you can choose and stuff your own bear and watch as it is completed for you.

BOAT EXCURSIONS

Anjin-San (772-7168), near town landing, South Freeport. A 34-foot sportfishing boat custom-built for Captain Greg Walts. Day trips for mackerel, bluefish, and shark. Also sight-seeing and diving trips, and charters.

Atlantic Seal/Arctic Seal (865-6112), Town Wharf, South Freeport. Memorial Day through mid-October. Daily narrated trips into Casco Bay include 3-hour cruises to Eagle Island, the former summer home of Admiral Robert E. Peary, the first man to reach the North Pole. Seal- and osprey-sighting trips and fall foliage cruises mid-September and October. Lobstering demonstrations are usually included, except Sunday, when lobstering is prohibited by Maine law.

Freeport Sailing Adventures (865-9225), P.O. Box 303, Freeport. Half- and full-day charters with crew. Longer charters available. You can learn to sail and help, or let them do the sailing while you relax.

CANOEING

The **Harraseeket River** in Freeport is particularly nice for canoeing. Start at Mast Landing, the northeastern end of the waterway; there are also launching sites at Winslow Memorial Park on Staples Point Road and at South Freeport Harbor. Phone the **Maine Audubon Society** in Falmouth (781-2330) for details about periodic, scheduled guided trips through the area. Nearby lake canoeing can be found at **Run Around Pond** in North Pownal (the parking lot is off Lawrence Road, 1 mile north of the intersection with Fickett Road).

GOLF
Freeport Country Club (865-4922), Old Country Road, Freeport. Nine holes.

CROSS-COUNTRY SKIING
The areas listed under *Green Space* are good cross-country skiing spots; rent or purchase equipment from L. L. Bean, which also offers classes in cross-country skiing (see *Special Learning Program*).

SPECIAL LEARNING PROGRAM
L. L. Bean Outdoor Discovery Schools (865-3111), Route 1, Freeport. An interesting series of lectures and lessons that cover everything from cross-country ski lessons (on weekends beginning in January) and golf to survival in the Maine woods, making soap, tanning hides, paddling sea kayaks, building fly-rods, cooking small game, and fishing for Atlantic salmon. Courses last from a couple of hours to weeklong trips. Call 1-800-341-4341, ext. 6666, for a free program guide.

GREEN SPACE

✎ **Winslow Memorial Park** (865-4198), Staples Point Road, South Freeport. Open Memorial Day through September. A 90-acre municipal park with a sandy beach and large, grassy picnicking area; also boating and 100-site campground. Facilities include rest rooms with showers. Admission fee.
✎ **Wolfe's Neck Woods State Park** (865-4465), Wolfe's Neck Road (take Bow Street, across from L. L. Bean), Freeport. Open Memorial Day through Labor Day. Day-use fee. A 244-acre park with shoreline hiking along Casco Bay, the Harraseeket River, and salt marshes. Guided nature walks are available; picnic tables and grills are scattered about.
Mast Landing Sanctuary (781-2330), Upper Mast Landing Road (take Bow Street south), Freeport. Maintained by the Maine Audubon Society, this 140-acre sanctuary offers trails through apple orchards, woods, and meadows and along a millstream. Several paths radiate from a 1-mile loop trail.
✎ **Bradbury Mountain State Park** (688-4712), Route 9, Hallowell Road, Pownal (just 6 miles from Freeport: from I-95, take exit 20 and follow signs). Open year-round. $2.50 per adult, $.50 children ages 5–11, under age 5 free. The summit, accessible by an easy (even for young children) ¼-mile hike, yields a splendid view of Casco Bay and New Hampshire's White Mountains. Facilities in the 297-acre park include a small playground, a softball field, hiking trails, toilets, and a 41-site overnight camping area.
Pettengill Farm (phone the Freeport Historical Society at 865-3170), Freeport. Open for periodic guided tours. A saltwater farm with 140

acres of open fields and woodland that overlook the Harraseeket Estuary, with a totally unmodernized, vintage 1810 saltbox house.

LODGING

All entries are for Freeport 04032 unless otherwise indicated.

INN

  ᴋ **Harraseeket Inn** (865-9377; 1-800-342-6423, harraseeke@aol.com), 162 Main Street. Just two blocks north of L. L. Bean, this luxury hotel is the largest in the area, with 84 rooms, including five suites. It has maintained the elegant atmosphere of the 1850 Greek Revival house next door, where this operation first began as a five-room B&B. Nancy and Paul Gray are native Mainers, but their family also owns the Inn at Mystic, Connecticut, and they definitely know the importance of attention to detail. Many of the rooms are decorated with antiques and reproductions and feature canopy beds and Jacuzzis or steam baths; 20 have fireplaces. The inn has formal dining rooms (see *Dining Out*), conference spaces (one with outdoor terrace), and the newly renovated casual Broad Arrow Tavern (see *Eating Out*). Other public spaces include a drawing room, library, and ballroom and a new indoor pool surrounded by glass walls overlooking the gardens. Rates in-season are $145–250; full breakfast and afternoon tea are included. Two-night minimum stay required on some holiday weekends. Package plans available.

BED & BREAKFASTS

The **Freeport Area Bed & Breakfast Association** (865-1500; 1-800-853-2727; mnetwork.com/freeportb&b), P.O. Box 267. Their 1998 brochure lists nine members, all of whom must meet certain standards established by the association. The majority of Freeport's B&Bs have opened since the shopping craze began. Many are in the handsome, old, white-clapboard Capes and Federal-style houses that stand side by side flanking Main Street just north of the shopping district.

🐾✎ **The Isaac Randall House** (865-9295; nkeepa@cybertours.com), 5 Independence Drive. Open year-round. Historically, this property has been a dairy farm, dance hall, and tourist court. The handsome farmhouse became the first bed & breakfast in Freeport in 1984. Twelve air-conditioned rooms with antiques, Oriental rugs, and lovely old quilts. Two have working fireplaces. The Loft, furnished all in wicker (including the king bed), is nice. We love the seasonal restored train caboose, a perfect place for families with children (who are welcome here). A full breakfast is served in the beam-ceilinged country kitchen; a playground out back can keep children entertained. Pets are also welcome. On a small street off Route 1, but within walking distance of the downtown shopping area. Doubles are $90–125, breakfast and snacks included.

One-Eighty-One Main Street (865-1226; 1-800-235-9750; bb181main @aol.com), 181 Main Street. Open year-round. This 1840s gray Cape with white trim and black shutters has been featured in *Country Home,* and it's easy to see why. The seven guest rooms, all with private baths (showers only), are attractive and cozy, especially the carpeted rooms in the back. Furnishings include American primitive antiques from the collections of hosts David Cates and Ed Hassett, Oriental rugs, and quilts made by David's mother. There are two parlors with books and games, gardens, a swimming pool, and a resident dog, May Elizabeth, who has appeared in an L. L. Bean catalog. Full breakfast, served at individual tables in the dining room, is included in the $95–110 high-season room rate.

White Cedar Inn (865-9099; 1-800-853-1269), 178 Main Street. Open year-round. This restored, white-clapboard Victorian house was once the home of Arctic explorer Donald B. MacMillan, who went to the North Pole with Admiral Peary. There are seven bedrooms with private baths and simple but pretty furnishings. Three have a single bed in addition to a double or queen. The cozy room up under the eaves offers a bit more privacy. A beautiful wooden spiral staircase leads to the newest room downstairs, which also has a private entrance, sitting area, and television, and can sleep four. Full breakfast, included, is served at small tables in the sunroom, adjacent to the country kitchen. Innkeepers Carla and Phil Kerber live in the remodeled ell and barn that extend from the back of the inn. Doubles $95–130.

The James Place Inn ((865-4486), 11 Holbrook Street. Darcy and Bill James have created a bright atmosphere with a happy feel. The five rooms, each with private bath, are decorated in peaceful pastel colors. All rooms have air-conditioning and cable TV; two have kitchenettes, and two have Jacuzzi baths. The deck with café tables and chairs looks like an inviting place to relax after an afternoon of shopping or sightseeing. A full breakfast is served in the glassed-in breakfast/social room. $90–135 double in-season.

Jacaranda House (865-9858), 8 Holbrook Street. New owners Jay Yilmaz and Jennifer Kelley have created a combination B&B and art gallery, with murals and interesting art ardorning the walls, all done by local artists and friends. Jennifer is an artist also, and her work hangs in one of the three guest rooms, each with a sleigh bed and private bath. The porch, with wicker furniture, is inviting. Well-behaved pets can be accommodated. Full breakfast included in the $90–125 in-season rates.

Atlantic Seal B&B (865-6112), Main Street, Box 146, South Freeport 04078. Open year-round. Just 5 minutes from downtown Freeport but eons from the bustle, this 1850 Cape in the village of South Freeport boasts views of the harbor from each of its three guest rooms. Owned and operated by the owners of the *Atlantic Seal* and *Arctic Seal* tour boats, it is furnished with antiques and nautical collections. One room has a wood-burning fireplace. There is a resident cat. Swimming off the private dock, row-boats and mountain bikes available for guest use. Summer rates, including "hearty sailor's breakfast," start at $95 and go to $135 (for a room with both a queen and a double bed, cable TV, refrigerator, and Jacuzzi). Guests also receive a discount on morning cruises.

  ♿ **The Bagley House Bed & Breakfast** (865-6566; 1-800-765-1772), 1290 Royalsborough Road, Durham 04222. Ten minutes from downtown Freeport in a serene country setting. This is the oldest house in town, built as a public house in 1772. The town's first worship services were held here, and it was the site of the first schoolhouse. Susan Backhouse and Suzanne O'Connor left the Boston area after many years in nursing, fulfilling a lifelong dream when they purchased the property in 1993. They have created an easy, welcoming atmosphere, furnished with antiques, custom-made pieces, and hand-sewn quilts. Details like fresh flowers, and cold drinks and cookies available anytime make guests feel right at home. The cozy nook has slanted ceilings, one double and one three-quarter bed, and wall-to-wall carpeting. Other rooms have queen or double beds. The new "barn" holds a suite and two additional guest rooms, each with a gas fireplace, and a small conference room with a wood-burning stove. $95–125 double in-season, including full breakfast and afternoon refreshments.

MOTELS

  ♿ On Route 1, south of Freeport near the Yarmouth town line, there are a number of modern motels. Among these is the **Freeport Inn** (865-3106; 1-800-99-VALUE). Set on 25 acres of lawns and nature trails, all rooms have wall-to-wall carpeting, cable TV, air-conditioning, and in-room phones. Doubles are $100–110 in-season. There's a swimming pool and a pond where you can ice skate in winter. Canoes are available for paddling on the Cousins River. The inn's café and bakery, the Freeport Café, serves all three meals (see *Eating Out*), and they also operate the Muddy Rudder (see *Eating Out*) just down the road.

CAMPGROUNDS

  ❋ **Cedar Haven Campground** (865-6254; reservations only 1-800-454-3403), Baker Road, Freeport. Fifty-eight mostly wooded sites, each with fireplace and picnic table. Water and electricity hook-ups, four with sewer as well. Twelve tent sites. Store with wood, ice, and groceries. Mini-golf, playground, and swimming pond. Two miles from Route 1 and downtown Freeport. $15–25 per night.

  ❋ **Desert Dunes of Maine Campgrounds** (865-6962; info@desertofmaine.com), 95 Desert Road, Freeport. Fifty wooded and open sites adjacent to this natural glacial sand deposit (see *To See and Do*). Hook-ups, hot showers, laundry, convenience store, propane, fire rings and picnic tables, horseshoe pits, nature trails, swimming pool. Campsites are $19–25 per night.

WHERE TO EAT

All entries are in Freeport unless otherwise indicated.

DINING OUT

  ♿ **Harraseeket Inn** (865-9377; 1-800-342-6423), 162 Main Street. Open year-round for breakfast, lunch, and dinner; Sunday brunch 11:30–2. Continental cuisine and elegant service in three formal dining rooms. The chef uses fresh ingredients from local gardeners and farmers in-season and creates mouthwatering entrées like tamarind-glazed duck confit or pan-roasted Maine salmon. The menu includes three dishes for two (one is châteaubriand, $57.50 for two) prepared at the table. Desserts are sure to please here, too. In addition to dinner, the Harraseeket is known for its outstanding Sunday brunch, which often features such delicacies as caviar, oysters on the half shell, and even venison. $16–25. The dress code at dinner is a collared shirt, and reservations are suggested.

✍ **Jameson Tavern** (865-4195), 115 Main Street. Lunch (11:30–2:30) and dinner (5 PM–closing) served in several inviting dining rooms in the 1779 tavern where the papers separating Maine from Massachusetts were signed in 1820. Specialties include fresh seafood, like bacon-wrapped scallops with maple cream, and chicken Aberdine. Children's menu and outside patio. $11.95–21.95.

15 Independence—An American Bistro, Independence Drive. Serves lunch and dinner daily, and a great Sunday brunch menu offers such items as roast of the day, special pastries, and more. Live music on the deck during brunch.

EATING OUT

✍& **The Broad Arrow Tavern** (865-9377), Harraseeket Inn, 162 Main Street. Recently moved to the ground floor overlooking a new terrace. Open from 11:30 daily. Open kitchen with wood-fired oven and grill, relaxed atmosphere, cozy decor, and a large, varied menu ranging from brick-oven pizzas and sandwiches to full dinners.

✍& **Crickets Restaurant** (865-4005), Lower Main Street. Open daily for lunch and dinner; opens for breakfast Saturday and Sunday at 7:30 AM. The almost overwhelming menu offers something for just about everyone, from generous specialty sandwiches ($6–9) to fajitas, pasta dishes, steak and seafood entrées ($9–15). Reservations appreciated.

Tap Room (865-4195), Jameson Tavern, 115 Main Street. This informal tavern to the rear of the building serves inexpensive snacks and sand-wiches from 11:30 AM until late in the evening.

& **Blue Onion** (865-9396), Lower Main Street. Open for lunch and dinner daily except Monday. A charming dining room in an old blue roadside house located south of Freeport's downtown traffic squeeze. Soups, salads, quiche for lunch; baked and broiled fish, lobster pie, and other fish, veal, and chicken dishes for supper. No liquor.

& **Gritty McDuff's** (865-4321), 183 Lower Main Street. The only brew pub in Freeport offers outdoor dining, lobster, seafood, pizza, and pub food. Great ales.

✍& **Muddy Rudder** (846-3082), Route 1. Operated by the nearby Freeport Inn, this popular restaurant overlooks the water and serves a wide selection of seafood dishes plus steaks, sandwiches, and salads; you can also have a full clambake on the deck. The atmosphere is relaxed, with piano music in the evening.

✒ **Harraseeket Lunch & Lobster Co.** (865-4888), South Freeport (turn off Route 1 at the giant wooden Indian outside Levinsky's, then turn right at a stop sign a few miles down). Open May through October. In the middle of the Harraseeket boatyard; you order lobsters and clams on one side, fried food on the other, and eat at picnic tables (of which there are never enough at peak hours) overlooking a boat-filled harbor. Lobsters are fresh from the pound's boats. Homemade desserts. There is also a small, inside dining room. Worth seeking out, but be aware that it is a busy place; you may have to wait a bit to eat.

✒ **The Corsican** (865-9421), 9 Mechanic Street. Lunch and dinner. Seafood, chicken, vegetarian entrées. Nonsmoking restaurant.

✒ **The Lobster Cooker** (865-4349), 39 Main Street. Steamed lobster, fresh-picked lobster and crabmeat rolls, sandwiches, chowders; dining on the outdoor patio. Beer and wine.

🏅 **The Freeport Café** (865-3106), Route 1. You might drive right by this small café, but you shouldn't. Open daily for all three meals. Extremely friendly service, great dinner specials, a cozy atmosphere, and great prices make it a spot worth finding.

SELECTIVE SHOPPING

FREEPORT FACTORY OUTLETS
🏅 As noted in the introduction to this chapter, Freeport's 125-plus factory outlets constitute what has probably become Maine's mightiest tourist magnet. *Boston Globe* writer Nathan Cobb described it well: "A shoppers' theme park spread out at the foot of L. L. Bean, the high church of country chic." Cobb quoted a local landlord: "The great American pastime now is shopping, not hiking."

Although hiking and hunting put L. L. Bean on the tourist map in the first place, tourists in Freeport are intently studying the map of shops these days. L. L. Bean has kept pace by selling fashionable, sporty clothing and an incredible range of sporting equipment, books, gourmet products, and gifts, as well as its golden boot.

L. L. Bean contends that it attracts at least 3½ million customers annually—almost three times the population of Maine. In the early 1980s, neighboring property owners began to claim a portion of this traffic. Instead of relegating the outlets to malls (see "Kittery and the Yorks"), they have deftly draped them in brick and clapboard, actually improving on the town's old looks (although longtime shopkeepers who were forced to move because of skyrocketing real estate prices might well disagree). Ample parking lots are sequestered behind the Main Street facade (it's still sometimes tough to find a space). In summer there is a festive atmosphere, with hot-dog and ice cream vendors on key corners. But it is the quality of the shops that ensures a year-round crowd. Just about any well-known clothing, accessory, and home furnishing line has a factory store here. The following is a selected list of some of the more interesting outlets. Many stores claim 20–70 percent off suggested retail prices, and even L. L. Bean has a separate outlet store, which you should check first for bargains before heading to the main store.

L. L. Bean (1-800-221-4221 for orders; 1-800-341-4341 for customer service), 95 Main Street. Open 24 hours a day, 365 days a year. More than a store—for millions it is the gateway to Maine. Most shoppers arrive having already studied the mail-order catalog (which accounts for 85–91 percent of sales) and are buying purposefully. The store has been expanded several times in recent years, to the point where it's hard to find the old boot factory—built by Leon Leonwood Bean—that is at its heart. With its outdoor waterfall, indoor trout pond, bookstore and café, and thousands of square feet of retail space, the building now resembles a fancy shopping mall more than it does a single store. It was back in 1912 that Mr. Bean developed his boot, a unique combination of rubber bottom and leather top. He originally sold it by mail order but gradually began catering to the hunters and fishermen who tended to pass through his town in the middle of the night. L. L. Bean himself died in 1967, but grandson Leon Gorman continues to sell nearly a quarter of a million pairs of the family boots each year. Gorman's leadership, together with an excellent marketing staff, has seen Bean grow substantially in the last few decades. Current stock ranges from canoes to weatherproof cameras to climbing gear. There is a wide variety of clothing as well as every conceivable gadget designed to keep you warm. It is the anchor store for all the outlets in town.

L. L. Bean Factory Store (1-800-341-4341), Depot Street (across the street and down the block from the main store). Seconds, samples, and irregular merchandise are offered here. You never know what you'll find, but it's always worth a look. Unlike the main store, the outlet is not open 24 hours a day.

Dooney & Bourke (865-1366), 52 Main Street (in back). Stylish pocketbooks, shoulder bags, belts, wallets, and portfolios in water-repellent, coarse-grained leather.

Cuddledown of Maine Factory Store (865-1713), Route 1 South. Comforters, pillows, gift items, all filled with goose down.

Maine Wreath & Flower Factory Outlet (865-3019), 13 Bow Street. Quality Maine dried flowers and wreaths at discount prices.

Buttons and Things Factory Outlet (865-4480), 24 Main Street. A warren of rooms chock-full of buttons, beads, bead books, and other findings.

Casey's Wood Products (865-3244), 15½ School Street. Bins full of wood turnings, craft materials, and toys. Free catalog.

Dansk Factory Outlet (865-6125), 92 Main Street (across from Bean's). Scandinavian-design tableware, cookware, and gifts.

Mikasa Factory Store (865-9441), 31 Main Street. Dinnerware, bone china, crystal, linens, and gifts. Three floors offering a large inventory.

SPECIAL SHOPS

Harrington House Museum Store (865-0477), 45 Main Street, Freeport. This charming house, right in the middle of all the outlet shops, is owned by the Freeport Historical Society. Faced with escalating property taxes, the preservationists came up with a unique way to hold onto their house and keep up with the times. Every room is furnished with 1830- to 1900-era reproductions, all of which are for sale. Pieces, all documented, range from handsome furniture and weavings to artwork, crafts, Shaker baskets, kitchen utensils, and toys. The historical society mounts changing exhibits in the newly renovated barn.

Edgecomb Potters/Hand in Hand Gallery (865-1705), 8 School Street, Freeport. Fine contemporary crafts. Displays colorful porcelain, jewelry, blown glass, and iron.

Brown Goldsmiths (865-4126), 1 Mechanic Street, Freeport. Open Monday through Saturday. Original designs in rings, earrings, and bracelets.

DeLorme's Map Store (865-4171), Route 1 (south of downtown Freeport). The publishing company's own maps, atlases, and pamphlets; also guidebooks and maps of the United States and the world. In a glassed-in lobby stands "Eartha," the largest rotating and revolving globe in the world.

Bridgham & Cook, Ltd. (865-1040), 8A Bow Street (behind Polo–Ralph Lauren). Packaged British and Irish foods, toiletries, teas, gifts—a must for the Anglophile.

Just Ship It (865-0421), 15 Bow Street, Freeport. If you've bought something you just can't fit into your suitcase, into the car, or onto the airplane, they'll ship it home for you. And if you forget to buy something while you're in Freeport, give them a call and they'll *buy* it and ship it for you!

20th Maine (865-4340), 49 West Street. Devoted to the Civil War—books, art, music, collectibles.

BOOKS

Sherman's Book & Stationery Store (869-9000), 128 Main Street. The newest branch of this Maine bookseller (also in Bar Harbor and Boothbay Harbor), featuring Maine books, cards, toys, and Maine gifts.

SPECIAL EVENTS

Early December: **Sparkle Weekend Celebration** brings caroling, horse-drawn wagons, Santa arriving in a Maine yacht, musical entertainment, holiday readings, storytelling, complimetary refreshment and hot cocoa stops, open houses at local inns, a talking Christmas tree, and, of course, plenty of holiday shopping. For more information call 1-800-865-1994.

III. MID COAST AND THE ISLANDS

A lobster boat heads through a channel on Bailey Island.

KIM GRANT

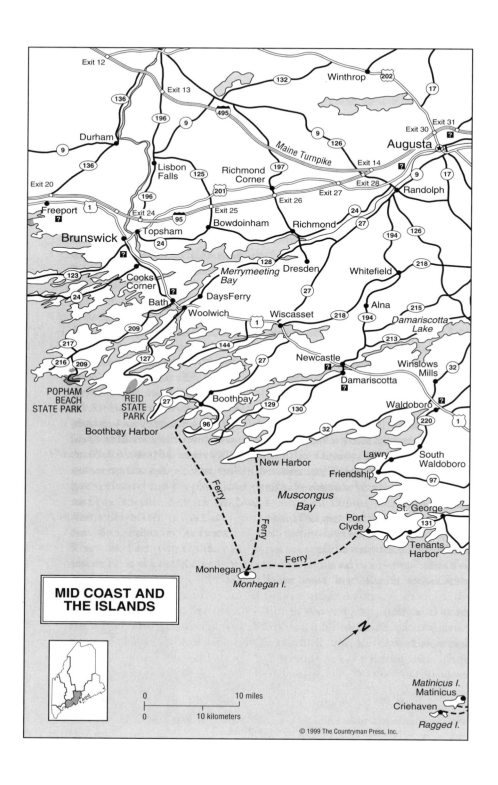

Exit 12

136

Exit 13

196

9

495

132

Winthrop

202

17

Durham

9

136

Lisbon
Falls

125

Richmond
Corner

197

Maine Turnpike

9

126

Exit 30

Exit 31

Augusta

Exit 14

9

17

Exit 28

Randolph

Exit 20

Freeport

1

196

201

Exit 26

Exit 27

24

194

126

Exit 24

95

Exit 25

Bowdoinham

Richmond

27

Brunswick

Topsham

24

128

Merrymeeting
Bay

Dresden

Whitefield

218

123

Cooks
Corner

DaysFerry

27

Alna

215

24

Bath

Woolwich

1

Wiscasset

218

194

Damariscotta
Lake

209

Newcastle

213

217

144

27

216

209

127

Damariscotta

Winslows
Mills

32

POPHAM
BEACH
STATE PARK

REID
STATE
PARK

27

Boothbay

129

130

Waldoboro

220

1

Boothbay Harbor

96

32

Lawry

South
Waldoboro

New Harbor

Friendship

97

Ferry

Muscongus
Bay

St. George

131

Port
Clyde

Tenants
Harbor

Ferry

Ferry

Monhegan

Monhegan I.

**MID COAST AND
THE ISLANDS**

N

0   10 miles

0   10 kilometers

Matinicus I.
Matinicus

Criehaven

Ragged I.

© 1999 The Countryman Press, Inc.

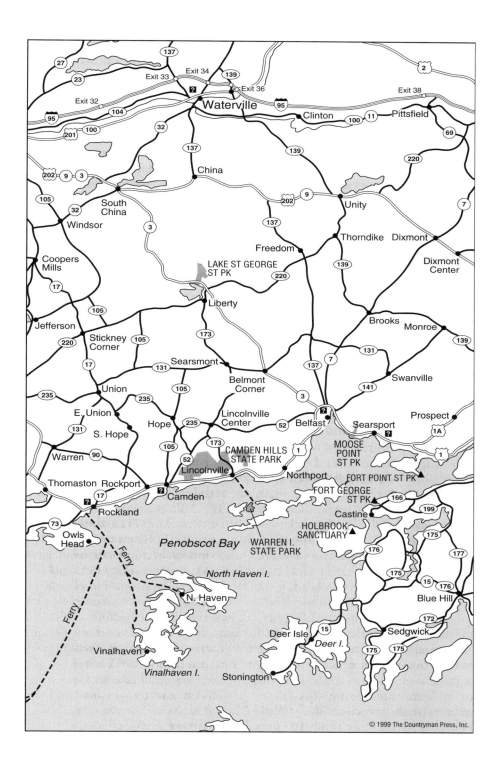

© 1999 The Countryman Press, Inc.

Mid Coast Area

Beyond Casco Bay the shape of Maine's coast changes—it shreds. In contrast to the even arc of shoreline stretching from Kittery to Cape Elizabeth, the coast between Brunswick and Rockland is composed of a series of more than a dozen ragged peninsulas extending like so many fingers south from Route 1, creating myriad big and small harbors, coves, and bays. Scientists tell us that these peninsulas and the offshore islands are mountains drowned by the melting of the same glaciers that sculpted the many shallow lakes and tidal rivers in this area.

The 70 miles of Route 1 between Brunswick and Lincolnville are generally equated with Maine's Mid Coast, but its depth is actually far greater and more difficult to define. It extends south of Route 1 to the tips of every peninsula, from Potts Point in South Harpswell and Land's End on Bailey Island to Popham Beach on the Phippsburg Peninsula and on through the Boothbays to Pemaquid Point, Friendship, Port Clyde, and Spruce Head. Along with Rockland, Camden, and the islands of Monhegan, Vinalhaven, North Haven, and Islesboro, these communities have all catered to summer visitors since steamboats began off-loading them in the mid–19th century. Each peninsula differs in character from the next, but all offer their share of places to stay and eat in settings you rarely find along Route 1.

North of Route 1, this midcoastal area also extends slightly inland. Above Bath, for instance, five rivers meld to form Merrymeeting Bay, and north of Newcastle the tidal Damariscotta River widens into 13-mile-long Damariscotta Lake. This gently rolling, river- and lake-laced backcountry harbors a number of picturesque villages and reasonably priced lodging places.

We would hope that no one who reads this book simply sticks to Route 1.

Brunswick and the Harpswells

The Civil War began and ended in Brunswick, or so say local historians. A case can be made. Harriet Beecher Stowe was attending a service in Brunwick's First Church when she is said to have had a vision of the death of Uncle Tom and hurried home to begin penning the book that has been credited with starting the war. Joshua Chamberlain, a longtime parishioner in this same church was, moreover, the Union general chosen for the honor of receiving General Lee's surrender at Appomattox.

Thanks largely to the Ken Burns PBS series *The Civil War,* Joshua Chamberlain has been rediscovered. Annual admissions to his house shot from 300 in 1993 to 5,000 in 1996 and have remained stable, fueling its restoration. A Brunswick restaurant is now named for "Joshua" and the historical society dispenses maps that pinpoint sites ranging from Chamberlain's student dorm rooms to his gravestone.

This scholar-soldier-governor is, in fact, an entirely appropriate figurehead for a town that's home to Brunswick Naval Air Station and to the current Maine governor, Angus King (who even bears an uncanny resemblance to Chamberlain), as well as to Bowdoin College, over which Chamberlain presided as president, after four terms as governor of Maine.

Brunswick began as an Indian village named "Pejepscot," at the base of the Androscoggin River's Great Falls. In 1688 this site became a Massachusetts outpost named Fort Andros and subsequently it has been occupied by a series of mills. Today, with a population of 21,500, this is Maine's largest town, a mix of Franco-Americans whose great-grandparents were recruited to work in the mills, of military and retired military families, of Bowdoin and retired Bowdoin faculty and alumni, of old seafaring families, and of an increasing number of professionals who commute the half hour to work in Portland or Augusta (Brunswick is halfway between).

Brunswick's Maine Street is the state's widest, laid out in 1717 with a grassy "mall" (scene of concerts and of farmer's markets) at one end, the other end now headed by the neo-Gothic First Parish Church and the Bowdoin College campus.

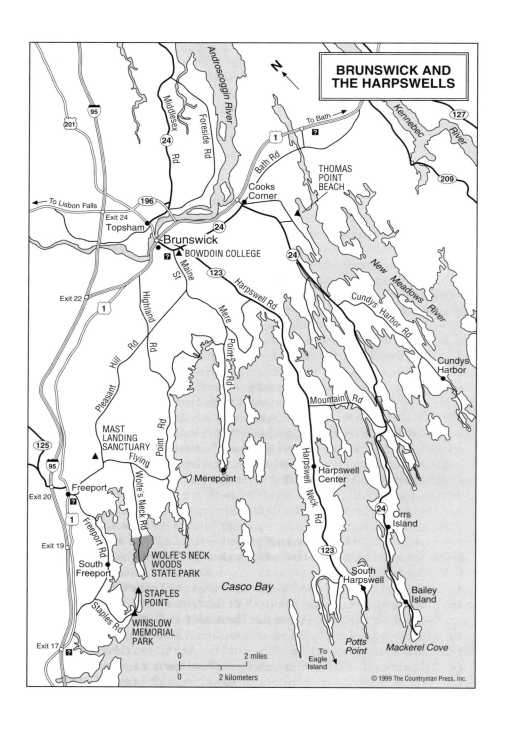

BRUNSWICK AND
THE HARPSWELLS

N

To Bath →

Kennebec River

127

209

Androscoggin River

Middlesex Rd

Foreside Rd

95

201

24

Bath Rd

Cooks Corner

THOMAS
POINT
BEACH

→ To Lisbon Falls

196

New Meadows River

Exit 24
Topsham

Brunswick

BOWDOIN COLLEGE

24

24

Cundys Harbor Rd

Exit 22

1

Maine St

123

Harpswell Rd

Cundys
Harbor

Highland Hill Rd

Mere Point Rd

Mountain Rd

Pleasant Hill Rd

125

MAST
LANDING
SANCTUARY

Point Rd

95

Flying

Harpswell Neck Rd

Harpswell
Center

Merepoint

Freeport

Wolfe's Neck Rd

24

Orrs
Island

Exit 20

1

Exit 19

Freeport Rd

South
Freeport

WOLFE'S NECK
WOODS
STATE PARK

Casco Bay

123

South
Harpswell

STAPLES
POINT

Bailey
Island

Staples Rd

WINSLOW
MEMORIAL
PARK

Exit 17

0   2 miles

0   2 kilometers

To
Eagle
Island

Potts
Point

Mackerel Cove

© 1999 The Countryman Press, Inc.

A small but prestigious college, chartered in 1794, Bowdoin is surprisingly welcoming to visitors, especially in July and August, when its buildings are filled with the practicing and the performing virtuoso musicians of the Bowdoin Summer Music Festival, and when Picard Theater is the stage for the Maine State Music Theater. The Bowdoin College Museum of Art and its Peary-MacMillan Arctic Museum are well worth a stop, as are the nearby Pejepscot Museum and Chamberlain House.

Brunswick is, however, no tourist town. No kiosk proclaims the schedule of plays and concerts because most patrons know enough to read about them in the Thursday edition of the *Times Record.* Maine Street's many shops, galleries, and restaurants also cater to residents and the Eveningstar Cinema screens art films for local consumption. Grand City is still a genuine five-and-dime with a lunch counter, a basement stocked with furniture and fabrics, and a summer supply of plastic sleds, found next to the boots and gloves that clammers also need. Freeport's 125-plus outlet stores are just miles yet light-years away.

South of Brunswick three narrow land fingers and several bridge-linked islands stretch seaward, defining the eastern rim of Casco Bay. Collectively they form the town of Harpswell, better known as "the Harpswells" because it includes so many coves, points, and islands (notably Orrs and Bailey). Widely known for its seafood restaurants, these peninsulas are surprisingly sleepy, salted with crafts, galleries, and some great places to stay. They are Maine's most convenient peninsulas, yet they seem much farther Down East.

GUIDANCE

Chamber of Commerce of the Bath-Brunswick Region (725-8797; www.midcoastmaine.com), 59 Pleasant Street, Brunswick 04011. Open weekdays year-round, 8:30–5; also open July through Labor Day on Fridays until 8 PM and Saturdays 3–7 PM. Staff members keep tabs on vacancies and send out lodging and dining information. The walk-in information center displays area menus and stocks a wide range of brochures. From Route 1 North follow Brunswick business district signs (these will take you down Pleasant Street).

GETTING THERE

By bus: Bus service to downtown Brunswick from Logan Airport and downtown Boston is unusually good: 2½ hours ($20–23) via **Concord Trailways.**

By car: I-95 to Route 1, which now doglegs around Brunswick, bypassing it entirely. Instead, continue straight ahead up Pleasant Street, which forms a T with Maine Street. Turn right for the Bowdoin College campus and the Harpswells.

MEDICAL EMERGENCY

Dial **911.**

KIM GRANT

Bowdoin College

Parkview Memorial Hospital (729-1641), 329 Main Street, Brunswick. **Mid Coast Hospital** (729-0181), 58 Baribeau Drive, Brunswick; and 1356 Washington Street, Bath (443-5524).

TO SEE

Bowdoin College (725-3000), Brunswick. Tours of the 110-acre campus with more than 50 buildings begin at the admissions office. Phone for current hours. Because Maine was part of Massachusetts when the college was founded in 1794, the school is named after a Massachusetts governor. Nathaniel Hawthorne and Henry Wadsworth Longfellow were classmates here in 1825; other notable graduates include Franklin Pierce and Robert Edwin Peary. Founded as a men's college, the school now also welcomes women among its 1,500 students. Bowdoin ranks among the nation's top colleges both in status and in cost. It isn't necessary to take a tour to see the sights.

MUSEUMS

Bowdoin College Museum of Art (725-3275), Walker Art Building. Open year-round, Tuesday through Saturday 10–5, Sunday 2–5; closed Monday and holidays. One of New England's outstanding art collections housed in a copper-domed building designed by McKim, Mead, and White with murals in its rotunda by Abott Thayer, Kenyon Cox, and John La Farge. Its core collection is one of the oldest in America (James Bowdoin III was an avid collector), and displays range from Assyrian bas reliefs and Far Eastern works through American portraits by Gilbert Charles Stuart, Robert Feke, John Singleton Copley and Thomas

Eakins; also paintings by Winslow Homer, Rockwell Kent, John Sloan, and Andrew Wyeth; special exhibits.

Peary-MacMillan Arctic Museum (725-3416), Hubbard Hall, Bowdoin College. Open same hours as the museum of art. A well-displayed collection of clothing, trophy walruses and seals, polar bears and caribou, and other mementos from expeditions to the North Pole by two Bowdoin alumni. Robert Edwin Peary (class of 1877) was the first man to reach the North Pole, and Donald Baxter MacMillan (class of 1898), who was Peary's chief assistant, went on to dedicate his life to exploring Arctic waters and terrain. Displays include an interactive touch screen, photo blowups, and artifacts to tell the story.

Pejepscot Historical Society Museums (729-6606). Founded in 1888 and named for an ancient Indian settlement (see "Brunswick" introduction), this is one of Maine's oldest historical societies. It maintains three downtown Brunswick museums, among which the **Joshua L. Chamberlain Museum** (226 Maine Street; open June through September, Tuesday through Saturday 10–4; $3 per adult, $1 per child) is by far the most popular. Thanks to the PBS series *The Civil War*, the entire country now seems to know about Joshua Chamberlain (1818–1914), the college professor who became the hero of Little Round Top in the Battle of Gettysburg and went on to serve four terms as governor of Maine and to become president of Bowdoin College. His formerly forgotten, decaying home—a fanciful mansion with two top floors dating from the 1820s and a Victorian first floor from 1871—has been partially restored over the past few years. Exhibits include his bullet-dented boots and his governor's chair and desk, and a museum store sells Civil War books and souvenirs. The **Pejepscot Museum,** 159 Park Row (open weekdays year-round, 9–4:30, summer Saturdays 1–4; free), is a massive, tower-topped mansion that includes an office and archives and also displays changing exhibits on the history of Brunswick, Topsham, and Harpswell. The **Skolfield-Whittier House,** part of the same mid-19th-century, Italianate double house (open for summer tours Tuesday through Friday 10–3, Saturday 1–4; $3 adults, $1 children ages 6–12), is virtually unchanged since the 1925 death of Dr. Frank Whittier. Its high-Victorian drawing room is hung with crystal chandeliers and heavy velvet drapes, furnished in wicker and brocade, filled with the photos, books, paintings, and clutter of three generations of a very real Maine family.

The First Parish Church (729-7331), Maine Street at Bath Road. Open for concerts and tours Tuesdays July through mid-August 12:10–12:50, for Sunday services, and by chance. This graceful neo-Gothic building was designed in the 1840s by Richard Upjohn, architect of New York City's Trinity Church. A dramatic departure from its Puritan predecessors, it is open-beamed, mildly cruciform in shape, and has deeply colored stained-glass windows. The large sanctuary window was donated by Joshua Chamberlain, one of the first men to be married here. The Hutchings-Plastid tracker organ was installed in 1883.

Brunswick Naval Air Station (921-2000). From Route 1, take the Cooks Corner exit just east of Brunswick, then follow Route 24 south to the entrance. Home of the navy's North Atlantic antisubmarine and general patrol squadrons, the base is now open for self-guided, drive-through tours. Pick up a map and directions at the kiosk just inside the gate.

✐ **Fishway Viewing Room** (795-4290), Brunswick-Topsham Hydro Station, next to Fort Andros (the former mill that's now a shopping complex), corner of Route 1 and Maine Street, Brunswick. Open during the spawning season: mid-May through June, Wednesday through Sunday 1–5. Watch salmon, smallmouth bass, and alewives climb the 40-foot-high fish ladder that leads to a holding tank beside the viewing room.

Also see Eagle Island under *Boat Excursions.*

SCENIC DRIVE

A tour of the Harpswells, including Orrs and Bailey Islands. Allow a day for this rewarding peninsula prowl. From Brunswick, follow Route 123 south past Bowdoin College 8 miles to the picturesque village of Harpswell Center. The white-clapboard Elijah Kellogg Church faces the matching Harpswell Town Meeting House built in 1757. The church is named for a former minister who was a prominent 19th-century children's book author. Continue south through West Harpswell to Pott's Point, where multicolored, 19th-century summer cottages cluster on the rocks like a flock of exotic birds that have wandered in among the gulls. Stop by the first crafts studio you see here and pick up a map/guide to other members of the Harpswell Craft Guild.

Retrace your way up Route 123, and 2 miles north of the church turn right onto Mountain Road, leading to busier Route 24 on Great (also known as Sebascodegan) Island. Drive south along Orrs Island across the only remaining cribstone bridge in the world. (Its granite blocks are laid in honeycomb fashion without cement to allow tidal flows.) This bridge brings you to Bailey Island, with its restaurants, lodging places, picturesque Mackerel Cove, and rocky Land's End (there's a small beach, gift shop, and parking lot). Return up Route 24.

TO DO

BICYCLING

The Androscoggin River Bicycle Path, a 2.5-mile, 14-foot-wide paved bicycle/pedestrian trail, begins at Lower Water Street in Brunswick and runs along the river to Grover Lane in Cooks Corner. It connects with Topsham along the way via a bicycle lane on the new Merrymeeting Bridge. **Center Street Bicycles** (729-5309) rents mountain bikes and serves as a source of local biking information.

BOAT EXCURSIONS

Casco Bay Boat Charters (833-2978) and **Sea Escape Charters** (833-5531) both offer fishing trips, scenic cruises, and excursions from Bailey Island to **Eagle Island.** A classic one-man's island, just 17 acres, Eagle

Island is the site of Admiral Robert E. Peary's shingled summer home where, on September 6, 1909, his wife received the news that her husband had become the first man to reach the North Pole. Peary positioned his house to face northeast on a rocky bluff that resembles the prow of a ship. He designed the three-sided living room hearth, which was made from island stones and Arctic quartz crystals, and stuffed many of the birds that occupy the mantel. The upstairs bedrooms appear as though someone has just stepped out for a walk, and the dining room is strewn with photos of men and dogs battling ice and snow. There is a small beach and a nature path that circles the island and takes you past the pine trees filled with seagulls on the ocean side.

Casco Bay Lines (774-7871) offers a daily seasonal excursion from Cook's Lobster House on Bailey Island. It takes 1½ hours—circles around Eagle Island and through this northern end of Casco Bay.

Symbion (725-0979) is Captain Ken Brigham's 37-foot sailboat; daysails and overnight charters.

GOLF

Brunswick Golf Club (725-8224), River Road, Brunswick. Incorporated in 1888, an 18-hole course known for its beauty and challenging nature. Snack bar, lounge, and cart rentals.

SEA KAYAKING

H2Outfitters (833-5257; 1-800-649-5257), P.O. Box 72, Orrs Island 04066. Located just north of the cribstone bridge on Orr's Island, this is one of Maine's oldest kayaking outfitters. No rentals. Lessons for all abilities from beginners to instructor certification; guided day trips and overnight excursions are also offered.

Bethel Point Oar and Paddle (725-6494), Cundys Harbor. Kayaks, Alden shells, and canoes by the half and full day, weather permitting.

GREEN SPACE

BEACHES AND SWIMMING HOLES

❧ **White's Beach** (729-0415), Durham Road, Brunswick. Open mid-May to mid-October. $2.50 per adult, $1.50 per child. A pond in a former gravel pit (water no deeper than 9 feet). Facilities include a small slide for children. Sandy beach, lifeguards, picnic tables, grills, and snack bar. Inquire about campsites.

❧ **Thomas Point Beach** (725-6009), off Thomas Point Road, marked from Route 24, Cooks Corner. Open Memorial Day through Labor Day, 9–sunset. $2.50 adults, $2 children under 12. The beach is part of an 80-acre private preserve on tidal water overlooking the New Meadows River. It includes groves for picnicking (more than 500 picnic tables plus snack bar, playground, and arcade), and 75 tent and RV sites. It's the scene of a series of special events, including the Maine Festival.

❧ **Coffin Pond** (725-6656), River Road, Brunswick. Open mid-June to Labor Day, 10–7. $3.50 per adult, $2 per child. A strip of sandy beach surround-

KIM GRANT

The Cribstone Bridge

ing a circular pool. Facilities include a 55-foot-long water slide, a playground, and changing rooms maintained by the town.

WALKS

Giant's Staircase. Turn off Route 24 at Washington Avenue, park at the Episcopal church, and walk down to Ocean Street; follow the path along the water and follow the small sign to the well-named "stairs."

Brunswick-Topsham Land Trust (729-7694), 108 Maine Street, Brunswick. The land trust has preserved some 700 acres in the area. Pick up map/ guides to the nature loops at **Skofield Nature Preserve,** Route 123, Brunswick (4 miles or so south of town), adjoining an ancient Indian portage between Middle Bay and Harpswell Cove and to the **Bradley Pond Farm Preserve** in Topsham.

LODGING

Brunswick Bed & Breakfast (729-4914; 1-800-299-4914), 165 Park Row, Brunswick 04011. Open year-round. Architect Steve Normand and quiltmaker Mercie Normand have beautifully restored this mid-1800s Greek Revival home in the historic district on the town green. It's within walking distance of shops, museums, and the Bowdoin College campus. The seven guest rooms are furnished with antiques and a collection of both new and antique quilts, and all have private baths. A carriage house unit, available in summer, has a full kitchen, bath, and sleeping area. The parlor's floor-to-ceiling windows overlook the mall. The breakfast (ours included perfect pancakes served with blueberries, strawberries, and melon) is included in the rate: $87–125 single or double occupancy. The

Normands are consummate hosts, tuned in to everything that's going on and eager to share the best of Brunswick with guests.

  ♿ **The Captain's Watch at Cundy's Harbor** (725-0979), 2476 Cundy's Harbor Road, Harpswell 04011. Open year-round. Built high on a bluff during the Civil War as the Union Hotel, this classic old building with an octagonal cupola has been restored by Donna Dillman and Ken Brigham. The five guest rooms include two with fireplaces, and one 2-room suite with a deck that can accommodate a family of five; all have private baths and water views; two rooms share access to the cupola. The Captain's Quarters is particularly romantic, with a high queen cherry pencil-post bed, antique dressers, a large Oriental rug, water views everywhere, and both a fireplace in the sitting area and access to the cupola for a 360-degree view. $95–130 per room and $120–180 for the suites includes a full breakfast featuring omelets or sour cream blueberry pancakes. Their 37-foot sloop *Symbion* is available for short sails and overnight cruises.

Harpswell Inn (833-5509; 1-800-843-5509), 141 Lookout Point Road, RR 1, Box 141, South Harpswell 04079. Built as the cookhouse for a boatyard across the way, this three-story white-clapboard has taken in guests under a number of names but has never been quite so gracious as now. Innkeepers Susan and Bill Menz have lived in Hawaii and Texas as well as the South, collecting antiques and furnishings to fill the house—much as though it were owned by a widely traveled sea captain. Guests enter a large living room with plenty of sitting space around a big hearth and windows overlooking Middle Bay. The nine guest rooms vary widely and come with and without baths and water views, and there are three suites with kitchens. Children must be over 10. No smoking. $76–125 for rooms, $135–165 for suites, breakfast is included.

☺🕷✈**Driftwood Inn and Cottages** (833-5461), Bailey Island 04003. Open June through mid-October; dining room (which is open to the public) is open late June through Labor Day. Sited on a rocky point within earshot of a foghorn are three gray-shingled, traditional Maine summer houses that contain a total of 16 doubles and eight singles (nine with half-baths); there are also six housekeeping cottages. Everyone dines in the pine-walled lodge dining room (so request a room away from the lodge). Almost all views are of the sea. There is a small saltwater swimming pool set in the rocks and plenty of room, both inside and out, to lounge. This is a rustic resort with the kind of atmosphere and value possible only under longtime (over 50 years) ownership by one family. Your hosts are Mr. and Mrs. Charles L. Conrad. $70–75 per couple, $45 single (no minimum stay, no meals). Housekeeping cottages, available by the week, are $475–550. Breakfast is $5; dinner, $13. Weekly MAP rates: $345 per person. No credit cards. Pets are accepted in the cottages.

  ♿ **Captain Daniel Stone Inn** (725-9898; 1-800-267-0525), 10 Water Street, Brunswick 04011. Twenty-five modern rooms and suites are annexed to a Federal mansion. All have color TV, telephone, VCR, alarm clock–

cassette player, and some feature whirlpool baths. Common space includes a handsome living room as well as large function rooms. Breakfast, lunch, dinner, and Sunday brunch are served in the **Narcissa Stone Restaurant.** Continental breakfast is included in the room rate. $89 off-season to $205 per room in-season; inquire about packages.

The Log Cabin (833-5546), Route 24, Bailey Island 04003. Better known as a restaurant, this old landmark was refitted in 1995 to offer six rooms, three with kitchens, several with Jacuzzis, all with private baths and waterside decks ($109–185).

Bethel Point Bed and Breakfast ((72(-1115; 1-888-238-8262), RR 5, Bethel Point Road, Box 2387, Brunswick 04011. Great views and a good launch site for kayakers, from $70 for Sunset Room to $95 for Bayview Room with private bath includes full breakfast served between 8 and 9; $750 per week for a self-contained apartment.

Captain York House (833-6224), P.O. Box 298, Bailey Island 04003. A turn-of-the century home on a hill overlooking Harpswell Sound. Four rooms with queen-sized beds; a small apartment with a kitchenette, a twin as well as a queen bed, and a den with TV and front parlor, both overlooking the water. $77 for rooms with shared bath, $90 with private bath, $95 for the apartment; children over 12 welcome.

The Black Lantern (725-4165; 1-888-306-4165), 6 Pleasant Street, Topsham 04086. A circa-1810 Federal-style house one block from the Androscoggin in the historic district. Tom and Judy Connelie offer two guest rooms with private baths and particularly welcome quilters. No children under 10, please. $70–85.

COTTAGES

The Bath-Brunswick Area Chamber of Commerce (see *Guidance*) lists a number of weekly cottage rentals, most on Orrs and Bailey Islands.

MOTELS

Little Island Motel (833-2392), RD 1, Box 15, Orrs Island 04066. Open mid-May to mid-October. An attractive motel with terrific views. Nine units, each with a small refrigerator and color TV; part of a complex that also includes a gift shop (the Gull's Nest) and a reception area where coffee and a buffet breakfast are served each morning. The complex is set on its own mini-island with a private beach, connected to other land by a narrow neck. $84–114 includes breakfast and use of boats, bicycles, and the outdoor picnic area.

Bailey Island Motel (833-2886), Route 24, Bailey Island 04003. Open early May to late October. Located just over the cribstone bridge. A pretty, gray-shingled building on the water's edge, offering ocean views and land-scaped lawns. The 11 rooms are clean and comfortable, with cable TV. No smoking. Morning coffee and muffins are included in the $84–114.

Note: If it happens to be a peak travel weekend and you are desperate for a bed, turn north on Route 24 into Topsham, then head up Route 196 toward Lisbon Falls. This truck route is lined with inexpensive motels that never seem to fill.

WHERE TO EAT

In Brunswick

Scarlet Begonias (721-0403), 212 Maine Street. Open Monday through Thursday 11–8, Friday 11–9, Saturday noon–9, closed Sunday. In their attractive storefront "bistro," Doug and Colleen Lavallee serve some great sandwiches (we recommend the turkey spinach with mozzarella and basil mayo, grilled on sourdough bread), pastas like Rose Begonia (bacon, chicken, mushrooms, tomato, cream sauce, and fresh herbs over penne), and unusual pizzas.

Joshua's Restaurant & Tavern (725-7981), 121 Maine Street. Open 8 PM–midnight in summer, until 10 in winter. Named for General Joshua Chamberlain (see *Museums*), this is a pubby, pleasant place with seasonal tables on a porch overlooking Maine Street. We can recommend the Chamberlain burger but it's a big menu—plenty of fried and broiled fish, soups, stews, and a wide choice of beers. Dinner entrées $10.95–13.95 but you can always get a burger, bowl of stew, or a salad.

Richard's German/American Cuisine (729-9673), 115 Maine Street. Open for lunch and dinner Monday through Saturday. Continental fare like veal Oscar and grilled New York sirloin, but also featuring very satisfying dishes like German farmer soup, *Gemischter salat,* Wiener schnitzel, and *Schlachtplatte.* Nightly specials include *Rindsrouladen* (thinly sliced beef rolled with onions, bacon, mustard, and pickles, braised in a brown sauce). The beer list is impressive. Dinner entrées $8–17. Hamburgers, quiche, and lighter fare served in the pub area. Specials like Swedish stuffed pork for $10; vegetarian specials too.

The Great Impasta (729-5858), 42 Maine Street. Open daily for lunch and dinner. A great stop even if you are simply traveling up or down Route 1 (it's at the Route 1 end of Maine Street), but you might want to get there early to get a booth; it's small, popular, and suffused with the aroma of garlic. The specialties are pasta dishes like seafood lasagna ($10.95); try the eggplant stuffed with smoked mozzarella, mushrooms, onions, and tomatoes and topped with roasted vegetables ($9.95, $5.95 at lunch). Wine and beer served.

Wild Oats Bakery and Cafe (725-6287), Tontine Mall, 149 Maine Street. Open Monday through Saturday 7:30–5, Sunday 8–2. Set back from Maine Street with tables on the terrace as well as inside, this is the town's meeting place: good coffees and teas, from-scratch pastries and breads, healthy sandwiches and salads.

The Big Top New York Style Delicatessen (721-8900), 70 Maine Street. Open 7 AM–8 PM most days, weekends from 8, closing at 4 PM on Sunday and Monday. When you've had one too many lobster or crab rolls, this is the place to come for a Reuben, a liverwurst sandwich, maybe even the Lion Tamer (roast beef, ham, turkey, Swiss, tomato, onion, etc.); try a bagel with pastrami for breakfast.

Bangkok Garden Restaurant (725-9708), 14 Maine Street (Fort Andros), Open daily for lunch and dinner, Sunday 4–9. This is an attractive restaurant and reviews for classic dishes like green curry and pad Thai are good. The menu is large and includes a number of tofu and vegetable dishes.

Fat Boy Drive-In (729-9431), Old Route 1, Brunswick. Open for lunch and dinner, late March through mid-October. This is no 1950s reconstruct, just a real drive-in with carhops that's survived because it's so good and incredibly reasonably priced. If you own a pre-1970 car inquire about the annual "sock hop," second Saturday in August. If you don't, you can't come.

First Wok (729-8660), 119 Maine Street. Open for lunch and dinner. Good Chinese food at reasonable prices.

Miss Brunswick Diner (729-5948), 101 Pleasant Street (Route 1, northbound). Open daily 5 AM–9 PM. A convenient road-food stop, a remake of a diner that originally stood in Norway (Maine) but has now been here several decades; the neon lights, booths, and jukebox are all new but the food is what it claims to be: "home cooking at a down-home good price." We ate at an outside table, but no one needs to be that close to Route 1. Hold out for an air-conditioned booth.

In the Harpswells

J. Hathaway's Restaurant and Tavern (833-5305), Route 123, Harpswell Center. Open from 5 PM for dinner daily except Monday. The Hathaways labor hard to create a casual country atmosphere and delectable dishes that may include honey-mustard chicken ($10.95), pan-seared salmon ($12.95), or a full brace of back ribs with the house sauce ($13.95); vegetarian, smaller suppers, and sandwiches also available.

Cribstone Restaurant (833-600), Route 24, Bailey's Island. This Thai restaurant got great reviews in the summer of 1998 for dishes like scallops in mango sauce, but off-season, judging from recent reports, we suspect that the chef takes a vacation. Entrées are higher than the going rate but so is the rent. This prime location has changed hands frequently and we hope this one succeeds.

Holbrook's Lobster Wharf & Snack Bar (725-0708), Cundy's Harbor (4.5 miles off Route 24). Open in-season for lunch and dinner. Lobsters and clams are steamed outdoors. Weekend clambakes; clams, crab rolls, fish-and-chips, homemade salads, and desserts like Barbara's chocolate bread pudding with ice cream. The window boxes are filled with petunias, and you sit at picnic tables overlooking buoys and lobster boats. You can get beer and wine in the shop next door.

✐ **The Original Log Cabin Restaurant** (833-5546), Route 24, Bailey Island. Open mid-March to mid-October, daily for lunch and dinner. A genuine log lodge built as an enormous summer cottage; the dining room is much smaller than in former years because much of the space has been preempted by guest rooms. Still the menu is extensive; dinner entrées range from $11.95 to $24.95 (surf and turf); a multicourse shore dinner is $28.95; children's meals. Specialties include chowders and vegetarian dishes.

The Dolphin Marina (833-6000), South Harpswell (marked from Route 123; also accessible by water). Open year-round, 8–8 daily (but not for breakfast in winter). The nicest kind of small Maine restaurant—family owned and run—with a combo chandlery/coffee shop partitioned from a more formal restaurant by a model of a ketch, overlooking a small but busy harbor. In the morning, fishermen occupy the six stools along the counter; the dining room fills for lunch and dinner (there's often a wait). Chowder, lobster stew, and homemade desserts are specialties, but there is a full dinner menu.

Cook's Lobster House (833-2818), Bailey Island. Open year-round, 11:30 AM–9 PM. A barn of a place, right on the water, adjacent to a working fishing pier. Save your leftover french fries and muffin crumbs to feed the seagulls on the dock out back. In July and August, try to get there before the Casco Bay Liner arrives with its load of day-trippers from Portland. $2.50–30.

Estes Lobster House (833-6340), Route 123, South Harpswell. Open mid-April through mid-October for lunch and dinner. Another large place on a causeway, with waterside picnic tables across the road. Entrées $2.95–19.95.

Lobster Village at Mackerel Cove Restaurant (833-6656), Bailey Island. Open April through mid-October; coffee shop remains open longer. This complex includes a marina, a coffee shop (6 AM–9 PM) that caters to fishermen, and a more formal restaurant (in the pine-paneled, seafood-barn tradition) that serves breakfast, lunch, and dinner. Under new ownership, it specializes in lobsters and homemade desserts.

Block & Tackle, Cundy's Harbor Road. Open mid-May to mid-October, 6:30 AM–8 PM. A family-run and -geared restaurant, a real find. Create your own omelet for breakfast; try shrimp stew or a real crabmeat roll for lunch, homemade clam cakes or seafood pie for dinner. The fried lobster platter is top of the menu.

ENTERTAINMENT

MUSIC

Bowdoin Summer Music Festival (725-3895). Famed in classical music circles, this chamber-music series brings together 200 talented young performers and 40 internationally acclaimed musicians, faculty members at the world's top music schools. It includes composers and choral artists as well as musicians, performing original and classical pieces. The Friday evening concerts (June through August) are staged in the new Crooker Theater at Brunswick High School. The Sunday "Upbeat" concerts, free Wednesday "Bach in the Chapel" concerts, and the Gamper Festival of Contemporary Music series are held in Bowdoin campus buildings.

Also see First Parish Church under *To See* and the Maine Arts Festival under *Special Events*.

THEATER

Maine State Music Theater (725-8769), Bowdoin College, Brunswick. Picard Hall, an 1873 memorial to the Bowdoin students who fought and died in the Civil War, ordered built, of course, by Joshua Chamberlain, is a relatively small (just 600 seats) stage for Maine's largest performing-arts group. This highly professional equity company strives for a mix of classics and new scripts and frequently gets rave reviews. Summer performances at 8 PM, Tuesday through Saturday, matinees Tuesday, Thursday, and Friday. Tickets: $15–30. Also special children's shows.

Theater Project of Brunswick (729-8584), 14 School Street, Brunswick. Serious drama presented year-round in a black-box theater, Wednesday through Sunday at 8. Inquire about late-night cabarets and about Thursday-night dinner theater.

Bowdoin College (725-3000). Performing arts groups from September to May. Concerts and theatrical performances.

FILM

Eveningstar Cinema (729-6796), Tontine Mall, 149 Main Street, Brunswick. The specialty is alternative films: foreign, art, biography, documentary, and educational. Also a monthly venue for folk, jazz, etc.

SELECTIVE SHOPPING

ANTIQUES

Cabot Mill Antiques (725-28555), Fort Andros, 14 Main Street (at Route 1), a vast 140-dealer space with quality antiques, flea markets on summer weekends.

ARTS AND CRAFTS GALLERIES

Quality galleries at the north end of Brunswick's Maine Street include **O'Farrell Gallery** (729-8228), 58 Maine Street, and **Icon Contemporary Art** (725-8157) is around the corner at 19 Mason Street. Check out **Spindleworks** (725-8820), 7 Lincoln Street, an artists' cooperative for people with disabilities that produces some striking handwoven fiber clothing and hangings, quilts, accessories, paintings, prints, etc. **Stone Soup Artisans** (798-5841), 102 Maine Street, Brunswick sells a wide variety of quality Maine crafts. **Wyler Gallery** (729-1321), 150 Maine Street, is a great mix of quality pottery, glassware, jewelry, clothing, and fun stuff.

In the Harpswells

Harpswell Craft Guild (833-6004) is an association of nine studios/galleries along Route 123 on Harpswell Neck. Pick up a copy of their leaflet guide. **Harpswell Schoolhouse Gallery** (729-8872), Route 123, Harpswell Neck, open May into December, Friday through Monday 10–5, features fine hand weavings, knitting, jewelry, and hand-painted glass ornaments. **Widgeon Cove Studios** (833-6081), open year-round, features the handmade papers and collages of Georgeann and the gold and silver jewelry of Condon Kuhl. It's a peaceful place with gardens overlooking the water. **The O'Hara Studio** (833-6871), Route 24, Bailey Island. Open mid-May to mid-October, 10–5, but call. Gail O'Hara's shop sells the artist's own oils and paintings on porcelain. Inquire about landscape classes and a weekly rental.

Hawke's Lobster (721-0472) in Cundy's Harbor is a source not only of live lobsters, clams, and smoked salmon but also the work of a dozen local craftpeople and of unusual container gardens.

BOOKSTORES

Gulf of Maine Books (729-5083), 134 Maine Street, Brunswick. A laid-back, full-service bookstore with a wide inventory, particularly rich in Maine titles, poetry, and "books that fall through the holes in bigger stores." Owner Gary Lawless is a founder of Blackberry Press (note the full line here), which has reissued many out-of-print Maine classics.

Maine Writers & Publishers Alliance (729-6333), 12 Pleasant Street, Brunswick. An inviting bookstore stocking Maine titles and authors, maintained by the state's nonprofit organization dedicated to promoting Maine literature. Frequent workshops, catalog listing, monthly newsletters.

Bookland (725-2313), Cooks Corner Shopping Center, Brunswick. A user-friendly superstore and café in southern Maine's largest bookstore chain.

Old Books (725-4524), 136 Maine Street, Brunswick. Closed Thursday. Upstairs from Gulf of Maine, Old Books features Clare Howell's floor-to-ceiling, well-arranged used books and a large stuffed couch, along with friendly nooks for reading.

SPECIAL EVENTS

Throughout the summer: **Farmer's market** *(Tuesday and Friday, May through November)* on the downtown Brunswick Mall (the town common). **Beanhole suppers** are staged during summer months by the Harpswell Neck Fire Department.

July: **Annual Lobster Luncheon,** Orrs Island United Methodist Church. **Bailey Island Fishing Tournament** (to register, phone Cook's Lobster House at 833-2818). **Great State of Maine Air Show** at the Brunswick Naval Air Station every other year (in 1999).

August: **Topsham Fair** *(early in the month),* a traditional agricultural fair complete with ox pulls, crafts and food competitions, carnival, and livestock; held at Topsham Fairgrounds, Route 24, Topsham. **The Maine Arts Festival** (772-9012), first weekend in the month. A four-day celebration of music, dance, crafts, and more, held at Thomas Point Beach, marked from Cook's Corners. **A weekend in Harpswell** *(late in the month)*—annual art show, garden club festival in historic homes, and beanhole supper. **Annual Bluegrass Festival,** Thomas Point Beach (off Route 24 near Cooks Corner). **Maine Highland Games,** Thomas Point Beach—a daylong celebration of Scottish heritage, with piping, country dancing, sheep dog demonstrations, and Highland fling competitions. **Joshua Chamberlain Days.**

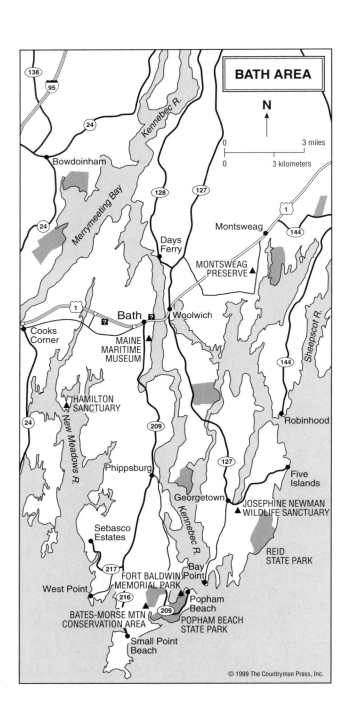

BATH AREA

N

0   3 miles

0   3 kilometers

138

95

24

Kennebec R.

Bowdoinham

Merrymeeting Bay

24

128

127

1

Days Ferry

Montsweag

144

MONTSWEAG PRESERVE ▲

1

Bath ?

? Woolwich

Cooks Corner

Sheepscot R.

MAINE MARITIME MUSEUM ▲

New Meadows R.

HAMILTON SANCTUARY ▲

144

24

209

Robinhood

Phippsburg

127

Georgetown

Kennebec R.

Five Islands

JOSEPHINE NEWMAN ▲ WILDLIFE SANCTUARY

Sebasco Estates

REID STATE PARK

217

Bay Point

West Point

FORT BALDWIN MEMORIAL PARK ▲

216

Popham Beach

209

BATES-MORSE MTN CONSERVATION AREA ▲

POPHAM BEACH STATE PARK

Small Point Beach

© 1999 The Countryman Press, Inc.

Bath Area

Over the years some 5,000 vessels have been built in Bath. Think about it: In contrast to most communities—which retain what they build— here an entire city's worth of imposing structures have sailed away. Perhaps that's why, with a population of fewer than 10,000, Bath is a city rather than a town, and why the granite city hall, with its rounded, pillared facade and cupola (with a Paul Revere bell and a three-masted schooner for a weather vane), seems meant for a far larger city.

American shipbuilding began downriver from Bath in 1607 when the 30-ton pinnace *Virginia* was launched by Popham Colony settlers. It continues with naval vessels that regularly slide off the ways at the Bath Iron Works (BIW).

With almost 9,000 workers, BIW employs about the same number of people who worked in Bath's shipyards in the 1850s. At its entrance, a sign proclaims: "Through these gates pass the world's best shipbuilders." This is no idle boast, for many current employees have inherited their skills from a long line of forebears.

Obviously, this is just the place for a museum about ships and shipbuilding, and the Maine Maritime Museum has one of the country's foremost collections of ship models, journals, logs, photographs, and other seafaring memorabilia. It even includes a 19th-century working shipyard. Both BIW and the Maine Maritime Museum are sited on a 4-mile-long reach of the Kennebec River where the banks slope at precisely the right gradient for laying keels. Offshore, a 35- to 150-foot-deep channel ensures safe launching. The open Atlantic is just 18 miles downriver.

In the 1850s Bath was the fourth-largest port in the United States in registered tonnage, and throughout the 19th century it consistently ranked among America's eight largest seaports. Its past prosperity is reflected in the blend of Greek Revival, Italianate, and Georgian Revival styles in the brick storefronts along Front Street and in the imposing wooden churches and mansions in similar styles along Washington, High, and Middle Streets.

Today, BIW dominates the city's economy as dramatically as its red-and-white, 400-foot-high construction crane—the biggest on the East

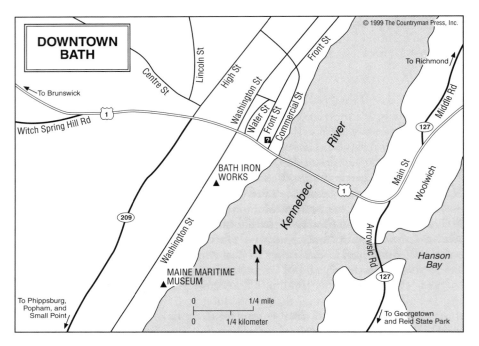

Coast—does the city's waterfront. The largest civilian employer in Maine, the company actually produced more destroyers during World War II than did all of Japan, and it continues to keep to its pledge to deliver naval ships ahead of schedule and under budget. Its story is one of many told in the Maine Maritime Museum—for which you should allow the better part of a day. Save another to explore the Phippsburg Peninsula south of Bath. Phippsburg's perimeter is notched with coves filled with fishing boats, and Popham Beach near its southern tip is a grand expanse of sand. Reid State Park on Georgetown Island, just across the Kennebec, is the Mid Coast's only other sandy strand. North of Bath, Merrymeeting Bay draws birders.

Traffic flow over the narrow Carlton bridge, which spans the Kennebec River from Bath to Woolwich, has long been an issue. In recent years, the concrete on the highway section of the bridge began to deteriorate, but a railroad bridge running underneath the highway makes repairs unfeasible. In 1998 construction began on a four-lane replacement bridge, which is expected to reduce traffic delays considerably. The new bridge, bid at $46.6 million, is currently slated to open in July of the year 2000.

GUIDANCE

Chamber of Commerce of the Bath-Brunswick Region (443-9751), 45 Front Street, Bath 04530. Open year-round, weekdays 8:30–5. From mid-June to mid-October, an information center on the northbound side of Route 1, at Witch Spring Hill, is one of the state's busiest. It marks the gateway to Maine's Mid Coast. There are also picnic tables and minimal rest rooms.

For a lodging referral service (including weekends and evenings), phone 389-1394.

GETTING THERE

By car: **Route 1** passes above the city with exits from the elevated road accessing the Carlton Bridge, a bottleneck twice daily when some 9,000 employees of BIW come and go to work.

By bus: **Concord Trailways** (1-800-639-3317) stops at the Coastal Plaza on Route 1.

By limo: **Mid-Coast Limo** (1-800-937-2424 outside of Maine; 1-800-834-5500 within Maine) makes runs from Portland International Jetport by reservation.

MEDICAL EMERGENCY

Mid Coast Hospital (443-5524), 1356 Washington Street, Bath. There is also an addiction resource center here.

TO SEE

MUSEUMS

Maine Maritime Museum (443-1316), 243 Washington Street, Bath. Open year-round; 9:30–5 daily; closed Thanksgiving, Christmas, and New Year's Day. Admission is $7.50 per adult and $4.75 per child ages 6–15 (family admission is $21). Sited just south of BIW on the banks of the Kennebec River, this extensive complex includes the brick-and-glass **Maritime History Building** and the **Percy & Small Shipyard,** the country's only surviving wooden shipbuilding yard (its turn-of-the-century belts for driving machinery have been restored). The size and solidity of the history building contrast with its setting and the low-slung wooden structures left from the old shipyards. Its exhibits focus, understandably, on the era beginning after the Civil War when 80 percent of this country's full-rigged ships were built in Maine, almost half of these in Bath.

The pride of Bath, you learn, were the Down Easters, a compromise between the clipper ship and old-style freighter that plied the globe during the 1870s through the 1890s, and the big, multimasted schooners designed to ferry coal and local exports like ice, granite, and lime. The museum's permanent collection of artwork, artifacts, and documents is now said to include more than a million pieces, and there is an extensive research library. Permanent exhibits range from displays on Maine's marine industries—fishing and canning as well as shipbuilding and fitting—to the story of BIW.

Did you realize that lobstering in Maine dates back to the 1820s? By the 1880s there were 23 "lobster factories" in Maine, all closed in the 1890s when a limit was imposed on the size of lobsters that could be canned. Visitors are invited to sit on the gunwale of a classic lobster boat and watch a documentary about lobstering narrated by E. B. White.

Woodworkers and wooden-boat buffs will appreciate the lofting models in the mold loft and the details of the cabinetwork in the joiners

Bath City Hall

shop, as well as watching the apprentices building wooden boats. Children find hands-on exhibits scattered throughout this sprawling museum—from the World Trade Game in the main gallery to the crow's nest in the sandbox boat near the water. Visitors of all ages should take advantage of the narrated boat rides.

Historic District. In the 18th and 19th centuries, Bath's successful shipbuilding and seafaring families built impressive mansions on and around upper Washington Street. Sagadahoc Preservation, Inc., offers "magical history tours," guided walks; ask for a schedule at the chamber of commerce (see *Guidance*). The historical society also produces an excellent brochure, "Architectural Tours—Self Guided Walking and Driving Tours of the City of Bath," available from the chamber of commerce.

1910 Farmhouse, Woolwich Historical Society Museum (443-4833), Route 1 and Nequasset Road, Woolwich. Open 10–4 daily, July through Labor Day. $2 per adult, $1 per child ages 6–12. An admirable, small museum run by volunteers, this rambling farmhouse displays an intriguing collection of antique clothing and quilts, plus seafaring memorabilia, all gleaned from local attics.

SCENIC DRIVE

The Phippsburg Peninsula. From the Maine Maritime Museum, drive south on Route 209, down the narrow peninsula making up the town of

Phippsburg, pausing at the first causeway you cross. This is **Winnegance Creek,** an ancient shortcut between Casco Bay and the Kennebec River; look closely to your left and you'll see traces of the 10 tidemills that once operated here.

Continue south on Route 209 until you come to the Phippsburg Center Store on your right. Turn left on Parker Head Road, into the tiny hamlet of **Phippsburg Center.** This is one of those magical places, far larger in memory than in fact—perhaps because it was once larger in fact, too. Notice the huge linden tree (planted in 1774) between the stark Congregational church (1802) and its small cemetery. Also look for the telltale stumps of piers on the shore beyond, remnants of a major shipyard. Just off Route 209, note the **Phippsburg Historical Museum** (open in summer Monday through Friday 2–4, and by appointment: 442-7606).

Continue along the peninsula's east shore on the Parker Head Road, past a former millpond where ice was once harvested. At the junction with Route 209, turn left. The road threads a salt marsh and the area at Hoss Ketch Point, from which all traces of the ill-fated **Popham Colony** have long since disappeared. Route 209 winds around Sabino Head and ends at the parking lot for **Fort Popham,** a granite Civil War–era fort (with picnic benches) at the mouth of the Kennebec River. A wooded road, for walking only, leads to World War I and II fortifications that constitute **Fort Baldwin Memorial Park;** a six-story tower yields views up the Kennebec and out to sea.

Along the shore at **Popham Beach,** note the pilings, in this case from vanished steamboat wharves. Around the turn of the century, two big hotels served the passengers who transferred here from Boston to Kennebec River steamers, or who simply stayed a spell to enjoy the town's spectacular beach. Now **Popham Beach State Park,** this immense expanse of sand remains a popular destination for fishermen, beach walkers, sunbathers, and even a few hardy swimmers. From Popham Beach return to Route 209 and follow it west to Route 217 and out to **Sebasco Harbor Resort,** then back up to Phippsburg Center.

TO DO

BICYCLING
Bath Cycle and Ski (442-7002), Route 1, Woolwich, rents bikes and cross-country skis.

BOAT EXCURSIONS
Maine Maritime Museum Cruises (443-1316). Mid-June to mid-October, the museum (see *To See*) offers periodic special-interest cruises along the Mid Coast, as well as up the Kennebec River and across Merrymeeting Bay. The fireworks cruise during Bath Heritage Days is also fun.

M/V *Ruth*, based at Sebasco Estates (389-1161), offers a variety of coastal excursions on the New Meadows River and into Casco Bay. **M/V *Yankee***

(389-1788) offers mid-June through Labor Day excursions from Hermit Island Campgrounds at Small Point. **Seguin Navigation Co.** (443-1677), Arrowsic, offers half- and full-day sails. **Lighthouse Lobsterboat Tours** (389-1838; 721-3629) offers fishing and sight-seeing, also lobster dinners aboard a 32-foot "lobster yacht," departing Fort Popham. **Kennebec Charters** (389-1883), Popham Beach, offers sightseeing trips on the Kennebec, Sheepscot, Sasasnoa, and New Meadows rivers, as well as island and lighthouse tours, and fishing trips.

CANOE AND KAYAK RENTALS

Taylor Rentals (725-7400), 271 Bath Road, Brunswick, rents canoes to explore Merrymeeting Bay. **Dragonworks, Inc.** (666-8481), in Bowdoinham on Merrymeeting Bay, sells white-water and sea kayaks and offers instruction.

FISHING

Surf fishing is popular at Popham Beach, and there's an annual mid-August Bluefish Tournament in Waterfront Park. Nearly 20 boats offer fishing on the river, and both **Kennebec Charters** (389-1883) and *Kayla D & Obsession* **Sportfishing Charters** (442-8581; 443-3316) offer deep-sea-fishing charters.

GOLF

Bath Country Club (442-8411), Whiskeag Road, Bath. Pro shop, 18 holes. **Sebasco Harbor Resort** (389-1161), Sebasco Estates. In the process of expansion to 18 holes. Primarily for hotel guests; open to the public by reservation. Late June to early September only.

SWIMMING

🐾 If you are traveling with a dog, it is important to know that they are allowed only in picnic areas, not on the beaches.

✍ **Charles Pond,** Route 27, Georgetown (about 0.5 mile past the turnoff for Reid State Park; 15 miles down the peninsula from the Carlton Bridge). Often considered the best all-around swimming hole in the area, this long and narrow pond has clear water and is surrounded by tall pines.

✍ **Pleasant Pond** (582-2813), Peacock Beach State Park, Richmond. Open Memorial Day through Labor Day. A sand and gravel beach with lifeguards on duty. Water depth drops off gradually to about 10 feet in a 30-by-50-foot swimming area removed from boating and enclosed by colored buoys. Picnic tables and barbecue grills. Admission is $1.50 adults, $.50 ages 5–11; under 5 free.

✍ **Popham Beach State Park** (389-1335), via Route 209 South from Bath to Phippsburg and beyond. One of the best state park beaches in the state. Three miles of sand at the mouth of the Kennebec River that never seem to be too crowded. Also a sandbar, tidal pools, and smooth rocks. It can be windy; extra layers are recommended. Day-use fees of $1.50 per adult and $.50 per child ages 5–11 (under 5 free) are charged from mid-April until mid-October.

✍ **Reid State Park** (371-2303), Route 127, Georgetown (14 miles south of Bath and Route 1). Open daily year-round. The bathhouse and snack bar overlook 1½ miles of sand in three distinct beaches that seldom become overcrowded, although the limited parking area does fill by noon on summer weekends. You can choose surf or slightly warmer sheltered backwater, especially good for children. Entrance fees of $2 per adult and $.50 per child ages 5–11 (under 5 free) are charged between mid-April and mid-October.

SPECIAL LEARNING PROGRAM

Shelter Institute (442-7938), 38 Center Street, Bath 04530. A year-round resource center for people who want to build or retrofit their own energy-efficient home. Two- and three-week daytime courses are offered May to October; Saturday-morning classes are given during the winter. Tuition varies according to course taken.

GREEN SPACE

- **Fort Baldwin Memorial Park,** Phippsburg. An undeveloped area with a six-story tower to climb for a beautiful view up the Kennebec and, downriver, out to sea. There are also remnants of fortifications from World Wars I and II. At the bottom of the hill is the site where the Popham Colony struggled to weather the winter of 1607–08, then built the pinnace *Virginia* and sailed away to Virginia.
- **Fort Popham Memorial Park** (389-1335 in-season) is located at one tip of Popham Beach. Open Memorial Day through Labor Day. Picnic sites are scattered around the ruins of the 1861 fort, which overlooks the beach.

Josephine Newman Wildlife Sanctuary, Georgetown. Bounded on two sides by salt marsh, 119 acres with 2 miles of walking trails. Look for the sign on Route 127, 9.1 miles south of Route 1.

Bates–Morse Mountain Conservation Area comprises some 600 acres extending from the Sprague to the Morse River and out to Seawall Beach. Allow 2 hours for the walk to and from this unspoiled private beach. Pack a picnic and towel, but please, no radios or beach paraphernalia. Seawall Beach is an important nesting area for piping plovers and least terns. There's a great view from the top of Morse Mountain, which is reached by an easy hike, just over a mile along a partially paved road and through river and marsh. Parking is very limited.

Hamilton Sanctuary, West Bath. Situated on a peninsula in the New Meadows River, offering a 1½-mile trail system and great bird-watching. Take the New Meadows exit off Route 1 in West Bath; turn left on New Meadows Road, which turns into Foster Point Road; follow it 4 miles to the sanctuary sign.

Montsweag Preserve, Montsweag Road, Woolwich. A 1½-mile trail takes visitors through woods, fields, a salt marsh, and along the water. This 45-acre preserve is owned by The Nature Conservancy (729-5181). You will have to watch carefully for the turns (right onto Montsweag Road about 6.5 miles from Bath on Route 1, then 1.3 miles and a left into the preserve).

LODGING

RESORTS

Sebasco Harbor Resort (389-1161; 1-800-225-3819), Sebasco Estates 04565. Open May through October. With new ownership in 1997, this traditional New England summer resort has been completely renovated. Though friends feel some of the "rusticity" has been lost, the old and new blend well, making good use of the property's prime ocean frontage with a dining room that overlooks the water and a lighthouse-shaped building with a beautiful top-floor sitting area. The 600-plus-acre, self-contained complex includes a saltwater pool and a golf course, in the process of being expanded to 18 holes. Other amenities include swimming at a private beach, hiking, boating, lobster cookouts, live entertainment, and special evening programs. Choose a cottage or a lodge room (115 rooms in all). Rates are MAP: $127–216 in July and August, $87–180 May, June, September, and October per person per night, double occupancy. B&B rates available; inquire about packages.

Rock Gardens Inn (389-1339), Sebasco Estates 04565. Open mid-June through late September. Next door to Sebasco Harbor Resort, Rock Gardens Inn accommodates just 60 guests, providing a more intimate atmosphere than the larger resort but offering access to all its facilities (see above). The inn perches on the edge of the water, banked, as you'd expect, in a handsome rock garden, and has its own heated swimming pool. Guests gather in the comfortable living room, library, and old-fashioned dining room with round tables and cornflower-blue wooden chairs. There's a welcoming Sunday cocktail party and a weekly lobster cookout. There are three rooms in the inn and 10 cottages, each with living room, fireplace, and sunporch. Most rooms have water views. $78–120 per person MAP; 5-night minimum in July and August. Inquire about weeklong art workshops offered in June, July, and September.

BED & BREAKFASTS

In Bath 04530

🐾🖌♿ **The Inn at Bath** (443-4294; innkeeper@innatbath.com), 969 Washington Street. Open year-round. In the historic district, Nick Bayard's rambling, elegantly restored 1810 mansion offers twin parlors with marble fireplaces and nine carefully decorated guest rooms with a choice of twin, double, queen, or king beds (all private baths), five rooms with working wood-burning fireplaces (two of these have two-person Jacuzzis overlooking the fireplaces). We especially like the old Hayloft, with its built-in bookshelves, window seat, and cozy nooks and crannies. All guest rooms have air-conditioning, phone, cable TV, VCR, and cassette-tape player with radio and alarm. On the grounds surrounding the house, a series of elaborate garden rooms is being developed. Rooms are $85–165, more for the suite. Fee for a third guest is $25. Children welcome and pets accepted selectively.

The Kennebec Inn (443-5202; 1-800-822-9393), 1024 Washington Street. Blanche and Ron Lutz have completely restored this beautiful Italianate mansion and offer seven luxurious guest rooms. Blanche's attention to detail is evident; the rooms are warm and comfortable with private baths, phones and data ports, color cable TV hidden inside armoires made specifically for each room, poster beds, and original light fixtures. Some rooms have gas fireplaces and Jacuzzis. Breakfast is served buffet-style at the convenience of the guests, in the spectacular tapestried dining room, which boasts a 9-foot solid walnut table and gas fireplace. $100 and up depending on room and season.

Benjamin F. Packard House (443-6069; 1-800-516-4578; packardhouse@clinic.net), 45 Pearl Street. Open year-round. A gracious 1790 Georgian home in the heart of the historic district, one block from the Kennebec. Once owned by Benjamin F. Packard, partner in one of the world's most successful shipbuilding companies (the captain's quarters of the clipper *Benjamin F. Packard* are displayed at Mystic Seaport in Connecticut). Three elegant guest rooms with period furnishings, one a suite with sitting room; all have private baths. Common space includes a fenced patio. $70–90 includes full breakfast.

Fairhaven Inn (443-4391, 1-888-443-4391; fairhvn@gwi.net), North Bath Road. Open year-round. Hidden away on the Kennebec River as it meanders down from Merrymeeting Bay, this 1790s house has eight pleasant guest rooms, six with private bath. Dave and Susie Reed stayed here as guests some 20 times before buying the place. The inn's 16 acres of meadow invite walking in summer and cross-country skiing in winter (the 10-acre golf course nearby makes for even more skiing). Two-night minimum stay on holidays and on weekends in July and August. In-season rates, including a full breakfast, are $80–120.

In Phippsburg 04562

Captain Drummond House (389-1394), Parker Head Road, P.O. Box 72. Open seasonally. Just off Route 209, halfway between Bath and Popham Beach, this historic, circa-1770 home sits on a secluded, 125-foot bluff above the Kennebec River with a spectacular view of woods and the cove. Although innkeepers Donna Dillman and Ken Brigham live at their Brunswick B&B, the Captain's Watch, this is still a homey but elegant retreat, with three guest rooms. One has a private, second-floor balcony; others have private entrances; there's also a small suite. $75–100 double; two-room suite $110–130 in-season. Inquire about renting the whole house by the week.

Stonehouse Manor (389-1141), HCR 32, Box 369, Route 209, Phippsburg 04563. Open year-round. Set off the road in a large field beside a small lake, this rambling old fieldstone-and-shingle house exudes the style of Maine's grand old cottages. Five large rooms, some with fireplaces and Jacuzzis, each with a lake or bay view and private bath. There is also a spectacular veranda with wicker furniture overlooking the bay and the

Varnish-prepping a Lawley yacht tender at the Maine Maritime Museum.

MAINE OFFICE OF TOURISM

well-groomed grounds. Jane and Tim Dennis serve a full breakfast. $100–175 per couple.

The 1774 Inn at Phippsburg Center (389-1774), Parker Head Road. Open year-round. Once the home of Maine's first congressman, later owned by the area's premier shipbuilder, this house dominates the road through the center of one of the Kennebec River's most picturesque villages. Debbie and Joe Braun offer four large Federal-style guest rooms furnished in antiques. There is also a beautifully proportioned main stairway you'll want to go up and down again and again. $75–115.

🐾🕊 **Small Point Bed & Breakfast** (389-1716), 312 Small Point Road. A comfortable, informal 1890s farmhouse with three guest rooms and one suite, handy to beaches, boats, and hiking; children and dogs accepted. The carriage house, with woodstove and additional loft sleeping area with twin beds, is rented on a weekly basis only. Rooms are $55–80, less off-season, full breakfast included.

♿ **Edgewater Farm Bed & Breakfast** (389-1322), 71 Small Point Road. A restored, circa-1800 farmhouse set in 4 acres of beautiful gardens and fruit trees. Bill and Carol Emerson continue to improve upon this wonderfully positioned place, just up the road from the entrance to the Bates–Morse Mountain Conservation area (see *Green Space*). Recent additions include an indoor lap pool open to guests and also shared with the community, and a large rec room over the garage. There are six rooms, a screened sunporch where breakfast is served in nice weather, and a 20-by-40-foot screened tent. $85 with shared bath, $95 with private.

Elsewhere

Coveside–Five Islands Bed and Breakfast (371-2807; 1-800-232-5490; coveside@gwi.net), Five Islands 04548. Open May through October. Ten miles down Route 127 from Route 1, beyond the turnoff for Reid State

Park. Coveside is a 100-year-old farmhouse with a deck. Carolyn and Tom Church purchased the pro refreshing the three guest rooms (all with private b They have plans for major renovations to the com dining room/atrium addition and a new guest roo suites (good for families) also available in the carria canoes for guest use. $95–115 includes full break

Popham Beach Bed & Breakfast (389-2409), Popham Beach 04562. Open year-round. Peggy Johannessen has restored this former Coast Guard station, built in 1883 right on Popham Beach, creating a B&B with as much character as the building itself. The four guest rooms (three with private bath) all have water views. The Captain's Quarters is decorated in white wicker, with a lovely sitting area, a private staircase, and large private bath. There is also a tastefully decorated suite, again with water views. $85–150 includes a full breakfast; $75–130 off-season.

Grey Havens (371-2616), Seguinland Road, P.O. Box 308, Georgetown 04548. Open mid-April to mid-December. The donor of the land for neighboring Reid State Park also built this turreted, gray-shingled summer hotel, opened in 1904, with a huge parlor window—said to have been Maine's first picture window. The large common room is hung with baskets, furnished comfortably, and warmed with a huge stone fireplace. The long porch, half screened and half open, is well equipped with rocking chairs from which to survey the sweep of islands and bay. The 12 rooms upstairs (private baths) range from small doubles to large, rounded turret rooms; half have water views and all have brass or iron beds and Victorian furniture. Call early, as it's usually booked with weddings on every summer weekend. $100–220 (half that off-season) for a two-room oceanfront suite with balcony. "Hearty continental" breakfast; 2-night minimum on weekends and holidays.

OTHER LODGING

New Meadows Inn (443-3921), Bath Road, West Bath 04530. Open year-round, with the exception of the cottages (open late May to mid-October). A good family place, with rooms for two, cottages for more, including two log cabins. Dining room with shore dinners, traditional family fare, snacks, salad bar, and buffets. Private docking and marina facilities. Rates: $30–40 for double rooms, $40–60 for cottages.

Hermit Island (443-2101), 42 Front Street, Bath 04530. This 255-acre, almost-island at Small Point offers 275 nicely scattered camping sites, 63 on the water with fantastic views. Only tents and pop-ups are permitted. Owned since 1953 by the Sewall family, Hermit Island also has a central lodge with a recreation room and snack bar where kids can meet. Beyond the camping area are acres of private beaches and unspoiled woods and meadows perfect for hiking and quiet exploration. Wildlife is abundant. $25.75–35.75 per night; less off-season.

Cottage listings are available from the Chamber of Commerce of the Bath-Brunswick Region (see *Guidance*) and in the Maine Tourism Association's

"Maine Guide to Camp and Cottage Rentals." (Also see *Cottage Rentals* in "What's Where in Maine.")

WHERE TO EAT

DINING OUT

The Robinhood Free Meetinghouse (371-2188), Robinhood Road, off Route 127, Robinhood. Open daily mid-May through mid-October for dinner (5:30–9) and Sunday brunch. Michael Gagne, the former chef at the nearby Osprey, has turned the vintage 1855 Robinhood Free Meetinghouse into an attractive dining space, decorated with local art, all for sale. The menu is so immense that it's academic to cite selections but the day we visited you could choose from wild mushroom with hazelnut or black bean soup ($4.25 per cup), and appetizers included asparagus in puff pastry ($5.75) and corn-fried oysters with fresh salsa and cream ($8). Among the 37 entrées ($16–23) were veal Oscar with Maine crabmeat, asparagus, and roasted red potatoes and grilled double breast of duck with beurre rouge and five herbs, wild rice, and lingonberry turnovers. The wine list is extensive, as is the choice of wine by the glass ($4–6).

The Osprey (371-2530), at Robinhood Marina, Robinhood (just off Route 127, near Reid State Park). Open spring through fall for lunch and dinner, Sunday brunch; fewer days off-season. Reservations appreciated and a must on summer weekends. Overlooks a boatyard and, yes, there is an osprey nest on the day marker; you can see it from the window. Atmosphere is minimal but the cuisine is elegant. The large menu changes often; it might include such appetizers as local shrimp and crab cakes, roast garlic aioli, and crispy vegetable salsa and entrées like blackened local tuna steak with roasted potatoes, cucumber salsa, and grilled vegetables. Leave room for raspberries with crème anglaise or dark chocolate mousse with Grand Marnier.

Kristina's (442-8577), corner of High and Center Streets, Bath. Closed in January and Mondays off-season. The rest of the year, open weekdays for all three meals, weekends for brunch and dinner. Very attractive dining room, outdoor dining on the tree-shaded deck in summer. What began as a simple room with booths and a bakery case has grown into a sophisticated, two-level restaurant with a small bar. You'll still find the same great quiche, cheesecake, and other incredible breads and pastries (which you can still buy to go at the bakery counter) for which it was first known (inquire about the bread of the day: anadama on Saturday, Swedish orange bread on Tuesday, etc.), plus such entrées as Maine crab cakes sautéed in red onion and lemon butter, or summer-vegetable lasagna with fresh herbs and mascarpone cheese. Entrées $10.95–16.95.

J. R. Maxwell's (443-4461), 122 Front Street, Bath. Open year-round for lunch and dinner daily. In the middle of the shopping district, in a renovated 1840s building that was originally a hotel. Predictable burgers, salads, crêpes, seafood sandwiches, also dinner steaks, prime rib, chicken, fresh seafood, and Sunday brunch. Children's menu. Exposed old brick walls, hanging plants. Downstairs is the **Boat Builder's Pub,** with live bands on weekends. Entrées $6.95–17.95.

EATING OUT

Beale Street Barbeque & Grill (442-9514), 215 Water Street, Bath. Open in summer 11 AM–10 PM; until 11 PM on weekends (until 9 in winter). Brothers Mark, Mike, and Patrick Quigg have built their slow-cooking pits and are delivering the real Tennessee (where Mark lived for six years) goods: pulled pork, ribs, sausage, a big Reuben, also nightly specials (frequently fish) to round out the menu. This place is well worth finding but you almost have to know it's there, in a renovated old BIW building behind Reny's (see *Special Shops*).

Kennebec Tavern and Marina (442-9636), 119 Commercial Street, Bath. On the riverfront, a great spot to watch bridge construction. Seafood, pub fare. Outside dining in-season.

Starlight Café (443-3005), 15 Lambard Street, Bath. Open for breakfast and lunch weekdays, breakfast only on Saturdays. This bright, funky place is a real find. Large, filling sandwiches, specials. Very popular with locals.

Front Street Deli/1840 Lounge (443-9815), 128 Front Street, Bath. Open year-round 8 AM–11 PM. A storefront with inviting booths and standard breakfast and lunch fare, soup of the day, good pies. Downstairs is the lounge with comfy, mismatched sofas and couches, same menu.

Sarah's Cafe (442-0996), Customs House, 1 Front Street, Bath. A branch of the popular Wiscasset restaurant, open for lunch 10–2, specializing in salads, sandwiches, and desserts; some seating on the lawn by the Kennebec.

Truffles Café (442-8474), 21 Elm Street, Bath. Open Wednesday through Saturday 7 AM–2 PM, Sunday 8 AM–noon. Chef-owner Ellen Spiegelman offers fresh, interesting breakfast and lunch choices.

Spinney's Restaurant and Guesthouse (389-1122), at the end of Route 209, Popham Beach. Open weekends in April and daily May to October for lunch and dinner. Our kind of beach restaurant: counter and tables, pleasant atmosphere with basic chowder-and-a-sandwich menu. Pete and Jean Hart specialize in fried fish and seafood but they also serve it steamed and broiled; good lobster and crabmeat rolls. Beer, wine, and cocktails.

Lobster House (389-1596), 395 Small Point Road (follow Route 1 to Route 209, then Route 209 to Route 216). Open summer season only, Tuesday through Saturday 5–9 PM, Sunday noon–8:30 PM. Mrs. Pye's is a classic lobster place specializing in seafood dinners and homemade pastry; it's down near Small Point, surrounded by salt marsh. Beer and wine are served.

The Love Nest (371-2950), 13 miles south of Route 1 on Route 127 at the Five Islands wharf in Georgetown. Run by the Georgetown Fisherman's Co-op. Open seasonally, specializing in steamed lobsters and clams, lobster rolls. No credit cards.

ENTERTAINMENT

✒ **Center for the Arts at the Chocolate Church** (442-8455), 804 Washington Street, Bath. Year-round presentations include plays, concerts, and a wide variety of guest artists. Special children's plays and other entertainment are included on the schedule. The handsome church has been completely restored inside. There is also a very nice gallery at the Chocolate Church (so-called because of the chocolate color of this Greek Revival building).

SELECTIVE SHOPPING

ART AND ARTISANS
Georgetown Pottery, Route 127, Georgetown (some 9 miles south of the Carlton Bridge). Jeff Peters produces an extensive selection of dishes, mugs, and other practical pottery pieces, including hummingbird feeders and soap dishes. **The Five Islands Gallery,** at the wharf at Five Islands at the end of Route 127. Open seasonally. This deceptively small gallery is cooperatively run by five genuinely interesting local artists; we especially like the fanciful wood carvings and ceramic pieces by Jack Schnider.

FLEA MARKET
Montsweag Flea Market (443-2809), Route 1, Woolwich. A field filled with tables weighted down by every sort of collectible and curiosity you could imagine. It is a beehive of activity every day during the summer and on weekends in spring and fall. Antiques, rather than flea-market finds, are featured on Wednesdays.

SPECIAL SHOPS
Bath's Front Street is lined with mid-19th-century, redbrick buildings. Among the gift shops, don't overlook **Reny's** (46 Front Street), one in a small chain of Maine department stores that are good for genuine bargains. **Yankee Artisan** (56 Front Street) offers a wide selection of Maine crafts and gifts. **Springer's Jewelers** (76 Front Street) is a vintage emporium with mosaic floors, chandeliers, and ornate glass sales cases.

Woodbutcher Tools (442-7938), 38 Centre Street, Bath. The Shelter Institute (see *Special Learning Programs*) maintains this woodworker's discovery, specializing in hard-to-find woodworking tools.

Kennebec Kiln (442-8024), 11 Centre Street, Bath. Choose your unfinished bisque piece ($3–30) and spend a few hours painting. When you are finished, leave it to be fired in their kiln, and pick it up in a few days. They also offer art classes and workshops, as well as cappuccino.

Dronmore Bay Farm (443-4228), Route 209, Phippsburg. Spread along the ridge above Cutting Creek, this cheerful spot offers a formal garden stroll and a wide variety of herbs, wildflowers, fruits, and vegetables. The shop is a nice mix of antiques, seasonal gifts crafted by local artisans, and Millie Clifford's arrangements of dried flowers.

SPECIAL EVENTS

Three days surrounding the Fourth of July: **Bath Heritage Days,** a grand celebration with an old-time parade of antique cars, marching bands, clowns, guided tours of the historic district, craft sales, art shows, musical entertainment in two parks, a triathlon, strawberry-shortcake festival, carnival, train, and Fireman's Follies featuring bed races, bucket relays, and demonstrations of equipment and fire-fighting techniques. Fireworks over the Kennebec.

Second Saturday in July: **Popham Circle Fair** at the Popham Chapel features the sale of birdfeeders (shaped like the chapel) that residents make all year; profits keep the chapel going.

July and August: Wednesday-evening concerts by the **Bath Municipal Band,** Library Park.

December: **"Old Fashioned Christmas"** (all month), with competitions and special events.

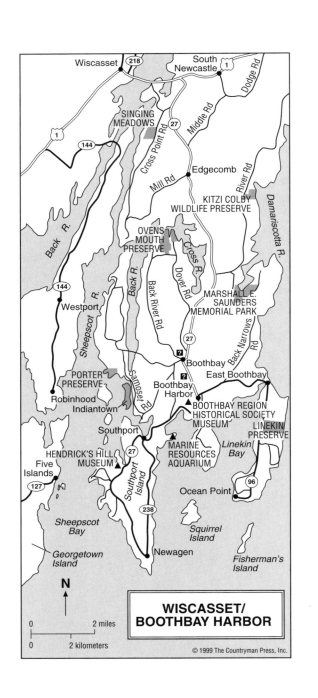

WISCASSET/
BOOTHBAY HARBOR

© 1999 The Countryman Press, Inc.

Wiscasset

Wiscasset is Maine's gift to motorists toiling up Route 1. After hours of ho-hum highways, here is finally a bit of what Maine is supposed to look like. Sea captains' mansions and mid-19th-century shops line the road as it slopes toward the Sheepscot River.

Still the shire town of Lincoln County, Wiscasset is only half as populous as it was in its shipping heyday, which—as the abundance of clapboard mansions attests—came after the American Revolution but before the Civil War. Several historic buildings are open to the public, and many more house shops, galleries, and restaurants. Though traffic on Route 1 can get extremely heavy, the village itself, which has been listed in the National Register as a historic district since 1973, is a peaceful place to explore even in the height of summer.

For 66 years, the weathered remains of two early-19th-century four-masted schooners, the *Hesper* and the *Luther Little,* were picturesquely positioned just offshore and often photographed. In May 1998, they were removed and salvaged by the town.

GUIDANCE

Wiscasset does not have a chamber of commerce, but **Wiscasset Hardware** (882-6622), on Water Street (to your left just before you cross the bridge from Wiscasset to Edgecomb), is a good source of information. Ask for a street map. Park at the Water Street entrance and walk up through the appliances; built in 1797 as a chandlery, this hospitable establishment also offers an upper deck on which to get your bearings with a cup of coffee and a river view. **Big Al's** on Route 1 just before town also stocks local brochures.

GETTING THERE

Concord Trailways (1-800-639-3317) stops here en route from Portland to Bangor. **Downeast Flying Service** (882-6752) offers air charters year-round. **Wiscasset Taxi** (758-1679) serves a 60-mile radius of town, including the airports in Portland, Damariscotta, and Boothbay Harbor.

PARKING

Parking is not a problem here. If you can't find a slot along Main Street, you can always find one in the parking lot or elsewhere along Water Street.

MEDICAL EMERGENCY
Mid Coast Hospital (443-5524), 1356 Washington Street, Bath.

VILLAGES

Sheepscot Village. Go north on Route 218 from Wiscasset; look for the sign in about 4 miles. An unusually picturesque gathering of 19th-century buildings.

Head Tide Village. Eight miles up Route 218 (follow sign), an early-19th-century village that was the birthplace of the poet Edward Arlington Robinson; note the Old Head Tide Church (1838), open Saturday 2–4. Watch for the swimming hole beneath the old milldam.

TO SEE

HISTORIC HOMES

Musical Wonder House (882-7163), 18 High Street. Open daily late May through October, 10–5. An intriguing collection covering two centuries of musical history. Music boxes, reed organs, pump organs, Victrolas, and other musical machines displayed in a fine 1852 sea captain's mansion. Visitors are taken on tours of the house, during which the various machines are played and demonstrated. Tours of just the ground floor are $10 per person (discounts for children and senior citizens); tours of the entire house are by reservation only. They take about 3 hours and are $30 per person, two for $50. The gift shop at the Musical Wonder House is open 10–6 every day that the museum is open (no admission charge).

Nickels-Sortwell House, corner of Main and Federal Streets. Open June 1 through September, Wednesday through Sunday noon–5 (last tour begins at 4). $4 adults, $3.50 seniors, $2 children 12 and under. This classic Federal-era mansion in the middle of town was built by a ship owner and trader. After he lost his fortune, the house became a hotel for many years. In 1895, a Cambridge, Massachusetts, mayor purchased the property; some of the furnishings date from that time. It is now one of six historic house museums in Maine operated by the Society for the Preservation of New England Antiquities. The elliptical staircase is outstanding.

Castle Tucker (603-436-3205). Open June 1 through October 15, Tuesday through Saturday 11–4; you're also welcome to walk around the grounds when the house is closed. Admission $4. An unusual mansion overlooking the Sheepscot River. It was built in 1807 by Judge Silas Lee, who overextended his resources to present his wife with this romantic house. After his death it fell into the hands of his neighbors, to whom it had been heavily mortgaged, and passed through several owners until it was acquired in 1858 by Captain Richard Holbrook Tucker. Captain Tucker, whose descendants owned the house until 1997, added the elegant portico. Castle Tucker is said to be named after a grand house in Scotland. Highlights include a freestanding elliptical staircase, Victorian furnishings, and original wall-papers. This house is also among the six in Maine operated by the Society for the Preservation of New England Antiquities.

HISTORIC SITES

✎ **Lincoln County Old Jail and Museum** (882-6817), Federal Street (Route 218), Wiscasset. Open July and August, Tuesday through Sunday 11–4:30 (last tour at 4). $2 per adult, $1 ages 12 and under. The museum comprises a chilling 1811 jail (in use until 1930) with damp, thick granite walls (some bearing interesting 19th-century graffiti), window bars, and heavy metal doors; plus the jailer's house (in use until 1953), with displays of tools and changing exhibits. Includes an antiques show in August.

✎ **Pownalborough Court House** (882-6817), Route 128, off Route 27, Dresden (8 miles north of Wiscasset). Open July and August, Wednesday through Saturday 10–4 and Sunday noon–4. $3 adults, $1 under 13. Worth the drive. The only surviving pre–Revolutionary War courthouse in Maine, it is maintained as a museum by the Lincoln County Historical Association. The three-story building, which includes living quarters for the judge upstairs, gives a sense of this countryside along the Kennebec in 1761, when it was built to serve as an outpost tavern as well as a courtroom. This site is still isolated, standing by a Revolutionary War–era cemetery and a picnic area; there are nature trails along the river. Special events include a mustering of the militia and wreath-laying ceremonies on Memorial Day and a cider pressing in October.

Lincoln County Courthouse. Open during business hours throughout the year. Built in 1824, this handsome redbrick building overlooking the town common is the oldest functioning courthouse in New England.

✎ **Fort Edgecomb State Memorial** (882-7777), Edgecomb (off Route 1; the turnoff is just across the Sheepscot River's Davey Bridge from Wiscasset, next to the Muddy Rudder restaurant). The fort is open May 30 through Labor Day, daily 9–6. $1; pay in the box. This 27-foot, two-story octagonal blockhouse (built in 1809) overlooks a narrow passage of the Sheepscot River. For the same reasons that it was an ideal site for a fort, it is today an ideal picnic site. Tables are provided on the grassy grounds.

Wiscasset, Waterville, & Farmington Railway Museum (882-6897), Sheepscot Station, Alna 04535 (about 5 miles north of Wiscasset, just off 218). Open Saturday year-round 9–5, Sunday in summer noon–5, or by appointment. Harry Percival and his friends are working hard to preserve the history of the 2-foot narrow-gauge railroads that were once a primary source of transportation for small Maine towns. This line stopped operations in 1933. The museum includes an engine house/shop, replicas of the original Sheepscot station and Weeks Mills freight house, an original flatcar, and the oldest 2-footer locomotive in the United States. Members have begun laying track on the original road-bed, with plans to rebuild as much as possible and restore the boxcar and locomotive to working order.

OTHER

Sunken Garden, Main Street, Wiscasset. Down a few steps, easy to miss, but a wonderful little garden surrounded by a stone wall. Planted by the Sortwell family in the foundation of an old inn, the property was donated to the town in 1959. Aside from the traffic sounds from Route 1, this is a pretty, peaceful place to relax and enjoy the many flower and tree varieties.

❧ **Morris Farm** (882-4080), Route 27, Wiscasset. A community working farm, open to the public during daylight hours for walking, hiking, and picnicking with rolling pastures, forest trails, a pond, waterfall, and streams. Also an education center, offering a day camp for children, farm tours, various workshops throughout the year, and special events. Farmer's market Saturday mornings from Memorial Day to Labor Day.

World's Smallest Church, Route 218. There is barely room for two worshipers in this tiny chapel, maintained as a memorial to a former Boston Baptist minister.

TO DO

❧ **Downeast Flying Service** (882-6752), Wiscasset, offers year-round sightseeing and fall foliage flights; $50 for up to three passengers.

📷❧ **Maine Coast Railroad** (882-8000; 1-800-795-5404), at the Wiscasset Town Landing (Water Street, next to Le Garage restaurant). Memorial Day through mid-October. Excursions through the coastal countryside to Bath or Damariscotta/Newcastle (depending on day of the week) and back aboard a bright red, restored 1920s train; $10 per adult, $5 per child ages 5–12, family packages. Ask about special events, fall foliage tours, and rail/sail packages.

Ledgewood Riding Stables (882-6346), Bradford Road. Trail rides Monday through Saturday beginning at 10 AM, Sunday by appointment only.

The Trading Post (882-9645) on Route 1 rents canoes and kayaks, and stocks a large line of canoe and kayak equipment for sale.

LODGING

All are in Wiscasset 04578 unless otherwise noted.

INNS

Squire Tarbox Inn (882-7693; squire@ime.net), 1181 Westport Island Road (Route 144; turn off Route 1 onto Route 144 just south of Wiscasset). Open mid-May to late October. The inn, located 8.5 miles down a winding country road from Route 1, is one of the quietest country locations we have found on the coast. The handsome Federal-style farmhouse (begun in 1763, completed in 1825) offers 11 inviting guest rooms and an atmosphere that's a mix of elegance (in the common rooms and dining room) and working goat farm. Guests are invited out to the barn to visit the goats and see how innkeepers Bill and Karen

Antiquing in Wiscasset

Mitman make their cheeses (Tellicherry pepper, herb and garlic, and jalapeño as well as plain). They can also take advantage of the swing hanging from the barn rafters. Other animals on the farm include a horse, two donkeys, laying hens, and a cat. A path leads through the woods to a saltwater inlet where a screened area is equipped with binoculars and a birding book, and where a rowboat awaits your pleasure. Four large, formally furnished guest rooms are in the original house, while seven more country-style rooms are in the 1820s converted barn. All have private baths and either king or queen beds. Goat cheese is served in the gracious parlor at the cocktail hour, and the player piano in the music room adds a lively touch. A five-course, candlelit dinner (see *Dining Out*) is served at 7 by the big, open fireplace in the attached ell, whose ceiling beams were once ship's timbers. Doubles $143–225, depending on the season, including breakfast and dinner; $85–167 for bed & breakfast; add 12 percent gratuity.

The Bailey Inn (882-4214), Main Street. A longtime landmark inn (formerly the Ledges), now named for a doctor who lived and practiced here in the early 1900s. The inn was renovated in recent years, and the seven rooms are pleasant, with private baths. Inquire about what's been done to eliminate road noise. $85 including breakfast; $75 off-season.

BED & BREAKFASTS

Marston House (882-6010; 1-800-852-4157), Main Street, P.O. Box 517. Open May through October. The front of the house is a shop featuring American antiques. In the carriage house behind this building—well away from the Route 1 traffic noise—are two exceptional rooms, each with private entrance, working fireplace, and private bath. They adjoin each other and can become a two-bedroom suite perfect for families. Breakfast is served in the beautiful gardens or in your room, and features fresh fruit, yogurt, home-baked muffins, and fresh orange juice. $90 double, $75 single. No smoking.

    ざ **Snow Squall** (882-6892; 1-800-775-7245), corner of Bradford Road and Route 1. Open year-round. New owners Anne and Steve Kornacki continue to offer elegant accommodations in this 1850s house, named for a clipper ship that was wrecked in the Falkland Islands. The six rooms, each named after a clipper ship built in Maine, offer private baths and king or queen beds. Two are large two-bedroom suites in the carriage house, ideal for families. Two guest rooms have fireplaces, as does the library. Doubles are $85–140; carriage house suites accommodating two to four people are $125–195. Full breakfast included. Rates reduced by 20 percent beginning November 1.

    Highnote Bed and Breakfast (882-9628), 32 Lee Street. Open year-round. No one was in when we dropped by, but the outside is very Victorian and appealing. Three rooms with shared bath. $65 double including European-style breakfast.

    Anniversary Farm (586-5590), 2282 Alna Road, Alna 04535. Open June through October. Beautiful grounds in a country setting offering hiking, nearby canoeing, gardens, and llama walks by arrangement. Just two rooms, nicely decorated, one with a private half-bath, the other with shared bath. Two-night minimum stay. Public tearoom on the porch in summer Wednesday through Saturday afternoons. $65–85.

OTHER LODGING

    🐾✿ **Edgecomb Inn** (882-6343; 1-800-437-5503; info@muddyrudder.com), 306 Eddy Road, Edgecomb 04556 (off Route 1, across the bridge from Wiscasset). Open all year. Commands a fine view of Wiscasset; 25 rooms (including efficiency suites) and 15 cottages. Tennis courts on the premises. Next door, the Muddy Rudder serves lunch and dinner daily (see *Eating Out*). Pets are accepted. Doubles $79–130 in-season, including continental breakfast buffet.

WHERE TO EAT

DINING OUT

Squire Tarbox Inn (882-7693), 1181 Westport Island Road (Route 144) (also see *Inns*). Open mid-May through late October, by reservation only. A candlelit, five-course dinner is served in an 18th-century former barn with a large fireplace reflecting off ceiling beams that were once ship's timbers. Dinner is preceded by a cocktail hour (6 PM) featuring a complimentary selection of savory goat cheeses (made here by innkeepers Karen and Bill Mitman), served variously in the living room, in the less formal game room, by the player piano, or out on the deck. Dinner begins at 7. The menu changes frequently but might include chicken chèvre patisserie, a boneless breast stuffed with herbed goat cheese, encased in pastry, and baked; swordfish in raisin basil butter; or pork tenderloin with a Dijon Tellicherry pepper sauce. The light-as-air whey rolls are made with goat's milk. After dessert, which might be a chocolate concoction or homemade vanilla ice cream with a fresh fruit sauce, guests are invited to visit the barn to pat the friendly Nubian goats as they line up for milking. The prix fixe is $33 per person.

Le Garage (882-5409), Water Street, Wiscasset. Open daily in summer for lunch and dinner (additional brunch features on Sunday). Closed for all of January, and Mondays off-season. A 1920s-era garage, now an exceptional restaurant with a glassed-in porch overlooking the Sheepscot River (when you make reservations, request a table on the porch). At dinner, many large, wrought-iron candelabra provide the illumination. The menu features plenty of seafood choices, steaks, and vegetarian meals. Specialties include traditional finnan haddie, charbroiled native lamb, and seafoods Newburg. Entrées are $7.25–18.25. "Light suppers" are also available for $7.25–8.95, giving you the option of smaller portions of many menu selections. The lunch menu features omelets and crêpes, soups and salads, as well as sandwiches. Lunch is $5.95–9.95.

The Bailey Inn (882-4214), Main Street, Wiscasset (see *Inns*). Serves breakfast and dinner daily. Light fare is offered in the pub in the attached carriage house. Dinner is served in the more formal dining rooms (linens and candles); a recent menu ranged from broiled or poached salmon with hollandaise sauce and shrimp scampi over egg-and-spinach fettuccine to Moroccan chicken served over a bed of rice with vegetables. $8.95–16.95.

EATING OUT

Red's Eats, Water Street, just before the bridge, Wiscasset. Open April through September until 2 AM on Friday and Saturday, until 11 PM weeknights, and noon–6 on Sunday. Al Gagnon has operated this classic hot-dog stand since 1977. Tables on the sidewalk and behind, overlooking the river. A Route 1 landmark for the past 60 years, good for a quick crab roll or pita pocket as well as a hot dog. Special children's meals.

Sarah's Pizza and Cafe (882-7504), Main Street, Wiscasset. Open Monday and Tuesday 11–9, the rest of the week 6:30 AM–9 PM. Recently renovated and expanded, this popular spot now offers an outside deck for summer dining. Everything is prepared from scratch, and the extensive menu includes exceptionally good pizza (try the Greek pizza with extra garlic), sandwiches in pita pockets or baked in dough, vegetarian dishes, Mexican fare, and lobster 12 different ways. Well known for their soup and bread bar, where seconds are only $1 extra. Fabulous desserts. Wine and a wide choice of beers, including Maine microbrews, are also served.

Muddy Rudder (882-7748), Route 1, North Edgecomb (across the bridge from Wiscasset). Open year-round 11–11 daily. Extensive menu includes sandwiches, steaks, and seafood specialties including lobster pie and lobster quesadillas, served in a riverside room. Children's menu. Piano entertainment nightly.

  ♿ **The Sea Basket** (882-6581), Route 1, south of Wiscasset. Open 11–8; closed Tuesday. A cheerful, family-operated diner with delicious lobster stew, lobster rolls, and scallops among the seafood choices.

SELECTIVE SHOPPING

ANTIQUES SHOPS

More than a dozen antiques shops (most carry an area map/guide) can be found in town (several just off the main road, in or attached to attractive houses) and just south on Route 1; many specialize in nautical pieces and country primitives.

ART GALLERIES

Maine Art Gallery (882-7511), Warren Street (in the old 1807 academy), Wiscasset. A historic schoolhouse with upper and lower galleries which house exhibits of Maine artists, including Andrew Wyeth, William Zorach, Dahlov Ipcar, and others.

Wiscasset Bay Gallery (882-7682), Water Street; changing exhibits in attractive spacious exhibit rooms. Specializes in 19th- and 20th-century Maine and New England marine and landscape paintings.

ARTISANS

Sheepscot River Pottery (pastel, floral designs), Route 1 just north of Wiscasset in Edgecomb. **Sirus Graphics,** Wiscasset; mostly made-in-Maine crafts, original-design T-shirts. **Feed the Birds,** Port Wiscasset Building, Water Street; birdhouses, feeders, accessories. **The Butterstamp Workshop,** 55 Middle Street, features exquisite hand-crafted folk art from antique chocolate and butter molds.

SPECIAL EVENTS

June: **Strawberry Festival and County Fair** features strawberries galore, crafts, and an auction.

Early July: **Morris Farm Fair**—animal exhibits, farm tours, crafts, games, and food.

Boothbay Harbor Region

The water surrounding the village of Boothbay Harbor brings with it more than just a view. You must cross it—via a footbridge—to get from one side of town to the other, and you can explore it on a wide choice of excursion boats and in sea kayaks. It is obvious from the very lay of this old fishing village that its people have always gotten around on foot or in boats. Cars—which have room neither to park nor to pass each other—are an obvious intrusion. The peninsula's other coastal villages, Southport and East Boothbay, also do not lend themselves to exploration by car. Roads are walled by pines, permitting only occasional glimpses of water.

Boats are what all three of the Boothbays have traditionally been about. Boats are built, repaired, and sold here, and sailing and fishing vessels fill the harbors. Excursions range from an hour-long sail around the outer harbor to a 90-minute crossing (each way) to Monhegan Island. Fishermen can pursue giant tuna, stripers, and blues, and nature lovers can cruise out to see seals, whales, and puffins.

In the middle of summer, Boothbay Harbor resembles a perpetual carnival, a place everyone plays tourist: Licking ice cream cones, chewing freshly made taffy and fudge, browsing in shops and looking into art galleries, listening to band concerts on the library lawn, and, of course, eating lobster. You get the feeling it's been like this every summer since the 1870s.

Boothbay Harbor is just a dozen miles south of Route 1 as the road (Route 27) runs, down the middle of the peninsula. The coastline is, however, a different story, measuring 100 miles as it wanders down the Sheepscot, around Southport Island and up into Boothbay Harbor, out around Spruce Head, around Linekin Bay, out Ocean Point, and back up along the Damariscotta River.

Thanks to the fervor of developers from the 1870s on, this entire coastline is distinguished by the quantity of its summer cottages, many of which can be rented by the week for much less than you might think. Still, thanks to the Boothbay Region Land Trust, there are now also easily accessible waterside preserves with many miles of trail meandering through hundreds of acres of spruce and pines, down to smooth rocks and tidepools.

KIM GRANT

Boothbay Harbor

It was precisely this landscape that inspired Rachel Carson, who first summered on the peninsula in 1946 and built a cottage on the Sheepscot River in 1953, to write much of *The Edge of the Sea* (1955) and then *Silent Spring*, the book that, when it was published in 1962, changed global thinking about man's relation to basic laws of nature.

GUIDANCE

Boothbay Harbor Region Chamber of Commerce (633-2353; www.boothbayharbor.com), P.O. Box 356, Boothbay Harbor 04538. Open year-round. Look for a satellite information booth at the Bay View Inn (882-5539), junction of Routes 1 and 12, open mid-May through October, weekends in fringe times, daily in high season. The chamber publishes an annual guide and maintains a Route 27 office stocked with brochures.

The Boothbay Information Center (633-4743), Route 27 (open daily, Memorial Day through Columbus Day), is an unusually friendly walk-in center that does its best to help people without reservations find places to stay. It keeps an illustrated scrapbook of options, also a cottage rental list.

Note: You can use the above numbers to find out who has current vacancies.

GETTING THERE

Boothbay Stage Line (633-7380) offers 24-hour, daily service from the Portland Jetport, from the nearest **Concord Trailways** bus stop (in Wiscasset, 14 miles away), and from anywhere else within reason.

GETTING AROUND

A **trolley-on-wheels** circulates between the Rocktide Motor Inn on the east side of the harbor and the shops on the west. Runs daily July and August, every 30 minutes, 7–11 AM (check current schedule).

PARKING

In-town parking has been substantially increased in the past few years. We had no trouble in August. Stop on your way into town at one of the information centers (see *Guidance*) and pick up a detailed map to downtown. The biggest public lot is at the municipal building.

MEDICAL EMERGENCY

St. Andrew's Hospital (633-2121), Hospital Point, Mill Cove, Route 27 South, Boothbay Harbor. A well-respected shoreside hospital, St. Andrew's serves the community by land and by water (the hospital has a pier).

TO SEE

Boothbay Region Historical Society Museum (633-3666), 70 Oak Street, Boothbay Harbor. Open July and August, Wednesday, Friday, and Saturday 10–4; off-season, Saturday 10–2 and by appointment (633-3462). This is a friendly museum filled with photos of hotels and cottage colonies.

✍ **Marine Resources Aquarium** (633-9542), McKown Point Road, West Boothbay Harbor. Open 10–5 daily from Memorial Day weekend through Columbus Day weekend. $2.50 adults; $2 ages 5–18 and over 60; 4 and under free. An octagonal waterside aquarium that's been expanded in recent years. We find it fascinating because, in contrast to the bright tropical fish you usually see in aquariums, here are fish you know by name because you are accustomed to eating them. We were fascinated with silver-and-black striped bass, the prettily dappled cod, and the silver alewife. The stars of the show are, of course, the sharks and skates in the large touch tank. Presentations several times a day in July and August. All the exhibits are the kind that the more you look at, the more you see. The grounds, overlooking the harbor, are set up for picnicking.

Hendricks Hill Museum (633-2370), Route 27, Southport Island. Open July and August, Tuesday, Thursday, Saturday 11–3. An old boardinghouse displays pictures of Southport's old boardinghouses and hotels as well as other village memorabilia, wooden boats, and farm implements. Try to time your visit to coincide with the open hours at the **Southport Memorial Library** (Tuesday, Thursday, and Saturday 1–4), which has an impressive butterfly collection. Southport happens to be in the narrow heart of the migratory route of the Monarch butterfly.

FOR FAMILIES

✍ **Boothbay Railway Village** (633-4727), Route 27 (1 mile north of Boothbay Harbor). Open daily 9:30–5, mid-June through Columbus Day; weekends beginning Memorial Day. Now operated as a museum, the 2-foot, narrow-gauge railway wends its way through a re-created, miniature, turn-of-the-century village made up of several restored buildings including vintage railroad stations, the Boothbay Town Hall (1847), and the Spruce Point chapel (1923). Displays include a general store and a doll museum. More than 50 antique autos (1907–1949) are also on display. Admission is $6 per adult and $3 per child. Many special events, including a large weekend antique auto meet (more than 250 cars) in the latter part of July.

✍ **The By-Way.** Don't miss Boothbay Harbor's old-fashioned harborside boardwalk area. See *To Do—Bowling* and *Where to Eat—Snacks*. Walk from the By-Way down to the footbridge across the harbor.

TO DO

BICYCLING
Harborside Bike Rental (633-4303; 1-800-734-7171) on Boothbay House Hill rents every kind of bike; **Tidal Transit Co.** (633-7140) rents mountain bikes. Our favorite bike route begins at Boothbay Village and follows relatively lightly trafficked Barter's Island Road, past Knickerbocker Lake and Knickerkane Island Park (see *Green Space*) to Hogdon Island and on to Barter Island and the Porter Preserve (again, see *Green Space*).

BOAT EXCURSIONS
✍ **Balmy Days Cruises** (633-2284; 1-800-298-2284), Pier 8, Boothbay Harbor. *Balmy Days II* offers supper cruises and sails every morning early June to late September and weekends in shoulder seasons to Monhegan (see "Mid-Coast Islands"); the crossing is 90 minutes each way, and you have close to 4 hours on the island. A half-hour boat ride around the island is sometimes offered. Bring a picnic and hit the trail. *Novelty* offers 1-hour harbor tours all day.

✍ **Boothbay Whale Watch** (633-4500; 1-888-942-5363), Fisherman's Wharf, offers whale-watches and sunset nature cruises daily, guided by naturalists; full bar and galley.

✍ **Cap'n Fish Boat Cruises** (633-3244/2626; 1-800-636-3244), Pier 1 (red ticket booth). Operates mid-May to mid-October, 7 days a week. A variety of cruises including whale-watches, puffin nature cruises, Pemaquid Point lighthouse trips, seal-watches, and sunset sails. Friday is senior citizens' day on 2-hour trips. Coffee, snacks, soft drinks, beer, wine, and cocktails are available on board (don't bring your own). Children under 12 are half price.

✍ *Miss Boothbay* (633-6445), Pier 5, is a lobster boat offering Tuesday through Sunday lobster-hauling cruises.

BOAT RENTALS
Midcoast Boat Rentals (882-6445), Pier 8, Boothbay Harbor, rents powerboats.

BOWLING
Romar Bowling Lanes (633-5721), at the By-Way, Boothbay Harbor. In business since 1929, under the same ownership since 1946, this log-sided pleasure hall with its sandwich bar, pool tables, and video games is a genuine throwback. A great rainy-day haven.

FISHING
Several deep-sea-fishing charters are based in Boothbay Harbor. Check with the chamber of commerce (see *Guidance*) The catch is mackerel, tuna, shark, bluefish, and stripers. Also see *Boat Rentals*.

Boothbay Fishing Rod Co. (633-3788) is one of the largest tackle shops on the Maine coast.

GOLF

Boothbay Region Country Club (633-6085), Country Club Road (off Route 27), Boothbay. Open spring through late autumn. Nine holes, restaurant and lounge, carts, clubs for rent.

✍ **Dolphin Mini-Golf** (633-4828), off Route 27 (turn at the lighthouse), Boothbay; 18 holes.

HORSEBACK RIDING

✍ **Ledgewood Riding Stables** (882-6346) in Wiscasset has horses and trails for all levels of expertise. Hourly rates.

SAILING

Several traditional sailing yachts offer to take passengers out for an hour or two, a half day, or a day. These include *Appledore V* (633-6598), a 60-foot windjammer that has sailed around the world; and the *Sylvaina W. Beal* (546-2927), a restored, 84-foot schooner built in 1911 in East Boothbay Harbor. *Tribute* (882-1020), a racing yacht, sails from Ocean Point.

SEA KAYAKING

Tidal Transit Co. (633-7140), 89 Townsend Avenue, offers guided tours.

TENNIS

✍ **Boothbay Region YMCA** (633-2855), Route 27 (on your left as you come down the stretch that leads to town). An exceptional facility open to nonmembers (use-fee charged) in July and August, with special swimming and other programs for children. Worth checking out if you will be in the area for a week or more. A wide variety of programs for all ages: tennis, racquetball, gymnastics, aerobics, soccer, swimming, and more. **Public tennis courts** are located across Route 27 from the YMCA.

GREEN SPACE

BEACHES

✍ Beaches are all private, but visitors are permitted in a number of spots. Here are four: (1) Follow Route 27 toward Southport, across the Townsend Gut Bridge to a circle (white church on your left, monument in the center, general store on your right); turn right and follow Beach Road to the beach, which offers roadside parking and calm, shallow water. (2) Right across from the Boothbay Harbor Yacht Club (Route 27 South), just beyond the post office and at the far end of the parking lot, is a property owned by the yacht club, which puts out a float by July. There are ropes to swing from on the far side of the inlet, a grassy area in which to sun, and a small sandy area beside the water; but the water is too deep for small children. (3) **Barrett Park,** Lobster Cove (turn at the Catholic church, east side of the harbor), is a place to picnic and get wet. (4) **Grimes Cove** has a little beach with rocks to climb at the very tip of Ocean Point, East Boothbay. (Also see Knickerkane Island Park under *Preserves*.)

PRESERVES

Boothbay Region Land Trust (633-4818) 2 McKown Street. Open Monday and Wednesday 9–noon. The chamber of commerce dispenses copies of the pamphlet guides to the six easily accessible properties. Inquire about Saturday morning guided walks. We walked down to the Sheepscot River in the **Porter Preserve** (19 wooded acres including a beach) on Barter's Island, accessible by bridge. An osprey peered from its nest atop a marker along a ledge just offshore and another ledge was so thick with seals that we assumed they were some kind of brown growth, until a dog barked and the entire ledge seemed to heave and rise, then flop and splash off in different directions. We also explored the **Ovens Mouth Preserve,** a narrow passage between the Sheepscot and Back Rivers and a tidal basin. In the mid-1700s, this area was settled by families from Dover, New Hampshire. They built ships and cleared pastures—still suggested by the white pines that obviously needed open space to grow so tall, and an occasional apple tree. Separating the two peninsulas that constitute this preserve is Ice House Cove, and across it are the remnants of the 1880s dam that once turned it into a freshwater pond. It's fascinating to think of schooners mooring just outside the dam and sailing for the Caribbean with their cargoes of ice. The former pond has reverted to salt marsh and teems with wildlife. The trust's other properties include **Linekin Preserve** (a 94.6-acre parcel with 2⅓ miles of hiking trails) on Route 96 south of East Boothbay; **Marshall E. Saunders Memorial Park** (22.5 acres) and **Kitzi Colby Wildlife Preserve** (12 acres), both on the Damariscotta River; and **Singing Meadows** (a 16-acre former saltwater farm in Edgecomb).

Knickerkane Island Park, Barter's Island Road, Boothbay. Paths lead from the parking lot onto a small island with picnic tables, swimming.

LODGING

The chamber of commerce lists upwards of 200 lodging places, from resorts to bed & breakfasts to campgrounds and cottages. Families should explore the possibilities of the area's many rental cottages. Because the chamber of commerce is open year-round, it's possible to contact the people there in time to reserve well in advance. See *Guidance* for the numbers you can call to check current vacancies in the area.

RESORTS

🐾🦽 **Spruce Point Inn** (633-4152; 1-800-553-0289), Boothbay Harbor 04538. Open Memorial Day to mid-October. A full-service 80-room resort at the end of a 100-acre wooded peninsula jutting into Boothbay harbor. Just eight guest rooms are in the main inn; the rest are in one- and two-bedroom cottages which are gradually being replaced with condo-style structures featuring unusually large bedrooms and baths (with whirlpool soaking tubs), TV, Vermont Castings fireplaces, and balconies with water views. Four family-sized units have full kitchens but no view. Common rooms in the main inn include a large living room, a TV room and study, and both formal and informal dining rooms. Grounds include a rec room (geared to kids) beside a freshwater pool, also a saltwater pool and whirlpool on the ocean, clay tennis courts, lawn games, and a private pier. $95–132 per person in a room MAP, more in suites and the one oceanside cottage; many packages; children free under age 4. A 25 percent service charge is added.

Newagen Seaside Inn (633-5242; 1-800-654-5242), Route 27, Southport Island, Cape Newagen 04552. Open mid-May through September. A boxy 1940s building (the original hotel was destroyed by fire) that Peter and Heidi Larsen rejuvenated. It stands at the seaward tip of Southport Island, just 6 miles "out to sea" from Boothbay Harbor, but feeling worlds away. Secluded among the pines, the inn's lawn sweeps down to a mile of bold coastline. Sunset Rock is a peaceful place to sit overlooking the water in the evening. There are 26 rooms in the main inn, all with private baths. The four new first-floor rooms all have private decks, and two are completely handicapped accessible. Heated freshwater pool, large saltwater pool, two tennis courts, many lawn games, and rowboats. Meals are served in the new screened dining area. Buffet breakfast is included in rates; lunch and dinner are also available. Doubles are $120–200 including a full breakfast, depending on room and season. Children are just $10–15 extra. Cottages begin at $800 per week; use of all facilities is included.

Ocean Point Inn (633-4200; 1-800-552-5554), P.O. Box 409, East Boothbay 04544. Open Memorial Day through Columbus Day. Set on 12 acres at the tip of Ocean Point Peninsula, but only 10 minutes from Boothbay Harbor. A cluster of traditional white clapboard buildings adorned with flower boxes filled with red geraniums, a total of 61 rooms, most with ocean views and porches. David and Beth Dudley have owned the historic inn since 1985, and David worked here for many years before they bought it, creating a real sense of continuity and traditions here. All rooms and cottages have private baths, cable TV, mini-refrigerators, phones; some have fireplaces. There is a heated pool and guests can relax in Adirondack chairs on the seawall overlooking the ocean. The inn offers an oceanfront dining room (see *Dining Out*). $96–152 in-season.

INNS AND BED & BREAKFASTS

Albonegon Inn (633-2521), Capitol Island 04538 (follow Route 27 to Route 238 in Southport; look for sign). Memorial Day to mid-October. "Determinedly old-fashioned" and proud of it, this inn is a true haven from the 20th century. It is an integral part of the 1880s gingerbread-style summer colony that fills Capitol Island, linked to the real world by a tiny bridge. Innkeeper Kim Peckham grew up summering on Capitol Island, and her great-grandfather stayed at the Albonegon in the 1890s (his signature is in the guest register); preserving its spirit as well as its structure is a labor of love. The summer's profits are visibly reinvested, most recently in storm

Albonegon Inn

CHRISTINA TREE

windows, new linens, and a new living room rug. The 11 rooms in the main inn are simple but inviting. From the bed in Room 35 you can lie on your side and watch a lobsterman setting his traps. Because this place was built as, rather than converted into, an inn, you find that the shared bath system works exceptionally well: Each room is fitted with a sink, and there are half- and full baths for every few rooms. Best of all are the porches, hung over the water and lined with classic green rockers. Guests are welcome to grill their own steaks or burgers right here if they would rather not budge from this incredible view at sunset. Fresh-baked muffins, coffeecake, and breads are served each morning in the informal dining room that shares this view. There are three rooms in separate buildings next to the inn (also on the water's edge) with private bathrooms. Two can be joined to form a cottage with two bedrooms, a kitchen, and a living room. The third, Barnacle, is smaller. $73–123 for a double.

Five Gables Inn (633-4551; 1-800-451-5048), Murray Hill Road (off Route 96), P.O. Box 335, East Boothbay 04544. Open mid-May through October. Built around 1890, this rambling building has been renovated into a luxurious B&B. Mike and Dee Kennedy are preserving the historic feel while offering guests 15 comfortable, thoughtfully furnished rooms, all with ocean view and private baths; most have queen-sized beds (many with handmade quilts), and five have working fireplaces. The rooms in the four smaller gables, the least expensive in the house, are very appealing. Mike has crafted some great built-in touches, ranging from beds to bookshelves. Almost all the guests are couples and the atmosphere is low-key and romantic. There are rocking chairs on the wraparound veranda and a welcoming fireplace in the common room; an extensive buffet breakfast, prepared by Mike, a Culinary Institute of America graduate, is included in $90–160 double. Afternoon tea is also offered.

Hodgdon Island Inn (633-7474), Barter's Island Road, Boothbay (mailing address: Box 492, Boothbay 04571). Open year-round. On a quiet road overlooking a cove, Peter Wilson and Peter Moran offer six attractive rooms with water views in a restored sea captain's house. All have private baths and ceiling fans, and two of the rooms share a porch. At breakfast guests are introduced to each other (but they don't necessarily have to sit together). It includes a hot dish like quiche or waffles, also fruit, granola, and muffins. The heated, chlorine-free swimming pool is set in a land-scaped garden and the living room has a gas fireplace, TV, VCR, books, and games; a large front porch with white wicker furniture is another space to relax, as are benches on the waterfront. $85–102 in high season (2-night minimum stay on holiday weekends); $70–85 off-season.

🐾 **Welch House** (633-3431; 1-800-279-7313), 56 McKown Street, Boothbay Harbor 04538. Open April through early December. A view of the harbor and islands beyond can be enjoyed from most of the 16 individually decorated rooms. Ownership had recently changed and while the entire place had been renovated when we visited, rooms were still being redone, so we cannot supply many details. The views from a third-floor observation deck, main deck, and glass-enclosed breakfast room are definitely hard to beat, especially combined with a downtown location. $60–125 in high season, $55–90 off-season includes a full breakfast. Small dogs are permitted in some rooms.

🐾 **Lawnmeer Inn** (633-2544; 1-800-633-7645), Box 505, West Boothbay Harbor 04575 (on Route 27 on Southport Island, 2 miles from downtown Boothbay Harbor). Open mid-May to mid-October. The location is difficult to beat, with broad lawns sloping to the water's edge. Most of the 13 comfortably decorated rooms in the main inn, and the 18 rooms (with decks) in the motel wing, have water views; there's also a small cottage. The Lawnmeer was built as a summer hotel in the 1890s. It has a small, personal feel with lots of attractive common space including the fireplace room with plenty of books, a small lounge, and a porch with a hammock. There is also a popular restaurant (see *Dining Out*). Small pets are accepted, depending on the room. $68–140 single or double occupancy, depending on season. Two-night minimum weekends in July and August.

1830 Admiral's Quarters Inn (633-2474), 71 Commercial Street, Boothbay Harbor 04538. Open most of the year. Les and Deb Hallstrom have done a great job, renovating this big old sea captain's house. The six tidy, bright (frill-free) rooms, most two-room suites, have private baths, phones, cable TV, and decks, with a seagull's-eye view of the waterfront. The sitting room is a solarium with that great view. $75–135 includes breakfast.

🐾 **Topside** (633-5404), 60 McKown Street, Boothbay Harbor 04538. Open May through October. This combination inn and motel has a lot going for it: its location at the top of McKown Hill with views over the harbor, its comfortable rooms with private baths, both in the 1876 house and the two 2-story motel-style annexes, and its reasonable rates: $65–85; $125–150 for two-bedroom units with kitchens, continental breakfast included; from $45 off-season.

Kenniston Hill Inn B&B (633-2159; 1-800-992-2915), Route 27, Boothbay 04537. Open year-round. A stately, 200-year-old pillared Colonial (one of Boothbay's oldest homes) set back from the road as it curves around to the Boothbay town green. Ten comfortable guest rooms, all with private baths; five have working fireplaces. There are also fireplaces in the dining room and the common area. Relax amid 4 acres of fields and perennial gardens, walk to the Boothbay Country Club for golf, or drive the couple of miles down to the harbor. The full country breakfast may include peaches-and-cream French toast, ham and Swiss in puff pastry, or three-cheese pie with tomato and sweet basil. $69–120 single or double in high season, $65–95 off-season, breakfast included. Inquire about dinner by reservation off-season.

Jonathan's (633-3588), 15 Eastern Avenue, Boothbay Harbor 04538. Open most of the year. Named for that famous seagull, this 100-year-old Cape offers three bedrooms, all with private baths, and either a double or twin beds (can be made into a king). In a quiet neighborhood, but just a few minutes' walk from downtown Boothbay Harbor. Grounds include a deck and beautiful gardens, and there is a fireplace in the parlor for colder weather. $65–95, including a full breakfast and afternoon refreshments and sherry. Inquire about special winter weekend packages.

Atlantic Ark Inn (633-5690), 64 Atlantic Avenue, Boothbay Harbor 04538. Open late May through late October. Furnished with antiques and Oriental rugs, this pleasant B&B is removed (but accessible by footbridge) from the bustle of the harbor. Six rooms; all have private baths and most have queen-sized beds (some mahogany four-posters). Some rooms have harbor views and private balconies. One of the third-floor rooms has a cathedral ceiling, an oak floor, a Jacuzzi with a view, and French doors opening onto a balcony. This room can be combined with the other third-floor room to form a suite with a private entrance. Full breakfast might include zucchini crescent pie or Scottish popovers. Beverages (spring water, for example) are served in the afternoon. $85–159. Two-night stays, major weekends.

Emma's Guesthouse and Cottages (633-5287; 1-888-881-9267), 110 Atlantic Avenue, Boothbay Harbor 04538. Open May through October. An old-fashioned guesthouse with five rooms (all with private bath), plus efficiency cottages on Spruce Point and in East Boothbay. A very homey atmosphere, like visiting an old friend. Each room accommodates three or four people. Water views. Pets are accepted in cottages. Rooms are $45–55, including continental breakfast.

COTTAGES

Note: Contact the chambers of commerce (see *Guidance*) for lists of rental cottages; quality is traditionally high and prices are affordable in the

Boothbays. In addition the locally based **Cottage Connection of Maine** (663-6545 or 800-823-9501) represents dozens of properties.

🐾✧ Ship Ahoy Motel (633-5222), Route 238, Southport (mailing address: Box 235, Boothbay Harbor 04538). Open late May to mid October. We are embarrassed that it took us so long to discover this fabulous find (and we never would have, had it not been for an English friend): a family-owned motel with tidy units, all with TV and AC, many with private balconies right on the water, also a pool and a coffee shop on a total three-quarters of a mile of waterfront. $39–59 per couple in high season, $29–49 off-season.

🐾✧✧ Hillside Acres Cabins and Motel (633-3411), Route 27 (Adams Pond Road), P.O. Box 300, Boothbay 04537. Open year-round. Seven cabins, including three efficiency units, and a motel building with four apartments and two B&B rooms. Electric heat, showers, color TVs. Swimming pool. Complimentary muffins, coffee cake, and coffee are served late June through Labor Day. $40–70; weekly rates.

Boothbay Harbor has a number of inviting motels, but we defer to the Mobil and AAA guides.

WHERE TO EAT

DINING OUT

The Black Orchid (633-6659), 5 By-Way, Boothbay Harbor. Seasonal; open daily for dinner except Tuesday. A chef-owned trattoria serving classic Italian dishes with a twist, like fettuccine Alfredo with fresh lobster meat and mushrooms, rolled stuffed scaloppine, and baked haddock with tomatoes and lemon pesto. In the less formal **Bocce Club Cafe** upstairs, there are seafood and raw oyster bars. No more than six people per table. No smoking. Entrées $10.95–18.95.

Lawnmeer Inn (633-2544; 1-800-633-7645), Route 27, Southport Island (just across the bridge). Open for dinner daily, mid-June through labor Day, closed Monday and Tuesday in spring and Monday in fall. Reservations appreciated. Large windows in this pleasant dining room overlook the water. The menu changes frequently but might include sautéed veal scallops with sun-dried tomato, balsamic vinegar, and pine nuts or fresh sole baked with spinach-mushroom stuffing and topped with a wine and cheese sauce. Some people come just for dessert. Entrées $14.50–19.

✧ **Andrew's Harborside Restaurant** (633-4074), Boothbay Harbor (downtown, next to the municipal parking lot and footbridge). Open daily, May through October, for breakfast, lunch, and dinner. The chef-owner specializes in creative seafood and traditional New England dishes. Wonderful cinnamon rolls at breakfast, the usual crab rolls and burgers at lunch, Round Top Ice Cream at the window and seafood entrées at dinner ranging from fish and chips ($9.95) to lobster pie ($16.95); also pasta, steak, salads and a great, informal waterside atmosphere.

✧ **Lobsterman's Wharf** (633-3443), Route 96, East Boothbay (adjacent to a boatyard). Open mid-May through Columbus Day, serving until midnight. Perhaps it's because we had a waterside table but this big old restaurant, decorated with lobster buoys, backlit stained-glass, snowshoes and ship models (for starters) rates high on our list. Just far enough off the beaten track to escape crowds, it's popular with locals. The large menu includes all the usual seafood, also pastas and pizzas. We dined well on lobster stew, crab cakes, spinach salad, and a decent house wine. Entrées from $4.50 for a burger to $18.25 for a mixed seafood grill, not counting lobster (market price).

Spruce Point Inn (633-4152), east side of outer harbor at Spruce Point. Open mid-June to mid-September; reservations advised. A gracious, old-fashioned inn with a sophisticated menu to match its decor. Entrées might include marinated breast of chicken with tropical salsa, north Atlantic salmon grilled or pan roasted in a dill sauce, or cioppino. $14.75–24.50.

Newagen Seaside Inn (633-5242), Cape Newagen, Southport Island. Open for breakfast, lunch, and dinner seasonally, closed for dinner on Tuesday. A pleasant, old-fashioned dining room with ocean and sunset views, and splendid grounds to walk off the entrées. Chef Alan Milchik delights diners with entrées like lobster thermidor, tournedos Rossini, and Cajun popcorn. Desserts are wonderful. Set price menu includes a cup of chowder, salad, entrée, and dessert, or you can order à la carte.

⚓ **Ocean Point Inn Restaurant** (633-4200), East Boothbay. Open mid-June through Columbus Day weekend. Serving dinner for over 100 years, three informal dining rooms with ocean views. Choices might include lobster brioche, wildberry chicken, or the house specialties: crab cakes, fresh Maine salmon (prepared four ways), and Black Angus steaks. Children's menu. $4.95–19.95.

EATING OUT

⚓ **Ebb Tide** (633-5692), Commercial Street, Boothbay Harbor. Open year-round. 6:30 AM–9 PM. Great breakfasts are served all day plus lobster rolls, club sandwiches, and fisherman's platters, reasonably priced specials. Homemade desserts like peach shortcake are wonderful. Old-fashioned, with knotty-pine walls, booths; look for the red-striped awning.

⚓ **Chowder House Restaurant** (633-5761), Granary Way, Boothbay Harbor (beside the municipal parking lot and footbridge). Serves lunch and dinner daily mid-June through Labor Day. A restored old building that also houses several small shops. Seating is around an open kitchen and on a waterside deck. There is also an outdoor boat bar. Chowders, lobster stew, salads, homemade breads, seafood, and full dinners. Homemade pies. Children's menu.

MacNab's (633-7222; 1-800-884-7222), Back River Road (first driveway on your left), Boothbay. Open Tuesday through Sunday 11–6. A Scottish-style tearoom, serving cock-a-leekie soup, scone sandwiches, and Highland pie as well as tea and scones; afternoon tea and high tea by reservation.

💲 **Everybody's** (633-6113), Route 27. Open year-round for breakfast, lunch, and dinner. A casual, inexpensive place that's popular with locals. Salad entrées plus light suppers and dinners. Sandwiches at lunchtime.

J. H. Hawk Ltd. (633-5589), Boothbay Harbor (right on the dock in the middle of town, upstairs). Liberally decorated with nautical artifacts, a large menu ranging from basic burgers to pastas and steaks, pan-blackened fish, and meat in Louisiana Cajun–style. Ask about live entertainment.

Carriage House (633-6025), Ocean Point Road, East Boothbay. Open year-round, daily 11–10. Entrées range from a fried fisherman's platter and charbroiled beef to pastas and sandwiches. Daily specials always include an all-you-can-eat haddock fry.

✍ **Brud's Hotdogs,** in the middle of the village and on the east side of the harbor. Keep an eye out for Brud's orange motorized cart—he has been selling juicy dogs around town for more than 50 summers.

Crump's (633-7655), 20A McKown Street, Boothbay Harbor. A tiny English dining room serving plowman's lunches, cappuccino and espresso, and Devonshire cream teas with scones and finger sandwiches. Everything on the menu can be packed for a picnic.

Dunton's Doghouse, Signal Point Marina, Boothbay Harbor. Open May through September, 11–8. Good, reasonably priced take-out food, including a decent $4.25 crabmeat roll.

LOBSTER POUNDS

🦞✍ **Robinson's Wharf** (633-3830), Route 27, Southport Island (just across Townsend Gut from West Boothbay Harbor). Open mid-June through Labor Day; lunch and dinner daily. Children's menu. Sit on the dock at picnic tables and watch the boats unload their catch. Pick out your lobster before it's cooked, or buy some live lobsters to prepare at home. Seafood rolls, fried shrimp, clams, scallops, fish chowder, lobster stew, sandwiches, and homemade desserts. Takeout available.

Boothbay Region Lobstermen's Co-op (633-4900), Atlantic Avenue (east side of the harbor). Open mid-May to mid-October, 11:30–8. Boiled lobsters and steamed clams to be eaten at picnic tables on an outside deck on the water or indoors. Corn on the cob, fried seafood dinners, desserts.

✍ **Clambake at Cabbage Island** (633-7200). The *Argo* departs Pier 6 at Fisherman's Wharf daily in summer, twice on Saturday and Sunday, carrying passengers to six-acre Cabbage Island for a clambake (including steamed lobsters), served on picnic tables. An old lodge, built in 1900, seats up to 100 people by a huge fireplace.

The Lobster Dock (633-7120), at the east end of the footbridge. Open seasonally noon–8:30. When downtown Boothbay restaurants are packed, you can walk across the footbridge to this relatively peaceful little place, offering both inside and outside lunches and dinners, fried fish, and the usual sandwiches plus lobster and shore dinners, steamed clams and mussels.

✍ **Sea Pier** (633-0627), 87 Atlantic Avenue. Check out the tanks of ocean creatures and what claims to be the biggest lobster roll in town; frequently the cheapest prices for lobster, too.

SNACKS

Downeast Ice Cream Factory (633-2816), the By-Way, Boothbay Harbor. Homemade ice cream and make-your-own sundae buffet; all sorts of toppings, including real hot fudge.

Daffy Taffy and Fudge Factory (633-5187), the By-Way, Boothbay Harbor. Watch taffy being pulled, designed and wrapped—then chew! The fudge is made with fresh cream and butter.

Cream teas are served at **Crumps** and **McNabs;** see *Eating Out.*

ENTERTAINMENT

Carousel Music Theatre (633-5297), Route 27, near Boothbay Harbor. Performances mid-May to late October. Doors open at 6:30 PM; show begins at 7. Closed Sunday. Light meals (sandwich baskets and such) and cocktails are served by the cast before they hop onto the stage to sing Broadway tunes cabaret-style and then to present a fully costumed and staged revue of a Broadway play.

Thursday-evening concerts by the Hallowell Band on the library lawn, Boothbay Harbor. July 4 through Labor Day, 8 PM.

Lincoln Arts Festival (633-4676). Concerts throughout the summer in varied locations.

SELECTIVE SHOPPING

ART GALLERIES

Gleason Fine Art (633-6849), 7 Oak Street, Boothbay Harbor. Tuesday through Saturday, 10–5. Museum-quality paintings by Farfield Porter and James Fitzgerald, as well as sculpture and paintings by some of Maine's best contemporary artists.

ARTISANS

Boothbay Region Art Foundation (633-2703), 7 Townsend Avenue, Boothbay Harbor. Open daily, 11–5 weekdays and Saturday, noon–5 on Sunday. Three juried shows are held each season in the 1807 Old Brick House. Works are selected from submissions by artists of the Boothbay region and Monhegan Island.

Andersen Studio (633-4397), Route 96 at Andersen Road, East Boothbay. Acclaimed stoneware animal sculptures of museum quality.

Footbridge Studio (633-0741), right in the middle of the footbridge, located in the old bridge tender's house. Open Memorial Day through October. Exclusive designs include a collection of miniature buildings by a local artist, pine needle baskets, and prints of Ethel Fowler artwork.

Nathaniel S. Wilson (633-5071), East Boothbay. A sailmaker who also fashions distinctive tote bags from canvas. Call for directions.

Hasenfus Glass Shop, Commercial Street, Boothbay Harbor. It's called glassblowing, but it's really the heating and bending of glass tubes into all sorts of imaginative ornaments, from sailing ships to tiny animals.

A Silver Lining, 21 Townsend Avenue, Boothbay Harbor. Working
metalsmiths. Original sculpture and jewelry in brass, sterling, and gold,
an exceptional store.

Edgecomb Potters, Route 27, Edgecomb. Open year-round. Also a seasonal shop on McKown Street in Boothbay Harbor. Maine's largest,
most famous pottery (with branches in Portland and Freeport), a two-
tiered gallery filled with deeply colored pots, vases, and table settings,
lamps, bowls, cookware, and jewelry. There's also a sculpture garden
and a small seconds corner.

Abacus Gallery, 12 McKown Street, Boothbay Harbor. Contemporary
crafts, fine furniture, whimsical pieces. Worth a look,

Gold/Smith Gallery, 41 Commercial Street, Boothbay Harbor. Contemporary art and an unusual selection of jewelry in gold and silver.

SPECIAL SHOPS

Palabra, 85 Commercial Street, Boothbay Harbor, across from Hasenfus
Glass. A warren of more than a dozen rooms offering everything from
kitschy souvenirs to valuable antiques. Upstairs (open by request) is a
Poland Spring Museum with an impressive collection of the Moses
bottles this natural spring water used to come in, plus other memorabilia from the heyday of the resort at Poland Spring.

Sherman's Book & Stationery Store, 7 Commercial Street, Boothbay
Harbor. A two-story emporium filled with souvenirs, kitchenware, and
games, as well as a full stock of books, specializing in nautical titles.

Sweet Woodruff Farm (633-6977), Route 27, Boothbay. Open May
through December. One of the oldest homes in Boothbay, this rambling 1767 Cape houses an antiques and herb shop that features herbs
that are grown and dried on the premises. Wreaths, potpourris, herb
vinegars, and more. Special open houses are held in May and at the end
of November.

SPECIAL EVENTS

April: **Fishermen's Festival**—contests for fishermen and lobstermen,
cabaret ball, crowning of the Shrimp Princess, tall-tale contest, boat
parade, and blessing of the fleet.

Late June–early July: **Windjammer Days**—parade of windjammers into
the harbor, fireworks, band concert, street dance, church suppers, parade of floats, bands, and beauty queens up Main Street. The big event
of the summer.

July: **Friendship Sloop Days**—parade and race of traditional fishing sloops
built nearby in Friendship. **Antique Auto Days,** Boothbay Railway
Village, Route 27. **Lobster Boat Races. Harbor Jazz Weekend**.

October: **Fall Foliage Festival**—boat cruises to view foliage, as well as
food booths, craft sales, live entertainment, antique auto museum,
steam train rides.

Early December: **Harbor Lights Festival**—parade, crafts, holiday shopping.

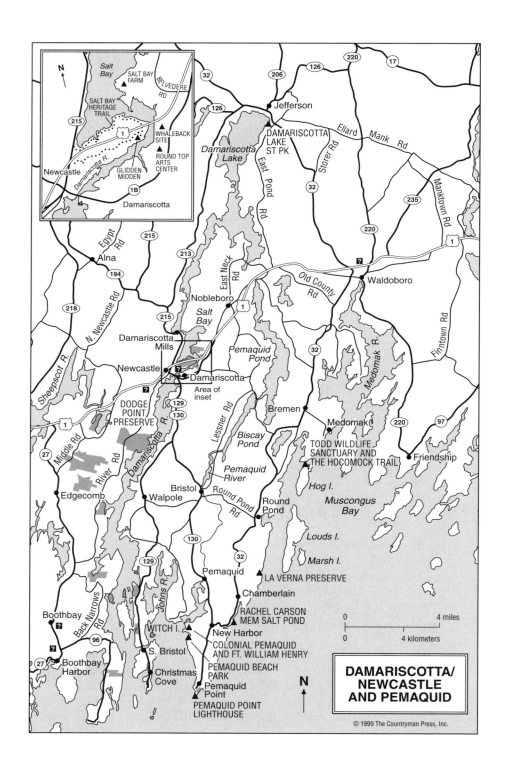

Inset map labels:

Salt Bay
SALT BAY FARM
SALT BAY HERITAGE TRAIL
BELVEDERE RD
215
1
WHALEBACK SITE
ROUND TOP ARTS CENTER
GLIDDEN MIDDEN
Damariscotta R.
Newcastle
1B
Damariscotta

N

Main map labels:

32
206
126
220
17
Jefferson
126
DAMARISCOTTA LAKE ST PK
Ellard Mank Rd
Storer Rd
Damariscotta Lake
East Pond Rd
32
32
235
220
Manktown Rd
215
Egypt Rd
Alna
194
215
213
East Neck Rd
Old County Rd
Waldoboro
1
218
N. Newcastle Rd
215
Nobleboro
1
Salt Bay
Pemaquid Pond
32
Medomak R.
Finntown Rd
Damariscotta Mills
Newcastle
Damariscotta
Area of inset
Sheepscot R.
DODGE POINT PRESERVE
129
130
Lessner Rd
Bremen
Medomak
220
97
1
27
Middle Rd
River Rd
Damariscotta R.
Biscay Pond
TODD WILDLIFE SANCTUARY AND THE HOCOMOCK TRAIL
Friendship
Edgecomb
Pemaquid River
Hog I.
Bristol
Walpole
Round Pond Rd
Round Pond
Muscongus Bay
130
Louds I.
129
Marsh I.
32
Pemaquid
LA VERNA PRESERVE
Boothbay
Back Narrows Rd
Johns R.
Chamberlain
RACHEL CARSON MEM SALT POND
96
WITCH I.
New Harbor
COLONIAL PEMAQUID AND FT. WILLIAM HENRY
27
Boothbay Harbor
S. Bristol
PEMAQUID BEACH PARK
Christmas Cove
Pemaquid Point
PEMAQUID POINT LIGHTHOUSE

0   4 miles
0   4 kilometers

N

DAMARISCOTTA/ NEWCASTLE AND PEMAQUID

© 1999 The Countryman Press, Inc.

Damariscotta/Newcastle and Pemaquid Area

Damariscotta is a small region of large, quiet lakes, long tidal rivers, and almost 100 miles of meandering coastline, all within easy striking distance of Route 1. It encompasses the Pemaquid peninsula communities of Bristol, Pemaquid, New Harbor, and Round Pond as well as communities around Lake Damariscotta, the exceptional twin villages of Damariscotta and Newcastle and neighboring Waldoboro.

Damariscotta's musical name means "meeting place of the alewives," and in spring spawning alewives can indeed be seen climbing more than 40 feet up a newly restored fish ladder, from Great Salt Bay to the fresh water in Damariscotta Lake.

The area's first residents must also have found an abundance of oysters here, judging from the shells they heaped, over the course of 1,500 years, on opposite banks of the river just below Salt Bay. Native Americans also had a name for the peninsula jutting 10 miles seaward from this spot: "Pemaquid," meaning "long finger."

Pemaquid loomed large on 16th- and 17th-century maps because its protected inner harbor was the nearest mainland haven for Monhegan, a busy fishing area for European fishermen. It was from these fishermen that the Pemaquid Native American Samoset learned the English with which he welcomed the Pilgrims at Plymouth in 1621. It was also from these fishermen that Plimoth Plantation, the following winter, secured supplies enough to see it through to spring. Pemaquid, however, lacked a Governor William Bradford. Although it is occasionally referred to as this country's first permanent settlement, its historical role remains murky.

The site of Maine's "Lost City" is a mini-peninsula bordered by the Pemaquid River and Johns Bay (named for Captain John Smith, who explored here in 1614). At one tip stands a round stone fort (a 1907 replica of vintage 1692 Fort William Henry). In recent years, more than 40,000 artifacts have been unearthed in the adjacent meadow, many of them now on display at the state-run museum that is part of the Colonial Pemaquid Restoration. An old cemetery full of crooked slate headstones completes the scene.

Since the late 19th century, when steamboats began to put into New Harbor and other ports in the area, this region has supported an abundance of summer inns and cottages. It is especially appealing to families with young children since it offers warm-water lakes, including 15-mile-long Damariscotta, which has the kind of clarity and largely wooded shore that you expect to find much farther inland.

Whether you have been there or not, you have undoubtedly seen Pemaquid Light. The vintage 1827 landmark is pictured in countless calendars and books because it not only looks just like a lighthouse should but stands atop dramatic but clamber-friendly rocks. Composed of varied seams of granite schist and softer volcanic rock, ridged in ways that invite climbing and pocked with tidal pools that demand stopping.

While there is plenty to see and to do (and to eat), it's all scattered just widely enough to disperse tourist traffic. The villages are small. Damariscotta, just a few streets built of mellow, old, local brick, is the region's compact shopping, dining, and entertainment hub.

GUIDANCE

Damariscotta Region Chamber of Commerce (563-8340; drcc@tidewater.net; www.drcc.org), P.O. Box 13, Damariscotta 04543. The chamber office, open year-round, weekdays 9–5, fronts on the parking lot just off Main Street beside the Salt Bay Cafe.

GETTING THERE

Concord Trailways (1-800-639-8080) stops in Damariscotta and Waldoboro en route from Portland to Bangor.

Mid Coast Limo runs to and from the Portland International Jetport (1-800-834-5500 within Maine; 1-800-937-2424 outside the state). Most inns on the peninsula will pick up guests in Damariscotta, but basically this is the kind of place where you will want to have a car—or a boat—to get around. **Wiscasset Taxi** (758-1679) also serves the Damariscotta area.

Parking in Damariscotta is much better than it first looks. Large lots are sequestered behind buildings on both sides of Main Street.

MEDICAL EMERGENCY

Miles Memorial Hospital (563-1234), Bristol Road, Damariscotta.

VILLAGES

Damariscotta/Newscastle. The twin villages of Newcastle and Damariscotta (connected by a bridge) form the commercial center of the region. The main street is flanked by fine examples of brick commercial buildings built after the fire of 1845. Shops and restaurants are tucked down alleyways. Note the towns' two exceptional churches and check the program of concerts and festivals at the Round Top Center for the Arts on Upper Main Street (see *Entertainment*). Damariscotta Mills, a short drive up Route 215 from Newcastle, has some elegant houses and a great picnic spot on Lake Damariscotta.

Waldoboro. An inscription in the cemetery of the Old German Church (see *To See*) relates the deceptive way in which landholder General Samuel Waldo lured the town's first German settlers here. The church and much of the town overlook the tidal Medomak (pronounced with the emphasis on "Med") River. Bypassed by Route 1, this village on the Medomak River includes some architecturally interesting buildings, one of the country's oldest continuously operating five-and-dimes, and a theater presenting films, concerts, and live performances. The **Waldoborough Historical Society Museum,** Route 220, just south of Route 1 (open daily 1–4:30 in summer months) includes a restored school, a barn and hall housing plenty of colorful local memorabilia, also a town pound. Free.

Round Pond. The name was obviously inspired by the village's almost circular harbor, said to have been a pirate base (Captain Kidd's treasure may be buried here in the Devil's Oven). It was once a major shipbuilding spot, and still is a working fishing and lobstering harbor. (Also see *Eating Out.*)

New Harbor. About as picturesque a working harbor as any in Maine. Take South Side Road to Back Cove and walk out on the wooden pedestrian bridge for a great harbor view. Note the Samoset Memorial, honoring the Native American who greeted the Pilgrims at Plymouth. It seems he also sold land here, creating the first deed executed in New England. The village itself is far bigger than it looks at first. **Hanna's Garage,** for instance, looks like a Mobil station but inside is a serious hardware and marine supply store with an upstairs (past the huge moosehead) stocked with clothing ranging from T-shirts and Woolrich jackets to clamming gear, and **Reilly & Sons Store** (established 1828) offers far more than most supermarkets (we scooped a quart of native blueberries for $1.98).

South Bristol. Be prepared to stop and find a parking space as you near this tiny village, a cluster of charming houses and shops around a busy drawbridge.

Jefferson, the village at the head of Damariscotta Lake, also at the junction of Routes 126, 32, and 206. Old farmhouses, a general store, and summer homes along the river now form the core of the village and Damariscotta Lake State Beach is on the fringe. Be sure to drive west a couple of miles on Route 213 to Bunker Hill with its old church commanding a superb panorama down the lake.

TO SEE

HISTORIC SITES

Colonial Pemaquid State Historic Site (677-2423), Pemaquid (off Route 130). Maintained by the state Bureau of Parks and Lands and open daily Memorial Day through Labor Day, 9:30–5. Admission, $1 per adult, also admits you to Fort William Henry and Old Fort House; free rest rooms. In the early 19th century, local farmers filled in the cellar holes of the

CHRISTINA TREE

Pemaquid Light

17th-century settlement that once stood here. Archaeologists have uncovered the foundations of early-17th-century homes, a customs house, a tavern, and the jail. Inside the museum you view dioramas of the original 1620s settlement and artifacts such as a 16th-century German wine jug and slightly less aged tools and pottery, Spanish oil jars, and wampum—all found in the cellar holes just outside. Nearby is the old burial ground, dating from 1695.

Fort William Henry, off Route 130, Pemaquid Harbor. Open daily Memorial Day through Labor Day, 9:30–5. (For admission see above.). This unlikely-looking round, crenellated stone fort, built in 1907, is one of New England's very few reminders of the French and Indian Wars. It replicates 1692 Fort William Henry, the third fort on this spot, built to be "the most expensive and strongest fortification that has ever been built on American soil," but destroyed by the French a year later. Fort Frederick, built in 1729, was never attacked, but during the American Revolution locals tore it down lest it fall into the hands of the British. The present building contains exhibits on the early explorations of Maine and enshrines the "Rock of Pemaquid," obviously meant as a rival Plymouth Rock, suggesting that settlers alighted on it a long time before the Pilgrims ever got to Plymouth. Both the proven and possible history of this place are fascinating: The stockade built on this spot in 1630 is said to have been sacked and burned by pirate Dixie Bull. In 1677 Governor Andros built a wooden redoubt manned by 50 men, but this was captured by Baron Castine and his Native allies (see "Castine"). The striking 1790 captain's house adjacent to the fort is also slated to be open to the public. Picnic tables on the grounds command water views.

☞ **Pemaquid Point Lighthouse** (677-2494/2726), Route 130 (at the end), Pemaquid Point. The point is owned by the town, which charges a $3.50 entrance fee during the summer (senior citizens $1; under 12 free). The lighthouse, built in 1824 and automated in 1934, is a beauty, looking even more impressive from the rocks below than from up in the parking lot. These rocks offer a wonderfully varied example of geological upheaval, with tilted strata and igneous intrusions. The tidal pools can occupy children and adults alike for an entire day, but take care not to get too close to the water; the waves can be dangerous, catching people off guard and pulling them into the water. The rocks stretch for half a mile to Kresge Point. The **Fishermen's Museum,** housed in the former lighthouse keeper's home, is open Memorial Day through Columbus Day, Monday through Saturday 10–5 and Sunday 11–5. It contains fine photographs, ship models, and other artifacts related to the Maine fishing industry, as well as a description of the coast's lighthouses. Voluntary donations are requested of visitors to the lighthouse and museum. The complex also includes the **Pemaquid Art Gallery,** picnic tables, and public toilets. Next door to the lighthouse is the Sea Gull Shop (see *Eating Out*).

Thompson's Ice House (644-8551 in summer; 729-1956 in winter), Route 129 in South Bristol, 12 miles south of Damariscotta. Open July and August, Wednesday, Friday, and Saturday 1–4. One of the few surviving commercial icehouses in New England, this 150-year-old family business uses traditional tools for cutting ice from an adjacent pond. In summer, a slide and video presentation shows how the ice is harvested (in February); tools are also on display.

☞ **Old Rock Schoolhouse,** Bristol (follow signs from Route 130 to Route 132). Open during summer months, Tuesday and Friday 2–4. Dank and haunting, this 1827 rural stone schoolhouse stands at a long-overgrown crossroads in the woods.

Shell Heaps. These ancient heaps of oyster shells, left by generations of Native Americans at their summer encampments in what are now Newcastle and Damariscotta, have become incorporated into the tall hillsides along the riverbank. A close look at the soil, however, reveals the presence of the shells. The heaps—or middens, as they are called—are accessible via the **Salt Bay Preserve Heritage Trail** (see *Green Space*).

Chapman-Hall House, corner of Main and Church Streets, Damariscotta (in the village, diagonally across from the First National Bank of Damariscotta). Open mid-June to mid-September, daily except Monday, 1–5. Built in 1754, this is the oldest homestead in the region. The house has been restored with its original kitchen. There is also an herb garden with 18th-century rosebushes.

HISTORIC CHURCHES

This particular part of the Maine coast possesses an unusual number of fine old meetinghouses and churches, all of which are open to the public.

Old German Church (832-5100), Route 32, Waldoboro. Open daily during July and August, 1–4. Built in 1772 with square-benched pews and a wineglass pulpit; note the inscription in the cemetery: "This town was settled in 1748 by Germans who immigrated to this place with the promise and expectation of finding a prosperous city, instead of which they found nothing but wilderness." Bostonian Samuel Waldo—owner of a large tract of land in this area—had not been straight with the 40 German families he brought to settle it. This was the first Lutheran church in Maine; it's maintained by the German Protestant Society. You may recognize this as the setting of one of Andrew Wyeth's most famous Helga paintings.

St. Patrick's Catholic Church, Academy Road, Newcastle (Route 215 north of Damariscotta Mills). Open year-round, daily, to sunset. This is the oldest surviving Catholic church (1808) in New England. It is an unusual building: brick construction, very narrow, and graced with a Paul Revere bell. The pews and stained glass date from 1896; and there is an old graveyard out back. Mass is frequently said in Latin.

St. Andrew's Episcopal Church (563-3533), Glidden Street, Newcastle. A charming, half-timbered building on the bank of the Damariscotta River. Set among gardens and trees, it was the first commission in this country for Henry Vaughan, the English architect who went on to design the National Cathedral in Washington, D.C.

Old Walpole Meeting House (563-5318), Route 129, South Bristol. Open during July and August, Sunday for 3 PM services, and by appointment. A 1772 meetinghouse with box pews and a pulpit with a sounding board.

Harrington Meeting House, Route 130, Pemaquid. Open during July and August, Monday, Wednesday, Friday, and Saturday 2–4:30. Donations accepted. The 1772 building has been restored and serves as a museum of Old Bristol. A nondenominational service is held here once a year, usually on the third Sunday in August.

SCENIC DRIVES

From Newcastle, Route 215 winds along **Damariscotta Lake** to Damariscotta Mills; continue along the lake and through farm country on Route 213 (note the scenic pullout across from the Bunker Hill Church, with a view down the lake) to Jefferson for a swim at **Damariscotta Lake State Park.**

Pemaquid Peninsula. Follow Route 129 south from Damariscotta, across the **South Bristol Bridge** to **Christmas Cove.** Backtrack and cross the peninsula via **Harrington Meeting House Road** to **Colonial Pemaquid** and **Pemaquid Beach** (this corner of the world is particularly beautiful at sunset). Turn south on Route 130 to **Pemaquid Point** and return via Route 32 and **Round Pond;** take Biscay Road back to Damariscotta or continue on Route 32 into Waldoboro.

TO DO

BOAT EXCURSIONS

✎ **Hardy Boat Cruises** (Stacie Davidson and Captain Al Crocetti: 677-2026; 1-800-278-3346), Shaw's Wharf, New Harbor. May through October the sleek, 60-foot, Maine-built *Hardy III* offers daily service to **Monhegan** (for a detailed description, see "Mid-Coast Islands"). Pick a calm day. It doesn't matter if it's foggy, but the passage is more than an hour and no fun if it's rough. A cruise also circles **Eastern Egg Rock,** one of only five Maine islands on which puffins breed; the tours are narrated by an Audubon naturalist (inquire about other special puffin-watching and birding trips). There are also sunset cruises to Pemaquid Point. Parking is free but roughly a quarter mile back up the road. The crew do everything they can to make the trip interesting, like the seal-watching detour on the way back from Monhegan.

Muscongus Bay Cruises (529-4474), Bremen. April to November Captain Chris Butler offers a variety of nature and pleasure cruises; inquire about rentals ranging from a classic "lobster yacht" to 25-foot Hunter sloop.

Cap'n Kurt's Lobster Boat Rides (563-2437) in John's Bay depart from the Colonial Pemaquid Restoration in Pemaquid Harbor.

Pax Scenic River Tours (677-2453). Jim and Darcy Austin's classic riverboat offers 1-hour tours of the Damariscotta River, frequently daily departures in summer, charters available.

BOAT RENTALS

Damariscotta Lake Farm (549-7953) in Jefferson rents boats and motors for use on 13-mile-long Damariscotta Lake. **Lake Pemaquid Camping** (563-5202), Egypt Road, Damariscotta, rents canoes. **Pemaquid River Canoe Rental** (563-5721), Route 130, Bristol (5 miles south of Damariscotta), has canoe sales and rentals. **Just for the Fun of It** (586-6752 or 563-1280), Route 130 in Bristol Mills, offers canoe rentals and shuttle service.

FISHING

Damariscotta Lake is a source of bass, landlocked salmon, and trout.

GOLF

Wawenock Country Club (563-3938), Route 129 (7 miles south of Damariscotta). Open May to November. Nine holes.

HORSEBACK RIDING

Hill-n-Dale Riding Stables (273-2511) in Warren offers trail rides.

Llama Backpacking (586-6752). Gary Hayward, based at Egypt Road in Alna, offers llama trekking in the Jefferson-Whitefield Game Preserve. Also inquire about guided canoe and fishing trips.

SWIMMING

On the peninsula there is public swimming at **Biscay Pond,** off Route 32, and at **Bristol Dam** on Route 130, 5 miles south of Damariscotta (also see Beaches under *Green Space*).

SPECIAL LEARNING PROGRAM

National Audubon Ecology Camp, Hog Island (a quarter mile offshore at the head of Muscongus Bay). June through August. One-week programs including family and adult camps and a 10-day Youth Camp (for 10- to 14-year-olds) focusing on the island's wildlife; also boat trips to see the puffins that were reintroduced to nearby Eastern Egg Rock by the

Audubon-related Puffin Project. There are 5 miles of spruce trails, wildflower and herb gardens, and mudflats surrounding rustic bungalows and a dining room in a restored 19th-century farmhouse. For more information and dates, call 203-869-2017, write to the National Audubon Society Ecology Camps and Workshops, 613 Riverville Road, Greenwich, CT 06831.

Damariscotta River Association (563-1393), P.O. Box 333, Belvedere Road, Damariscotta 04543, offers archeology field schools, mid-July through mid-August.

GREEN SPACE

BEACHES
Pemaquid Beach Park (677-2754), Route 130, Pemaquid. A town-owned area open Memorial Day through Labor Day, 9–5. Admission is $1 per adult, under 12 free. Bathhouse, rest rooms, refreshment stand, and picnic tables. Pleasant, but it can be windy, in which case try the more pebbly but more sheltered (and free) beach down the road. This is also a great place to walk and watch the sunset in the evening.

Damariscotta Lake State Park, Route 32, Jefferson. A fine, sandy beach with changing facilities, picnic tables, and grills at the northern end of the lake. Nominal admission.

Also see **Dodge Point Preserve** under *Green Space*.

NATURE PRESERVES
Rachel Carson Memorial Salt Pond, at the side of Route 32, just north of New Harbor. The Salt Pond is on the opposite side of the road from the parking lot. There's a beautiful view of the open ocean from here, and at low tide the tidal pools are filled with tiny sea creatures. Look for blue mussels, hermit crabs, starfish, and green sea urchins. Here Rachel Carson researched part of her book *The Edge of the Sea.* Inland from the pond, the preserve includes fields and forest.

La Verna Preserve, Route 32, 3 miles north of New Harbor. Walk the half mile down a gravel road to the preserve, which includes 3,600 feet on Muscongus Bay, maintained by the Maine Chapter of The Nature Conservancy.

Todd Wildlife Sanctuary and the Hocomock Trail, Medomak (take Keene Neck Road off Route 32). A visitors center is open daily, June through August, 1–4. The nature trail leads down to the beach.

Damariscotta River Association (563-1393), based at 100-acre **Heritage Center Farm** (P.O. Box 333, Belvedere Road, Damariscotta 04543), publishes a free map/guide to the properties which it maintains, frequently in conjunction with other landowners. These total more than a thousand acres in more than a dozen easily accessible places. They include **Great Salt Bay Preserve Heritage Trail** (see Shell Heaps under *To See*), which loops around Glidden Point, first hugging the shore of Great Salt Bay (look for horseshoe crabs, great blue herons,

Damariscotta Lake State Park

and eagles) and then tunnels right under Route 1 and leads down to the "Glidden Midden" of oyster shells that's now on the National Register and said to date back 2,400 years. The trail begins beside the Newcastle post office.

Dodge Point Preserve is a 506-acre property on Newcastle's River Road (2.6 miles south of Route 1). It includes a sand beach as well as a fresh-water pond, beaver bog, and trails.

Witch Island, South Bristol. An 18-acre wooded island lies a quarter mile offshore at the east end of the Gut, the narrow channel that serves as South Bristol's harbor. A perimeter trail around the island threads through oaks and pines, allowing views of Johns Bay. Two sheltered beaches offer swimming, picnicking, and access to a small skiff, kayak, or canoe.

Inquire locally about the **Whaleback** midden site and **Plummer Point Preserve.**

LODGING

INNS

The Newcastle Inn (563-5685; 1-800-832-8669), River Road, Newcastle 04553. Open year-round. Howard and Rebecca Levitan continue to renovate and improve this inn, which is already fairly luxurious. The 14 rooms are tasteful and comfortable, all with private baths, several with canopy beds, six with fireplaces, and two with Jacuzzis. The several common spaces, including a sunporch with a woodstove and French doors opening on a deck with water views, are particularly appealing. Howard has schooled himself in culinary arts in Paris, the better to prepare four-course dinners (see *Dining Out*) that are the centerpiece of a stay here. Rates are $95–225 double MAP (including a three-course breakfast). Inquire about special wine-tasting and holiday weekends. No smoking.

✒&. **Gosnold Arms** (677-3727), 146 Route 32, New Harbor 04554. Open mid-May through mid-October (restaurant opens Memorial Day weekend). Just across the road from the water (and from the *Hardy* boat offering day trips to Monhegan and puffin cruises around Egg Rock), this friendly, family-owned and -run inn has been welcoming summer guests since 1925. Nothing fancy, it's a rambling, white-clapboard farmhouse with a long, welcoming porch, an attached barn, and scattered cottages. Eleven guest rooms with unstained pine walls, pleasant furnishings, and firm beds (all with private bath) have been fitted into the barn, above a gathering room with a huge fireplace. There are 14 cottages, some with kitchenettes, fireplaces, and/or water views. Guests breakfast and sup on the enclosed porch overlooking the water; the dining room is also open to the public and has a reputation for fresh, local, simply prepared food (see *Dining Out*). The inn is named for Bartholomew Gosnold, who is said to have sailed into the harbor in 1602. All rates include breakfast. $79–102 double B&B in the inn, $98–144 for cottages; less off-season.

&. **Bradley Inn** (677-2105; 1-800-492-5560), 3063 Pemaquid Point, New Harbor 04554. Open year-round. Warren and Beth Busteed are energetic young innkeepers who have brought new zip and a culinary reputation to this turn-of-the-century inn (see *Dining Out*). The 16 guest rooms are divided between the main house, the carriage house, and a cottage, all nicely furnished (private baths), and the grounds have been nicely land-scaped. Request one of the third-floor rooms with a view of Johns Bay. The entry area also serves two dining rooms but there is a living room with a fireplace, wing chairs, and a library of nautical books for guests. Old clunker bicycles are free, and the inn is less than a mile from Pemaquid Lighthouse in one direction and from Kresge Point in the other. From $95 off-season to $185 in-season; also inquire about the Garden Cottage and the carriage house and about special birding weekends.

Coveside Inn (644-8282), Christmas Cove, South Bristol 04568. Motel units are open late May to mid-October; the restaurant and inn rooms, from early June to mid-September. Five old-fashioned guest rooms are in the holly-berry red Victorian inn (all have private baths but some are across the hall), which also has a big living room with a woodstove and plenty of books, shared with guests in the 10 shorefront motel units (private decks, pine paneling, and cathedral ceilings with skylights). The complex also includes a restaurant, serving all three meals, and a yacht brokerage. $65–95 includes continental breakfast.

&. **The Hotel Pemaquid** (677-2312), Pemaquid 04554. Open mid-May to mid-October. A century-old classic summer hotel just 150 feet from Pemaquid Point but without water views. The 25 rooms are neat and tidy, divided between the main house and new annexes. The decor is high Victorian, the living room has a big stone fireplace, and the long porch is lined with wicker chairs. Rooms in the inn itself come with and without private baths, but all rooms in the annex, the bungalows, and the motel units have private baths; there are also handicapped-access rooms and several reserved for smokers. The hotel does not have a restaurant, but coffee is set out at 6:30 AM, and the nearby Sea Gull Shop (see *Eating Out*) overlooks the ocean. From $49 off-season with shared bath to $125 for a suite in August; a four-bedroom housekeeping cottage is $650–695 per week. Inquire about art workshops.

BED & BREAKFASTS

∂ **Mill Pond Inn** (563-8014), Route 215, Damariscotta Mills (mailing address: 50 Main Street, Nobleboro 04555). Open year-round. A quiet spot with a wide terrace overlooking a pond. On the other side of the house Damariscotta Lake is just across the road. You can canoe or kayak out from the pond into the lake, where you might well see a resident bald eagle. Temptations not to budge, however, include two-person hammocks under the willow trees, a beach and (relatively) warm water. The 1780 gray-clapboard house with a red door offers six double rooms (all private baths), all so different from each other that you might want to ask for descriptions. Request a pond view. Breakfast might be pancakes with fresh blueberries or omelets with crabmeat and vegetables from the inn's garden, served in the dining room, which has a fireplace and a picture window overlooking the lake. In winter, pack a picnic lunch and skate across the lake to a miniature island. In summer, ask for a ride in the 16-foot, restored, antique motorboat on Damariscotta Lake. You can also paddle out in a canoe or explore the rolling countryside on one of the inn's mountain bikes. Owner Bobby Whear, a Registered Maine Guide, also will arrange fishing trips; the catch is landlocked salmon, brown trout, and smallmouth bass. $80.

⚲∂ **Brannon-Bunker Inn** (563-5941), 349 Slat Street, Route 129, Walpole 04573. Open March to December. An 1820s Cape and a barn that was a Prohibition-era dance hall before it became an inn. The upstairs sitting area walls are hung with memorabilia from World War I, and there are plenty of antiques and collectibles around (the adjoining antiques shop is open May through October). This is an unusually relaxed B&B. Your hosts are the Hovance family; children are welcome. Rooms with private baths are $70; the two that share are $60; a suite with a kitchen, living room, and bathroom is $80–100. A path leads to the river. Breakfast features muffins and fruit, and the kitchen is available for guests' use at other times of the day.

The Flying Cloud (563-2484), River Road, Newcastle 04553. Open most of the year. An 1840s sea captain's home, expanding on a 1790s Cape. The elegance of the furniture matches that of the floor-to-ceiling windows and fine detailing. We have not had a chance to visit since ownership changed in 1998 but are assured it's as good as ever. $75–95 includes a full breakfast, less off-season.

Broad Bay Inn & Gallery (832-6668; 1-800-736-6769), 1014 Main Street, Waldoboro 04572. Closed January. Within walking distance of village restaurants, shops, and performances at the Waldo Theatre, this is a pleasant, 1830s home with Victorian furnishings and canopy beds. The five guest rooms share three baths. Afternoon tea and sherry are served on the sun deck in summer and by the fire in winter. The art gallery in the barn exhibits works by well-known Maine artists, and also sells limited-edition prints, crafts, and gifts. Host Libby Hopkins offers art workshops. Rates include a full breakfast; on Saturday evenings, candlelight dinners may be arranged in advance (for guests and the public). Two-night minimum stay required in July and August. Ask about Thanksgiving, Christmas, and New Year's Eve packages. $50–75 double.

Oak Gables (563-1476), P.O. Box 276, Pleasant Street, Damariscotta 04543. Open year-round. Set on its own 13 acres overlooking the Damariscotta River, minutes from village shopping and dining, Martha Scudder's gracious house has four second-floor rooms that share a bath and a first-floor room (summers only). The grounds include a heated swimming pool and a studio cottage. $65–95 with breakfast.

Glidden House (563-1859), 24 Glidden Street, Newcastle 04553. Open most of the year. This Victorian house on a quiet street lined with elegant old homes is a convenient walk to the shops of both Newcastle and Damariscotta. Doris Miller offers four guest rooms with private baths. There is also a three-room apartment. Exceptional breakfasts, included in the lodging, are served in the dining room or in the garden. $55 double with shared bath; $60 with private bath; $70 for third-floor suite; $75 for the apartment.

The Harbor View Inn at Newcastle (563-2900), P.O. Box 791, Newcastle 04553. A handsome old house set above Main Street in Newcastle was opened in 1998 as a luxurious B&B by Joe McEntee, a former corporate executive turned chef. Common space includes a large beamed living room with windows overlooking the harbor; two upstairs guest rooms have fireplaces, river views, and private decks. Breakfast is a production. $105–140.

The Roaring Lion (832-4038) 995 Main Street, Waldoboro 04572. Open year-round. A 1905 home with tin ceilings, fireplaces, and a big screened porch. The kitchen can cater to special, vegetarian, and macrobiotic diets. One room with private bath; three with shared bath. $60–70 double, $10 less for single occupancy. No smoking.

La Va Tout B&B, Gallery, and Gardens (832-4969), 218 Kalers Corner Road, Waldoboro. Open year-round. Elizabeth Sweet took on this long-established B&B in 1996 and infused it with an air of hospitality. There are five guest rooms, one with private bath, and a hot tub in the garden (at this writing a sauna is also planned). $75–85 includes a full breakfast. The gallery exhibits contemporary art (no lobster boats).

Inland

🏵️ **The Jefferson House** (549-5768), Route 126, Jefferson (
  Barbara O'Halloron's comfortable 1835 farmhouse feel:
  moment you walk in. The large, bright kitchen with its big
  is the center of the house, or you can breakfast on the dec
  the village and millpond. Guests can use the canoe on the ⸱⸱⸱ᴏᴍꜱ
  are homey and comfortable; shared baths. $50 double, $40 single.

Snow Drift Farm Bed & Breakfast (845-2476), 117 Fitch Road, Washington 04574. Open year-round. George and Arlene VanDeventer's restored, mid-1800s farmhouse set in the country with a garden, deck,
  fields, nature trails, a trout stream, and pond (skating in winter). There's
  even a professional massage therapist available. From $45 with shared
  bath to $55 with private bath.

COTTAGES

🏵️ Many rental properties are listed with the Damariscotta area chamber (see
  Guidance); for cottages and apartments down on the peninsula, also
  request a copy of the current "Map & Guide" published by the Pemaquid
  Area Association (Chamberlain 04541).

The Thompson House and Cottages (677-2317), with 14 cottages, many
  with ocean views and facing New Harbor or Back Cove; they run $750–
  1,000 a week, less off-season.

MOTEL

🖋️ **The Oyster Shell Motel** (563-3747; 1-800-874-3747). Open all year. A
  condo-style motel complex on Business Route 1, north of Damariscotta
  Village. No view but clean and comfortable, good for a family for a night
  or two. One-bedroom or two-bedroom suites with cooking facilities,
  from $69 off-season to $129 in-season.

CAMPING

🖋️♿ **Lake Pemaquid Camping** (563-5202), Box 967, Damariscotta 04543. Off
  Biscay Road. Many tent and RV sites are right on 7-mile Lake Pemaquid,
  and canoe and boat rentals are available. Facilities also include tennis, a
  pool, swimming, a playground, game room, laundry, sauna, and store.

WHERE TO EAT

DINING OUT

The Newcastle Inn (563-5685), River Road, Newcastle. Open nightly June
  through October; Friday and Saturday off-season. Chef-owner Howard
  Levitan recently studied culinary arts in Paris to sharpen his cooking skills.
  Candlelight and the flowery dining rooms with their fine china are the
  romantic setting for a dinner that might begin with local mussels steamed
  in a broth of cream, garlic, saffron, and ouzo and feature entrées like
  grilled boneless duck breast served with a raspberry cassis glaze or a bouillabaisse of lobster and seafood in a classic, French spicy fish broth. The

four-course prix fixe dinner includes appetizer or soup, salad, entrée, dessert, and coffee. $39 plus 15 percent gratuity. The wine list is extensive.

Bradley Inn (677-2105; 1-800-942-5560), Pemaquid Point Road, New Harbor. Open for dinner year-round; nightly in-season, Thursday through Sunday November to March. There's live jazz or folk music on Friday and Saturday nights, frequently piano music other nights, but fine dining is what these two attractive dining rooms are about. The rooms are decorated in nautical antiques and soothing greens and tables are well-spaced, candlelit. The à la carte menu might include rock crab and lobster spring roll for starters and entrées like pan-seared Ahi tuna with Asian vinaigrette. We dined on an indescribably light seafood in puff pastry and scallops with duck, topped off with a chocolate hazelnut terrine. Entrées $17–23.

✐ **Anchor Inn** (529-5584), Round Pond. Open daily for lunch and dinner, mid-May through Columbus Day. A real find. Jean and Rick Hirch offer a tiered dining room overlooking the harbor in this small fishing village. Try the native crab cakes for either lunch or dinner. Dinner options include Italian seafood stew (loaded with fish, shrimp, scallops, and mussels), grilled seafood, and linguine with black olives, feta, and roasted vegetables in a sherried tomato sauce. Daily specials. Children's menu. Dinner entrées $12–16.

Gosnold Arms (677-3727), Route 32, New Harbor. Open Memorial Day weekend through mid-October, 5:30–8. An old-fashioned summer hostelry (see *Inns*) with a public dining room that seats 80. The kitchen specializes in the freshest local seafood in straightforward preparations, such as broiled salmon steak with dill, seafood casserole, and sea scallops broiled or deep fried. Dinner is served on the enclosed porch with a view of the harbor. From $8.95 for a fried boneless chicken breast to daily pricing for the salmon or lobster. The blackboard specials always include roast lamb on Sundays. Full liquor and beer list.

Coveside Waterfront Restaurant (644-8282), Christmas Cove, South Bristol. Open June through mid-September; three meals daily. This is a large waterside dining room; accessible by boat. At lunch your best bet is a Cove crab burger served with *rémoulade* ($8.50); the dinner ranges from Mike's Pasta ($8.50) to seafood Alfredo (shrimps, scallops, and lobster on spinach pasta, $21.95).

EATING OUT
On or just off Route 1

Backstreet Landing (563-5666), Elm Street Plaza, Damariscotta. Open daily, year-round. Back of Main Street, overlooking the Damariscotta River, this very pleasant, low-key restaurant and gathering place has good, dependable food. Three meals are served each day, plus Sunday brunch. Seafood entrées, homemade soups and chowders, quiches, lunch specials, and light late-evening snacks.

✐ **King Eider's Pub** (563-6008), 2 Elm Street, Damariscotta. Open year-round 11–11. A family-run favorite among locals and visitors alike. The downstairs pub is the perfect foggy-evening spot for light grub and a boutique brew and the pleasant upstairs restaurant, with a moderately priced menu featuring local produce and seafood, gets rave reviews. Go with a special of the day.

Salt Bay Cafe (563-1666), Main Street, Damariscotta. Open year-round for lunch and dinner. A pleasant, chef-owned and locally liked restaurant with booths and a fireplace. At lunch the choice of salads is wide, along with the soup and sandwich combos. The dinner menu is large, ranging from crab cakes and fried oysters to Oriental-style ribs to plenty of pasta. Entrées $12.95–17.95.

S. Fernald's Country Store (563-8484), 29 Main Street, Damariscotta. A self-conscious but fun old-fashioned store featuring penny candy up front and a deli in back with some seating in between. Basically, however, this is a great source of picnic sandwiches, like smoked turkey with provolone, tomato, onion, pickle, black olives, and house dressing. A "half" ($2.99) was plenty for us. Soups, salads, and Round Top ice cream.

Moody's Diner (832-7468), Route 1, Waldoboro. Open 24 hours (except closed midnight–5 AM on Friday and Saturday). A clean and warm, classic old diner run by several generations of the Moody family along with other employees who have been there so long they have become part of the family. Recently renovated and expanded, it still retains all the old atmosphere and specialties like cream pies and family-style food; corned beef hash, meat loaf, stews, at digestible prices.

Pine Cone Cafe (832-6337), 13 Friendship Street, Waldoboro. Open for breakfast, lunch, and dinner. Laura Cabot's attractive restaurant has evolved over the years from a small café/bakery to a 135-seat restaurant with a bar (wine and beer). Stained-glass insets in the booths and paintings on the brick walls are by noted North Haven artist Eric Hopkins, and a back deck overlooks the Medomak River. Peasant breads, salads, soups and sandwiches; full menu at dinner.

The Sea Gull Shop (677-2374), next to the Pemaquid Lighthouse at Pemaquid Point. Open daily in-season, 8–8. The shop's Monhegan Room is what this place is all about. Standard menu. BYOB.

Captain's Catch Seafood (677-2600), 74 Snowball Hill Road, New Harbor. Open throughout the summer season, 11–8 daily. Indoor and outdoor picnic-style dining. Lobsters, clams (steamed or fried), seafood baskets, and dinners; fish fry every Friday; homemade desserts. Take a truly succulent crab roll or fish sandwich down to Pemaquid Beach (just up the road) for a sunset picnic.

The Cupboard (677-3911), Route 130, New Harbor village. Open May into October, Monday through Saturday 8–4. A real resource where you need it: sandwiches served on homemade bread, haddock chowder and soup of the day, espresso, and breakfast sandwiches.

Samoset Restaurant (677-2142), Route 10, New Harbor. Open daily, year-round, 11–11. No view but great on a foggy or rainy day, geared to locals with homemade specials, good chowder, fresh seafood, reasonably priced

Sunday brunch (10–1). A recently added pub features live entertainment on weekends and other selected nights.

✐ **Osier's Wharf** (644-8101), Route 129 at "the Gut" in South Bristol. Open 8–8. Another classic spot from which to savor a lobstering atmosphere. This complex includes a general store and fish market, and the dining deck is upstairs overlooking the water; a place for a morning "clucker muffin," a crabmeat or lobster roll at lunch, or fresh-dough pizza all day.

✐ **Bullwinkle's Family Steakhouse** (832-6272), Route 1, Waldoboro. Locally loved and a good bet for road food. Steaks are the specialty along with baby back ribs, seafood baskets, and subs.

LOBSTER POUNDS

Note: Muscongus Bay is a particularly prime lobster source and genuine lobster pounds are plentiful around the harbors of the Pemaquid peninsula.

✐ **Shaw's** (677-2200), New Harbor (next to the New Harbor Co-op). Open late May to mid-October, daily for lunch and supper. You can't get nearer to a working harbor than this very popular dockside spot. In addition to lobster and steamed clams, the menu includes a variety of basic foods like meat loaf, fish cakes, stews, shrimp, roast turkey, scallops, and sandwiches. Liquor is also served. Choose to sit at a picnic table either out on the dock over the water or in the inside dining room.

New Harbor Co-op (677-2791), New Harbor. Open daily noon–8. Serves boiled lobsters and clams, inside and outside dining. BYOB.

At the picture-perfect harbor in **Round Pond,** two competing companies share the town wharf, resulting in satisfying prices. **Muscongus Bay Lobster Company** (529-5528), open daily from 10 AM, has an outdoor sink, and **Round Pond Lobster** (529-5725), open daily 10–7, has a slightly better view. Both offer no-frills (no toilets) facilities.

Pemaquid Fisherman's Co-op (677-2801), Pemaquid Harbor. Open Saturday and Sunday 11–6. Lobster, steamed clams and mussels, and shrimp to be enjoyed at outdoor tables over the harbor.

✐ **Round Top Ice Cream** (563-5307), Business Route 1, Damariscotta. Open Memorial Day through Columbus Day. You'll find delicious Round Top ice cream offered at restaurants throughout the region, but this is the original Round Top; the shop recently expanded and moved just up the road from the farm where it all began in 1924 (that property is now Round Top Center for the Arts; see *Entertainment*). The ice cream comes in 36 flavors, including raspberry, Almond Joy, and fresh blueberry. The shop offers a deck overlooking a sloping meadow, also rest rooms.

ENTERTAINMENT

Round Top Center for the Arts (563-1507), Upper Main Street, Damariscotta. On the grounds of the old Round Top Farm, this energetic, nonprofit organization offers an ambitious schedule of concerts, exhibitions, classes, and festivals. Check locally for evening outdoor concerts in summer—it could be anything from the Portland Symphony Orchestra to rousing ethnic music by Mama Tongue. Bring a blanket and a picnic and enjoy both the music and the lovely setting.

Lincoln Theater (563-3424), entrance off Main Street, Damariscotta. The biggest hall east of Boston in 1875 when it was completed, later boasting the largest motion-picture screen in the state, recently restored by the Lincoln County Community Theater, which stages its own productions here in winter and spring. Also offers first-run films and special programs.

Waldo Theatre (832-6060), Main Street, Waldoboro. March through December, a schedule of films, concerts, and live performances. Inquire about outlets for advance sales of concert tickets in Damariscotta, Rockland, and Thomaston.

SELECTIVE SHOPPING

ANTIQUES
"Antiquing in the Newcastle, Damariscotta, Pemaquid Region," a free pamphlet guide, lists more than 30 dealers in this small area. Check local papers for auctions or call Robert Foster (563-8110), based at his auction gallery on Route 1, Newcastle. Kaja Veilleux Antiques (563-1002; 1-800-924-1032) is the area dean in quality art and antiques, also organizes occasional auctions.

ART AND CRAFT GALLERIES AND STUDIOS
Victorian Stable Gallery (563-3548), Water Street, Damariscotta. Open June through October, 10–5. Handsome stalls in this carriage house behind a white Victorian mansion are filled with a collection of Maine craftswork at its best: original designs in natural materials—clay, straw, slate, and wood. Barbara Briggs seems to know all the possibilities from which she can pick and choose. The display is a stunning selection of hand-blown glass, colorful enamels, silver, iron, porcelain, and wood, examples of needlework, rugs, and some original furniture.

Gallery House at Holly Hill (564-8598), Route 1 at the turnoff for Nobleboro, 3 miles north of Damariscotta. Open daily, 10–5. Easy to miss but worth finding, Marcia Stewart's gallery is several rooms in a small house that doubles as a garden shop and is surrounded by serious gardens. Shows change but the 30 contemporary Maine artists Stewart represents are among the state's best. They include Philip Barter, Jane Dahmen, Heidi Daub, and Eric Hopkins. Inquire about gallery talks.

David Margonelli (633-3326), 780 River Road, Edgecomb. Open year-round 10–5 weekdays, 10–3 Saturday. Exquisite, completely handmade furniture with a classic influence. David and Susan make it all themselves.

Ax Wood Products (563-5884), Route 129, Walpole. Open year-round. Owner Barnaby Porter is an internationally recognized wood sculptor best known for his whimsical miniature houses and "wild contraptions" built inside tree stumps.

Damariscotta Pottery (563-8843), Northey Square, around back of Weatherbird, Damariscotta. Majolica ware, decorated in floral designs. You won't see this advertised. It doesn't have to be. Watch it being shaped and painted.

Sheepscot Pottery (882-9410; 1-800-659-4794). The big shop is on Route 1 in Edgecomb, but this shop stocks a range of distinctive hand-painted dinnerware, plates, and ovenwear as well as lamps and tiles.

River Gallery (563-6330), Main Street, Damariscotta. Open in-season Monday through Saturday 10–3; features 19th- and early-20th-century landscapes.

Brown's Cove Handweavers (529-5796), Brown's Cove Road, Round Pond. Jenny Cleaves makes contemporary 100 percent woolen rag rugs, also weaves coverlets; special orders.

SPECIAL SHOPS

Reny's (563-3177), Main Street, Damariscotta. First opened in Camden in 1949, Reny's has since become a small-town, Maine institution from Biddeford to Fort Kent. Operated by Robert H. Reny and his two sons, Robert D. and John E., the stores sell quality items—ranging from TVs to sheets and towels and whatever "the boys" happen to have found to stock this week. "We don't know what to call ourselves," Robert H. tells us, "but we have a lot of fun doing it." We enjoy shopping at Reny's too; it's not just the unexpected quality and prices, it's a certain something that's still distinctly Maine. The headquarters for the 15-store chain are in Damariscotta's former grade school; on Main Street look for **Reny's** and the recently expanded **Reny's Underground.**

Maine Coast Book Shop (563-3207), Main Street, Damariscotta. One of Maine's best bookstores, with knowledgeable staff members who delight in making suggestions and helping customers shop for others.

Weatherbird, Northey Square, Damariscotta. Open Monday through Saturday 8:30–5:30. A combination café and gift shop with mouthwatering pastries and specialty foods, wines, home accessories, clothing, gifts, toys, and cards.

Granite Hall Store (529-5864), Route 32, Round Pond. Open Tuesday through Sunday 10–5. A general store filled with Scottish-, Irish-, and Maine-made woolens, Eskimo sculptures, a few antiques and baskets, toys, books, a good selection of greeting cards, penny candy, hot roasted peanuts, homemade fudge, and, at an outdoor window, ice cream.

Carriage House (529-5555), Route 32 south of the village of Round Pond. Jean Gillespie continues to run this exceptional antiquarian bookstore, which she established with her husband, Roy, in 1961. Some 15,000 titles line shelves in a barnlike annex to the house. We recently found here a 19th-century Maine guidebook that we had been hunting high and low for, reasonably priced.

Old Post Office Shop, New Harbor center. Open May to December; good selection of gifts, local crafts.

The Roserie at Bayfields (832-6330; 1-800-933-4508), Route 32, just 1.7 miles south of the light on Route 1 in Waldoboro. Open daily April 19 until late July, then Tuesday through Saturday through the growing season. Rose lovers across the country are aware of this unusual nursery, specializing in hundreds of varieties of "practical roses for hard places."

SPECIAL EVENTS

Second weekend in July: **Damariscotta River Oyster Festival,** Damariscotta—a celebration of the oyster aquaculture conducted in the river. Oysters fixed every way (especially au naturel), music, crafts, and a canoe race through the rapids of the Damariscotta River.

Early August: **Olde Bristol Days,** Old Fort Grounds, Pemaquid Beach— parade, fish fry, chicken barbecue, bands, bagpipers, concerts, pancake breakfast, road race, boat race, firemen's muster, crafts, and the annual **Bristol Footlighters Show** (which has been going on for more than 40 years).

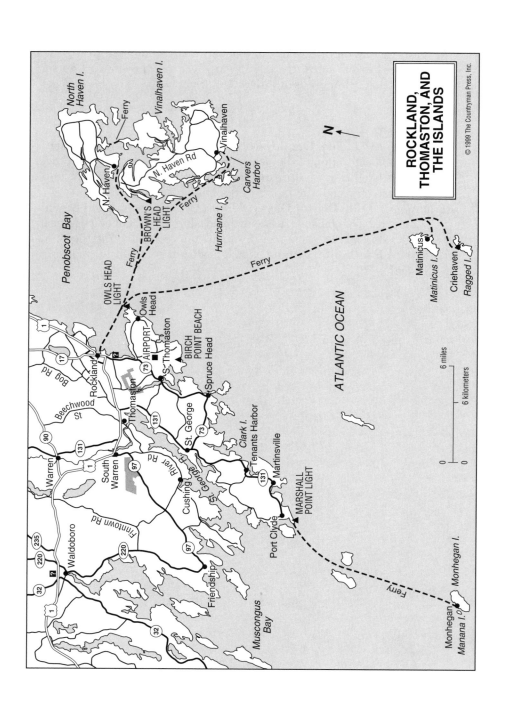

ROCKLAND,
THOMASTON, AND
THE ISLANDS

© 1999 The Countryman Press, Inc.

Rockland/Thomaston Area

Rockland's brick downtown is the commercial center for a wide scattering of towns and islands. Long "Lobster Capital of the World," this small city is now recognized as home port for the majority of Maine's windjammers and best known as home of the Farnsworth Museum, with its exceptional collection of Maine-based paintings, including works by three generations of Wyeths. Still a workaday place, it has attracted a year-round population of artists and musicians. It is also departure point for ferries to the islands of Vinalhaven, North Haven, and Matinicus (see "Mid-Coast Islands").

A century ago summer people heading for Bar Harbor as well as the islands took the train as far as Rockland, switching here to steamboats. Today a similar summer crowd fly into Knox County Airport on Owls Head, just south of town, here transferring to rental cars, air taxis, or windjammers, to charter boats as well as ferries. Wide, deep, and protected by a 4,436-foot-long granite breakwater, Rockland's harbor is now clean and amply equipped to accommodate pleasure as well as lobster and fishing boats.

Southwest of Rockland, two peninsulas separate Muscongus Bay from Penobscot Bay. One is the fat arm of land on which the villages of Friendship and Cushing doze. The other is the skinnier St. George Peninsula with Port Clyde at its tip, the departure point for the year-round mail boat to Monhegan Island (again, see "Mid-Coast Islands").

The peninsulas are divided by the 10-mile-long St. George River, on which past residents of Thomaston launched their share of wooden ships. Although its Main Street mansions stand today in white-clapboard testimony to the shipbuilders' success, and Thomaston is a beautiful town, it's best known as the site of the state prison—and its popular prison shop.

GUIDANCE

Rockland-Thomaston Chamber of Commerce (596-0376 or leave a message at 1-800-562-2529; www.midcoast.com/~rtacc/index.html), Public Landing, Rockland (write P.O. Box 508, Rockland 04841). Open daily Memorial Day to Labor Day, 9–5; weekdays and Saturdays (10–2) until Columbus Day, then just weekdays. The chamber's large, comfortable information center in Harbor Park serves the entire Rockland area, which includes Thomaston, the peninsula villages, and the islands.

It has cottage listings for North Haven, Vinalhaven, and the area from Owls Head to Cushing.

GETTING THERE

By air: **Knox County Airport** (594-4131), at Owls Head, just south of Rockland, daily service via Continental Connection (1-888-265-4267) to Boston, Bar Harbor, Augusta, and New York. Inquire about charter services to the islands. **Angel Air** (1-800-780-6071) offers charter service from throughout the mid-Atlantic region. **Penobscot Air** (1-800-780-6071), and **Gray Webster Aviation** (1-800-504-2651) all serve the islands from a variety of mainland points. Rental cars are available at the airport. Also see taxi service under *Getting Around*; all offer service to **Portland International Jetport** (see "Portland").

By bus: **Concord Trailways** (1-800-639-3317) offers service to Rockland with a stop at the ferry terminal.

GETTING AROUND

By taxi: **Schooner Bay Limo** (1-800-539-5001) and **Midcoast Limo** (1-800-937-2424) are the old reliables; **Hit the Road Driver Service** (230-0095) will get you there too. Rockland's role as transportation hub of Penobscot Bay was underscored in 1996 with the opening of a spacious new **Maine State Ferry Service Terminal** (596-2022), along with the bus stop (see above).

MEDICAL EMERGENCY

Penobscot Bay Medical Center (596-8000), Route 1, Glen Cove, Rockland.

VILLAGES AND ISLANDS

Friendship. Best known as the birthplace of the classic Friendship sloop, first built by local lobstermen to haul their traps (originals and reproductions of this sturdy vessel hold races here every summer). Friendship remains a quiet fishing village with a museum in a former schoolhouse on Martin's Point (it's open July through Labor Day).

Tenants Harbor has a good little library and, beyond, rock cliffs, tidal pools, old cemeteries, and the kind of countryside described by Sarah Orne Jewett in *Country of the Pointed Firs.* Jewett lived just a few bends down Route 131 in Martinville while she wrote the book.

Union is a short ride from the coast but surrounded by gentle hills and farm country (the Union Fair and Blueberry Festival is a big event; see *Special Events*). This place is also a good spot to swim, eat, and explore the unusually interesting Matthews Museum of Maine Heritage at the fairgrounds (open July 1 through Labor Day, daily except Monday, noon–5).

Islands. An overnight or longer stay on an island is far preferable to a day trip. From Rockland you can take a Maine State (car) Ferry to **Vinalhaven** and **North Haven.** Together these form the Fox Islands, with just a narrow passage between them. Yet the islands are very different. On Vinalhaven, summer homes are hidden away along the shore, and what visitors see is the fabulously funky old fishing village of Carver's Harbor. On North Haven, most of the clapboard homes (mainly owned by wealthy summer people) are set in open fields. **Matinicus,** also accessible from Rockland, is the most remote Maine island and quietly beautiful. Tiny **Monhegan,** accessible from Port Clyde, offers the most dramatic cliff scenery and the most hospitable welcome to visitors. For details, see the descriptions of each island in the next chapter.

TO SEE

MUSEUMS AND HISTORIC HOMES
Farnsworth Art Museum (596-6457), 352 Main Street, Rockland. Open year-round, daily June through Columbus Day 9–5, otherwise closed on Monday and open Sunday 1–5. Admission to the museums, the homestead, and the Olsen House (see next entries) is $9 adults, $8 senior citizens, $5 students ages 12 and under; less, interestingly enough, off-season. This exceptional art museum was established by Lucy Farnsworth, an eccentric spinster who lived frugally in just three rooms of her family mansion. When she died in 1935 at age 96, neighbors were amazed to find that she had left $1.3 million to preserve her house and build the handsome museum next door.

"People come to a museum like this to see what makes Maine unique," observes Chris Crosman, the Farnsworth director credited with catapulting the museum from a way stop to a destination for art lovers.

The depth and quality of the Farnsworth's 7,000-piece collection is impressive. A permanent exhibit, "Maine in America," traces the evolution of Maine landscape paintings. The museum features Hudson River School artists like Thomas Cole, and 19th-century marine artist Fitz Hugh Lane; American impressionists Frank Benson, Willard Metcalf, Childe Hassam, and Maurice Prendergast; early-20th-century greats like George Bellows, Rockwell Kent, and Charles Woodbury; and such "modernists" as John Marin and Marsden Hartley. It is also well known for its collection of works by three generations of Wyeths: Look for *Eight Bells at Port Clyde* by N. C., *Her Room* by Andrew, and *Portrait of Orca Bates* by Jamie (who worked on nearby peninsulas and islands). Rockland-raised painter and sculptor Louise Nevelson is also well represented. Note the changing exhibit gallery and Main Street museum store.

In 1998 to all this was added **Farnsworth Museum Center for the Wyeth Family in Maine,** a major new two-story exhibit space in a former church with holdings of some 4,500 works of arts and objects—paintings, drawings, studies, photographs, and archival materials—from America's most prominent artistic dynasty: N. C. Wyeth (1882–1945), Andrew Wyeth (born 1917), and Jamie Wyeth (born 1946). Exhibits vary.

The Farnsworth's original Georgian Revival library houses an extensive collection of reference materials and serves as the site for regularly scheduled lectures and concerts. A sculpture garden connects the main museum with the Wyeth Center.

Farnsworth Homestead (596-6457), Elm Street, Rockland. Open Memorial Day through Columbus Day museum hours and weekends in December (when it's decorated for Christmas and free). Included in museum admission. The Farnsworth Homestead was built in 1850 by Miss Lucy's father, a tycoon who was very successful in the lime industry and also owned a fleet of ships. Brimming with lavish, colorful Victorian furnishings (all original), it remains—according to a stipulation in Miss Lucy's will—just as it was when she died at the age of 96. Curious details of the decor include draperies so long that they drag on the floor, to indicate that the family could afford to buy more fabric than was required. Nevertheless, the walls are hung with inexpensive copies of oil paintings known as chromolithographs, a fireplace mantel is glass painted to resemble marble, and doors are not made of fine wood grains but, rather, have been painted to imitate them. How strange that a woman whose home shows so little appreciation for the fine arts should leave all her money for the establishment of an art museum.

The Olson House (596-6457), Hathron Point Road, Cushing. Open Memorial Day through Columbus Day, daily 11–4. See museum for admission rates. Administered by the Farnsworth Art Museum, this house served as a backdrop for many works by Andrew Wyeth, including *Christina's World.*

Montpelier (354-8062), Thomaston. Open June to mid-October, Tuesday through Saturday 10–4, Sunday 1–4. Admission $5 adults, $4 seniors, $3 children ages 5–11. A 1926 re-creation of the grand mansion (financed by *Saturday Evening Post* publisher and Camden summer resident Cyrus Curtis) built on this spot in 1794 by General Henry Knox, the portly (5-foot-6-inch, 300-pound) Boston bookseller who became a Revolutionary War hero, then our first secretary of war. He married a granddaughter of Samuel Waldo, the Boston developer who owned all of this area (and for whom the county is named). Inquire about concerts, lectures, and special events.

Owls Head Transportation Museum (594-4418), adjacent to the Knox County Airport off Route 73, Owls Head (just south of Rockland). Open daily year-round. April through October, 10–5; November through March, 10–4. Regular admission is $6 adults, $4 under 12, under 5 free, $5 for senior citizens; $16 family admission, more for the frequent special weekend events staged spring through fall. One of the country's outstanding collections of antique planes and automobiles, and unique because everything works. On weekends there are special demonstrations of such magnificent machines as a 1901 Oldsmobile and a 1918 "Jenny" airplane; and sometimes rides are offered in a spiffy Model T. In the exhibition hall, you can take a 100-year journey through the evolution of transportation, from horse-drawn carriages to World War I fighter planes; from a 16-cylinder Cadillac to a Rolls Royce; from the Red

Baron's Fokker triplane to a Ford trimotor. There are also wagons, motorcycles, and bikes. All vehicles have been donated or lent to the museum.

✐ **Shore Village Museum** (594-4950), 104 Limerock Street, Rockland. Open June 1 to September 30, 10–4 daily; by appointment the rest of the year. Free but donations welcome. A large and fascinating collection of historic artifacts of the US Coast Guard, including one of the most extensive collections of lighthouse materials (working foghorns, flashing lights, search-and-rescue gear, buoys, bells, and boats), plus Civil War memorabilia and changing exhibits.

Thomaston Historical Society Museum. Knox Street, Thomaston, down near the river. This is a great-looking 1790s brick "tenant building" constructed as part of the Knox estate. It's theoretically open in June, July, and August 2–4, but we have never found it open during those times. We will, however, keep trying.

Antique Boats/Maine Watercraft Museum (354-0444), 4 Knox Street Landing, Thomaston. Open Memorial Day through September. This is a great idea—a collection of antique smallcraft that you can actually get into the water in. But in the summer of 1998 we found little here, certainly nothing worth the admission price of $4 per adult, $2 per senior and student.

The Old Homestead (594-7647), Ash Point Drive, Owls Head. Open mid-July through August, 1–4. A 1700s house that's under restoration by the Mussel Ridge Historical Society; displays include vintage photos and artifacts.

LIGHTHOUSES

✐ Maine has more lighthouses (63) than any other state, and Penobscot Bay boasts the largest number of lighthouses of all. Three in the Rockland area are accessible by land. One is the **Rockland Light,** perched at the end of the almost mile-long granite breakwater (turn off Route 1 onto Waldo Avenue just north of Rockland, then follow Samoset Road to the end); the breakwater is a good spot for a picnic. The second lighthouse is the **Owls Head Light,** built in 1825 atop sheer cliffs, but with safe trails down one side to the rocks below—good for scrambling and picnicking. From Rockland or the Owls Head Transportation Museum, take Route 73 to North Shore Drive Road. After about 2 miles you come to a small post office at an intersection. Go down Main Street for a quarter mile and make a left onto Lighthouse Drive (the road turns to dirt). Just north of the village of Port Clyde (turn off Route 131 onto Marshall Point Road) is the **Marshall Point Lighthouse Museum** (372-6450), open June through September, weekdays 1–5 and Saturday 10–5; also weekends in May and October, 1–5. Built in 1885, deactivated in 1971, this is a small light on a scenic point; part of the former lighthouse keeper's home is now a lively museum dedicated to the history of the town of St. George in general and the Light Station (established in 1832) in particular. Even if the lighthouse isn't open, this is a great spot to sit, walk, and picnic.

Lighthouse buffs should also be sure to visit the **Shore Village Museum** (see *Museums and Historic Homes*).

Rockland Breakwater Be sure to walk out on this pleasant promentory, the ideal vantage point for watching the windjammers sail in and out.

TO DO

BICYCLING
"Georges River Bikeways" is the name of a free map/guide tracing routes along the river and in its watershed area from Thomaston north into Liberty. Check with the **Georges River Land Trust** (594-5166), 328 Main Street, Studio 206, Rockland. See "Camden/Rockport" for the nearest bike rentals.

BOAT EXCURSIONS
Check with the chamber of commerce (see *Guidance*) for current excursions. Also see the **Maine State Ferry Service** described above (under *Getting Around*). Ferry passage to North Haven and Vinalhaven is cheap and takes you the distance. Also see **Monhegan** in the "Mid-Coast Islands" chapter. The **Monhegan Boat Line** (372-8848) offers dinner, lighthouse, and nature cruises from Port Clyde.

BOAT RENTALS
Midcoast Boat Rentals (594-7714), 5 Commercial Street, Rockland, rents powerboats.

WINDJAMMERS
Note: All these vessels are members of the **Maine Windjammer Association** (1-800-807-WIND; www.sailmainecoast.com). Also see *Windjammers* in "What's Where" and described in the next chapter. In 3 days aboard a windjammer you can explore islands and remote mainland harbors that would take hundreds of miles of driving and several ferries to reach. Three- and 6-day cruises range from $335 to $750 (slightly less early and late in the season). All the vessels are inspected and certified each year by the Coast Guard.

American Eagle (594-1001; 1-800-648-4544), North End Shipyard, Rockland. One of the last classic Gloucester fishing schooners to be launched (in 1930), this 92-foot vessel continued to fish (minus its original stern and masts, plus a pilothouse) off Gloucester until 1983, when Captain John Foss brought her to Rockland's North End Shipyard and spent the next two years restoring and refitting her. The *Eagle* was built with an engine (so she still has one) as well as sails, and she offers some comfortable belowdecks spaces, well stocked with the captain's favorite books about Maine. The *Eagle* sails farther out to sea (to see whales and seabirds) than other windjammers, also offers a 10-day July cruise to New Brunswick and a Labor Day sail to Gloucester (Mass.) to participate in a race which she won in both 1997 and 1998. She offers 3- and 6-day cruises, accommodating 28 guests in 14 double cabins.

© GREIG CRANNA

Schooner American Eagle, a national historic landmark

Heritage (1-800-648-4544; 1-800-542-5030 outside Maine), North End Shipyard, Rockland. Captain Doug Lee likes to describe his graceful, 95-foot,
33-passenger vessel as "the next generation of coasting schooner rather
than a replica." He notes that schooners were modified over the years to
suit whatever cargo they carried. Here headroom in the cabins and the
top of companionways was raised to accommodate upright cargo, and the
main cabin is an unusually airy, bright space in which to gather. Captain
Lee is a marine historian who, with his wife and co-captain, Linda, designed and built the *Heritage* in Rockland's North End Shipyard. Their
two daughters, Clara and Rachel, have always summered aboard ship
and now sail as crew. Both captains are unusually warm hosts.

J&E Riggin (594-2923; 1-800-869-0604) was built in 1927 for the oyster-
dredging trade. A speedy 90-footer, she was extensively rebuilt in the
1970s before joining the windjammer trade. Captain Jon Finger and
Ann Mahle take 26 passengers in 10 double, 2 triple cabins; no children
under 16.

Stephen Taber (236-3520; 1-800-999-7352), Windjammer Wharf (at the
State Ferry Landing), Box 1050, Rockland, was launched in 1871 and is
the oldest documented US sailing vessel in continuous use. She is 68
feet long and accommodates 22 passengers. She has a hand-held, hot-
water shower on deck. Ken and Ellen Barnes, both licensed captains,
bought, restored, and continue to sail the *Taber* after careers as (among
other things) drama professors. Their enthusiastic following proves that
they approach each cruise as a new production, throwing their (considerable) all into each sail. This tends to be the most music-filled cruise.

Victory Chimes (594-0755; 1-800-745-5651), P.O. Box 1401, Rockland. "There was nothing special about this boat in 1900 when she was built," Captain Kip Files is fond of telling his passengers at their first breakfast aboard. "But now she's the only three-masted American-built schooner left. And she's the largest commercial sailing vessel in the United States." The *Chimes* is 170 feet long, accommodating 44 passengers in a variety of cabins (4 singles, 2 quads, 1 triple, 12 doubles). In 1991 the vessel returned to the Maine windjammer fleet in which she had served for more than 30 years, before an interlude on the Great Lakes.

Nathaniel Bowditch (273-4062; 1-800-288-4098) comes by her speed honestly: She was built in East Boothbay as a racing yacht in 1922. Eighty-two feet long, she took special honors in the 1923 Bermuda Race and served in the Coast Guard during World War II. She was rebuilt in the early 1970s. A Maine guide from Rangeley, Captain Gib Philbrick came to the coast to sail aboard a windjammer in 1966 and has been at it ever since. He and his wife, Terry, met aboard the *Bowditch* (she was a passenger). They remain a great team. Twenty-four passengers in 11 double-bunked cabins, two single "Pullmans"; in-cabin sinks. Children ages 10 and up; 3-, 4-, and 6-day cruises, some geared to whale-watching.

OTHER SCHOONER CRUISES

Wendameen (236-3472), a classic 67-foot schooner, has been beautifully restored by owner-captain Neal Parker, who takes passengers on overnight cruises from Rockland.

Summertime (359-2067; 1-800-562-8290 outside Maine), 115 South Street, Rockland, is a 53-foot pinky schooner offering 3- and 6-day cruises for up to six passengers throughout the summer. In the spring and autumn, she offers daysails out of Stonington, Castine, and Bucks Harbor.

Kathryn B (1-800-500-6077), a 105-foot, three-masted, steel-hulled schooner. A luxury version of the traditional windjammer, launched in 1996, accommodating just 10 passengers in five luxurious cabins. Sailing only July through September. Staterooms have private or shared (just two on a head) baths, Victorian detailing and furnishings, and working portholes; the saloon (with fireplace) and dining area (where five-course gourmet meals are served by candlelight) are topside. Three-day cruises $495–575; 6-day, $1,000–1,295.

GOLF

Rockland Golf Club (594-9322), 606 Old County Road, Rockland. Open April through October, an 18-hole public course that gets high marks from pros, complete with a modern clubhouse serving meals from 7 AM. For the local resort specializing in golf, see the **Samoset** in "Rockport."

SPECIAL LEARNING PROGRAMS

Hurricane Island Outward Bound School (594-1401), Box 429, Rockland 04841. An international program begun in Wales, Outward Bound challenges participants to do things they never thought they could and then push themselves just a little further. Founded in 1964, this is the largest of the five Outward Bound Schools and two Outward Bound Urban Centers in this country. Courses are May to October, 5 to 26 days on Hurricane Island (near Vinalhaven). Tailored to age and sex, the courses focus on sailing, rock climbing, and outdoor problem solving.

Merle Donovan's Maine Coast Art Workshops (372-8200), P.O. Box 236, Port Clyde 04855-0326. Mid-June through September. A well-established program of weeklong landscape workshops (both oil and watercolor) taught by a series of prominent artists from throughout the country. Lodging is in the Ocean House and its Seaside annex in the village of Port Clyde, on a working harbor at the tip of the St. George Peninsula. The ample, attractive studio space is in a converted barn.

GREEN SPACE

BEACHES

Johnson Memorial Park, Chickawaukee Lake, Route 17 (toward Augusta); **Birch Point Park,** Owls Head; and **Ayer Park,** Union.

Birch State Park, also known as Lucia Beach, off Ash Point Road in Owls Head. Sandy, with smooth boulders for sunning, wooded walking trails, and picnic benches. Marked from Route 73.

Drift Inn Beach in Port Clyde, down Drift Inn Road by the Harpoon Restaurant, just off Route 31; a small beach in a great spot.

Clark Island Cove Beach. A nice little beach but lots of NO PARKING signs.

BIRDING

Waldo Tyler Wildlife Sanctuary, Buttermilk Lane off Route 73, South Thomaston, is a birding spot on the Weskeag River.

HIKING

The Georges River Land Trust (594-5166), 328 Main Street, Studio 206, Rockland, publishes a map/guide to the Georges Highland Path, a foot trail through the hills and mountains of the Georges River watershed. Maps are available at the chamber of commerce (see *Guidance*).

PICNICKING

Route 1 picnic area overlooking Glen Cove, between the towns of Rockland and Camden.

LODGING

INNS

Craignair Inn (594-7644; 1-800-320-9997), Clark Island, Spruce Head 04859. Open mid-May to October. Steve and Neva Joseph have breathed new life into this old inn, an unusual building that was originally erected for workers at a nearby granite quarry. Sited on four shorefront acres, it offers 24 guest rooms, divided between the main house (all shared baths) and more luxurious units (private baths) in the Vestry, set in gardens in the rear. In the main house bedrooms are small but pleasing, furnished with antiques, some with water views. The dining room overlooks the water and is open to the public for dinner (see

Dining Out). Common space includes a pleasant living room, but it's the outside that beckons here: Walk across the causeway and the path to Clark Island's quarry. There's good bird-watching along the way and swimming in the quarry. From $88 (less off-season) including a full breakfast. Two-night minimum stay on holiday weekends. Weekly rates are available.

Ocean House (372-6691; 1-800-269-6691), P.O. Box 66, Port Clyde 04855. Open May through mid-October. The logical place to spend the night before boarding the morning ferry to Monhegan, a friendly old village inn run by former islander Bud Murdock. Eight of the 10 upstairs guest rooms in this building have private baths (two share) and several have water views (also available from the upstairs porch); every year a couple get redone. This is a good place for a single traveler thanks to the pleasant single rooms and rates and the ease with which you can dine with others. A reasonably priced, family-style dinner is by reservation (BYOB) and the breakfast is served to both guests and the public, 7–noon. Rooms are $80 double, less single and off-season. **Merle Donovan's Maine Coast Art Workshops** (see *To Do—Special Learning Programs*) is partially based here.

East Wind Inn (372-6366; 1-800-241-VIEW), P.O. Box 149, Tenants Harbor 04860. Open April through November; for special functions the remainder of the year. Under longtime ownership of Tim Watts, this is a very tidy and rather formal waterside inn. The parlor is large, with a piano that guests are welcome to play, but the best seats in the house are on the wraparound porch, overlooking Tenants Harbor. Rooms vary from tired-looking singles with shared baths, which seem overpriced at $57–75, to suites ($118–188) and apartments ($136–275) divided among the main inn, the waterside Meeting House, and the Wheeler Cottage (a two-story apartment, a studio apartment, and a two-bedroom housekeeping suite). Rates for double rooms are $72–132. All rates include continental breakfast. The dining room, open to the public, serves breakfast and dinner in-season (see *Dining Out*).

(In the "Camden/Rockport" chapter, also see the Samoset Resort, which overlooks Rockland Harbor.)

BED & BREAKFASTS

The Captain Lindsey House (596-7950; 1-800-523-2145), 5 Lindsey Street, Rockland 04841. Built in 1837 as one of Rockland's first inns, this sturdy brick building just off Main Street was eventually converted into offices and labs by the Camden-Rockland Water Company. By the 1990s it took real imagination to envision, let alone restore it to, its original use. Ken and Ellen Barnes, who have also restored the windjammer *Stephen Taber* and turned a former sardine carrier into the luxury motor vessel *Pauline*, have created a gem of a small hotel with richly paneled public rooms and nine spacious guest rooms (one handicapped accessible). All rooms have air-conditioning, phones, TVs in cabinets, and baths equipped with hair dryers. Rates are $95–160, including continental breakfast; lunch and dinner are served next door at the Water Works (see *Eating Out*). Ask about discounts for windjammer passengers and value packages in conjunction with the *Taber* and *Pauline*.

✎ **Weskeag Inn** (596-6676; 1-800-596-5576), Route 73, P.O. Box 213, South Thomaston 04858. Open year-round (weekends-only in winter). Convenient to Owls Head Transportation Museum and the Knox County Airport (where they'll gladly pick you up, perhaps in an antique car). A hospitable 1830s home overlooking the Weskeag estuary (there is good fishing for stripers in the rapids), within walking distance of shops in the village of South Thomaston, also handy to a public boat landing. From the dining room and deck, you can watch lobstermen hauling their traps. Six guest rooms have private baths; two share. Request a water view. There's a comfortable living room but guests are drawn to the sunny sitting room/dining area off the kitchen where Lynn Smith usually presides, dispensing advice on the best local dining, shopping, swimming, and birding spots. Gray Smith is an antique car enthusiast and one or two vintage autos are usually parked out front. $80–100 in high season, otherwise $55–70 includes a full breakfast.

🦞&️ **Old Granite Inn** (594-9036; 1-800-386-9036) Main Street, Rockland 04841. An 1840s mansion built of local granite, attached to a 1790 house, set in a flower and sculpture garden, right across from the Maine State Ferry Terminal (also the Concord Trailways stop). The obvious place to stay before boarding a ferry to Vinalhaven, North Haven, or Matinicus (see "Mid-Coast Islands"). New innkeepers Ragan and John Cary have lived and worked in the area many years and this remains an unusually welcoming and interesting B&B. The living room and dining room feature rich woodwork, and the 12 guest rooms (8 with private bath) are hung with art and furnished with antiques. Five rooms are on the ground floor (some are wheelchair accessible), six are on the second floor (one single, two with harbor views), and the most expensive is on the third floor, with a queen bed, private bath, and harbor view. $65–130 per night includes a full breakfast.

LimeRock Inn (594-2257; 1-800-LIME-ROC), 96 Limerock Street, Rockland 04841. An 1890s Queen Anne–style mansion on a quiet residential street within walking distance of the Farnsworth Museum, restaurants, and the harbor, the inn has been thoroughly restored, its eight guest rooms (all with private baths) furnished with splendid reproduction antiques (the innkeepers own a furniture store in Intervale, New Hampshire). Rates range from $95 for a small room decorated in floral prints to $185 for a large room with a mahogany four-poster and whirlpool bath or for a turret room with a "wedding canopy" bed. Rates include a full breakfast and afternoon tea.

✎ **The Outsiders' Inn** (832-5197), corner of Routes 97 and 220, 4 Main Street, Friendship 04547. Open year-round, except for a few weeks in midwinter. Comfortable atmosphere in an 1830 house. Guests can take advantage of Bill Michaud's kayaking expertise; eight kayaks are available for rent and guided expeditions in nearby Muscongus Bay. Pleasant doubles with private bath are $65; $50 with shared. A small cottage in the garden is $350 per week. Facilities include a sauna.

❧ **Harbor Hill** (832-6646), Town Landing Road, P.O. Box 35, 5 Harbor Hill Lane, Friendship 04547. Open July and August, also spring and autumn weekends by arrangement. Liga and Len Jahnke's 1800s farmhouse is set on a hillside sloping to the sea, with views of the islands in Muscongus Bay. The three suites all have water views and private baths; $90–95 includes a Scandinavian-style breakfast. A two-bedroom cottage is $550 per week.

Lakeshore Inn (594-4209), 184 Lakeview Drive, Rockland 04841. A much modified 1767 home above Route 17, overlooking Lake Chickawaukee (good swimming), 2 miles north of downtown Rockland. Paula Nicols and Joseph McCluskey offer four air-conditioned guest rooms (private baths) at $95–125, breakfast included. Facilities include a spa room with a hot tub. Inquire about spa weekends.

Friendship Harbor House Bed & Breakfast (832-7447), P.O. Box 189, Friendship 04547. This B&B opened in 1998 with four guest rooms, an apartment, and a cottage. Facilities include a beach, dock, and kayak rental. $95–125; $600 per week for the cottage.

MOTEL

Navigator Motor Inn (594-2131; 1-800-8026). 520 Main Street, Rockland 04841. Open all year. Geared to families bound for the islands of Vinalhaven, North Haven, and Matinicus. The Maine State Ferry terminal is across the street so you can park your car in line for the early-morning ferry and walk back to your room. This is a five-story, 80-room motel with cable TV and a restaurant that serves from 6:30 AM.

COTTAGES AND EFFICIENCIES

A list of cottages, primarily in the Owls Head and Spruce Head areas, is available from the Rockland-Thomaston Chamber of Commerce (see *Guidance*).

WHERE TO EAT

DINING OUT

Jessica's, a European Bistro (596-0770), 2 South Main Street (Route 73), Rockland. Open year-round, nightly for dinner in summer, closed Tuesday in shoulder seasons, also Monday in winter. Reservations are a must. In a restored Victorian home, chef-owner Hans Bucher serves nicely prepared Swiss and generally Continental cuisine including a wide variety of meat entrées and pastas as well as seafoods. We celebrated our anniversary here this year, dining on baked stuffed shrimp filled with crabmeat stuffing. The menu changes quarterly but always includes Wiener schnitzel ($16.50) and veal Zürich ($18.50); entrées $13.50–19.50; extensive wine list and full bar.

Cafe Miranda (594-2034), 15 Oak Street, Rockland. Open Tuesday through Sunday 5:30–9:30; the patio is open for lunch in summer, 11–1:30. Be sure to reserve for dinner because chef Kerry Altiero's small, bright dining room—in an array of southwestern colors and flavors—is usually filled with savvy locals. The open kitchen features a brick oven and seafood grill, and the menu, fresh pastas and herbs. Our pink-pottery platter of curried mussels and shrimp (both in the shell) served on polenta with sweet peppers and onions, mopped up with flatbread (olive oil provided), was a bargain at $12.50. Wine and beer, espresso and cappuccino are served. The handwritten menu of 45 items changes daily. Entrées $9.50–15.

Craignair Inn (594-7644), Clark Island, Spruce Head, off Route 73. Open for lunch and dinner in summer months. This water-view dining room has had an up-and-down reputation over the past few years, but it's definitely up under the recent change in ownership and supervision by a locally respected chef. Dinner entrées might include a bouillabaisse of local mussels, shrimp, and fish ($17.95) and pasta primavera with chicken ($13.95) or shrimp ($15.95).

Harbor View Restaurant (354-8173). Open year-round for lunch and dinner. Chef-owner Bernard Davodet's restaurant in a former boathouse is a local standby, hidden away on the harbor on Snow's Pier, Thomaston. Photographs and memorabilia ornament the walls. At dinner try the broiled scallops ($14.95), mussels and cream ($9.95), or a baker's dozen of stuffed shrimp ($15.95). Nightly specials. Full license.

The Harpoon (372-6304), corner of Drift Inn and Marshall Point Road, Port Clyde. Open May through mid-October. In July and August, open for lunch and dinner every day. Spring and fall, dinner only, Wednesday through Sunday. This engaging little seafood restaurant in the seaside village of Port Clyde (just off Route 131, around the corner from the harbor) specializes in the local catch. Try the Cajun seafood, lazy lobster, fried combo plate, or prime rib. Full bar.

East Wind Inn (372-6366), Tenants Harbor. Open for dinner and Sunday brunch. Reservations suggested. A dining room overlooking the working harbor with a porch on which cocktails are served in summer. The menu features local seafood and produce. Dinners might include pan-seared Maine salmon with a soy glaze ($14.95) or grilled medallions of beef tenderloin ($17.95).

(Also see Marcel's at the Samoset Resort, under *Dining Out*, in the "Camden/Rockport" chapter.)

EATING OUT

In Rockland

   The Water Works (596-7950), Lindsey Street, Rockland. Serving lunch and dinner daily, late light fare. The Barnes family have converted a former eight-bay garage for the Camden-Rockland Water Company into an attractive meeting spot with two distinct atmospheres: a dining area with a striking fountain sculpture (by Captain Ken Barnes) at one end and a pub with congenial, shared tables at the other. Former windjammer chef Susan Barnes is the hand behind the large and satisfying menu. Staples include shepherd's pie, Bermudian fish stew, and pub sausages (Irish bangers wrapped in puff pastry and baked, served with homemade mustard and salad); the blackboard dinner menu changes nightly. The brew list is extensive. Children's menu.

Schooner Fare (596-0012), 421 Main Street. A good bet for lunch, also for dinner Thursday through Sunday: chowders, sandwiches, seafood, steak, pasta, Cajun dishes. A storefront restaurant that's friendly and reliable. Entrées $3–15.

The Brown Bag (596-6372), 606 Main Street (north of downtown). Open Monday through Saturday 6:30 AM–4 PM, Sunday 7–2. This expanded storefront restaurant offers an extensive breakfast and sandwich menu. Make your selection at the counter and carry it to your table when it's ready.

Second Read Bookstore (594-4123), 328 Main Street. Open 8–5:30, much later on music nights, noon–4 on Sunday. Patrick Reilley and Susanne Ward's recently expanded café seems to serve as a living room for the city's sizable creative community as well as the obvious place for museumgoers to pause for cappuccino and croissants. Try the curried chicken salad or a pastry. There's frequently folksinging or jazz on Friday and Saturday nights.

The Landings Restaurant & Pub (596-6563), 1 Commercial Street. Open May to October, on the harbor with outside as well as inside seating, serves 11–9:30 from a menu that ranges from a hot dog to steak, lobster, and a full-scale clambake. Fried clams, fish-and-chips, and a good selection of sandwiches. Entrées $5–16.

Kate's Seafood (594-2626), Route 1, south of Rockland. April to October. A standby for fried, boiled, and steamed seafood, chowder, and lobster rolls.

Dave's Restaurant (594-5424), Route 1, between Thomaston and Rockland. Seafood dinners and the area's only smorgasbord, with old-fashioned classics such as macaroni and cheese and beans and franks. Breakfast and lunch buffets, plus a large salad bar. Breakfast is served all day; sandwiches, pizza, seafood dinner, too.

Wasses Wagon (found either at 2 North Main Street or the corner of Park and Union Streets); a local institution for hot dogs.

In Thomaston

Thomaston Cafe and Bakery (354-8589), 88 Main Street. Open 7–2, also for dinner Friday and Saturday and for Sunday brunch. Homemade soups, great sandwiches, specials like fish cakes with homefries, salads, and a wicked quesadilla with Maine shrimp, goat cheese, and salad.

ELSEWHERE

Dip Net Coffee Shop, Port Clyde. Seasonal. Offers counter service and table seating, good food, and access to the harborside deck, but it seems to be closed more than it is open. The neighboring **Port Clyde General Store** makes good sandwiches and has picnic benches on the deck, and the **Ocean House,** just up the road, serves breakfast, a real convenience if you have driven from a distance to catch the Monhegan ferry.

Hannibal's Café on the Common (785-3663), Union. Open year-round from 10 AM Tuesday through Friday; from 7 AM Saturday; Sunday brunch 8–2. Good lunch and dinner; specializing in "classical, ethnic, and vegetarian cuisine," now in an 1839 farmhouse with views of Seven Trees Pond.

LOBSTER POUNDS

Cod End (372-6782), on the Wharf, Tenants Harbor. Open mid-June to mid-September daily 7 AM–9 PM; spring and fall 8–6. Hidden down a lane, a particularly appealing longtime family-owned combination fish shop and informal wharfside eatery (tables inside and out) right on Tenants Harbor with a separate cook house: breakfast muffins and eggs, lunch chowders and lobster rolls, dinner lobsters and clams. We recommend the strawberry-rhubarb pie with ice cream. BYOB.

Miller's Lobster Company (594-7406), Wheeler's Bay, Route 73, Spruce Head. Open 10–7, Memorial Day through Labor Day. On a working harbor, old-fashioned, family-owned and -operated, with a loyal following. Tables are on the wharf; lobsters and clams are cooked in seawater.

Waterman's Beach Lobsters (594-2489), off Route 73, South Thomaston. Open daily 11–7 in the summertime. Oceanfront feasting on the deck: lobster and clam dinners, seafood rolls, homemade pies.

ENTERTAINMENT

The Farnsworth Museum (596-6457) stages a year-round series of Sunday concerts, free with museum admission; reservations advised.

Second Read Bookstore (594-4123), 328 Main Street, Rockland, has live music, usually jazz or folksinging, on many Friday and Saturday evenings; also poetry readings.

Strand Cinema (594-7266), Main Street, Rockland. A classic old downtown theater showing first-run films. We hope it weathers the competition from the Flagship Cinemas (594-2100) with its seven screens on Route 1, the Rockland-Thomaston line.

Down East Singers (354-2262), Thomaston. The Mid Coast's largest community chorus performs throughout the year.

SELECTIVE SHOPPING

Rockland's Main Street is a relatively well-preserved example of 19th-century commercial architecture, with department, hardware, and furniture stores. Note especially: **The Store,** featuring a wide selection of cooking supplies; **Coffin's,** a family clothing store; **The Reading Corner,** a full-service bookstore with an interesting interior. Since the

You can admire the work of local artists in the many Rockland galleries.

Farnsworth Museum Store opened in 1994 (corner of Main and Elm Streets), boutique-style stores have proliferated. They include: **The Grasshopper Shop,** a major link in a Maine chain; **Black Parrot,** a Maine-based outerwear company known for colorful fleece-lined reversible garments, and **Peabody & King,** another mix of things you have never thought of needing.

ANTIQUES

More than a dozen antiques stores, scattered between Rockland and Thomaston, publish their own guides, which are available locally.

ART AND CRAFT GALLERIES

So many galleries have opened around the Farnsworth area that an "Arts in Rockland" map is available at most. They include **Atlantis Gallery** (596-6509), 30 Elm Street; the prestigious **Caldbeck Gallery** (12 Elm Street across from the museum); **Between the Mews** (8 Elm Street); **Gallery One** (365 Main Street); and Thomas O'Donovan's **Harbor Square Gallery,** filling a former bank building (374 Main Street). Be sure to check out the **Islands of Maine Gallery** (596-0701), 412 Main Street, Rockland. Open Monday through Saturday 10–6, Sunday 1–5. It features quality art and folk art, books, ceramics, quilts and clothing, furnishings, sculpture, jewelry, and much more, representing 70 artists and artisans on 18 Maine islands.

Along Route 131 to Port Clyde

Noble Clay (372-6468; 1-800-851-4957), Route 131, Tenants Harbor. Open year-round, Monday through Saturday 10–5. Trish Inman and Steve Barnes produce functional white-and-blue-glazed porcelain pottery—

plates, lamps, bowls, and vases—with whimsical and botanical designs. Also on Tenant's Harbor: **Harbor Frame Shop & Gallery** (372-8274) on Barter's Point Road (look for the totem pole out front), displaying both established and upcoming artists; and **Cindy McIntyre Images/ Scalawags Gallery**, Route 131 across from Farmer's Restaurant. Be sure to stop at the **Gallery-by-the Sea** in the village of Port Clyde (372-8671), open daily June through October and by appointment. Sally MacVane knows her Maine artists and carries the best.

In South Thomaston

Keag River Pottery (594-7915), Westbrook Street, South Thomaston. Open July through Labor Day; otherwise by appointment. Toni Oliveri looks more like the urban planner he studied to be than the potter he has been since 1968. We love his work, and even splurged on a unusually shaped and glazed vase with inner ribbons of pottery that make it easier to artistically display flowers. Each piece is individually crafted, and surprisingly reasonably priced.

The Old Postoffice Gallery & Art of the Sea (594-9396), Route 73, South Thomaston. Nearly 100 museum-quality full-rigged ship models are displayed in a series of rooms on two floors; also half models and nautical paintings.

BOOKSTORES

The Reading Corner (596-6651), Main Street, Rockland. A full-service bookstore filling two unusual storefronts; note the bargain book section.

Thomaston Books & Prints (354-0001), 105 Main Street, Thomaston. Open daily. An attractive full-service bookstore.

✎ **The Personal Book Shop** (354-8056), 78 Main Street, Thomaston. Open year-round, 10–6. Marti Reed's shop is more like a book-lined living room than your ordinary bookstore: plenty of places to sit and read but also a large selection of titles; many Maine authors, including out-of-print John Gould and Elisabeth Ogilvie books and a well-stocked children's room. Special orders and out-of-print searches.

Lobster Lane Book Shop (594-7520), Spruce Head. Marked from the Off-Island Store. Open June to September, Thursday through Sunday and weekends through October, 12:30–5. Vivian York's stock of 50,000 titles is well known in bookish circles. Specialties include fiction and Maine.

(Also see Second Read Bookstore under *Eating Out* and *Entertainment*.)

SPECIAL STORES

Prison Shop at the Maine State Prison in Thomaston, Main Street (Route 1), at the southern end of town. A variety of wooden furniture—coffee tables, stools, lamps, and trays—and small souvenirs, all carved by inmates. Prices are reasonable and profits go to the craftsmen.

Local Talents of Maine (354-0013), 119 Main Street, Thomaston. A consignment shop for 160 local craftspeople with the stress on variety: jams, dried flowers, quilts, etc.

SPECIAL EVENTS

June: **Warren Day**—a pancake breakfast, parade, art and quilt shows, chicken barbecue, and auction.

July: **Fourth of July** celebrations in most towns, with parades. Thomaston's festivities include a big parade, foot races, live entertainment, a craft fair, barbecue, and fireworks. **Schooner Days and the North Atlantic Blues Festival,** Harbor Park, Rockland *(Friday, Saturday, and Sunday after July 4)*—see the wonderful windjammers vie for first place in a spectacular race that recalls bygone days. The best vantage point is the Rockland breakwater. **Friendship Sloop Days,** Rockland. **Full Circle Summer Fair,** at the Union Fairgrounds sponsored by WERU-FM—the emphasis is on everything natural and on crafts.

August: **Maine Lobster Festival** *(first weekend, plus the preceding Wednesday and Thursday)*—this is probably the world's biggest lobster feed, prepared in the world's largest lobster boiler. Patrons queue up on the public landing to heap their plates with lobsters, clams, corn, and all the fixings. King Neptune and the Maine Sea Goddess reign over the event, which includes a parade down Main Street, concerts, an art exhibit, contests such as clam shucking and sardine packing, and a race across a string of lobster crates floating in the harbor. Annual **Transportation Spectacular and Aerobatic Show** at the Owls Head Transportation Museum. **Union Fair and Blueberry Festival** *(third week)*—a real agricultural fair with tractor- and ox-pulling contests, livestock and food shows, a midway, the crowning of the Blueberry Queen, and, on one day during the week, free mini blueberry pies for all comers.

October: **Farnsworth Festival of Scarecrows**—Rockland community scarecrow contest, dance, related events.

November–December: **Christmas celebrations** beginning Thanksgiving; parade, Santa's Village, sleigh rides.

Mid Coast Islands

Monhegan; The Fox Islands: Vinalhaven and North Haven;
and Matinicus

MONHEGAN

Eleven miles at sea and barely a mile square, Monhegan is a micro-cosm of Maine landscapes, everything from 150-foot sheer headlands to Cathedral Woods, from inland meadows filled with deer to the smooth, low rocks along Lobster Cove. "Beached like a whale" is the way one mariner in 1590 described the island's shape: headlands slop-ing down to Lobster Cove, a low and quiet tail.

Monhegan is known for the quality (also quantity) of its artists and the grit of its fishermen—who lobster only from January through June. The island's first recorded artist arrived in 1858, and by the 1890s a mansard-roofed hotel and several boardinghouses were filled with sum-mer guests, many of them artists. In 1903 Robert Henri, a founder of New York's Ashcan school and a well-known art teacher, discovered Monhegan and soon introduced it to his students, among them George Bellows and Rockwell Kent. Monhegan remains a genuine art colony. Jamie Wyeth owns a house built by Rockwell Kent. Some 20 artists open their studios to visitors (hours are posted on "The Barn" and printed in handouts) during summer weeks.

The island continues to draw artists in good part because its beauty not only survives but also remains accessible to all. Prospect Hill, the only attempted development, foundered around 1900. It was Theodore Edison, son of the inventor, who amassed property enough to erase its traces and keep the island's cottages (which still number just 130) bunched along the sheltered Eastern Harbor, the rest preserved as common space and laced with 17 miles of footpaths.

In 1954 Edison helped to organize Monhegan Associates, a non-profit corporation dedicated to preserving the "natural, wild beauty" of the island. Ironically, this is one of the country's few communities to shun electricity until relatively recently. A number of homes and one inn still use kerosene lamps. Vehicles are limited to a few trucks to haul lobstering gear and visitors' luggage to and from the dock. Deer saun-ter through the village.

Monhegan has three inns, several bed & breakfasts, and a number of rental cottages; it is also a summer day's destination for day-trippers from Boothbay Harbor and New Harbor as well as Port Clyde—obvi-ously a heavy tide of tourists for such a small, fragile island. Luckily the fog and frequently rough passage, not to mention limited public plumbing, discourage casual visitors. The island's year-round population of substantially less than 100 swells to a little more than 400 (not counting day-trippers) in summer; visitors come to walk, to paint, and to reflect. An unusual number come alone.

GETTING THERE

For details about the *Balmy Days II,* see "Boothbay Harbor," and for the *Hardy III,* see "Damariscotta/Newcastle." The **Monhegan-Thomaston Boat Line** operates both the sleek new *Elizabeth Ann* and the beloved old *Laura B* from Port Clyde (reservations are necessary: Monhegan Boat Line, P.O. Box 238, Port Clyde 04855; or call 372-8848); parking is $4 per day; the ticket is $25 round-trip per adult, $12 per child, $2 per pet. Service is three times daily in-season, less frequent in spring and fall, and only Monday, Wednesday, and Friday in winter.

EQUIPMENT AND RULES

Come properly shod for the precipitous paths, and bring sweaters and windbreakers. Wading or swimming from any of the tempting coves on the back side of the island can be lethal. Flashlights, heavy rubber boots, and rain gear are also good ideas. There is no bank, let alone ATM, on the island. Public phones are few and most require phone cards. Camping is prohibited. Do not bring bicycles or dogs (which must be leashed at all times). No smoking outside the village, and please don't pick the flowers.

PUBLIC REST ROOM

Hidden up a lane behind the Monhegan House at the bottom of Horn Hill, this overpriced ($1) facility was a hard-fought concession to day-trippers.

GETTING AROUND

Several trucks meet each boat as it arrives and provide baggage service for a fee. Otherwise visitors have no access to motorized transport; you need none because distances are all short and there are no paved roads.

MEDICAL EMERGENCY

Dial 911 (most private homes as well as island businesses now have phones). Unfortunately, the island's Emergency Rescue Squad gets plenty of practice and is a highly skilled group.

TO SEE

The Lighthouse, built in 1824 and automated in 1959, offers a good view from its perch on the crest of a hill. The former keeper's cottage is now the **Monhegan Museum** (open daily July through mid-September, 11:30–3:30), a spellbinding display of island art, artifacts, flora, fauna, some geology, lobstering, and an artistic history of the island, including documents dating back to the 16th century. One upstairs room is dedicated each summer to a show devoted to one of the island's deceased artists. A separate art museum, opened in 1998, preserves the invaluable paintings that have accrued to the museum and offers space for

Monhegan Island

special exhibits like that of the opening year, appropriately dedicated to
Rockwell Kent, the artist whose turn-of-the-century Monhegan paintings (when he lived here year-round, working as a fisherman and serving as the island game warden) and 1950s work still add up to some of
the best the island has ever inspired.

Manana Island (across the harbor from Monhegan) is the site of a famous
runic stone with inscriptions purported to be Norse or Phoenician. At
Middle Beach on Monhegan, you may be able to find someone willing
to take you over in a skiff.

TO DO

BIRDING

During migratory season, especially mid- through late September, it's difficult to find a room on the island because Monhegan is well known
among birders as one of the best birding places on the East Coast. Your
local Audubon society may have a trip going. Whenever you come, be
sure to bring a copy of *Birder's Guide to Maine* by Jan Erik Pierson.

HIKING

Pick up a trail map to the island's 17-mile network before setting out. Day-
trippers should take the **Burnt Head Trail** and loop back by the village via
Lobster Cove rather than trying a longer circuit; allow at least 5 hours
(bring a picnic) to go around the island. Our favorite hike is **Burnt Head** to
White Head along high bluffs, with a pause to explore the unusual rocks in
Gull Cove, and back through **Cathedral Woods.** On another day head
for **Blackhead** and **Pulpit Rock,** then back along the shore to **Green
Point** and **Pebble Beach** to watch the action on **Seal Ledges.**

LODGING

INNS

Monhegan House (594-7983; 1-800-599-7983), Box 345, Monhegan 04852. Open Memorial Day through Columbus Day. An 1888 summer inn with 33 rooms, family owned and operated for five generations. No closets, shared baths, but clean, comfortable, and bright; rooms are furnished with antique oak pieces and many have water views. The downstairs lobby is often warmed by a glowing fireplace, and has ample seating for foggy mornings; on sunny days guests tend to opt for the rockers along the porch, a vantage point from which you can watch the comings and goings of just about everyone on the island. The café is a popular spot for all three meals with locals as well as guests of the inn. Singles are $52; doubles $85; $105 for three people.

Island Inn (596-0371; fax, 596-5577), Monhegan Island 04852. Open late May to mid-October. Owners Howard Weilbacker and Philip Truelove continue to struggle to raise the comfort level in this vintage wooden hotel to reflect the prices they need to charge. In the two small living rooms (part of the original circa-1850 house that is the nucleus of the 1906 inn), note the hand-painted murals. The large, old-fashioned dining room serves three meals a day to the public as well as to overnight guests. The 32 rooms and four suites are small, typically with a sink, plainly furnished; just seven have private baths (five more are planned); $110–165 double (the low end is for shared bath, "meadow" view), $185 for a one-bedroom suite, $98 single including a full breakfast.

The Trailing Yew (596-0440; 1-800-592-2520), Monhegan Island 04852. Open mid-May through mid-October. In 1996 Josephine Day died, having operated the Yew since 1926. At present it is being run as a trust, the idea being to preserve this quirky institution: 40 very basic rooms divided among the main house, adjacent buildings, and cottages on the grounds and up the road. Unfortunately, in 1998 we received several complaints and checked ourselves to confirm that the place is dirty. We trust that management will literally clean up their act because this place deserves to survive, complete with its shared baths, a combination of electricity (in the bathrooms) and kerosene lamps, and simple food (usually there's some form of cod). Before meals, guests gather around the flagpole outside the main building to pitch horseshoes and compare notes; family-style dining at shared tables features lots of conversation. Birders tend to have their own table. The dining room is open to the public. The rate is $58 per person per day, including breakfast and dinner and all taxes and tips; under age 10, $15–35. No credit cards.

BED & BREAKFASTS

🐾 **Shining Sails Guesthouse** (596-0041; fax, 596-7611), Box 346, Monhegan Island 04852. Open year-round. John and Winnie Murdock maintain this charming, renovated old Monhegan home on the edge of the village

Boats of Monhegan by James Fitzgerald

and water. There are three rooms, two with views of the meadow and one of the ocean (our favorite guest room on the entire island); also four efficiencies, three with ocean views and private decks. All rooms are tastefully decorated, as is the common room, which has a water view and Franklin stove. An ample continental breakfast is served May through Columbus Day. John Murdock is an island lobsterman and the couple are knowledgeable, helpful hosts. Rooms are $70–95, $470–610 per week; apartments are $575–765 per week.

Hitchcock House (594-8137), Horn's Hill, Monhegan Island 04852. Open year-round. Hidden away on top of Horn's Hill with a pleasant garden and deck. Barbara Hitchcock offers several rooms and efficiencies with views of the meadows. The studio, a separate cabin, has a kitchen and bedroom. Rooms are $55 per night, $350 per week; efficiencies are $80 per night, $510 per week.

COTTAGES AND EFFICIENCIES

Cooking facilities come in handy here: You can buy lobster and good fresh and smoked fish (bring meat and staples) and a limited line of vegetables. **Shining Sails Real Estate** (596-0041; fax 596-7166) manages two dozen or so rental cottages, available by the weekend as well as by the week.

WHERE TO EAT

Monhegan House Cafe at the Monhegan House is an attractive and informal place to eat: The long, many-windowed dining room with its blue-painted tables is in the back of the inn, overlooking the village and meadow. Homemade breads and omelets for breakfast; luncheon sandwiches like cheese, lettuce, tomato, and avocado on homemade bread; fresh-ground peanut butter, or "the ultimate burger"; dinner entrées include vegetarian choices as well as seafood and steak ($9–18). BYOB.

The Island Inn (mid-June to mid-September). Open to the public for all three meals. The traditional hotel dining room offers a large à la carte dinner menu; entrées range from $10.95 for spinach and caramelized onion lasagna to $21.95 for jumbo lobster and spinach ravioli with red and green pepper diamonds in sun-dried tomato broth; $4 service charge for BYOB wine. The inn also operates the **Barnacle** across the road, a good bet for take-out sandwiches, pastries, coffees.

The Trailing Yew (mid-May to mid-October). Open to the public by reservation. Under $15 for fruit cup, entrée, salad, and dessert, whatever is being served that night. Ask when you reserve. The big attraction here is the conversation around communal tables. BYOB.

The Periwinkle, open seasonally, serves breakfast, lunch, and dinner. A two-floor restaurant with water views, varied menu, beer and wine. Outside seating at lunch.

Not North End Pizza (594-5546), open seasonally 11–7 for lunch and dinner. After years of serving pizza, the focus here is now a variety of daily specials: soups, sandwiches, rice dishes.

The Monhegan Store (594-4126), open daily until 6 PM. All the staples, including beer and wine and sandwiches, at convenience-store prices.

At the **Fish "R" Us Fish Market,** you'll find smoked products and picnic fixings as well as lobsters.

SELECTIVE SHOPPING

ART GALLERIES

The Lupine Gallery (594-8131). Bill Boynton and Jackie Bogel offer original works by 60 artists who paint regularly on the island. This is a very special gallery, showcasing the work of many professional artists within walking distance. You can pick out work that you like and then check the artist's hours on the island's "open studio" list.

Open studios: Many of the resident artists welcome visitors to their studios; pick up a schedule, check "The Barn," or look for shingles hung outside listing the hours they're open. To see works by James Fitzgerald, contact his longtime patron, Anne Hubert. In addition, some of the island's most prestigious artists do not post hours, but still welcome visitors by appointment. Several of these, notably Don Stone and Guy Corriero, give occasional workshops.

SPECIAL SHOPS

Carina. The spiritual successor of the old Island Spa, with booths, books, quality crafted items, wines, and fresh-baked goods and vegetables.

Winter's Work. Open Memorial Day to Labor Day, by the ferry dock. A former fish house filled with work produced by the island's 20 craftspeople: a surprising variety and quality of knitted goods, jewelry, Christmas decorations, etc.

Black Duck. Open Memorial Day to Columbus Day, a gift store hidden behind the general store on Fish Beach, selling imaginative T-shirts, and the like.

THE FOX ISLANDS:

VINALHAVEN AND NORTH HAVEN

The Fox Islands Thoroughfare is a rowable stretch of yacht-filled water that separates Vinalhaven and North Haven, two islands that differ deeply.

Vinalhaven is heavily wooded and marked by granite quarries that include two public swimming holes. Life eddies around the village of Carver's Harbor, home to Maine's largest lobster fleet. In 1880, when granite was being cut on Vinalhaven to build Boston's Museum of Fine Arts and New York's Brooklyn Bridge, 3,380 people were living here on the island, a number now reduced to about 1,200—a mix of descendants of 18th-century settlers and the stonecutters who came here from Sweden, Norway, Finland, and Scotland. In recent years the island has also attracted a number of artists, including Robert Indiana. Summer visitors far outnumber year-round residents, but there is no yacht club or golf course, and even in August, this is still clearly a working island, not an island resort.

By contrast, North Haven is half as big, with just 325 year-round residents. It's rolling and open, spotted with idyllic farmhouses, summer homes for some of the country's wealthiest and most influential families. Pastimes include wagon rides and golf. Many children sail in the same distinctive dinghies their grandparents sailed.

It was British explorer Martin Pring who named the Fox Islands in 1603, ostensibly for the silver foxes he saw on both. A dozen miles out in Penobscot Bay, both islands are still understandably protective of their considerable beauty, especially in view of their unusual—by Maine island standards—accessibility by Maine State Ferry.

Be it said that there is no overnight lodging on North Haven and only 30 or so beds on Vinalhaven for visitors in August. Neither is there an excursion boat, an ATM, a kayaking outfitter, or on-island transport. In-season the hurdles for bringing your car onto these islands can also be high.

Still, for the kind of tourist who loves islands, especially less crowded islands with ample places to walk, Vinalhaven is a real find. And contrary to rumor, it's very possible to cross the Thoroughfare (see *Getting Around*) to spend the day on North Haven, but you may have to wait a little while. These islands dictate their own terms.

Vinalhaven makes sense as a day-trip destination only if it's a nice day and if you take the early boat. Pick up the first map you find and don't be discouraged by the walk into Carver's Harbor, along the island's ugliest quarter mile. Don't miss the Historical Society Museum, and walk or bike out to Lane's Island. This is a great place to be on the Fourth of July.

GUIDANCE

Town offices on **North Haven** (867-4433) and **Vinalhaven** (863-4471/4393) field most questions; the chamber of commerce web site is www.foxislands.net/vhc.

GETTING THERE

In the past couple of years, the nightmare quality of taking a car to Vinalhaven has eased thanks to the addition of a second ferry, but it can still be enough of a hassle in July or August to cancel out the relaxing effect of the island itself. **The Maine State Ferry Service** (in Rockland: 596-2202) has its own system: Each ferry takes a set number of cars and only a handful of these spaces can be reserved (reservations must be made at least 30 days in advance). Cars are taken in order of their position in line. For the morning boats you must be in line the night before. During the summer season, getting off the island can entail lining up a day in advance and then moving your car for every ferry (five times a day). It's $26 round trip for car and driver; $9 per adult and $4 per child; for bicycles, it's $8 per adult, $4 per child.

Penobscot Air Service (596-6211; 1-800-780-6071) will fly you in from Portland or Boston as well as Rockland to either Vinalhaven or North Haven.

GETTING AROUND

Fox Islands Thoroughfare Water Taxi (867-4621/4894). Dock Shields, a former ferry captain based at the J. O. Brown Boatyard on North Haven, offers regular shuttle service between North Haven and Vinalhaven in summer months. There's a phone on the Vinalhaven shore next to the boat landing.

Bicycles. Given the lack of public transport and rental multigear bikes, many visitors bring their own. Be advised, however, that islanders frown on visiting bicyclists because they frequently wheel down the middle of the road, oblivious to local traffic and to the lobster trucks that are as much king of these island roads as lumber trucks are in the North Woods. *Note:* **Day-trippers** to North Haven will find shopping and food within walking distance of the ferry dock, but on Vinalhaven the distances from the ferry to Carver's Harbor and from there to quarries and nature preserves is a bit far on foot. The Tidewater Motel in Carver's Harbor rents clunker bikes.

Tour: Retired fisherman–turned restaurateur–turned tour guide John Morton (863-4315) offers a 1½-hour car tour of the southern end of Vinalhaven for $25.

MEDICAL EMERGENCY

Islands Community Medical Services (863-4341) is based on Atlantic Avenue in Carver's Harbor, Vinalhaven. For the ambulance call 594-5656.

TO SEE

On Vinalhaven

The Victorian-style town of **Carver's Harbor** is picturesque and interesting, its downtown a single street straddling a causeway and narrow land strip between the harbor and Carver's Pond. A boom town dating from the 1880s when Vinalhaven was synonymous with granite, the village is built almost entirely of wood, the reason why many of the best of its golden-era buildings are missing. The strikingly Victorian Star of Hope Lodge, owned by artist Robert Indiana, is the sole survivor of three such amazing buildings that once marked the center of town.

The Vinalhaven Historical Society Museum (863-4410/4318), top of High Street. Open mid-June though early September, daily 11–3. Volunteer staffers Esther Bissell and Roy Heisler maintain one of Maine's most welcoming and extensive community museums. It's housed in the former town hall, which has also served as a theater and skating rink, built in 1838 in Rockland as a Universalist church, brought over in 1878. Displays, including striking photographs, feature the island's granite industry. The first order for Vinalhaven granite, you learn, was shipped to Boston in 1826 to build a jail, but production really skyrocketed after the Civil War when granite was the preferred building material for the country's building boom. On an island map, 40 red pins mark the sites of major quarries, but there are also countless "motions," or backyard pits. Museum displays also depict island life and other industries, like fishing (the Lane-Libby Fisheries Co. was once one of Maine's largest fish-processing companies) and lobstering (in the 1880s the Basin, a large saltwater lake here, was used as a giant holding tank, penning as many as 150,000 lobsters until prices peaked). Knitting horse nets (to keep off flies) in intricate designs was yet another island industry. Check out the nearby **Carver Cemetery.** At the opposite end of town note the **Galamander,** a huge wagon such as those used to carry stone from island quarries to schooners, which stands in the small park at the top of the hill (junction of Main, Chestnut, Carver, and School Streets and Atlantic Avenue).

Brown's Head Lighthouse, now automated, commands the entrance to the thoroughfare from the northern end of Vinalhaven, more than 8 miles from Carver's Harbor.

On North Haven

North Haven Village is of most interest to visitors. While it has no museum or sight-to-see as such, the village itself is charming and several shops, notably North Haven Gift Shop and the Eric Hopkins Gallery (see *Selective Shopping*) are destinations in their own right. **Pulpit Harbor** is the island's other community, a low-key cluster of homes with a general store and the **North Island Historical Museum**, theoretically open Tuesdays in summer months, 9:30–11:30.

TO DO

BICYCLING

See *Getting There* and *Getting Around* on the logistics of bringing/renting/
riding bikes. The truth is that if you take care to keep to the roadside,
both North Haven (with 30 miles of paved road, including a shore loop)
and Vinalhaven (with at least 40) are suited to bicycling. We recommend the **Granite Island Road** out along the **Basin** or following Main
Street the other direction out to Geary's Beach (see *Green Space*). The
North Haven Road is an 8-mile slog up the middle of Vinalhaven but
the rewards are great: **Browns Head Light**, the **Perry Creek Preserve,** and views of North Haven.

GOLF

North Haven Golf Club (867-2061), Waterman Cove, North Haven, is
open to the public, accessible by foot from North Haven Village and
surprisingly visitor friendly (nine holes). Call before coming.

SWIMMING

Lawson's Quarry. From the middle of Carver's Harbor, turn (uphill) at the
Bank Building and continue up and up High Street, past the Historical
Society, and then turn right on the North Haven road for a half mile.
We prefer this public swimming hole to the Booth Quarry.

Booth Quarry. Continue east (uphill) on Main Street 1.5 miles past the
Union Church to the Booth Brothers granite quarry. A town park and
swimming hole.

GREEN SPACE

On Vinalhaven

The Vinalhaven Land Trust (863-2543) maintains most of the preserves
mapped on island handouts. These include:

Lane's Island Preserve, on the southern side of Carver's Harbor (cross
the Indian Creek Bridge and look for the sign on your left). It includes
45 acres of fields, marsh, moor, and beach. This is a great spot to picnic
or to come in the evening. Stroll out along the beach and up into the
meadows facing open ocean, filled with wild roses and beach peas.
Armrust Hill is on the way to Lane's Island, hidden behind the medical center. The first place in which the island's granite was commercially quarried, it remained one of the most active sites on the island for
many decades. Notice the many small pits ("motions") as well as four
major quarries. The main path winds up the hill for a splendid view.

Grimes Park, just west of the ferry terminal, is a 2-acre point of rocky land
with two small beaches. Note the rough granite watering trough once
used by horses and oxen.

Geary's Beach. Turn right off Main Street a bit farther than the Booth
Quarry (see *To Do—Swimming*); just after the Coke Statue of Liberty

Booth Quarry

CHRISTINA TREE

(you'll see), and bear left for this stony beach, its trails and picnic table. The view is off to Isle au Haut, Brimstone, and Matinicus.

Note: This list is just a sampling of possibilities. If you stay on the island for a week, you will not begin to exhaust the variety of hiking possibilities.

LODGING

Fox Island Inn (863-2122), P.O. Box 451, Carver Street, Vinalhaven 04863. Open Memorial Day through September. A restored, century-old town house near the library, just a 10-minute walk from the ferry landing, through the village and up the hill. Gail Reinertsen, a competitive long-distance runner, is a warm and helpful host, knowledgeable about the island and happy to dispense directions to her favorite beauty spots. Several bikes are available to guests. Rooms are nicely decorated, and the living room is well stocked with books. Breakfast is buffet-style, and guests are welcome to use the kitchen to prepare picnics, light meals, and snacks. There are six rooms, shared (immaculate) baths, and one suite (private bath). Doubles are $55–75; there's also a three-room suite; rates include breakfast. To reserve off-season, call Gail at 850-425-5095.

Tidewater Inn (863-4618), Carver's Harbor, Vinalhaven 04863. Open year-round. Phil and Elaine Crossman's outstanding little motel is located on the water in the heart of the village. There are 11 units and one apartment; some have waterside decks, others kitchens, some both. In July and August: $85 double; $95 for waterfront units with kitchens; $69–85 single. The Tidewater also rents bicycles. Off-season: waterfront units from $53 double. Pickup service from ferry available.

Libby House (863-4696; winter, 516-369-9172), Water Street, Vinalhaven 04863. Open July and August. Built in 1869, this handsome, rambling home is furnished with Victorian pieces, including heavily carved beds. The comfortable common rooms are often filled with music; innkeeper Philip Roberts is a music teacher. It's a short walk from here to Lane's Island Preserve. Breakfast is included; $52–100.

Payne Homestead at the Moses Webster House (863-9963), Atlantic Avenue, Vinalhaven 04863, a high-Victorian mansion, is open year-round; $75–80 in-season, less off, but a $10 surcharge for just one night.

COTTAGES

Vinalhaven Rentals (863-2241) specializes in summer rentals. **The Island Group** (863-2554) offers both sales and rentals for both islands.

WHERE TO EAT

On Vinalhaven

The Haven (863-4969), Main Street. Open year-round. In summer for dinner Tuesday through Saturday; call for days and hours off-season. Two dining rooms—an open-beamed room overlooking the water and a smaller streetside café—flank a kitchen. Dinner in the waterside room is elegant and by reservation for sittings at 6 and 8:15; lighter meals are served in the pub-style street side; frequent live music. Liquor served. No smoking.

☞ **Candlepin Lodge** (863-2730), Roberts Cemetery Road. Open from 5 PM daily except Monday, dinner 6–9, Sunday noon–10. Rusty Warren's restaurant is geared to both island and visiting families. This rustic cedar lodge is the island's real community center, a place to come in the evening to eat—either in the booths near the soda fountain and a grill, within earshot of the jukebox and sight of the pool tables (probably the only public pool tables with quilts decorating the wall behind them), or in the more formal (still informal) dining room, where the specialty is reasonably priced seafood, including freshly dug steamers. The attached candlepin bowling alley is another great family amenity.

The Island Restaurant (863-2028), East Main Street. Open daily for breakfast, Monday through Saturday 4:30–10:30 and Sunday 6–10:30; lunch, Monday through Saturday; dinner, Wednesday through Saturday. Pub night, with music and drink specials on Tuesday. An attractive restaurant in a former pharmacy, retaining the ornate woodwork and tin ceilings. Good food, moderately priced, fully licensed.

The Harbor Gawked (863-9365), Main Street, middle of the village. Open daily, early and late, good for chowder, seafood rolls, and baskets of just about anything.

Surfside (863-2767), Harbor Wharf, West Main Street. Donna Webster opens at 4 AM for the lobstermen and technically closes at 10:30 AM. A great harborside breakfast spot with tables on the deck, specials like a zucchini and cream cheese omelet with homefries.

On North Haven

Cooper's Landing, North Haven Village across from the ferry landing. Open seasonally for light fare and ice cream 11–7. Truly great burgers.

Coal Wharf Restaurant (867-4739), down on the water next to Brown's Boatshop, open for dinner daily in July and August, weekends in spring and fall. Call. No credit cards. Good food. Reservations advised.

SELECTIVE SHOPPING

In Carver's Harbor on Vinalhaven

The Paper Store (863-4826) is the nerve center of the island, the place everyone drops by at least once a day. Carlene Michael is as generous about dispensing directions to visitors as she is news to residents. This is also the place to check for current happenings like plays and concerts.

Vinalhaven Press Gallery (863-9320), School Street, features Maine artists.

The Fog Gallery, at Harbor Wharf, features the work of Fox Islands artists.

The Island Gift Shop, West Main Street. Open June until Christmas. Amy Durant's shop, in the front room of her house, is the oldest gift shop on the island: clothespins bags, "stop puffin" signs, buoy key chains, assorted gifts. Amy enjoys people, even if you just stop by to talk.

Vinalhaven Fisherman's Coop, West Main Street, is the place to buy seafood.

Vinalhaven knot-knitting (see Vinalhaven Historical Museum under *To See*) is available at Hidden Treasure on East Main Street in Carver's Harbor and from Stephanie Crossman (863-2176). Years ago we commissioned Crossman to make a curtain that we still treasure.

In North Haven Village

Eric Hopkins Gallery (867-2229/4401). Open June until Labor Day daily 10–6; Sunday 11–4; otherwise by appointment. This gallery is the reason many people come to North Haven. One of Maine's best-known artists, Hopkins is the son of a North Haven fisherman and a graduate of prestigious art schools. The waterside gallery is hung with bold, distinctive paintings ranging from large canvases (selling for megabucks) to small watercolors (we bought a very small one). Most Hopkins paintings are of clouds, deep blue water, and spiky green islands, all seemingly in motion.

North Haven Gift Shop (876-4444). Open Memorial Day to the middle of September, but closed Sunday. Since 1954 June Hopkins (mother of Eric) has been running this classic island gift shop with rooms that meander on and on, filled with pottery, nautical books and accessories, jewelry, much more.

Calderwood Hall Gallery (867-2265). Open Memorial Day to Columbus Day in a weathered building that has served as movie theater and dance hall, featuring paintings by owner Herbert Parsons; also offering an interesting mix of clothing and gifts.

SPECIAL EVENTS

Warm-weather months: **Saturday Flea Market,** 10 AM in the field next to the Galamander, Carver's Harbor, Vinalhaven. **Union Church Baked Bean Supper,** every other Thursday, Vinalhaven.

Year-round: **North Haven Community School Dramatic Presentations** are exceptional. For details, phone 867-2008. For details about **Fox Island Concerts** and other regular occurrences on both islands, consult *The Wind,* a weekly newsletter published on Vinalhaven.

MATINICUS

Home to about 70 hardy souls in winter, most of whom make their living lobstering, Matinicus's population grows to about 200 in summer. A very quiet, unspoiled island, 23 miles at sea on the outer edge of Penobscot Bay. Walking trails thread the meadows and shore and there are two sand beaches, one at each end of the island. **Matinicus Rock** is a protected nesting site for puffins, a lure for birders in June and July.

GETTING THERE

The Maine State Ferry (see "The Fox Islands," above; 624-777) takes 2 hours and 15 minutes to ply between Matinicus and Rockland, several times a month May through October, once a month the rest of the year. The ***Mary and Donna*** (366-3700) takes the same amount of time, runs sporadically June through September ($40 round-trip) and also offers day trips to Matinicus Rock to see the puffins. The flying time via **Penobscot Air Service Ltd.** (596-6211) from Owls Head is 12 minutes, but flights are often canceled because of weather. Check with Tuckanuck Lodge about the island-based water taxi that makes the trip from Rockland in 1 hour.

LODGING

🐾✦ **Tuckanuck Lodge** (366-3830), Box 217, Shag Hollow Road, Matinicus 04851. Open year-round. Pets and well-behaved children welcome. Nantucket islander Bill Hoadley offers five rooms (two shared baths), some with a view of Old Cove and the ocean. $45–80 double, $40–55 single, including breakfast; half rate for children. Lunch and supper are available at the Pirates Galley when it's open; when it's not, guests have kitchen privileges for lunch (bring your own fixings); the lodge offers supper ($12–15, BYOB).

For **cottage rentals:** Write or call the Matinicus Chamber of Commerce (366-3868), Box 212, Matinicus 04851.

Camden/Rockport Area

All I could see from where I stood
Was three long mountains and a wood;
I turned and looked another way,
And saw three islands in a bay.
   —Edna St. Vincent Millay

These opening lines from "Renascence" suggest the view from the top of Mount Battie. Millay's hometown—Camden—lies below the mountain on a narrow, curving shelf between the hills and bay.

Smack on Route 1, Camden is the most popular way station between Kennebunkport or Boothbay Harbor and Bar Harbor. Seemingly half its 19th-century captains' homes are now B&Bs. Shops and restaurants line a photogenic harbor filled with private sailing and motor yachts. It's also a poor man's yacht haven.

Here, in 1935, artist Frank Swift refitted a few former fishing and cargo schooners to carry passengers around the islands in Penobscot Bay. He called the boats windjammers. A half-dozen members of Maine's current windjammer fleet are still based here (the rest are in neighboring ports) and several schooners offer daysails. You can also get out on the water in an excursion boat or a sea kayak.

From the water you can see two aspects of Camden that you can't see from land. The first is the size and extent of the Camden Hills. The second is the size and number of the palatial old waterside "cottages" along Beauchamp Point, the rocky promontory separating Camden from Rockport. Here, as in Bar Harbor, summer residents were wise and powerful enough to preserve the local mountains, seeding the creation of the present 6,500-acre Camden Hills State Park, one of Maine's more spectacular places to hike.

Camden's first resort era coincided with those colorful decades during which steam and sail overlapped. As a stop on the Boston–Bangor steamboat line, Camden acquired a couple of big (now vanished) hotels. In 1900, when Bean's boatyard launched the world's first six-masted schooner, onlookers crowded the neighboring ornate steamboat wharf to watch.

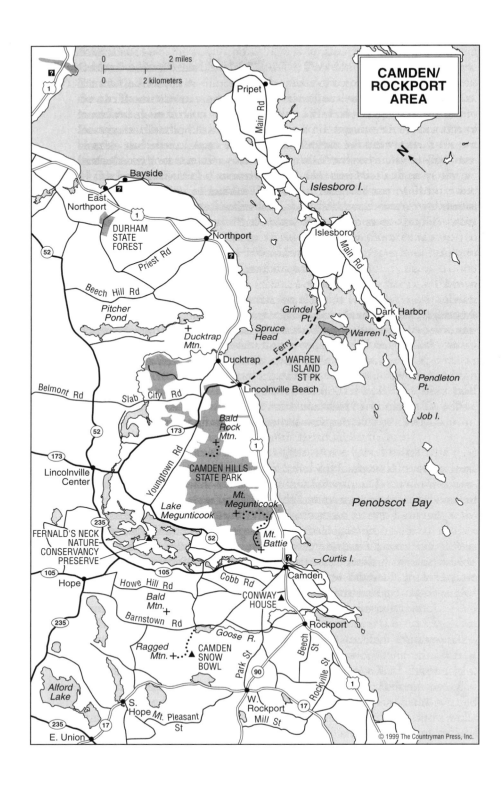

CAMDEN/ ROCKPORT AREA

0   2 miles
0   2 kilometers

Pripet

Bayside

East Northport

Islesboro I.

Northport

Islesboro

DURHAM STATE FOREST

52

Priest Rd

Dark Harbor

Beech Hill Rd

Pitcher Pond

Main Rd

Grindel Pt.

Warren I.

Spruce Head

Ducktrap Mtn.

Ferry

Ducktrap

WARREN ISLAND ST PK

Pendleton Pt.

Belmont Rd

Slab City Rd

Lincolnville Beach

Job I.

52

173

Bald Rock Mtn.

Lincolnville Center

Youngtown Rd

CAMDEN HILLS STATE PARK

Penobscot Bay

173

Lake Megunticook

Mt. Megunticook

FERNALD'S NECK NATURE CONSERVANCY PRESERVE

235

52

Mt. Battie

Curtis I.

105

Camden

105

Hope

Howe Hill Rd

Cobb Rd

CONWAY HOUSE

235

Bald Mtn.

Barnstown Rd

Goose R.

Rockport

Beech St

Ragged Mtn.

CAMDEN SNOW BOWL

Park St

Rockville St

90

Alford Lake

W. Rockport

17

235

S. Hope

Mt. Pleasant St

Mill St

1

17

E. Union

© 1999 The Countryman Press, Inc.

In contrast to Boothbay and Bar Harbor, Camden has always been a year-round town that's never been overdependent on tourism. Camden's early business was, of course, building and sailing ships. By the mid-1800s, a half-dozen mills lined the series of falls on the Megunticook River, just a block or two from the waterfront. The vast wooden Knox Woolen Company—the "Harrington Mill" portrayed in the movie *Peyton Place*—made the felts used by Maine's paper mills to absorb water from paper stock. It operated until 1988, and the complex is now the New England headquarters for a major credit card company, the most recent among dozens of companies to locate in Camden.

Culturally enriched by its sophisticated populace—workaday residents, retirees, and summer people alike—Camden (along with Rockport) offers a bonanza of music, art, and theatrical productions surprising in quality. There are also programs in filmmaking, computer science, and photography, as well as the long-acclaimed summertime Salzedo Harp School.

Ironically, only a small fraction of the thousands of tourists who stream through Camden every summer take the time to discover the extent of its beauty. The tourist tide eddies around the harborside restaurants, shops, and galleries and continues to flow on up Route 1 toward Bar Harbor. Even in August you are likely to find yourself alone atop Mount Battie (accessible by car as well as on foot) or Mount Megunticook (highest point in the Camden Hills), or in the open-sided Vesper Hill Chapel, with its flowers and sea view. Few visitors see, let alone swim in, Megunticook Lake or set foot on the nearby island of Islesboro.

A dozen years ago you could count on your fingers the number of places to stay here, but Camden has since become synonymous with bed & breakfasts, which, at last count, totaled more than 20. A total of some 500 rooms can now be found in hotels, motels, inns, and cottages as well as the B&B's between Camden and neighboring Lincolnville and Rockport.

GUIDANCE

Rockport-Camden-Lincolnville Chamber of Commerce (236-4404; www.camdenme.org), P.O. Box 919, Public Landing, Camden 04843. Open year-round, Monday through Friday 9–5 and Saturday 10–5; also open Sunday noon–4, mid-May through mid-October. You'll find all sorts of helpful brochures here, plus maps of Camden, Rockport, and Lincolnville, along with knowledgeable people to send you in the right direction. The chamber keeps tabs on vacancies during the high season, as well as on what is open off-season and cottages available to rent (a list is ready for requests each year by January). Be sure to secure their booklet, as well as the Camden-Rockport Historical Society's "A Visitor's Tour," which outlines tours of historic districts in Camden and Rockport.

Rockport harbor

GETTING THERE

By air: **Knox County Airport,** at Owls Head, about 10 miles from Camden (see the "Rockland" chapter), offers daily flights to and from Boston. **Bangor International Airport** (see the "Bangor" chapter) and **Portland International Jetport** (see the "Portland" chapter) offer connections to all parts of the country.

By bus: **Concord Trailways** stops on Route 1 south of Camden en route from Bangor to Portland and Boston.

By limo: **Mid Coast Limo** (1-800-937-2424 outside of Maine; 1-800-834-5500 within Maine) makes runs from Portland International Jetport by reservation.

PARKING

Parking is a problem in July and August. In-town parking has a stringently enforced 2-hour limit (just 15 minutes in a few spots, so be sure to read the signs). There are a few lots outside the center of town (try the Camden Marketplace and a lot on Mechanic Street). There's an advantage here to finding lodging within walking distance of the village.

GETTING AROUND

The Camden Shuttle (596-6605) is a good alternative to hassling with parking. The shuttle runs from Megunticook by the Sea Campground (south of town) to Lincolnville Beach. It makes sense to use this service—especially since the ride is only $.50 (free for children under 12 who are accompanied by an adult). In summer, the shuttle runs daily. Schedules are posted at stops, and available at the chamber or on the shuttle upon request.

MEDICAL EMERGENCY
Penobscot Bay Medical Center (596-8000), Route 1, Rockport.

VILLAGES

Rockport's harbor is as picturesque as Camden's, and the tiny village is set high above it. Steps lead down to Marine Park, a departure point in 1816 for 300 casks of lime shipped to Washington, D.C., to help construct the capitol building. A granite sculpture of Andre the Seal recalls the legendary performer who drew crowds every summer in the early and mid-1980s. The village (part of Camden until 1891) includes the restored Rockport Opera House, site of the summer Bay Chamber Concerts, the noted Maine Coast Artists Gallery, the Maine Photographic Workshop program, and a salting of restaurants and shops.

Lincolnville is larger than it looks as you drive through. The village's landmarks—the Lobster Pound Restaurant and Maine State Ferry to Islesboro (see "Mid-Coast Islands")—serve as centerpieces for proliferating shops, restaurants, and B&Bs.

TO SEE

MUSEUMS
Old Conway House Complex (236-2257), Conway Road (off Route 1 just south of Camden). Open during July and August, Tuesday through Friday 10–4; admission $2 for adults, $1 for students, $.50 for children over 6. Administered by the Camden-Rockport Historical Society, this restored, early-18th-century farmhouse has been furnished to represent several periods. The barn holds collections of carriages, sleighs, and early farm tools, and there is a Victorian privy, a blacksmith shop, and an 1820 maple sugar house where sugaring demonstrations are held each spring.

Knox Mill Museum, MBNA offices, Mechanic Street, Camden. Open weekdays 9–5. A sophisticated little museum dramatizes the 125 years of operation of the Knox Woolen Mill. Exhibits include a video, many photographs, and some machinery. The mill was the prime supplier of felts for the endless belts used in paper manufacturing.

SCENIC DRIVE
Drive or, better yet, bicycle (see *To Do—Bicycling*) around **Beauchamp Point.** Begin on Chestnut Street in Camden and follow this peaceful road by the lily pond and on by the herd of belted Galloway cows (black on both ends and white in the middle). Take Calderwood Lane through the woods and by the **Vesper Hill Children's Chapel,** built on the site of a former hotel and banked with flowers, a great spot to get married or simply to sit. Continue along Beauchamp Avenue to Rockport Village to lunch or picnic by the harbor, and return via Union Street to Camden.

OTHER

✒ **Kelmscott Farm** (763-4088), RR 2, Box 365, Lincolnville. Open Tuesday through Sunday 10–5 from May through October, 10–3 November through April. Adults $5, children $3, under 4 free. A delightful farm dedicated to the conservation of rare livestock breeds. Wander through the farm buildings at your leisure, stopping to read the informative signs about the various breeds on stalls and fences. A peaceful, interesting place worth the short drive. Tours, special events and learning programs, gift shop, and exhibits.

TO DO

BICYCLING

✒ **Brown Dog Bikes** (236-6664), 53 Chestnut Street, Camden, across from the YMCA, rents a variety of mountain and road bikes, Kiddie Kart trailers, and accessories, and delivers them to inns and B&Bs. Ask about evening group rides. They also have rental locations in Rockport at the Samoset Resort and at Lincolnville Beach.

Mainely Mountain Bike Tours (785-2703), Union, offers 2- and 3-hour guided mountain bike tours.

Maine Sport Outfitters (236-8797; 1-800-722-0826) rents Specialized Crossroads and Specialized Rockhoppers, as well as bike trailers and car racks for a day or extended periods. Rentals include helmet, lock, and cable.

BOAT EXCURSIONS

(See also *Windjammer Cruises.*)

Yacht charters are offered spring to autumn along the Maine coast. Most charters run for a week, although sometimes it is possible to charter a boat just for a long weekend, with or without crew. For more information, contact **Windward Mark Yacht Charters** (236-4300; 1-800-633-7900 outside Maine). **Bay Island Yacht Charters** (236-2776; 1-800-421-2492) has yachts available for bare-boat skippered or crewed charters out of Rockland as well as other ports the length of Maine's coast. **Blue Seas Adventure Co.** (236-6904) rents a variety of power- and sailboats by the day or longer.

It would be a shame to be in Camden and not spend some time on the water. The **2-hour sailing excursions** are a wonderful way to get a taste of what the harbor has to offer if your time is limited. Remember to bring a jacket, as the air can get chilly once you are offshore, even on a sunny day.

✒ *Appledore* (236-8353), an 86-foot schooner (the largest of the daysailing fleet), has sailed around the world and now offers several trips daily, including sunset cruises.

Surprise (236-4687), a traditional, historic, 57-foot schooner, offers entertaining, informative 2-hour sails. Captain Jack and wife, Barbara Moore, spent seven years cruising between Maine and the Caribbean, educating their four children on board in the process.

Olad and *Northwind* (236-2323), 55- and 75-foot schooners, respectively, offer 2-hour sails.

Shantih II (236-8605; 1-800-599-8605) offers full-day, half-day, and sunset sails out of Rockport for a maximum of six passengers.

Betselma (236-2101), a motor launch, provides 1- and 2-hour sightseeing trips (owner Les Bex was a longtime windjammer captain) around the harbor and nearby coast.

Lively Lady and *Lively Lady Too* (236-6672), traditional lobster boats, take passengers on 2- and 3-hour cruises that can include watching lobster traps being hauled or an island lobster bake and sunset cruise.

🦞 **Maine State Ferry** from Lincolnville Beach to Islesboro (789-5611). At $4.50 round-trip per passenger and $4 per bicycle, this is the bargain of the local boating scene; see Islesboro under "Mid-Coast Islands."

GOLF

Goose River Golf Club (236-8488), Simonton Road, Camden. Nine holes, but you can play through twice using different starting tees. Cart rentals. Clubhouse. Tee times recommended for weekends and holidays.

Samoset Golf Course (594-2511; 1-800-341-1650), Rockport, has 18 holes on a course that *Golf Digest* selected as the seventh most beautiful in the country. Many of the fairways skirt the water, and the views are lovely. There is a new clubhouse with a pro shop, locker rooms, video golf simulator and the Clubhouse Grille. Carts are available.

HIKING

The Camden Hills are far less recognized than Acadia National Park as a hiking haven, but for the average once-or-twice-a-year hiker, they offer ample challenge and some spectacular views. Mount Battie, accessible by a moderate and sometimes steep half-mile trail just off Route 52, is the only peak also accessible by car. The 1-mile Maiden Cliff Trail (park off Route 52, 2.9 miles from Route 1) is favored by locals for its views from the top of 800-foot sheer cliffs overlooking Lake Megunticook; it connects with the 2½-mile Ridge Trail to the summit of Mount Megunticook (1,380 feet). A complete trail map is available from most B&Bs and at Camden Hills State Park (see *Green Space*).

SEA KAYAKING

Ducktrap Sea Kayak Tours (236-8608), Lincolnville Beach, offers 2-hour and half-day guided tours in Penobscot Bay. No experience is necessary, in fact most patrons are first-time kayakers. Group and family tours also available.

Maine Sport Outfitters (236-8797; 1-800-722-0826), on Route 1 just south of Rockport, is a phenomenon rather than merely an outfitter. Be sure to stop. They offer courses in kayaking and canoeing, guided excursions around Camden Harbor and out into Penobscot Bay, and island-based workshops. They also rent kayaks and canoes. Contact them for their catalog of activities.

Mt. Pleasant Canoe and Kayak (785-4309), West Rockport, offers a 2-hour sunset trip on Megunticook Lake as well as guided coastal tours.

SWIMMING

Saltwater swimming from Camden's **Laite Memorial Park and Beach,** upper Bayview Street; at **Lincolnville Beach,** Route 1 north of Camden; and in Rockport at **Walker Park.** Freshwater swimming at Megunticook Lake (**Barret Cove Memorial Park and Beach;** turn left off Route 52 northwest of Camden), where you will also find picnic grounds and a parking area; **Shirttail Beach** on Route 105; and at the **Willis Hodson Park** on the Megunticook River (Molyneaux Road). At the **Camden YMCA** (236-3375), Chestnut Street, visitors can pay a day-use fee that entitles them to swim in the Olympic-sized pool (check hours for family swimming, lap swimming, etc.), use the weight rooms, and play basketball in the gym.

TENNIS

There are two public tennis courts at the **Camden Snow Bowl** on Hosmer's Pond Road. In addition, **Samoset Resort** (594-2511), Rockport, has outdoor courts, as do the Whitehall Inn and the **Rockport Recreation Area.**

WINDJAMMER CRUISES

Windjammer cruises are offered mid-June to mid-October. A half-dozen schooners and a ketch sail from Camden and Rockport on 3- to 6-day cruises through Penobscot Bay. For brochures and sailing schedules, contact the **Maine Windjammers Association** (374-2952; 1-800-807-WIND). (See also *Windjammer Cruises* under *To Do* in the "Rockland" chapter and under "What's Where.")

Angelique (236-8873; 1-800-282-9989), P.O. Box 736, Camden, is a 95-foot ketch that was built expressly for the windjammer trade in 1980. Patterned after 19th-century English fishing vessels, she offers a pleasant deck-level salon and belowdecks showers.

Timberwind (236-0801; 1-800-759-9250), P.O. Box 247, Rockport, was built in Portland in 1931 as a pilot schooner. This pretty, 75-foot vessel was converted to a passenger vessel in 1969. She has an enclosed, hand-held shower on deck. The *Timberwind* is the only windjammer sailing out of Rockport Harbor.

Roseway (236-4449; 1-800-255-4449), Yankee Schooner Cruises, P.O. Box 696, Camden, was built in 1925 as a fishing schooner and later spent 32 years as a pilot vessel, escorting ships in and out of Boston Harbor. She was the last pilot schooner active in the United States. *Roseway* has been a passenger vessel sailing out of Camden since 1975. There are enclosed, hot, freshwater showers on deck.

Lewis R. French (236-2463; 1-800-469-4635), P.O. Box 992 CC, Camden, was launched on the Damariscotta River in 1871. Before becoming a passenger vessel, she carried cargo along the coast. She had three major rebuilds, the most recent in 1976 when she was brought into passenger service. Sixty-five feet long, she accommodates 23 passengers. Hot, freshwater shower on board. Native Maine Captain Dan Pease met his wife, Kathy, when she came aboard for a vacation. Now their sons, Joe and Bill, come along every chance they get. No smoking.

Mary Day (1-800-540-2750 in Maine; 1-800-992-2218 from elsewhere in the US and Canada), Box 798, Camden, was the first schooner built specifically for carrying passengers. She's among the swiftest; Captains Barry King and Jen Martin have extensive sailing experience. Features include a fireplace and parlor organ and hot, freshwater showers on the deck.

Grace Bailey, Mercantile, and **Mistress** (236-2938; 1-800-736-7981), Maine Windjammer Cruises, P.O. Box 617, Camden. For years known as the *Mattie, Grace Bailey* took back her original name following a thorough restoration in 1990. Built in 1882 in New York, she once carried cargo along the Atlantic coast and to the West Indies. She has belowdecks showers. **Mercantile** was built in Maine in 1916 as a shallow-draft coasting schooner; 78 feet long, she has been in the windjammer trade since its beginning in 1942. Each cabin has its own private head, and there are belowdecks showers nearby. **Mistress,** the smallest of the fleet, carries just six passengers. A topsail schooner built along the lines of the old coasting schooners, she is also available for private charter. All three cabins have private heads, but there is no shower on board.

SKIING

  Camden Snow Bowl (236-3438), Hosmer's Pond Road, Camden. With a 950-foot vertical drop, nine runs for beginner through expert, and night skiing, this is a comfortably sized area where everyone seems to know everyone else. Facilities include a base lodge, a rental and repair shop, and a cafeteria.

Camden Hills State Park also marks and maintains some trails for cross-country skiing, and there's a ski hut on Mount Battie (see *Green Space*).

Tanglewood 4-H Camp (789-5868), off Route 1 near Lincolnville Beach. Ungroomed scenic trails. Map and description of trails available at the chamber (see *Guidance*).

SPECIAL LEARNING PROGRAMS

  Camden Yacht Club Sailing Program (236-3014), Bayview Street, provides sailing classes for children and adults, boat owners and non–boat owners, during July and August; among them is an excellent weeklong course just for women. There is also a lecture series open to the public.

Bay Island Sailing School (236-2776; 1-800-421-2492), headquartered in Camden but based at Journey's End Marina in Rockland, an ASA-certified sailing school offering beginner, coastal cruising, and bareboat certification programs ranging from intensive weekend workshops to 5-day hands-on cruises. $395–995.

Maine Photographic Workshops (236-8581), Rockport. A nationally respected, year-round school that offers a choice of 200 programs that vary in length from 1 week to 3 months for every level of skill in photography, cinematography, television production, and related fields. Teachers are established, recognized professionals who come from across the country, as do the students. There is also a gallery with changing exhibitions open to the public. The school provides housing for most of its students and helps to arrange accommodations for others.

Maine Sport Outfitters (236-8797), P.O. Box 956, Rockport. This Route 1 complex is worth a stop whether you are up for adventure sports or not. This place is more than simply a store or kayaking, canoeing, mountain biking center; it has evolved over the years from a fly-fishing and canvas shop into a multitiered store that's a home base for adventure tours. Inquire about a wide variety of local kayaking tours and multiday kayaking workshops geared to all levels of ability, based at its facilities on Gay Island.

Center for Furniture Craftsmanship (594-5611), 25 Mill Street, Rockport. June through October. Hands-on, 1- and 2-week workshops for novice, intermediate, and advanced woodworkers. Twelve-week intensive courses also offered a couple of times a year.

GREEN SPACE

Camden Hills State Park (236-3109), Route 1, Camden. In addition to Mount Battie, this 6,500-acre park includes Mount Megunticook, one of the highest points on the Atlantic seaboard, and a shoreside picnic site. You can drive to the top of Mount Battie on the road that starts at the park entrance, just north of town. Admission through the gate is $2 adults; $.50 ages 6–12; 5 and under free. At the entrance, pick up a "Camden Hills State Park" brochure which outlines 19 trails, with distance and difficulty level. For highlights of this 25-mile network, see *Hiking*. In winter many of the trails are suitable for cross-country skiing, given snow. There are 112 campsites here.

Warren Island State Park, also administered by Camden Hills State Park, is just a stone's throw off the island of Islesboro. There are picnic tables, trails, and tent sites here. Accessibility is the problem: You can arrange to have a private boat carry you over from the mainland, rent your own boat in Camden, or paddle out in a sea kayak (see *Sea Kayaking*). Because of this, the island is seldom used and always peaceful.

Marine Park, Rockport. A nicely landscaped waterside area with sheltered picnic tables. Restored lime kilns and a train caboose are reminders of the era when the town's chief industry was processing and exporting lime.

Merryspring Horticultural Nature Park and Learning Center (236-2239), Camden. A 66-acre preserve with walking trails, an herb garden, a lily garden, a rose garden, raised beds, a demonstration garden, and an arboretum. The preserve is bisected by the Goose River and is accessible by way of Conway Road from Route 1 in Camden. Weekly talks in summer. The organization is dedicated to planting and preserving flowers, shrubs, and trees in this natural setting and to interpreting them through workshops and special events. Donations are encouraged.

Fernald's Neck Nature Conservancy Preserve. Near the junction of Route 52 and the Youngtown Road, 315 acres cover most of a heavily wooded peninsula that juts into Lake Megunticook. A brochure of walk-

ing trails is available at the registration box near
leads to 60-foot cliffs. Trails can be boggy: Wea1

Camden Amphitheatre, Atlantic Avenue, Camde1
summertime plays and concerts and a good plac€
anytime. Tucked behind the library and across th
bor park—a gentle, manicured slope down to the

Curtis Island, in the outer harbor. A small island w
marks the entrance to Camden. It is a public picn
sea-kayaking destination.

LODGING

All listings are Camden 04843 unless otherwise indicated. Rates are for high
season; most have off-season rates as well. *Note:* If you choose one of
the many B&Bs in historic houses on Elm, Main, or High Streets (all
are Route 1), you might want to ask what pains have been taken to
muffle the sound of passing traffic.

Camden Accommodations (1-800-236-1920) is a reservations service representing most places to stay in the Camden area. It also coordinates
rentals for some six dozen cottages and condos.

Camden Bed & Breakfast Association (www.camdeninns.com), P.O. Box
553. The brochure lists 14 members with descriptions of each, and contact information.

RESORT

✐⛶ **Samoset Resort** (594-2511; 1-800-341-1650), 220 Warrenton Street, Rockport 04856. Open year-round, a full-service resort set on 230 oceanside
acres, with 132 rooms and 18 suites, some handicapped accessible, many
with ocean views, all with balconies or patios, private baths, color TVs, and
climate-controlled air-conditioning and heat; 72 time-share units with full
kitchens and washers and dryers are also available for nightly rentals. The
two-bedroom Flume Cottage, perched on a rocky outcropping above the
water, is available by the week in-season and nightly off-season. A scenic,
peaceful spot with many amenities, including an outstanding 18-hole golf
course, indoor golf center, four outdoor tennis courts, a Nautilus-equipped
fitness club, racquetball courts, and indoor and outdoor pools. A clubhouse
for the golf course opened in April 1997, with a pro shop, locker rooms,
indoor golf center with video golf simulator, and the Clubhouse Grille. A
children's program is offered during the summer months and other school
holiday periods. This is a popular meeting and convention site, especially
with the addition of a 7,000-square-foot exhibit hall. The dining room,
Marcel's (see *Dining Out*), is generally rated among the best on the Mid
Coast. The adjacent Breakwater Cafe has a large fireplace and floor-to-
ceiling windows overlooking the water. $135–315 in summer; $99–175 in
winter. Time-share units are $290–345 (one bedroom), $335–410 (two
bedrooms) in summer, less by the week and off-season. Ask about packages.

e Belmont (236-8053; 1-800-238-8053; foodeez@midcoast.com), 6
Belmont Avenue. Open mid-May through October. An 1890s
Edwardian house with a wraparound veranda. The four guest rooms
and two suites are each attentively furnished with careful details. All
have private baths. Our favorite is the third-floor room with the canopy
bed. In the living room, accented by Oriental rugs on shining wood
floors, guests are invited to relax in comfortable wing chairs and chat
about the day's adventures or enjoy a cocktail from the bar. Chef Gerald
Clare (one of the owners) offers imaginative "New American" fare (see
Dining Out) in an inviting dining room that's recognized as one of the
best on the Maine coast. A full country breakfast—egg dishes or perhaps blueberry pancakes—is included in lodging, and breakfast in bed
is available. $290–390 in high season for 2 nights, including breakfast
both mornings, and one dinner for two. Single-night stays with dinner
are accepted when space is available.

✆& **Whitehall Inn** (236-3391, 1-800-789-6565), 52 High Street (Route 1). Open
Memorial Day through Columbus Day weekend. There's an air of easy
elegance and comfort to this rambling inn on Route 1, east of the village.
The Dewing family has owned and operated the inn for more than 25
years. The large, low-beamed lobby and adjoining parlors are fitted with
Oriental rugs and sofas, games, and puzzles. The Millay Room, with its
vintage 1904 Steinway, looks much the way it did on the summer evening
in 1909 when a local girl, Edna St. Vincent Millay, read a poem,
"Renascence," to assembled guests, one of whom was so impressed that
she undertook to educate the young woman at Vassar. The inn offers 40
guest rooms in the main inn, 5 more in both the Maine House and the
Wicker House across Route 1. These rooms are simpler than most to be
found in neighboring B&Bs, but each has its appeal. Most have private
baths. All have the kind of heavy, old phones your children have never
seen. There is a tennis court and shuffleboard, and it's just a short walk
to the Salzedo Harp Colony (summer concerts) and a "sneaker" beach
(wear shoes because of the rocks) on Camden's outer harbor. Families
are welcome but asked to dine early. Doubles are $135–175 MAP, $105–
145 B&B July through mid-October; off-season rates Memorial Day
through June. Add 15 percent service for MAP, 10 percent for B&B.

♞🐾✆**The Blue Harbor House** (236-3196; 1-800-248-3196; balidog@
midcoast.com), 67 Elm Street. Open year-round. This place has the feel
of a friendly B&B, but they serve dinner to guests as well as breakfast on
the spacious sunporch. We haven't sampled dinner, but guests have
raved about it in the logbook. The dinners are multicourse ($35 per
person) and might include entrées like beef Wellington or stuffed rack
of lamb, or the ever popular Down East lobster dinner. Breakfast is just
as delectable, and might be a lobster quiche, Dutch babies (custard-type
pancakes with fresh fruit, Maine maple syrup, almonds, and powdered
sugar), or blueberry pancakes with blueberry butter. The eight guest

rooms vary, pleasantly decorated with country antiques, stenciling, and handmade quilts; all have private baths and telephones, some have air-conditioning and/or TV with VCR. The two carriage house suites are warm and cozy, with whirlpool tubs. Children and pets can be accommodated in one room with advance reservations. Bicycles are available to guests. Hosts Jody Schmoll and Dennis Hayden are warm, fun to talk to, and eager to help. Doubles $85–145. Call for "quiet season" packages.

Youngtown Inn (763-4290; 1-800-291-8438; info@youngtowninn.com), Route 52 and Youngtown Road, Lincolnville 04849. This 1810 farmhouse is 4 miles from Camden Harbor at the end of Megunticook Lake, near Lincolnville Center. Five rooms plus a suite are furnished in a simple, dainty, country style. All rooms have private decks and air-conditioning. The larger upstairs rooms also offer TVs with VCRs. The suite has a bedroom and a sitting area with a fireplace. The dining room (see *Dining Out*) and pub downstairs have a genuinely hospitable atmosphere, complete with pumpkin-pine floors, beamed ceilings, and fireplaces. $99–140 double occupancy in summer, $85–120 in winter includes a full country breakfast: maybe fresh fruit, muffins, or croissants, French toast stuffed with apples and walnuts, or an egg dish. Ask about packages.

Hartstone Inn (236-4259; hrtstone@midcoast.com), 41 Elm Street. Open year-round. Mary Jo and Michael Salmon each worked in the hotel industry for more than 10 years before buying this inn in 1998. Their experience shows in the attention to detail, both in the decor of the inn and the quality of the dinner offered to guests. Guest rooms are pretty, some with fireplaces and lace canopy beds. The new porch is a perfect spot for dinner, an elegant affair served by candlelight. Our meal began with crusty olive bread drizzled in olive oil, followed by pork tenderloin with a mango salsa, a salad of fresh Maine greens, then the main course, a delicious pan-seared halibut with lobster and mussels, couscous, and fresh vegetables. The chocolate amaretto soufflé was a perfect end to a delightful meal. The presentation of the food and the friendly conversation from the hosts left us feeling spoiled and very content. $85–135 double with breakfast in-season. Dinner is $35 prix fixe per person.

BED & BREAKFASTS

The Maine Stay (236-9636), 22 High Street (Route 1). Open year-round. This Greek Revival house is one of the oldest in Camden's High Street Historic District, and innkeepers Peter Smith, his wife Donny, and her twin sister, Diana Robson, take on a new project each year to improve upon it. The most extensive changes ever were taking place in 1998, as they built new owners' quarters in the barn and renovated the inn space accordingly. When the project is complete, all eight rooms (two are suites) will offer private baths. The lower-level carriage house room is especially appealing, with well-stocked, built-in bookshelves, a woodstove, and French doors opening onto a private patio with lawn and woods beyond (the 2-acre property includes an extensive, well-tended wildflower garden and benches). The Clark Suite features a queen-sized brass bed with private bath and a sitting room with a gas fireplace overlooking historic High Street. The two parlors (with fireplaces), the TV den, and the dining room are all salted with interesting furnishings and curiosities collected during Peter's wide-ranging naval career. The innkeepers are warm and unusually helpful, offering a personalized area map to each guest, as well as computer printouts of things to do, day trips, and more. A hot breakfast is served at the formal dining room table; afternoon tea is also included in the $100–145 (less off-season) double room rate. Needlepointers should inquire about the March Stitch-Inn weekend.

The Hawthorn (236-8842; hawthorn@midcoast.com), 9 High Street (Route 1). Open year-round. Nick and Patty Wharton strive to operate an elegant, comfortable inn, and they are doing a beautiful job. Their attention to detail is evident, from the bottled water and cookies in the rooms to the hand-painted napkin rings at breakfast. Two elegant parlors available for quiet relaxation. Each guest room has a theme to its decor; some have views of the harbor. The four carriage house rooms are more modern, with Jacuzzis, TVs and VCRs, fireplaces, and private decks. $80–140 includes a delicious full breakfast, served on the porch overlooking the harbor in nice weather.

Norumbega (236-4646), 61 High Street (Route 1). Open year-round. With one of the most imposing facades of any B&B anywhere, this turreted stone "castle" has long been a landmark just north of Camden. Inside, the ornate staircase with fireplace and love seat on the landing, formal parlor with fireplace, and dining room capture all the opulence of the Victorian era. Eleven guest rooms and two suites, some with fireplaces and all with king-sized beds and private baths. Rooms are located both upstairs and downstairs, the latter with private terrace entrances. We are intrigued by the Library Suite, two rooms with a loft balcony full of books, which was the original castle library. There is a billiard room open to guests until 9 PM. Doubles are $155–450 (penthouse) in high season, including full breakfast and afternoon wine and cheese reception. Two-night minimum on weekends. Inquire about special Murder Mystery weekends.

Windward House (236-9656; bnb@windwardhouse.com), 6 High Street (Route 1). Open year-round. Tim and Sandy Laplante continually upgrade the rooms in this handsome Greek Revival clapboard home surrounded by lawn and gardens. Each of the eight welcoming guest rooms have private baths and are carefully furnished with antiques and many little touches. The airy Garden Room is delightful, with its Vermont Castings gas stove, skylights, and gardening decor. The Carriage Room is beautiful, with blue and white decor, pine-board floors, a gas stove, queen canopy bed, claw-foot tub, great window seat, private entrance, and private parking. The common rooms and back porch are comfortable and inviting, and the game room is stocked with a wide variety of board and card games. Coffee and tea are available any time, and light refreshments are offered upon check-in. Doubles $105–175, including a delicious gourmet breakfast served in the sunny dining room.

✐ **The Blackberry Inn** (236-6060; 1-800-388-6000; blkberry@midcoast.com), 82 Elm Street. Open year-round. New owners Cindy and Jim Ostrowski had only been at the inn one week when we dropped in, but the changes they have planned were already apparent. The common rooms are comfortable, relaxing places guests will really want to use. Small changes—an Amish quilt on one bed, new curtains—have been made in the 10 guest rooms, with larger changes planned for the off-season. All rooms have private baths; some are air-conditioned and others feature king-sized beds, whirlpool baths, TV, wood-burning fireplaces, and ceiling fans. Children are welcome, and the carriage house is a good place for families. The garden rooms are private and cozy, with fireplaces and whirlpool baths. Rates are $95–155 in high season, with a full breakfast served in the dining room or alfresco in the courtyard included.

Inn at Ocean's Edge (236-0945; ray@innatoceansedge.com), P.O. Box 704. Ray and Marie Donner, former owners of The Victorian, built this literally ocean's-edge B&B from scratch in 1998. From the outside it resembles a shingled Maine summer mansion. Designed inside with plenty of common space and windows on the water, it offers 15 guest rooms, each equipped with all the bells and whistles (Jacuzzi, gas fireplace, TV, VCR, stereo, etc.), and facilities include an exercise room. Steps lead down to a private "shingle" beach. The property is seven landscaped acres in all, accessible via a private drive off Route 1, a couple miles north of the Camden line in Lincolnville. Needless to say, weddings are a specialty. Mid-June to mid-October, $220–250 includes a full breakfast; off-season $150.

The Inn at Sunrise Point (236-7716; 1-800-435-6278), P.O. Box 1344, Lincolnville 04849. Open May through October. Set on a 4-acre waterfront estate just over the town line in Lincolnville, this small, luxurious B&B is owned by Jerry Levitin, author of the *Country Inns and Back Roads* guidebooks. Levitin himself tends to be on the road in summer, but an affable innkeeper is on hand to welcome guests. The location is a definite asset here. The cottages have large picture windows with an incredible view, fireplaces, and Jacuzzis. The three rooms in the main house have fireplaces and water views, and the sound of the waves will lull you to sleep. All accommodations have queen- or king-sized beds, phones, and color TVs with VCRs; plush robes are also provided in each bath. Common rooms include a glass conservatory that lets the sun shine in, plus a snug, wood-paneled library with fireplace that's just right for cooler days. Rooms are $160–350, with full breakfast and afternoon appetizers included.

⛴ **The Spouter Inn** (789-5171), Route 1, P.O. Box 270, Lincolnville Beach 04849. Open year-round. Just across the road from the beach and the ferry to Islesboro, this unpretentious early-1800s home invites guests to enjoy the view from a rocker on the front porch or to relax by the fire in the attractive library and parlor. There are seven rooms, named for naval ranks and increasing in luxury accordingly. The Admiral's Quarters on the third floor has ocean and mountain views, a deck, fireplace, and Jacuzzi. All but two rooms have wood-burning fireplaces, and three also have Jacuzzis. Doubles $85–175 depending on room and season. Full breakfast included. Two-night minimum during high season.

The Victorian by the Sea (236-3785; 1-800-382-9817; victbb@midcoast.com), Lincolnville Beach 04849. Open year-round. Ginny and Greg Ciraldo are the new owners of this quiet, romantic spot overlooking the water, away from the bustle of Route 1. As the name suggests, decor is Victorian, but subtle. The spacious 1800s house offers seven guest rooms, all with queen beds and private baths; most have fireplaces. The third-floor suite has a bathroom sink set into an antique library table, a claw-foot tub, sitting area, and loft with twin beds. The newest room is decorated in bright blues and yellows, white wicker, and has a claw-foot tub. The $135–205 rate includes full breakfast and afternoon sweets.

A Little Dream (236-8742), 66 High Street (Route 1). Open year-round. If you like ruffles and furbelows, you will love this Victorian confection: all ribbons and collectibles, with a touch of English country. There are tiny details everywhere, with each room's decor telling a little story. We especially like the first-floor room with a turret sitting area and working fireplace. A full breakfast, served in the dining room, may include a smoked-salmon or an apple-Brie omelet, banana-pecan waffles, or lemon-ricotta soufflé pancakes. Doubles $95–185; includes breakfast and an afternoon snack. Two-night minimum on holiday weekends.

OTHER LODGING
All listings are in Camden 04843 unless otherwise indicated.

🐾 **High Tide Inn** (236-3724, 1-800-778-7068 outside of Maine), Route 1. Open May through October. Set far enough back from Route 1 to preclude traffic noise, this friendly complex appeals to singles and couples (who tend to choose one of the five rooms in the inn) and families, who opt for one of the six cottages or 19 motel units (some with connecting, separate sleeping rooms). Most accommodations have views. The complex is set on 7 quiet acres—formerly a private estate—of landscaped grounds and meadow that slope to the water, where there's more than 250 feet of private beach. Home-baked continental breakfast is served on the glass-enclosed porch; the living room also has ample windows with views of the bay. The porch, living room, and bar all have working fireplaces. Rates: $60–175 in-season, less May through late June; 2-night minimum weekends in July and August and over holidays.

🏅 **The Owl and Turtle Harbor View Guest Rooms** (236-9014), P.O. Box 1265, 8 Bayview Street. Open year-round. In the middle of all the harbor hubbub but high above it, with the best harbor view in town. Just three rooms (limit of two people per room), and repeat business is heavy, so book early for the summer months. Each room has air-conditioning, TV, telephone, and private bath; two face directly over the water. Private parking is provided. Downstairs is one of the state's best bookstores. No smoking; no pets. Rates include continental breakfast brought to the room. $90–105 plus tax; less off-season.

✐ **Lord Camden Inn** (236-4325; 1-800-336-4325), 24 Main Street. Open year-round. In a restored, 1893 brick Masonic hall, the "inn" occupies several floors above a row of Main Street shops. Restored antique furnishings, including some canopy beds, blend with modern amenities: color cable TV, private baths, in-room telephones, and elevator service. Most rooms have two double beds and balconies overlooking the town and harbor or the river and hills beyond; there are also three luxury suites on the first floor. Rates include a full continental breakfast buffet with fresh muffins, juices, cereals, breads, and coffee. $128–175, depending on the view, in summer; $88–118 off-season. Children 16 and younger stay free.

🐾✐ **Quiet Cottages and Bayview Cottages** (236-8608), RR 3, Box 3315, Lincolnville Beach 04849. Five cottages just outside of Camden tucked behind Ducktrap Sea Kayak, among trees, with a nature trail leading to a secluded rocky beach. Great for families, and the rates are extremely reasonable at $39–69 per night in-season.

WHERE TO EAT

DINING OUT

♿ **Marcel's** (594-0774), Rockport (at the Samoset Resort). Open every day year-round for breakfast, dinner, and Sunday brunch. The fare merits the formality it receives; the wait staff wear tuxedos, and jackets are suggested for gentlemen at dinner. Specialties include tableside service of Caesar salad, steak Diane, rack of lamb for two or châteaubriand for two. Extensive selection of beer and wine. The children's menu ($5.25–6) features fish-and-chips and fettuccine Alfredo prepared tableside among its choices. There's piano music at dinner and entertainment in the adjacent Breakwater Cafe. $14.50–28. Reservations suggested.

✐ **The Sail Loft** (236-2330), Rockport. Open year-round for lunch and dinner daily and Sunday brunch. A family-owned restaurant since 1962, this is a favorite of residents and visitors alike. The Sail Loft overlooks Rockport Harbor and the activities of the boatyard below (owned by the same family). The lunch menu might include scallop Thai pasta, or crabmeat and lobster quiche. At dinner, fresh seafood selections are the specialty, and one option is a shore dinner of clam chowder, steamed clams or mussels, and a steamed lobster. Small, melt-in-your-mouth blueberry muffins come with every meal. Children's menu ($3.50–8) includes green eggs and ham. Dinner entrées run $5.95–38.50 (the shore dinner with a 2-pound lobster).

Youngtown Inn (763-4290; 1-800-298-8438 outside of Maine), corner of Route 52 and Youngtown Road, Lincolnville. Open for dinner 6–9, daily June 15 through October 15; closed Sunday and Monday the rest of the year. Four miles from Camden, this inn's (see *Inns*) dining rooms are warmed by fireplaces on cool evenings. The French chef and owner, Manuel Mercier, serves up a wide variety of French cuisine, which might include lobster ravioli, rack of lamb, and salmon *en croute*. There is also a small, cozy lounge. $12–23 or a three-course prix fixe menu for $32.

🏵 **Chez Michel** (789-5600), Lincolnville Beach (across the road from the beach). Open for dinner Tuesday through Saturday, lunch and dinner on Sunday. This pleasant restaurant serves exceptional food with a French flair. Moderately priced entrées include bouillabaisse, beef bourguignon, and lamb kabobs. Outside dining in-season. A well-kept secret among loyal regulars. Dinner entrées run $8.75–14.95.

Frogwater Cafe (236-8998), 31 Elm Street, Camden. Open for dinner at 5 PM daily June through September; closed Sunday the rest of the year. Highly recommended by local innkeepers. Entrées include garlic ziti, pesto-crusted lamb, and vegetable strudel over saffron couscous. Breads and desserts are made fresh by the pasty chef. The dessert menu changes every 2 or 3 weeks, and may include chocolate cake baked to order, served warm. $10–20.

Rathbone's (236-3272) 21 Bayview Street. Open Tuesday through Sunday 11 AM–10 PM (bar stays open until 1 AM). This location has seen a number of restaurants in recent years, but the newest one is among the favorites of local innkeepers. Menu choices in this elegant setting include fresh seafood and beef. $9–16.

Cork-Bistro, Wine Café & Gallery (230-0533), 37 Bayview Street (second floor), Camden. Started as a wine and espresso café, this has evolved into a gourmet dining spot serving dinner Tuesday through Saturday 5–9. The atmosphere continues to be warm and relaxing. The menu changes nightly, with specialties like châteaubraind with béarnaise sauce, herbed chicken breast, or Atlantic salmon poached in white wine. Dozens of wines are offered by the glass, even more by the bottle. Desserts might include cannoli and chocolate truffle cake. $12–22. Reservations suggested.

The Belmont (236-8053; 1-800-238-8053), 6 Belmont Avenue, Camden. While chef Gerald Clare has received great reviews, we have had recent complaints. Entrées ($14–28) might include salmon, crisply seared and served in lime-scented broth; desserts are around $6. Reservations recommended.

EATING OUT

In Camden

✎ **Cappy's Chowder House** (236-2254), Main Street. Open year-round: 8 AM–midnight from May to October; call for winter hours. An extremely popular pub—they claim that "sooner or later, everyone shows up at Cappy's," and it's true. Good food with reasonable price tags: eggs, granola, treats from the on-premises bakery for breakfast; croissant sandwiches, burgers, full meals for lunch; seafood entrées, special pasta dishes, meat dishes for dinner. The seafood stew with Maine kielbasa is a big hit and the chowder has been written up in *Gourmet*. Upstairs in the Crow's Nest (open in the summertime only), you will find a quieter setting, a harbor view, and the same menu. Kids get their own menu with selections served in a souvenir carrying box; a place mat with puzzles, crayons for coloring, and sometimes even balloons are provided. This is also a good bet if you're in a hurry and just want a chowder and beer at the bar. Bakery, coffeehouse, and company store downstairs.

The Waterfront (236-3747), Bayview Street. Terrific waterfront dining where you can watch the activity in the harbor. It fills up fast, and they don't take reservations, so be prepared to wait.

✒ **Sea Dog Brewing Co.** (236-6863), 43 Mechanic Street. Housed in the former Knox mill with views of the waterfall; a large, cheerful, family-run brew pub decorated with windjammer and other nautical paraphernalia, featuring a large, moderately priced menu and generous portions. Though there are many choices, your best bet here is the pub food; fish-and-chips, burgers, and the like. The specialty brews are lagers and ales with a half-dozen staples and several monthly specials.

✒ᛣ **Village Restaurant** (236-3232), Main Street. Open year-round for lunch and dinner, daily from July through October, closed Tuesday the rest of the year. Family owned for more than 40 years, this is long a favorite with locals. Emphasis on broiled and sautéed seafood, home-baked desserts. Children's menu. The two dining rooms overlook Camden Harbor.

✒ **Gilbert's Public House** (236-4320), Bayview Street. Tucked underneath the shops along Bayview Street (you enter through a side door just off the road), this is a good place for a beer and a sandwich, snacks or light meals for the kids, or a simple supper before the evening's activities. There's an international flavor to the "pub food" offered: Mediterranean shrimp salad, wurst platter, egg rolls, and nachos are among the favorites. There's also a frozen drink machine here, plus frothy and colorful daiquiris, margaritas, and the like. Live music for dancing in the evening.

✒ᛣ **Fitzpatrick's Cafe** (236-6011), Bayview Landing, Bayview Street. Open year-round for breakfast, lunch, and dinner. Fitzi's is easy to miss as you walk to the public landing. But it's a find: a wide variety of sandwiches and salads plus daily specials. You order at the counter, and they call you by name when it's time to pick up your food. Popular with locals. Nonsmoking facility with outside patio for summertime dining.

✒ᛣ **Camden Deli** (236-8343), 37 Main Street. All three meals served daily. Over 35 sandwich choices, combining all of the regular deli meats and cheeses, as well as some less-expected choices, like chicken broccoli salad or hummus. Large selection of homemade soups, salads, and desserts also. The back room overlooks the waterfall in downtown Camden.

In Rockport

✒ **The Helm** (236-4337), Route 1 (1.5 miles south of Camden). Open for lunch and dinner April to late October; closed Monday. There's a French accent to the menu, with such dishes as coquilles Saint-Jacques and bouillabaisse, plus Maine shore dinners. The menu offers about 50 entrées. One dining room overlooks the Goose River. Children's menu. At the take-out window you can order real onion soup, fresh rabbit paté, among other treats, plus delicious crabmeat rolls and sandwiches on French bread.

Rockport Corner Shop (236-8361). Open daily year-round for breakfast and lunch. Regulars greet each other warmly at this spot in the heart of the village, but newcomers are made to feel welcome, too. Help yourself to coffee. An exceptional find with almost no decor but plenty of atmosphere. Fresh coffeecakes are baked each morning; all salads are made with garden-grown vegetables. Breakfast specialties include eggs Benedict and Swedish pancakes; lunch offers pocket sandwiches, lobster and crabmeat rolls, and daily specials. No liquor. Very reasonable prices.

Miss Plum's (596-6946), Route 1. Open year-round, for all three meals from April through October; breakfast and lunch only from November to March. Painted deep plum, this is a real, old-fashioned ice cream parlor with all flavors made on the premises. There are homemade cones and edible dishes and nostalgic treats such as egg creams and extra-thick frappes. The menu includes hash-and-eggs and omelets at breakfast, a variety of sandwiches at lunch, and several choices like meat loaf and gravy or chicken potpie available at lunch or dinner.

LOBSTER POUNDS

Lobster Pound Restaurant (789-5550), Route 1, Lincolnville Beach. Open every day for lunch and dinner, the first Sunday in May through Columbus Day. Also serves breakfast from July 4 through Labor Day. This is a mecca for lobster lovers—some people plan their trips around a meal here. Features lobster, steamed or baked, also clams, other fresh seafood, roast turkey, ham, steaks, and chicken. This is a family-style restaurant that seats 260 inside and has picnic tables near a sandy beach and take-out window. Always popular (always crowded).

Captain Andy's (236-2312), Upper Washington Street, Route 105, Camden. Call and order your lobsters with all the fixings, and they'll be delivered right to you at the harbor park or town landing for a delicious picnic.

TAKEOUT

The Market Basket (236-4371), Routes 1 and 90, Rockport. Open daily, 7:30 AM to 6:30 PM Monday through Friday, 9 AM to 6:30 PM weekends. Under new ownership, this specialty-food store still offers a wide variety of creative salads, delicious French bread, soups, and sandwich specials for take out, as well as catering services.

Scott's Place (236-8751), Elm Street, Camden. For 25 years, this tiny building in the parking lot of a small shopping center has served hundreds of toasted crabmeat and lobster rolls, chicken sandwiches, burgers, veggie burgers, hot dogs, and chips. Prices are among the best around: $1 for a hot dog, under $6 for a lobster roll. This is one of several small take-out buildings around town, but it's the only one open year-round.

Also see The Helm under *Eating Out* and Captain Andy's under *Lobster Pounds*.

ENTERTAINMENT

Bay Chamber Concerts (236-2823), Rockport Opera House, Rockport. Thursday- and Friday-evening concerts during July and August (some concerts off-season also) in this beautifully restored opera house with its gilded interior. Outstanding chamber music presented for more than 30 years. Summer concerts are preceded by free lectures, and there are postconcert receptions at the Maine Coast Artists Gallery on Thursdays, and the Opera House on Fridays.

Camden Civic Theatre (236-2281), Camden Opera House, P.O. Box 362, Main Street, Camden. A variety of theatrical performances are presented in this restored, second-floor theater with plum seats and cream-and-gold walls. Tickets are reasonably priced.

Camerata Singers (Sandra Jerome, director: 236-8704). This award-winning, 15-member, a cappella singing group presents a summer series in July and a Twelfth Night concert in January. Performances are given in Camden, Belfast, and Waldoboro.

Maine Coast Artists (236-2875; see *Art Galleries*) sponsors a series of lectures and live performances June through September.

Bayview Street Cinema (236-8722), 10 Bayview Street, Camden. Showings daily. A mixed bag of old favorites, foreign and art films, and current movies.

SELECTIVE SHOPPING

ANTIQUES
At the chamber of commerce (see *Guidance*), pick up the leaflet guide to antiques shops scattered among Camden, Rockport, and Lincolnville.

ART GALLERIES
Maine Coast Artists Gallery (236-2875), 162 Russell Avenue, Rockport. Major exhibitions April through October; open Monday through Saturday 10–5; Sunday noon–5. Ongoing special exhibits off-season; call for details. $2 admission. A late-19th-century livery stable, then a firehouse, then the town hall, and, since 1968, one of Maine's outstanding art centers. Showcasing contemporary Maine art, the gallery sponsors several shows each season, an art auction, a crafts show, gallery talks, and an evening lecture series.

Maine's Massachusetts House Galleries (789-5705), Route 1, Lincolnville (2 miles north of Lincolnville Beach). Open year-round Monday through Saturday 9–5; Sunday in summer and fall, noon–5. A large barn gallery that's been a landmark since 1949, exhibiting works by Maine artists: oils, watercolors, and sculpture.

Art of the Sea (236-3939), 12 Bayview Street, Camden. Full- and half-rigged ship models, prints, scrimshaw, nautical jewelery, and more.

Shopping in Camden

Bay View Gallery (236-4534), Bayview Street, Camden. One of the largest galleries in the Mid Coast area. Original paintings and sculptures by contemporary Maine artists plus several thousand posters and prints. Expert custom framing, too.

A Small Wonder Gallery (236-6005), Commercial Street (across from the Camden Chamber of Commerce), Camden. A small gallery with well-chosen, limited-edition graphics, watercolors, hand-painted tiles, porcelain, and original sculpture.

ARTISANS

Anne Kilham Designs (236-0962), 165 Russell Avenue, Rockport. Anne Kilham's distinctive designs on postcards, note cards, and prints are now distributed throughout the country. She is frequently here in her studio and in the shop that sells her watercolors and oils, as well as paper products, place mats, and more.

Windsor Chairmakers (789-5188), Route 1, Lincolnville Beach. Filling two floors of an old farmhouse, the inviting display encompasses not only Windsor chairs but also tables, highboys, and four-poster beds, all offered in a selection of finishes including "distressed" (instant antique). The owner welcomes commissions—he's always ready to make a few sketches as you describe your ideas—and enjoys chatting with visitors and showing them around the workshop.

Brass Foundry (236-3200), Park Street, West Rockport (diagonally across from Mystic Woodworks). Custom metal castings in bronze and aluminum. Also handblown glass vases, bowls, and goblets.

James Lea (236-3632), 9 West Street, Rockport. Showroom is open by appointment Monday through Friday. Jim Lea is a third-generation craftsman fashioning museum-quality furniture reproductions using antique tools as well as more modern devices; all work is done on commission.

BOOKSTORES

ABCDef Books (236-3903), 23 Bayview Street, Camden. Open daily except Sunday from July 4 through Labor Day; also closed Monday April through December; closed January through March. A Camden literary landmark: an unusually extensive and organized collection of rare and used books featuring maritime, art, New England, and history titles.

Down East (594-9544), Route 1, Rockport. The headquarters for Down East Enterprises (publishers of *Down East, Fly Rod & Reel, Fly Tackle Dealer,* and *Shooting Sportsman* magazines, as well as a line of New England books) is a fine old mansion that includes a book and gift shop.

✐ **The Owl and Turtle Bookshop,** Bayview Street, Camden. One of Maine's best bookstores. Six rooms full of books, including special ones devoted to arts and crafts, boats, sports, and young adults and children. Special orders and searches for out-of-print books. Great for browsing.

SPECIAL SHOPS

All shops are in Camden and open year-round unless otherwise indicated.

✐ **Camden 5 & 10.** The Camden Store. "Yes you can buy underwear in downtown Camden!" is the slogan of this huge old five-and-dime on Mechanic Street, just off Main.

Unique 1, Bayview Street. Woolen items made from Maine wool, designed and hand loomed locally. Also some pottery.

Once a Tree, Bayview Street. Wooden crafts including beautiful clocks, kitchen utensils, desk sets; a large game and toy section.

✐ **The Smiling Cow,** Main Street. Seasonal. Three generations ago, a mother and five children converted this stable into a classic gift shop, one with unusual warmth and scope. Customers help themselves to coffee on the back porch overlooking a waterfall and the harbor.

Ducktrap Bay Trading Company, Bayview Street. Decoys and wildlife art. Many of these really special pieces have earned awards for their creators. There are also some less expensive carvings, plus jewelry.

Etienne Fine Jewelry, Main Street. Gallery of designer jewelry in 14- and 18-carat gold; contemporary and unusual pieces made on the premises.

L. E. Leonard, 67 Pascal Avenue, Rockport. An old general store with a fine selection of antique and contemporary furnishings from Indonesia and India; pieces range from jewelry to carved beds.

Danica Candleworks (236-3060), Route 90, West Rockport. In a striking building of Scandinavian design, a candle factory and shop.

SPECIAL EVENTS

Late June: **Down East Jazz Festival,** Camden Opera House.

Late July: **Annual Open House and Garden Day,** sponsored by the Camden Garden Club. Very popular tour of homes and gardens in Camden and Rockport held every year for five decades. **Arts and Crafts**

Show, Camden Amphitheatre *(third Saturday and Sunday in July).*

Early August: **Maine Coast Artists Annual Art Auction,** Maine's largest exhibit and auction of quality, contemporary Maine art.

Late August: **Union Fair and Blueberry Festival,** Union Fairgrounds (see "Rockland/Thomaston Area").

Labor Day weekend: **Windjammer Weekend,** Camden Harbor—a celebration of the windjammer industry.

First weekend in October: **Fall Festival of Arts and Crafts,** Camden Amphitheatre—75 artisans displaying work for sale.

First weekend in December: **Christmas by the Sea**—tree lighting, Santa's arrival, caroling, holiday house tour, refreshments in shops, Christmas Tree Jubilee at the Samoset Resort.

ISLESBORO

A 12-mile-long, stringbean-shaped island just 3 miles off Lincolnville Beach (a 20-minute ferry ride), Islesboro is a private kind of place. Its two communities are Dark Harbor (described by Sidney Sheldon in his best-seller *Master of the Game* as the "jealously guarded colony of the super-rich") and Pripet, a thriving, year-round neighborhood of boatbuilders and fishermen.

GETTING THERE

The car-carrying **Maine State Ferry** (789-5611; 596-2202; $4.50 per passenger, $13.50 per car (with driver), $4 per bicycle) from Lincolnville Beach lands mid-island, at Grindle Point. At the landing, there is a clean ferry terminal with public rest rooms.

TO SEE AND DO

The old lighthouse on Grindle Point (built in 1850, now automated) and keeper's cottage is now the seasonal **Sailors' Memorial Museum** (734-2253), open 9–4:30 Tuesday through Sunday, July through Labor Day. There are summer musical and theatrical performances at the **Free Will Baptist Church.** Check out the **Up Island Church,** a fine old structure with some beautiful wall stencils and fascinating old headstones in the adjacent graveyard.

The layout of the island really makes a vehicle necessary to get a real feel for the place. You can do it on a bicycle, but the roads are narrow with no shoulder, not great for biking. A drive from one end of the island to the other is a nice way to spend a couple of hours. In Dark Harbor, you will see huge "cottages" and impressive architecture. A picnic area and town beach at Pendelton Point have spectacular water views. The drive down the other side of the island will take you past the **Islesboro Historical Society** (734-6733) in the former town hall, which houses rotating exhibits on the first floor and a permanent collec-

Grindle Point Lighthouse

RICK WEBB

tion upstairs. There is a smattering of shops on the island, but they seem to be closed up come early autumn.

LODGING

The **Islesboro Town Office** (734-2253 is a friendly source of information and can refer you to local real estate agents who handle cottage rentals.

Dark Harbor House (734-6669), Box 185, Main Road, Dark Harbor, Islesboro 04848. Open mid-May to mid-October. The only place to stay on Islesboro and one of the most pleasant inns along the Maine coast. Built on a hilltop at the turn of the century as a summer cottage for the president of the First National Bank of Philadelphia, this imposing, yellow-clapboard inn offers elegance from a past era. The gardens and landscaping are outstanding. Inside you'll find a summery living room with glass French doors opening onto a porch and a cozier library with a fireplace just right for crisp autumn afternoons. The staircases to the second floor are wonderful. New owners Jerry Ames and Chris Dickman brought many fine antiques with them from California, and have carefully placed them throughout the inn. All 10 guest rooms have private baths, some feature balconies. There's also a two-room suite with a wet bar and a fold-out sofa bed in its living room, as well as a two-room master suite complete with an enclosed sunporch sitting room, fireplace, and canopied queen-sized mahogany bed. An à la carte dining and full wine service is offered to guests and to the public by reservation, upon availability. Entrées might be *paupiettes* of sole with native crabmeat, chicken roulades with leek, Gruyère, and prosciutto, or locally caught steamed lobster. Dessert might be lemon mousse, raspberry-blueberry crisp, or chocolate caramel walnut torte. Picnic baskets can be prepared for day trips. Doubles are $115–275 including a full, four-course breakfast; 2-night minimum on holiday weekends. Dinner entrées run $17.95–26.95.

WHERE TO EAT

You can pick up a snack (breakfast specials, burgers, lobster rolls, etc for lunch and dinner) at the **Islander** (734-2270), a takeout stand at the far end of the ferry terminal parking lot, open 7–5 daily, until 7 PM Friday and Saturday. The luncheonette in the **Dark Harbor Shop** is the local gathering place. The **Dark Harbor House** (see *Lodging*) offers dinner by reservation upon availability. **Oliver's,** open May through October (734-6543) in Dark Harbor, offers fine dining and lighter fare in a second-floor pub.

Belfast, Searsport, and Stockton Springs

Belfast has a history of unusual commercial diversification, including a highly successful sarsaparilla company, a rum distillery, and a city-owned railroad, not to mention poultry and shoe enterprises. Belfast can also boast 11 shipyards and over 360 vessels raised in its shipbuilding past. Many sea captains made their homes here, and the streets are lined with a number of their fine old houses, many of which have become bed & breakfasts in recent years. The Victorian brick downtown is now a genuinely interesting place to shop.

East of Belfast, Route 1 follows the shore of Penobscot Bay as it narrows and seems more like a mighty river. With its sheltered harbors, this area was once prime shipbuilding country.

In 1845 Searsport alone managed to launch eight brigs and six schooners. In Searsport's Penobscot Marine Museum you learn that more than 3,000 different vessels have been built in and around Penobscot Bay since 1770. Searsport also once boasted more sea captains than any other town its size, explaining the dozens of 19th-century mansions, many now B&Bs, still lining the Searsport stretch of Route 1.

Just north of Searsport lies Stockton Springs, a small town with neither a large shopping area nor a business district. It does have some good restaurants, inns, and Sandy Point, offering great views and a nice little beach.

Pleasant lodging places are scattered along the bay between Belfast and Bucksport, making this a logical hub from which to explore the entire region, from Camden to Bar Harbor.

Waldo County is mainly made up of quaint small towns that are a real pleasure to explore when you are not in a hurry to get somewhere. If you have the time, take the scenic route to this region from Augusta, poking through the communities of Unity, Thorndike, and Brooks, detouring to Liberty then down to Belfast (see *Scenic Drive*).

GUIDANCE

Belfast Area Chamber of Commerce (338-5900; www.acadia.net/Belfast/), P.O. Box 58, Belfast 4915 maintains a year-round office (write to request information) and seasonal information booth on the waterfront.

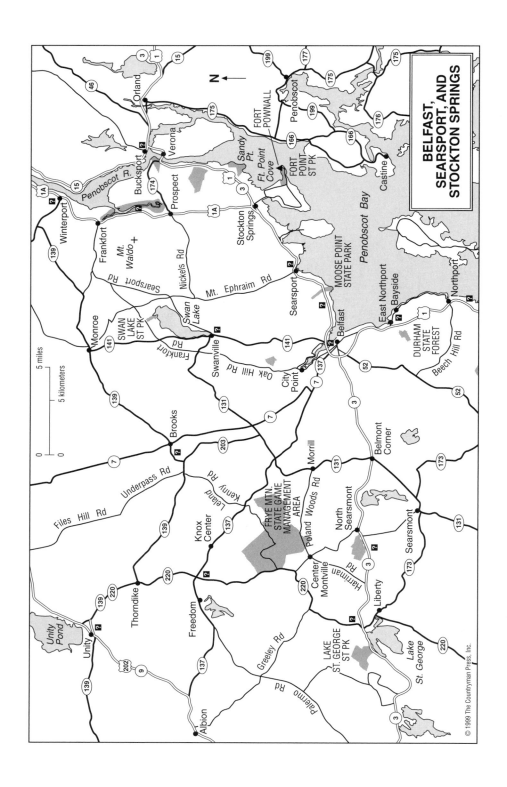

BELFAST,
SEARSPORT, AND
STOCKTON SPRINGS

© 1999 The Countryman Press, Inc.

Waldo County Regional Chamber of Commerce (948-5050), P.O. Box 577, Unity 04988. Publishes a nice guide covering all communities in the county.

GETTING THERE

By air: **Ace Aviation** (338-2970) in Belfast offers charter service to all points.

By car: The most direct route to this region from points south and west is via I-95, exiting in Augusta and taking Route 3 to Belfast.

By bus: Concord Trailways stops at the Big Apple in Searsport seasonally.

MEDICAL EMERGENCY

Waldo County General Hospital (338-2500; 1-800-649-2536), 118 Northport Avenue, Belfast.

VILLAGES

Brooks. In the center of this quiet county, surrounded by hills, this town has the most scenic golf course around, and a new summer theater group.

Liberty is home to Lake St. George State Park, and the Liberty Tool Company on Main Street draws large crowds with its bizarre mix of antiques and items found in an old-fashioned hardware store. The octagonal post office houses the historical society and is itself a museum with all of its original equipment. It is open on weekends in the summer.

Northport. A deceptively sleepy-looking little town has a yacht club, a golf club, pretty gingerbread cottages lining the bay, a popular Saturday-night dance club, and a well-known Mexican restaurant.

Unity. Home to the headquarters of the Belfast & Moosehead railroad, a rural college, a raceway, and the new fairgrounds for the popular Common Ground Fair.

TO SEE

MUSEUMS

Penobscot Marine Museum (548-2529; pmmuseum@acadia.net), Route 1, Searsport. Open Memorial Day to mid-October, Monday through Saturday 10–5, Sunday noon–5; year-round by appointment. Adults $6, seniors $5, children 7–15, $2. Family rate $14. (The library is open weekdays year-round, except closed on Monday, December through March.) Recently expanded to 13 buildings, eight of which are on the National Historic Register. The museum shop is now on Route 1, and the entrance to the complex is more visible and attractive. Displays in the 1845 town hall trace the evolution of sailing vessels from 17th-century mast ships to the Down Easters of the 1870s and 1880s—graceful, square-rigged vessels that were both fast and sturdy cargo carriers. In other buildings there are fine marine paintings, scrimshaw, a variety of lacquerware, Chinese imports, and more. You learn that Searsport didn't just build ships; townspeople owned the ships they built and sailed off in them to the far reaches of the compass, taking their families along. In 1889 Searsport boasted 77 deep-sea captains, 33 of whom manned full-rigged Cape Horners. There are pictures of Searsport families meeting in distant ports, and, of course, there is the exotica they brought home—much of which is still being sold in local antiques shops. The **Fowler-True-Ross house** tells the story of two prominent captains' families. Not everyone led the life of a sea captain, however, and the museum's exhibit "Working the Bay: The Ports and People of Penobscot Bay" focuses on the working-class people who made their living here in the granite, lime, ice, fishing, and lobstering industries. The galleries in the **Captain Jeremiah Merithew House** have been refurbished and now hold a collection of paintings by father and son marine artists Thomas and James Buttersworth. The museum sponsors lecture, film, and concert series and operates a gift store.

Searsport Historical Society (548-6663), Route 1, Searsport. Open July through September, Wednesday through Sunday 1–5. A collection of local artifacts, photos, maps, clothing, and town records.

Belfast Museum (338-2078/1875), 6 Market Street, Belfast. Open Thursday and Sunday in summer, 1–4, and by appointment year-round. A small but interesting museum, featuring local area artifacts, paintings, scrapbooks full of newspaper clippings about the area, and other displays.

Second Congregational Church, Route 1, Searsport. Pick up the key at the Harbor House across the street and check out the fabulous Tiffany windows in this church, built in 1815.

Bryant Museum (568-3665), Rich Road, Thorndike. What began as a stove shop has evolved into a fascinating museum, chock-full of things to look at. The front is crammed with restored woodstoves. Walk through these to the doll circus, with its amazing array of mechanical, musical dolls from Barbie to Disney characters and everything in between. The back room houses a wonderful collection of player pianos, nickelodeons, and vintage automobiles. Hardly what you would expect to find in this quiet little town, but worth the drive.

SCENIC DRIVE

Route 3, past Lake St. George and Sheepscot Pond, through the China Lakes region, is the most direct path between Belfast and Augusta, but take time to detour down Route 173 to **Liberty** to see the octagonal post office and the **Liberty Tool Company.** For a leisurely tour of the villages between Belfast and Augusta, head north from East Belfast on Route 141 to Monroe. Ask for directions to **Stone Soup Farm** to see their gardens, then check out **Monroe Falls,** just off Route 139, and maybe have a picnic. Head out on Route 139, through Brooks, and then on toward Thorndike, where you will want to be sure and stop at the **Bryant Museum** (see *To See*). Continue on Route 139 to Unity, where you will pass the new home of the Common Ground Fair and the pretty station for the **Belfast & Moosehead Lake Railroad** (see *To Do*). Follow Route 139 into Kennebec County to Fairfield to meet up with I-95, or detour yet again onto Route 202, which will bring you through the China Lakes region to Augusta.

TO DO

AIRPLANE RIDE
Ace Aviation Inc. (338-2970) offers scenic flights from Belfast Municipal Airport for one to three people.

BERRY PICKING
Staples Homestead Blueberries (567-3393/3703), County Road, Stockton Springs. Turn at the ball field on Routes 1/3, then drive 3 miles until the T at County Road; turn right. Or ask directions in Stockton Springs village. Open 8–5 daily while berries are in-season (mid-August). Friendly owners Basil and Mary Staples will instruct you in the mysteries of blueberry raking then let you go to it, or you can pick by hand; 85 cents per quart, and everyone gets a recipe booklet with their berries. Martha Stewart's crew was there the day we stopped by, capturing the picking tradition on film.

BOAT EXCURSIONS
Balmy Days (338-4652) offers coastal cruises and trips to Castine, also daysails aboard the wooden yacht *Jessamyn Rose*. The **Chippewa**, built as a freight and passenger ferry in 1923 and rebuilt in 1994, offers excursions in conjunction with the Belfast & Moosehead Lake Railroad. Check with the Belfast Chamber of Commerce (see *Guidance*) for information about other cruises of the bay.

GOLF
Country View Golf Course (722-3161) in Brooks is the most scenic in the area: nine holes, par 36, cart rental, club rentals, lessons, clubhouse.

KAYAKING
Harvey Schiller (282-6204) offers guided tours from Belfast City Pier using double kayaks; beginners and families welcome.

SWIMMING
Lake St. George State Park (589-4255), Route 3, Liberty. Open May 15 through October 15. A great way station for travelers going to or from Down East. A deep, clear lake with a small beach, lifeguard, bathhouse, parking facilities, 31 campsites, and a boat launch. **Swan Lake State Park,** Route 141, Swanville (north of town; follow signs). This beach has picnicking facilities on Swan Lake. **Belfast City Park,** Route 1, Belfast (south of town). Swimming pool, tennis courts, picnicking facilities, and a gravel beach. **Sandy Point Beach,** off Route 1 north of Stockton Springs (it's posted HERSEY RETREAT; turn toward the water directly across from the Rocky Ridge Motel). **Mosman Beach Park,** Searsport. There's a town dock, boat ramp, swimming, fishing.

TRAIN EXCURSION

Belfast & Moosehead Lake Railroad Co. (338-2330; 1-800-392-5500), May through October, operates 1½-hour excursions from the Belfast waterfront along the Passagassawakeag River to the inland village of Waldo and back. Inquire about Rail & Sail combos. The Unity station, at One Depot Square, is painted bright red with green and white trim, hardly what you expect to see as you drive down the quiet roads of this area. There is a gift shop, rest rooms, snack bar, and waiting area with a stuffed black bear, plenty of cushioned seats, and historical photos on the walls. A Swedish steam engine carries passengers on a 1½-hour narrated journey from Unity to Burnham Junction. Pre-ride demonstration as the engine is turned on the old Armstrong turntable. $14 adults, $7 children. Several special events and packages throughout the season.

GREEN SPACE

Also see *Swimming.*

Moose Point State Park, Route 1, south of Searsport. Open May 30 to October 15. A good spot for picnicking; cookout facilities are in an evergreen grove and an open field overlooking Penobscot Bay.

Fort Pownall and **Fort Point State Park,** Stockton Springs (marked from Route 1; accessible via a 3.5-mile access road). The 1759 fort built to defend the British claim to Maine (the Kennebec River was the actual boundary between the English and French territories) was burned twice to prevent its being taken; only earthworks remain. The adjacent park, on the tip of a peninsula jutting into Penobscot Bay, is a fine fishing and picnic spot. A pier accommodates visitors who arrive by boat. The lighthouse is another great spot. Views from the point are back down to the Camden Hills.

LODGING

INNS AND BED & BREAKFASTS
In Belfast 04915

The Jeweled Turret Inn (338-2304; 1-800-696-2304), 40 Pearl Street. Open year-round. A handsome gabled and turreted house built ornately inside and out in the 1890s. The fireplace in the den is said to be made of stones from every state in the Union at that time, from the collection of the original owner. Each of the seven guest rooms has a private bath, is decorated in shades reminiscent of the gem it is named for, and is furnished with antiques and plenty of knickknacks. We especially like the romantic Amethyst Room in the turret. Carl and Cathy Heffentrager serve a full breakfast and tea and take time to visit with guests, perhaps on one of two verandas that overlook the historic district. $70–100 double.

Downtown Belfast

The White House (338-1901), 1 Church Street. This distinct gracious house set on a triangle of lawn and gardens has been renovated into an elegant bed & breakfast with many amenities. The eight guest rooms all have private baths, king, queen, or twin beds, and telephones, and are decorated with antique and reproduction furnishings. We especially like the Belfast Bay Room with its fireplace, king-sized poster bed, and whirlpool bath. Common areas include formal parlors, a comfortable library with plenty of books and games, and the terrace and gardens. Rooms are $75–125 in-season, including gourmet breakfast and afternoon tea.

The Alden House (338-2151), 63 Church Street. Another great new addition to the area. Jessica Jahnke and Marla Stickle saved this Greek Revival house from its state of disrepair, reviving it so thoroughly that it was filmed for the Oprah Winfrey show. Amazing architectual details from Italian marble mantels and sinks to a wonderful circular staircase to the seven guest rooms (five with private baths). One guest room has a working fireplace, and there are three other fireplaces in the common areas. A great porch overlooks the lawns, where guests can also play croquet. $63–110 includes a candlelight breakfast.

Belfast Bay Meadows (338-5715; 1-800-335-2370), 90 Northport Avenue. John and Patty Lebowitz offer a variety of accomodations set on 17 acres of fields, waterfront, and woods. Six rooms upstairs in the shingle-style cottage are great for couples. Two have woodstoves, two have bay views. The 14 rooms of various sizes in the renovated barn are more modern, with TVs; two have whirlpool tubs. Children and dogs are welcome in these rooms.

Thomas Pitcher House (338-6454; 1-888-338-6454), 19 Franklin Street. Open year-round. Set just off the main drag, this is a comfortable, friendly place. Fran and Ron Kresge are warm hosts, eager to help guests enjoy the area. Each of the four guest rooms has a private bath and a speaker (which guests control) for the music which is piped throughout the house. We especially like the Thomas Pitcher Room with its four-poster bed, bay window reading area, and claw-foot tub. Downstairs is a cozy common room with a TV and VCR available. $65–85 includes breakfast served family-style in the dining room.

In Searsport 04974

Homeport Inn (548-2259; 1-800-742-5814), Route 1. Open year-round. An 1861 captain's mansion complete with widow's walk overlooking the bay. Dr. and Mrs. George Johnson were the first Searsport B&B hosts. Rooms in front are old-fashioned and three of the four have shared baths, but the six downstairs rooms in the back are modern and elegantly decorated, with private baths and bay views. Also offered are two 2-bedroom cottages. The landscaped grounds, with lovely flower gardens, slope to the water. A full breakfast is included in the rates, which range from $35 (single with shared bath) to $90 (double with private bath); lower rates November through April. The cottages are $600–750 per week.

❄ Captain Green Pendleton B&B (548-6523; 1-800-949-4403), Route 1. Open year-round. Another fine old captain's home with 80 acres set well back from Route 1. The three bedrooms, one downstairs (with private bath) and two upstairs, are comfortably furnished, with a welcoming feel. All have working fireplaces, and there's a Franklin fireplace in the guest parlor. A path circles the meadow, a cross-country ski trail goes through the woods, and there's a large, spring-fed trout pond. The Greiners are warm and helpful hosts. Dogs are allowed for an additional fee. $65 per night downstairs, $55 upstairs, includes tax as well as a full breakfast; less off-season.

❀ Thurston House B&B Inn (548-2213; 1-800-240-2213), 8 Elm Street. Open year-round. Carl and Beverly Eppig offer four guest rooms in an attractive 1830s house on a side street in the village, originally built as a parsonage. The two upstairs rooms have private baths; the two on the first floor of the carriage house share a bath and have a private entrance (good for a family of five). "Forget-about-lunch" breakfasts and state tax are included in $50–65 high season ($45 single); reduced rates off-season.

Watchtide (548-6575; 1-800-698-6575), Route 1. This is a bright house with a 60-foot-long, 19-windowed, wicker- and flower-filled sunporch with a periwinkle blue floor, overlooking fields stretching to the bay. Nancy-Linn Nellis and Jack Elliott are warm, welcoming hosts. Nancy-Linn also operates **Angels to Antiques**—a gift store specializing in angels—in the adjacent barn. The four guest rooms are furnished with antiques and attention is paid to small details. Two of the bedrooms have been recently renovated, and one now offers a Jacuzzi. Staying here is like staying with old friends. The "bog beans" (chocolate-covered dried cranberries with a touch of raspberry flavor) Nancy puts in guest rooms are positively addictive (she also sells them in the gift shop). $70–135, depending on the season.

❀♿ The Captain Butman Homestead (548-2506), Route 1. A classic 1830s farmhouse on 5½ acres. It's open summers only because hosts Lee and

Wilson Flight teach school in Massachusetts. This was home for two generations of Searsport deep-water captains, and there's a right-of-way down to Penobscot Bay. The four guest rooms share 1½ baths. A full breakfast is included in $45 double. If you have high-school-aged children, you might want to ask about the Downeast Outdoor Education School, an exciting 2- to 4-week program run by the Flights. In 1998, a spotless, spacious International Youth Hostel was added with five dorm-style beds each for men and women, a large sitting and kitchen area, and a fully handicapped-accessible private room. A bargain at $15 for members, $18 for nonmembers (more for the private room).

McGilvery House (548-6289), Route 1. Sue Omness is the hostess of this elegant Victorian with 11-foot ceilings. Open and spacious, the parlors (the front with a piano, copies of museum portraits, and its original light fixture; the back a less formal TV room) are inviting. Three rooms are rented at a time, on a first-come, first-pick basis. All have queen beds and private baths. Continental breakfast served family-style in the dining room is included.

In Stockton Springs 04981

The Hichborn Inn (567-4183; 1-800-346-1522; hichborn@aol.com), Church Street, P.O. Box 115. Open year-round except Christmas. This stately Victorian Italianate mansion complete with widow's walk is up a side street in an old shipbuilding village that's now bypassed by Route 1. Built by a prolific shipbuilder (N. G. Hichborn launched 42 vessels) and prominent politician, it remained in the family, preserved by his daughters (there's a tale!), until 1939. For Nancy and Bruce Suppes, restoring this house has meant deep involvement in its story—and its friendly ghosts. Bruce, an engineer on supertankers, has done much of the exceptional restoration work himself. There's a comfortable "gent's parlor," where evening fires burn; also a music room and an elegant library. Elaborate breakfasts are served either in the dining room or on the sunporch. There are four rooms, two with private baths; niceties include books and magazines by all the beds, a pitcher of ice water on the dresser, and chocolates on the night stand. Your hosts will pick you up at the dock in Searsport or Belfast, and provide transport to dinner or for supplies. $60–95 per night, $51–81 off-season.

WHERE TO EAT

DINING OUT

Rhumb Line (548-2600), 200 East Main Street (Route 1), Searsport. Fine dining in a relaxed atmosphere. Owners Charles and Diana Evans ran a successful restaurant on Martha's Vineyard before coming to Searsport. Dinner guests are invited into the parlor for drinks before heading to one of the oversized tables for dinner. The menu changes daily, but some favorites, such as roast rack of lamb or horseradish-crusted salmon are usually offered. Everything is made fresh, and the wine list is also a work in progress. Dessert choices may include French bread pudding or chocolate temptation (a flourless cake filled with raspberry hazelnut ganache). Entrées are $16–24.

Nickerson Tavern (548-2220), Route 1, Searsport. Open Tuesday through Sunday 5:30–9. The tavern's elegance and quality inspires patrons to drive from Bar Harbor and Bangor to this handsome 1838 sea captain's house. Everything is fresh and made in-house, from appetizers to dessert. Appetizers include oysters on the half shell and Brie baked in puff pastry. Entreés include chicken coated in hazelnuts with a raspberry, shallot, and sweet butter sauce, and pork medallions sautéed with a wild mushroom, bell pepper, and Brandy Hunters sauce. Reservations are a must. Entrées are $14.95–19.95.

90 Main (338-1106), Belfast. Open daily for lunch and dinner; Sunday brunch. A reasonably priced dining-out alternative—a storefront with atmosphere and a menu featuring the likes of blueberry chicken (grilled breast in a sauce laced with Bartlett's blueberry wine and Dijon mustard, $11.95), vegetarian dishes, and a variety of fresh pastas as well as a lamb of the day and local salmon (market price). The downstairs deli/bakery (open 7 AM–6 PM) features fabulous breads, soups, and sandwiches.

EATING OUT

Darby's Restaurant and Pub (338-2339), 155 High Street, Belfast. Open daily for lunch and dinner. A friendly storefront café with interesting tin ceilings and local art work featured. Salads, burgers, and upscale lunch sandwiches. A reasonably priced dinner find: Entrées might include pad Thai or Moroccan lamb. Soups and sandwiches are served all day.

Young's Lobster Pound (338-1160), Mitchell Avenue (posted from Route 1 just across the bridge from Belfast), East Belfast. Open in-season 7–6:30. A pound with as many as 30,000 lobsters, and seating (indoor and outdoor) to accommodate 500. Order and enjoy the view of Belfast across the Passagassawakeag River while you wait.

Seafarer's Tavern (548-2465), Route 1, Searsport. Open for lunch and dinner except Sunday. The real heart of Searsport where locals gather. Friendly, casual, and fun. A great little restaurant with a full bar, sandwiches, pizza, excellent crab cakes, and reasonably priced entrées including scallops with pasta and chicken potpie.

COFFEE SHOP

Bell the Cat (338-2081), Church Street, Belfast. A spacious, friendly place with one brick wall displaying local art, small wooden tables, and a comfy couch and chair. Plenty of coffee choices, sandwiches, ice cream, and computers with Internet access.

ENTERTAINMENT

The Belfast Maskers (338-9668). A year-round community theater that puts on several shows each season at the Railroad Theater on the waterfront.

Schedule available at the theater. They also offer acting workshops and classes for adults and children.

The Playhouse (338-5777), Church Street, Belfast. A cozy 36-seat theater offering shows by the Assembled Players company. Founder Mary Weaver also offers after-school and Saturday workshops for actors of all ages.

The Colonial Theater (338-1930), Belfast. The new home of the outsized carved elephants from Belfast's now-closed landmark, Perry's Nut House; three screens with nightly showings in a restored theater in downtown Belfast.

SELECTIVE SHOPPING

ANTIQUES SHOPS

Searsport claims to be the "Antiques Capital of Maine." After counting 29 shops on Route 1, we may be inclined to agree: The **Searsport Antique Mall,** open daily year-round, is a cooperative of 74 dealers. Everything from 18th-century furniture to 1960s collectibles is spread over two floors. Next door, **Hickson's Flea Market** has both indoor shops (most have specialties) rented for the season and outdoor tables where anyone can set up. **The Pumpkin Patch,** we're told by an experienced dealer, is one of the best shops in the state. They've been in business close to 20 years and have 26 dealers represented. Mary Harriman ran a truck stop until 1989. When it closed, she opened the **Hobby Horse,** which has since grown to house 20 shops, 30 tables, and a lunch wagon. **The Searsport Flea Market,** held weekends in-season, is also big. Antiques at **Hillman's** (Route 1 across from the Nickerson Tavern): good linens, china, glassware.

ART GALLERIES

Artfellows (338-5776), 104 Main Street, Belfast. Open Monday through Saturday 9–5. A cooperative gallery that represents the work of 40 artists working in a variety of media. Changing exhibits; annual **Invitational Painters Show.**

M. H. Jacobs Art Gallery (338-3324), 44 Main Street, Belfast. Original paintings, framing, art supplies.

Spring Street Gallery (338-5315), 28 Spring Street, Belfast. Open Tuesday through Sunday 1–5:30. Contemporary Maine art.

BOOKSTORES

Victorian House/Book Barn (567-3351), Stockton Springs. Open April through December, 8–8; otherwise by chance or appointment. A large collection of old, out-of-print, and rare books. **Fertile Mind Bookshop** (338-2498), 13 Main Street, Belfast. An outstanding browsing and buying place featuring Maine and regional books and guides, maps, records, and cards. **Canterbury Tales** (338-1171), 52 Main Street, Belfast. A full-service bookstore with great selection of Maine and children's books. **Mr. Paperback** (338-2735), Belmont Avenue, Belfast.

SPECIAL SHOPS

Coyote Moon (338-5659), 54 Main Street, Belfast. A nifty, reasonably priced women's clothing and gift store. **Waldo County Co-op,** Route 1, Searsport Harbor. Open June to October, daily 9–5. A showcase for the local extension service. Dolls, needlework, wooden crafts, quilts, pillows, jams, and ceramics—and lots of them. **Silkweeds** (548-6501), Route 1, Searsport. Specializes in "country gifts": tinware, cotton afghans, rugs, wreaths. **Monroe Saltworks** (338-3460), Route 1, Belfast. This distinctive pottery has a wide following around the country. There are seconds and unusual pieces both here and in the Ellsworth outlets. **Ducktrap River Fish Farms, Inc.** (338-6280), 57 Little River Drive, Belfast. This company produces more than 25 varieties of smoked seafood, sold nationwide. Visitors may view (through windows) the processes involved, and purchase the products in the store. It's best to call first. **All About Games** (338-9984), 171 High Street, Belfast, is a great place to buy and play traditional board games, as well as some more unusual nonautomated games. **Birdworks of Maine** (567-3030), School Street, Stockton Springs. Open weekdays 9–5. Decorative pottery bird feeders, nesting roosts, suet keepers, and much more, all made on the premises.

SPECIAL EVENTS

July and August: Free Thursday-night **street concerts** in downtown Belfast.

Mid-July: **Belfast Bay Festival**—a week of events, including a giant chicken barbecue, midway, races, and parade.

August: **Searsport Lobster Boat Races** and related events.

September: **Common Ground Fair** at new fairgrounds in Unity—organic farm products, demonstrations, children's activities, sheep-dog round-up, crafts, entertainment. The Belfast & Moosehead Lake Railroad runs to the fairgrounds.

Second weekend in December: **Searsport Victorian Christmas:** open houses at museum, homes, and B&Bs.

IV. DOWN EAST

East Penobscot Bay Region
Acadia Area
Washington County, Campobello, and St. Andrews

Bass Harbor Head Lighthouse, Acadia National Park

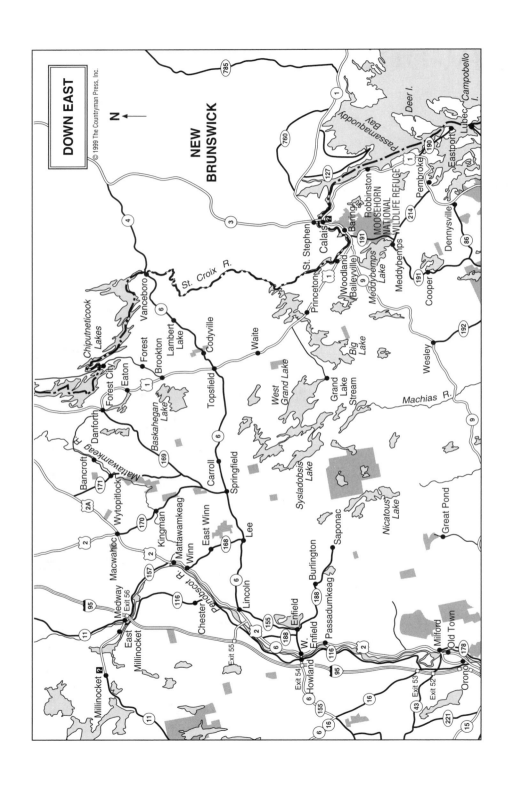

DOWN EAST

N

NEW BRUNSWICK

Passamaquoddy Bay

Deer I.

Lubec

Campobello I.

Eastport

Pembroke

Robbinston

Baring

Calais

St. Stephen

Princeton

Woodland

Baileyville

MOOSEHORN NATIONAL WILDLIFE REFUGE

Meddybemps Lake

Meddybemps

Dennysville

Cooper

Wesley

St. Croix R.

Vanceboro

Chiputneticook Lakes

Forest

Lambert Lake

Codyville

Waite

West Grand Lake

Grand Lake Stream

Big Lake

Machias R.

Brookton

Forest City

Eaton

Topsfield

Danforth

Baskahegan Lake

Carroll

Springfield

Sysladobsis Lake

Nicatous Lake

Great Pond

Bancroft

Wytopitlock

Kingman

Mattawamkeag

East Winn

Winn

Lee

Burlington

Saponac

Macwahoc

Medway

Mattawamkeag R.

Chester

Lincoln

Enfield

W. Enfield

Passadumkeag

Milford

Old Town

East Millinocket

Exit 55

Exit 54

Howland

Exit 53

Exit 52

Orono

Millinocket

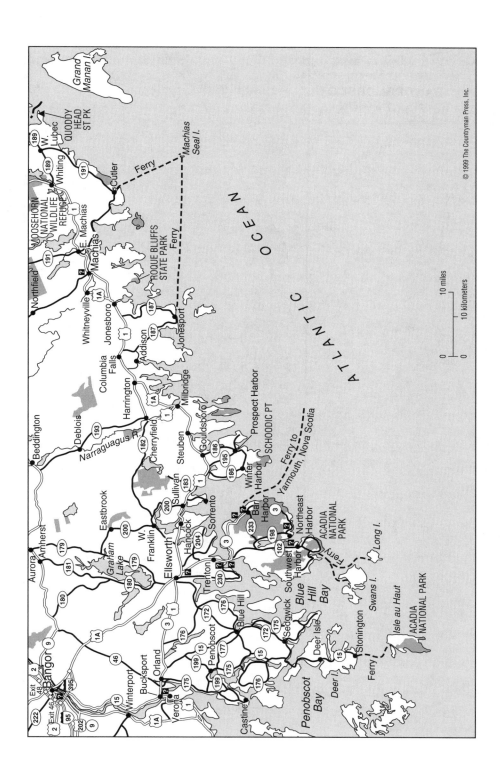

© 1999 The Countryman Press, Inc.

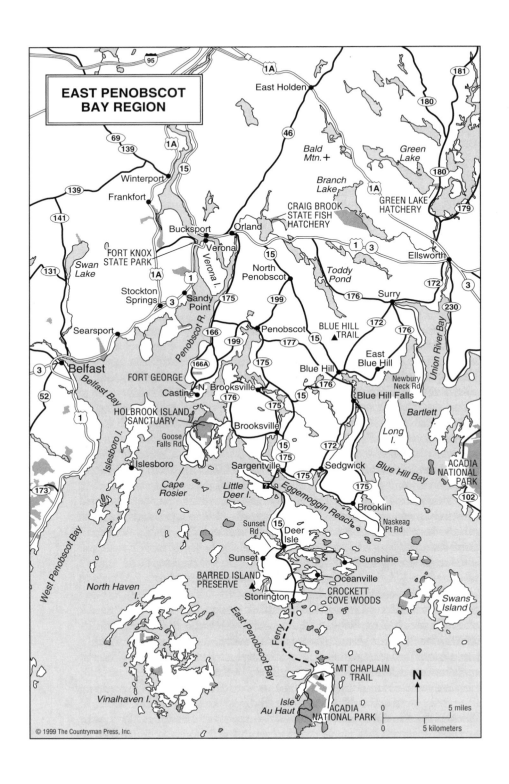

EAST PENOBSCOT
BAY REGION

95

1A

East Holden

181

180

69
139

1A

46

Bald
Mtn. +

Green
Lake

15

Winterport

Branch
Lake

1A

180

139

Frankfort

CRAIG BROOK
STATE FISH
HATCHERY

GREEN LAKE
HATCHERY

179

141

Bucksport

Orland

1 3

Ellsworth

Verona

FORT KNOX
STATE PARK

Swan
Lake

15

North
Penobscot

Toddy
Pond

176

Surry

172

3

131

1A

1

199

230

Stockton
Springs

3

Sandy
Point

175

BLUE HILL
TRAIL

172

Searsport

166

Penobscot

15

East
Blue Hill

176

199

177

Belfast

3

166A

175

Blue Hill

176

Newbury
Neck Rd

FORT GEORGE

N. Brooksville

15

Blue Hill Falls

52

Castine

176

175

Bartlett

1

HOLBROOK ISLAND
SANCTUARY

Brooksville

Long
I.

ACADIA
NATIONAL
PARK

Goose
Falls Rd

15

172

Islesboro

Sargentville

175

Sedgwick

Blue Hill Bay

102

173

Cape
Rosier

Little
Deer I.

175

Eggemoggin Reach

Brooklin

Naskeag
Pt Rd

15

Sunset
Rd

Deer
Isle

North Haven

Sunset

Sunshine

BARRED ISLAND
PRESERVE

Oceanville

Vinalhaven I.

Stonington

CROCKETT
COVE WOODS

Swans
Island

West Penobscot Bay

East Penobscot Bay

Ferry

MT CHAPLAIN
TRAIL

N

Isle
Au Haut

ACADIA
NATIONAL PARK

0   5 miles

0   5 kilometers

© 1999 The Countryman Press, Inc.

East Penobscot Bay Region

Bucksport; Blue Hill Area; Castine; Deer Isle, Stonington, and Isle au Haut

BUCKSPORT

"Gateway" is a much overused touring term, but crossing the high, narrow Waldo–Hancock County suspension bridge (vintage 1931) above the confluence of the Penobscot River and Bay, you can't escape the sense of turning a corner in the coast. Beyond is Bucksport, a workaday river and paper-mill town with a couple of very good places to eat and a 1916 movie theater/museum showcasing New England films dating back to the turn of the century.

Bucksport began as a major shipping port in 1764. After the British burned it, settlers rebuilt, and it is still a strong shipping force today. Bucksport overlooks New England's biggest fort, a memorial to its smallest war.

GUIDANCE

Bucksport Area Chamber of Commerce (469-6818), Main Street 04416, next to the town offices, is open Monday through Friday 9–1. It publishes a brochure with a map, and a "source book" that includes Orland and Verona Islands. Public rest rooms are at the town dock.

TO SEE AND DO

✎ **Fort Knox State Park** (469-7719), Route 174 (off Route 1), Prospect (just across the Penobscot from Bucksport). Open daily May 1 through November 1, 9 AM–sunset. $2 per adult, $.50 for children ages 5–11. Built in 1844 of granite cut from nearby Mount Waldo, it includes barracks, storehouses, a labyrinth of passageways, and even a granite spiral staircase. There are also picnic facilities. The fort was to be a defense against Canada during the boundary dispute with New Brunswick called the Aroostook War. The dispute was ignored in Washington, and so in 1839 the new, lumber-rich state took matters into its own hands by arming its northern forts. Daniel Webster represented Maine in the 1842 treaty that formally ended the war, but Maine built this fort two years later, just in case. It was never entirely completed and never saw battle.

Bucksport Historical Society Museum (469-2464), Main Street, Bucksport. Open July and August, Wednesday through Friday 1–4, and other announced times. Admission $.50. Housed in the former Maine Central Railroad Station; local memorabilia.

Northeast Historic Film/The Alamo Theatre (469-0924; oldfilm@acadia.net), 379 Main Street, Bucksport. Open year-round, Monday through Saturday 9–4. Housed in the vintage 1916 Alamo Theatre is New England's only "moving image" archives—source of silent, Maine-made films. The museum is devoted to collecting and preserving films depicting New England life, from 1901 to the present. Check out the daily matinees. The gift shop features videos and classic posters.

At **Buck Cemetery**, near the Verona Bridge (across from the Shop & Save), a granite obelisk marks the grave of Colonel Jonathan Buck, founder of Bucksport. The outline of a leg on the stone has spurred many legends, the most popular being that a woman whom Judge Buck sentenced to death for witchcraft is carrying through a promise to dance on his grave. Attempts to remove the imprint have failed, and it is still there.

Craig Brook National Fish Hatchery (469-2803), East Orland (turn off Route 1 in Orland, just east of Bucksport). Open daily 8–8. Opened in 1871, this is the country's oldest salmon hatchery. Situated on the shore of a lake, it offers a visitors center (open 8–5) with aquariums, a display pool, nature trail, boat launch, picnic areas, and a 19th-century icehouse.

SPECIAL LEARNING PROGRAM

Verna Cox (469-6402; fax, 469-6243) offers multiday rug-braiding and rug-hooking seminars at the River Inn; also inquire about spinning, weaving, crewel, cross-stitching, tatting, and wool-felting workshops.

LODGING

The River Inn Bed & Breakfast (469-3783), 210 Main Street, Bucksport 04416. Open year-round. A sea captain's house with three pleasant guest rooms, $55 with private bath, $50 for a private deck but shared bath. The parlor is equipped with color TV, books, and a player piano. No smoking.

Allamoosook Lodge (469-6393), P.O. Box 16, Orland. Open year-round. Down a secluded road, on the banks of Allamoosook Lake, this is a wonderful find. Beautiful common room with plenty of windows overlooking the water, white wicker furniture, and a woodstove. Six clean, simple rooms with private bath. Swimming, canoeing, and fishing are among activities for guests in summer, and winter brings ice skating, cross-country skiing, ice fishing, and snowmobiling. $78 single, $93 double in summer; less off-season; includes full breakfast.

WHERE TO EAT

MacLeods (469-3963), Main Street, Bucksport. Open weekdays 11–9, weekends 5–9. A pubby bar with booths, informal atmosphere, dependable dining. Good lunch specials. Dinner entrées might include grilled crab cakes with a roasted red pepper sauce, or ratatouille. Save room for dessert, maybe their delicious French silk pie. Entrées $8.95–12.95.

L'Ermitage (469-3361), 219 Main Street, Bucksport. Open for dinner by reservation, Tuesday through Sunday. Enjoy traditional French fare in the dining rooms of a Victorian house. It may be the only place in Maine you will find blueberry trifle. Entrées begin at $12.95.

Sail Inn, Route 1 in Prospect just before the bridge. The name always makes us laugh since there is no way you could sail into this classic diner, perched as it is atop a high bluff. Blackboard specials supplement a menu featuring fried chicken, sandwiches, pizza, seafood chowders, and stews.

Riverview (469-7600), Main Street, Bucksport. Open for all three meals. Adjacent to the public landing, overlooking the Penobscot and Fort Knox. Good road food, casual lounge.

SPECIAL EVENTS

Last week in June: **Orland River Days**—an "anything goes" raft contest, live music, crafts in a classic New England town on the Narramissic River.

August: **Fort Knox Bay Festival**, a celebration of the Fort Knox restoration project and the revitalization of the Bucksport waterfront. Arts and crafts, live music, garden tours, tours of the fort, living-history demonstrations.

BLUE HILL AREA

In Maine, "Blue Hill" refers to a specific hill, a village, a town, a peninsula—and also to an unusual gathering of artists, musicians, and craftspeople.

The high, rounded hill overlooks Blue Hill Bay. The white wooden village is graced with no fewer than 76 buildings on the National Register of Historic Places: old mansions, an 1840s academy, a fine town hall, a busy music hall, a music library, gourmet restaurants, lively cafés, many galleries, and two potteries.

Blue Hill is a shade off the beaten path, one peninsula west of Mount Desert and nowhere near a beach, but it always has had its own following—especially among creative people. Over the entrance of the Bagaduce (sheet music) Lending Library a mural depicts Blue Hill as the center of concentric creative circles, radiating out over the peninsula. Helen and Scott Nearing, searching for a new place to live "the Good Life" in the 1950s (when a ski area encroached on their seclusion in southern Vermont) swung a dowsing pendulum over a map of coastal Maine. It came to rest on Cape Rosier. For many decades the tiny town of Brooklin was a familiar byline in *The New Yorker* thanks to E. B. White, the same decades during which millions of children were reading about "Blueberry Hill" in Robert McCloskey's *Blueberries for Sal* and about Condon's Garage (still a South Brooksville family-owned landmark) in the 1940s classic *One Morning in Maine*.

Energy lines or not, this peninsula's intermingling of land and water—along lakes and tidal rivers as well as bays—creates a landscape that's exceptional, even in coastal Maine. Pause at the turnout on Caterpillar Hill, the height-of-land on Route 15/175 (just north of the Deer Isle bridge) to appreciate the extent of this phenomenon. Then plunge down the hill to that improbably narrow, soaring suspension bridge.

Across the bridge, Deer Isle is a chapter in its own right (see "Deer Isle, Stonington, and Isle au Haut"); it is both physically and otherwise distinct from the Blue Hill Peninsula, but both are distinguished by their number of narrow roads threading numerous land fingers, leading to studios of local craftspeople and artists. What you remember afterward is the beauty of clouds over fields of wildflowers, quiet coves, the loveliness of things woven, painted, and blown, and conversations with the people who made them.

The 1939 bridge spans Eggemoggin Reach, a 10-mile long passage dividing the Blue Hill peninsula from Deer Isle but linking Penobscot and Jericho Bays. A century ago this was a busy thoroughfare, a shortcut from Rockland to points Down East for freight-carrying schooners and passenger steamboats. It remains a popular route for windjammers, yachts, and, increasingly, for sea kayakers. Route 175 hugs "the Reach" on its way through Sedgwick to Brooklin.

Castine, the tip of an arm of the Blue Hill peninsula with its own history and feel, has its own chapter too. Once positioned in the thick of traffic—the pivotal point at the mouth of the Penobscot River and head of Penobscot Bay—it's still the home of the Maine Maritime Academy.

GUIDANCE

There is no Blue Hill Chamber of Commerce. A map/guide is available from P.O. Box 520, Blue Hill 04614, or by calling the Liros Gallery at 374-5370 (see *Selective Shopping*). Also pick up the current copy of the *Browser's Trail*, published by the Penobscot Bay Press.

GETTING THERE

By air: See the "Bangor" and "Bar Harbor and Ellsworth" chapters.

By car: The obvious way is Route 1 to Route 15 to Blue Hill, but there are many shortcuts through the confusing web of roads on this peninsula; ask directions to your lodging place.

MEDICAL EMERGENCY

Blue Hill Memorial Hospital (374-2836), Water Street, Blue Hill, the largest facility in the area, has a 24-hour emergency room. **The Peninsula Ambulance Corps** (374-9955) serves Blue Hill.

TO SEE

Parson Fisher House (374-2001), 0.5 mile south of Blue Hill Village on Route 15/176. Open July through mid-September, Monday through Saturday 2–5. A house built in 1814 by Blue Hill's first pastor, a Harvard graduate who augmented his meager salary with a varied line of crafts and by teaching (he founded Blue Hill Academy), farming, and writing. His furniture, paintings, books, journals, and woodcuts are exhibited. $2 admission.

Holt House, Water Street, Blue Hill. Open during July and August, Tuesday and Friday 1–4. Donation. The Blue Hill Historical Society collection is housed in this restored 1815 Federal mansion near the harbor, noted for its stenciled walls. The annual quilt show is held here.

Blue Hill Library (374-5515), Main Street. Open daily except Sunday. A handsome WPA-project building with periodicals and ample reading space; changing art shows in summer.

Bagaduce Lending Library (374-5454), Blue Hill. Open Tuesday, Wednesday, and Friday, 10–3. This is another Blue Hill phenomenon: some 625,000 volumes of sheet music, some more than a century old, most of it special for one reason or another, all available for borrowing. The collection includes 1,400 pieces about Maine, by Maine composers, or published in Maine. Stop by just to see the mural over the entrance depicting Blue Hill at the center of concentric, creative circles.

Forest Farm: The Good Life Center (326-8211), on the loop road, facing Orr's Cove (opposite side of the road), Harborside, on Cape Rosier. Open year-round, Thursday through Tuesday, 1–5 and by appointment. The stone home built in 1953 by Helen and Scott Nearing, coauthors of

Living the Good Life and seven other books based on their simple, purposeful lifestyle, is now maintained by a trust, and through a stewardship program a couple maintains the property year-round just as the Nearings did. Inquire about weekly programs in summer and periodic workshops. The grounds include an intensively cultivated organic garden, a greenhouse, and a yurt. Inquire about tours and workshops.

MERI Resource Center (359-8078), Brooklin. Open May through August, weekdays 9–5, Saturday 10–4. The Marine Environmental Research Institute, based in a storefront in the middle of Brooklin village, offers frequent family-geared cruises as well as weeklong programs for youngsters to tune them in to shore and sea life. The center has a small aquarium and a "sea library."

Reverend Daniel Merrill House (359-2537), Route 172, Sedgwick. Open July and August, Sunday 2–4. This complex includes the town's original parsonage, a restored schoolhouse, and an 1820s cattle pound. This is part of a Sedgwick Historic District that includes an 18th-century town house. Check out the large old Rural Cemetery.

Also see *Art Galleries* under *Selective Shopping.*

SCENIC DRIVES

To come as far as Blue Hill and go no farther would be like walking up to a door and not opening it. The beauty of the peninsula lies beyond—via roads that wander west to **Brooksville** by taking Route 15 South to Route 176/175 North to Route 176 (yes, that's right) and across the **Bagaduce River** and south on Route 176 (never mind). Turn off at the sign for **Cape Rosier** to see **Holbrook Island Sanctuary** (see *Green Space*) and **Forest Farm** (above). Return to Route 176 and continue into the village of South Brooksville (be sure not to miss **Buck's Harbor**). Route 176 rejoins Route 175 and then Route 15; turn south and follow Route 15 South over **Caterpillar Hill** (be sure to pull out for the view) and then down to **Eggemoggin Reach**. The alternate scenic route is 175 south to **Brooklin** and back along the Reach through Sedgwick. These two routes meet at the **Little Deer Isle Bridge.** Be sure to cross the bridge (see "Deer Isle, Stonington, and Isle au Haut").

TO DO

SAILING

Buck's Harbor Marine (326-8839), South Brooksville, is the place from which daysail charters leave. Captain Gil Perkins (326-4167) offers half- and full-day cruises on his 30-foot sailboat *2nd Fiddle* and power cruiser *Queen Mary*. *Summertime* (359-2067; 1-800-562-8290 outside the state), a 53-foot pinky schooner, offers daysails and longer cruises from several ports around Penobscot Bay.

SEA KAYAKING

The Phoenix Center (374-2113), Route 175, Blue Hill Falls. With a salt pond on its acreage, the center is well positioned to teach and guide half-day and full-day sea kayaking on both sides of the Blue Hill peninsula. Wilderness canoe camping, backpacking, and rock-climbing trips are also offered. Inquire about the Fantasy Island Escape (a guide paddles with you to a private island, prepares your dinner, and disappears to return in the morning to make breakfast).

The Activity Shop (374-3600), Green's Hill, Route 172, Blue Hill. Kayak rentals start at $25 a day including a free pickup from the water.

Also see "Deer Isle, Stonington, and Isle au Haut."

SPECIAL LEARNING PROGRAM

Wooden Boat School (359-4651), off Naskeag Point Road, south of the village of Brooklin. A spinoff from *Wooden Boat* magazine more than 14 years ago, this seafaring institute of national fame offers more than 75 summer courses between June and October, ranging from building your own sailboat, canoe, or kayak to navigation and drawing and painting. Facilities are a former estate on Eggemoggin Reach, and visitors are encouraged to come to the library and to shop in the Big House. The former brick barn now houses three separate boatbuilding spaces, and you can wander down to the Boathouse, now a classroom and evening gathering spot. For a course catalog write: Wooden Boat School, P.O. Box 78, Brooklin 04616. Accommodations available.

Also see "Deer Isle, Stonington, and Isle au Haut."

GREEN SPACE

Blue Hill. Our friends at the Blue Hill Bookstore tell us that this was not the setting for the children's classic *Blueberries for Sal,* by Robert McClosky—a longtime summer resident of the area. But we choose to disbelieve them. It looks just like the hill in the book and has its share of in-season blueberries. The big attraction, however, is the view of the Mount Desert mountains. To find the mile-long trail to the top, drive north from Blue Hill Village on Route 172 and take a left across from the Blue Hill Fairgrounds; after 0.8 mile, a sign on your right marks the start of the path.

CONSERVATION AREA

Holbrook Island Sanctuary (326-4012), Route 176 in West Brooksville (on Cape Rosier) is a state wildlife sanctuary of 1,350 acres, including 2.3 miles of shore and 115-acre Holbrook Island. No camping is permitted, but a lovely picnic area adjoins a pebble beach. A network of old roads, paths, and animal trails leads along the shore and through marshes and forest. It's the creation as well as the gift of Anita Harris, who died in 1885 at age 92, the sole resident of Holbrook Island. Her will stipulated that her mansion and all the other buildings on the island be demolished. She was also responsible for destroying all homes within the sanctuary. Wildlife is plentiful and birding is exceptional, especially during spring and fall migrations. Great blue herons nest around the pond and the estuary. Bald eagles and peregrine falcons and an eagle's nest may also be seen. Inquire about guided nature walks, Tuesdays and Thursdays in July and August.

LODGING

RUSTIC RESORTS

🐾♥ **Oakland House** (359-8521; 1-800-359-RELAX), Brooksville 04617. Off the Herrick Road. Most cottages open May through October with Lone Pine Cottage open year-round. The picturesque old mansard-roofed hotel opened by Jim Littlefield's forebears in 1889 now houses only the dining rooms and serves as a centerpiece for this unusually extensive property, with a half mile of frontage on Eggemoggin Reach, and lake as well as saltwater beaches. Fifteen cottages (each different, most with living rooms and fireplaces) are scattered through the woods and along the shore, each accommodating two to nine people. Some accept pets and smokers. There are no TVs (with the exception of Lone Pine, which has satellite TV and a VCR) and firewood is free. Families feel particularly welcome. Facilities include a dock, rowboats, badminton, croquet, a rec hall full of games, and some spectacular hiking trails. Breakfast and dinner are served in the old-fashioned dining rooms, one reserved for families, the other adults-only. After a century of "plain Maine cooking," the menu is now up to par (see *Dining Out*); wine and beer are served. Thursday is lobster picnic night. Cottages rent by the week: $597–835 MAP per adult in-season (children's rates slide) and $373–761 per week (housekeeping) in shoulder seasons. This is a great spot for a wedding or family reunion. (Also see Shore Oaks Seaside Inn under *Inns and Bed & Breakfasts*.)

🐾♥ **Hiram Blake Camp** (326-4951), Cape Rosier, Harborside 04642. Open mid-May to mid-October. Well off the beaten track, operated by the same family since 1916, this is the kind of place you come to stay put. All cottages are situated within 200 feet of the shore, with views of Penobscot Bay. There are 6 one-bedroom cottages, 5 cottages with two bedrooms, and 3 with three bedrooms; each has a living room with a wood-burning stove; some have a fireplace as well. Each has a kitchen, a shower, and a porch. Guests with housekeeping cottages cook for themselves in the four shoulder months, but in July and August everyone eats in the dining room, which doubles as a library because thousands of books are ingeniously filed away by category in the ceiling. There are rowboats at the dock, a playground, and a recreation room with table tennis and board games; also ample hiking trails. The camp is run by the children, grandchildren, and great-grandchildren of Captain Hiram Blake. From $225 per week for the one-room Acorn Cottage to $775 for a three-bedroom cottage (up to six guests, plus $180 per week per adult for meals, $130 for children ages 12 and under. Rates drop during "housekeeping months" to $150–550 per week.

INNS AND BED & BREAKFASTS
In Blue Hill 04614

John Peters Inn (374-2116), Peters Point. Open May through October. An imposing mansion, a fantasy place with columns, fine Oriental rugs and a grand piano in the living room, and airy, superbly furnished guest rooms (many with fireplaces), set on 25 shorefront acres, a mile from the center of town. The 14 guest rooms are divided between the mansion and the Carriage House in which four suites have kitchens, fireplaces, and decks. There's a glassed-in breakfast room, a pool, and lawns sloping down to the water. A canoe, rowboat, and small sailboat are available to guests. $130–165 per couple includes a fabulous breakfast. Children over age 12. Rick and Barbara Seeger are warm, helpful hosts.

Blue Hill Farm (374-5126), Box 437. Open year-round. An attractive old farmhouse on 48 acres laced with walking/cross-country ski trails. The former barn has been reworked as an open-beamed combination breakfast room, dining and living room with plenty of light and space to read quietly alone or mingle with other guests. Innkeepers Jim and Marcia Schatz are usually around, manning the desk or the adjoining kitchen. Upstairs are seven small guest rooms, each with a private bath. The attached farmhouse offers seven more guest rooms with shared baths (including one appealing single) and more comfortable common rooms, one with a woodstove. $80–95 double (less off-season) includes a very full breakfast. Dinner, with live music, is also served; see *Dining Out*.

Blue Hill Inn (374-2844), near the junction of Main Street and Route 177. Open mid-May through Thanksgiving. A classic 1830s inn on a quiet, elm-lined street in the village. The 11 guest rooms, some with sitting rooms and/or working fireplaces, are all carefully furnished with antiques and have private baths. A pine-floored suite with kitchen, sitting areas, deck, fireplace, and handicapped-access bath is next door in the Cape House. Common rooms are ample and tasteful. In good weather guests gather for cocktails in the garden. A full breakfast, five-course candlelight dinner, and hors d'oeuvres are included in $150–190 double, plus 15 percent service charge; B&B rates also available. Inquire about kayaking and sailing packages. (Also see *Dining Out*.)

Elsewhere on the Blue Hill Peninsula

Buck's Harbor Inn (326-8660; fax, 326-0730), Box 268, South Brooksville 04617. Open year-round. In the lively little village of South Brooksville, the inn derives its name from the delightful yachting harbor at the end of its street. Built in 1901 as an annex to a larger, long-vanished hotel, Peter and Ann Ebeling's mansard-roofed inn offers six bedrooms, 2½ baths, and pleasant common rooms. The dining room is open to the public November to April 1 on Saturday nights, and in summer the neighboring Landing Restaurant (see *Dining Out*) offers fine food and views. We like the feel of this place, from the sea-bright rooms to the glass-faced breakfast room; a full breakfast (Swedish pancake trees if you're lucky) features fresh fruit. Pets are accepted off-season. $50 single, $65 double; $75 for the suite with an attached room, ideal for a family with one child.

Eggemoggin Reach Bed & Breakfast (359-5073), RR 1, Box 33A, Herrick Road, Brooksville 04673. Closed mid-October to mid-May. Susie and Mike Canon built this many-windowed waterside house as a retirement retreat but have transformed it into an unusually luxurious B&B, one that just keeps growing bigger and better. What you see from the suite that fills the whole third floor, and also from the equally luxurious second-floor suites, is one of the better views along the Maine coast. A cottage in the pines is divided into two attractive "studio" units, each with stove, cathedral ceiling, sitting area, and private screened porch overlooking Deadman's Cove. Bay Lodge, added in 1997, offers two more pine-walled units with efficiency kitchens, porches or decks, and water views. Rooms in the main house and common space are more formal than the cottages: Oriental rugs, wing chairs, a gracious dining room table, the setting for breakfasts both innovative and substantial. The partially screened porch with its view is a place you could easily spend entire days. Inquire about Tuckaway Cottage, also waterfront. A dock with rowboat and canoe await. Children must be 12. $160–175 per couple.

Shore Oaks Seaside Inn (359-8521; 1-800-359-RELAX), part of the Oakland House property (see *Rustic Resorts*) and one of the best-kept secrets of the region. Built at the turn of the century as a private "cottage," it eventually became absorbed into the resort complex—where it dozed until Sally, a trained designer, married Jim (Littlefield) and focused her considerable energy on this 10-bedroom stone and shingle building, renovating it totally but preserving the old simple feel of summer life centered on the water (the porch and lawn command sweeping views of the entrance to Eggemoggin Reach) and the big stone hearth. We also appreciated the bedtime reading light and the deep old tub. Guests have full use of all Oakland House facilities and can breakfast as well as dine in the hotel dining room, but this is a place apart. Coffee and tea are available from early morning in the dining room (where breakfast is also frequently served), and the living room and library are delightful. Our favorite is Number 7, a corner room overlooking the water with no less than six windows and a working fireplace, mission oak furniture and a sense of space and comfort. $60–95 per person MAP in-season; B&B rates available, less in shoulder seasons. The entire house can be rented for family reunions and weddings.

🐾✍ **Seaside Bed and Breakfast** (359-2792), RR-01, Box 6800, Sedgwick 04676. Open May through September. Wally and Darcy Campbell built their classic Cape on Eggemoggin Reach in 1982 when the Maine couple returned from Saudi Arabia, where Wally was maintenance chief of an oil field and Darcy taught. With their daughter now launched on her own career, the Campbells offer three rooms, two upstairs (each with a bath), and a basement-level garden apartment with a canopied double bed, a full kitchen, and living and dining areas. All rooms have water views and the common rooms are attractive. Well sited for kayakers (within walking distance of the boat landing on the Benjamin River). Worth noting: Until recently both Darcy and Wally taught in the Stonington Junior High School, but now they spend the winters on the road—in a vintage 1958 Greyhound bus that they have fitted out as a vehicle for touring North America's "blue highways." From $65 double to $145 for five in the two upstairs rooms.

Breezemere Farm Inn (326-8628; 1-888-223-FARM), Box 290, Brooksville 04617. Open year-round. An 1850s farmhouse overlooking Orcutt's Harbor that's been taking in guests since 1917, recently revitalized by innkeepers Laura Johns and Carolyn Heller. Gradually they have been tastefully redoing the seven guest rooms in the house itself (five share baths) and have done a job on the cottages (sleeping two to six), good for families: resident animals include sheep, goats, and chickens. Buffet breakfast included in the rates: $55–65 shared bath, $85 private bath, $400 per week for "studio cottages," $475–675 for housekeeping cottages sleeping two to six. Dinner is served.

The Brooklin Inn (359-2777), Route 175, Brooklin 04616. A casual, friendly old inn on the edge of the village. Lorraine Duffy charges $70 and serves breakfast and dinner.

WHERE TO EAT

DINING OUT

Firepond (374-9970), Main Street, Blue Hill. Open mid-May through October for dinner, lunch most of the year. Although long revered as the best restaurant around, Firepond received mixed reviews the summer of 1998. But chef Craig Rodenheiser is still in charge of the kitchen, and while the dining room has been substantially expanded, reservations remain a must for dinner in August. Request a table on the porch, within earshot of an old millstream (recently added sliding glass windows now keep you warm if needed). The specialties are delicately flavored veal, maybe with shiitake mushrooms and sun-dried tomatoes, and seafood dishes like local scallops with leeks; also roast duckling or tournedos of beef with the chef's sauce of the day. Dinner entrées run $14.95–29.95.

Jonathan's (374-5226), Main Street, Blue Hill. Open daily year-round for lunch and dinner. Now owned by the same New York restaurateur who owns Firepond, but at this writing still a dependably good bet for seafood prepared imaginatively and well. Entrées $16.95–18.95)

The Landing Restaurant (326-8483), Buck's Harbor, South Brooksville. Open May to October, Tuesday through Sunday from 5 PM. Kurt and Verena Stoll, from Zurich (Switzerland), have enhanced the decor and view of the harbor and reports of the food here are excellent. The menu might include veal saltimbocca ($20) and roasted rack of Australian range lamb with caramelized onion and sun-dried tomato ($24). Wines run $10–42.

Blue Hill Farm (374-5126), Route 15, north of Blue Hill. Open for dinner, nightly in-season, fewer nights off-season. Check. Innkeeper Jim Schatz thoroughly enjoys cooking, as evidenced by the quality of the fare served in the inn's large common room (it's the interior of a barn). Specialties include Maine bouillabaisse, locally raised chicken, and seafood pastas. You can almost always count on live music, usually a jazz trio. $25 prix fixe. BYOB at this writing but wine and beer is planned. Reserve.

Surry Inn (667-5091), Route 172, Contention Cove, Surry. Open nightly for dinner. This pleasant dining room overlooking a cove is well known locally for reasonably priced fine dining. The menu changes often but always includes interesting soups—maybe Hungarian mushroom or lentil vegetable—and a wide selection that might include veal tarragon, medallions of pork sautéed with herbs and red wine vinegar, spicy garlic frogs' legs, and scallops with pesto and cream. Entrées $14–17.

Blue Hill Inn (374-2844), Union Street, Blue Hill. Dinner served June through October, Wednesday through Sunday (Tuesday in July) by reservation only. The candlelit dining room is large and there is a choice of two dinner entrées. The $30 prix fixe menu changes nightly. You might begin with a salad of lobster, potatoes, and peas, then dine on salmon with Pernod or beef fillet with blue-cheese sauce, and finish with parfait glacé. The wine list includes over 100 labels and has received *Wine Spectator*'s Award of Excellence.

The Lookout (359-2188), Flye Point (2 miles off Route 175), North Brooklin. Memorial to Columbus Day, dinner from 5:30; Sunday brunch. Reserve a table on the porch for the best view. This 1890s summer hotel (still in the family that built the house) has a spectacular view of Herrick Bay on one side and the Acadia Range on Mount Desert beyond Blue Hill Bay on the other. The menu might include grilled salmon with cucumber dill sauce or seared venison, finished with port wine and boysenberry. Entrées $13–20.

Oakland House (359-8521), off Herrick Road, Brooksville. Open mid-June through September. Reservations requested. This old-fashioned dining room is one of the hidden gems of the peninsula because, while it has been here more than a century, its fare has changed radically and wine and beer have been added within the past couple of years. Portions are still huge (too much!). Entrées change nightly but might include native salmon in white wine butter and lightly crumbled lemon ($16.95) and penne pasta with sautéed artichoke hearts, mushrooms, garlic, and fresh, sweet cream ($14.95); price includes salad and vegetables. Saturday is still prime rib night and desserts are time-tried specialties like the house steamed chocolate pudding with Sunshine Sauce, Bucksport bread and raisin custard, and Maine blueberry buckle with freshly whipped sweet cream.

Also see *Dining Out* in "Deer Isle, Stonington, and Isle au Haut."

LUNCHING OUT

Jean-Paul's Bistro (374-5852), Main Street, Blue Hill Village. Open just July and August, 11–4 for lunch and then for tea until 5. Fitting neither into "dining out" or simply "eating out," this bistro is a category in its own right. The view of Blue Hill Bay is unbeatable and the food is summer light, with a French accent as thick and authentic as Jean-Paul's. "Les Sandwiches" include *croque monsieur,* a walnut tarragon chicken salad with watercress on whole-grain bread and "quiche du jour." A prix fixe lunch: soup, Caesar salad, and chicken with tea or lemonade is $12.95. Of course many people come specifically for the fresh baked desserts. We came for tea on a sunny afternoon and sampled the exquisite chocolate truffle terrine with delicate wild strawberries, and the taste will forever be mixed in memory with the view. The preferred seats are outside under umbrellas or, better yet, in one of the Adirondack chairs that can be grouped together around tables on the lawn overlooking the water. Wine and beer served.

EATING OUT

The Left Bank Bakery and Cafe (374-2201), Route 172, Blue Hill. Open daily 7 AM–10 PM. A sensational success as a place both to eat and to hear nationally known musicians (see *Entertainment*). Exceptional baked goods, soups, freshly picked salads, spinach pie, fruit pies, and reasonably priced dinners like mushroom bean Stroganoff and apricot chicken. In summer, frequent nightly programs pack the place.

Cafe Out Back (COB) at the Buck's Harbor Market (326-8683), center of Brooksville village, Route 176. The market has a lunch counter and the fully licensed café is a very attractive space, open in summer months 8–11, noon–2, and 5–9, except Sunday night, shorter hours off-season. Check. All baking is done here and the stuffed croissants and breads are exceptional (great picnic fare); the menu ranges from pizzas to full seafood dinners; also a lunch counter in the store.

Captain Isaac Merrill Inn & Cafe, middle of Blue Hill, next to the general store, a new café in an old house. Daytime chowders, baguette sandwiches, soda fountain, moderately priced evening meals like roast Maine turkey and local haddock broiled in herb lemon butter, also Portuguese seafood stew.

Bagaduce Lunch, Route 176, North Brooksville (at the Reversing Falls). Seasonal. A great spot with picnic tables by the river.

Morning Moon Cafe (359-2373), Brooklin. Open daily 7 AM–2 PM, except Monday, also for dinner Thursday through Sunday 5–8. A tiny oasis in the middle of Brooklin Village. Fresh-dough pizza, full menu: traditional American fare like a really good BLT, fine fish-and-chips.

Merrill & Hinckley (374-2821), Union Street, middle of Blue Hill. If Blue Hill has a center, this is it: a great old-fashioned general store and a source of picnic fixings. Don't waste a nice day by eating inside!

Also see *Eating Out* in "Deer Isle, Stonington, and Isle au Haut."

ENTERTAINMENT

MUSIC

✎ **Kneisel Hall Summer Music School** (374-2811), Pleasant Street, Route 15, Blue Hill. Faculty and students at this prominent old summer school for string and ensemble music present a series of Sunday afternoon and Friday evening concerts, early July through mid-August. Also inquire about student concerts, open rehearsals, and children's concerts.

The Left Bank Bakery and Cafe (374-2201), Route 172, northern fringe of the village of Blue Hill. A 60-seat café that's become a stop on the national folk music, humor, jazz, and poetry circuit. It stages the likes of Tom Rush, Dave Mallet, and Bill Morrissey, also many less well known but promising performers. Pick up a copy of the entertainment roster; reservations advised for big names.

WERU (469-6600), a nonprofit community radio station based on Route 1 in East Orland (89.9 FM), is known for folk and Celtic music, jazz, and reggae.

Bagaduce Chorale (326-8532), Blue Hill. A community chorus staging several concerts yearly ranging from Bach to show tunes.

Surry Opera Company (667-2629), Morgan Bay Road, Surry. Zen master Walter Nowick founded this company in 1984 and mounts fairly spectacular productions most (but not all) summers, often incorporating performers from Russia and other countries. Performances are held throughout the area, but home base is Walter Nowick's Concert Barn.

Flash in the Pan Steel Band, Brooksville, a community steel drum band that performs Monday nights in summer months in the middle of South Brooksville.

Also see Blue Hill Farm under *Dining Out.*

SELECTIVE SHOPPING

ART GALLERIES

In Blue Hill: **Leighton Gallery** (374-5001), Parker Point Road. Open June to mid-October. Exhibits in the three-floor gallery change every few weeks, but there are some striking staples: Judith Leighton's own oils, the wonderful variety of sculpted shapes in the garden out back, and the unforgettable wooden animal carvings by local sculptor Eliot Sweet. **Liros Gallery** (374-5370), Main Street, specializes in fine paintings, old prints, maps, and Russian icons. **Jud Hartman Gallery and Sculpture Studio** (374-9917), Main Street, exhibits Hartman's own realistic bronze sculptures of northeastern Native Americans. **Randy Eckard** (374-2510), 4 Pleasant Street, displays and sells limited edition prints of his precise, luminous landscapes. **The Gallery at Caterpillar Hill** (359-6577) is yet another reason to stop at the area's most panoramic view. Positioned right next to the scenic pullout (Route 15/17), it features changing works featuring local landscapes. **Quinn Gallery** (667-8490), Route 172, Surry. A truly eclectic and quality collection of paintings, photography, jewelry, pottery, blown glass.

Also see "Deer Isle, Stonington, and Isle au Haut."

ARTISANS

Rowantrees Pottery (374-5535), Union Street, Blue Hill. Open year-round, daily in summer (8:30–5, Sunday from noon) and weekdays in winter (7–3:30). Find your way back behind the friendly white house into the large studio. It was a conversation with Mahatma Gandhi in India that got Adelaide Pearson going on the idea of pottery in Blue Hill by using glazes gathered from the town's abandoned copper mines, quarries, and bogs. More than 50 years later, Sheila Varnum continues to make the deeply colored glazes from local granite and feldspar. She invites visitors to watch tableware being hand thrown and to browse through the upstairs showroom filled with plates, cups, vases, and jam pots. Note the prints and original work by a longtime Blue Hill summer resident, artist Frank Hamabe.

Rackliffe Pottery (374-2297), Route 172, Blue Hill. Open Monday through Saturday 9–5, also Sunday afternoon. Phyllis and Phil Rackliffe worked at Rowantrees for 22 years before establishing their own business. They also use local glazes, and their emphasis is on individual small pieces rather than on sets. Visitors are welcome to watch.

Handworks Gallery (374-5613), Main Street, Blue Hill. Open Memorial Day to late December, Monday through Saturday 10–5. A middle-of-town space filled with unusual handwoven clothing, jewelry, furniture, rugs, and blown glass.

North Country Textiles, Route 175, South Penobscot (326-4131), and Main Street, Blue Hill (374-2715). Open May through December in Blue Hill, summer months on Route 175. A partnership of three designer/weavers: Sheila Denny-Brown, Carole Ann Larson, and Ron King. The shop displays jackets and tops, mohair throws, guest towels, and coasters, all in bright colors and irresistible textures.

Scott Goldberg Pottery, Route 176, Brooksville. Open daily May to October. Scott Goldberg and Jeff Oestreich display their own stoneware pottery as well as work by others.

Peninsula Weavers (374-2760), Green's Hill, Blue Hill. Open Monday through Saturday. Weavers share a studio in the Bagaduce Library complex, using Swedish looms and techniques. Woven rugs, scarves, weaving supplies. Inquire about weaving classes.

Gail Disney (326-4649), Route 176 between North Brooksville and Brooksville Corners. Visitors are welcome year-round. Handwoven cotton and wool rag rugs, custom made.

ANTIQUES

Roughly a dozen antiques shops are scattered through the peninsula, described in a pamphlet guide available at all. Anyone with a serious interest in early American and European painted country furniture should stop by **Anne Wells Antiques** (374-1093) just north of Blue Hill Village on Route 172. Open Monday through Saturday 10:30–5 and by appointment.

BOOKSTORES

Blue Hill Books (374-5632), 2 Pleasant Street (two doors up from the post office), Blue Hill. A long-established, full-service, family-run bookstore.

North Light Books (374-5422), Main Street, Blue Hill. A full-service, family-run bookstore.

Wayward Books (359-2397), Route 15, Sargentville; mid-May through December, 10–5, Saturday noon–5. A good used-book store.

SPECIAL SHOPS

Blue Hill Tea & Tobacco Shop (374-2161), Main Street. Open Monday through Saturday 10–5:30. An appealing shop dedicated to the perfect cup of tea or coffee, a well-chosen wine, and the right blend of tobacco.

Blue Hill Yarn Shop (374-5631), Route 172 north of Blue Hill Village. Open Monday through Saturday 10–4. A mecca for knitters in search of a variety of wools and needles. Lessons and original hand knits are sold.

H.O.M.E. Co-op (469-7961), Route 1, Orland. Open daily in-season 9–5. A remarkable complex that includes a crafts village (visitors may watch pottery making, weaving, leatherwork, woodworking); a museum of old handicrafts and farm implements; a large crafts shop featuring handmade coverlets, toys, and clothing; a market stand with fresh vegetables, herbs, and other garden produce; and a chapel with services open to the public on Wednesday afternoons. There is a story behind this nonprofit enterprise, which has filled an amazing variety of local needs. Be sure to stop.

SPECIAL EVENTS

Last weekend in July: **Blue Hill Days**—arts and crafts fair, parade, farmer's market, antique car rally, shore dinner, boat races.

August: **St. Francis Annual Summer Fair.**

Labor Day weekend: **Blue Hill Fair,** at the fairgrounds—harness racing, a midway, livestock competitions; one of the most colorful old-style fairs in New England.

December: a weekend of Christmas celebrations.

CASTINE

Sited at the tip of a finger of the Blue Hill peninsula, Castine is one of Maine's most photogenic coastal villages, the kind writers describe as "perfectly preserved." Even the trees that arch high above Main Street's clapboard homes and shops have managed to escape the blight that has felled elms elsewhere, and Castine's post office, said to be the oldest operating post office in the country, has recently been restored, painted a tasteful tan and mulberry.

Situated on a peninsula at the confluence of the Penobscot and Bagaduce Rivers, the town still looms larger on nautical charts than on road maps. Yacht clubs from Portland to New York visit annually. Castine has always had a sense of its own importance. According to the historical markers that pepper its tranquil streets, Castine has been claimed by four different countries since its early-17th-century founding as Fort Pentagoet. It was an early trading post for the Pilgrims but soon fell into the hands of Baron de Saint Castine, a young French nobleman who married a Penobscot Indian princess and reigned as a combination feudal lord and Indian chief over Maine's eastern coast for many decades.

Since no two accounts agree, we won't attempt to describe the outpost's constantly shifting fortunes—even the Dutch owned it briefly. Nobody denies that in 1779 residents (mostly Tories who fled here from Boston and Portland) welcomed the invading British. The Commonwealth of Massachusetts retaliated by mounting a fleet of 18 armed vessels and 24 transports with 1,000 troops and 400 marines aboard. This small navy disgraced itself absurdly when it sailed into town in 1779. The British Fort George was barely in the making, manned by 750 soldiers with the backup of two sloops, but the American privateers refused to attack and hung around in the bay long enough for several British men-of-war to come along and destroy them. The surviving patriots had to walk back to Boston, and many of their officers, Paul Revere included, were court-martialed for their part in the disgrace. The town was occupied by the British again in 1814.

Perhaps it was to spur young men on to avenge this affair that Castine was picked (150 years later) as the home of the Maine Maritime Academy, which occupies the actual site of the British barracks and keeps a training ship anchored at the town dock, incongruously huge beside the graceful, white-clapboard buildings of a very different maritime era.

In the mid–19th century, thanks to shipbuilding, Castine claimed to be the second-wealthiest town per capita in the United States. Its genteel qualities were recognized by summer visitors, who later came by steamboat to stay in the eight hotels. Many built their own seasonal mansions.

Only two of the hotels survive. But the town dock is an unusually welcoming one, complete with picnic tables, parking, and rest rooms. It remains the heart of this walking town, where you can amble uphill past shops or down along Perkins Street to the Wilson Museum. Like many of New England's most beautiful villages, Castine's danger seems to lie in the perfect preservation of its beauty, a shell unconnected to the lives that built it. Few visitors complain, however. Castine is exquisite.

GUIDANCE

Castine Merchants Association (326-4884), P.O. Box 329, Castine 04421. Request the helpful map/guide, available by mail or around town. The obvious place to begin exploring is the Castine Historical Society on the common.

GETTING THERE

By air: See the "Bar Harbor" and "Portland" chapters for air service.

By car: The quickest route is the Maine Turnpike to Augusta, then Route 3 to Belfast, then Route 1 to Orland, then 15 miles down Route 175.

MEDICAL EMERGENCY

Blue Hill Memorial Hospital (374-2836), the largest facility in the area, has a 24-hour emergency room. **Castine Community Health Services** (326-4348) has a doctor on call.

TO SEE

MUSEUMS

Castine Historical Society (326-4118), Abbott School Building, Castine Town Common. July through Labor Day 10–4, from 1 on Sunday; closed Monday. The former high school, converted to a historical society and welcome center for the town's bicentennial in 1996. Center stage is a stunning quilted mural designed by artist Margaret Hodesh and stitched by more than 50 townspeople. An ornate chair, said to be carved from the wood of a sunken English warship, is also displayed, along with vintage photos.

Wilson Museum (326-8545), Perkins Street. Open May 27 through September 30, Tuesday through Sunday 2–5. Housed in a fine waterside building donated by anthropologist J. Howard Wilson, a summer resident who amassed many of the displayed Native American artifacts as well as ancient ones from around the world. There are also changing art exhibits, collections of minerals, old tools and farm equipment, an 1805 kitchen, and a Victorian parlor. **Hearse House** and a blacksmith shop are open Wednesday and Sunday afternoons in July and August, 2–5. The complex also includes the **John Perkins House,** open only during July and August, Wednesday and Sunday 2–5 ($4 admission); a pre–Revolutionary War home, restored and furnished in period style. Guided tours and crafts and fireside cooking demonstrations.

HISTORIC SITES

Fort George. Open May 30 through Labor Day, daylight hours. The sorry tale of its capture by the British during the American Revolution (see above) and again during the War of 1812, when redcoats occupied the town for eight months, is told on panels at the fort—an earthworks complex of grassy walls (great to roll down) and a flat interior where you may find Maine Maritime Academy cadets being put through their paces.

State of Maine (326-4311). The current training vessel for Maine Maritime Academy cadets, a 498-foot former US Navy hydrographic survey ship, is open to visitors weekdays in July and August; 30-minute tours are conducted by midshipmen.

TO DO

BOAT EXCURSION
Balmy Days (338-4652; 596-9041), a 1932 coastal Maine workboat, offers tours of Castine Harbor and around Islesboro, also sunset cruises and trips to Belfast; bicycles and kayaks welcome.

FISHING
We are told that you can catch flounder off the town dock and mackerel at Dyce's Head, below the lighthouse.

KAYAKING
New England Outdoor Center (800-766-7238), Dennett's Wharf. As the annual site of L. L. Bean's Sea Kayaking Symposium, Castine has long been associated with sea kayaking—recognized as a great place to paddle out from—so it was just a matter of time before a savvy outfitter located here. NEOC, with elaborate base camps on the Kennebec and Penobscot, is better known for its white-water-rafting programs, but it is well respected as an all-around outfitter. Half-day ($55), full-day ($90) and sunset ($35) tours are offered.

GOLF AND TENNIS
Castine Golf Club (326-4311), Battle Avenue. Offers nine holes and four clay courts.

SWIMMING
British Canal, Backshore Road. During the War of 1812, the British dug a canal across the narrow neck of land above town, thus turning Castine into an island. Much of the canal is still visible.

Maine Maritime Academy (326-4311) offers, for a nominal fee, gymnasium facilities to local inn guests. This includes the pool, weight room, and squash and racquetball courts.

GREEN SPACE

Witherle Woods is an extensive wooded area webbed with paths at the western end of town. The ledges below **Dyce's Head Light,** also at the western end of town, are great for clambering. The **Castine Conservation Commission** sponsors nature walks occasionally in July and August. Check local bulletin boards.

KIM GRANT

Castine Harbor

LODGING

All lodging listings are for Castine 04421.

❉ **Castine Inn** (326-4365), P.O. Box 41, Main Street. Open May through mid-December. A rare bird among Maine's current plethora of B&Bs and inns: a genuine, 1890s summer hotel that's been lovingly and deftly restored, right down to the frieze beneath its roof. It offers 19 light and airy, but unfrilly (the furniture is Maine made—solid but not fancy), guest rooms, all with private baths and many with harbor views. Guests enter a wide, welcoming hallway and find a pleasant sitting room and a pub, both with frequently lit fireplaces. A mural of Castine by the previous innkeeper covers all four walls of the dining room—a delightful room with French doors leading out to a broad veranda overlooking the inn's terraced, formal gardens (a popular place for weddings) and the town sloping to the harbor beyond. Children over 8 welcome. In 1997

Tom and Amy Gutow acquired the inn. A Paris-trained chef who has cooked in some of New York's finest restaurants, Tom has even improved on the inn's long-established culinary fame. (See *Dining Out*.) Rates: $85–135 (more for two-room suites if occupied by four) includes a full breakfast; less off-season. Minimum 2-day stay in July and August.

Pentagoet Inn (326-8616; 1-800-845-1701), P.O. Box 4, Main Street. Open May to October. The main inn is a very Victorian summer hotel with a turret, gables, and a wraparound porch. The rooms in the inn itself are unusually shaped, nicely furnished, and cozy; one room in neighboring **Ten Perkins Street** (a 200-year-old home) has a working fireplace. In all there are 16 guest rooms, each with private bath. There are two sitting rooms and a pink-walled dining room that opens onto the garden. $99–129 per couple B&B includes early-morning coffee, a full buffet-style breakfast, afternoon tea, and evening wine and cheese; children over 12 are welcome.

WHERE TO EAT

DINING OUT

Castine Inn (326-4365), Main Street. Open daily for breakfast and dinner. The ambiance, quality, and value of this dining room are well known locally, filling it most nights. Crabmeat cakes in mustard sauce and chicken and leek potpie have been the house specialty for so long that current, Paris-trained chef-owner Tom Gutow has had to continue the tradition or face mutiny. However, Gutow has already established his own reputation for dishes like beef tenderloin carpaccio seasoned with coriander and cumin with tarragon goat cheese and greens for starters ($7), entrées like Kalamata olive–crusted salmon with caponata and yellow pepper–grapefruit sauce ($19) and lobster with wild mushrooms, leeks, corn, and a tarragon-shallot sauce ($24). Local seafood and produce are featured. Save room for the flourless chocolate cake with fromage blanc and raspberry sauce or Earl Grey mousse with a hazelnut orange tuile and laurel syrup (both $5). The wine list is well priced and balanced.

EATING OUT

Bah's Bake House (326-9510), Water Street. Open 7 AM–9 PM daily, until 8 PM on Sunday. A few tables and a great deli counter featuring sandwiches on baguette bread, daily-made soups, salads, and baked goods.

Dennett's Wharf (326-9045), Sea Street (off the town dock). Open daily spring through fall for lunch and dinner. An open-framed, waterside structure said to have been built as a bowling alley after the Civil War. Seafood, smoked fish, and seafood pasta salads, and waterside dining.

The Breeze (326-9034), town dock. Seasonal. When the summer sun shines, this is the best place in town to eat: fried clams, hot dogs, onion rings, and soft ice cream. The public facilities are next door and, with luck, you can dine at the picnic tables on the dock.

SELECTIVE SHOPPING

Leila Day Antiques (326-8786), Main Street. An outstanding selection of early American furniture, also paintings, quilts, and Maine-made Shard Pottery. The shop is in the historic Parson Mason House and the approach is through a formal garden.

McGrath-Dunham Gallery (326-9938), Main Street. Open daily May through October. Thirty artists.

✐ **Compass Rose** (326-9366; 1-800-698-9366), Main Street. Frances Kimball's fully stocked bookstore features children's titles, summer reading, regional books, and Penguin classics.

Water Witch (326-4884), Main Street. Jean de Raat sells original designs made from Dutch Java batiks, English paisley prints, and Maine-made woolens. This is a totally standout store. This store alone is worth the trip.

SPECIAL EVENTS

June through October: Windjammers usually in port on Tuesdays.

✐ *Third weekend in June:* **Summer Festival**—craft show, ethnic food, children's activities.

July: **Sea Kayaking Symposium** sponsored by L. L. Bean.

DEER ISLE, STONINGTON, AND ISLE AU HAUT

The narrow suspension bridge across Eggemoggin Reach connects the Blue Hill peninsula with a series of wandering land fingers linked by causeways and bridges. These are known collectively as Deer Isle and include the towns of Deer Isle and Stonington, the villages of Sunset and Sunshine, and the campus of the nationally respected Haystack Mountain School of Crafts. Many prominent artisans have come here to teach or study—and stayed. Galleries in the village of Deer Isle display outstanding work by dozens of artists and craftspeople who live, or at least summer, in town. Stonington, a full 40 miles south of Route 1, remains a working fishing harbor, but it too now has its share of galleries. Most buildings, which are scattered on smooth rocks around the harbor, date from the 1880s to World War I boom years, during which Deer Isle's pink granite was shipped off to face buildings from Rockefeller Center to Boston's Museum of Fine Arts.

In Stonington life still eddies around Bartlett's Supermarket, Billings Diesel and Marine, and the Commercial Pier, home base for one of Maine's largest fishing/lobstering fleets. But the tourist tide is obviously rising. Galleries and seasonal, visitor-geared shops are multiplying along Main Street and the downtown, upscale Inn on the Harbor and the Atlantic Cafe (same ownership) are now open year-round.

Stonington

CHRISTINA TREE

Why not? Deer Isle offers the kind of coves and lupine-fringed inlets usually equated with "the real Maine," and Isle au Haut, a mountainous island 8 miles off Stonington, is accessible by mail boat. It's a glorious place to walk trails maintained by the National Park Service.

GUIDANCE

Deer Isle–Stonington Chamber of Commerce (348-6124) maintains a spacious new information booth on Route 15 at Little Deer Isle, just this side of the bridge. Open 10–4 mid-June to Labor Day, sporadically after that for a few weeks.

The *Annual Bay Community Register,* listing some useful touring information, is available from **Penobscot Bay Press** (367-2200), Box 36, Stonington 04681. The press also publishes *Island Advantages* and the *Weekly Packet.*

GETTING THERE

Follow directions for Blue Hill; continue down Route 15 to Deer Isle.

MEDICAL EMERGENCY

Island Medical Center (367-2311), Airport Road, Stonington. (Also see "Blue Hill Area.")

TO SEE

Deer Isle Granite Museum (367-6331), Main Street, Stonington. Open Memorial Day through Labor Day, Monday through Saturday 10–5, Sunday 1–5. Housed in the former pharmacy, this beautifully conceived and executed small museum features an 8-by-15-foot working model of quarrying operations on Crotch Island and the town of Stonington in 1900.

Derricks move and trains carry granite to waiting ships. Photo blowups and a video also dramatize the story of the quarryman's life during the height of the boom (see the introduction to this chapter, above).

Salome Sellers House (348-2897), Route 15A, Sunset. Open late June through late September, Wednesday and Friday 2–5. This is the home of the Deer Isle–Stonington Historical Society, an 1830 house displaying ship models, Native American artifacts, and old photos; interesting and friendly.

Lighthouses. Pick up a copy of the *Deer Isle Lighthouse Trail* at the chamber booth on Little Deer Isle or at the Island Heritage Trust office in Deer Isle Village. **Pumpkin Island Light**, near enough to the old ferry landing for a good photo (it's 3 miles from the chamber booth, down Eggemoggin Road), is now a private home. **The Eagle Island Light** can be viewed from Sylvester Cove in Sunset or, better yet, from the Eagle Island Mailboat (see *Boat Excursions*), from which you can also see the **Heron Neck, Brown's Head,** and **Goose Rocks Lights.** From Goose Cove Lodge in Sunset you can see and hear the now-automated **Mark Island Light** (its old bronze bell sits on the resort's lawn); the **Saddleback Ledge Light** is also visible on the horizon. (For details about reaching the **Isle au Haut light** see *Boat Excursions* and *Lodging.*)

Haystack Mountain School of Crafts (348-2306), Deer Isle (south of Deer Isle Village; turn left off Route 15 at the Mobil station, follow signs 7 miles). Visitors are welcome to join campus tours offered Wednesday at 1 PM, June through August, and to shop at the school store, the campus source of art supplies and craft books. Phone to check when visitors are also welcome to view student shows and to attend lectures and concerts. The school itself is a work of art: a series of small, spare buildings clinging to a steep, wooded hillside above Jericho Bay.

TO DO

BOAT EXCURSIONS

🐾 **Isle-au-Haut Company** (367-5193) departs Stonington at least twice daily except Sunday, year-round. See *Green Space* for a description of the island; note that the island's famous hiking trails cluster around Duck Harbor, a mail-boat stop only in summer; a ranger usually meets the morning boat to orient passengers to the seven hiking trails, the picnic area, and drinking-water sources (otherwise a pamphlet guide serves this purpose). Be sure to check the schedule, and in July and August come as early as possible for the first ferry. The boat tends to fill up, and it's first come, first served; if you miss the first boat, you can at least make a later one. The boat takes kayaks and canoes for a fee, but not to Duck Harbor. $12 adult, $5 per child, $3 per pet one-way to Duck Harbor.

The Eagle Island mail boat. Operated by the Sunset Bay Company (348-9316), the *Katherine* leaves Sylvester's Cove in Sunset, mid-June through mid-September, Monday through Saturday, 8:30 AM. A half mile off Sunset, Eagle Island is roughly a mile long with rocky ledges, sandy beach, and an abandoned lighthouse. Inquire about island rentals. The round-trip mailboat run is $15 per person, $10 per kayak or canoe.

Charter boats. Jericho Bay Charters (348-6614) and Old Quarry Charters (367-8977) both offer charter fishing, sightseeing cruises, also serve as water taxis.

KAYAKING AND CANOEING

Granite Island Guide Service (348-2668). Deer Isle. Dana Douglas, who is a Registered Maine Guide, a former white-water canoe racer, and a Congregational minister who has biked around the world, and his wife, Anne, a veteran schoolteacher, offer guided kayaking and canoeing ranging from $45 for a half day ($35 under age 13) to $200 for 2 days with overnight island camping ($125 per child). Full-day and 3-day expeditions also offered. Inquire about canoeing trips in northern Maine.

Finest Kind Restaurant (348-7714) at Joyce's Crossroad (off 15 and 15A) rents canoes and kayaks: $35 per day for a solo, $45 for tandem.

GOLF AND TENNIS

Island Country Club (348-2379), Deer Isle, welcomes guests mid-June through Labor Day; nine holes.

✐ **Finest Kind Restaurant** (348-7714) operates an 18-hole mini-golf course.

SPECIAL LEARNING PROGRAMS

Haystack Mountain School of Crafts (348-2306), Deer Isle. Offers 2- and 3-week sessions June through Labor Day, attracting some of the country's top artisans in a variety of crafts. See directions and details under *To See*.

The Stonington Painter's Workshop (367-2368 mid-June through September; otherwise, 617-776-3102). Nationally prominent artist and art teacher Jon Imber coordinates and is one of several instructors at this July series of weeklong landscape workshops. The current fee is $400 per week plus lodging.

SWIMMING

✐ **Lily Pond,** off Route 15 north of Deer Isle Village. Mothers congregate here with small children.

GREEN SPACE

Island Heritage Trust (348-2455), P.O. Box 42, Deer Isle 04627. Write ahead or stop by the trust's office in Deer Isle Village for detailed maps to walking trails, which include Settlement Quarry and several offshore islands.

Ames Pond, east of town on Indian Point Road, is full of pink-and-white water lilies in bloom June to early September.

Holt Mill Pond Preserve. A walk through unspoiled woodland and marsh. The entrance is on Stonington Cross Road (Airport Road)—look for a sign several hundred feet beyond the medical center. Park on the shoulder and walk the dirt road to the beginning of the trail, then follow the yellow signs.

Isle au Haut (pronounced *eye-la-ho*) is 6 miles long and 3 miles wide; all of it is private except for the 2,800 acres of national park that are wooded and webbed with hiking trails. More than half the island is preserved as part of Acadia National Park (see "Acadia Area"). Camping is forbidden everywhere except in the five Adirondack-style shelters at Duck Harbor (each accommodating six people), which are available by reservation only. For a reservation form, phone 288-3338 or write to Acadia National Park, P.O. Box 177, Bar Harbor 04609; the form must be sent on or as soon after April 1 as possible. Camping is permitted mid-May through mid-October, but in the shoulder season you have to walk 5 miles from the town landing to Duck Harbor. In summer months the mail boat arrives at Duck Harbor at 11 AM, allowing plenty of time to hike the island's dramatic Western Head and Cliff trails before returning on the 5:30 boat. Longer trips, like that to the summit of Mount Champlain near the northern end of the island, are also possible. Trails are pine carpeted and shaded, with water views. For more about day trips to the island, see *Boat Excursions*.

Crockett Cove Woods Preserve (a Maine Nature Conservancy property) comprises 100 acres along the water, with a nature trail. Take Route 15 to Deer Isle, then the Sunset Road; 2.5 miles beyond the post office, bear right onto Whitman Road; a right turn at the end of the road brings you to the entrance, marked by a small sign and registration box. From Stonington, take the Sunset Road through the village of Burnt Cove and turn left on Whitman Road.

Barred Island Preserve is a 2-acre island just off Stinson Point, accessible by a wide sandbar; request permission for access from Goose Cove Lodge (see *Rustic Resort*).

LODGING

RUSTIC RESORT

✎♿ **Goose Cove Lodge** (348-2508; 1-800-728-2508), Sunset 04683. Open mid-May to mid-October. Sited on a secluded cove, this many-windowed lodge with its fine library and dining, unusually attractive common space and cabins, and waterside/island trails, is a real standout. Joanne and Dom Paris have retained the rustic feel but brightened both the lodge and nine cottages (sleeping four to eight) with well-chosen art, quilts, hooked rugs, and attractive fabrics. Just 15 minutes from Stonington, Goose Cove is at the end of its own 1½-mile road, set in a 21-acre preserve with trails along the shore and low-tide passage to Barred Island, a Nature Conservancy property well known to birders. Guests congregate for evening cocktails and hors d'oeuvres and frequently team up for dinner, although there is no pressure to do so. Children are given a special menu and dine early. Dinners are exceptional (see *Dining Out*) and breakfast might include potato latkes with sweet pepper relish and crème fraîche or baked egg in a dilled crêpe nest with smoked salmon and chèvre. You might want to pack a flashlight if you book one of the more secluded cabins (we recommend Bunchberry); the evening walk through the firs can be inky black despite the stars. Widely scattered, most cottages have water views. Four attached to the lodge also have water views (one doesn't) and rooms in the lodge include a suite. Late June through August, a week's reservation is requested but shorter stays are frequently available due to cancellations. $90–143 per person MAP or $100–190 per couple B&B; sliding rates for children; a three-person minimum is required in high season for some cottages; a 2-night minimum is required during July and August. Service charge added.

INNS

In Stonington 04681

The Inn on the Harbor (367-2420; 1-800-942-2420), P.O. Box 69. Open year-round. The old Captain's Quarters has been transformed into an upscale inn with 14 comfortable rooms (private baths, phones, cable TV), each named for a different windjammer (the passenger schooners usually visit Stonington in the course of a summer week). While the inn is smack on Main Street, rooms face the ample deck and working harbor, one of Maine's most photographed views. Request this view, if possible from a second-floor room like the Heritage (with a working hearth made of local granite) or the American Eagle (with a full kitchen and private deck). The Stephen Taber is a freestanding room retaining its tin walls and ceiling (it used to be a barber shop), and the Shipps House is a two-bedroom suite in the proprietor's own vintage 1850 house. Innkeeper Christina Shipps, a New York–based jeweler, also now owns the town's waterside restaurant, Cafe Atlantic (see *Dining Out*). Rates are $100–125 with continental breakfast.

Burnt Cove Bed & Breakfast (367-2392), RFD 1, Box 2905, Whitman Road. Open late May through Columbus Day weekend. A modern, year-round home designed to maximize its view of Burnt Cove, both from the large, open central room and from the inviting deck. This is the comfortable, genuinely hospitable home of local fisherman Bob Williams and Diane Berlew, a good breakfast chef. It's within walking distance of the Crockett Cove Woods Preserve and a few steps from a beach on which kayakers can put in. The large downstairs bedroom with a cathedral ceiling, full bath, and private entrance is $90 and the two upstairs bedrooms (shared bath) are $55 single, $65 double. $12 for extra person in a room.

Pres du Port (367-5007), Box 319, West Main and Highland Avenue. Open May through October—a find. A cheery, comfortable B&B with three imaginatively furnished guest rooms. The one in back has a cathedral ceiling and loft, kitchenette, deck access, and private bath; the other two share a bath (but each has its own sink) and have screened and glassed-in porches with harbor views, plus there's an outdoor hot tub with water views. Charlotte Casgrain is a warm, knowledgeable hostess who enjoys speaking French. $75–80 double with a buffet breakfast, less for a single; price includes tax. Inquire about cottages.

Island House (367-5900), Weedfield Road, RD 1, Box 3227. Open June through September. An ultramodern redwood home with water views, furnished in pastels and southwestern decor. The five rooms (three with private bath) range from the large, balconied Merchants Room to the tiny top-floor Lookout Room, an enclosed cupola above the trees. Rates $110–120 per room, $200 for the neighboring two-bedroom guesthouse; full breakfast and tea included. Amenities include a hot tub and laundry facilities.

Ocean View House (367-5114), Main Street, Box 261. Open July and August only. A white-clapboard, Victorian inn set on a knoll near the dock, built to board quarry workers employed on Crotch Island. Midwesterners Christine and Jack Custer have created bright, cheerful rooms; the three guest rooms share baths, but all have bay views. $70 per room; breakfast of homemade pastries.

In Deer Isle 04627

🐾 **The Inn at Ferry Landing** (348-7760), Old Ferry Road, RR 1, Box 163. Overlooking Eggemoggin Reach is this 1840s seaside farmhouse with magnificent water views, spacious rooms, patchwork quilts, and a great common room with huge windows and two grand pianos which innkeeper-musician Gerald Wheeler plays and uses for summer recitals and spontaneous music sessions. The six guest rooms include a huge master suite with a woodstove and skylights. The Mooring, a two-story, two-bedroom fully equipped housekeeping cottage, is perfect for families. $95–100 for double rooms, $140 for the suite, and $1,000 per week ($200 per night) for the Mooring. Rates include a full breakfast; minimum of 2 days in high season.

Pilgrim's Inn (348-6615). Open mid-May through mid-October. Squire Ignatius Haskell built this house in 1793 for his wife, who came from Newburyport, Massachusetts, and demanded an elegant home. The story goes that he built the house in Newburyport and had it shipped up to Deer Isle, where it stands in the middle of the village overlooking Northwest Harbor and his millpond. Of the 15 guest rooms, 12 have private baths and 3 on the top floor share one. All rooms have water views, and many have fireplaces. Downstairs there are four common rooms, and a dining room is in the old barn, known for its gourmet fare (see *Dining Out*). Eighteenth-century colors predominate, and the inn is furnished throughout with carefully chosen curtains and rugs, antiques, and local art; $160–215, plus 15 percent service charge, double MAP. The one-bedroom cottages next door are $135 EP. Weekly rates.

The Haskell House (348-2496), P.O. Box 595, Route 15. Open year-round. Margaret Haskell Logus is a pleasant host who genuinely welcomes guests to the gracious house a seafaring forebear built in 1899. Two attractive upstairs guest rooms share a bath; $60 includes a full breakfast.

Holden Homestead (348-6832), P.O. Box 221, Route 15. Open May to November. A former church parsonage, this is an 1850s house, owned since the 1860s by the Holden family and restored by Cynthia Bancroft

Melnikas, a fifth-generation Holden. Three rooms, the back one (by far the most attractive, and the quietest) has a private entrance and deck. $43–48 single, $53–65 double.

On Isle au Haut 04645

The Keeper's House (367-2261), P.O. Box 26. This turn-of-the-century lighthouse keeper's house sits back in firs behind its small lighthouse on a point surrounded on three sides by water. Guests arrive on the mail boat from Stonington just in time for a glass of sparkling cider before dinner (guests who want something stronger are advised to bring it). Dinner is by candlelight, and guests tend to sit together, four to a table, and after dinner wander down to the smooth rocks to gaze at the pinpoints of light from other lighthouses and communities in Penobscot Bay. There are four guest rooms in the main house, a self-contained room in the tiny Oil House. It's a hike to the island's most scenic trails in Duck Harbor on the southeastern end of the island. $289–296 per couple, $180–221 single, and $50 per child includes all meals and use of bikes; add $20 per person round-trip for the ferry plus $4 per night for parking.

MOTEL

Eggemoggin Landing (348-6115), Little Deer Isle 04650. Open mid-April through mid-October. A nicely sited motel just beyond the Deer Isle suspension bridge, overlooking Eggemoggin Reach. The 20 rooms are clean, the Sisters Restaurant next door (same owners) serves breakfast, lunch, and dinner, and moorings and a marina are part of the complex. Rooms: $59–69 per unit.

COTTAGE RENTALS

Reasonably priced rentals are available on both Deer Isle and Isle au Haut. Check with **Island Vacation Rentals** (367-5095) and **Edgewater Rentals** (348-6612), both in Stonington.

CAMPGROUND

Sunshine Campground (348-6681), RR 1, Box 521D, Deer Isle 04627. Open Memorial Day weekend to mid-October. Long established and the only campground in the area; wooded RV and tent sites.

WHERE TO EAT

DINING OUT

Pilgrim's Inn (348-6615), Main Street, Deer Isle Village. Open mid-May to late October. Dinner is by reservation only. Guests congregate at 6 for hors d'oeuvres served in the living room or on the deck, and the five-course meal begins at 7, including soup, salad, an entrée that varies with the night: maybe halibut with artichokes and cream, poached salmon with beurre blanc, or paella. Lettuce is from the backyard, chickens from Deer Isle, breads and desserts are baked daily. The dining room is a converted goat barn; tables are covered with checked cloths and lighted by candles. Wine is served. Prix fixe $29.50.

The Cafe Atlantic (367-2420), Main Street, Stonington. Open year-round for lunch and dinner. Innkeeper Christina Shipman (of the Inn on the Harbor) opened this much-needed middle-of-town restaurant in 1998. In summer it doubles in size with a big harborside deck (the Atlantic Deck) and opens an ice cream window, but the core of the place is an attractive dining room serving staples like broiled haddock with native crab studding and a light Dijon sauce ($12.95) and prime rib (served Friday through Sunday, $13.95).

Goose Cove Lodge (348-2508), Route 15A, Sunset. Open May to mid-October. Outside guests are welcome by reservation, gathering for cock-tails and hors d'oeuvres at 6. Friday night always features lobster and one Saturday night we dined on potato-and-horseradish-crusted salmon fillet with chive and pink peppercorn beurre blanc, served with fresh asparagus and greens. Dessert was a chocolate almond terrine with a trio of sauces. Wine is served. Dinner is $30. No reservations are necessary for lunch or tea at the **Outdoor Cafe at Goose Cove Lodge,** open Monday through Saturday in-season 1:30–3:30, weather permitting.

Eaton's Lobster Pool Restaurant (348-2383), Deer Isle. Seasonal. Mon-day through Saturday 5–9, Sunday noon–9. A barn of a place with a great view. For the best value, be sure to order lobster à la carte and by the pound instead of the higher-priced "lobster dinner." The restaurant is still in the family that settled the spot, and it is the area's premier lobster pound. BYOB. We've received both rave reviews and complaints from readers.

EATING OUT

Lily's Cafe (397-5936), Route 15, Stonington. Open in summer 8 AM–8 PM, in winter Tuesday through Thursday 10 AM–7 PM, Friday until 8 PM, Saturday 5 PM–8 PM. A Route 15 house is the area's newest hot restaurant (Julia Child was spotted lunching here, summer of 1998) with a series of dining rooms, upstairs and down. The table we lunched on was a sheet of glass over a fascinating collection of shells, and the lunch was "Russell's Special": hard salami, melted Havarti cheese, ar-tichoke hearts, lettuce, and vinaigrette dressing on French bread ($4.95). Yum. The dinner specials vary widely, so call after 2 PM to check; it varies from penne with shiitake mushrooms to roast beef ($4.95–9.95). BYOB.

Finest Kind (348-7714), marked from Route 15 between Stonington and Deer Isle Village. Open April through November, lunch and dinner; Sunday breakfast from 8 AM. Neat as a pin, a log cabin with counter and booths. Dinner from $6.25 for chopped steak to $12.95 for prime rib. Pizzas, fried seafood, salad bar, calzones, draft and imported beers.

Sisters Restaurant (348-6115), Little Deer Isle. Open April 15 through October 15 for breakfast, lunch, and dinner. Sisters Robin Rosenquist and Patty Show now operate the restuarant just the Little Deer Isle side of Eggemoggin Reach. Lunch inside or take out to the picnic benches by the water, but dinner is an inside affair (unless you want your steamed lobster by the water) and it's an interesting menu: cashew-crusted chicken ($13.95), seaood tossed with tomatoes and cream on angelhair pasta ($14.95), or salmon in puff pastry ($15.95). Draft beer and wine ($4.95 per glass). Sail-in guests welcome; the 15-acre complex includes the Eggemoggin Landing marina.

Eaton's Pier (348-6036), Sunshine Road, Deer Isle. Open mid-May through October, Monday through Saturday 11–8. No relation to the Lobster Pool Eatons (see *Dining Out*). A small waterside restaurant with a screened porch, picnic tables, reasonably priced lobster plus corn, steamed shrimp. No alcohol permitted.

The Lobster Deck & Restaurant at North Atlantic Seafood, Stonington. Open year-round, daily 5 AM–9 PM, from 6 AM on Sunday. All inside and sometimes smoky, featuring steamed and fried seafood, lobster, scallop, and crabmeat stews.

Fisherman's Friend Restaurant (367-2442), School Street, Stonington (just up the hill from the harbor). Open daily 11–9, BYOB. Simple decor, reasonably priced food, varied reviews in recent years but not about the pies.

SELECTIVE SHOPPING

ART GALLERIES AND ARTISANS

Pick up a current (free) copy of the *Maine Cultural Guide* published by the **Maine Crafts Association** (348-9943), which maintains its own gallery featuring the work of over 70 members at 6 Dow Road, marked off Route 15 just before Deer Isle Village. The registry represents 300 members but is particularly helpful in tracking down the art galleries and crafts studios, which are most plentiful here. It's available at most local galleries.

Deer Isle Artists Association, 6 Dow Road, Deer Isle Village. Open mid-June to Labor Day. A 150-member cooperative gallery with exhibits changing every 2 weeks.

Turtle Gallery (348-2538), Route 15, north of Deer Isle Village. Open June through September, Monday through Saturday 10–5 and Sunday 2–6. Newly relocated in the Old Centennial House Barn, this choice gallery now fills two levels with paintings, photographs, prints, sculpture, and outstanding craftswork.

Hoy Gallery (367-6339/5628), East Main Street, Stonington. Open daily July through September, 10–5. A big, white barn set back from the street, filled with Jill Hoy's bold, bright Maine landscapes.

Eastern Bay Gallery (367-5006), West Main Street, Stonington. Open May through October, daily. Janet Chaytor now owns this fine crafts gallery, featuring fine clothing, jewelry, pottery, and such, most made within 40 miles of Stonington.

The Blue Heron (348-6051), Route 15, Deer Isle (near the center of the village). Open daily June through September. An old barn attached to Mary Nyburg's pottery studio is filled with fine contemporary crafts featuring work by Haystack Mountain School's faculty (see *To See*).

© JILL ANISE HOY

October Glare *by Jill Hoy*

Dockside Quilt Gallery (348-2531), Church Street, Deer Isle Village. Tacked by hand, finished by machine; stunning quilts.

Rugosa Rose (348-6615), at the Pilgrim's Inn, Deer Isle Village. Open mid-May to mid-October. A highly selective gallery showing the work of 40 local artists: pottery, jewelry, woodcarving, clothing, notecards, more.

Pearson's Jewelry (348-2535), Old Ferry Road (off Route 15), Deer Isle. Ron Pearson has an international reputation for creative designs in gold and silver jewelry as well as delicately wrought tabletop sculpture in other metals. The shop also displays work by local blacksmith/sculptor Douglas Wilson.

William Mor (348-2822), Reach Road, Deer Isle. Open mid-June through October. Hand-thrown pottery in interesting shapes, functional and handsome. Designs are based on Oriental folk pottery; the studio, kiln, and shop are in a garden setting. Oriental rugs are also sold.

Jutta Graf (348-7751) weaves stunning one-of-a-kind rugs usually on view in local galleries, also at her studio by appointment.

Terrell S. Lester Photography (348-2676), East Main Street, Deer Isle Village. Open in-season Monday through Saturday 10–5; otherwise by appointment. Popular, sharply detailed local landscapes.

G. Watson Gallery (367-0983), Main Street (above the Grasshopper Shop), Stonington. Open June through October, daily. Ron Watson operates a serious gallery.

SPECIAL SHOPS

Old Deerfield Parish House (348-9964), Route 15, Deer Isle Village. Open daily mid-June through October. Mother and daughter Genevieve Bakala and Janice Glenn operate a combination antiques, crafts, and whatever shop that's a phenomenon in its own right: hand-made quilts, used books, rag rugs, whatever. Browser's heaven.

Dockside Books and Gifts (367-2652), West Main Street, Stonington. Seasonal. Al Webber's waterside bookstore has an exceptional selection of Maine and marine books, also gifts and a great view with a harbor balcony where you can sit and read, or not read.

✎ **Nervous Nellie's Jams and Jellies and Mountainville Cafe** (348-6182; 1-800-777-6845), Sunshine Road, halfway between Deer Isle and Sunshine. Open daily mid-June to mid-October, 10–5, café open July and August. Sculptor Peter Beerits displays his whimsical life-sized sculptures and sells his jams and jellies (wild blueberry preserves, blackberry peach conserve, hot tomato chutney) and serves tea, coffee, and scones. Children of all ages love the sculptures, like the big red lobster playing checkers as a 7-foot alligator looks on. Follow directions for Haystack.

The Dry Dock (367-5528), Main Street, Stonington. Open daily mid-May through Christmas. A varied trove of craftswork and mostly New England–made products.

The Periwinkle, Deer Isle. A tiny shop crammed with books and carefully selected gifts.

The Grasshopper Shop (367-5070), Main Street, Stonington. A Maine chain with a mix of clothing, gifts, and gadgets that you usually don't get away from without buying something.

SPECIAL EVENTS

July: **Independence Day** parade and fireworks in Deer Isle Village.
August: Lobster-boat races and **Stonington Fisherman's Festival.**

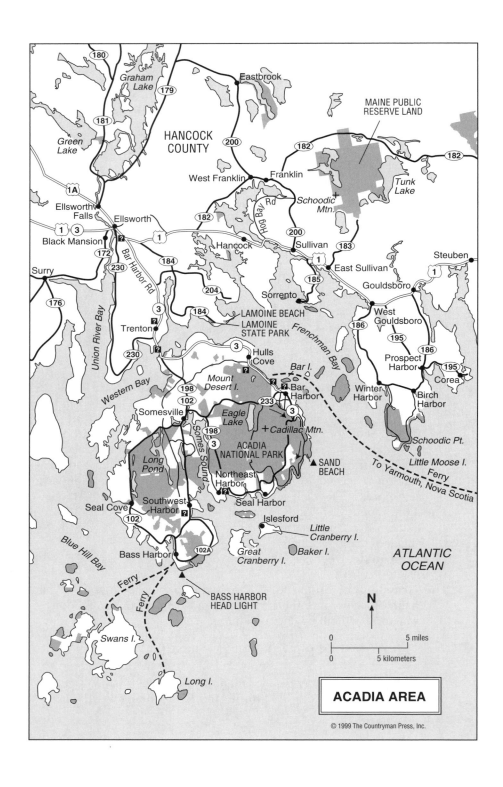

ACADIA AREA

© 1999 The Countryman Press, Inc.

Acadia Area

Acadia National Park; Bar Harbor and Ellsworth;
The Quiet Side of Mount Desert; East Hancock County

MOUNT DESERT ISLAND

Mount Desert is New England's second-largest island, one conveniently linked to the mainland. Two-fifths of its 108 square miles are maintained as Acadia National Park, laced with roads ideally suited for touring by car, 51 miles of "Carriage Roads" specifically for biking and skiing, and 120 miles of hiking trails.

The island's beauty cannot be overstated. Seventeen mountains rise abruptly from the sea and from the shores of four large lakes. There are also countless ponds and streams, an unusual variety of flora, and more than 300 species of birds.

Native Americans first populated the area, using it as hunting and fishing grounds. Samuel de Champlain named it L'Isle de Monts Deserts in 1604. Although it was settled in the 18th century, this remained a peaceful, out-of-the-way island even after a bridge was built in 1836 connecting it to the mainland. In the 1840s, however, landscape painters Thomas Cole and Frederic Church began summering here, and their images of the rugged shore were widely circulated. Summer visitors began arriving by steamboat, and they were soon joined by travelers taking express trains from Philadelphia and New York to Hancock Point, bringing guests enough to fill more than a dozen huge hotels that mushroomed in Bar Harbor. By the 1880s, many of these hotel patrons had already built their own mansion-sized "cottages" in and around Bar Harbor. These grandiose summer mansions numbered more than 200 by the time the stock market crashed. Many are now inns.

Mount Desert Island seems far larger than it is because it is almost bisected by Somes Sound, the only natural fjord on the East Coast, and because its communities vary so in atmosphere. Bar Harbor lost its old hotels and many of its mansions in the devastating fire of 1947, which also destroyed 17,000 acres of woodland, but both the forest and Bar Harbor have recouped, and then some, in recent decades.

Northeast Harbor, Southwest Harbor, and the remaining villages on the island—which also enjoy easy access to hiking, swimming, and boating within the park—are relatively quiet, even in July and August, and the several accessible offshore islands are quieter still.

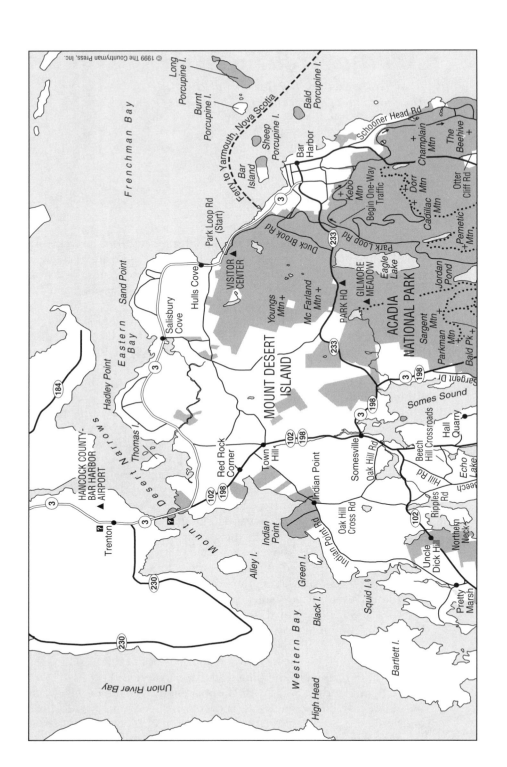

© 1999 The Countryman Press, Inc.

Long Porcupine I.

Burnt Porcupine I.

Sheep Porcupine I.

Bald Porcupine I.

Frenchman Bay

Ferry to Yarmouth, Nova Scotia

Bar Island

Bar Harbor

Schooner Head Rd

Champlain Mtn +

The Beehive +

3

Kebo Mtn +

Dorr Mtn +

Begin One-Way Traffic

Cadillac Mtn +

Otter Cliff Rd

Pemetic Mtn. +

Park Loop Rd (Start)

Duck Brook Rd

Park Loop Rd

233

VISITOR CENTER ▲

Hulls Cove

Eastern Sand Point

Youngs Mtn +

Mc Farland Mtn +

PARK HQ ▲

GILMORE MEADOW ▲

Eagle Lake

ACADIA

NATIONAL PARK

Jordan Pond

Sargent Mtn +

Parkman Mtn +

Bald Pk +

Salisbury Cove

Eastern Bay

3

233

198

3

Sargent Dr

MOUNT DESERT ISLAND

198

Somes Sound

102

198

Somesville

Oak Hill Rd

Beech Hill Crossroads

Hall Quarry

Hadley Point

The Narrows

Red Rock Corner

Town Hill

Indian Point

Oak Hill Cross Rd

Indian Point Rd

Beech Hill Rd

Echo Lake

Beech

Mount   Thomas

Desert

184

HANCOCK COUNTY-
BAR HARBOR
AIRPORT ▲

102

198

3

102

Ripples Rd

Uncle Dick Hill

Northern Neck

Trenton

3

230

Alley I.

Green I.

Indian Point

Squid I.

Pretty Marsh

Western Bay

Black I.

Bartlett I.

High Head

Union River Bay

230

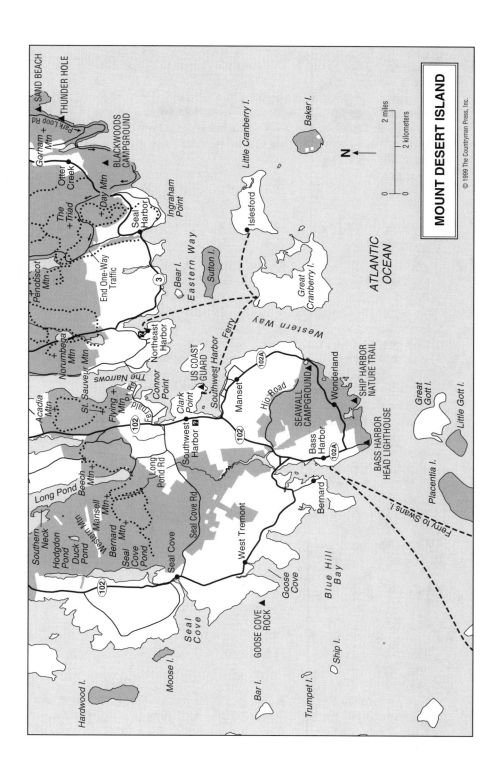

MOUNT DESERT ISLAND

© 1999 The Countryman Press, Inc.

N

0 ____ 2 miles
0 ____ 2 kilometers

SAND BEACH
THUNDER HOLE
Park Loop Rd
Gorham Mtn
BLACKWOODS CAMPGROUND
Otter Creek
Day Mtn
The Triad
Seal Harbor
Ingraham Point
Penobscot Mtn
End One-Way Traffic
3
Bear I.
Eastern Way
Sutton I.
Little Cranberry I.
Islesford
Great Cranberry I.
Baker I.
ATLANTIC OCEAN
Norumbega Mtn
Northeast Harbor
The Narrows
Connor Point
US COAST GUARD
Clark Point
Southwest Harbor
Manset
Hio Road
Ferry
Western Way
Acadia Mtn
St. Sauveur Mtn
Flying Mtn
Fernald Point
102
Southwest Harbor
Long Pond Rd
102
SEAWALL CAMPGROUND
Wonderland
SHIP HARBOR NATURE TRAIL
Bass Harbor
BASS HARBOR HEAD LIGHTHOUSE
Great Gott I.
Little Gott I.
Long Pond
Beech Mtn
Western Mtn
Mansell Mtn
Bernard Mtn
Southern Neck
Hodgdon Pond
Duck Pond
Seal Cove Pond
Seal Cove Rd
Seal Cove
West Tremont
Bernard
102A
102A
Placentia I.
Seal Cove
Goose Cove
GOOSE COVE ROCK
Blue Hill Bay
Moose I.
Hardwood I.
Bar I.
Trumpet I.
Ship I.
Ferry to Swans I.

Mount Desert's mountains with "their grey coats and rounded backs look like a herd of elephants, marching majestically across the island," travel writer Samuel Adams Drake wrote in 1891, describing the first impression visitors then received of the island. They were, of course, arriving by steamboat instead of down the unimpressive commercial strip that's Route 3. Today it's a shade harder to get beyond the clutter and crowds but still not that hard. The memorable march of rounded mountains is still what you see from excursion boats and from Little Cranberry Island, as well as from the eastern shore of Frenchman Bay, the area described in this chapter as "East Hancock County."

ACADIA NATIONAL PARK

The legacy of Bar Harbor's wealthy "rusticators" is Acadia National Park. A cadre of influential citizens, which included Harvard University President Charles W. Eliot, began to assemble parcels of land for public use in 1901, thus protecting the forests from the portable sawmill. Boston textile heir George Dorr devoted his fortune and energy to amassing a total of 11,000 acres and persuading the federal government to accept it. In 1919 Acadia became the first national park east of the Mississippi. It is now a 40,000-acre preserve, encompassing almost half of Mount Desert Island.

It's a shame that four-fifths of the park's 3 million annual visitors limit their tour to the introductory film in the visitors center and to the 27-mile Park Loop Road. The Loop Road is a good place to begin (see below), but the park has much more to offer, from simple hikes to rock climbing, horse-drawn carriage rides to swimming, bicycling, canoeing, and kayaking.

Within the park are 45 miles of carriage roads donated by John D. Rockefeller. These incredible gravel roads take bikers, hikers, joggers, and cross-country skiers through woods, up mountains, past lakes and streams. The paths also lead over and under 17 spectacular stone bridges. In recent years, volunteers have rallied to refurbish and improve this truly spectacular network.

Isle au Haut (see the "Deer Isle" chapter) and the Schoodic Peninsula (see "East Hancock County") are also part of Acadia National Park, but they are not located on Mount Desert Island, and are much quieter, less traveled areas.

FEES
The entrance fee for vehicles is $10 for a weekly pass. For individuals on foot or bicycle the fee is $5 for a weekly pass.

GUIDANCE
The park maintains its own visitors center (288-3338) at Hulls Cove, open mid-April through October. From mid-June to August 31, hours are 8–6 daily; during shoulder seasons, hours are 8–4:30. The park head-quarters at Eagle Lake on Route 233 (288-3338) is open daily through-

KIM GRANT

The rugged coastline of Acadia National Park

out the winter 8–4:30. For more information about the park, write to Superintendent, P.O. Box 177, Bar Harbor 04609. The glass-and-stone visitors center, set atop 50 steps, shows its 15-minute introductory film every half hour. Books, guides, and postcards may be purchased here. This is also the place to pick up a free map and a copy of the current "Acadia's Beaver Log" (a listing of all naturalist activities), to rent a cassette-tape tour, and to sign up for the various programs offered. Special evening programs are scheduled by the national park staff nightly, June through September, at the amphitheaters in Blackwoods and Seawall campgrounds. Children of all ages are eligible to join the park's Junior Ranger Program; inquire at the visitors center.

TO SEE

PARK LOOP ROAD

The 27-mile Loop Road is the prime tourist route within the park. There is a weekly fee of $10 per car on the road. It is possible, however, to get to mountain trails and some popular spots, such as the drive up Cadillac, without charge.

The Loop Road officially begins at the visitors center, but may be entered at many points along the way. Most of the road is one-way, so be alert to how traffic is flowing. Places of interest along the Loop Road include **Sieur de Monts Spring,** a stop that could include the Wild Gardens of Acadia, the Abbe museum, and Park Nature Center (see *Museum and Gardens*) as well as the covered spring itself; **Sand Beach,** which is actually made up of ground shells and sand and is a great beach to walk down and from which to take a dip, if you don't mind 50-degree water (there are changing rooms and lifeguards); **Thunder Hole,** where the water rushes in and out of a small cave, which you can view from behind a railing (the adjacent rocks can keep small children scrambling for hours); **Jordan Pond House,** popular for afternoon tea and popovers; and **Cadillac Mountain.** From Cadillac's smooth summit (accessible by car) you look out across Frenchman Bay dotted with the Porcupine Islands, which look like giant stepping-stones.

MUSEUM AND GARDENS

Robert Abbe Museum at Sieur de Monts Spring (288-3519), posted from both Route 3 (south of Jackson Laboratory) and the Park Loop Road. Open May to October, 9–5 daily during July and August, otherwise 10–4. Don't miss this exceptional collection of New England Native American artifacts: sweet-grass baskets, jewelry, moccasins, a birch-bark canoe, dioramas of Native American life during all seasons, an authentic wigwam. Changing exhibits teach about early life on Mount Desert Island, recent archaeological excavations, culture and traditions, and more. $2 per adult, $.50 per child. The museum overlooks the Park Nature Center and the Wild Gardens of Acadia, a pleasant walk where more than 300 species of native plants are on display with labels.

TO DO

BIKING

The 50-plus miles of broken-stone carriage roads make for some good mountain biking. Several outfitters in Bar Harbor (see *To Do—Bicycling* in the "Bar Harbor" chapter) rent equipment and can help you find good trails.

CAMPING

There are two campgrounds within the park, both in woods and close to the ocean. One vehicle, up to six people, and two tents are allowed on each site. Neither campground has utility hook-ups. Facilities include com-

Bicycling on the carriage roads in Acadia National Park

KIM GRANT

fort stations, cold running water, a dump station, picnic tables, and fire rings. Showers and a camping store are within half a mile of each. There are also five group campsites at each campground, which can be used by educational organizations and other formally organized groups. These must be reserved through the park, by writing to the superintendent after January 1 for a park reservation form. The two campgrounds within Acadia National Park are:

Blackwoods (288-3274), open all year. Reservations can be made for the period between June 15 and September 15 through the National Park Reservation Service (1-800-365-2267) at least 8 weeks in advance. Cost of sites is $16 per night during the reservation period, $14 per night in shoulder seasons; varying fees off-season.

Seawall (244-3600), near Southwest Harbor, open late May to late September. Sites at Seawall are meted out on a first-come, first-served basis. Get there early because a line forms, and as campers check out, others are checked in. Cost is $14 with a vehicle; $10 if you walk in.

HIKING

The park is a mecca for hikers. Several detailed maps are sold at the visitors center, which is also the source of an information sheet that profiles two dozen trails within the park. These range in diffculty from the **Jordan Pond Loop Trail** (a 3⅓-mile path around the pond) to the **Precipice Trail** (1½ miles, very steep, with iron rungs as ladders). There are 17 trails to mountain summits on Mount Desert. **Acadia Mountain** on the island's west side (2 miles round-trip) commands the best view of Somes Sound and the islands. **The Ship Harbor** on Route 102A (near Bass Harbor) offers a nature trail that winds along the shore and into the woods; it is also a great birding spot.

HORSE-DRAWN TOURS

Wildwood Stables (276-3622). Follow the Park Loop Road from the visitors center; turn left at the sign a half mile beyond Jordan Pond House. Two-hour horse-drawn tours in multiple-seat carriages are offered six times a day.

RANGER PROGRAMS

A wide variety of programs—from guided nature walks and hikes, to birding talks, sea cruises, and evening lectures—are offered throughout the season. Ask at the visitors center for current schedule.

ROCK CLIMBING

Acadia National Park is the most popular place to climb in Maine; famous climbs include the Precipice, Goat Head, and Otter Cliffs. See *To Do—Rock Climbing* in the "Bar Harbor" chapter for guide services.

SWIMMING

Within Acadia there is supervised swimming at **Sand Beach,** 4 miles south of Bar Harbor, and at **Echo Lake,** a warmer, quieter option, 11 miles west.

WINTER SPORTS

More than 43 miles of carriage roads at Acadia National Park are maintained as ski-touring and snowshoeing trails. Request the "Winter Activities" leaflet from the park headquarters (write to Superintendent, P.O. Box 177, Bar Harbor 04609).

BAR HARBOR AND ELLSWORTH

Bar Harbor is the island's big town, one of New England's largest clusters of hotels, motels, inns, B&Bs, restaurants, and shops—all within easy reach of the park visitors center on the one hand, and ferries to Nova Scotia on the other.

Ellsworth is the shire town and shopping hub of Hancock County, a pass-through place with a split personality: the old brick downtown blocks along and around the Union River and its 60-foot falls, and the unmitigated strip of malls and outlets along the mile or so along which Route 1A and 1 converge. Unfortunately, if you are coming down Route 1A from Bangor you miss the old part of town entirely, and it's well worth backtracking. Downtown Ellsworth offers the restored art deco Grand Theater, several good restaurants, and rewarding shopping, as well a sense of the lumbering-boom era in which the Colonel Black Mansion, arguably the most elegant in Maine, was built.

The 6 miles of Route 3 between Ellsworth and Bar Harbor are lined with a mix of commercial attractions (some of which are vacation savers if you are here with children in fog or rain), 1920s motor courts and 1960s motels, newer motor inns and hotels.

In Bar Harbor itself shops and restaurants line Cottage, Mount Desert, West, and Main Streets, which slope to the Town Pier and to

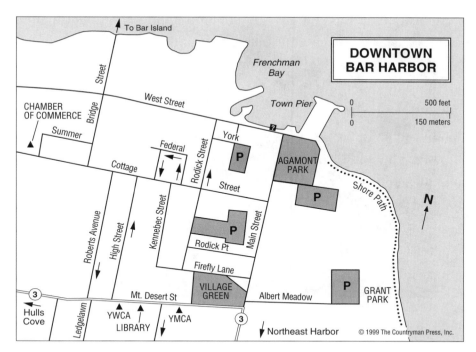

the Shore Path, a mile walk between mansions and the bay. During July and August, Bar Harbor is expensive and crowded. Between Labor Day and Columbus Day it is cheaper, less crowded, and Mount Desert is still beautiful. The rest of the year is off-season. If you take advantage of the solitude and bargains available in June or February (when there may be cross-country skiing), be sure you have access to a fireplace.

GUIDANCE

Bar Harbor Chamber of Commerce (year-round, 288-5103; 1-800-288-5103; bhcc@acadia.net; www.acadia.net/bhcoc), P.O. Box 158, 93 Cottage Street, Bar Harbor 04609, maintains seasonal information booths. Write for the free visitor's guide.

Mount Desert Island Regional Visitors Center (288-3411) is open daily May to mid-October (9–8 during high season) on Route 3, just after you cross the bridge. It is a walk-in center that offers rest rooms, national park information, and help with lodging reservations on all parts of the island.

Ellsworth Chamber of Commerce (667-5584/2617), 163 High Street, Ellsworth 04605 (in the Ellsworth Shopping Center; look for the Burger King), also maintains a well-stocked, friendly information center.

Also see "Acadia National Park."

GETTING THERE

By air: **Colgan Air** (1-800-272-5488) serves the Hancock County–Bar Harbor Airport in Trenton (between Ellsworth and Bar Harbor) from

Downtown Bar Harbor

Boston and Rockland. Avis, Hertz, and Budget rental cars are available at the airport. (Also see Bangor International Airport in the "Bangor" chapter of "Northern Maine" for connections with most American cities.)

By boat: **"The Cat"** (288-3395; 1-888-249-7245), a high-speed ferry to Nova Scotia, has introduced its share of problems (the speed creates very rough waters), but the trip from Nova Scotia now takes just 2½ hours (the old *Bluenose* ferry took 6 hours), and the boat departs both Bar Harbor and Yarmouth twice daily, making a day trip feasible (though rather pricey). One-way summer fares are $45 for adults, $20 children ages 5–16. Group fares available.

By private boat: A number of visitors arrive under their own sail; contact the Mount Desert or Bar Harbor Chamber of Commerce (see *Guidance*) for details about moorings, or contact the Bar Harbor harbormaster at 288-5571.

By bus: **Vermont Transit** serves Bar Harbor May through October. **Concord Trailways** also operates seasonal shuttle service to Bar Harbor.

By car: Take Route 3 East from Ellsworth to Bar Harbor. From Boston and New York to Ellsworth, there are three routes. The longest is Route 1 from Kittery. The shortest is I-95 to Bangor to I-395, then to Route 1A North to Ellsworth. The third is a compromise, and the most interesting: I-95 to Augusta, then Route 3 East to Belfast, and Route 1 North to Ellsworth.

GETTING AROUND

Both **Acadia National Park Tours** (288-3327) and **Oli's Trolley** (288-9899) offer narrated, 2½-hour bus tours through Bar Harbor and along the Park Loop Road, and 1-hour trolley tours, daily in-season.

MEDICAL EMERGENCY

Maine Coast Memorial Hospital (667-4520), Ellsworth. **Mount Desert Island Hospital** (288-5081), Bar Harbor, provides 24-hour emergency care.

TO SEE

✍ **Bar Harbor Oceanarium** (288-5005), Route 3 at the entrance to the island. Open 9–5 daily, except Sunday, mid-May to late October. Large seal exhibit and everything you ever wanted to know about a lobster; also the Thomas Bay Marsh Walk. $5.50 adults, $4 children ages 4–12. Tour the lobster hatchery for an additional fee.

College of the Atlantic (288-5015), Route 3, Bar Harbor. The **Ethel H. Blum Gallery**, Gates Community Center, open Monday through Saturday 9–5, is outstanding. The **Natural History Museum** (9–5 daily in summer, weekdays 10–4 Labor Day through Columbus Day) is housed in the original Acadia National Park headquarters, which has been moved to the college campus. It showcases the skeleton of a rare true-beaked whale; detailed dioramas depict plants and animals of coastal Maine. Note the hands-on discovery room, self-guided nature trail, Wednesday-evening lecture series, and museum shop. Admission is $2.50 adults, $1.20 seniors and teens, $.50 per child above age 3. Founded in 1969, the College of the Atlantic (COA) is a liberal arts college with a curriculum based on the study of "human ecology." Its 26 waterside acres, an amalgam of four large summer estates, are now a handsome campus for 230 students.

Bar Harbor Historical Society (288-0000), 33 Ledgelawn Avenue, Bar Harbor. Open mid-June through September, Monday through Saturday 1–4. Free. A fascinating collection of early photographs of local hotels, steamers, cottages, the cog railroad, and the big fire of 1947. Microfilm collection of area newspapers.

The Shore Path. This mile-long path runs from Agamont Park near the Bar Harbor Town Pier and along the bay. It's also accessible from Grant Park, off Albert Meadow at the corner of Main and Mount Desert Streets.

In Otter Creek

Jackson Laboratory (288-3371), Route 3. June to September, Monday and Wednesday, an audiovisual presentation about one of the world's largest mammalian-genetics research facilities. Cancer, diabetes, and birth defects are among the problems studied.

In Ellsworth

Colonel Black Mansion (Woodlawn), West Main Street. Open June to mid-October, Monday through Saturday 10–5 (last tour starts at 4:30). An outstanding Georgian mansion built as a wedding present in 1862 by John Black, who had just married the daughter of the local agent for a Philadelphia land developer, owner of this region. Supposedly, the bricks were brought by sea from Philadelphia, and it took Boston workmen three years to complete it. It is now open to the public, furnished just as it was when the Black family used it (three generations lived there). Besides the fine period furniture and spiral staircase, there is a lovely garden and a carriage house full of old carriages and sleighs. $5 per adult, $2 per child.

Stanwood Homestead Sanctuary and Museum (667-8460), Route 3. Open daily mid-June to mid-October, 10–4; sanctuary open year-round. Don't miss this exceptional place: a 130-acre nature preserve that is a memorial to Cordelia Stanwood (1865–1958), a pioneer ornithologist, nature photographer, and writer. The old homestead (1850) contains family furnishings and a collection of Stanwood's photos. There are gardens, a picnic area, and a gift shop. $2 per adult, $1.50 for seniors, and $.50 per child for the museum; no admission charge for the sanctuary.

FOR FAMILIES

There are several attractions along Route 3: the **Acadia Zoological Park** ($5 per adult, $4 per child) has 15 acres that house native and exotic animals, as well as a rain forest display. Along Route 3 there are waterslides, and many elaborate mini-golf and go-cart options.

TO DO

AIRPLANE RIDES

Acadia Air (667-5534), Route 3 at Trenton Airport. Flight instruction, aircraft rentals, and a number of well-worth-it sightseeing and whale-sighting flights.

Island Soaring Glider Rides (667-SOAR), also at the airport, offers motorless soaring flights daily.

BICYCLING

The 50-mile network of gravel carriage roads (see "Acadia National Park") constructed by John D. Rockefeller in 1915 lends itself particularly well to mountain biking.

In Bar Harbor, **Acadia Bike & Canoe Company** (288-9605) rents child trailers and every kind of bike; also provides detailed maps. **Bar Harbor Bicycle Shop** (288-3886) also rents a wide variety of bikes and offers handy access to the park. **Acadia Outfitters** (288-8118) also offers rentals. Companies offering sunrise rides from the top of Cadillac Mountain seem to vary each season.

BIRDING

For special programs led by park naturalists, consult "Acadia's Beaver Log," available at the park visitors center (see "Acadia National Park").

BOAT EXCURSIONS

There are a number of cruises available daily; **Frenchman Bay Nature Cruise** (288-3322) is narrated by a naturalist from Acadia National Park; check local listings for other options.

Kebo Valley Club, Bar Harbor

BOAT RENTALS
In Bar Harbor, **Harbor Boat Rentals** (288-3757) rents powerboats and sailboats.

BREWERY TOURS
Atlantic Brewing Company (288-9513), 30 Rodick Street, Bar Harbor, offers daily tours at 4 PM. The Brewer's Shop is open daily 10–6.

Bar Harbor Brewing Co. and Sodaworks (288-4592), Route 3, one mile north of Blackwoods campground, offers tours every 20 minutes on Tuesday and Thursday, 3:30–5 PM.

CANOEING AND KAYAKING
Most ponds on Mount Desert offer easy access. Long Pond, the largest lake on the island, has three access points. Boats can be launched at Echo Lake from Ike's Point, just off Route 102. Seal Cove Pond is less used, accessible from fire roads north of Seal Cove. Bass Harbor Marsh is another possibility at high tide. Canoe rental sources offer suggestions and directions. Kayaking is a recent but booming sport, easier to master than saltwater canoeing. More companies are offering guided tours and rentals each year. Outfitters include **Acadia Bike & Canoe Company** (288-9605), **Coastal Kayaking Tours** (288-9605), **Island Adventures** (288-3886), and **National Park Sea Kayak Tours** (288-0342) in Bar Harbor; **National Park Canoe Rentals** (244-5854) on Long Pond near Somesville; **Loon Bay Kayaking** (266-8888) in Trenton (they specialize in family outings); and **Life Sports** (667-7819) in Ellsworth.

DEEP-SEA FISHING
M/V Seal (288-4585) offers 4-hour fishing excursions; check local listings for other options.

GOLF

Kebo Valley Club (288-3000), Route 233, Bar Harbor. Open daily May through October. Eighteen holes; "oldest golf grounds in America," since 1892. **Bar Harbor Golf Course** (667-7505), Routes 3 and 204, Trenton. Eighteen holes.

HIKING

See "Acadia National Park."

LUMBERJACK SHOW

✎ **The Maine Lumberjack Show** (667-0067), Route 3 in Trenton. The 1¼-hour show includes events like ax throwing, log rolling, speed climbing, and more. Nightly show at 7 PM, rain or shine, late June through early September.

ROCK CLIMBING

Acadia Mountain Guides (288-8186) and **Atlantic Climbing** (288-2521) offer instruction and guiding for beginner through advanced climbers. (Also see *To Do—Rock Climbing* in "Acadia National Park.")

SAILING

The *Margaret Todd* (288-4585) sails from the Bar Harbor pier, late June through early October. This new 151-foot four-masted schooner offers 2-hour cruises through Frenchman Bay several times a day in high season, less frequently in slower weeks. The *Bay Lady* also offers 2-hour sails on an 85-foot schooner. Check current handouts for other daysails.

SWIMMING

✎ **Lake Wood** near Hull's Cove is a pleasant freshwater beach, ideal for children. The trick is finding it: Turn off Route 3 at the Cove Motel and take your second left up a dirt road (there is a small official sign); park and walk the short way to the beach. No facilities or lifeguard, but warm water.

Also see **Molasses Pond** in "East Hancock County."

Also see "Acadia National Park."

WALKING TOUR

Bar Harbor Tour Company offers "a step back in time," a historical tour led by a costumed guide from a bygone era. Approximately 1 hour. $10.

WHALE-WATCHING

Whale-watching is offered by a number of Bar Harbor–based companies including **Acadian Whale Watcher Co.** (288-9794), **Bar Harbor Whale Watch Co.** (288-2386), **Sea Bird Watcher Company** (288-5033), and **Whale Watcher Inc.** (288-3322). Remember to bring a jacket, sunblock, and your camera.

LODGING

The majority of Bar Harbor's nearly 3,000 beds, ranging from 1920s motor courts to large chain hotels and motels, are strung along Route 3, north of the walkaround town—where 30 or so surviving summer mansions are now B&Bs, commanding top dollar. Be warned: Never come to Bar Harbor in July or August without a reservation. You will find a room, but it may well cost more than $300. We cannot claim to have inspected every room in town, but we offer this partial listing of places that we have actually checked out.

BED AND BREAKFASTS

All listings are for Bar Harbor 04609.

Inn at Canoe Point (288-9511), Box 216. Open year-round. Two miles north of Bar Harbor near the entrance to the Acadia National Park visitors center. Tom and Nancy Cervelli have refurbished this lovely inn overlooking the bay, separated from Route 3 by a small pine forest. The five guest rooms have water views and private baths. The master suite, with its fireplace and French doors onto a deck, is ideal for a romantic getaway. The garret suite occupies the whole third floor; the garden room exudes the charm of a traditional Bar Harbor cottage guest room. All rooms have been imaginatively, elegantly furnished. Guests gather in the Ocean Room for breakfast to enjoy the fireplace, grand piano, and 180-degree view. $150–245 in-season.

Nannau Seaside B&B (288-5575), Box 710, 396 Main Street. Open May through October. Sited on peaceful Compass Harbor a mile from downtown Bar Harbor and abutting the national park, this vintage 1904, shingled, 20-room "cottage" offers four guest rooms ranging from a third-floor double to one with a fireplace and a large bay window on the ocean. There is also a two-bedroom suite for four with ocean views. A large breakfast, maybe eggs Florentine or almond French toast, is served, and Vikki and Ron Evers invite guests to make themselves at home in the parlor and living room. The couple pride themselves on their organic vegetable garden, young orchard, and perennial flower beds. A path leads down to the water, and there is an easy walk to a point with wonderful views. No smoking. $125–175 (for suite).

Ivy Manor Inn (288-2138; ivymano@acadia.net), 194 Main Street. Robert and Judith Stanley created this spectacular place from scratch in this Tudor-style former insurance building. Judy designed the layout, woodwork, and interior decorating on her own, and the result is an elegant, "brand new old" inn with mahogany in the lobby, imported European tile, antique sconces throughout, antique tubs in the rooms, and more. The seven rooms and the suite are each exquisitely decorated, romantic and warm, with phones, cable TV, and gas fireplaces. $150–250 includes a breakfast buffet with choice of entrée, and afternoon cordials and spirits. Dining room open to the public (see *Dining Out*).

    Mira Monte Inn and Suites (288-4263; 1-800-553-5109), 69 Mount Desert Street. Open May to mid-October. For 18 years, Marian Burns has offered comfortable guest rooms in her gracious 1865 mansion. Thirteen rooms, many with private balconies overlooking the deep, peaceful lawn in back or the formal gardens on the side; plus two suites with kitchenettes, whirlpool tubs, and private decks; and a four-room housekeeping apartment great for families. A native of Bar Harbor, Marian is an avid hiker who likes to steer her guests off the park's beaten paths. All units have private baths; 13 have fireplaces. All are furnished with antiques and equipped with phones, clock radios, and TVs. Common space includes the inviting library and sitting room with fireplaces as well as the formal Victorian flower garden. Rates include full breakfast and afternoon refreshments. $135–165 per room, $200–215 for suites. Discounts for longer stays and special spring and fall packages.

Ullikana Bed & Breakfast (288-9552), 16 The Field. An 1885 Tudor-style summer cottage with 10 guest rooms, all with private baths, 3 with fireplaces, each decorated with unusual imagination and taste by innkeeper Helene Harton, who obviously has a way with paint and an eye for art (the artwork throughout was done by friends from all over the world). An exquisite breakfast (maybe poached pears and light pancakes stuffed with fresh berries) is served on the terrace overlooking the water in nice weather. The "cottage" is handy both to the Shore Path and to downtown shops and restaurants, yet has a secluded feel. Helene and her husband, Roy Kasindorf, recently purchased the "Yellow House" across the street and have redone it to offer four additional rooms, each with private bath and claw-foot tub. The parlors have been redone with furniture that is original to the house, and there is a great front porch. $120–205.

The Tides (288-4968), 119 West Street. Open year-round. A vintage 1887 mansion overlooking the "bar" and the harbor, just a short walk from shops and restaurants. At low tide you can walk out to Bar Island. Three two-room suites, with sitting rooms, queen or king four-poster beds, fireplaces, cable TV, and window seats with water views. The veranda, with its wicker chairs, fireplace, and water views overlooks the gardens and is the gathering spot for afternoon hors d'oeuvres. The upstairs sitting room is casual, with gas fireplaces and a rainy-day closet full of games and puzzles. $150–300 includes a full breakfast.

Manor House Inn (288-3759; 1-800-437-0088 for reservations), 106 West Street. Open May through mid-November. All 14 rooms in this 1887 "cottage" have private baths, and most are furnished with Victorian pieces. Six have working fireplaces. Rare woodwork and nicely preserved details add elegance, as does the full acre of landscaped grounds. We particularly like the guest room and two suites in the Chauffeur's Cottage and the two cottages (with gas fireplaces) in the garden. $85–175 per room (less off-season) includes full breakfast and afternoon tea.

Canterbury Cottage (288-2112), 12 Roberts Avenue. Open year-round. Armando and Maria Ribeiro have pleasantly renovated this architecturally interesting (its original owner was the B&M stationmaster, and its architect specialized in railroad stations) Victorian house. Rooms are comfortably decorated, each with private bath. We especially like the room with a balcony and view of Cadillac mountain. No pets or smoking. $85–100 double in-season includes breakfast served in the pretty formal dining room.

Coach Stop Inn (288-9886), P.O. Box 266, Route 3. Open May through late October. A shingled house that rambles back from an 1804 Cape, through the slightly later section that now houses the common room (with fireplace) and dining room to the former barn. There are three attractive guest rooms with private baths and two suites with sitting rooms, one with a private bath. Hosts Kathy and Ted Combs are skilled at turning guests on to the best Acadia has to offer (Kathy is a past chamber of commerce president and Ted is a field biologist/naturalist. From $49 for a room before June 30 to $129 for the best suite in high season. Rates include a full breakfast.

The Maples Inn (288-3443), 16 Roberts Avenue. Tom Palumbo is the new owner-innkeeper at this pleasant 1903 house. Six rooms with private baths on a quiet side street within walking distance of shops and restaurants. He has a similar approach to innkeeping as the former owner, with whom he stayed several times before purchasing the inn. He still uses her recipes at breakfast (maybe blueberry-stuffed French toast). His attention to detail is apparent in the common areas as well as the guest rooms. $90–150 per couple; $60–95 mid-October through mid-June.

Hatfield (288-9655; hatfield@hatfieldinn.com), 20 Roberts Avenue. Sandy and Jeff Miller have received rave reviews on their warmth and hospitality from guests. The six rooms (four with private bath) are beautifully decorated, each with a personality of its own, from the John Wayne room with a queen four-poster bed and large private bathroom to the Corner, a cozy room with full-sized high-back bed and shared bath. Hayley is the resident dog, but she is only in the common area if guests ask for her. A full country breakfast is included.

Anne's White Columns Inn (288-5357; 1-800-321-6379; anneswci@aol.com), 57 Mount Desert Street. Built in the 1930s as a Christian Science church, hence the columns, the interior of the building was redesigned as a B&B. Each of the 10 rooms, each named for an old mansion on the island, has a private bath and cable TV. Innkeeper Anne Bahr delights in helping guests explore the park and area. $80–120 in July and August, otherwise $75–100; includes continental breakfast.

Bass Cottage in the Field (288-3705), The Field. Open late May to mid-October. This grand old home, just off Main Street but in a quiet byway, has been in Ann Jean Turner's family since 1928. Her niece now assists her in running the guesthouse. The large, enclosed porch is stacked with magazines and local menus, furnished with wicker. Nine rooms with high ceilings and one suite simply, traditionally furnished; six have private baths. Smoking on porches only. Morning coffee and tea served on the porch. $55–95 double; the $45 single (in-season) is a real find.

COTTAGES

"Maine Guide to Camp & Cottage Rentals," available free from the Maine Tourism Association (623-0363), lists some great rental cottages within easy striking distance of Mount Desert.

Emery's Cottages on the Shore (288-3432; emeryscottages@acadia.net), Sand Point Road, Bar Harbor 04609. Open May to late October. Twenty-two cottages on Frenchman Bay (14 with kitchens), electric heat, showers, cable TVs. Linens, dishes, and cooking utensils provided. Private pebble beach. Telephone available for local calls. No pets. $460–730 per week, $75–115 per day; less off-season.

Eden Village Motel and Cottages (288-4670), Box 1930 (10 minutes north of Bar Harbor on Route 3), Bar Harbor 04609. The housekeeping cottages, set on 25 acres, accommodate two to six people and are equipped with fireplaces and screened porches. $375–659 per week; nightly and lower off-season rates. Motel rooms are $54–72. Inquire about the honeymoon cottage.

HOTELS AND MOTELS

✍️♿ **Bar Harbor Inn** (288-3351; 1-800-248-3351), Newport Drive, Bar Harbor 04609. With 153 units, this landmark hotel get its share of tour groups, but its downtown waterside location is unbeatable and it's a good value at Bar Harbor prices, especially for families. It's also a genuinely gracious hotel, with a 24-hour front desk, bellmen, a restaurant open for all three meals, and room service. The lobby with its formal check-in desk is grand, and the Reading Room (dining room) began as an elite men's social club in 1887. The 51 guest rooms in the main inn were the first new hotel rooms available in town after the 1947 fire, 43 of these rooms were recently renovated, adding balconies and fireplaces to some, and putting suites in where the attic space used to be. The three-bedroom unit on the end has two balconies and a view from both sides. Also a 64-unit Oceanfront Lodge with private balconies on the bay and the Newport Building: 38 equally comfortable rooms without views. All rooms have phone, cable TV, and access to the pool, Jacuzzi, fitness room, and 7 acres of manicured lawns on the water. The lodge is open year-round. In winter rates begin at $59; in summer the range is $115–255, continental breakfast included. Children 15 and under are free; ask about 2- to 4-night packages, which bring the rack rates down.

Atlantic Oakes By-the-Sea (288-5801; 1-800-33-MAINE), Box 3, Eden Street (Route 3, next to the *Cat* ferry terminal), Bar Harbor 04609. Open year-round. This is a modern facility on the site of Sir Harry Oakes's 10-acre estate: The eight different buildings house 152 units, many with balconies, 12 with kitchens. There's also an eight-room bed & breakfast in the original Oakes summer mansion. Facilities include a pebble beach, heated outdoor pool, indoor pool, five tennis courts, and pier and float. Under the same ownership are the **Bayview** and **Atlantic Eyrie Lodge,** each a little different but equally nice properties. Rates range $99–275 in high season, depending on which facility and the type of room you choose.

✍️ **Wonder View Inn** (288-3358; 1-888-439-8439), P.O. Box 25, 50 Eden Street, Bar Harbor 04609. Open mid-May to mid-October. Children are welcome in the 79-unit motel built on 14 acres, the site of an estate once owned by Mary Roberts Rinehart, author of popular mystery stories. Near both the ferry terminal and downtown Bar Harbor, the motel overlooks Frenchman Bay. Its extensive grounds are nicely landscaped.

Includes a swimming pool and the Rinehart Dining Pavilion, which serves breakfast and dinner. $87–135.

PUBLIC CAMPGROUNDS

Aside from the camping in the park (see *To Do—Camping* in "Acadia National Park") there are more than a dozen commercial campgrounds in this area; check local listings.

OTHER LODGING

Bar Harbor Youth Hostel (288-5587; 1-800-444-6111), 41 Mount Desert Street (behind St. Savior's Episcopal Church), P.O. Box 32, Bar Harbor 04609. Open mid-June through August to AYH members. Two dorms with a total of 20 cheery red and white bunks in a clean, cozy building, kitchen facilities. $15 per person for nonmembers.

WHERE TO EAT

DINING OUT

All listings are in Bar Harbor unless otherwise indicated.

Jordan Pond House (276-3316), Park Loop Road, Seal Harbor. Open mid-May to mid-October for lunch 11:30–2:30, for tea on the lawn 2:30–5:30, and for dinner 5:30–9. First opened in the 1870s, this landmark was beautifully rebuilt after a 1979 fire, with dining rooms overlooking the pond and with a view to the mountains. It's best known for popovers and outdoor tea, but is most pleasant and least crowded at dinner (jackets suggested). Specialties include crabmeat au gratin, prime rib, and crabmeat and havarti quiche. Children's menu and half portions available. $14–18.

George's Restaurant (288-4505), 7 Stephen's Lane (just off Main Street behind the First National Bank). Open mid-June through October. Dinner 5:30–10 PM. Creative, fresh, vaguely Greek cuisine in a summery house with organdy curtains. Extensive choice of appetizers, grazers, and entrées. You might dine on lamb in a phyllo shell and lobster strudel. All entrées are $24 and the prix fixe for a three-course meal is $33 or $36 depending on appetizer choice. You can also just go with appetizers, choosing four for $33.

The Burning Tree (288-9331), Route 3, Otter Creek. Open 5–10; closed Tuesday. Admired for its fresh fish and organically grown produce, imaginatively prepared. Dine inside or on a lattice-enclosed porch on a wide choice of seafood, chicken, and vegetable entrées like Cajun crab and lobster ($20), grilled scallop kabobs ($17), and a cashew, brown rice, and Gruyère terrine ($16).

Galyn's (288-9706), 17 Main Street. Easy to miss among the shops near the bottom of Main Street, this is one of the best bets in town for seafood at either lunch or dinner. Try the Frenchman Bay stew. The large menu actually ranges from pasta Galyn (linguine with chicken, ham, mushroom, garlic, and herbs) to filet mignon. There is lighter fare in the Galley Lounge, featuring weekend jazz until 11 PM. $8.95–18.95.

The Porcupine Grill (288-3884), 123 Cottage Street. Open most of the year for dinner, daily from 6 PM. Reservations recommended. Well-chosen antiques, photos of the Porcupine Islands, and fresh flowers complement imaginative dishes that range from free-range chicken in a red pepper barbecue sauce to steamed lobster out of the shell in Thai lemon grass broth. $18–23. Extensive wine list, cocktails a specialty.

Cafe Bluefish (288-3696), 122 Cottage Street. Dark wood, books, cloth napkins patterned with different designs, and mismatched antique china create a pleasant atmosphere. Chef-owner Bobbie Lynn Hutchins, a fourth-generation Bar Harbor native, specializes in chicken, vegetarian, seafood entrées, and dinner strudels. $14.95–20.95.

The Reading Room (288-3351), Bar Harbor Inn, Newport Drive. Opened in 1887 as an elite men's club, the horseshoe-shaped, formal dining room commands a splendid harbor view; frequent piano music at dinner. Open for all three meals, specializing in daily lobster bakes on the outdoor terrace. Dinner entrées range from herbed veal saltimbocca to steak-and-lobster pie (market price). $16.95–22.95. A Sunday champagne-brunch buffet is served 11:30–2:30 ($17.95 adults, $9.95 children).

124 Cottage Street (288-4383). Pleasant, flowery atmosphere, a large vegetarian salad bar (included in all meals), and genuine early-bird specials (5–6 PM): a three-course dinner for $12.95. The extensive menu includes haddock almondine, a broiled seafood sampler, and steaks. $13.95–20.95.

Poor Boy's Gourmet (288-4148), 1 Stanwood Place, Lower Main Street. Open for dinner nightly. Chef-owner Kathleen Field is dedicated to providing a decent dining experience at reasonable prices. Choices include lobster, seafood, veal, beef, chicken, pasta, and vegetarian entrées. $7.95–16.95. An early-bird menu with entrées like apricot chicken and shrimp marinara is $7.95. Wine and beer served.

Testa's at Bayside Landing (288-3327), 53 Main Street. Open 7 AM–midnight, June 15 through September, when the family moves to its Palm Beach restaurant. In Bar Harbor since 1934, serving three daily meals. Extensive menu, including Italian and seafood specialties. Children's menu. $11.95–18.95.

Michelle's (288-2138; ivymano@acadia.net), 194 Main Street. Located in the Ivy Manor Inn, this dining room is cozy and elegant. Entrées like scallops *l'ermitage*, châteaubriand for two, and roast rack of lamb. $24–32 (more for the dishes for two). Michelle's Bag of Chocolate for Two sounds like a deliciously sinful dessert choice.

LOBSTER

Lobster pounds are the best as well as the traditional places to eat lobster—as everyone should. The easiest to find are the clutch around the Trenton Bridge on Route 3. The **Trenton Bridge Lobster Pound** (667-2977), open in-season 8:30–8, has been in George Gascon's family a long time, and the view is great. (Also see "The Quiet Side of Mount Desert" for lobster-pound options).

    Bar Harbor Lobster Bakes (288-5031), Route 3, Hulls Cove, is a twist on the traditional lobster pound. One seating nightly in this spacious, attractive dining room. Reservations are a must. Your choices are lobster or steak, and you can watch the lobsters steamed with your potatoes and corn in the large steel cookers. $23 per person.

Also see Union River Restaurant in "Bar Harbor."

EATING OUT

In Bar Harbor

Elaine's Vegetarian Café (288-3287), 78 West Street. A truly vegetarian restaurant with several creative choices, fantastic desserts.

Anthony's Cucina Italiana (288-3377), 191 Main Street. Open for lunch and dinner. Highly recommended by local innkeepers as a great new place. Menu ranges from pizza to pasta and other Italian specialties.

    Fisherman's Landing (288-4632), 47 West Street. Open in-season 11:30–8. Right on the dock. Boiled lobster dinner, steamed clams, hamburgers, hot dogs, and fried foods; liquor license.

    Epi Sub & Pizza (288-5853), 8 Cottage Street. Open 7 AM–11 PM. Tops for food and value but zero atmosphere. Cafeteria-style salads, freshly baked calzone, pizza, quiche, pasta, and crabmeat rolls. Clean and friendly; game machines in back.

Bubba's (288-5871), 30 Cottage Street. Open 11:30 AM–1 AM but serving food to 8:30 PM only. Steam-bent oak and mahogany in art deco style creates a comfortable atmosphere. Soup and sandwiches, full bar.

Island Chowder House (288-4905), 38 Cottage Street. Open 11–11. A toy train circles just below the ceiling and the atmosphere is bright; good service, homemade soups, thick chowder, seafood pasta, and chicken. Bar. Lunch and dinner specials.

Miguel's Mexican Restaurant (288-5117), 51 Rodick Street. Open 5–10 nightly. Best Mexican food Down East: fajitas, blue-corn crab cakes with roasted red pepper sauce.

Lompoc Cafe & Brew Pub (288-9392), 34 Rodick Street. Open daily for lunch, dinner, and late-night dining, specializing in house-made beer, espresso, international and vegetarian entrées; live entertainment.

Nakorn Thai Restaurant (288-4060), 30 Rodick Street. Open daily for lunch and dinner, closing Saturday and Sunday at 4 PM. Locally liked, reasonably priced.

In Hulls Cove

Chart Room (288-9740), Route 3. Open for breakfast, lunch, and dinner. A dependable, family-geared, waterside restaurant with seafood specialties.

In Ellsworth

    Union River Restaurant (667-5077), behind Rooster Brothers at the western edge of Ellsworth. Open daily June through October, 11:30–9. Brian Langley established his reputation as operator of the Oak Point Lobster Pound (which we can no longer recommend). This pleasant riverside restaurant serves a full menu including St. Louis–style ribs and chicken coated in Raye's mustard, but the specialty is seafood. Try the

"Mess of Mussels" and the steamed clams, broiled or fried. The fish is fabulous and lobster is (relatively) reasonably priced. Leave room for pie. Beer and wine served.

The Mex (667-4494), 185 Main Street. Open daily for lunch and dinner. Tiled booths in front; the inner dining room has white stucco walls, beaded curtains, heavy wooden chairs and tables. The Mex serves standard Mexican food—we always order too much. (The bean soup is a meal in itself.) Sangria, margaritas, and Mexican beer.

Maidee's (667-6554), Main Street, Ellsworth. A good road-food bet: a former diner with Oriental and standard American fare.

SNACKS

Jordan Pond House (276-3316), Park Loop Road. Tea on the lawn at the Jordan Pond House (served 2:30–5:30) has been de rigueur for island visitors since 1895. The tea comes with freshly baked popovers and homemade ice cream. Reservations suggested.

J. H. Butterfield Co. (288-3386), 152 Main Street, Bar Harbor. FANCY FOODS SINCE 1887, the sign says, and John Butterfield preserves the quality and atmosphere of the grocery that once delivered to every one of Bar Harbor's summer mansions. The reasonably priced sandwiches are the best takeout we've found in town, and the chocolate and lemon cakes are legendary. Carry your order to a bench across the way on the town green or around the corner to Grant Park, overlooking the Shore Path and the bay.

Rooster Brothers (667-8675), Route 1, Ellsworth. Just south of the bridge. Gourmet groceries, cheese, fresh-roasted coffee blends, takeout.

ENTERTAINMENT

MUSIC

Bar Harbor Music Festival (288-5744), the Rodick Building, 59 Cottage Street, Bar Harbor. Mid-July to mid-August. For more than 30 years this annual series has brought top performers to the island. The 8:30 PM concerts are staged at a variety of sites around town.

Arcady Music Festival (288-3151/2141). Late July through August. A relative newcomer (this is its 14th season) on the Mount Desert music scene. A series of concerts held at the College of the Atlantic (each concert performed in Bangor and Dover-Foxcroft as well).

Also see *Theater,* below; and *Entertainment* in "The Quiet Side of Mount Desert."

FILM

Criterion Theater (288-3441), Cottage Street, Bar Harbor. A vintage 1932, art deco, 891-seat theater, gorgeous but musty (asthmatics, beware); first-run and art films nightly. Rainy-day matinees.

Reel Pizza Cinema (288-3828), 22 Kennebec Place, Bar Harbor. Gourmet pizza and first-run art, foreign and independent films in a funky setting (beanbag chairs and big sofas). Films at 6 and 8:30 nightly, year-round.

The Grand Theater (667-9500), Main Street, Ellsworth. A classic old theater. When not in use for live performances, first-run and art films are shown.

Ellsworth Cinemas (667-3251), Maine Coast Mall, Route 1A, Ellsworth. Two evening shows; matinees on weekends, holidays, and rainy days. First-run films.

THEATER

See Acadia Repertory Theatre in "The Quiet Side of Mount Desert."

The Grand Theater (667-9500), Main Street, Ellsworth. Live performances by singers, comedians, and theatrical groups. Check current listings.

Also see **The Maine Lumberjack Show** under *To Do*.

SELECTIVE SHOPPING

ART AND FINE CRAFTS GALLERIES

Eclipse Gallery (288-9048), 12 Mount Desert Street, Bar Harbor. Seasonal. A quality gallery specializing in hand-blown glass, ceramics, and fine furniture; also showing metal sculpture, fine jewelry, and art photography.

Island Artisans, (288-4214), 99 Main Street, Bar Harbor. A cooperative run by area craftspeople.

Lone Moose (288-4229), 78 West Street, Bar Harbor. A long-established collection of "made in Maine" craftswork.

Birds Nest (288-4054), 12 Mount Desert Street, Bar Harbor. A beautiful collection of oils and watercolors.

Spruce Grove Gallery (288-2002), 29 Cottage Street, Bar Harbor. Work by a group of Maine artists, including Salt Marsh Pottery and fine jewelry.

BOOKSTORES

Sherman's Bookstore and Stationery (288-3161), Main Street, Bar Harbor. A great browsing emporium; really a combination five-and-dime, stationery store, gift shop, and well-stocked bookshop.

Mr. Paperback, Maine Mall, Route 1A, Ellsworth. Fully stocked bookstore with popular titles and magazines.

Main Street Books (667-0089), 165 Main Street, Ellsworth. An appealing bookstore-café.

SPECIAL SHOPS

Bowl and Board, Main Street, Bar Harbor. A unique selection of wood products, including bowls from Pakistan, puzzles, and games.

L. L. Bean Outlet, High Street, Ellsworth. Clothing, sporting equipment, and a wide variety of discounted items from Maine's most famous store.

Big Chicken Barn (667-7308), Route 1 south of Ellsworth. Maine's largest used-book store fills the vast innards of a former chicken house on Route 1. Annegret and Mike Cukierski have 80,000 books in stock: hardbacks, paperbacks, magazines, and comics; also used furniture and collectibles. Browsers are welcome.

SPECIAL EVENTS

May: **Celebrate Bar Harbor** *(Memorial Day weekend).*
Throughout the summer: **Band concerts**—Bar Harbor village green (check current listings).
June: **Antique Auto Rally, Lobster Races,** Bar Harbor.
July: **Independence Day**—midnight square dance with breakfast for dancers, followed by sunrise dance on top of Cadillac Mountain, street parade, and seafood festival. **Art Show**—Bar Harbor's Agamont Park *(later in the month).* **Dulcimer and Harp Festival,** Bar Harbor. **Ellsworth Craft Show** (end of month).
August: **Crafts Show** and **Art Show,** Bar Harbor.
September: **Marathon road race, bicycle race,** Bar Harbor.

THE QUIET SIDE OF MOUNT DESERT

A Southwest Harbor innkeeper claims to have coined the term "Quiet Side" for the longer, thinner arm of land that's divided by Somes Sound from the part of Mount Desert on which Bar Harbor and the busier part of Acadia National Park (including its visitors center and Park Loop) are found. The name has stuck and generally also applies to Northeast Harbor and the offshore islands as well.

Northeast is the island's yachting center, with a large marina geared to visiting yachtsmen and summer residents. Beyond a brief lineup of boutiques and art galleries, summer mansions trail off and away along Somes Sound. The village also offers splendid public gardens and a wide choice of ways onto the water. Try to get to Islesford (Little Cranberry Island) and be sure to follow Sargent Drive (rather than Route 3/198) along the Sound. The Mount Desert Historical Society in Somesville is well worth a stop. Some of Acadia's best hiking, as well as its best public swimming beach (at Echo Lake) and canoeing (on Long Pond) are found west of Somes Sound.

Southwest Harbor, while it hums in the summer, is less seasonal than the island's other major villages. It's still a boatbuilding center, home of Hinckley, the Rolls Royce of yachts. Nearby Bass Harbor is the island's genuine fishing and lobstering village, departure point for Swan's and several other islands that were once far busier.

Ironically, back in the 1840s Mount Desert's first summer visitors—artists in search of solitude—headed for the Bar Harbor area precisely because it was then far less peopled than the boatbuilding and fishing villages on this western side of the island. Much as the Route 1 town of Ellsworth is today, Southwest Harbor back then marked the crossroads of Down East Maine and several island harbors were as busy as any on the mainland.

GUIDANCE

Mount Desert Chamber of Commerce (276-5040), Sea Street, Northeast Harbor. A walk-in cottage (with showers), geared to visitors arriving by water, is open daily mid-June to mid-October at the town dock. Pick up a copy of the current "Mount Desert Guide & Northeast Harbor Port Directory."

Southwest Harbor/Tremont Chamber of Commerce (244-9264; 1-800-423-9264), P.O. Box 1143, Southwest Harbor 04679, maintains a seasonal office in Harbor House, Main Street. Pick up copies of the "Southwest Harbor & Tremont Visitors Guide" and "Southwest Harbor Port Directory."

GETTING THERE

By air and bus: See "Bar Harbor."

Note: **Airport & Harbor Taxi** (667-5995; 1-888-814-5995) meets planes, buses, and boats, serves the entire area.

By car: **From Ellsworth:** Fork right off Route 3 as soon as it crosses the Mount Desert narrows, just after the Thompson Island Information Center; follow Route 102/198 to Somesville and Route 198 to Northeast Harbor or Route 102 to Southwest Harbor.

From Bar Harbor: Follow Route 3 south to Northeast Harbor and on along Somes Sound on Sargent Drive to Somesville, back down along Echo Lake on Route 102 to Bass Harbor and back up through Pretty Marsh to Route 3.

GETTING AROUND

This is one place in Maine where water transport is still as important as land. **MDI Water Taxi** (244-7312) supplements the services out of Northeast and Southwest Harbors listed under *Boat Excursions* (see *To Do*) and the **Maine State Ferry Service** (244-4353; 1-800-491-4883) services Swan's Island and Frenchboro. **Airport and Harbor Taxi** (667-5995; 1-888-814-5995) meets boats, planes, and buses.

MEDICAL EMERGENCY

Maine Coast Memorial Hospital (667-4520), Ellsworth. **Mount Desert Island Hospital** (288-5081), Bar Harbor, provides 24-hour emergency care. **Southwest Harbor** (244-5513). **Northeast Harbor** (276-3331).

TO SEE

In Northeast Harbor

Asticou Terraces, Thuya Garden, and **Thuya Lodge** (276-5130). Parking for the Asticou Terraces (open July to Labor Day, 7–7; $2 donation) is marked on Route 3, just east of the junction with Route 198. The exquisite, 215-acre garden, begun by landscape artist Joseph Henry Curtis around 1900, features a system of paths and shelters on Asticou Hill. It's now open to the public along with his home, Thuya Lodge (open late June through Labor Day, 10–5), which houses an important

Asticou Azalea Gardens, Northeast Harbor

collection of botanical books and floral paintings. Thuya Garden behind the lodge was designed by the landscaper and artist Charles Savage; it's semiformal, with perennial beds and a reflecting pool. The gardens descend in terraces, then through wooded paths to the harbor's edge.

Asticou Azalea Gardens, Route 3 (near the junction of Route 198). Open April through October. Also designed by Charles Savage. A delightful place to stroll down winding paths and over ornamental bridges. Azaleas (usually in bloom mid-May until mid-June), rhododendrons, laurel, and Japanese-style plantings.

Petite Plaisance (276-3940), South Shore Road. Open mid-June through August by appointment. The former home of French author Marguerite Yourcenar has long been a pilgrimage destination for her fans. English translations of her books are available in local bookstores.

Great Harbor Maritime Museum (276-5262), the Old Firehouse, Main Street. Open June through Columbus Day, Monday through Saturday 10–5. $1 per person, $2 per family. A collection of model shops, small boats, and historical artifacts ranging from an early fire engine to a parlor room, a kitchen, photographs, clothing, sleighs, and a player piano; demonstrations.

From Northeast Harbor

Little Cranberry Island. Also known as Islesford, this 400-acre island, 20 minutes offshore, is exceptionally appealing, both naturally and in the ways visitors can interact with the people who live and summer here. The official "sight-to-see" is the incongruously brick and formal **Islesford Historical Museum** (244-9224; open daily mid-June through September, 10:45–4:30), built in 1928 with funds raised by Bangor-born, MIT-educated summer resident William Otis Sawtelle, to house his fascinating local historical collection. Acadia National Park now maintains the museum, one reason why the island enjoys such good boat service from both Northeast and Southwest Harbors (see *To Do*). **Islesford Market** (244-7667) is the island's living room. Chairs and counter stools are within easy reach of coffeepots, pizza and light lunches are served year-round, and island-bred postmistress Joy Sprague dispenses cream puffs (every 25th Express Mail customer receives a dozen) as well as stamps. Frequently Islesford sells more stamps per year than any other post office in Maine, despite the fact that it has just 80 year-round and some 400 summer residents. Requests for Sprague's "Stamps by Mail" come from as far as Fiji, Iceland, and Istanbul—perhaps because with each order she encloses one of her fine island photos and a monthly newsletter (her address is USPO, Islesford 04646). Ask directions in the market to the home studio of nationally known artist and folklorist **Ashley Bryan,** and to lobsterman-artist Danny Furnald's **Islesford Artists Gallery,** exhibiting some of Maine's top artists. Be sure to lunch or dine at **Islesford Dock** (see *Dining Out*), and at the dock also check out Marian Baker's **Islesford Pottery** (244-5686). Consider spending the night on Little Cranberry at Frances Bartlett's **Braided Rug Inn** (244-5943): four attractive guest rooms, $65 with shared bath, $70 with private. Rooms are hung with extraordinary turn-of-the-century photos taken by Bartlett's grandfather Fred Morse (published in 1998 as *Maine Island* by the Maine Folklife Center).

In Somesville

Almost all of this tiny white wooden village at the head of Somes Sound is part of a National Historic District; be sure to check out **Brookside Cemetery** and the **Mount Desert Historical Society** (244-7334), Route 102. Open June through October, Tuesday through Saturday 10–5 ($1 per adult), the historical society maintains a lively museum: two tidy buildings, one dating back to 1780, connected by a moon bridge, house many artifacts and photographs of the island's vanished hotels and the shipyards for which this village was once widely known. Inquire about special programs.

In Southwest Harbor

🖉 **Oceanarium** (244-7330), Clark Point Road. Open mid-May to mid-October, 9–5 daily except Sunday. A large, old, waterside building filled with exhibits, including 20 tanks displaying sea life, whale songs, a "lobster room," and a touch tank. $6 per adult, $4.50 per child.

Wendell Gilley Museum (244-7555), Route 102. Open May through December, 10–4 (10–5 July and August), daily except Monday; Friday through Sunday only in May, November, and December. A collection of more than 200 bird carvings by the late woodcarver and painter Wendell Gilley. $3 per adult, $1 per child under age 12.

Also see the Ship Harbor trail under *To Do—Hiking* in "Acadia National Park."

🖉 **Seal Cove Auto Museum** (244-9242), Pretty Marsh Road, off Route 102, between Bass Harbor and Somesville. Open daily June to September, 10–5. Squirreled away in an unpromising-looking warehouse in the foggiest, least trafficked corner of the island, this collection is a real find: over 100 gleaming antique cars and 30 motorcycles, including the country's largest assemblage of pre-1915 cars—the life's work of a private collector; $5 per adult, $2 per child.

Indian Point Blagden Preserve, a 110-acre Nature Conservancy preserve in the northwestern corner of the island, includes 1,000 feet of shorefront and paths that wander through the woods. It offers a view of Blue Hill Bay and is a tried-and-true seal-watching spot. From Route 198 north of Somesville, turn right on Indian Point Road, bear right at the fork, and look for the entrance; sign in and pick up a map at the caretaker's house.

From Bass Harbor

Swan's Island. At the mouth of Blue Hill Bay, 6 miles out of Bass Harbor with frequent car ferry service (see *Getting Around*), this is a large lobstering and fishing island with a year-round population of 350, a library, general store (no alcohol), three seasonal restaurants, **Quarry Pond** to swim in, and **Fine Sand Beach** to walk. With a bike it's a possible day trip but be forewarned: the ferry docks 5 hilly miles from **Burnt Coat Harbor,** the picturesque island center with **Hockamock Light** (built 1872) at its entrance. **Swan's Island Educational Society** (526-4350), a historic complex that includes a store, school, old tools, and photographs is less than a mile from the dock. Swan's, however, works better as an overnight. Jeannie Joyce offers three rooms (**Jeannie's Place,** 526-4116), open year-round at Burnt Coat Harbor ($45 double, $35 single). September through May, Maili Mailey coordinates rentals for cottages, houses, and apartments (**Swan's Island Vacations,** 526-4350 or 474-7370; off-season, 474-7370). The big annual event is the **Sweet Chariot Festival** (526-4443), usually the first weekend in August. Folk singers gather from throughout the East and serenade boats in the harbor at dusk, then perform in the big old-fashioned hall. Unfortunately it's all after the ferry stops running, so you have to come by boat or reserve lodging far ahead.

Frenchboro is accessible via **Island Cruises** (244-5785), which offers a lunch cruise daily in-season (weather permitting) that includes an island walking tour. **Frenchboro Historical Society** (334-2929), open seasonally, displays old tools, furniture, local memorabilia. A good excuse to explore this very private island 8 miles offshore. Bring a bike. *Note:* One day a year (early in August) the island welcomes visitors with a lobster feed, plenty of chicken salad, and pies. Ferry service: 244-3254.

SCENIC DRIVES

Sargent Drive, obviously built for carriages, runs from Northeast Harbor north a half dozen miles right along Somes Sound.

Route 102A Loop. This isn't the quickest way between Southwest and

Bass Harbors but it's beautiful, threading National Park shoreline at the **Sea Wall** with its oceanside picnic tables and the **Ship Harbor Nature Trail** down to gorgeous, flat pink rocks (see "Acadia National Park"). Be sure to turn onto Lighthouse Road to see **Bass Harbor Light** and continue on into Bass Harbor and Bernard (see *Where to Eat* and *Selective Shopping*).

TO DO

ℰ **Acadia Ranger Programs.** Pick up a copy of the Acadia National Park "Beaver Log" at Seawall Campground (Route 102A) if you cannot find it in local chambers (see *Guidance*) or shops. The free handout "Acadia Weekly," more widely distributed, also lists programs ranging from guided walks and cruises to evening programs offered in the Seawall Amphitheater.

BICYCLING

The 57-mile network of gravel carriage roads (see *To Do—Biking* in "Acadia National Park") constructed by John D. Rockefeller in 1915 lends itself particularly well to mountain biking. (Also see Swan's Island under *To See*.)

Northeast Harbor Bike Shop (276-5480), Main Street, Northeast Harbor, offers rentals.

ℰ **Southwest Cycle** (244-5856; 1-800-649-5856) in Southwest Harbor rents mountain and touring bicycles, children's bikes, baby seats, car racks, and jog strollers.

BIRDING

For special programs led by park naturalists, consult the "Beaver Log;" also see the **Wendell Gilley Museum** (see *To See—In Southwest Harbor*).

BOAT EXCURSIONS

See Little Cranberry Island, Swan's Island, and Frenchboro under *To See*.

From Bass Harbor: The year-round, car-carrying **Maine State Ferry** (244-3254) runs to Swan's Island several times a day, twice weekly to Frenchboro.

Island Cruises (244-5785), Little Island Marine, Bass Harbor. Eric and Kim Strauss offer daily (weather dependent) lunch cruises to Frenchboro and around Placentia and Black Islands as well as Great and Little Gott islands. all depicted in novels by Great Gott native Ruth Moore (1903–1989). In *The Weir, Speak to the Winds,* and *Spoonhandle,* Moore describes the poignant ebb of life from these islands in the 1930s and '40s.

Bass Harbor Cruise (244-5365) also offers nature cruises and a cruise with dinner served at the Boat House Restaurant on **Swan's Island** (see *To See*).

From Northeast Harbor: **Beal & Bunker** (244-3575) offers year-round mail-boat and ferry service aboard *Island Queen* to the Cranberries (see *To See*) and Sutton Island. The excursion boat *Islesford Ferry* (276-3717) offers a lunch cruise to Little Cranberry, and a park naturalist–led nature cruise to Baker Island. *Sea Princess* (276-5352) offers a dinner cruise to Little Cranberry. For water-taxi service, call 244-7312 or 244-5724. See Little Cranberry Island under *To See* and Islesford Dock under *Dining Out.*

From Southwest Harbor: **Cranberry Cove Boating** (244-5882) offers frequent service to the Cranberries and Sutton Island.

BOAT RENTALS

In Southwest Harbor, both **Manset Yacht Service** (244-4040) and **Mansell Boat Co., Inc.** (244-5625) rent power- and sailboats.

CANOEING AND KAYAKING

Long Pond, the largest lake on any Maine island, has three access points. Boats can be launched at Echo Lake from Ike's Point, just off Route 102. **Seal Cove Pond** is less used, accessible from fire roads north of Seal Cove. Bass Harbor Marsh is another possibility at high tide. Canoe-rental sources offer suggestions and directions. Outfitters include **National Park Canoe Rentals** (244-5854) on Long Pond near Somesville; inquire about guided evening paddles and instruction.

GOLF

Causeway Golf Club (244-3780), Southwest Harbor. Nine-hole course, club and pull-carts, pro shop.

FISHING

Deep-sea fishing is offered aboard the party boat *Mosako Queen* (667-1912), departing Beal's Lobster Pier in Southwest Harbor June through September.

HIKING

The highest mountains on the western side of Somes Sound are Bernard and Mansett, but both summits are wooded. The more popular hikes are up **Acadia Mountain** (3½ miles round-trip, off Route 102) with an east-west summit trail commanding a spectacular view of the Sound and islands. Admittedly we have only climbed **Flying Mountain,** a quick hit with a great view too. The trail begins at the Fernald Cove parking area.

SAILING

Mansell Boat Company (244-5625), Route 102A, Manset (near Southwest Harbor), offers sailing lessons; also rents small sailboats. For sailboat charters contact **Classic Charters** (244-7312), Northeast Harbor; **Hinckley Yacht Charters** (244-5008), Southwest Harbor; or **Manset Yacht Service** (244-4040). Several daysails are offered out of Southwest Harbor: check Eastern Sailing Company ("harbor tours, island picnics": 497-2807). Check with local chambers (see *Guidance*) about current daysails.

SWIMMING

Echo Lake offers the warmest water, a beach with lifeguard, rest room, and parking; accessed from Route 102 between Somesville and Southwest Harbor.

WHALE-WATCHING

Northeast Whale Watch (288-9794) departs from Northeast Harbor.

LODGING

GRAND OLD RESORTS

🚲⚓ **The Claremont** (244-5036; 1-800-244-5036), Claremont Road, Southwest Harbor 04679. Open May to mid-October. Mount Desert's oldest hotel, first opened in 1884; it has the grace and dignity but not the size of a grand hotel and the best views on the island. Never attempting to compete in size and glitz with all those Bar Harbor hotels that burned in the fire of 1947, the Claremont has remained low-key and gracious but not stuffy. It's been lucky in its owners, just three couples, who have preserved its appeal for families. Current owner Gertrude McQue's family has been summering on Mount Desert since 1871. Her grandfather discovered the island while at Harvard, subsequently built a "cottage" and was among the island's elite who met in 1901 to first discuss the idea of preserving "points of interest on the Island for the perpetual use of the public." "We didn't expect to make money, just to keep it going and to improve it" is the way Gertrude McQue explains how she and her late husband Allen happened to buy the hotel in 1968, as a retirement project. All 24 guest rooms in the four-story hotel have new plumbing, wiring, and phones and each is carefully furnished in cottage furniture and wicker. Wild flowers brighten bureaus, wood floors gleam around Oriental carpets in sitting rooms, the wraparound porch is lined with rockers and every table in the dining room (renovated in 1998) has a view. Visitors are welcome to dine (or to lunch) in the boathouse and to attend Thursday-evening lectures. There are large suites in Phillips and Clark Houses, also 12 cottages, each with living room and fireplace. Recreation options include tennis on clay courts, croquet, badminton, and water sports; rowboats are available. The Croquet Classic in August is the social high point of the season. A room in the hotel is $125–200 double MAP in-season; $85–180 EP off-season. *Note:* Water-view rooms must be MAP in-season but others need not be; children's rates, discounts for longer stays. Cottages from $158, $100–140 off-season. A 15 percent gratuity is added in the hotel, 19 percent in cottages.

Asticou Inn (276-3344; 258-3373), Route 3, Northeast Harbor 04662. Mid-May to mid-October. The elegant Asticou Inn offers superb food, simply furnished rooms with water views, luxurious public rooms with Oriental rugs and wing chairs by the hearth, and a vast porch overlooking formal gardens. In all, there are 46 rooms and suites, all with private baths, divided among the main house and annexes, which include Cranberry Lodge across the road and the Topsider suites in modern water-view cottages. In recent years the mood has lightened here: bellboys are now in shirtsleeves so as not to intimidate guests, and nonguests in shorts feel far more welcome at lunch, served on the deck, overlooking the harbor; see *Dining Out*). Facilities include a cocktail lounge, tennis courts, and a heated swimming pool. Music many summer nights. $264–364 double MAP in July and August, $166–297 EP; from $117 per couple EP off-season. Add 15 percent gratuity.

INNS AND BED & BREAKFASTS

In Northeast Harbor 04662

Harbourside Inn (276-3272). Open June through September. An 1880s, shingle-style inn set in 4 wooded acres, with 11 guest rooms and three suites on three floors, all with private baths, some kitchens. There are also working fireplaces in all the first- and second-floor rooms. All are large and bright with interesting antiques and fine rugs. This is a very special place, as only an inn with long-term family management and a returning clientele can be. The flower garden and its yield in every guest room is a special feature. Guests mingle over breakfast muffins served on wicker-furnished sunporches. There is also a comfortable living room, but most guests spend their days in adjacent Acadia National Park (its wooded paths are within walking distance) or on boat excursions out of Northeast Harbor, also just down the road. Your hosts, the Sweet family, are longtime island residents. $100 (low off-season) to $185 for a suite in August.

The Maison Suisse Inn (276-5223; 1-800-624-7668), Main Street at Kimball Lane, P.O. Box 1090. Open late May to late October. A gracious 19th-century Acadia summer mansion, right in the middle of Northeast Harbor's shops and restaurants but set back behind its large garden and backing, in turn, into its own small forest of firs. Three large, adjoining common rooms are sparely, elegantly furnished, hung with Audubon prints, warmed with fireplaces and, in the study, a big, bay window filled with flowers. The 10 guest rooms are simply but comfortably furnished in antiques and have private baths, phones, and cable TV; a ground-floor efficiency with a separate entrance is good for families. The $105–125 ($185–195 for two-room suites) includes breakfast at a bakery/café across the street.

In Southwest Harbor 04679

Penury Hall (244-7102), Box 68, Main Street. Open year-round. An attractive village house with three guest rooms (private baths), all nicely decorated with interesting art and tempting reading material salted about. This was the first bed & breakfast on the island. Toby and Gretchen Strong take their job as hosts seriously and make guests feel part of the family. Breakfast includes juice, fresh fruit, a choice of eggs Benedict, blueberry pancakes, or a "penurious omelet." $85 also includes use of the canoe and sauna and feline welcomes from Widget and Patches.

The Birches (244-5182), Fernald Point Road, P.O. Box 178. "Great-Grandma bought these 8 acres for $50 and for another $50 she could have had 20 more," Dick Homer quips. The Homer home, built in 1916, commands a splendid water view from its spacious, bright, tongue-and-groove paneled living room and ample grounds (which include a croquet court). There are three guest rooms furnished in family antiques (private baths) and you feel like a guest in a gracious but informal home. $90 includes a full breakfast.

The Island House (244-5180), Box 1006. Open all year. Across from the harbor, this large 1850s house is part of an early summer hotel (ask to see the scrapbook of historical memoirs). Ann and Charlie Bradford offer four double rooms with two shared baths, also an attractive efficiency apartment with a loft in the carriage house, large enough for a family of four. $70–95 double in high season, includes a breakfast that might be fresh fruit crêpes or eggs Florentine; 2-night minimum in July and August.

The Inn at Southwest (244-3835), P.O. Box 593, Main Street. Open May through October. Built in 1884 as a high-Victorian-style annex to a now-vanished hotel. A carved fireplace with couches grouped around it is the heart of the house. Of the nine guest rooms, all with private baths and named for lighthouses, we particularly like Moose Peak, decorated in deep rose with a chapel-style window and a window seat. Innkeeper Jill Lewis obviously enjoys preparing breakfasts such as crab potato bake with poached pears in wine sauce and blueberry gingerbread, included in $90–135 per couple in high season; from $50 in shoulder seasons.

Lindenwood Inn (244-5335; 1-800-307-5335), 118 Clark Point Road, Box 1328. Open all year. A turn-of-the century sea captain's home set by the harbor among stately linden trees, this is a pleasing fusion of old and new. Australian-born owner Jim Kind has a sure decorating touch, reflected in the rich colors of rooms and intriguing artwork. Many of the nine rooms (all private baths) have water views, as do the six housekeeping units with balconies and fireplaces in the annex. There are three cottages, one at water's edge. An in-ground heated pool and hot tub are appreciated after a day's hiking or biking. A full breakfast is served in the paneled dining room (where the fire is lit most mornings). $95–250 double in-season; $20 per extra person.

The Kingsleigh Inn 1904 (244-5302), 373 Main Street. Open year-round. The check-in desk is the counter of a country kitchen and the living room is comfortable, with a wood-burning fireplace; wicker chairs fill the wraparound porch. We would opt for one of the quiet back rooms on the second floor, such as Room 5, which has a balcony overlooking the harbor. A three-room suite on the third floor has a fireplace and a telescope, positioned in a turret window overlooking the harbor. Hosts Ken and Cyd Collins serve an elaborate candlelit breakfast: homemade granola, freshly baked pastries, plus the day's specials, which might include ricotta-filled crêpes or lemon French toast. In-season $95–125, $175 for the suite.

The Heron House (244-0221), 1 Fernald Point Road. Open year-round. After 16 years of vacationing in the area, Sue and Bob Bonkowski redecorated this comfortable house into a B&B of their own. Three pleasant guest rooms with private baths. Guests are welcome to use the living room and den and to enjoy the large greenhouse off the kitchen; the grounds include a flower garden and small pond. $85–95 depending on season ($15 per extra person), includes full breakfast served family-style.

In Bass Harbor 04653

Pointy Head Inn and Antiques (244-7261), HC 33, Box 2A. Open late May to late fall. This 1780 sea captain's home on Route 102A overlooks the harbor. Doris and Warren Townsend offer six guest rooms, some with views of water, mountains, or both, two with private baths, the rest sharing baths. "Mature" children only. An antiques shop with wood carvings by Warren is on the premises. $45–105 per room, $20 per extra person; includes full breakfast.

Bass Harbor Inn (244-5157), P.O. Box 326. Open May through October. In an 1860 house with harbor views, within walking distance of village restaurants, Barbara and Alan Graff offer eight rooms ranging from doubles with shared baths to a top-floor studio with kitchenette. One room with half-bath has a fireplace. $65–110 in-season, $45–90 off-season; includes breakfast.

✍ **Bass Harbor Cottages and Country Inn** (244-3460), Route 102A, P.O. Box 40. Open year-round. This is a family find. The inn itself is a friendly, informal old house and guest rooms have private baths and fridges; one has a full kitchen. The cottages vary in size but all have water views, kitchens, and decks; the carriage house accommodates six. Guest rooms and cottages start at $70 in high season; cottages are available by the day when not rented. $450–950 per week depending on cottage and week. In winter the inn caters to cross-country skiers.

Elsewhere

West of Eden (244-9695), P.O. Box 65, Route 102 and Kelleytown Road, Seal Cove 04695. Open May to mid-October. The only place to stay in the quietest corner of "the Quiet Side." The 1872 farmhouse is right on Route 102 but it's surrounded by gardens and the three upstairs rooms are light and airy; Room 3 is especially large and inviting, with a queen-sized bed, a private bath, a skylight, and a sleeping loft with futons, good for a family. Regina Ploucquet and George Urbanneck keep a vegetarian kitchen; breakfasts include homemade granola, fresh fruit, and specialties like pear-pecan waffles and sweet-potato pancakes. $55–75 single, $70–90 double, $10 per extra child, $15 per extra adult.

The MacDonald's Bed & Breakfast (244-3316), 111 Main Street, Somesville 04660. Open year-round. Right in the middle of the oldest and most central village on Mount Desert, Stan and Binnie MacDonald's 1850 house offers three rooms with private baths (request a view of Somes Harbor), a screened porch, and a garden, as well as attractive common rooms. $75–85 in-season, $50 off-season.

OTHER LODGING

✍ **Appalachian Mountain Club's Echo Lake Camp** (244-3747), AMC/Echo Lake Camp, Mount Desert 04660. Open late June through August.

Accommodations are platform tents; family-style meals are served in a central hall. There is a rustic library reading room and an indoor game room. The focus, however, is outdoors: There are boats for use on the lake, daily hikes, and evening activities. Reservations should be made on April 1. Rates for the minimum 1-week stay (Saturday to Saturday) are inexpensive per person but add up for a family. All meals included. For a brochure, write to Echo Lake Camp, AMC, 5 Joy Street, Boston, MA 02108.

COTTAGES AND EFFICIENCIES
Both chambers of commerce listed under *Guidance* keep and publish lists of available rentals.

WHERE TO EAT

DINING OUT
Redfield's (276-5283), Main Street, Northeast Harbor. Open for dinner daily in summer, weekends in the off-season. Reservations a must. Chef Scott Redfield's trendy café is *the* place to dine in Northeast Harbor. You might begin with sautéed lobster meat with a chartreuse cream sauce in pastry ($11) followed by grilled veal rib chop with wild mushroom glaze ($25). Entrées from $19.

The Claremont (244-5036), Clark Point Road, Southwest Harbor. Open late June through Labor Day; lunch at the Boathouse, mid-July through August, also the place for a drink before dinner, with a view that's as spectacular as any on the island. In the handsome dining room, redone in deep rose in 1998, most tables have some water view and both food and service are traditional (jacket and tie are required). Dinner entrées might range from lemon Thai pasta ($16) to grilled lamb in a cranberry demiglaze and baked stuffed lobster (both $19).

Seafood Ketch (244-7463), on Bass Harbor. Open May to November, 7 AM–9:30 PM daily. Lisa, Stuart, and Ed Branch work hard to make this place special. Known for homemade breads and desserts, and fresh, fresh seafood. Dinner specialties include baked lobster-seafood casserole and baked halibut with lobster sauce; luncheon fare includes burgers, BLTs, and crabmeat rolls. Dinner entrées $12.95–16.95.

Asticou Inn (276-3344), Northeast Harbor. Open mid-May to mid-October for breakfast, lunch, and dinner. The Thursday-night buffet and dance is an island tradition. Grand old hotel atmosphere with a waterside formal dining room (window seats, however, are reserved for longtime guests). In 1998 the kitchen was staffed by chefs and students of the Vermont-based New England Culinary Institute (NECI). Dinner entrées might include breast of duck with merit syrup or roasted rack of lamb and barley risotto with mushroom and artichoke compote ($16–27). Reservations required.

XYZ Restaurant & Gallery (244-5221), Shore Road, Manset. Open for dinner nightly except Tuesday. Mexican food aficionados alert: Billed as "classical food from the Mexican interior," the fare is authentic and good. Try the sampler plate. Entrées are $11–16. Across the road from the water, this is the dining room of the Dockside Motel, decorated in the white, red, and green of the Mexican flag.

The Preble Grill (244-3034), 14 Clark Point Road, Southwest Harbor. Open 5:30–10. The specialty here as in Terry Preble's popular Fin Back in Bar Harbor is regional cuisine with a Mediterranean touch. It's an à la carte menu with entrées ranging from manicotti filled with spinach, caramelized onions and much more ($11.95) or eggplant layered with fresh vegetables ($13.75) to lobster with Seal Cove chèvre and a tarragon cream sauce over grilled polenta (market price). Reservations suggested.

The Islesford Dock (244-7494), Little Cranberry Island. Open mid-June to Labor Day. Destination dining. Cynthia and Dan Leif's restaurant, sited right at the island dock, serves lunch (11–3) but it's really the place to watch the sun set behind the entire line of Mount Desert's mountains. The Leifs grow their herbs and tomatoes, and secure most of their seafood and produce within a boat ride of their dock. Specialties include nicely seasoned steamed mahogany quahogs, clams, or mussels, also tuna and salmon. Crab cakes are the big seller ($14.95 as a dinner entrée) and the menu also includes hamburgers and pasta. "A Summer Night's Dream" is a cold plate of lobster tail, crab claws, locally smoked salmon, fresh tomato, and salmon tartare ($21). For lunch try the lobster club sandwich with homemade carrot chips. Sunday brunch is also special. See *Boat Excursions* under *To Do* and Little Cranberry under *To See*.

EATING OUT

Lobster pounds: Thurston's Lobster Pound (244-7600), Steamboat Wharf Road, Bernard. Open Memorial Day through September daily 11–8:30. Our favorite. Expanded and weatherproofed in 1998. On a working wharf overlooking Bass Harbor. Fresh and tender as lobster can be, plus corn and pie, also seafood stew, sandwiches, chowder. Wine and beer. **Beal's Lobster Pier** (244-7178; 244-3202), Clark Point Road, Southwest Harbor. Dock dining, also a weatherproofed area on picnic tables at the oldest lobster pound in the area. Crabmeat rolls, chowder, fresh fish specialties, and lobster. (Both pounds pack and ship too.)

🦞 **Keenan's Restaurant** (244-3404), junction of Routes 102 and Route 102A. Open for dinner year-round, in summer Tuesday through Sunday, in winter Thursday through Sunday. Funky exterior, great casual hideaway atmosphere. Seafood gumbo and barbecued back ribs are the house specialty, served with house corn bread. The crab cakes, pan-fired and topped with a light seafood sauce, are also great. Wine and beer. Children's menu.

🦞 **Docksider** (276-3965), Sea Street, Northeast Harbor. Open 11–9. Bigger than it looks, with a no-frills, knotty-pine interior and great chowder; also salads, burgers, sandwiches, clam rolls, seafoods, and shore dinner. Wine and beer; lunch menu all day, early-bird specials 4:30–6.

☙ **The Deacon Seat** (244-9229), Clark Point Road, Southwest Harbor. Open daily 5 AM–4:30 PM except Sunday. A great place for breakfast and the local gathering spot, near the middle of the village. A choice of 22 sandwiches to take out for picnics.

Little Notch Cafe (244-3357), 340 Main Street, Southwest Harbor. Open year-round 11–8 except Sundays, specializing in freshly made soups and sandwiches like grilled tuna salad with cheddar on wheat ($3.95) and grilled chicken on focaccia with onions and garlic aioli ($4.95). Cheese, fresh-roasted coffee blends, takeout.

Eat-a-Pita (244-4344), 326 Main Street, Southwest Harbor. Open Monday through Saturday for breakfast (at 7), lunch, and dinner. A lively, bright café with soups, salads and pastas, specialty coffees, and pastries.

ENTERTAINMENT

MUSIC

Mount Desert Festival of Chamber Music (276-5039), Neighborhood House, Main Street, Northeast Harbor. A series of six concerts presented for more than 35 seasons mid-July through mid-August.

THEATER

Acadia Repertory Theatre (244-7260), Route 102, Somesville. Performances during July and August, Tuesday through Sunday at 8:15 PM, Sunday matinees at 2. A resident theater group based in the Somesville Masonic Hall (8 miles from Bar Harbor) performs a half-dozen popular plays in the course of the season.

Deck House Cabaret Theatre (244-5044), Great Harbor Marina, Southwest Harbor. July and August. After 26 years in Bass Harbor, this dining/entertainment landmark relocated in 1997 to a refurbished sardine canning factory, a great spot with an excellent view and menu, nightly cabaret theater by the serving staff, beginning at 8:30 PM. Entertainment cover. Full bar. Reservations are a must.

SELECTIVE SHOPPING

In Somesville

Port in a Storm Bookstore (244-4114), Route 102. Open year-round, Monday through Saturday 9:30–5:30 and Sunday 1–5. A 19th-century general-store building with water views, two floors of books, disks and cassettes, soft music, reading nooks, coffee. Linda Lewis and Marilyn Mays have created a real oasis for book lovers.

Along Main Street in Northeast Harbor

The quality of the artwork showcased in this small yachting haven is amazing. **The Wingspread Gallery** (276-3910) has changing exhibits in the main gallery and a selection by well-established artists like Rockwell Kent (for a mere $40,000). **Redfield Artisans Gallery** (276-3609) offers a mix of high-end and affordable works. **Shaw Contemporary**

Wicker is the specialty at E. L. Higgins Antiques.

Jewelry (276-5000), 100 Main Street, open year-round, is an outstanding shop featuring Sam Shaw's own work; check out the exquisite beachstone jewelry.

In Southwest Harbor

Aylen & Son Jewelry, Main Street, open year-round. Peter Aylen fashions gold, silver, and Maine gemstone jewelry with a signature leaf and berry motif, and Judy Aylen's hand-carved bead necklaces are also distinctive. **Christine's Gallery** (244-3850), Clark Point Road, features the owner's own etchings and watercolors.

In Bernard

E. L. Higgins (244-3983) Bernard Road (the way to Thurston's), mid-April to mid-October, 10–5 or by appointment; an 1890s schoolhouse filled with Maine's largest stock of antique wicker (ask to see the coffin basket), also a variety of antique furniture, glassware, and Ruth Moore titles.

Also see Little Cranberry Island under *To See* for galleries and studios.

SPECIAL EVENTS

July: **Southwest Harbor Days**—crafts show, parade, sidewalk sales.

Early August: **Sweet Chariot Festival** on Swan's Island. **Frenchboro Days** in Frenchboro.

EAST HANCOCK COUNTY

At the junction of Route 3 and 1 in Ellsworth it's Route 3 that continues straight ahead and Route 1 that angles off abruptly, obviously the road less taken. Within a few miles you notice the absence of commercial clutter. The first major turnoff is to Hancock Point, a former railroad terminus at which summer visitors transferred to steamers for Bar Harbor. It's a quiet old summer colony with a tiny octagonal post office and an 1880s inn.

Continue along Route 1 and across the new bridge (replacing the notoriously old, slippery, iron "Singing Bridge") that spans the tidal Taunton River between Hancock and Sullivan Harbor. Stop to notice the lay of the land and the signs pointing to nearby galleries. For the next 10 miles Route 1 shadows the curve of Frenchman Bay, offering spectacular views back across the bay of Mount Desert's rounded, pink-shouldered mountains. Be sure to stop at the scenic turnout (the site of a former inn) just before Dunbar's Store.

It's said that on a clear day you can see Katahdin as well as the Acadia peaks from the top of Schoodic Mountain, accessible from East Sullivan. Most travelers who come this far are, however, bound for the Schoodic Point loop, an oceanside drive that's one of the most dramatic parts of Acadia National Park. The village of Winter Harbor, just before the entrance to the park, has an old-money feel and serves an old summer colony on adjacent Grindstone Neck. Prospect Harbor, at the eastern end of the park, is more of a fishing village, the site of one of Maine's last sardine-processing plants (Stinson Seafood) and of red-flashing Prospect Harbor Light. Corea, beyond on Sand Cove, is another much painted and photographed fishing village and the village of Gouldsboro, just off Route 1, is another beauty.

Too many visitors simply day-trip to this area, perhaps ending the day with a visit to the Bartlett Maine Estate Winery in Gouldsboro. Given the choice of attractive places to stay and to eat, to shop and to hike, not to mention the kayaking and mountain biking and distinctive beauty of this area—which harbors many old estates—East Hancock County should be viewed as a destination in its own right.

GUIDANCE
Schoodic Peninsula Chamber of Commerce (963-7658; 1-800-231-3008), P.O. Box 381, Winter Harbor 04693; request the helpful pamphlet guide; it's available at the Ellsworth Chamber of Commerce information booth (see "Bar Harbor") and in most local businesses.

GETTING THERE
From Bar Harbor, take Route 3 north to Route 204, posted for Lamoine State Park and Marlboro. Turn left at the Marlboro Meeting House and then follow Mud Creek Road to Route 1 at Hancock. Turn right (east) on Route 1.

TO SEE

Acadia National Park: Schoodic Peninsula. Allow 2 to 3 hours. The park's 6-mile one-way loop road begins beyond Winter Harbor. **Frazier Point Picnic Area** is a good first stop, a place to unload bikes if you want to tour on two wheels. A little more than 2 miles farther along, look for the unpaved road on your left that leads up to **Schoodic Head,** where a short trail leads to a rocky summit with long views. The loop road continues to **Schoodic Point,** where the smooth rocks with tidal pools between them invite clambering. **Little Moose Island,** with its arctic flora, is accessible at low tide. This is one corner of the park that is as popular in stormy as in fair weather because the roiled surf here is magnificent. *Warning:* The road is one-way so if you see something you want to look at, stop.

The **Winter Harbor Historical Society** (963-2370), just off Main Street, is in the old schoolhouse; it's open noon–2 Saturdays in July and August. Route 186 continues through Birch Harbor and Prospect Harbor. Inquire about monthly meetings with speakers and about dramatic productions by the Hammed Hall Players in June and August.

TO DO

GOLF

Grindstone Neck Golf Course (963-7760), Gerrishville. A nine-hole course, open to the public.

HIKING

Schoodic Mountain, off Route 183 north of Sullivan, provides one of eastern Maine's most spectacular and least known hikes, with 360-degree views (see introduction). The Bureau of Parks and Lands (287-5936) has improved the parking area and trail system here. Take your first left (it's unpaved) after crossing the railroad tracks on Route 183; bear left at the Y and in 0.8 mile bear right to the parking lot. The hike to the top of Schoodic Mountain (1069 feet) should take less than 45 minutes; a marked trail from the summit leads down to sandy Schoodic Beach at the southern end of Donnell Pond (good swimming and a half-dozen primitive campsites); return to the parking lot on the old road that's now a footpath (½ mile). From the same parking lot you can also hike to the bluffs on Black Mountain; from here the trail continues to other peaks, and another trail descends to Schoodic Beach. This is now part of 14,000 acres known as Donnell Pond Public Preserved Land, which also includes Tunk and Spring River Lakes and primitive campsites.

KAYAKING

Atlantic Kayak Tours (422-3213) just across the Singing Bridge in Sullivan.

Moose Look Guide Service (963-7720), in Gouldsboro, offers guided fishing trips as well as rental canoes and kayaks.

Acadia Mountains from across Frenchman Bay

SWIMMING

The clearest water and softest sand we have found in the area are at **Molasses Pond** in Eastbrook.

LODGING

Crocker House Country Inn (422-6806), Hancock Point 04640. Open daily mid-April through Columbus Day, weekends (Thursday through Sunday) late October to New Year's Eve. Just 30 minutes north of Bar Harbor, Hancock Point has a different feel entirely: quiet, with easy access to water, hiking trails, crafts shops, and concerts. The three-story, 1880s inn has 11 guest rooms, 9 in the inn itself and 2 on the second floor of the carriage house. All rooms have private baths (new and nicely done with natural woods) and country antiques, quilts, and stenciling. There is a pleasant, unpretentious air to this inn, and families feel welcome; the common rooms are spacious, and there's more lounging space on the ground floor of the carriage barn near the hot tub. The second-smallest post office in the United States sits across the road next to the tennis courts, and the nearby dock is maintained by the Hancock Improvement Association. Breakfast and dinner are served in the dining room, which is open to the public (see *Dining Out*). $90–130 double includes breakfast.

❧ **Le Domaine** (422-3395/3916; 1-800-554-8498), HC 77, Box 496, Hancock 04640. Best known for the French fare of its dining room (see *Dining Out*), this European-style inn also has seven rooms, each with private bath. Guests arrive in plenty of time for dinner (check-in ends promptly at 5:30), ideally early enough to stroll through the woods to the tranquil trout pond. Each room is named for an herb and each has obviously been designed and furnished with care for closet, writing, and reading space. There are fresh flowers and interesting books. Request a room facing the wide deck (where your breakfast of fresh croissants and fruit can be served), overlooking the flower garden and lawns stretching to 80 acres with paths through woods to a small pond. $200 per couple MAP, plus tax and 15 percent gratuity; $140 B&B, plus 8 percent gratuity.

Island View Inn (422-3031), HCR 32, Box 24, Sullivan Harbor 04664. Open Memorial Day to mid-October. This is a spacious, gracious, turn-of-the-century summer "cottage" set well back from Route 1 with splendid views of Frenchman Bay and the dome-shaped mountains on Mount Desert. The six guest rooms, all with private baths and three with water views, are nicely decorated, and there is ample and comfortable common space; a full breakfast is included. $70–105; no charge for children 5 years and younger, otherwise $10 per extra person in room. An 18-foot sailboat is available for guests to rent and a canoe and rowboat are available at no charge.

Sullivan Harbor Farm (422-3735), Route 1, Sullivan Harbor 04664. Built in 1820 by Captain James Urann, who launched his vessels from the shingle beach across the road. The house, overlooking Frenchman Bay, is cheerfully, tastefully decorated and includes a library and an enclosed porch on which breakfast is served. The three guest rooms with double beds are simply, sparely furnished with exquisite taste and sense of color, private baths ($65). Cupcake, a particularly bright year-round cottage with working fireplaces, also has water views and can sleep six ($750 per week, less off-season). Another great cottage, Milo, sleeps four ($575 per week). A canoe is available, and hosts Joel Franztman and Leslie Harlow delight in tuning guests in to local hiking, kayaking, biking, and paddling possibilities. Their award-winning salmon smokehouse is on the premises (see *Selective Shopping*).

🐾♿ **Oceanside Meadows Inn** (963-5557), P.O. Box 90, Prospect Harbor 04669. Open May through October, off-season by special arrangement. This 200-acre property/nature preserve includes an 1860s sea captain's home and neighboring 1830 farmhouse overlooking well-named Sand Cove. Sonja Sundaram and Ben Walter (who met at an environmental research center in Bermuda) have spiffed up the guest rooms (there are seven in each building, including several suites good for small families) and gracious common rooms. The farmhouse, in particular, lends itself to rental as a whole, ideal for family reunions. The meadows and woods are webbed with trails leading to salt marsh and a rehabbed open-timbered barn used as a theater, conference, or wedding reception center. $80–105 per room, $115 per suite during July and August, includes a three-course breakfast.

The Black Duck (963-2689), P.O. Box 39, Corea 04624. Overlooking picturesque Corea Harbor. Barry Canner and Robert Travers offer four guest rooms, comfortably furnished with antiques, contemporary art, and Oriental rugs. Common areas display collections of antique toys and lamps, and the living room has a cozy fireplace. Twelve acres of land and waterfront property invite hiking, photography, artistic pursuits, and quiet relaxation. Two dogs, three cats, and Dolly the potbellied pig will welcome you, so please leave your pets at home. Two waterfront cottages are also available. $70–145.

Sunset House Bed & Breakfast (963-7156; 1-800-233-7156). Route 186 (a quarter mile south of Route 1), West Gouldsboro 04607. Open year-round. Carl and Kathy Johnson's Victorian farmhouse offers six attractive guest rooms, views of Flanders Bay on one side and of Jones Pond, good for swimming, fishing, and canoeing, on the other. Common space includes a double parlor and sunporch as well as the dining room, where ample breakfasts are served. $69–89, less in winter.

COTTAGES

✍ **Albee's Shoreline Cottages** (963-2336; 1-800-963-2336), Route 186, Prospect Harbor 04669. Open Memorial Day through mid-September. The 10 waterside cottages are classic old Maine motor-court vintage but each has been painstakingly rehabbed and all but four are right on the water; all have woodstoves or fireplaces. Larry Caldwell and Richard Rieth enjoy orienting guests to the best of what's around. $322–476 per week includes towels and sheets.

Black Duck Properties (963-7495) in Corea handles local seasonal rentals. "Maine Guide to Camp & Cottage Rentals," free from the **Maine Tourism Association** (623-0363), lists rentals in this area.

CAMPING

Lamoine State Park (667-4778), Route 184, Lamoine. Open mid-May to mid-October. Actually just minutes from busy Route 3 (between Ellsworth and Bar Harbor), this 55-acre waterside park offers a boat launch and 61 campsites (no hook-ups, no hot showers, 2-night minimum), $15 per night for nonresidents. Neighboring Lamoine Beach is great for skipping stones. *Note:* There are frequently vacancies here in July and August when Acadia National Park campsites are full.

Ocean Woods Campground (963-7194), P.O. Box 111, Birch Harbor 04613. Open early May to late October. Wooded, mostly oceanside campsites, some with hook-ups, some wilderness, hot showers.

WHERE TO EAT

DINING OUT

Le Domaine (422-3395), Route 1, Hancock (9 miles east of Ellsworth). Open nightly in August; the rest of the year, open nightly except Tuesday. Nicole

Purslow, *propriétaire et chef,* prepares very French entrées, generally rated the best cuisine Down East. The atmosphere is that of a European-style country bistro. Nicole's mother, Marianne Purslow-Dumas, established the restaurant in the 1940s. She fled France during World War II and came to live with a relative, Pierre Monteux, who had established a conducting school—which still thrives and holds summer concerts—in Hancock. Every summer resident in and around Bar Harbor knows this story, along with the shortcut to Le Domaine from Mount Desert. Dinner should begin with drinks in the lounge, with its bright provençale prints, then proceed into one of the two softly lit dining rooms where a fire frequently glows. The meal might begin with steamed mussels and poached Maine scallops on sorrel or a tart filled with spring vegetables and eggplant, and move on to fresh salmon lightly sautéed with sorrel and shallot sauce of rabbit served in a rich prune sauce. Dessert choices include crème brûlée and Nicole's bread pudding. Needless to say the wine list is extensive. Entrées $20.50–26.

Crocker House Country Inn (422-6806), Hancock Point. Open nightly for dinner, 5:30–9. A pleasant country inn atmosphere and varied menu; the specialty is Crocker House scallops, sautéed with mushrooms, scallions, garlic, and tomatoes with lemon and wine sauce ($17.50). In summer request the sunporch. Sunday brunch is big here, as are desserts. Entrées $16.95–21.95.

Oceanwood Gallery (963-2653), Birch Harbor. Open seasonally. Sited just north of the Park Loop Road on the Schoodic Peninsula, with water views. A great place, especially for lunch. Restaurant profits benefit the Pajaro Jai Foundation, dedicated to practical solutions to rain forest destruction. The gallery features top local artists and Native American baskets, carvings. Lunch ranges from a peanut butter sandwich ($3.50) to crab salad ($8.50); dinner, from roast chicken ($9.50) to steak (17.50). Try the finnan haddie pie ($13.50).

LOBSTER

Tidal Falls Lobster Pound (422-6818), Hancock, a half mile off Route 1 (take East Side Road). Open June to Labor Day, 5-9. It's getting so that local summer people cannot find a table overlooking the reversing falls. Bring your own wine, salad, and dessert, feast on steamers, lobster, mussels, crabs and the view. There's a weather-proofed pavilion.

West Bay Lobsters in the Rough (963-7021), Route 186, north of Prospect Harbor. Look for the greenhouses. Seasonal. Joan and Vince Smirz let you pick your own lobster, serve it up with steamers and local corn, slaw, and beans that are baked daily.

EATING OUT

Chase's Restaurant (963-7171), 193 Main Street, Winter Harbor. Open all year for all three meals. A convenient, no-nonsense eatery on Route 186 near the entrance to the park. Booths, salad bar, fried lobsters and clams, good chowder; will pack a picnic.

Fisherman's Inn Restaurant (963-5585), Route 186, Winter Harbor. Open April to October, then weekends until Christmas, dinner only; 4:30–9 on weekdays and Saturday; noon–9 on Sunday. Tony and Linda Coelho have made this old landmark a bit more formal and expensive but kept the food fine.

Gerrish's Store (963-5575), Winter Harbor. Open May through October. An old-fashioned village store with an ice cream parlor, light lunches, and penny candy.

Ruth & Wimpy's Kitchen (422-3723), Route 1 at the junction with Route 182. Open year-round, for lunch and dinner, breakfast too on weekends. Reasonably priced road food, pizza, cocktails.

ENTERTAINMENT

Pierre Monteux Memorial Concert Hall (546-4495), Hancock, is the setting for a series of summer concerts presented by faculty and students at the respected Pierre Monteux School for Conductors.

SELECTIVE SHOPPING

ART AND FINE CRAFTS GALLERIES

Worth the trip: The **Barter Family Gallery and Shop** (422-3190), North Sullivan. Open mid-May through December, Monday through Saturday 9–5, or by appointment. We put this one first, although it's way off the beaten track, because it's our favorite. You will find Philip Barter's paintings in the best galleries (we first saw them in a Massachusetts museum). Mostly landscapes, they are primitive, bold, and evocative of northern Maine. The artist's furniture creations are also displayed in this extension of the Barter home, and the gallery shop also features Maine woolens, crafts, and Priscilla Barter's original hooked and braided rugs. Marked from Route 1 not far beyond the Sullivan bridge, less than 15 miles from Ellsworth.

Hog Bay Pottery (565-2282), 4 miles north of Route 1 on Route 200 in Franklin. Susanne Grosjean's award-winning rugs and the distinctive table and ovenware by Charles Grosjean are well worth the pleasant drive.

Spring Woods Gallery (442-3007), Route 200, off Route 1 in Sullivan. Open daily 10–5 except Sunday. This gallery represents five members of the Breeden family. It features fine arts, jewelry, and sculpture.

Gull Rock Pottery (422-3990), Eastside Road, Hancock; 1.5 miles off Route 1. Open year-round. Torj and Kurt Wray wheel-throw blue and white stoneware with hand-brushed designs.

Pine Tree Kiln, Route 1, West Sullivan. Ruth and Denis Vibert have made this shop standing behind an easy-to-miss clapboard home into an insider's landmark. Their own ovenproof stoneware is outstanding, as is the selection of prints. Books and cards are also sold.

The Harbor Shop (963-4117), Route 186, Winter Harbor. The custom-made hardwood furniture by owner John Jandik is center stage in this crafts shop.

Lee Art Glass Studio (963-7004), Main Street, Winter Harbor. It's difficult to describe this fused-glass tableware, which incorporates ground enamels and crochet doilies or stencils. It works.

U.S. Bells (963-7184), Route 186, Prospect Harbor. Open daily 8–5 except Sunday. Richard Fisher creates (designs and casts) superb and distinctive wind-bells.

SPECIAL SHOPS

✎ **Darthia Farm** (963-7771), West Bay Road (marked from Route 1), Gouldsboro. Open May through October, 8–6. A 133-acre organic farm with resident sheep, Scottish Highland cattle, turkeys, collies, and cows. Visitors are welcome to inspect the farm as well as the farm stand, justly famed for its vinegars, jams, and cheeses (there's even crème fraîche); **Hattie's Shed,** a weaving shop also at the farm, features coats, jackets, scarves, and shawls.

Sullivan Harbor Salmon (422-3735), Route 1, Sullivan Harbor. The salmon is local and visitors are welcome to tour the smokehouse in which the fish are cured in a blend of salt and brown sugar, then cold smoked in the traditional Scottish way, using hickory and applewood.

Bartlett Maine Estate Winery (546-2408), off Route 1, Gouldsboro. Open June to mid-October, Monday through Saturday 10–5; other times by appointment. Maine's first winery, specializing in blueberry, apple, and pear wines, also limited raspberry, strawberry, and honey dessert wines. An attractive complex in the pines, just off Route 1. Guided tours, tasting rooms, and gift packs. Call for tour times.

SPECIAL EVENTS

May: **Annual Trade Day and Benefit Auction**—peninsula-wide yard sales climaxed by an auction at the Winter Harbor Grammar School.

August (second Saturday): **Winter Harbor Lobster Festival,** Winter Harbor—includes road race, lobster feed, and lobster-boat races.

Washington County, Campobello, and St. Andrews

The Atlantic Coast: Milbridge to Campobello; Eastport and Cobscook Bay; Calais and the St. Croix Valley; St. Andrews, New Brunswick

As Down East as you can get in this country, Washington County is a ruggedly beautiful and lonely land unto itself. Its 921-mile coast harbors some of the most dramatic cliffs and deepest coves—certainly the highest tides—on the eastern seaboard, but relatively few tourists. Lobster boats and trawlers still outnumber pleasure craft.

Created in 1789 by order of the General Court of Massachusetts, Washington County is as large as the states of Delaware and Rhode Island combined. Yet it is home to just 32,000 people, widely scattered among fishing villages, canning towns, logging outposts, Native American reservations, and saltwater farms. Many people (not just some) survive here by raking blueberries in August, making balsam wreaths in winter, and lobstering, clamming, digging sea worms, and diving for sea urchins the remainder of the year.

Less than 10 percent of the visitors who get as far as Bar Harbor come this much farther. The only "groups" you see are scouting for American bald eagles or ospreys in the Moosehorn National Wildlife Refuge, for puffins, auks, and arctic terns on Machias Seal Island, or for whales in the Bay of Fundy. You may also see fishermen angling for Atlantic salmon in the tidal rivers or for landlocked salmon and smallmouth bass in the lakes.

Recently word has begun to spread that you don't drop off the end of the world beyond Eastport or Campobello, despite the fact that since 1842—when a boundary was drawn across the face of Passamaquoddy Bay—New England maps have included only the Maine shore and Campobello Island (linked to Lubec, Maine, by a bridge), and Canadian maps have detailed only New Brunswick. In summer when the ferries are running, the crossing from either Eastport or Campobello to the resort town of St. Andrews, New Brunswick is, in fact, one of the most scenic in the East. This circuit, which is best done driving one way and taking ferries the other, has come to be known as the "Quoddy Loop." The drive is up along the St. Croix River to Calais and the ferry involves transferring from a small to a larger (free) Canadian ferry on Deer Island in the middle of Passamaquoddy Bay. Because St. Andrews

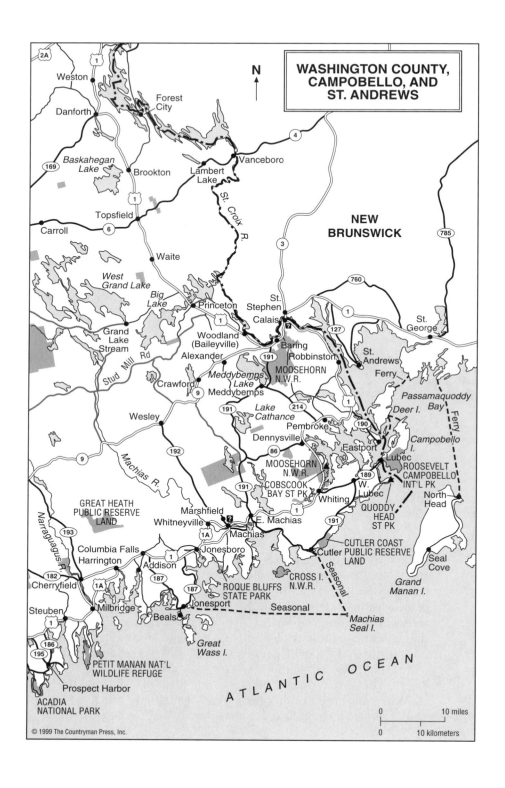

WASHINGTON COUNTY, CAMPOBELLO, AND ST. ANDREWS

N

NEW BRUNSWICK

Weston
Forest City
Danforth
Vanceboro
Baskahegan Lake
Brookton
Lambert Lake
Topsfield
Carroll
Waite
West Grand Lake
Big Lake
Princeton
St. Stephen
Calais
St. George
Woodland (Baileyville)
Grand Lake Stream
Alexander
Baring
Robbinston
St. Andrews
Ferry
MOOSEHORN N.W.R.
Stud Mill Rd
Crawford
Meddybemps Lake
Meddybemps
Passamaquoddy Bay
Deer I.
Wesley
Lake Cathance
Pembroke
Campobello I.
Dennysville
Eastport
MOOSEHORN N.W.R.
Lubec
ROOSEVELT CAMPOBELLO INT'L PK
Machias R.
COBSCOOK BAY ST PK
Whiting
W. Lubec
QUODDY HEAD ST PK
North Head
GREAT HEATH PUBLIC RESERVE LAND
Marshfield
Whitneyville
E. Machias
Seal Cove
Machias
CUTLER COAST PUBLIC RESERVE LAND
Columbia Falls
Harrington
Jonesboro
Addison
Cutler
CROSS I. N.W.R.
Grand Manan I.
Cherryfield
ROQUE BLUFFS STATE PARK
Steuben
Milbridge
Beals
Jonesport
Seasonal
Machias Seal I.
Great Wass I.
PETIT MANAN NAT'L WILDLIFE REFUGE
Prospect Harbor
ACADIA NATIONAL PARK

St. Croix R.
Narraguagus R.

ATLANTIC OCEAN

0   10 miles
0   10 kilometers

© 1999 The Countryman Press, Inc.

itself probably offers a greater number and variety of "rooms" and dining than all Washington County combined and because the exchange rate (at this writing) favors Americans, it is a logical place to spend the night.

For exploring purposes, Washington County is divided into four distinct regions: (1) the 60-mile stretch of Route 1 between Steuben and Lubec (this actually includes some 600 miles of rugged coast), an area for which Machias is the shopping, dining, and information center; (2) Eastport and Cobscook Bay, the area of the highest tides and an end-of-the-world feel (by water, Lubec and Eastport—both of which claim to be the country's easternmost community—are just 3 miles apart, but separated by 40 land miles); (3) Calais and the St. Croix Valley, including the lake-splotched backwoods and the fishermen's havens at Grand Lake Stream; and (4) St. Andrews, New Brunswick.

Wherever you explore in Washington County—from the old sardine-canning towns of Eastport and Lubec to the coastal fishing villages of Jonesport and Cutler and the even smaller villages on the immense inland lakes—you find a Maine you thought had disappeared decades ago. You are surprised by the beauty of old buildings such as the 18th-century Burnham Tavern in Machias and Ruggles Mansion in Columbia Falls. You learn that the first naval battle of the Revolution was won by Machias men; that some local 18th-century women were buried in rum casks (because they were shipped home that way from the Caribbean); and that pirate Captain Richard Bellamy's loot is believed to be buried around Machias.

And if any proof were needed that this has always been one isolated piece of coast, there is Bailey's Mistake. Captain Bailey, it seems, wrecked his four-masted schooner one foggy night in a fine little bay 7 miles south of Lubec (which is where he should have put in). Considering the beauty of the spot and how far he was from the Boston ship-owner, Bailey and his crew unpacked their cargo of lumber and settled right down on the shore. That was in 1830, and many of their descendants have had the sense to stay put.

Local historians will also tell you why Deer Island and Campobello now belong to Canada rather than to the United States. Daniel Webster, the story goes, drank a few too many toasts the night Lord Ashburton sailed him out to check the boundaries. The islands were barely visible to Webster when he conceded them.

GUIDANCE

Washington County (1-800-377-9748); call to request printed information. Request a copy of "Maine's Washington County." A web site detailing the region's natural and historical sights and possibilities for hiking, kayaking, fishing, etc. is: www.quoddyloop.com/sunrise.htm.

The Machias Bay Area Chamber of Commerce (255-4402), P.O. Box 606, Machias 04654.

Lubec Chamber of Commerce (733-4522), P.O. Box 123, Lubec 04652, publishes a an information sheet on Lubec and maintains a volunteer-staffed office on Route 189, open sporadically in summer.

The **Calais Information Center** (454-2211), 7 Union Street, Calais 04619. Open year-round and staffed by the Maine Tourism Association, summers 8–6, after Columbus Day 9–5.

New Brunswick information of all kinds is available by phoning (within North America) 1-800-561-0123; locally in summer, 506-752-7018; winter, 506-752-7043. Request a copy of the "New Brunswick Travel Guide."

GETTING THERE

By air: See the "Bar Harbor and Ellsworth" chapter, along with the "Bangor" chapter in "Northern Maine," for scheduled airline service. Charter service is available to the following airports: **Eastport Municipal** (853-2951); **Machias Valley** (255-8709); **Lubec Municipal** (733-5532); and **Princeton Municipal** (796-2744).

By bus: **Vermont Transit** (1-800-451-3292) and **Concord Trailways** (1-800-639-3317) both serve Bangor year-round; some summers Vermont Transit comes as close as Ellsworth.

By car: There are three equally slow ways to come: (1) I-95 to Augusta, then Route 3 to Belfast (stop at Lake St. George for a swim), then Route 1; (2) I-95 to Bangor, then Route 1A North to Ellsworth, then Route 1 (*note:* For coastal points east of Harrington, you save 9 miles by cutting inland on Route 182 from Hancock to Cherryfield); (3) for eastern Washington County, take I-95 to Bangor, then the Airline Highway (Route 9) for 100 miles straight through the blueberry barrens and woods to Calais. The state maintains camping and picnic sites at intervals along this stretch, and food and lodging can be found in Beddington, Wesley, Alexander, and Baring.

GETTING AROUND

East Coast Ferries (506-747-2159), based on Deer Island, serves both Campobello (45 minutes) and Eastport (30 minutes). Generally these run every hour from around 9 AM to around 7 PM, mid-June to mid-September, but call Stan Lord to check. The Campobello ferry takes 15 cars, and the Eastport ferry (a fishing boat lashed to a barge) takes 12 but gets fewer passengers. **Deer Island** itself is more than a mere stepping-stone in the bay. Roughly 9 miles long and more than 3 miles wide, it's popular with bicyclists and bird-watchers. It boasts the world's three largest lobster pounds, the original salmon aquaculture site, a staffed lighthouse, and several B&Bs. The free, 18-car **Deer Island–L'Etete (New Brunswick mainland) Ferry** (506-453-2600) crossing takes 20 minutes, departing April through September every hour, 7–7, but call to confirm. This ride across Cobscook Bay is one of the most dramatic ferry rides in the country. Don't miss it. See *Boat Excursions* under *To Do*.

MEDICAL EMERGENCY

Calais Regional Hospital (454-7531); **Down East Community Hosptial** (255-3356), Machias. In case of emergency—fire, human or wildlife injury—call the **Washington County Regional Communication Center,** 1-800-432-703; or the **State Police,** 1-800-432-7381.

MONEY

This is the part of coastal Maine in which you may have to drive an hour to find an ATM. Look in Milbridge, Columbia Four Corners Mall on Route 1, Machias, Lubec, Pembroke, Eastport, and Calais.

THE ATLANTIC COAST: MILBRIDGE TO CAMPOBELLO

GUIDANCE

The **Machias Bay Area Chamber of Commerce** (255-4402); see *Guidance* in the introduction to this chapter. The **Campobello Tourist Bureau** (506-752-7043), at the entrance to the island, is open daily May through Columbus Day.

TO SEE

Entries are listed geographically, traveling east.

Steuben, the first town in Washington County, is known as the site of the 6,000-acre **Petit Manan National Wildlife Refuge** (546-2124). The preserve actually includes two coastal peninsulas and 24 offshore islands. (For details about two trails on Petit Manan Point, see *Hiking*.)

Milbridge, a Route 1 town with a wandering coastline, is the administrative home of one of the oldest wild-blueberry processors (Jasper Wyman and Sons). The town also supports one of the county's surviving sardine canneries, a Christmas wreath factory, a commercial center, and a great little movie theater. **McClellan Park,** overlooking Narraguagus (pronounced *nair-a-gway-gus*) Bay, offers picnic tables, fireplaces, campsites, rest rooms, and drinking water. The **Milbridge Society and Museum** (546-4471), open late May through September, Saturday and Sunday 1–4, also Tuesday 1–4 in July and August and by appointment, is a delightful window into this spirited community, with ambitious changing exhibits and displays on past shipyards, canneries, and 19th-century life. **Milbridge Days** (late July) has attracted national coverage in recent years; the highlight is a greased cod contest (see *Special Events*).

Cherryfield. A few miles up the Narraguagus River, Cherryfield boasts stately houses and a fine Atlantic salmon pool. The **Cherryfield-Narraguagus Historical Society** (546-7979), Main Street (just off

Ruggles Mansion in Columbia Falls

KIM GRANT

Route 1), is open July and August, Wednesday and Friday 1–4, otherwise by appointment May through October. Picnic tables in **Stewart Park** on Main Street and in **Forest Mill Dam Park** on River Road, a good place for a swim. Cherryfield (why isn't it called *Berryfield*?) bills itself "Blueberry Capital of Maine"; there are two processing plants in town.

Columbia Falls is an unusually picturesque village with one of Maine's most notable houses at its center. The **Ruggles House** (0.25 mile off Route 1; open June to mid-October, Monday through Saturday 9:30–4:30, Sunday 11–4:30; suggested donation is $3 adults, $1.50 children) is a Federal-style mansion built by wealthy lumber dealer Thomas Ruggles in 1818. It is a beauty, with a graceful flying staircase, a fine Palladian window, and superb woodwork. Legend has it that a woodcarver was imprisoned in the house for three years with a penknife. There is an unmistakably tragic feel to the place. Mr. Ruggles died soon after its completion. The house had fallen into disrepair by the 1920s and major museums were eyeing its exquisite "flying staircase" when local pharmacist Mary Chandler, a Ruggles descendant, galvanized local and summer people to save and restore the old place.

Jonesport and **Beals Island.** Jonesport and Beals are both lobstering and fishing villages. Beals is the home of the **Beals Island Regional Shellfish Hatchery** (497-5769), open to the public May through November, daily 9–4, where up to 10 million clams are annually seeded for distribution to local clam flats and old photos depict the history of local clamming. Beal's Island, still populated largely by Allens and Beals, is known for the design of its lobster boats, and it's not hard to find one under construction. Beals is connected by a bridge to Jonesport and by a shorter bridge to **Great Wass Island,** one of the county's most popular places to walk (see *Hiking*). Jonesport is the kind of village that seems small the first time you drive through but grows in dimensions as you slow down. Look closely and you will find a colorful marina, several restaurants, grocery stores, antiques shops, bed & breakfasts, chandleries, a hardware/clothing store, an art gallery, and more. Together the towns are home for eastern Maine's largest lobstering fleet, but the big buy at the cooperative in Jonesport is crabmeat.

Jonesboro is represented on Route 1 by a general store, a church, and a post office. The beauty of this town, however, is in its shoreline, which wanders in and out of points and coves along the tidal Chandler River and Chandler Bay on the way to **Roque Bluffs State Park** (see *Swimming*), 6 miles south of Route 1. A public boat launch with picnic tables is 5 minutes south of Route 1; take the Roque Bluffs Road but turn right onto Evergreen Point Road.

Machias is the county seat, an interesting old commercial center with the Machias River running through town and over the Bad Little Falls. **The Burnham Tavern** (255-4432), tucked up behind the old-fashioned five-and-dime, is open early June through mid-September, Monday through Friday 9–5 and by appointment. A 1770s, gambrel-roofed tavern, it's filled with period furnishings and tells the story of British man-of-war *Margaretta*, captured on June 12, 1775, by townspeople in the small sloop *Unity*. This was the first naval battle of the American Revolution. Unfortunately, the British retaliated by burning Portland.

Machias was a hotbed of patriotic zeal at the outbreak of the Revolution, an era that can also be savored at **Micmac Farm** in Machiasport. Micmac Farm contains one of Maine's best restaurants (see *Dining Out*), filling two rooms of a low-beamed house built in 1772 by a patriot who fled here from Nova Scotia.

The **University of Maine at Machias** maintains an interesting art gallery featuring paintings by John Marin and sponsors weeklong (live-in) summer workshops for birders. There is summer theater and music, including concerts in the graceful 1836 **Congregational church** (centerpiece of the annual Wild Blueberry Festival). Also note the picnic tables and suspension bridge at the falls and the many headstones worth pondering in neighboring **O'Brien Cemetery.**

Early in the 19th century, Machias was second only to Bangor among Maine lumber ports. In 1912 the town boasted an opera house, two newspapers, three hotels, and a trotting park. Today Machias retains its share of fine houses and is home to the **Maine Wild Blueberry Company,** which processes 250,000 pounds of berries a day and ships them as far as Japan. Billed as the world's largest processor of wild blueberries, Maine Wild is the brainchild of Dr. Amir Ismail, a courtly and portly Egyptian who is generally recognized as Maine's most colorful and effective blueberry promoter.

Machiasport. Turn down Route 92 at Bad Little Falls Park in Machias. This picturesque village includes the **Gates House** (255-8461, open mid-June to early September, Tuesday through Saturday 12:30–4:30, adults $1), a Federal-style home with maritime exhibits and period rooms. **Fort O'Brien** is an earthwork mound used as an ammunitions magazine during the American Revolution and the War of 1812. We recommend that you continue on down this road to the fishing village of Bucks Harbor and on to **Jasper Beach,** so named for the wave-tumbled and polished pebbles of jasper and rhyolite that give it a distinctive color. The road ends with great views and a beach to walk in **Starboard.**

Cutler. From East Machias, follow Route 191 south to this small fishing village that's happily shielded from a view of the Cutler navy communications station—said to be the world's most powerful radio station. Its 26 antenna towers (800–980 feet tall) light up red at night and can be seen from much of the county's coast. Cutler is the departure point for Captain Andy Patterson's excursions to see the puffins on Machias Seal Island (see *Boat Excursions*) and the home of a **Marine Lobster Hatchery** (259-3693), open to visitors June through September. Beyond Cutler, Route 191 follows the shoreline through moorlike blueberry and cranberry country, with disappointingly few views. Much of this land is now publicly owned and the high bluffs can be accessed via the **Bold Coast Trail** (see *To Do—Hiking*). In South Trescott, bear right onto the unmarked road instead of continuing north on Route 191 and follow the coast through Bailey's Mistake (see chapter introduction) to West Quoddy Light.

West Quoddy Light State Park, South Lubec Road, Lubec. Open mid-April through October, sunrise to sunset. Marking the easternmost tip of the United States, the red-and-white-striped lighthouse dates back to 1858. The park, adjacent to the lighthouse, offers benches from which you are invited to be the first person in the United States to see the sunrise. There is also a fine view of Grand Manan Island, a pleasant picnic area, and a 2-mile hiking trail along the cliffs to Carrying Place Cove. Between the cove and the bay, roughly a mile back down the road from the light, is an unusual coastal, raised-plateau bog with dense sphagnum moss and heath.

Lubec. Most visitors now pass through this "easternmost town" on their way over the FDR Memorial Bridge to Campobello Island. Take a minute to find the old town landing, where there's a public boat launch and a breakwater and a view of the Sparkplug, as the distinctive little Lubec channel light is known. It is just offshore amid very fast-moving currents. Once there were 20 sardine-canning plants in Lubec; the wonder is that there are still two, one now processing salmon (farmed in pens in the bay). The **Lubec Historical Society Museum** (733-4696), open summer months, Tuesday through Thursday and Saturday, 9–3, fills an old storefront on the edge of town and doubles as an information center. Also check out the **Downeast Interpretive Center,** corner of School and Water Streets: local videos, photographs, and artifacts.

✐ **Roosevelt Campobello International Park** (506-752-2922), Welshpool, Campobello Island, New Brunswick, Canada (for a brochure write Box 121, Lubec 04652; the web site is www.fdr.net). Open daily Memorial Day weekend to mid-October, 9–5 eastern daylight time (10–6 Canadian Atlantic daylight time). Although technically in New Brunswick, this manicured, 2800-acre park with a visitors center and shingled "cottages" is the number-one sight to see east of Bar Harbor. You turn down a side street in Lubec, and there is the bridge (built in 1962) and Canadian customs. The house in which Franklin Delano Roosevelt summered as a boy has disappeared, but the airy 34-room **Roosevelt Cottage,** a wedding gift to Franklin and Eleanor, is sensitively maintained just as the family left it, charged with the spirit of the dynamic man who contracted polio here on August 25, 1921. It's filled with many poignant objects like the toy boat FDR carved for his children. During his subsequent stints as governor of New York and then as president of the United States, FDR returned only three times. Neighboring **Hubbard Cottage,** with its oval picture window, gives another slant on this turn-of-the-century resort. There's a visitors center here with an excellent new historical exhibit that compensates for the vapid 15-minute introductory film. Beyond stretch more than 8 miles of trails to the shore and then inland through woods to lakes and ponds. There are also 15.4 miles of park drives, modified from the network of carriage drives that the wealthy "cottagers" maintained on the island. Beyond the park is **East Quoddy Head Lighthouse,** accessible at low tide, a popular whale-watching station but a real adventure to get to (attempt only if you are physically fit). Note the small car ferry to Deer Island that runs during July and August (see *Getting Around*) and the description of the Owen House under *Inns and Bed & Breakfasts.* Campobello Park was granted to Captain William Owen in the 1760s and remained in the family until 1881, when it was sold to Boston developers, who built large (long-gone) hotels.

TO DO

AIRPLANE RIDES
Sunrise Air–Lubec (733-2124), Lubec. Scenic rides, photos, and fish spotting.

BIRDING
Summer Workshops for Birders and Ornithologists at the University of Maine at Machias (255-3313). Three 1-week sessions are presently offered, one in early July, focusing on warblers, the others in August, each taught by prominent ornithologists. The workshops include field- and boat trips and dorm lodging.

BOAT EXCURSIONS AND PUFFIN-WATCHING
Note: Birders and naturalists should be aware that the area's many offshore islands, such as **Cross Island, Petit Manan, Bois Bubert, Seal,** and

Pond Islands, as well as **Machias Seal,** are what the following excursions are all about; inquire about exploring the islands themselves.

Machias Seal Island is a prime nesting spot for puffins in June and July, also a place to see razor-billed auks and arctic terns in August and September. Although just 9 miles off Cutler, the island is maintained by Canada as a lighthouse station and wildlife refuge. But **Captain Barna Norton** (497-5933) of Jonesport, who has been offering bird-watching cruises to Machias Seal since the 1940s, refuses to concede the island. Since it was never mentioned in the 1842 Webster-Ashburton Treaty, he insists that it was claimed by his grandfather in 1865. Thus he continues to offer puffin-watching and other birding trips to the island, ably assisted by his son John, emphasizing his views on the island by shading himself with an umbrella displaying an American flag on top.

Captain Andrew Patterson's **Bold Coast Charter Company** (259-4484) is based in Cutler, just 9 miles from Machias Seal Island, to which he also offers frequent bird-watching trips from May to August. Captain Patterson also uses his 40-foot passenger vessel *Barbara Frost* to cruise the coast, to visit the **Cross Island Wildlife Refuge** at the mouth of Machias Bay, and, on special request, to go to Grand Manan Island.

Idle Tours (546-2136), Milbridge. A 45-foot tour boat offers cruises past the 123-foot high, granite Petit Manan Light (1855), on Petit Manan Island.

Machias Bay Boat Tours (259-3338), Route 191, East Machias, Captain Martha Jordan offers tours aboard the six-passenger, 34-foot, fiberglass, diesel-powered *Martha Ann*. Destinations include Cross Island and one of several 1,700-year-old petroglyph sites in the area.

Captain Laura Fish (497-3064/2445), Kelley Point Road, Jonesport. From May to mid-October daily (weather permitting), the 23-foot *Aaron Thomas*, named for Jonesport's first settler—from whom the captain and first mate are descended—offers 3-hour cruises around the islands, lighthouses, beaches, and salmon farms; also a walk around **Mistake Island,** site of 72-foot-high Moose Peak Light.

East Coast Ferries. See *Getting Around.* Departing from Eastport every hour or Campobello every 90 minutes, this is the bargain cruise of the eastern seaboard: a car ferry that's a workboat attached to a barge that sails out into Cobscook Bay, past Old Sow, a whirlpool that's billed as the world's second-largest. Drive across Deer Island and take the free Canadian ferry from Lord's Cove to the New Brunswick mainland.

CANOEING AND SEA KAYAKING

The **Machias River,** fed by the five Machias Lakes, drops through the backwoods with technically demanding rapids and takes 3 to 6 days to run. The Narraguagus and East Machias Rivers are also good for trips of 2 to 4 days. For rentals, lessons, advice, and guided tours, see **Sunrise County Canoe Expeditions** (454-7708) in the "Calais and the St. Croix Valley" part of this chapter.

Machias Bay Sea Kayaking (259-3338). Registered guides Martha and Rick Jordan (see *Boat Excursions*) offer year-round guided kayaking tours, specializing in tours of the Machias Bay petroglyphs near their base at Holmes Bay (Route 191). Guided freshwater trips are also offered.

Eastern Outdoor Adventures (255-4210; 1-800-396-7664), Machias, offers guided tours to a choice of destinations from Bucks Harbor, Roque Bluffs, Cobscook Bay, and Great Wass and Head Harbor Islands. Beginners welcome.

FISHING

Salmon fishing is the reason many people come to this area (see Cherryfield under *To See*); the Narraguagus and Machias Rivers are popular places to fish mid-May through early June. Six Mile Lake in Marshfield (6 miles north of Machias on Route 192), with picnic facilities, shelters, and a boat ramp, is known for trout. **Eastern Outdoor Adventures** (see *Canoeing and Sea Kayaking*) offers guided fishing expeditions. For information about licenses, guides, and fish, write to the regional headquarters of the **Inland Fisheries and Wildlife Department,** Machias 04654.

GOLF

Great Cove Golf Course (434-2981), Jonesboro Road, Roque Bluffs, offers nine holes, water views, clubhouse, rental clubs, and carts.

Herring Cove Golf Course (506-752-2449), in the Herring Cove Provincial Park (open mid-May to mid-November), has nine holes, a clubhouse restaurant, and rentals.

HIKING

Also see West Quoddy Light State Park under *To See* and Schoodic Mountain in the "East Hancock County" chapter.

Petit Manan Point, Steuben (6 miles off Route 1 on Pigeon Hill Road), a 2,166-acre preserve with over 10 miles of shoreline. A varied area with pine stands, cedar swamps, blueberry barrens, marshes, and great birding (more than 250 species have been identified here). Maps are posted at the parking lot, showing the two hiking trails. A 5-mile shore path hugs the woods and coastline. For details about the entire 6,000-acre **Petit Manan National Wildlife Refuge,** contact Refuge Headquarters, Main Street, Millbridge (546-2124).

Great Wass Island. The Maine chapter of The Nature Conservancy owns this 1,579-acre tract at the southern tip of the Jonesport-Addison peninsula. Trail maps are posted at the parking lot (simply follow the main road to its logical end). The interior of the island supports one of Maine's largest stands of jack pine and has coastal peat lands. We prefer the 2-mile trek along the shore to Little Cape Point, where children can clamber on the smooth rocks for hours. Wear rubber-soled shoes and bring a picnic.

Western Head, off Route 191, 11 miles south of East Machias, maintained by the Maine Coast Heritage Trust, Brunswick (276-5156). Take your first right after the Baptist church onto Destiny Bay Road and follow it to the end. Parking is minimal but there is a sign. The loop trail is

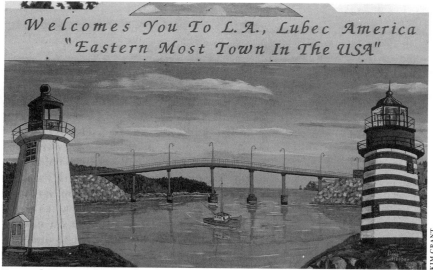

East and West Quoddy Head Lights as depicted on a billboard

KIM GRANT

through mixed-growth woods and some dense stands of spruce to the shore, with views of the entrance of Cutler Harbor and high ledges with crashing surf, large expanses of open ocean, as well as the high sheer ledges of Grand Manan, approximately 14 miles to the northeast, and Machias Seal Island, about 10 miles to the southeast. The loop takes a good hiker 35 minutes.

The Bold Coast Trail. Look for the trailhead some 4 miles east of Cutler Harbor. Maine's Bureau of Parks and Lands (287-4920) has constructed inner and outer loop trails from Route 191 to the rugged cliffs and along the shore, overlooking Grand Manan Channel. It's a 5.4-mile loop. The Coastal Trail begins in spruce-fir forest, bridges a cedar swamp and climbs to a promontory, continuing along the cliffs to Black Point Cove, a cobble beach. At this point the Black Point Brook Cut-Off Trail turns inland. *Note:* The cliffs are high and sheer, not good for children or shaky adults. Bring a picnic, allow at least 4 hours. The trail continues from Black Point Cove to Fairy Head, site of three primitive campsites.

For the hiking guide "Cobscook Trails," which includes the Bold Coast, contact the **Quoddy Regional Land Trust** (733-5509), P.O. Box 49, Whiting 04691. It details hikes in Lubec to **Horan Head** (6 miles round-trip, to the **Boot Head Preserve** (less than 2 miles round-trip), along the **South Lubec Sand Bar,** and to **Commissary Point in Trescott.**

Roosevelt Campobello International Park. At the tourist information center, pick up a trail map. We recommend the trail from Southern Head to the Duck Ponds. Seals frequently sun on the ledges off Lower Duck Pond and loons are often seen off Liberty Point. Along this dramatic shoreline at the southern end of the island, also look for whales

July through September. At Eagle Hill Bog a boardwalk spans a peat bog with interpretive panels.

Also see Quoddy Light under *To See.*

PICNICKING

McClellan Park in Milbridge, 5 miles south of town at Baldwin's Head, overlooking the Atlantic and Narraguagus Bay (from Route 1, follow Wyman Road to the park gates). A town park on 10½ acres donated in 1926 by George McClellan, a one-time mayor of New York City and later a professor of economic history at Princeton. There's no charge for walking or picnicking. (Also see *Hiking* and *Campgrounds.*)

SPECIAL LEARNING PROGRAMS (ADULT)

SummerKeys (733-2316; winter, 201-451-2338), 6 Bayview Street, Lubec. July through mid-August. New York piano teacher Bruce Potterton offers a series of programs in jazz, voice, classical, and flamenco guitar as well as piano. Beginners to more advanced are welcome. Lodging is at local B&Bs.

SWIMMING

Roque Bluffs State Park, Roque Bluffs (6 miles off Route 1). There is a pebble beach on the ocean, frequently too windy to use even in August. A sheltered sand beach on a freshwater pond is the ideal place for children. But the water is COLD. Tables, grills, changing areas with vault toilets, and a children's playground.

Gardner Lake, Chases Mills Road, East Machias, offers freshwater swimming, a picnic area, and a boat launch. **Six Mile Lake,** Route 192, in Marshfield (north of Machias), is also good for a dip. On Beals Island, the **Backfield Area,** Alley's Bay, offers saltwater swimming.

WHALE-WATCHING

The unusually high tides in the Bay of Fundy seem to foster ideal feeding grounds for right, minke, and humpback whales and for porpoises and dolphins. East Quoddy Head on Campobello and West Quoddy Head in Lubec are favored viewing spots. Two father-and-son teams, the Nortons (see *Boat Excursions and Puffin-Watching*) and the Harrises (see *To Do—Boat Excursions* under "Eastport"), offer whale-watching cruises. **Cline Marine** (506-529-4188) also offers 2-hour whale-watching cruises from Head Harbour on Campobello Island.

LODGING

INNS AND BED & BREAKFASTS

Entries are listed geographically, heading east.

Ricker House (546-2780), Cherryfield 04622. Open May to November. A classic Federal house built in 1803 with a double parlor, furnished comfortably with plenty of books and an inviting country kitchen. There are three guest rooms (two with river views), nicely furnished with antiques and old quilts, sharing one bath. A path leads to a picnic table by the river, and the tennis courts across the road are free. There are also lawn games: horseshoes and croquet. Jean and Bill Conway keep a two-volume photo album, "Adventures from Ricker House," on their coffee table and are delighted to help guests explore the area, especially on foot, or by bicycle or canoe (both are available to guests). Many guests, however, see no reason to explore farther than the comfortable wicker on the screened-in pine porch. $60 per couple ($10 per extra person), $50 single, includes a full breakfast.

Pleasant Bay Bed & Breakfast (483-4490), P.O. Box 222, West Side Road, Addison 04606. Open year-round. After raising six children and a number of llamas in New Hampshire, Leon and Joan Eaton returned to Joan's girlhood turf, cleared this land, and built themselves a large, gracious house with many windows and a deck and porch overlooking the Pleasant River. Opening onto the deck is a large, sunny room with couches, a piano, and a fireplace, and an adjoining open kitchen and dining room, all with water views. A more formal living room is well stocked with puzzles and books for foggy days. This is a 110-acre working llama farm, and guests are invited to meander the wooded trails down to the bay, either accompanied or unaccompanied by llamas. The three upstairs guest rooms include the corner green room with an old book-keeper's desk and a private bath; it's big enough for a small family; all have water views and there are moorings for guests arriving by water. $45–70 per couple ($10 per additional child) includes a splendid breakfast of fresh fruit and, if you're lucky, Joan's popover/pancake. Evening meals are available by prior arrangement off-season.

Harbor House on Sawyer Cove (497-5417; fax, 497-3211), P.O. Box 468, Sawyer Square, Jonesport 04649. Open year-round. An 1880s building that housed the telegraph office, general store, and ship's chandlery (owned by 4-foot-6 "Little Charlie" Mansfield). Maureen and Gene Hart have turned it into a combination antiques store and restaurant downstairs, with two attractive guest rooms upstairs. One room has a king-sized (or twin) iron bed and windows overlooking the marina and harbor, the other has a queen-sized bed with cottage-style headboard and in-room binoculars to focus in on the water view. $95 in-season, $85 off, $5 discount each additional night, complimentary lobster dinner for two with 3 nights.

Tootsie's Bed and Breakfast (497-5414; fax, 483-4653), RFD 1, RRO, Box 252, Jonesport 04649. This was the first bed & breakfast in Washington County, and it is still one of the nicest. Charlotte Beal (Tootsie, as her grandchildren call her) offers two rooms—nothing fancy, but homey and spanking clean—and routinely makes a 6 AM breakfast for guests who need to leave at 6:45 to catch Barna Norton's boat (see *To Do—Boat Excursions and Puffin-Watching*). The Beals raised eight children in this shipshape house that sits in a cluster of lobstermen's homes on the fringe of this fishing village, handy to Great Wass Island. $25 single, $45 double includes a full breakfast. Children are $5 extra if over 5 years old. Pets are occasionally accommodated if they are small and well behaved.

Raspberry Shores B&B (497-2463), Route 187, Jonesport 04649. Geri Taylor's Victorian home in the middle of town offers three rooms with shared bath, water views, and full breakfasts; steps lead from the back down to a picnic table by the water. It's right next door to Barna Norton, an obvious place to stay if you are puffin-watching with the captain. $60 per couple.

Riverside Inn & Restaurant (255-4134), Route 1, East Machias 04630. Open year-round. Built originally in 1805, Victorianized in the 1890s from its fanlights (white glass was replaced with red) to tin ceilings. Tom and Carol Paul, antiques dealers specializing in Victoriana, have authentically restored and expanded it, right down to the antique linens. Note the old train-baggage rack over the claw-foot tub in the bath for one of the two upstairs guest rooms and the woodwork in the common rooms, all deftly restored or installed by Tom. The house sits right on Route 1 but a terraced garden overlooks the river and two suites (with kitchen facilities) in the Carriage House have balconies with river views. $58–85 includes a full breakfast; the specialty is blueberry-stuffed French toast. Carol is well known in the area for the quality of her dinners (see *Dining Out*).

Downeast Farm House (733-2496), Route 189, Trescott (mailing address: RR 1, Box 3860, Lubec 04652). Open year-round. Just one guest room but a real find. Priscilla and Henry Merrill summered in this circa-1800 Cape, set way back from Route 189, for many years before retiring here and converting a wing—a living room furnished with well chosen art and antiques as well as bedroom facing the meadow and bath—into guest quarters. Avid sailors who are knowledgeable about local boating and birding (windows outside the dining room are hung with feeders), they also maintain a small antiques shop. $65 includes a full country breakfast.

Home Port Inn (733-2077; 1-800-457-2077), 45 Main Street, Lubec 04652. Open June through October. Tim and Miyoko Carman offer seven antiques-furnished rooms (two on the ground floor, all with private baths) in a gracious 1880s hilltop home. Each room is individually furnished and one, with twin beds and a water view, is quite grand. While the dining room is popular (see *Dining Out*), guests have their own common space, an inviting living room with TV. $75–85 includes continental breakfast.

Peacock House (733-2403; fax: 733-2403), 27 Summer Street, Lubec 04652. Open May 15 to October 15. An 1860s house on a quiet side street, home to four generations of the Peacock family (owners of the major local cannery). The two guest rooms and three suites, like the formal common rooms, are immaculate and furnished with souvenirs from the far-flung places where Chet and Veda Childs previously lived; one of two ground-floor suites is handicapped accessible. No children under 7. $60–90 with a full breakfast.

Lubecker Gast Haus (733-4385), 31 Main Street, Lubec 04652. Open June through September. Sited on a hilltop with water views and rear deck overlooking the garden. Robert and Irmgard Swiecicki hail originally from Lubec, Germany, and have furnished their four guest rooms with flair. $68 includes a full breakfast.

The Owen House (506-752-2977), Welshpool, Campobello, New Brunswick EOG 3HO, Canada. Open May through September. Probably the most historic house on the island, it was built in 1835 by Admiral William Fitzwilliam Owen, son of the British captain to whom the island was granted in 1769. Joyce Morrell, an artist who maintains one room as her gallery, has furnished the nine guest rooms (five with private baths) with friendly antiques, handmade quilts, and good art. Guests gather around an immense breakfast table in the formal dining room, and also around one of the many fireplaces in the evening. There are 10 acres of land, and you can walk to the Welshpool dock and take the ferry to Deer Island. Birders are particularly welcome. $78–115 Canadian plus 15 percent tax (no GST) includes a full breakfast.

COTTAGES

The choice of rental cottages in Washington County has increased substantially in recent years. Check with the Machias Bay Chamber of Commerce (see *Guidance*); a number of additional listings are in the booklet "Maine Guide to Camp & Cottage Rentals," available from the **Maine Tourism Association** (see *Information* in "What's Where in Maine"). Summer rentals in this area still begin at around $300 per week.

Micmac Farm Guest Cabins (255-3008), Machiasport 04655. Open May to mid-October. Best known for her restaurant (see *Dining Out*), Barbara Dunn also offers several housekeeping cabins. Each has two double beds and a view of the Machias River through sliding glass doors. A real find at $50–60 daily per unit, $300–375 per week.

MOTELS

Blueberry Patch Inn (434-5411), Route 1, Jonesboro 04648. This spick-and-span motel is next to the White House restaurant (see *Eating Out*). Each unit has a refrigerator, air-conditioning, phone, TV, and coffee; two efficiencies, a pool, and sun deck surrounded by berries. $32–58 in-season.

Machias Motor Inn (255-4861), Route 1 next to Helen's Restaurant, Machias 04654. Bob and Joan Carter maintain a two-story, 35-unit motel; most rooms are standard units, each with two double, extra-long beds, cable TV, and a phone. Rooms feature decks overlooking the Machias River. There are six efficiency units, and **Helen's Restaurant,** serving all three meals, is part of the complex. A new indoor pool is a welcome addition if you are traveling this foggy coast with kids. Pets are an extra $5. $50–65 double, $85 for efficiencies.

Eastland Motel (733-5501), Lubec 04652. A good bet if you are taking the kids to Campobello and want a clean, comfortable room with TV; $52–62 in summer, less off-season.

CAMPGROUNDS

McClellan Park, Milbridge. Open Memorial through Columbus Day. See *To Do—Picnicking* for more on this dramatically sited, town-owned park. Free for day use but $3 for tenting, $5 for full campsites; 18 campsites and water are available, but no showers. For details, call the town hall at 546-2422.

Henry Point Campground, Kelly Point Road, Jonesport. Open April through November. Surrounded on three sides by water, this is another great town-owned campground that's usually got space (its crunch weekend is July 4). Neither showers nor water is available, but you can shower and use the coin-operated laundry at the Jonesport Shipyard across the cove. Good water is also available from an outside faucet at the town hall. This is a put-in place for sea kayaks. Turn off Route 187 at the purple house.

Herring Cove Provincial Park (506-752-2396), Campobello Island. Adjoining the Roosevelt Campobello International Park is this campground offering 87 campsites; there's a beach, a golf course, and extensive hiking trails.

Also see Cobscook Bay State Park in "Eastport and Cobscook Bay."

WHERE TO EAT

DINING OUT

Entries are listed geographically, heading east.

Kitchen Garden Restaurant (546-2708). Just off Route 1 in Steuben. Open most of the year for dinner 6–8, weekends-only off-season. Call. Everything is organic and, rumor has it, delicious. Entrées might include curried goat with leeks and Jamaican crab cakes. From $27 per person.

Riverside Inn (255-4134), East Machias. Dinner Monday, Wednesday, Friday, and Saturday by reservation. Tables line the sunporch overlooking the East Machias River and fill a lacy, flowery dining room. Innkeeper Carol Paul's reputation as a chef is well deserved. The four-course meals include appetizers, homemade strawberry nut bread, starch, vegetable, rolls, and beverage and a choice of five entrées, always fish, perhaps pork tenderloin marinated in orange wine sauce, beef, a boneless breast of chicken, or seafood pasta. $14.95–17.95, BYOB.

Seafarer's Wife (497-2365), 9 miles down Route 187 from Route 1 (after the high school look for a small sign on the left), or 3 miles north of Jonesport. The Ol' Salt Room is open for lunch and dinner, the Down East fine dining room is open 5:30–8:30, reservations required. Long-skirted waitresses and a choice of entrées ranging from a vegetarian plate and stuffed baked chicken to Fisherman's Bounty, a baked medley of shrimp, lobster, halibut, scallops, and more. The entrée price ($14.95–19.95) includes hors d'oeuvres, soup, salad, bread, dessert, and tea or coffee. Faye Carver is the owner-chef and her local reputation is sterling. BYOB.

Micmac Farm Restaurant (255-3008), Machiasport. Open year-round (except for 2 weeks at Christmas), Tuesday through Saturday 6–9, by reservation. Located down a dirt road off Route 92. You wouldn't think anyone could find it, but it tends to be full most summer evenings. The restaurant is in an exquisite riverside house built in 1776 by Ebenezer Gardner, a patriot-refugee from Nova Scotia. Just 25 diners can be seated in the low-beamed dining room, and meals are served by candle-light. From her minute kitchen, Barbara Dunn produces a choice of four entrées, which might include tenderloin Stroganoff, lobster Graziella, and filet mignon bordelaise. Full dinners run $16–18. BYOB, since the town is dry. Service may be slow.

The Home Port Inn Restaurant (733-2077), 45 Main Street, Lubec. Open nightly Memorial Day weekend through September. Recognized as the best place to dine in the Campobello/Lubec area, this attractive sunken dining room in the back of an inn is small, so it may be wise to reserve. The menu is large and reasonably priced. Specialties include Down East scampi (a seafood medley of fresh lobster, scallops, and salmon sautéed in a scampi butter with artichoke hearts and black ol-ive, $13.59) and fresh poached salmon ($12.99). Wine (there's an exten-sive list) and beer are served.

EATING OUT

Entries are listed geographically, heading east.

Milbridge House (546-2020), Main Street, Milbridge. Open 10:30–8, a great family-owned restaurant that's bigger and more attractive than it looks from the road. Don't pass up the pies. Beer and wine are served.

✎ **The Red Barn** (546-7721), Main Street (junction of Routes 1 and 1A), Milbridge. Open daily year-round, 6 AM until 9 PM in summer. There is a counter in the back, an abundance of deep booths in the main, pine-paneled dining room, and more seating in the overflow "banquet" room. The menu is large: pastas, burgers, steak, seafood, and fried chicken. Most dinners include access to the extensive salad bar. Fully licensed. Children's menu, great cream pies.

The Blue Beary (546-2052), Route 1, Cherryfield. Open 11–9, a friendly dining room; also a picnic area featuring fresh-dough pizza (try the gar-lic and cheese), homemade soups and pies.

Perry's Seafood, Route 1, Columbia. Open daily 11–9. Easy to pass without noticing, favored by locals for dinner as well as other meals; try the clam pizza, homemade soups and onion rings, and the special of the day.

Harbor House on Sawyer Cove (497-5417), Sawyer Square, Jonesport. Open May through October, 11–8. The town's 19th-century telegraph office with tongue-and-groove woodwork is now an informal dining room, complementing the screened porch and picnic tables overlook-ing the water. You can get a hot dog with sauerkraut ($1.50) and lemon pepper chicken with corn and chips ($9.95), but this place is about lob-ster and crabmeat, stews and rolls, as well as steamed lobster and clams.

River's Edge Café in Machias

Tall Barney, Main Street, Jonesport. Open 4:30 AM–7 PM weekdays, 5:30 AM–7 PM Sunday. Don't be put off by the exterior of this local gathering spot, set back behind its parking lot across from the access to the big bridge. Particularly welcoming for breakfast on a foggy morning (papers are stacked on the counter). *Note:* The long table down the middle of the front room is reserved for the local lobstermen, who come drifting in one by one.

The White House (434-2792), Route 1, Jonesboro. Open 5 AM–9 PM. It's not white but still a great place. Inside are cheery blue booths, a counter, and friendly service. Memorable breakfasts, outstanding fish chowder (better than the lobster); specialties include fried seafood platters and delectable pies.

River's Edge, Main Street, Machias. Open year-round, daily 9–7. Finally, a café that suggests this is a college town, also that it has a riverfront. Opened in 1998 with coffees, a blackboard menu, specials such as enchiladas with refried beans and key lime tuna on a bagel. Adjacent and related to Obidiah's, a used-book store; summer seating on the back deck overlooking the river. At this writing dinner is still a promise.

Melanie's Chowder House, Dublin Street, Machias. Open for lunch (11–2) and dinner (5–8). Approaching Machias from the south on Route 1, it's easy to miss this small restaurant, housed in the former fish market across from Napa Auto Parts. Melanie Colbeth frequently alters the blackboard menu. It might include salmon chowder and carrot cashew soup, mini crab and lobster quiches, and shepherd's pie. Dinner entrées run $7–11. Homemade breads come with soups like 15-bean (bread and soup is under $3). The cheery decor features plants, flowered tablecloths made by Melanie's mother, and two booths allegedly from a 1920s Machias speakeasy. Just opened in fall 1998; we hope this lasts.

Helen's Restaurant (255-6506), 32 Main Street, Machias (north of town on the water). Open 6 AM–8 PM. Geared to bus groups en route from Campobello to Bar Harbor, but there's plenty of room for everybody. Generous servings: a wide choice of seafood, meat entrées, salads, fish stews, and sandwiches. "Whipped" pies are a specialty: strawberry, blueberry, and a dozen more. Children's plates.

Blue Bird Ranch (255-3351), Lower Main Street (Route 1), Machias. Open year-round for all three meals. A diner atmosphere for breakfast and lunch, but the dining room (with banquet room) features lobster, fried seafood, salad bar, homemade pies, specials like baby ribs ($6.95) or beans and franks ($4.95); fully licensed. This is high on our family dining list.

Michelle's (255-5801), Route 1, Machias (north of town). Open daily year-round for lunch and dinner. The menu includes an antipasto salad and eggplant parmigiana, good fish chowder, pleasant atmosphere.

Phinney's Seaview (733-0941), Route 189, Lubec. Open year-round, 6:30 AM–9 PM in summer, 7 AM–8 PM the remainder of the year. Recently remodeled with an outside deck overlooking Johnson's Bay, a full menu but specializing in seafood dishes (a fish market is part of the complex); good chowder, but we waited forever.

The Waterside Restaurant (733-2500), the Landing, Lubec. Open May through Labor Day, 11 until sunset. Home Port Inn owner Tim Carman has turned a former sardine-packing warehouse into a waterside eatery with picnic tables on the water. We found the prices higher than at other local places but what the heck: good crab rolls, lobster, chowder, specials like ribs; beer served. If all the outdoor tables are taken it's customary to share, and you can always request that another table be moved out (this is still a warehouse with machinery for moving boxes of sea urchins). Inquire about live music.

The Cafe Kontinental (733-4385), 31 Main Street, Lubec. German pastries, sandwiches, soups, beer and wine; by reservation off-season.

Lupine Lodge (752-2555), Campobello. Open noon–9. Under new ownership, this former log "cottage" features a great hearth and has regained its old charm. The dinner menu ranges from $6.95 to $16.95 and friends recommend the sautéed Fundy haddock. Full license.

Herring Cove Restaurant (752-2467), Campobello. A café at the golf club, good for breakfast, lunch, and informal dinner, specializing in fish-and-chips; vague views of the water.

ENTERTAINMENT

Milbridge Theater (546-2038), Main Street, Milbridge. Open nightly May through November, 7:30 show time; Saturday and Sunday matinees for children's films; all seats $3.75. A very special theater: a refurbished movie house featuring first-run and art films with truly affordable prices. Fresh popcorn, ice cream parlor.

University of Maine, Machias (255-3313, ext. 284), offers both a winter and summer series of plays, performances, and concerts.

Downriver Theater Productions (255-4997) stages plays June through August at Gay's Wreath Building, Marshfield Ridge Road, Machias. Productions are a mix of safe musicals (*The Sound of Music, Cabaret*) and original plays. Tickets are $8 per adult, $7 for seniors and students.

Machias Bay Chamber Concerts (255-3889), Center Street Congregational Church, Machias. A series of six chamber music concerts, July through early August, Tuesday at 8 PM. Top groups such as the Kneisel Hall Chamber Players and the Vermeer Quartet are featured.

Mary Potterton Memorial Piano Concerts, Sacred Heart Church Parish Hall, Lubec. Wednesday evenings (7:30 PM) all summer, free. Featuring SummerKeys faculty (see *To Do—Special Learning Programs*) and guest artists.

SELECTIVE SHOPPING

Entries are listed geographically, heading east.

Jonesport offers six antiques shops, all within walking distance of each other.

Sea-Witch (546-7495), Milbridge. Describing itself as "the biggest little gift shop in Washington County," this is a trove of trinkets and treasures: collector dolls, spatterware, stuffed animals, seafood, and berry products.

Columbia Falls Pottery (483-4075; 1-800-235-2512), Main Street, Columbia Falls. Open year-round. Striking, bright, sophisticated creations by April Adams: mugs, platters, kitchenware, lamps, wind chimes, and more, featuring lupine and sunflower designs; catalog.

Crossroads Vegetables (497-2641), posted from Route 187 (off Route 1), Jonesport. Open daily except Saturday, 9–5:30 in-season. Bonnie and Arnold Pearlman built their house, windmill, sauna, and barn, and have reclaimed acres of productive vegetable garden from the surrounding woods. In addition to their outstanding vegetables (salad lovers get their greens picked to order; Bonnie adds edible flowers like nasturtium), they also sell the hand-hollowed wooden bowls that Arnold carves all winter and the dried-flower wreaths that Bonnie makes.

Whitney Originals (255-3392; 1-800-562-7963), 5 Bridge Street, Machias. While Washington County is studded with Christmas-wreath makers, David Whitney is the first to also make decorative year-round wreaths. Tasteful and fragrant, they range from a "woodland wreath" on a blueberry-vine base ($28.95) to an elaborate Floral Fantasy ($56.95). Look for the display on Route 1 just south of the bridge.

The Sow's Ear (255-4066), 7 Water Street, Machias. A mix of cards, jewelry, toys, clothing, and things "from away."

Country Duckling (255-8063), 1 Water Street, Machias. Locally made hand-crafted gifts.

Downeast 5 & 10 Cents (255-8850), Water Street, Machias. Open Monday through Saturday 9–5 and until 8 on Friday. A superb, old-fashioned Ben Franklin store: two stories of crammed aisles.

Obidiah's, Main Street, Machias. A great used-book, antiques store.

Machias Hardware Co. (255-6581; 1-800-543-2250), 26 Main Street. An unexpected source of reasonably priced herbs and spices in 2-ounce and 1-pound packages, also local products like those by A.M. Look Canning (see below).

A.M. Look Canning Co., Route 191, East Machias (259-3341; 1-800-962-6258). Retail shop open weekdays, 8–4. A former sardine-processing plant now processes Atlantic and Bar Harbor brand seafoods, also New England specialty foods like Indian Pudding.

Connie's Clay of Fundy (255-4574), Route 1, East Machias. Open year-round. Connie Harter-Bagley's combination studio/shop is filled with her distinctive glazed earthenware in deep colors with minimal design. Bowls, pie plates, platters, lamps, and a variety of small essentials like garlic jars and ring boxes.

Cottage Garden (733-2902), North Lubec Road, Lubec. Open in-season Wednesday through Sunday 10–5; 4.5 miles from Lubec. Gretchen Mead welcomes visitors to her steadily expanding perennial gardens. A short trail through woods leads to a picnic meadow, and a deck behind the shop (herbs, flower wreaths, toys, Christmas ornaments, birdhouses) overlooks the garden and a small pond.

CHRISTMAS WREATHS

Wreath-making is a major industry in this area. You can order in the fall and take delivery of a freshly made wreath right before Christmas. Prices quoted include delivery. Sources are: **Cape Split Wreaths** (483-2983), Box 447, Route 1, Addison 04606; **Simplicity Wreath** (483-2780), Sunset Point, Harrington 04643; **The Wreath Shoppe** (483-4598), Box 358, Oak Point Road, Harrington 04643 (wreaths decorated with cones, berries, and reindeer moss); and **Maine Coast Balsam** (255-3301), Box 458, Machias 04654 (decorations include cones, red berries, and bow). Also see Whitney Originals, above.

SPECIAL EVENTS

June (last weekend): the **Down East Rodeo,** Machias fairgrounds.

July: **Independence Day** celebrations in **Jonesport/Beals** (lobster-boat races, easily viewed from the bridge); **Cherryfield** (parade and fireworks); and **Steuben** (firemen's lobster picnic and parade); also in **Cutler** and **Machias.**

Last weekend in July: **Milbridge Days** (546-2406) include a parade, a dance, a lobster dinner, and the big feature: the greased codfish relay race.

August: **Wild Blueberry Festival** and **Machias Craft Festival** (*third weekend*) in downtown Machias, sponsored by Penobscot Valley Crafts and Center Street Congregational Church: concerts, food, major crafts fair, and live entertainment.

EASTPORT AND COBSCOOK BAY

With its flat, haunting light and blank, staring storefronts, Eastport has an end-of-the-world feel and suggests an Edward Hopper painting. The town was occupied by the British for four years during the War of 1812, a tale told in the Barracks Museum. One of the old cannons used to fend off the enemy still stands in front of the Peavey Library. But the town's big claim to fame remains the fact that the sardine-canning process was invented here by Julius Wolfe in 1875, and not long thereafter 18 canneries were operating here.

A "city" of 2,500 people (less than half its turn-of-the-century population), Eastport remains a working deep-water port, and large freighters frequently dock at the municipal pier to take on woodland products. The town is also a base for salmon farming, but there are many gaps in the old waterfront, now walled in pink granite to form Overlook Park.

This is a good spot from which to get out on Passamaquoddy Bay in an excursion boat, to watch the area's summer gathering of whales, and to view Old Sow, a whirlpool off Deer Island that's billed as the world's second-largest. If nothing else, take the small ferry that runs every hour to Deer Island and back.

Eastport is on Moose Island, connected to the mainland by a series of causeways linking other islands. In the center of the Pleasant Point Indian Reservation, situated on one of these islands, the Waponahki Museum tells the story of the Passamaquoddy tribe, past and present.

GUIDANCE
Eastport Chamber of Commerce (853-4644; www.nemaine.com/ eastportcc), Eastport 04631. Open late May to mid-September.

TO SEE

Waponahki Museum & Resource Center (853-4001), Route 190, Pleasant Point. Open weekdays 8:30–11 and noon–4. Easy to miss, a small red building near the big (closed) IGA. Curator Joseph Nicholas has created an outstanding museum with photos, tools, baskets, and crafts that tell the story of the Passamaquoddy tribe. A good place to inquire about where to shop for Native American crafts.

Barracks Museum (853-4674/6630) 74 Washington Street, Eastport. Open Memorial Day through Labor Day, Tuesday through Saturday 1–4. Originally part of Fort Sullivan, occupied by the British during the War of 1812, this house has been restored to its 1820s appearance as an officers' quarters and displays old photos and memorabilia about Eastport in its golden era.

Deer Island Ferry and Landing at Eastport

Reversing Salt Water Falls. From Route 1 in West Pembroke, take the local road out along Leighton Neck, which brings you to a 140-acre park with hiking trails and picnic sites that view the incoming tidal current as it passes between Mahar's Point and Falls Island. As the salt water flows along at upward of 25 knots, it strikes a series of rocks, resulting in rapids.

TO DO

AIRPLANE RIDES
Quoddy Air (853-0997) offers scenic rides, whale-watching, and charters.
BIRDING
Birding is what Moosehorn National Wildlife Refuge is about. See *Green Space*.
BOAT EXCURSIONS
Whale-watching (853-4303), out of Eastport. Captain George Harris and his son Butch offer 3-hour cruises of Passamaquoddy Bay.
Ferry to Deer Island. For details about **East Coast Ferries Ltd.** (506-747-2159) see *Getting Around* in the introduction to "Washington County." Mid-June to mid-September the ferry departs every hour from the beach beside Eastport Lobster and Fish House. Be sure to take it at least to Deer Island ($10 for car and passenger, less for walk-ons or bikes). We strongly suggest you go the whole way around the "Quoddy Loop" (see the "Washington County" introduction).
Moose Island Tours (853-831), 37 Washington Street, Eastport. Jim Blankman of smoked salmon fame (see *Selective Shopping*) has bought

himself a 1947 genuine wood-paneled station wagon in which he offers island tours with a picnic (smoked salmon or roasted chicken). $15 per adult, $10 per child.

KAYAKING, CANOEING, AND RAFTING

Tidal Trails (853-7373 in Eastport; 726-4079 in Pembroke). Amy and Tim Sheehan view the Cobscook and Passamaquoddy Bay area as one of the last coastal frontiers on the East Coast and are offering a variety of ways of exploring it: kayak and canoe rentals, guided tours, charter-fishing boats, raft float trips through the Reversing Falls; also cottage rentals.

GREEN SPACE

The Quoddy Regional Land Trust (733-5509), with the help of the Maine Coast Heritage Trust, publishes a 36-page booklet entitled "Cobscook Trails: A Guide to Walking Opportunities around Cobscook Bay and the Bold Coast." It details 13 trails open to walkers.

WALKS

Shackford Head (posted from Route 190 south of Eastport) is a 90-acre peninsula with a half-mile-long trail from the parking lot to a 173-foot high headland overlooking Campobello and Lubec in one direction and Cobscook Bay in the other. An additional quarter-mile-long trail leads down the headland and permits access to the shore.

Moosehorn National Wildlife Refuge, Edmunds, off Route 1 between Dennysville and Whiting. Some 7,200 acres bounded by Cobscook Bay and the mouth of the Dennys and Whiting Rivers, with several miles of rocky shoreline. North Trail Road is 2.5 miles and leads to a parking area from which canoes can be launched into Hobart Stream. South Trail Road is 0.9 miles and leads to a parking area for a 10-mile unmaintained trail network. Trails in the Baring section of the refuge (see "Calais and the St. Croix Valley") are maintained.

Cobscook State Park (726-4412), off Route 1 between Dennysville and Whiting, is 888 acres with a 2-mile nature trail with water views and a ½-mile (round-trip) Shore Trail. Wildlife and birds are plentiful.

Gleason Point, Perry. Take the right just before the Wigwam on Route 1 (see *Selective Shopping*) and follow signs to the beach and boat landing.

LODGING

INNS AND BED & BREAKFASTS

Weston House (853-2907; 1-800-853-2907), 26 Boynton Street, Eastport 04631. Open year-round. An elegant, Federal-style house built in 1810 by a Harvard graduate who became a local politician. There are five large guest rooms, one with a working fireplace and tall four-poster with a brocade spread, views of the bay and gardens, antiques. You can have the room in which John James Audubon slept on his way to Labrador in 1833. Rooms in the back ell are smaller but still inviting. When they first opened, fresh from California, we gave Jett and John Peterson one winter. That was 15 years ago and the couple continue to add "rooms"— a bricked terrace here and a rose garden there—to the ever-expanding grounds. Rates are $50–75 double, including state tax, a sumptuous breakfast in the formal dining room, maybe Eastport-raised and -smoked salmon and eggs Benedict. Jett's four-course dinner ($35) or a picnic lunch can be arranged. The common rooms are furnished with Oriental rugs and wing chairs; but if you want to put your feet up, there is a very comfortable back room with books and a TV.

Todd House (853-2328), Todd's Head, Eastport 04631. Open year-round. A restored 1775 Cape with great water views. Breakfast is served in the common room in front of the huge old fireplace. In 1801, men met here to charter a Masonic Order, and in 1861 the house became a temporary barracks when Todd's Head was fortified. The house has changed little in a century. The four large double rooms (shared baths) vary in feel, view, and access to baths. Our favorites are the ground-floor Cornerstone Room (but its bath is across the common room) and the Masonic Room, both with working fireplaces ($45–55). There are also two efficiency suites ($70–85.60), both with water views. Guests are welcome to use the deck and barbecue. Innkeeper Ruth McInnis welcomes well-behaved children and pets; her own pets include a Maine Coon cat, a cockatiel, and a pet seagull that keeps his eye on the goldfish in the ornamental pond.

The Inn at Eastport (853-4307), 13 Washington Street, Eastport 04631. An early-19th-century house built by the owner of a schooner fleet, now a comfortable, welcoming B&B with four rooms, one with a canopy bed, all with antiques and private baths. Guests can gather in two front parlors (one with a TV) or in the outdoor hot tub. $55–65 includes inn-keeper Brenda Booker's very full breakfast, maybe Belgian waffles or scrambled eggs with salmon.

The Milliken House (853-2955), 29 Washington Street, Eastport 04631. The 1840s house built by a wharf owner retains Victorian detailing and some original furniture. Artist/innkeeper Joyce Weber maintains a large studio that guests are welcome to use. The five guest rooms share two baths. $50 single, $60 per couple, $10 per extra guest.

Kilby House Inn (853-0889; 1-800-435-4529), 122 Water Street. A spotless Victorian house on the waterfront with an attractive double parlor and formal dining room, five pleasant upstairs guest rooms, private baths. $55–75.

MOTEL

The Motel East (853-4747), 23A Water Street, Eastport 04631. This two-story motel has 14 units, some handicapped accessible, all with water views, some with balconies. Amenities include direct-dial phones, cable TV, 10 kitchenettes. $80 per night, $95 for a suite, $125 for five people.

COTTAGES AND MORE

Cinqueterre Farm Cottage (726-4766), RR 1, Box 1264, Ox Cove Road, Pembroke 04666. Les Prickett and Gloria Christie, two of the area's outstanding chefs, offer a waterside cottage with choice of catered or cook-your-own meals.

✐ **Yellow Birch Farm** (726-5807), Young's Cove Road, Pembroke 04666. Studio open May through October; cottage, May through September. Bunny Richards and Gretchen Gordon maintain a 200-year-old working farm on a dirt road leading to the Reversing Falls. A second-floor studio with a wood-burning stove, queen-sized bed and skylight, and private bath, fridge, and hot plate (a great base for a couple; cooking facilities available) and a two-room cottage with a fully equipped kitchen, outdoor hot shower, and outhouse (hot water, electricity but no septic) are both available by the day ($55 double) or week ($300). The cottage is good for families; farm animals include pigs, lambs, and a flock of hens.

Note: Tidal Trails (see *To Do*) serves as a referral service for local cottages.

CAMPGROUND

Cobscook Bay State Park (726-4412), Route 1, Dennysville. Open mid-May to mid-October. Offers 150 camping sites, most of them for tents and many with water views. There are even showers (unusual in Maine state campgrounds). The 880-acre park also offers a boat-launch area, picnicking benches, and a hiking and cross-country ski trail. (*Cobscook* means "boiling tides.")

WHERE TO EAT

The Baywatch Cafe (853-6030), 75 Water Street, Eastport. Open daily 11–9, closed Sundays off-season. Homemade chowders are the specialty, along with baked haddock with lobster sauce and baked scallops. As we lunched we watched paper products being loaded onto a giant Norwegian freighter at the municipal pier.

Eastport Lobster and Fish House (853-9663), 167 Water Street, Eastport. Open May through September, daily 11:30–9. An unbeatable location, on the site of the country's first fish and sardine cannery. The two top-floor dining rooms are fairly formal with tablecloths, fresh flowers, and a menu that runs from sandwiches through smoked salmon and bouillabaisse with a wide choice of seafood dishes. Entrées $11.95–17.95. The downstairs pub is informal and it's possible to get take-out (thus park in line) for the ferry that departs from the adjacent beach. The complex includes a lobster pound and picnic tables on the dock, also a gift shop. Inquire about leasing your own lobster trap.

La Sardina Loca (853-2739), 28 Water Street, Eastport. Open daily 4–10 except Tuesday. "The crazy sardine" is so flashy, cheerful, and out-of-character with the rest of Water Street that you figure it's a mirage, or at best somebody's one-season stand. But it's been there for years in the former A&P with its Christmas lights, patio furniture, and posters, and a menu that's technically Mexican, including "la Sardina Loca" with hot chiles and sour cream. Where else can you get fresh crabmeat enchiladas? Entrées $5.50–14. Fully licensed.

New Waco Diner, Water Street, Eastport. Open year-round, Monday through Saturday 6 AM–9 PM. A friendly haven with booths and a long shiny counter; menu choices are posted on the wall behind. You can get a full roast turkey dinner; there is also beer, pizza, and great squash pie.

Crossroads Restaurant (726-5053), Route 1, "at the Waterfall," Pembroke. Open 11–9 daily. Bigger than it looks from outside, a great road-food stop, serving the best lobster roll in the area; deep-fried seafood pies are specialties; liquor served.

The New Friendly Restaurant (853-6610), Route 1, Perry. Great road food. Known for the most lobster in a lobster sandwich around ($7.25).

ENTERTAINMENT

Stage East (726-4670), a 100-seat theater in the 1887 Masonic Hall at the corner of Water and Dana Streets; summer-season performances.

SELECTIVE SHOPPING

Raye's Mustard Mill (853-4451; 1-800-853-1903), Route 190 (Washington Street), Eastport. Open daily 9–5 in summer; winter hours vary. In business since 1903, this company is billed as the country's last remaining stone-ground-mustard mill. This is the mustard in which Washington County's sardines were once packed, and it's sensational. Try the samples in **The Pantry,** which has evolved into a full gift store selling Maine products; tours in July and August.

Cinqueterre Farm Bakery (726-4766), Ox Cove Road, off Route 1, Pembroke. Open May through October Monday–Saturday. Les Prickett and Gloria Christie, both locally respected chefs, operate a bakery specializing in 5-grain breads, pizza, and rolls; soups and eggs, honey, jams, and pickles also available along with a selection of wines.

The Eastport Gallery (853-4166), 69 Water Street. Eastport. Open daily in summer. A cooperative gallery representing more than 40 local artists. Note the upstairs back balcony over the harbor.

Earth Forms Pottery, corner of Water and Dana Streets. Daily in-season. Nationally known potter Donald Sutherland specializes in large garden and patio pots.

Jim's Smoked Salmon (853-4831), 37 Washington Street, Eastport. Jim Blankman uses an old method to process the town's newest product; also rainbow steelhead trout. Will ship anywhere.

The **Wigwam** and the **Trading Post,** both on Route 1 in Perry, are outlets for local Passamaquoddy crafts.

At the Pleasant Point Reservation: **Clara and Rocky Neptune Keezer** (853-4322) make traditional Passamaquoddy ash and sweet-grass baskets and **Richard Neptune** fashions drums and carvings. **Theresa Neptune Gardner** (853-4613) also makes baskets. **Joe's Basket Shop** (853-2840), Route 190, Pleasant Point, features baskets and handmade jewelry.

Fountain Books, Main Street, Eastport. A funky former pharmacy filled with books, retaining the old soda fountain, adding cappuccino.

SPECIAL EVENTS

July: **Independence Day** is celebrated in **Pembroke** (parade, canoe races) and for a week in **Eastport,** with parades, an air show, and fireworks. Eastport's is the first flag in the United States to be raised on July 4 itself (at dawn). **Cannery Wharf Boat Race** *(last weekend).*

Mid-August: **Annual Indian Ceremonial Days,** Pleasant Point Reservation—a celebration of Passamaquoddy culture climaxing with dances in full regalia.

September: **Eastport Salmon Festival** *(the weekend after Labor Day)*—a celebration of Eastport's salmon industry; salmon, trout, and Maine potatoes are grilled dockside, and free tours of fish farms in the bay are offered, along with live entertainment, games, and an art show, antiques auction, fishing derby.

CALAIS AND THE ST. CROIX VALLEY

GUIDANCE

Calais Information Center (454-2211), 7 Union Street, Calais. Open year-round, daily 8–6 July through October 15, otherwise 9–5 (rest rooms). Operated by the Maine Tourism Association, a source of brochures for all of Maine as well as the local area. Though it's not set up as a walk-in information center, the **Greater Calais Area Chamber of Commerce** (454-2308) is also helpful.

Grand Lake Stream Chamber of Commerce, P.O. Box 124, Grand Lake Stream 04637. Request the brochure listing local accommodations and outfitters and get a map showing hiking and mountain biking trails.

GETTING THERE

By car: The direct route to Calais from points west of Washington County is Route 9, the Airline Highway. From the Machias area, take Route 191.

TO SEE

Calais. The largest city in Washington County, Calais (pronounced *cal-us*) is a busy border-crossing point and shopping center for eastern Washington County. Its present population is 4,000, roughly 2,000 less than it was in the 1870s, the decade in which its fleet of sailing vessels numbered 176.

Moosehorn National Wildlife Refuge (454-3521), P.O. Box 1077, Calais. Established in 1937, this area is the northeast end of a chain of wildlife and migratory bird refuges extending from Florida to Maine, managed by the US Fish and Wildlife Service. The refuge comprises two units, some 20 miles apart. The larger, 16,000-acre area is in Baring, 5 miles north of Calais on Route 1. Look for eagles, which seem to be nesting each spring at the intersection of Charlotte Road and Route 1. Inquire about special programs—guided hikes, bike and van tours—offered late June through August.

Grand Lake Stream. A remote but famous resort community on West Grand Lake, with access to the Grand Lake chain. Grand Lake Stream claims to have been the world's biggest tannery town for some decades before 1874. Fishing is the big lure now: landlocked salmon, lake trout, smallmouth bass, also pickerel and white perch. Some of the state's outstanding fishing lodges and camps are clustered here and there are many good and affordable lakeside rental camps, a find for families. Local innkeepers can get you into the historical museum, a trove of Native American artifacts, cannery-era photos, and canoe molding. Inquire about hiking and biking trails and guided kayaking.

St. Croix Island Overlook, Red Beach. Eight miles south of Calais on Route 1, the view is of the island on which Samuel de Champlain and Sieur de Monts established the first white settlement in North America north of Florida. That was in 1604. Using the island as a base, Champlain explored and mapped the coast of New England as far south as Cape Cod. The rest area here is a beauty, a great spot for a picnic.

TO DO

CANOEING

Sunrise Canoe Expeditions (454-7708), Cathance Lake, Grove Post Office 04638. March to October. Offers advice, canoe rentals, and guided trips down the Grand Lake chain of lakes and the St. Croix River along the Maine–New Brunswick border; good for a 3- to 6-day run spring through fall. We did this trip with Sunrise (putting in at Vanceboro) and highly recommend it. In business more than 20 years, Sunrise is headed by photographer and naturalist Martin Brown; expeditions to the Arctic and Rio Grande are offered as well as to the Machias, St. John, and St. Croix Rivers. Canoes for local use are $25 per day.

FISHING

Salmon is the big lure. Ranging from 8 to 20 pounds, Atlantic salmon are taken by fly-anglers in the Dennys and St. Croix Rivers, mid-May through early July. **Grand Lake Stream** is the focal point for dozens of lakes, ponds, and streams known for smallmouth bass and landlocked salmon (May through mid-June). There are also chain pickerel, lake trout, and brook trout. Fishing licenses, available for 3 days to a season, are also necessary for ice fishing. For information on fishing guides, lodges, and rules, write to the **Regional Headquarters of the Inland Fisheries and Wildlife Department,** Machias 04653.

GOLF

St. Croix Golf Club, Calais. A tricky nine-hole course on the banks of the St. Croix River.

SWIMMING

Reynolds Beach on Meddybemps Lake by the town pier in Meddybemps (Route 191) is open daily 9 AM–sunset. Meddybemps is a very small, white, wooden village with a church, general store, and pier; a good spot for a picnic and a swim. **Red Beach** at Calais on the St. Croix River is named for the sand on these strands, which is deep red. There is also swimming in dozens of crystal-clear lakes. Inquire about access at local lodges and general stores.

LODGING

BED & BREAKFAST

Brewer House (454-2385; 1-800-821-2028), Route 1, P.O. Box 94, Robbinston 04671. Open year-round on Route 1, 12 miles south of Calais, this is a striking 1828 mansion with graceful Ionic pillars. The interior, filled with treasures amassed by antiques dealers David and Estelle Holloway, is very Victorian, a mix of fun and formality. A life-sized saint stands in the deep blue living room, next to a marble fireplace. Each of the five bedrooms is named for one of David and Estelle's children and each is different, most featuring massive antique beds and fanciful baths, with views of Passamaquoddy Bay across the road. The Servants Quarters, a small apartment furnished in cottage furniture (two beds, a TV and VCR, efficiency kitchen) has an outside entrance, suited to families. $60–85 in summer (less in winter) includes a very full breakfast, not the kind you probably eat at home, served with silver and crystal in the sunny breakfast room. Estelle sells antiques next door at the Landing.

SPORTING LODGES

Weatherby's (796-5558), Grand Lake Stream 04637. Open early May through October 15. A rambling, white, 1870s lodge with flowers along the porch, set in roses and birches by Grand Lake Stream, the small river that connects West Grand Lake with Big Lake. Ken and Charlene Sassi have been welcoming guests more than 25 years, and their experience shows. There is a big sitting room—with piano, TV, and hearth—in the lodge; also a homey, newly redecorated dining room with a tin ceiling and better than down-home cooking (served by the owner-chef). Each of the 16 cottages is unique, but most are log-style with screened porches, bath, and a Franklin stove or fireplace. *Fishing* is what this place is about, and it's a great place for children. $94 per person double occupancy, $115 single MAP (family rates available); motorboats are $42 per day, and a guide, $140; 15 percent gratuity added. Inquire about the canoe-camping option and fly-fishing.

Leen's Lodge (796-5575; 1-800-995-3367), Box 40, Grand Lake Stream 04637. November 1 through April 30 write to P.O. Box 92, Newport 04953 or call 368-5699. A peaceful cluster of cottages on the shore of West Grand Lake. Dick and E. J. Beaulieu offer 10 cabins, nicely scattered through the woods. Ranging in size from one to eight bedrooms, each has a full bath, fireplace or Franklin stove (with gas heat as a backup), and fridge. The spacious dining room overlooks the water. The Tannery room, a pine-paneled gathering space with picture window, is equipped with games, books, and a TV, a good spot to relax before dinner (BYOB). $90 per person per day MAP. Family rates available in non-peak periods. 15 percent gratuity; lunch, boat rentals, and guide service are extra.

Indian Rocks Camps (796-2822; 1-800-498-2821), Grand Lake Stream 04637. Open year-round. The Canells offer five, century-old log cabins and a central lodge. It's a friendly compound that caters to families in summer as well as to fishermen, cross-country skiers, snowmobilers, and ice fishermen in winter. Amenities include miniature golf as well as a store on the premises. $62 per person includes all meals; $25 per person (no meals) in the housekeeping cabins. Summer rates in cabins: $375. Inquire about fly-fishing school; guide service.

Lakeside Inn and Cabins (796-2324), Princeton 04668. Open year-round; cabins May through November. A handsome old inn with twin chimneys and seven guest rooms; also five basic housekeeping cabins on Lewy Lake (the outlet to Big Lake, also a source for the St. Croix River). Rooms in the inn are simple and nicely furnished; each has a sink. Although baths are shared, there are plenty. Common areas are inviting, especially the front porch and the sporting room with a pool table. Rooms are $31 double; meals are available at additional cost.

Shoreline Camps (796-5539), P.O. Box 127, Grand Lake Stream 04637. Open ice-out until mid-October. A very attractive set of camps on the banks of Big Lake. Peaceful and remote, offering hiking, swimming, boating, and fishing. Ten cabins range from one to three bedrooms, each with bath and private deck. Boat rental, guides, fishing licenses available. Facilities also include a coin-operated laundry and the Last Cast Lounge (open to the public). $30 per person per day with a $60–85 minimum depending on the cottage. Children under 12 are half price; under 3, free.

CAMPGROUND

Georgia Pacific's woodland office in Millinocket (723-5232) dispenses a sportsman's map and information about camping on its extensive woodland holdings ($3).

Also see Cobscook Bay State Park in "Eastport and Cobscook Bay."

WHERE TO EAT

DINING OUT

The Chandler House (454-7922), 20 Chandler Street, Calais. Open 4–11 daily except Monday. Chef-owned, specializing in seafood like blackened whitefish and known for the best prime rib around. Entrées $9–18.95.

Bernardini's (454-2237), 89 Main Street, Calais. Open year-round for lunch and dinner except Sunday. An attractive storefront trattoria; traditional Italian entrées, pasta specials, and desserts. Entrées $11–15.

The Townhouse Restaurant (454-8021), 84 Main Street, Calais. Open mid-April to mid-October, daily 11–9 except Sunday. Seafood specialties include haddock with lobster sauce ($12.95), prime rib.

Redclyffe Dining Room (454-3279), Route 1, Robbinston. Open 5–10 for dinner. The view of the bay is superb through the solarium windows. The vast menu offers pasta, steaks, chicken, and seafood; the specialty is baked haddock with lobster sauce. Entrées $8.50–18.50.

Heslin's (454-3762), Route 1, Calais (south of the village). Open May through October, 5–9. A popular local dining room specializing in steak and seafood entrées and "French cooking." Moderate.

EATING OUT

Wickachee (454-3400), 282 Main Street, Calais. Open year-round, 6 AM–10 PM. Steak and seafood with a big salad bar are the dinner specialties; even dinner entrées start at just $7. Spacious, clean, and friendly, but the rest rooms are tiny.

SELECTIVE SHOPPING

Pine Tree Store, Grand Lake Stream. Open daily, year-round. A general store that also carries many sportsmen's essentials.

Pandora's Box (454-3604), 5 Lowell Street, Calais. Open 10–4. Seven rooms of a former boardinghouse are filled with an unpredictable assortment of clothing, furniture, jewelry, books, whatever Nellie Walton finds at auctions and estate sales. Special orders are happily filled.

SPECIAL EVENTS

July: **Indian Festival** at **Indian Township,** near Princeton. **Grand Lake Stream Folk Art Festival** *(last weekend)*—bluegrass and folk music, woodsmen's skills demonstrations featuring canoe-building, crafts, dinner cooked by Maine guides.

August: **North Country Festival,** Danforth. **International Festival,** Calais—a week of events (parade, suppers, canoe and raft races).

ST. ANDREWS, NEW BRUNSWICK

St. Andrews is much like Bar Harbor, but with the genteel charm and big hotels that Bar Harbor lost in the 1947 fire. The big hotel in St. Andrews is the Algonquin, a 200-room, many-gabled, neo-Tudor resort dating from 1915 and still managed by the Canadian Pacific Railroad. The Algonquin sits enthroned like a queen mother above this tidy town with loyalist street names like Queen, King, and Princess Royal. St. Andrews was founded in 1783 by British Empire loyalists, American colonists who so strongly opposed breaking away from the mother country that they had to leave the new United States after independence was won. Most came from what is now Castine, many of them unpegging their houses and bringing them along in the 1780s. Impressed by this display of loyalty, the British government made the founding of St. Andrews as painless as possible, granting the settlers a superb site. British army engineers dug wells, built a dock, constructed a fort, and laid out the town on its present grid. Each loyalist family was also given a house lot twice the usual size. The result is an unusually gracious, largely 19th-century town, hauntingly reminiscent of Castine. The focal point remains Market Wharf, where the first settlers stepped ashore—now the cluster point for outfitters offering whale-watching, sailing, and kayaking tours—and Water Street, lined with shops specializing in British woolens and china.

GUIDANCE

St. Andrews Chamber of Commerce (506-529-2555), Reed Avenue, St. Andrews, New Brunswick EOG 2XO, Canada; office open year-round, information center, May through October.

Complete lodging listings for both St. Andrews and Grand Manan are detailed in the **"New Brunswick Travel Guide,"** available toll-free in Canada and the United States (1-800-561-0123), or by writing to Economic Development & Tourism, P.O. Box 12345, Fredericton, New Brunswick E3B 5C3, Canada.

GETTING THERE

By car: Route 1 via Calais. From the border crossing at Calais, it's just 19 miles to St. Andrews.

By car ferry: See *Getting Around* in the Washington County introduction, also *To Do* in the previous sections. The ferry docks in L'Etete and the road curves up he peninsula through the town of St. George, where you pick up the Canadian Route 1, following it 13 unremarkable miles to the turnoff (Route 127) for St. Andrews.)

TIME

Note that New Brunswick's Atlantic time is 1 hour ahead of Maine.

TAXES

The Canadian Goods and Services Tax (GST) is a 7 percent tax imposed on food, lodging, and just about everything else in Canada. Visitors who spend more than $100 on goods and short-term accommodations will get most of it back by mailing in a Revenue Canada application and appending all receipts. New Brunswick also tacks on a food and lodging tax; the latter does not apply to smaller B&Bs.

TO SEE

Ross Memorial Museum (506-529-1824), corner of King and Montague Streets, St. Andrews, open daily mid-June through Labor Day 10–4:30, then closed Monday until Thanksgiving. An 1824 mansion displaying the fine decorative art collection of the Reverend and Mrs. Henry Phipps Ross of Ohio.

Sheriff Andrews House Historic Site, 63 King Street, St. Andrews. Open June to October, Monday through Saturday 9:30–4:30, Sunday from 1. An 1820 house with fine detailing, nicely interpreted by costumed guides.

Ministers Island Historic Site (506-529-5081), Chamcook. Open June to mid-October. One of the grandest estates, built around 1890 on an island connected by a "tidal road" (accessible only at low tide) to St. Andrews, **Covenhoven** is a 50-room mansion with 17 bedrooms, a vast drawing room, a bathhouse, and a gigantic and ornate livestock barn. The builder was Sir William Van Horne, the driving force in constructing the Canadian Pacific Railway. Because of the tides and nature of the island, only set, 2-hour guided tours are offered. Phone before coming.

Huntsman Marine Science Centre (506-529-1200), off Route 127, Brandy Cove Road, St. Andrews. Open daily. A nonprofit aquaculture research center sponsoring educational programs and cruises; the aquarium-museum features hundreds of living plants and animals found in the Quoddy region, including resident harbor seals.

Atlantic Salmon Centre (506-529-4581), in Chamcook, 5 miles east of St. Andrews on Route 127. Open spring to fall, 10–5, until 6 in July and August. A staffed interpretation area dramatizes the history of Atlantic salmon and current conservation efforts. A nature trail threads the salmon nursery area and adjoining woods.

Kingsbrae Horticultural Garden (506-529-3335), 220 King Street, St. Andrews. Ten-acre, elaborately re-created formal gardens.

TO DO

GOLF

Algonquin golf course (see *Resort*) is New Brunswick's oldest (it dates from 1894) and is considered its best. The 18-hole seaside course was designed by Donald Ross. There is also a nine-hole "Woodland" course. Both are open to the public.

HORSEBACK RIDING

Kerrs Ridge Riding Stables (506-529-4698), St. Andrews, offers trail rides, pony rides, riding lessons.

KAYAK AND CANOE TOURS

In St. Andrews, **Seascape** (506-529-4012) and **Eastern Outdoors** (1-800-56-KAYAK) offer guided half- and full-day tours, beginners welcome.

SAILING

S/V Cory (506-529-8116), a 72-foot gaff and square-rigged cutter built by her captain in New Zealand, offers 3-hour sails in Passamaquoddy Bay and up the St. Croix River.

SWIMMING

Katy's Cove, Acadia Road, has (relatively) warm water, a sandy beach, and a clubhouse; nominal admission.

WHALE-WATCHING

In St. Andrews along King Street and the adjacent waterfront you can comparison shop: **Cline Marine** (506-526-4188) is the local pioneer in bird- and whale-watching tours; **Fundy Tide Runners** (506-529-4481) features fast, 24-foot, rigid-hulled Zodiac Hurricane boats, and clients wear flashy orange, full-length flotation suits; **Quoddy Link Marine** (506-529-2600) offers Whale Search and Island Cruises aboard a larger (40-passenger), slower vessel.

LODGING

All entries are in St. Andrews, New Brunswick EOG 2XO, Canada.

RESORT

The Algonquin (506-529-8823; in the United States, 1-800-441-1414). Open year-round in the 54-room "new" wing. The last of the truly grand coastal resorts in northeastern America; a 200-room, Tudor-style hotel with formal common and dining rooms, also banquet space geared to the many groups that keep it in business. Although the golf course is the big draw, amenities include tennis courts, a pool, and spa. The rack rate averages $119–369 (Canadian) per couple, but special packages, including golf, romance, and others, can bring the price down, and children are free.

Kingsbrae Arms (506-529-1897), 219 King Street. Canada's first five-star inn (decreed by Canada Select) opened in 1997, after a two-year remake of a splendid old mansion at the top of King Street, by Harry Chancey Jr. and David Oxford, owners of the deluxe Centennial House in East Hampton. All guest rooms were filled on the day we visited but we were impressed with the elegance of the softly colored drawing room with its grand piano and gardens beyond; there is also a comfortable, beamed study and a formal dining room. We have no doubt that a similar sense of luxury pervades the five guest rooms and three suites with gas fireplaces, all with private bath, most with Jacuzzis. We were assured that a guest's every need is met and anonymity preserved. Rates in 1998 were $175–280 US (but going up), including a full breakfast. Dinner is also served.

The Hiram Walker Estate (506-529-4210; 1-800-470-4088), 109 Reed Avenue. Built in the grand manner in 1912 as a summer retreat, set in

St. Andrews

11 wooded acres for the Walker (as in Johnny Walker whiskey) family, the châteaulike mansion became Canada's second five-star inn in 1997. The formal drawing room, library, music room, and dining room, and the upstairs suites, are opulent by today's standards (seven with king-sized beds and whirlpool tubs). This is a distinctly romantic inn, ideal for honeymoons and anniversaries. Breakfast is served with crystal, silver, and candlelight, and English tea is laid midafternoon. Dinner is by reservation. Innkeeper Elisabeth Cooney, who was born in St. Andrews, is the chef. $175–295 US includes breakfast and tea. Facilities include a pool and outside hot tub.

The Windsor House of St. Andrews (506-519-3834; 1-888-726-7972), 132 Water Street. Fully open for its first season in 1999, this small (six-room) hotel is a gem, furnished in antiques and artwork from the private collection of American owners Jay Remer (who has worked at Sotheby's) and Greg Cohane. The building dates to 1810 and includes a (public) dining room and a billiards room (the table is from a Newport mansion). Guest rooms all have phones and concealed TV/VCRs. $175–225 Canadian includes a full breakfast.

BED & BREAKFASTS

Check with the chamber of commerce for other reasonably priced B&Bs, which seem to change each season.

Pansy Patch (506-529-3834; 1-888-726-7972), 59 Carleton Street. Open mid-May to mid-October. Built fancifully in 1912 to resemble a Norman cottage, right across from the Algonquin. Michael O'Connor offers five guest rooms with private baths, water views, and antiques in the house itself (an attic suite has a kitchenette) and four more in the adjacent Cory Cottage. Breakfast, served in the sunroom, is included in $120–175 per couple Canadian. An art gallery and tea garden are also on the premises and guests have access to an outdoor pool, tennis, and other resort facilities at the Algonquin. Lunch and dinner are served, open to the public.

❦ **Treadwell Inn** (506-529-1011; 1-888-529-1011), 129 Water Street. Open practically year-round, a real find, with four spacious guest rooms, private baths, furnished in antiques, two with balconies overlooking the water (35 feet away). A third-floor efficiency suite has a sitting area and whirlpool bath with a private waterside balcony. At $95–165 Canadian ($75–125 off-season), this is great value.

MOTEL
St. Andrews Motor Inn (506-529-4571), 111 Water Street. A three-story motel with 33 units and a heated swimming pool. All rooms have two queen-sized beds and color TVs, some have kitchenettes, and all have private balconies overlooking Passamaquoddy Bay; $100 plus tax Canadian includes coffee and doughnuts.

CAMPING
Passamaquoddy Park Campground (506-529-3439), Indian Point Road. Maintained by the Kiwanis Club of St. Andrews, this is a beautifully sited campground with full hook-up as well as tent sites.

WHERE TO EAT

All listings are in St. Andrews, unless otherwise noted.

DINING OUT
L'Europe Dining Room and Lounge (506-529-3818), 63 King Street. Open for dinner daily except Monday in-season. Chef-owner Alexander Ludwig's specialties are a pleasing mix of French and German classics ranging from Wiener schnitzel ($16.50) to duck à l'orange ($26.70) to rack of lamb ($26.90); seafood entrées range from broiled sea bass ($17.50) to lobster with morel mushrooms ($34.50); prices are Canadian and include homemade pâté and salad as well as breads and vegetable. Candlelight and fine linen but no view.

The Passamaquoddy Dining Room at the Algonquin (506-529-8823), 184 Adolphus Street. The dining room is huge and its most pleasant corner is in the Veranda, with windows overlooking formal gardens. The menu is large, featuring local salmon and lobster. Entrées $17.95–23.50 plus tax. The hugely popular Sunday buffet is $8.95 Canadian.

The Gables (506-529-3440), 143 Water Street. Open 11–10. Reasonably priced, good food, and a tiered, shaded deck with a water view; what more can you ask, especially with wine by the glass and a wide selection of beers? Specialties include fresh fish ranging from fried haddock and chips to a seafood platter. We recommend the mussels. Entrées $9.50–17.95.

EATING OUT
The Pickled Herring (506-529-3766), 211 Water Street. Open year-round for lunch and dinner, an inviting, pubby place with a basics-all-day menu: burgers, fish or clams and chips, salads, chili, and Bay of Fundy

pickled herring served with cheese on rye, with a dill pickle. Spirits served.

Lighthouse Restaurant (506-529-3082), Lower Patrick Street. Open for lunch and dinner May through October. The best weatherproof view of the bay from a restaurant.

SELECTIVE SHOPPING

Cottage Craft Ltd., Town Square, St. Andrews. Open year-round, Monday through Saturday. Dating back to the 1940s, Cottage Craft showcases yarns, tweeds, and finished jackets, sweaters, and skirts; also distinctive handwoven throws made in homes throughout Charlotte County. Skirt and sweater kits as well as the finished products are the specialties.

V. WESTERN MOUNTAINS
AND LAKES REGION

Sebago and Long Lakes Region
Oxford Hills and Lewiston/Auburn
Bethel Area
Rangeley Lakes Region
Sugarloaf and the Carrabassett Valley

Bethel, with Sunday River and the Mahoosuc Range in the distance.

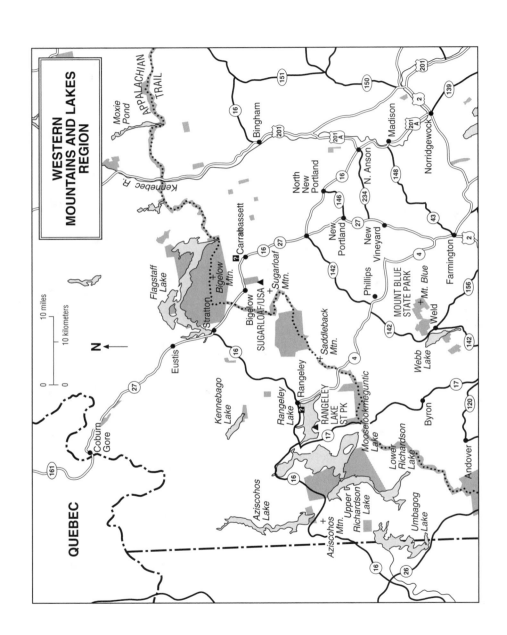

WESTERN
MOUNTAINS AND LAKES
REGION

N

10 miles
10 kilometers
0
0

QUEBEC

APPALACHIAN TRAIL

Moxie Pond

Kennebec R.

Bingham

151

150

201

2

139

Madison

201 A

Norridgewock

16

201

201 A

148

N. Anson

North New Portland

16

234

43

146

New Portland

27

New Vineyard

2

Carrabassett

16

27

27

Farmington

16

27

Flagstaff Lake

Bigelow Mtn.

Sugarloaf Mtn.

4

156

Bigelow

SUGARLOAF/USA

142

Phillips

MOUNT BLUE STATE PARK

Mt. Blue

Stratton

Saddleback Mtn.

Weld

Eustis

16

4

142

Webb Lake

142

Rangeley

Kennebago Lake

Rangeley Lake

27

17

120

RANGELEY LAKE ST PK

Mooselookmeguntic Lake

Byron

Andover

17

Coburn Gore

161

16

Aziscohos Lake

Lower Richardson Lake

Aziscohos Mtn.

Upper Richardson Lake

Umbagog Lake

16

26

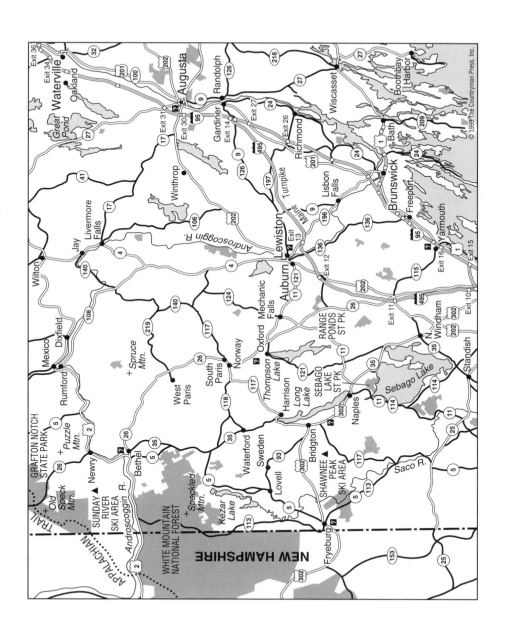

© 1999 The Countryman Press, Inc.

Western Mountains and Lakes Region

Inland Maine is the most underrated, least explored piece of New England, frequently perceived as an uninterrupted flat carpet of firs.

Larger than Vermont and New Hampshire combined, it is actually composed of several very different regions and distinguished by a series of almost continuous mountain ranges, more extensive than New Hampshire's White Mountains and higher than Vermont's Green Mountains, but lacking a name (why aren't they the Blue Mountains?).

In contrast to the coast, inland Maine was actually more of a resort area a century ago than it is today. By the 1880s, trains connected Philadelphia, New York, and Boston with large resort hotels in Rangeley and Greenville, and steamboats ferried "sports" to "sporting camps" in the far corners of lakes. Many of these historic resorts survive but today require far more time to reach, unless you fly in.

Today inland Maine seems even larger than it is because almost a third of it lies beyond the public highway system, a phenomenon for which we can blame Massachusetts and its insistence that Maine sell off the "unorganized townships" (and divide the profits) before it would be permitted to secede in 1820. In the interim, most of this land has been owned and managed by lumber and paper companies, and while debate currently rages about the future of these woodlands (somewhere between a third and almost a half of inland Maine), the reality of the way public roads run—and don't run—continues to physically divide Maine's mountainous interior into several distinct pieces.

One of these pieces is the Western Mountains and Lakes Region, extending from the rural farmland surrounding the lakes of southwestern Maine, up through the Oxford Hills and into the foothills of the White Mountains and the Mahoosuc Range around Bethel, and into the wilderness (as high and remote as any to be found in the North Woods) around the Rangeley lakes and the Sugarloaf area—east of which public roads cease, forcing traffic bound for the Moosehead Lake Region to detour south into the farmland of the Lower Kennebec Valley.

The five distinct areas within the Western Mountains and Lakes Region are connected by some of Maine's most scenic roads, a fact not generally appreciated because the area is best known to skiers, accustomed to racing up to Sunday River and Sugarloaf (Maine's most popular ski resorts) by the shortest routes from the interstate.

In summer and fall we suggest following Route 113 through Evans Notch or heading north from Bridgton to Bethel by the series of roads that thread woods and skirt lakes, heading east along Route 2, continuing north to Rangeley via Route 17 through Coos Canyon and over the spectacular height-of-land from which you can see all five Rangeley lakes and the surrounding mountains. From Rangeley it's just another 19 scenic miles on Route 16 (better known as Moose Alley) to the Sugarloaf area. You can return to Route 2 by continuing along Route 16 to Kingfield, then taking Route 142 through Phillips and Weld. (Also see *Scenic Drives* in "Rangeley Lakes Region.")

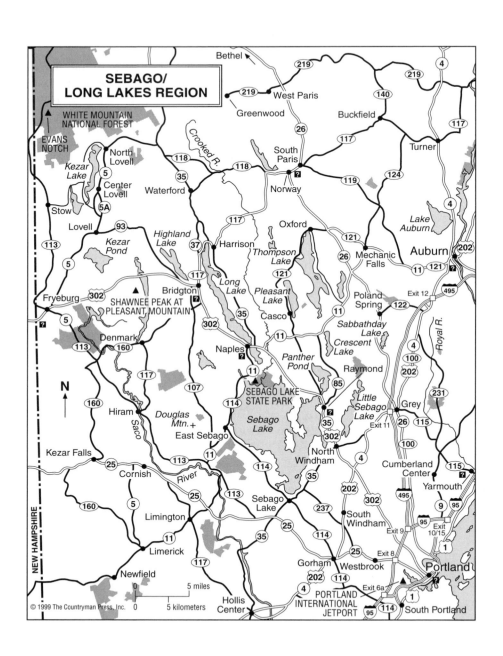

SEBAGO/
LONG LAKES REGION

WHITE MOUNTAIN
NATIONAL FOREST

EVANS
NOTCH

Bethel

Crooked R.

219 West Paris
219
Greenwood

219
140
Buckfield

4

219

4

117

26

South
Paris
118
118
Norway
117
Turner

North
Lovell
Kezar
Lake
5
Center
Lovell
5A
Stow
Lovell
35
Waterford

119
124

Oxford
121
Mechanic
Falls
26
Auburn
202
Lake
Auburn
4

93
Kezar
Pond
Highland
Lake
37
Harrison
117
Thompson
Lake
121
Pleasant
Lake
11
121

5

113

Fryeburg
302
SHAWNEE PEAK AT
PLEASANT MOUNTAIN
Bridgton
117
Long
Lake
Casco
302
35

Poland
Spring
Exit 12
122
495

Denmark
113
160
Naples
11
302
11
Panther
Pond
Sabbathday
Lake
Crescent
Lake
Raymond
4
100
202

N

160
107
SEBAGO LAKE
STATE PARK
114
Sebago
Lake
85
Little
Sebago
Lake
Exit 11
35
302
Grey
26
115
231

Hiram
Douglas
Mtn.
East Sebago
100

Saco

Kezar Falls
25
Cornish
River
113
11
113
114
North
Windham
35
4
202
Cumberland
Center
115
Yarmouth

160
5
Limington
25
113
Sebago
Lake
25
237
302
495
95
Exit 10/15
9
95
1

11
Limerick
35
South
Windham
114
Exit 9
95

117
Newfield
25
Gorham
202
114
Westbrook
Exit 8
Exit 6a
Portland
1

© 1999 The Countryman Press, Inc.
0   5 kilometers
0   5 miles
Hollis
Center
4
PORTLAND
INTERNATIONAL
JETPORT
95
114
South Portland

NEW HAMPSHIRE

Sebago and Long Lakes Region

Fifty lakes can be seen from the summit of Pleasant Mountain, 10 within the town of Bridgton itself.

These lakes are what draw summer visitors. They swim and fish, fish and swim. They cruise out in powerboats or paddle canoes. On rainy days, they browse through the area's abundant antiques and crafts stores. In winter, visitors ski, downhill at Shawnee Peak (alias Pleasant Mountain) or cross-country almost anywhere.

Before the Civil War, visitors could actually come by boat all the way to Bridgton from Boston. From Portland, they would ride 20 miles through 28 locks on the Cumberland and Oxford Canal, then across Sebago Lake, up the Songo River, Brandy Pond, and Long Lake to Bridgton. The first hotel atop Pleasant Mountain opened in 1850, and in 1882 the "2-footer" narrow-gauge opened between Hiram and Bridgton, enabling summer visitors to come by train as well.

Today, as in the 1880s, most visitors waste little time getting onto or into water. The Naples Causeway is the base for water sports and departure point for cruises on Long Lake and through the only surviving canal lock. Sebago, Maine's second-largest lake, is its most popular waterskiing area.

This southwestern corner of the state offers plenty on land too: golf, tennis, mineral collecting, and such fascinating historic sights as Willowbrook in Newfield.

Fryeburg, just west of the lakes in the Saco River Valley, is the region's oldest community and the site of the state's largest agricultural fair. It is also headquarters for canoeing the Saco River. Sandy-bottomed and clear, the Saco meanders for more than 40 miles through woods and fields, rarely passing a house. Too shallow for powerboats, it is perfect for canoes. There is usually just enough current to nudge along the limpest paddler, and the ubiquitous sandbars serve as gentle bumpers. Tenting is permitted most places along the river, and there are public campgrounds. Outfitters rent canoes and provide shuttle service.

In summer most families come for a week to stay in lakeside cottages—of which there seem to be thousands. The few motels and scattered inns and bed & breakfasts tend to fill on weekends with parents visiting their children at camps—of which there seem to be hundreds.

GUIDANCE

Bridgton–Lakes Region Chamber of Commerce (647-3472), Box 236, Bridgton 04009. The chamber maintains a walk-in information bureau on Route 302. Request a copy of the "Bridgton–Lakes Region Map and Guide." Year-round information is also available from the town office (647-8786).

Naples Business Association (693-3285), P.O. Box 412, Naples 04055, publishes a map/guide to the Sebago–Long Lakes region just south of Bridgton; it also maintains a seasonal information bureau next to the town's historical society museum on Route 302.

Windham Chamber of Commerce (892-8265), P.O. Box 1015, Windham 04062, maintains a seasonal information booth on Route 302 and publishes a booklet guide.

Fryeburg Information Center (935-3639), Route 302, Fryeburg. The Maine Tourism Association staffs this state-owned log cabin on the New Hampshire line. Pamphlets on the state in general, western Maine in particular.

GETTING THERE

By air: The **Portland International Jetport,** served by five minor carriers, is a half-hour to an hour drive from most points in this area. **Rental cars** are available at the airport.

By car: From New York and Boston, take I-95 to the Westbrook exit (exit 8), then Route 302, the high road of the lakes region. For Newfield and south of Sebago area, take Route 25 from I-95 at Westbrook (exit 8).

MEDICAL EMERGENCY

Northern Cumberland Memorial Hospital (647-8841), South High Street, Bridgton. **Stephens Memorial Hospital** (743-5933), Norway.

VILLAGES

Bridgton has experienced a wave of antiques shop openings, including two country auction houses, making it a good way stop for browsers.

Cornish. The *Maine Sunday Telegram* rated this pretty, quiet little town Maine's second-best small town. The Colonial and Victorian homes lining Main and Maple Streets were moved there by teams of about 80 oxen in the 1850s after the arrival of a new stagecoach route. The little town has a county inn, some nice shops, and restaurants to offer.

Harrison. Another quaint little town with a good restaurant, a peaceful inn, and the DeerTrees Theater. The tower clock in the center of town is currently being restored.

TO SEE

MUSEUMS

Willowbrook at Newfield (793-2784), Newfield (off Route 11). Open May 15 to September 30, daily 10–5. Admission charged. This is a quiet, peaceful place that shouldn't be missed. Although it's off the beaten track, the drive through the quiet countryside is easy and relaxing, and, once you get there, well worth it. Devastated by fire in 1947, the village was almost a ghost town when Donald King began buying buildings in the 1960s. The complex now includes 37 buildings displaying more than 11,000 items: horse-drawn vehicles, tools, toys, a vintage 1894 carousel, and many other artifacts of late-19th-century life. Linger in the ballroom, ring the schoolhouse bell, picnic in the area provided. This is a perfect place to get away from it all. A restaurant and ice cream parlor for light lunches, an old-time country store, and a Christmas gift shop open most of the year are located on the premises.

The Jones Museum of Glass and Ceramics (787-3370), Douglas Hill (off Route 107), Sebago. Open mid-May to mid-November, Monday through Saturday 10–5 and Sunday 1–5. $5 per adult, $3 per student. More than 7,000 works in glass and china. Displays include ancient Egyptian glass, Chinese porcelains, Wedgwood teapots, and French paperweights. There are also gallery tours, frequent lecture-luncheon seminars, and identification days (visitors bring their own pieces to be identified).

HISTORIC BUILDINGS AND MUSEUMS

Daniel Marrett House, Route 25, Standish. Tours mid-June to September 1, Tuesday, Thursday, Saturday, and Sunday noon–5. Admission charged. Money from Portland banks was stored in this Georgian mansion for safekeeping during the War of 1812. Built in 1789, it remained in the Marrett family until 1944; architecture and furnishings reflect the changing styles over 150 years, and the formal gardens bloom throughout the summer.

Parson Smith House (892-5315), 89 River Road, South Windham. Open mid-June through Labor Day, Tuesday, Thursday, and Sunday noon–5; admission. A Georgian farmhouse with an exceptional stairway and hall; some original furnishings.

Narramissic, Ingalls Road (2 miles south of the junction of Routes 107 and 117), Bridgton. Open July and August, Wednesday–Saturday, 10–3; other hours by special arrangement. $3 adults, $1 children. A Federal-period home and a Temperance Barn in a rural setting; includes a blacksmith shop, the scene of frequent special events; check with the **Bridgton Historical Society Museum** (647-3699), Gibbs Avenue, which also maintains a 1902 former fire station. The collection (open same hours) includes slide images of the old narrow-gauge railroad.

Naples Historical Society Museum (693-6790), Village Green, Route 302, Naples. Open July and August, Tuesday through Friday 10–3. The old brick complex includes the old jail, some great memorabilia, and slide presentations on the Cumberland and Oxford Canal, the Sebago and Long Lake steamboats, and vanished hotels like the Chute Homestead.

Hopalong Cassidy in the Fryeburg Public Library (935-2731), 98 Main Street, Fryeburg. Open year-round, varying days; the library is housed in an 1832 stone schoolhouse and is decorated with many paintings by local artists. It also contains a collection of books, guns, and other memorabilia belonging to Clarence Mulford, creator of Hopalong Cassidy. The **Fryeburg Historical Society Museum** is next door, also open seasonally and by request at the library.

OTHER

Songo Locks, Naples (2.5 miles off Route 302). Dating from 1830, the last of the 27 hand-operated locks that once enabled people to come by boat from Portland to Harrison. It still enables you to travel some 40 watery miles. The boat traffic is constant in summer.

TO DO

AIR RIDES

Western Maine Flying Service (693-3129), Naples. Operates daily in-season, scenic flights.

Parasailing (693-3888), Naples Causeway.

Destinations Unlimited (743-9781; 1-800-526-TOUR), Norway. Hot-air-balloon rides.

BICYCLING

Shawnee Peak (647-8444), Route 302, Bridgton, offers lift-accessed riding, a terrain park, and rental mountain bikes, weekends in-season.

BOAT EXCURSIONS

Songo River Queen II (693-6861), Naples Causeway. Operates daily July through Labor Day; weekends during June and September. Offers a 2½-hour Songo River ride and a 1-hour Long Lake cruise. The 90-foot-long stern-wheeler was built in 1982; snack bar and rest rooms. The ride is across Brandy Pond and through the only surviving lock from the 1830 canal. It is a pleasant ride to the mouth of Sebago Lake down the Songo River, which is about as winding as a river can be. The distance is just 1.5 miles as the crow flies, but 6 miles as the Songo twists and turns. **Mail Boat Rides** cruises (1½ hours) are also offered daily in-season except Sunday. This pontoon boat offers varied rides on Songo and Long Lakes (no toilets on board).

BOAT RENTALS

Available region-wide. Inquire at local chambers. (See also *Canoeing.*)

CANOEING

Saco River Canoe and Kayak (935-2369), P.O. Box 111, Route 5, Fryeburg (across from the access at Swan's Falls). "For canoeing, the Saco is the number-one river east of the Mississippi," enthuses Fred Westerberg. "Nowhere else can you canoe so far without having to portage. Nowhere else can you find this kind of wilderness camping experience without the danger of remoteness. Nowhere on the river are you far from help if you need it." Westerberg, a Registered Maine Guide, runs Saco River Canoe and Kayak with the help of his wife, Prudy, and daughters, Beth and Chris. They also offer shuttle service and canoe rentals, which come with a map and careful instructions geared to the day's river conditions.

Saco Bound (603-447-2177/3801), Route 302, Center Conway, New Hampshire (just over the state line, south of Fryeburg). The largest canoe outfitter around. Offers rentals, guided day trips during the summer (Tuesday and Thursday in July and August), white-water canoeing on the Androscoggin River, a campground at Canal Bridge in Fryeburg, and a shuttle service. Its base is a big, glass-faced store stocked with kayaks and canoes, trail food, and lip balm. Staff members are young and enthusiastic.

Canal Bridge Canoes (935-2605), Route 302, Fryeburg Village. Pat and Carl Anderson offer rentals and a shuttle service.

Woodland Acres (935-2529), Route 160, Brownfield. Full-facility camping, canoe rentals, and a shuttle service.

FISHING

Fishing licenses are available at town offices and other local outlets; check marinas for information. Salmon, lake trout, pickerel, and bass abound.

GOLF AND TENNIS

Bridgton Highlands Country Club (647-3491), Bridgton, has an 18-hole course, snack bar, carts, and tennis courts. Nine-hole courses include **Lake Kezar Country Club** (925-2462), Route 5, Lovell; and **Naples Country Club** (693-6424), Route 114, Naples.

Tennis at Brandy Pond Camps (693-6333), old Route 114, Naples; also at **Bridgton Highlands Country Club.**

HIKING

Douglas Mountain, Sebago. A Nature Conservancy preserve with great views of Sebago and the White Mountains. The trail to the top is a 20-minute walk, and there's a ¾-mile nature trail at the summit; also a stone tower with an observation platform. Take Route 107 south from the town of Sebago and turn right on Douglas Mountain Road; go to the end of the road to find limited parking.

Pleasant Mountain, Bridgton. Several summits and interconnecting trails, the most popular of which is the Firewarden's Trail to the main summit: a relatively easy, 2½-mile climb from base to peak through rocky woods.

✐ **Jockey Cap,** Route 302, Fryeburg. Watch for the Jockey Cap Motel beside a general store. The arch between them is the entrance to one of New England's shortest hikes to one of its biggest rewards. A 10-minute climb up the path (steep near the top) accesses a bald, garnet-studded summit with a sweeping view of the White Mountains to the west, lesser peaks and lakes to the east and south, all ingeniously identified on a circular bronze monument designed by Arctic explorer Admiral Peary (see *Lodging—Bed & Breakfasts*).

HORSEBACK RIDING

Sunny Brook Stables (787-2905), Sebago, offers trail rides pitched to beginners and intermediate riders. $15–18 per hour. **Secret Acres Stables** (693-3441), Lambs Mill Road, Naples (1 mile off Route 302), offers trail rides and lessons.

MINI-GOLF

Steamboat Landing (693-6429), Route 114, Naples. Open weekends Memorial Day to late June, then daily through Labor Day 10–10 (1–10 Sunday). A lovely 19-hole course with a Maine theme in a wooded setting.

Maplewood Miniature Golf and Arcade (655-7586), Route 302 across from State Park Road, Casco. Eighteen holes and a full arcade with video games, pinball, snacks.

Seacoast Adventure Park (892-5952), Route 302, Windham. Elaborate mini-golf, go-carts, bumper boats, arcade, and the Skycoaster, a ride that hauls you high into the air harnessed in on a bungee cord, then lets you swing.

SWIMMING

Sebago Lake State Park (693-6613, June 20 through Labor Day; 693-6231 otherwise), off Route 302 (between Naples and South Casco). A great family beach, with picnic tables, grills, boat ramp, lifeguards, and bathhouses. There is a separate camping area (see *Campgrounds*) with its own beach; also a summer program of conducted hikes on nature trails and presentations in the amphitheater. Songo Lock is nearby.

The town of Bridgton maintains a tidy little beach on **Long Lake** just off Main Street, another on **Woods Lake** (Route 117), and another on **Highland Lake.** The town of Fryeburg maintains a beach, with float, on the **Saco River,** and **Casco** maintains a small, inviting beach in its picturesque village.

DOWNHILL SKIING

Shawnee Peak at Pleasant Mountain (647-8444), Route 302, Bridgton. An isolated, 1,900-foot hump, 1 mile west of the center of town. Maine's oldest ski area, it has a vertical drop of 1,300 feet, 30 trails, 98 percent snowmaking, and extensive night skiing. Lifts include one triple chair and three double chairs. Other amenities include ski school, rentals, and child care.

LODGING

RUSTIC RESORTS

The Western Lakes area offers some unusual old resort complexes, each with cabin accommodations, dining, and relaxing space in a central, distinctively Maine lodge. In contrast to similar complexes found farther north, these are all geared to families or to those who vacation here for reasons other than hunting and fishing.

Migis Lodge (655-4524), P.O. Box 40, South Casco 04077 (off Route 302). Open early June through Columbus Day weekend. Seven rooms in the two-story main lodge, and 30 cottages scattered throughout the pines on 97 acres. All cottages have fireplaces, and guests enjoy use of the private beach, tennis, lawn games, waterskiing, sailboats, canoes, and boat excursions. Children under 4 are not permitted in the dining room during the high season (July through Labor Day), so the resort provides a supervised dining and play time 6:30–8:30; older children are also welcome to join in. $230–360 per couple includes three meals; children's rates; 15 percent service charge.

Quisisana (925-3500; off-season, 914-833-0293), Lake Kezar, Center Lovell 04016. Late June through Labor Day. One-week minimum stay in high season. Founded in 1917 as a place for music students and music lovers to relax in the pines by one of Maine's clearest lakes. Each evening climaxes with performances in the lakeside hall: musical theater, opera, and concerts performed by staff recruited from top music schools. There are 75 guest rooms in all, from rooms in two lodges to one- to three-room cottages (some with fireplaces) scattered through the woods and around the soft beach, which curves to a grassy point. Waterskiing, boats, and fishing guides are available, and other recreation includes croquet, tennis and swimming. The white-frame central lodge includes a big, homey sitting room and the kind of dining room you don't mind sitting in three times a day, especially given the quality of the food. $118–160 per person double occupancy with all three meals in high season.

  ﺥ **Northern Pines** (655-7624), 559 Route 85, Raymond 04071. Open Memorial Day weekend through Labor Day; September and October weekends; Christmas, New Year's week, and 2 weeks in February. A very pleasant holistic health resort housed in an expanded rustic women's camp on the shores of Crescent Lake. A total of 50 rooms are divided between the lodge and cottages. The daily regimen includes aerobics and yoga, meditation and stretch, and frequently there are evening lectures. Meals are vegetarian and delicious. Summer facilities include sailboats, canoes, paddleboats, and a lakeside hot tub; cross-country skiing and ice skating January through March. There are two lodges, one closed in winter. Personal services such as massage, seaweed wraps, and flotation tank are available. Ten percent service added.

  ✐ **Aimhi Lodge** (892-6538; aimhilodge@aol.com), North Windham 04062. Open summer season. For some 80 years, this classic complex has operated in the same family. Twenty-three cottages on Little Sebago Lake have one to three rooms, Franklin stoves, screened porches, and a dock. Down-home cooking; turkey every summer Sunday since the 1930s (at least), and Friday lobster picnics. Facilities include game rooms, lawn games, a beach, sailboats, canoes, tennis, supervised children's activities, and fishing. $111–152 per person per day (children less) with all three meals.

INNS

  ✐ﺥ **Tarry-a-While** (647-2522; 1-800-451-9076; tarryayl@megalink.net), Ridge Road, Bridgton 04009. Open June through Columbus Day. Marc and Nancy Stretch have redone this turreted, vintage 1897 summer hotel, giving it a classic Maine ambience. Set on 25 lakeside acres, it offers 27 rooms (22 with private baths) divided among the inn, cottages, and a two-bedroom apartment. A beach, social hall, canoes, rowboats, pedal boats, and tennis are all part of the resort, and an 18-hole golf course is next door. $80–130 double includes a large continental breakfast. Dinner is served in the restaurant (see *Dining Out*) and picnic lunches are available.

Oxford House Inn (935-3442; 1-800-261-7206), Fryeburg 04037. Open year-round, this spacious 1913 house in the middle of Fryeburg has a view across the Saco River to the White Mountains. The public restaurant is popular for dinner (see *Dining Out*), but there is ample space for inn guests to relax. John and Phyllis Morris offer five upstairs guest rooms, all large and nicely decorated, with private baths. Request one with a view. $75–125, includes a full breakfast.

Center Lovell Inn (925-1575; 1-800-777-2698), Route 5, Center Lovell 04016. Closed November and April. A striking old inn with a cupola and a busy public dining room (see *Dining Out*). Janice and Richard Cox saw their dream come true when they won the inn in an essay contest in May 1993. They run the inn with the help of Janice's mother, Harriet, and her husband, Earle (known to guests as Mom and Pop). There are four guest rooms on the second floor (the two with shared bath are a suite), nicely furnished with antiques and art. In the 1835 Harmon House there are five cozy rooms, some with private bath. $68–158 MAP.

The Cornish Inn (625-8501), P.O. Box 266, Main Street, Cornish 04020. Right in the center of this quaint town, this inn has been recently renovated. Sixteen guest rooms with private baths and cozy furnishings reminiscent of a simpler time. Common areas include a parlor and tavern, and a great front porch. Dinner is open to guests and the public; reservations suggested. $75–125 in-season; less in winter and spring.

BED & BREAKFASTS

  ♿ **Noble House** (647-3733), Box 180, Bridgton 04009. Open year-round, but October 15 to June 15 by reservation only. There is a suitably formal feel to the grand piano, crystal, and Oriental rugs in the parlor of this former senator's manor, set among stately oaks and pines. Back beyond the kitchen, however, is a comfortable den/breakfast room, and the welcome guests receive from Jane and Dick Staret is anything but stiff. The nine guest rooms (six with private baths) are divided between the original house (ranging from a single to a family suite under the eaves) and newer doubles and suites in the former ell (three with whirlpool bath); all are furnished with antiques. The private beach (with a hammock, canoe, and dock) on Highland Lake is just across the road; in winter, both downhill and cross-country skiing are nearby. $78–125 double includes full breakfast and use of a canoe and pedal boats. Singles are $5–10 less; $15 more per child.

Acres of Austria (1-800-988-4391), RR1, Box 177, Fryeburg 04037. Candice and Franz Redl have created a wonderful haven at the end of a secluded dirt road on 65 acres, including river frontage. When you drive up, the first thing you see is the goats in a pen in the front. A very Austrian feel, as the name might suggest. The common rooms include a dining area with a wonderful central fireplace, a spiral staircase, and window seats; the cozy lounge is another inviting place to relax. Four guest rooms, all with private bath. Many of the inn's furnishings and decorative touches are from Vienna. A wide variety of special packages is offered as well, including eating celebrations, an Austrian Thanksgiving dinner (with roasted goose), murder-mystery weekends, and more. Dinner is available to guests with advance notice. $75–105 includes full breakfast.

Admiral Peary House (935-3365; 1-800-237-8080), 9 Elm Street, Fryeburg 04037. If he returned today we suspect that Robert E. Peary, Maine's famed Arctic explorer, would be pleased with what's happened to the house in which he lived with his mother after graduating from Bowdoin College and before surveying the Panama Canal. The large old home stands on a leafy side street and guests enter from the back, through a large, wicker-filled screened porch overlooking a perennial garden. Next comes a spacious informal living room with barnboard walls and a large hearth, equipped with TV, a billiards table, a stereo, and games. The more formal spaces (a handsome dining room, living room, and library) are off in the front of the house, beyond an open kitchen. The six large guest rooms, each with private bath and air-conditioning, are furnished with oversized beds and antiques. The top-floor North Pole Room, with its king brass bed, features mountain views. Amenities include an outdoor spa, bicycles, and well-maintained clay tennis courts; innkeepers Nancy and Ed Greenberg are both tennis pros and offer tennis lessons to guests. $98–128 in-season includes a full breakfast; from $70 off-season. In winter, a 7-night contract can be used anytime except holidays (not necessarily consecutive nights) for $385, and a romantic 2-night package is $129. Snowshoe rentals are available and there is a complimentary trail.

Sebago Lake Lodge (892-2698), P.O. Box 110, White's Bridge Road, North Windham 04062. A rambling, old white inn on a narrows between Jordan Bay and the Basin, seemingly surrounded by water. Debra and Chip Lougee, both Maine natives, have refurbished the rooms to create eight units with their own kitchens (one is a suite with an enclosed porch) and four standard rooms with kitchen privileges. A light buffet breakfast is set out in the gathering room, a pleasant space to read, play games, or watch TV. There are also nine moderately priced cottages. Facilities include an inviting beach, picnic tables, and grills; there is also a fishing boat, rowboat, canoe, and motorboat rentals. Fishing licenses are available. $48 for a room, $98–120 per housekeeping unit; cheaper off-season. Cottages $395–695 per week.

The Inn at Long Lake (693-6226), P.O. Box 806, Naples 04055. Built in 1906 as an annex to the (vanished) Lake House Resort, this four-story, clapboard building is now a warm, romantic inn. Irene and Maynard Hincks offer 16 guest rooms from "cozy deluxe" to two-room suites. Each has private bath, TV, and air conditioner. Rooms are decorated with many small touches, like chantilly lace and pretty flower arrangements. The fourth-floor rooms are spacious and quiet, with great views and an additional library common area. The Great Room on the ground floor has a magnificent fieldstone fireplace. $95–150 in summer; $59–95 off-season, includes expanded continental breakfast.

Tolman House Inn (583-4445), P.O. Box 551, Tolman Road, Harrison 04040. Open year-round. A former carriage barn with nine guest rooms (private baths) and a dining and lounging area overlooking gardens. The inn is situated on a hillside sloping to the tip of Long Lake. There is a game room in a former icehouse. Children under 2 stay free, but there are no cribs. $115 double, $90 single, includes full breakfast.

COTTAGES

The **Bridgton–Lakes Region Chamber of Commerce** (see *Guidance*) publishes a list of more than two dozen rental cottages, and many in this area are also listed in the "Maine Guide to Camp & Cottage Rentals," free from the **Maine Tourism Association** (see *Information* in "What's Where").

One set of cottages that deserves special mention is **Hewnoaks** (925-6051), Center Lovell 04016. Six unusually attractive, distinctive cottages built as an artists' colony and imaginatively furnished (in no way are these your usual summer camps) are scattered on a landscaped hillside above pristine Lake Kezar. Moderately priced.

CAMPGROUNDS

See *Canoeing* for information about camping along the Saco River. In addition to those mentioned, the **Appalachian Mountain Club** maintains a campground at Swan's Falls. The "Maine Camping Guide," available from the **Maine Campground Owners Association** (782-5874), 655 Main Street, Lewiston 04240, lists dozens of private campgrounds in the area.

Sebago Lake State Park (693-6613; 693-6611 before June 20 and after Labor Day), off Route 302 (between Naples and South Casco). Open through mid-October. On the northern shore of the lake are 1,300 thickly wooded acres with 250 campsites, many on the water; the camping area has its own beach, hot showers, a program of evening presentations, and nature hikes. For information about reservations, call 1-800-332-1501, or 207-287-3824 from outside the state.

Point Sebago (655-3821), RR 1, Box 712, Casco 04015. More than just a campground: 500 campsites, most with trailer hook-ups, on a 300-acre lakeside site, plus 160 rental trailers ranging from small trailers to large models of near mobile-home size. Campers have access to the beach, marina, dance pavilion, children's daycare, teen center, excursion boats, soccer and softball fields, horseshoe pitches, 10 tennis courts, video-game arcade, general store, and combination restaurant/nightclub/gambling casino, as well as a full daily program beginning with 8 AM exercises and ending at 1 AM when the club closes.

WHERE TO EAT

DINING OUT

Center Lovell Inn (925-1575), Center Lovell. Open for breakfast and dinner daily in high season, Friday through Sunday off-season (reservations requested.) Chef-owner Richard Cox's specialties include an appetizer of smoked pheasant ravioli and entrées like veal Picatta. There are two pleasant dining rooms, and the wraparound porch is also used in summer. $13.95–23.95.

✐ **Tarry-a-While Restaurant** (647-2522), Highland Road, Bridgton. The timber-beamed dining room in this old lakeside summer hotel is the setting for dining from a menu which includes a wild mushroom ragout appetizer and a variety of entrées, including crispy curried crab and squiddly diddly (sautéed calamari in a fresh basil, garlic, and plum tomato sauce). Children's menu available. Entrées $12.95–19.95.

The Olde House (655-7841), just off Route 302 on Route 85, Raymond. Open for dinner daily year-round. Candlelight dining in a 1790 home. Menu options are widely varied, and include Wiener schnitzel (sautéed veal with lemon sauce) and grilled balsamic and honey duckling breast. $11.95–19.95.

Venezia Ristorante (647-5333), Bridgton Corners, Routes 302 and 93. Open Tuesday through Sunday, 5–10. Dependable, moderately priced Italian dishes.

Oxford House Inn (935-3442; 1-800-261-7206), 105 Main Street, Fryeburg. Open nightly in summer and fall, Thursday through Sunday in winter and spring. Reservations required. Appetizers like hot buttered Brie with fresh fruit; specialties include veal Oxford and scallops à l'orange. The setting is the former living room and dining room of a handsome 1913 house, with mountain views from the back dining rooms. $17–23.

Cornish Inn (625-8501), Main Street, Cornish. Open for dinner nightly in summer, inquire off-season. A pleasant old inn with a prix fixe ($28 per person) menu including a choice of several appetiers and frequently changing entrées (one is always vegetarian) and desserts. Full bar service and a bar menu are also offered; wines are reasonably priced.

EATING OUT

Bray's Brew Pub (693-6806), Routes 302 and 35, Naples. Open year-round for lunch and dinner daily. A mansard-roofed landmark formerly housing a gourmet restaurant is now an inviting way stop. Mike and Rich Bray brew American ales as they are known in the Pacific Northwest, using North American grains and malted barley, Oregon yeast, and Washington hops. Specials might include lobster stew, Maine crab cakes, and mussels stewed in beer. The dinner menu runs from grilled salmon ($12.95) to petit filet mignon ($14.95); pub menu served all day.

Mountain View Family Restaurant (935-2909), 107 Main Street, Fryeburg. Open from 6 AM through dinner. The Mutrie family have tacked this pine-paneled dining room onto the back of their Village Variety, with large windows overlooking the White Mountains. For breakfast try the Belgian waffles with blueberries; go with a special like fried haddock at dinner. Burgers and sandwiches are fine, and don't pass up the pies.

Olde Mill Tavern (583-4992), Maine Street, Harrison. Open daily, 11–11. This slick eatery opened in 1996 and was an instant success with local residents, featuring "family-style dinners" (for two or more) like whole roasted chicken at $7.95 per person and a choice of "big plates" (which run as high as $19.95 for rack of lamb) and "small plates" like mill tavern meat loaf and fajita chicken salad; also "hand-carved sandwiches," flat breads, and Sunday brunch.

ENTERTAINMENT

FILM

Magic Lantern, Main Street, Bridgton, presents film classics and first-run cartoons. **Windham Hill Mall,** Route 302, has a cinema that shows first-run movies. **Bridgton Drive-In,** Route 302, shows first-run movies in summer.

MUSIC

Sebago–Long Lakes Region Chamber Music Festival (627-4939), DeerTrees Theater, Harrison. A series of concerts held mid-July through mid-August.

THEATER

DeerTrees Theater (583-6747), Harrison. Once a popular 1930s summer theater, abandoned until the 1980s, when the town of Harrison and volunteers turned it into a nonprofit organization. It is once again becoming a cultural center for the area, with the chamber music festival, comedians, and shows by the resident theater company, the Dear Deer Players.

SELECTIVE SHOPPING

ANTIQUES SHOPS

Route 302 seems to be regaining its 1950s and 1960s reputation as an antiques alley, and Bridgton has had nine new shops open in the past year, giving browsers plenty of choices.

BOOKSTORES

Bridgton Books (647-2122), 74 Main Street. Extensive stock, books on tape, stationery, music.

CRAFTS SHOPS

Craftworks (647-5436), Upper Village, Bridgton. Open daily. Filling a former church and two neighboring buildings, selective women's clothing, pottery, books, linens, handmade pillows, crafted jewelry, and more.

Cry of the Loon (655-5060), Route 302, South Casco. Ten rooms of gifts, crafts, sculpture garden.

Frances Riecken Pottery (928-2411), Center Lovell. Ceramic cookware, porcelain, and other functional pots, made for more than 40 years in this studio on Kezar Lake.

The Maine Theme (647-2161), 36 Main Street, Bridgton. Open daily. Two floors of New England–crafted work and widely assorted gifts.

SPECIAL SHOPS

Sportshaus (647-5100), 61 Main Street, Bridgton. Open daily. Known for its original Maine T-shirts; also a selection of casual clothes, canvas bags, tennis rackets, downhill and cross-country skis, athletic footwear, swimwear, and golf accessories. Canoe, kayak, sailboat, and sailboard rentals.

SPECIAL EVENTS

July: **Independence Day** is big in both Bridgton and Naples. **Bridgton** events include a lobster/clambake at the town hall, a road race, a concert, arts and crafts fair, and fireworks. In **Naples,** the fireworks over the lake are spectacular. In late July, a major **crafts fair** at the town hall is sponsored by the Bridgton Arts and Crafts Society, and the 3-day **Lakes Region Antique Show** is held at the high school.

August: **Windham Old Home Days** *(beginning of the month)* include a parade, contests, and public feeds. In Lovell, the **Annual Arts and Artisans Fair** *(midmonth)* is held on the library grounds; chicken barbecue, book and crafts sale.

October: **Fryeburg Fair,** Maine's largest agricultural fair, is held for a week in early October, climaxing with the Columbus Day weekend. This is an old-fashioned agricultural happening—one of the most colorful in the country.

December: **Christmas open house and festivals** in Harrison and Naples. Also see "Oxford Hills and Lewiston/Auburn."

Oxford Hills and Lewiston/ Auburn

One particularly rolling, gem- and lake-studded swatch of Oxford County is known as the Oxford Hills. Its commercial center is the community composed of both Norway and South Paris, towns divided by the Little Androscoggin River but joined by Route 26, the region's traffic spine. Most visitors are simply passing through, up or down Route 26, from Gray (an exit on the Maine Turnpike) to the summer and ski resort area around Bethel.

Off Route 26, this is a quiet part of the Western Lakes and Mountains Region, with some startlingly beautiful villages like Waterford and Paris Hill, and genuinely interesting places to see such as the country's last living Shaker community at Sabbathday Lake.

The Oxford Hills are best known for their mineral diversity. The area's bedrock is a granite composed of pegmatite studded with semiprecious gemstones, including tourmaline and rose quartz. Several local mines invite visitors to explore their "tailings" or rubble and take what they find.

Lewiston and Auburn (Maine's "L.A."), just east of the Oxford Hills, are the "cities of the Androscoggin," but for most visitors are seen as "the cities on the Turnpike," the exits accessing routes to the Rangeley and Sugarloaf areas. Both are worth a stop. By the 1850s, mills on both sides of the river had harnessed the power of the Androscoggin's Great Falls and the Bates Mill boomed with the Civil War, supplying fabric for most of the Union's tents.

Today Lewiston is best known as the home of prestigious Bates College (founded 1855), an attractive campus that's the summer site of the nationally recognized Bates Dance Festival. The Bates Mill is now a visitor-friendly complex, housing shops and restaurants, and both Lewiston and Auburn offer interesting restaurants, shopping, and a number of colorful festivals, some like Festival de Joie, reflecting the rich cultural diversity of the residents.

GUIDANCE

Oxford Hills Chamber of Commerce (743-2281), P.O. Box 167, South Paris 04281, publishes a directory to the area and maintains a seasonal information booth on Route 26 in South Paris across from Mario's Pizza.

Androscoggin Country Chamber of Commerce (783-2249; www.androscoggincountry.com), 179 Lisbon Street, Lewiston 04243.

GETTING THERE

For the Sabbathday Lake–Poland Spring–Oxford area, take I-95 to Gray (exit 11) and Route 26 North. Auburn is exit 12 and Lewiston is exit 13 on the Maine Turnpike.

MEDICAL EMERGENCY

Northern Cumberland Memorial Hospital (647-8841), South High Street, Bridgton.

Stephens Memorial Hospital (743-5933), Norway.

Central Maine Medical Center (795-2200), 300 Main Street, Lewiston, and **St. Mary's Regional Medical Center** (777-8120) both have 24-hour emergency rooms. Dial 911 for police or ambulance.

TO SEE

The International Sign. At the junction of Routes 5 and 35 in the village of Lynchville, some 14 miles west of Norway, stands Maine's most photographed roadside marker, pointing variously to Norway, Paris, Denmark, Naples, Sweden, Poland, Mexico, and Peru—all towns within 94 miles of the sign.

MUSEUMS

Sabbathday Lake Shaker Community and Museum (926-4597), Route 26, New Gloucester (8 miles north of Gray). Open Memorial Day through Columbus Day, daily except Sunday, 10–4:30. Guided tours (admission charged). Welcoming the "world's people" has been part of summer at Sabbathday Lake since the community's inception in 1794.

Founded by Englishwoman Ann Lee in 1775, Shakers numbered 6,000 Americans in 18 communities by the Civil War. Today, with fewer than 10 Shaker Sisters and Brothers, this village is the only one that still functions as a religious community rather than as a museum. These men and women still follow the injunction of Mother Ann Lee to "put your hands to work and your heart to God." Guided tours are offered of the 17 white-clapboard buildings; rooms are either furnished or filled with exhibits to illustrate periods or products of Shaker life. The Shaker Store sells Shaker-made goods including oval boxes, knitted and sewn goods, homemade fudge, yarns, souvenirs, antiques, Shaker-style furniture, and Shaker herbs. During warm-weather months, services are held at 10 AM on Sundays in the 18th-century meetinghouse on Route 26. Sit in the World's People's benches and listen as the Shakers speak in response to the psalms and gospel readings. Each observation is affirmed with a Shaker song—of which there are said to be 10,000. This complex includes an extensive research library housing Shaker books, writings, and records open to scholars by appointment. Inquire about special workshops, fairs, and concerts.

Sabbathday Lake Shaker Community and Museum

Orlin Arts Center at Bates College (786-6255), Campus Avenue, Lewiston. Open Tuesday through Saturday 10–3, Sunday 1–5. Hosts a variety of performances, exhibitions, and special programs. Also inside the building, the museum houses a fine collection of artwork, including the Marsden Hartley Memorial Collection. Lovers of the artist won't want to miss this small but excellent collection of bold, bright canvases by Hartley, a Lewiston native (call ahead to find out what's on display).

HISTORIC BUILDINGS

State of Maine Building from the 1893 World's Columbian Exposition in Chicago, Route 26, Poland Spring. Open July and August, daily 9–1; June and September, weekends 9–1. Admission. A very Victorian building that was brought back from the 1893 World's Columbian Exposition in Chicago to serve as a library and art gallery for the now-vanished Poland Spring Resort (the water is now commercially bottled in an efficient, unromantic plant down the road). Houses the **Poland Spring Preservation Society,** with museum displays from the resort era on the second floor and art on the third. While you are there, peek into the **All Souls Chapel** next door for a look at its nine stained-glass windows and the 1921 Skinner pipe organ.

Hamlin Memorial Library and Museum (743-2980), Paris Hill, off Route 26. Open year-round, Tuesday through Friday 11:30–5:30, Saturday 10–2; also Wednesday 7–9. The old stone Oxford County Jail now houses the public library and museum. Worth a stop for the American primitive art; also local minerals and displays about Hannibal Hamlin (who lived next door), vice president during Abraham Lincoln's first term. This stop may not sound very exciting, but the setting is superb: a ridgetop of spectacular, early-19th-century houses with views west to the White Mountains.

FOR FAMILIES

🖉 **Maine Wildlife Park** (657-4977), Route 26, Gray. Open mid-April through Veteran's Day, daily 9:30–5:30 (no one admitted after 4 PM). $3.50 admission, $2 ages 4–12, ages 3 and under free. From exit 11, turn right onto Route 115 and drive into Gray (0.1 mile). Turn north onto Route 26 and drive 3.5 miles. The park is on the right. What started as a pheasant farm has evolved into a wonderful haven for animals who have been injured and cannot survive in the wild. The goal is to try to prepare them to return to the wild, but while they are here, it is a great opportunity to see animals you might otherwise never see. The park provides habitats that are as natural as possible to the animals, allowing visitors to observe them as they might be in the wild. Nature trails and picnic facilities round out the experience. Animals you may see include moose, lynx, deer, black bears, wild turkeys, eagles, and many more.

RACING

Oxford Plains Speedway (539-8865), Route 26, Oxford. Weekend stock-car racing, late April through September.

SCENIC DRIVES

Along Route 26. Patched with ugly as well as beautiful stretches, the 46 miles between Gray (Maine Turnpike exit 11) and West Paris don't constitute your ordinary "scenic drive," but this is the way most people head for Bethel and the White Mountains. The following sights are described in order of appearance, heading north:

Sabathday Lake Shaker Community and Museum, New Gloucester (8 miles north of Gray), both sides of the road, a must stop (see *Museums*).

State of Maine Building from the 1893 World's Colombian Exposition in Chicago (see *Historic Buildings* for details). An abrupt right, up through the pillars of the old Poland Spring resort.

🖉 In Oxford two exceptional **farm stands** make ice cream from the milk of their own cows. Northbound don't miss hilltop **Crestholm Farm Stand and Ice Cream** (on your right), which has a petting zoo (sheep, goats, pigs, ducks, more) as well as cheeses, honey, and great ice cream, also a nice view. Southbound it's **Smedberg's Crystal Spring Farm** (see *Snacks*).

🖉 In South Paris, road rash sets in big-time after the light; it's easy to miss **Shaner's Family Dining** (see *Eating Out*).

Across from Ripley Ford, look for the **McLaughlin Garden & Horticultural Center** (743-882) at 97 Main Street, open May through October, dawn to dusk. A 3-acre floral oasis begun by Bernard McLaughlin in 1936 and preserved since 1997 by a nonprofit foundation, it's especially beautiful during lilac season (98 varieties). The perennial garden is also known for its hostas, daylilies, phlox, and sempervivums. The **Oxford Hills Chamber of Commerce** (743-2281), two houses up at 6 Western Avenue, open year-round, maintains an information booth across from Mario's Pizza, where you can pick up the magazine guide to this area.

Paris Hill is posted just beyond the second light in South Paris. The road climbs steadily up to Paris Hill common, a spacious green surrounded on three sides by early-19th-century mansions, with the fourth commanding a panoramic view of hills and valley on the White Mountains in the distance. Look for **Hamlin Memorial Library and Museum** (see *Historic Buildings*).

Christian Ridge Pottery (see *Selective Shopping*) is marked from Christian Ridge Road, a way back to Route 26.

✐ **Snow Falls Gorge,** 6 miles south of the center of West Paris on Route 26, left as you are heading north. A great picnic and walk-around spot, a rest area with tables and trail by a waterfall that cascades into a 300-foot gorge carved by the Little Androscoggin. The **River Restaurant** (see *Dining Out*), just across the way, is recognized as one of the best "dining out" as well as "eating out" bets in the area.

✐ **Trap Corner** in West Paris (junction, Route 219) is rockhounding central. (See Perham's of West Paris under *To Do—Rockhounding*.)

✐ **Trap Corner Store and Restaurant** (674-2482) open daily from 5 AM (6 AM on Sunday) is a good road-food stop.

Greenwood Shore Rest Area, Route 26 just north of Bryant Pond. A good waterside spot for a picnic.

TO DO

GOLF

Paris Hill Country Club (743-2371), nine holes, founded in 1899, is the epitome of old-shoe; rental carts, snack bar. **Norway Country Club** (743-9840), off Route 117, nine holes, long views. **Summit Golf Course** (998-4515), Poland Spring.

HIKING

Streaked Mountain. This is a relatively easy hike with a panoramic view, good for kids. From Route 26 take Route 117 to the right-hand turnoff for Streaked Mountain Road and look for the trailhead on your left. The trail follows a power line up to an old fire tower at just 800 feet. The round trip takes about 1½ hours. Look for blueberries in season.

Singlepole Mountain. Also off Route 117, nearer South Paris (see the *Maine Atlas*), is a walk up a dirt road (bear left) through the woods to a summit with a view of Mount Washington and the Mahoosuc Mountains.

Also see **Bear Mountain Inn** under *Lodging—Bed & Breakfasts*.

MOUNTAIN BIKING

Paris Hill Area Park, near the common. You can bike the ridge roads radiating from here; inquire about routes in Hamlin Memorial Library (see *Historic Buildings*).

Lost Valley Ski Area (784-1561), Auburn, opens its trails to bikers and organizes events in biking season.

ROCKHOUNDING

Perham's of West Paris (674-2341; 1-800-371-GEMS), open 9–5 daily. Looking deceptively small in its yellow-clapboard, green-trim building (right side of Route 26, heading north), this business has been selling gemstones since 1919. Aside from displaying an array of locally mined amethyst, tourmaline, topaz, and many other minerals, as well as selling gem jewelry, Perham's offers maps to five local quarries in which treasure seekers are welcome to try their luck. Whether you're a rockhound or not, you'll want to stop by this mini-museum, said to attract 90,000 visitors per year.

Rochester's Eclectic Emporium (539-4631), Route 26, Oxford. Nick Rochester displays a 54-carat amethyst that he found locally and steers visitors to local mines.

SWIMMING

✍ **Range Pond State Park** (998-4104), Poland, another great family beach, which offers a grass lawn above the beach, perfect for spreading out a picnic blanket. Snack bar, changing rooms, bathrooms, swimming, and fishing.

Pennesseewasee Lake in Norway is well off the road, but public and equipped with lifeguards.

In addition, most camps, cottages, and lodges have their own waterfront beaches and docks, and there are numerous local swimming holes.

WINTER SPORTS

CROSS-COUNTRY SKIING

Carter's Farm Market (539-4848), Route 26, Oxford. Extensive acreage used to grow summer vegetables is transformed into a ski center during the winter. Equipment rentals, lessons, 10 km of groomed trails, some lighted trails for night skiing, and food.

Lost Valley Ski Area (764-1561), Auburn. Mid-September to mid-March, trails and rentals. $8 fee.

SNOW TUBING

✍ **Mountain View Sports Park** (539-2454), Route 26, Oxford. Open Thursday through Sunday. A lighted 1,000-foot slope, tubes, helmets, and a T-bar are the ingredients of this low-tech, low-cost sport.

LODGING

INNS

♿ **The Waterford Inne** (583-4037), Box 149, Waterford 04088. This striking, mustard-colored, 1825 farmhouse with its double porch is sequestered up a back road, set on 25 acres of fields and woods. Mother and daughter Rosalie and Barbara Vanderzanden have been welcoming guests since 1978, offering tasteful, spacious rooms (four in the old house and five more carved into the old ell). Common rooms are ample and tastefully furnished; the standout is the Chesapeake Room, with a fireplace and the second-story porch. A full breakfast is included in $74–105 per room; dinner, available to the public (see *Dining Out*), is $31.

Kedarburn Inn (583-6182), Route 35, Waterford 04088. London natives Margaret and Derek Gibson offer olde English hospitality in their seven guest rooms, five with private baths. Decor in their 1850s home is warm and pretty, with Margaret's specialty quilts throughout. We particularly like the room with a double bed and loft with two twin beds, a nice spot for families. The crafts shop on the ground floor is filled with items made by local artists as well as Margaret's quilts and crafts. $75–125 double in-season, including breakfast. Dinner is available in the restaurant, Peter's (see *Dining Out*), and English afternoon tea is served by reservation.

Lake House (583-4182; 1-800-223-4182; mjum@aol.com), Routes 35 and 37, Waterford 04088. Open year-round. A graceful old stagecoach tavern and inn, the first building in Waterford "flat." It has been an inn, a sanatorium for ladies, a hotel, and a private residence. In 1984 it was reopened as a country inn. Michael Myers offers five spacious guest rooms, including a two-room suite and a one-room cottage, all with private baths. The Grand Ballroom is particularly nice, with soft green walls, hardwood floors, and a claw-foot tub on a raised floor surrounded by a curtain. Rooms have phones, coffeemakers, hair dryers, and bathrobes, among other amenities. The whole place has an elegant 1700s feel. Lake Keoka is across the street. $84–130.

BED & BREAKFASTS

Bear Mountain Inn (583-4404), Routes 35 and 37, South Waterford 04081. Open year-round. Set on 52 acres on Bear Pond, this farmhouse has welcomed guests for more than 150 years. Lorraine Blais purchased the property and completely renovated all the rooms in 1997. Seven rooms in the main house range from the "Polo Bear" room decorated in Ralph Lauren, with a shared bath, to the Family Cub Den with two adjoining rooms and a large private bath. The top-floor suite offers a Jacuzzi, gas fireplace, private entrance, and deck. The Sugar Bear Cottage has a wood-burning fireplace, kitchenette, and claw-foot tub. A 45-minute hiking trail to the top of Bear Mountain begins across the street. Private beach with docks and canoes available to guests. $85–125 per room includes a full breakfast.

Farnham House B&B (782-9495), 520 Main Street, Lewiston 04240. Open year-round. Barbara Fournier offers five rooms with a touch of elegance in this pleasant house built in 1900. Her main business comes from Bates College, but anyone is welcome. The second-floor Deck Room is particularly nice, with (as you might suspect) a private deck. $50–100.

OTHER LODGING

☜✍ **Wadsworth Blanchard Farm Hostel** (625-7509), RR 2, Box 5992, Hiram 04041. Open May through October. An attractive Hosteling International (HI) facility that's an 18th-century farmstead, and handy to canoeing on both the Saco and Ossippee Rivers. Sally Whitcher and Edward Bradley offer two dorms with four beds each, one family room with a queen bed; access to the kitchen is included in all rates. $10 per person, $30 per family, half price for children 12 and under.

✒ **Papoose Pond Resort and Campground** (583-4470), RR 1, Box 2480, Route 118, North Waterford 04267-9600 (10 miles west of Norway). Family-geared for 40 years, this facility is on 1,000 wooded acres with a half mile of sandy beach on mile-long Papoose Pond; facilities include 25 cabins with baths, 18 cabins without baths, 10 housekeeping cottages, 8 bunkhouse trailers, 13 tent sites, 59 tent sites with electricity and water, 28 more with sewage as well, a dining shelter, and a kitchen and bathhouse. Amenities include a recreation hall, store, café, movie tent, sports area, 50 boats (canoes, rowboats, sailboats, paddleboats, kayaks), fishing equipment, and a vintage 1916 merry-go-round.

WHERE TO EAT

DINING OUT

The Waterford Inne (583-4037), Waterford. Ask for directions when you call to reserve. Dinner by reservation only in the common rooms of a classic country inn. Our dinner began with mini-popovers and a squash-orange soup, followed by greens and chopped walnuts, then perfectly grilled lamb chops with fresh mint, roasted potatoes, and grilled tomato, topped with a glorious pear dessert. Wine can be purchased at Springer's Store down the road.

Peter's (583-6265), Route 35, Waterford. Peter and Emma Bodwell offer good fare in the dining rooms of the 1858 Kedarburn Inn. Specialties include stuffed artichoke hearts, steak au poivre, and fresh seafood specials. Entrées $8–19.

Lake House (583-4182; 1-800-223-4182; mjum@aol.com), Routes 35 and 37, Waterford. Open from 5:30 PM daily. The atmosphere is casual, but the dining is elegant, with all the little touches that make a meal an event. Two cozy dining rooms set with linen cloths, fresh flowers, and oil lamps. The menu is varied and the wine list extensive. Owner and chef Michael Myers prepares all meals to order. This is a place to linger and enjoy, from the breadsticks to coffee and dessert. Order the bananas Foster for two just for the pleasure of watching it prepared tableside.

& **Maurice Restaurant** (743-2532), 109 Main Street, South Paris. Open for dinner daily, lunch weekdays, Sunday brunch. Though the main focus here is French cuisine, they also offer pasta and beef dishes. Entrées include scampi, veal flambé, and roast duck à l'orange. Extensive wine list. Reservations recommended. $12–17.

🎗 **The River Restaurant** (743-7816), just across from Snow Falls, Route 26, Norway. Open for lunch and dinner, daily except Monday. Known for its Sunday brunch buffet and creative menu, fine dining at "eating out" prices. Entrées $6.95–14.95.

    Sedgley Place (946-5990), off Route 202, Greene. Reservations required. A lovely Federal-style house with a well-known dining room. Five-course dinners with entrées that change weekly, but always include prime rib, a fish, a poultry, and a fourth selection. Prix fixe.

Trolley House Restaurant (743-2211), 110 Main Street, Norway. Open for lunch and dinner daily except Sunday. Two attractive, high-ceilinged dining rooms decorated with old photo blowups. The menu features Angus beef and seafood. Dinner entrées $8.95–16.95.

Village Inn (782-7796), 165 High Street, Auburn. Casual dining. Seafood is the specialty here, especially their fried clams. $7.95–14.95.

Korn Haus Keller (786-2379), 1472 Lisbon Street, Lewiston. The specialty here is chicken cordon bleu. Other menu options include lobster pie, seafood, and beef. $8.95–16.95.

Marois (782-9055), 249 Lisbon Street, Lewiston. It is a surprise to find this fine dining spot smack in the middle of downtown Lewiston. Well known and popular among locals. Greek and French specialties. $7–15.

EATING OUT

Cole Farms (657-4714), Route 100/202, Gray. Open 5 AM–10:30 PM daily except Monday. Maine cooking from family recipes. Specialties include the fried fish plate and seafood Newburg. Everything from soups and chowders to ice cream and pastries made on the premises. No liquor.

Chopsticks (783-6300), 37 Park Street, Lewiston. One of the best Chinese restaurants we have found, with all the usual choices.

Val's Root Beer (784-5592), 925 Sabattus Street, Lewiston. Seasonal drive-up stand where the wait staff still serves you in your car. Burgers, hot dogs, and the like, and their specialty, homemade root beer. Popular summer hangout among locals.

Shaners Family Dining (743-6367), 193 Main Street, South Paris. Open for breakfast, lunch, and dinner. A large, cheerful family restaurant with booths; specials like fried chicken, liver and onions, and chicken pie; creamy homemade ice cream in a big choice of flavors.

SNACKS

Crestholm Farm Stand and Ice Cream (539-2616), Route 26, Oxford. Farm stand, cheeses, honey, ice cream, and a petting zoo: sheep, goats, pigs, ducks, more.

Smedberg's Crystal Spring Farm (743-6723) sells its One Cow Ice Cream (there are actually a couple of dozen cows) in a dozen flavors; try the black raspberry.

ENTERTAINMENT

Celebration Barn Theater (743-8452), 190 Stock Farm, off Route 117 north of South Paris. In 1972 theater and mime master Tony Montanaro founded a performance arts school in this big red old racing-horse barn high on Christian Ridge. Summer workshops in acrobatics, mime, and juggling by resident New Vaudeville artists, Fridays and Saturdays in July and August; tickets are reasonably priced.

The Public Theater (782-3200; 1-800-639-9575), 2 Great Falls Plaza, Auburn. Professional theater with equity actors.

Bates Dance Festival (786-6161), mid-July to mid-August, Schaeffer Theater, Bates College, Lewiston. Student and faculty performances.

SELECTIVE SHOPPING

ANTIQUES
Mollyockett Marketplace (674-3939), Route 26, junction Route 219, West Paris. Open Thursday through Monday May through November, winter weekends. A two-story group shop, priced to sell.

BOOKSTORES
Books 'n' Things (743-7197), Oxford Plaza, Route 26, Oxford. Billing itself as "Western Maine's Complete Bookstore," a fully stocked store with a full children's section.

Downtown Bookshop (743-7245), 200 Main Street, Norway. Closed Sunday. A source of general titles, stationery, cards, and magazines.

GEM SHOPS
See *Rockhounding*.

SPECIAL SHOPS
United Society of Shakers (926-4597), Route 26, New Gloucester. Open Memorial Day through Columbus Day; sells Shaker herbs, teas, handcrafted items.

Christian Ridge Pottery (743-8419), 210 Stock Farm Road, Paris Hill, marked from Route 26 and from Christian Ridge Road. Open Memorial Day weekend through December, 10–5 daily, except noon–5 Sunday. One of Maine's major potters, known for its functional, distinctive stippleware in ovenproof, microwavable designs: coffee- and teapots, bowls, etc.; also specialty items like apple-baking dishes. Seconds.

Stone Soup Artisans (783-4281), Vernon and Center Streets, Auburn. Open Tuesday through Saturday 10–5. An outstanding artist's and artisan's cooperative.

OUTLETS
Bates Mill Store (784-7626; 1-800-552-2837), 49 Canal Street, Lewiston. Open year-round; weekdays 9–4, Saturday 9–1. A genuine outlet for Bates bedspreads, towels, sheets, blankets.

Marden's (786-0313), Northwood Shopping Center, Route 202, Lewiston. Like Reny's (*see* "Damariscotta/Newcastle and Pemaquid Area") this is a Maine original, the first store in a Maine chain; a mix of clothing, staples, furnishings, whatever happens to be in stock, and always worth checking.

SPECIAL EVENTS

May: **Maine State Parade** *(first Saturday)*—The state's biggest parade; theme varies annually.

July: The **Oxford 250 NASCAR Race** draws entrants from throughout the world to the Oxford Plains Speedway; **Harrison** celebrates **Old Home Days. Founders Day** on **Paris Hill** is observed *(midmonth)*. **Bean Hole Bean Festival** in Oxford draws thousands. **The Moxie Festival** *(second weekend)*, downtown Lisbon, features live entertainment, plenty of food, and Moxie (Maine's own soft drink).

August: **Gray Old Home Days** *(beginning of the month)* includes a parade, contests, and public feeds. **Festival de Joie** *(first weekend)*, Lewiston—music, dancing, cultural and crafts displays. **Great Falls Balloon Festival** *(fourth weekend)*, Lewiston—music, games, hot-air launches.

September: **Oxford County Agricultural Fair** in West Paris *(usually held during the second week)*.

December: **Christmas open house and festivals** in Paris Hill.

Bethel Area

Bethel is a natural farming and trading site on the Androscoggin River. Its town common is the junction for routes west to the White Mountains, north to the Mahoosucs, east to the Oxford Hills, and south to the lakes.

When the trains from Portland to Montreal began stopping here in 1851, Bethel also became an obvious summer retreat for city people. But unlike many summer resorts of that era, it was nothing fancy. Families stayed the season in the big, white farmhouses, of which there are still plenty. They feasted on home-grown and home-cooked food, then walked it off on nearby mountain trails.

Hiking remains a big lure for summer and fall visitors. The White Mountain National Forest comes within a few miles of town, and trails radiate from nearby Evans Notch. Just 12 miles northwest of Bethel, Grafton Notch State Park also offers some short hikes to spectacles such as Screw Auger Falls and to a wealth of well-equipped picnic sites. Blueberrying and rockhounding are local pastimes, and the hills are also good pickings for history buffs.

The hills were once far more peopled than they are today—entire villages have vanished. Hastings, for example, now just the name of a national forest campground, was once a thriving community complete with post office, stores, and a wood alcohol mill that shipped its product by rail to Portland, thence to England.

The Bethel Inn, born of the railroad era, is still going strong. Opened in 1913 by millionaire William Bingham II and dedicated to a prominent neurologist (who came to Bethel to recuperate from a breakdown), it originally featured a program of strenuous exercise—one admired by the locals (wealthy clients actually paid the doctor to chop down his trees) as well as by the medical profession. The inn is still known for at least two forms of exercise—golf and cross-country skiing.

Bethel is best known these days as a ski town. Sunday River, 6 miles to the north, claims to offer "the most dependable snow in North America" and, despite its relatively low altitude, has managed to produce reliably good snow conditions on its eight mountains throughout the season. Powered by its snow guns (powered in turn by water from the Androscoggin), the family-geared resort has doubled and redoubled its trails, lifts, and lodging regularly since 1980 when it was acquired by Les Otten, whose

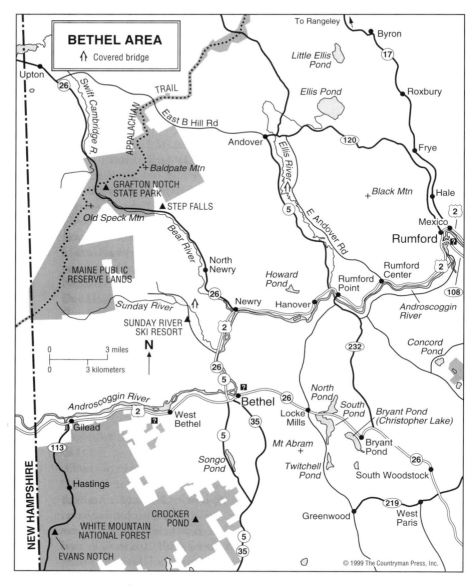

American Skiing Company now also owns six of the region's major ski resorts, including Killington in Vermont (by far the East's largest ski resort) and Sunday River's longtime Maine competitor, Sugarloaf, as well as major western resorts in Utah, Colorado and California. So it happens that Bethel is now the address of one of the world's largest ski-resort-operating companies. Mount Abram, a few miles south of the village, by contrast remains an old-fashioned family ski area.

Skiers tend to see Bethel as "a quick hit" that you simply get to—and out of—without stopping on the way to the snow-covered trails. In summer, it's a very different story. As it has been since settlement, Bethel is a natural way station—between the White Mountains and the coast, and between the lake resorts and children's camps to the south and Rangeley to the north. See the "Western Mountains and Lakes Region" introduction.

Bethel is also home to Gould Academy, a coed prep school with a handsome campus, and is the summer home of NTL Institute for Applied Behavioral Science, enrolling roughly 1,000 participants from around the world. Hidden away in the Newry woods, Outward Bound's "Mountain Center" also contributes to the mix that's Bethel: several former instructors now offer visitors outdoors-geared activities such as dogsledding, llama trekking, kayaking, and horseback riding.

For Bethel, tourism has remained the icing rather than the cake. Its lumber mills manufacture pine boards, furniture parts, and broom handles. Three dairy farms ship 7,000 gallons of milk per week. Brooks Brothers is still the name of the hardware store, not a men's clothier.

GUIDANCE

Bethel Area Chamber of Commerce (824-2282; bethelcc@nxi.com; www.bethelmaine.com), P.O. Box 439, 30 Cross Street, Bethel 04217, publishes an excellent area guide and maintains a large walk-in information center with rest rooms in the depot-style Bethel Station, off Lower Main Street (Route 26). Open year-round, weekdays 9–5, varying hours on weekends. See *Lodging* for reservations services.

The Maine Tourism Association (824-4582) and **White Mountain National Forest Service** (824-2134) also maintain a joint information center (rest rooms too) on Route 2/5/26 just outside town; open most days, but hours vary. It's stocked with information on all areas in Maine and offers detailed information about camping, hiking, and other outdoor activities in the national forest and other nearby natural areas.

GETTING THERE

By air: The **Portland International Jetport,** served by Continental Express, United, Delta, USAir, and TWA Express, is 75 miles from Bethel. All major car rentals are available at the airport. **Bethel Air Service** (824-4321) offers air taxi/charter service; the **Bethel Airport** (824-4321) has a paved 3,150-foot runway.

Bethel Express (824-4646). Van limo shuttle will pick up at Portland Jetport or other transportation hubs.

By car: Bethel is a convenient way stop between New Hampshire's White Mountains (via Route 2) and the Maine coast. From Boston, take the Maine Turnpike to Gray, exit 11; Bethel is 55 miles north on Route 26. For more than a dozen suggested stops along the way, see *Scenic Drives* in "Oxford Hills and Lewiston/Auburn."

MEDICAL EMERGENCY
    Bethel Family Health Center (824-2193).
    Sheriff's Department/Bethel Rescue: 911.

TO SEE

HISTORIC HOUSES AND MUSEUMS
Dr. Moses Mason House Museum (824-2908), 15 Mason Street, Bethel.
    Open July to Labor Day, 1–4 daily except Monday, and by appointment
    the rest of the year; $2 per adult, $1 per child. This exquisite Federal-
    style mansion built in 1813, home of the Bethel Historical Society, is
    proof of the town's early prosperity. Restored to its original grandeur
    when it was owned by Dr. Moses Mason, one of Bethel's most promi-
    nent citizens in the 1800s, it has Rufus Porter murals in the front hall,
    fine furnishings in nine period rooms, woodwork, and special exhibits
    and extensive archives for the area. This is an unusually lively, visitor-
    friendly historical museum that's in the process of expanding.

COVERED BRIDGES
Artist's Covered Bridge, Newry (across the Sunday River, 5 miles north-
    west of Bethel). A weathered town bridge built in 1872 and painted by
    numerous 19th-century landscape artists, notably John Enneking. A
    great spot to sun and swim. Other swimming holes can be found at
    intervals along the road above the bridge.
Lovejoy Covered Bridge, South Andover, roughly a quarter mile east of
    Route 5. Built across the Ellis River in 1867, another local swimming
    hole (it's more than 7 miles north of Route 2).

SCENIC DRIVES
Evans Notch. Follow Route 2 west to Gilead and turn south on Route 113,
    following the Wild and then the Cold River south through one of the
    most spectacular mountain passes in northern New England. (Also see
    To Do—Camping and *Hiking*.)
Grafton Notch State Park. A beautiful drive even if you don't hike (see
    Hiking). Continue on beyond Upton for views of Lake Umbagog; note
    the loop you can make back from Upton along the old road to Andover
    (look for the vintage 1867 **Lovejoy Covered Bridge** across the Ellis
    River), then south on Route 5 to Route 2.
Patte Brook Multiple-Use Management Demonstration Area, a 4-
    mile, self-guided tour with stops at 11 areas along Patte Brook near the
    national forest's **Crocker Pond** campground in West Bethel. The tour
    begins on Forest Road No. 7 (Patte Brook Road), 5 miles south of
    Bethel on Route 5. A glacial bog, former orchards and homesites, and
    an old dam and pond are among the clearly marked sites.
Rangeley and **Weld Loops.** See the introduction to "Western Mountains
    and Lakes Region" for a description of these rewarding drives. You can
    access both by following Route 2 north from Bethel along the
    Androscoggin, but back-road buffs may prefer cutting up the narrow

rural valleys threaded by Rumford Road or Route 232 from Locke Mills; both join Route 2 at Rumford Point.

TO DO

AIRPLANE RIDES
Bethel Air Service (824-4321). Steve Whitney and Dan Bilodeau offer daily scenic flights of the area with views of the Bethel and Appalachian Mountain areas year-round. They also offer flight instruction, air taxi/charter, and a public lounge.

BICYCLING
See *Mountain Biking*.

CAMPING
In the **Evans Notch area** of the White Mountain National Forest there are five campgrounds: **Basin** (21 sites), **Cold River** (12 sites), **Crocker Pond** (7 sites), **Hastings** (24 sites), and **Wild River** (11 sites). All accept reservations for May 13 through October 11 through the National Recreation Reservation Service: 1-800-280-2267, Monday through Friday (Pacific time, so from the East Coast, phone weekdays between noon and 9 PM or Saturday and Sunday 1–6). For information, phone the **Evans Notch Ranger Station** (824-2134), Bridge Street, Bethel.

Also check with the **White Mountain National Forest** information center (see *Guidance*) about wilderness campsites, and under *Lodging* for commercial campgrounds.

CANOEING AND KAYAKING
Popular local routes include the **Ellis River** in Andover (13 easy miles from the covered bridge in South Andover to Rumford Point); the **Androscoggin River** has become far more accessible in recent years with 10 put-in points mapped and shuttle service offered between Shelburne on the New Hampshire line and the Rumford boat landing; the **Sunday River** (beginning at the covered bridge) also offers great white water in spring. A chain of water connects **North, South,** and **Round Ponds** and offers a day of rewarding paddling, with swimming holes and picnic stops en route. See the "Upper Androscoggin Valley Interpretive Map" produced by the Appalachian Mountain Club and available at no charge from the White Mountain National Forest information center (see *Guidance*).

Bethel Outdoor Adventures (836-3607; 1-800-533-3607), Route 2 in West Bethel, offers shuttle service, canoe and kayak rentals, guided trips, and kayak clinics; also operates **Riverside Campground** in Bethel. The locally based **Mahoosuc Guide Service** (824-3092) offers guided trips on the Allagash, Penobscot, and St. John Rivers. **The Telemark Inn** (836-2703) also offers guided canoeing (see *Lodging*).

CHAIRLIFT RIDES
Sunday River Ski Resort (824-3000) offers scenic chairlift rides. Weather permitting, Memorial Day through Columbus Day weekend.

NORWAY 14 MI.

PARIS 15 MI.

DENMARK 23 MI.

NAPLES 23 MI.

SWEDEN 25 MI.

POLAND 27 MI.

MEXICO 37 MI.

CHINA 94 MI.

PERU 46 MI.

International Sign, Route 5 south of Bethel

KIM GRANT

FISHING

Temporary nonresident licenses are available at the **Bethel, Newry,** and **Woodstock Town Offices;** also at **Dave's Store** in Andover, **Bob's Corner Store** in Locke Mills, **Bethel Outdoor Adventures** in Bethel, and **Sun Valley Sports** (824-753), Sunday River Road. Fly-fishing is a growing sport here, especially along the Androscoggin, increasingly known for the size of its trout. Also see L'Auberge under *Bed & Breakfasts*.

FOR FAMILIES

✐ **Sunday River Adventure Center** (824-3000), White Cap Base Lodge, Sunday River Ski Area, Newry. The Tempest Lagoon water slide (two lanes), a skateboard/in-line skate park, and a climbing wall are all open daily through summer months.

✐ **The BIG Adventure Center,** Route 2 and Northwest Road (just beyond the Norseman), Bethel. Open 10–10 daily. Indoor laser tag, climbing wall and climbing gym, outdoor 18-hole miniature golf.

GOLF

Bethel Inn and Country Club (824-2175), Bethel. An 18-hole, championship-length course and driving range. Mid-May to October the inn's **Guaranteed Performance School of Golf** offers 3- and 5-day sessions (classes limited to three students per PGA instructor); golf cart rentals are available.

HIKING

White Mountain National Forest, although primarily in New Hampshire, includes 41,943 acres in Maine. A number of the trails in the Evans Notch area are spectacular. Trail maps for the Baldface Circle Trail, Basin Trail, Bickford Brook Trail, and Caribou Trail are available from the **Evans Notch Ranger District** (824-2134), Bridge Street, Bethel, open Monday through Friday 8–4. Pick up detailed maps from the chamber of commerce (see *Guidance*).

Grafton Notch State Park, Route 26, between Newry and Upton. From Bethel, take Route 2 East to Route 26 North for 7.8 miles. Turn left at the Getty station (Newry Corner) and go toward New Hampshire for 8.7 miles. **Screw Auger Falls** is 1 mile farther—a spectacular area at the end of the Mahoosuc Range. Other sights include **Mother Walker Falls** and **Moose Cave,** a ¼-mile nature walk. The big hike is up **Old Speck,** the third-highest mountain in the state; up Old Speck Trail and back down the Firewarden's Trail is 5½ miles.

Step Falls can be found just before the entrance to Grafton Notch State Park. From Newry Corner, go 7.9 miles. On your right will be a white farmhouse, followed by a field just before a bridge. There is a road leading to the rear left of the field, where you may park. The well-marked trail is just behind the trees at the back. Please respect the private property adjoining the trail and falls. This scenic area on Wight's

Brook, maintained by The Nature Conservancy, has been enjoyed by local families for generations.

In Shelburne there are hiking trails on **Mount Crag, Mount Cabot,** and **Ingalls Mountain,** and there are more trails in **Evans Notch.** For details, check the AMC *White Mountain Guide,* and *50 Hikes in Southern and Coastal Maine* by John Gibson, published by Backcountry Publications, Woodstock, VT 05091.

Mount Will Trail. Recently developed by the Bethel Conservation Commission, this 3¼-mile loop is a good family trip; many people choose to climb only to the North Ledges (640 vertical feet in ¾ mile), yielding a view of the Androscoggin Valley, which only gets better over the next 1½ miles—climbing over ledges to 1,450 feet and then descending the South Cliffs. The trailhead is a chained-off logging road on Route 2 just 1.9 miles beyond the Riverside Rest Area (which is just beyond the turnoff for Sunday River).

HORSEBACK RIDING

Speckled Mountain Ranch (836-2908), Flat Road, West Bethel. We are grateful to the reader who tipped us off to the full beauty of this place, one of the few in New England that offer this combination of responsive horses, beautiful trails, and friendly, effective teaching. Leo Joost has worked both with racing horses and handicapped students, and her way with both people and horses is exceptional. The "ranch" consists of a handsome red barn and a white farmhouse set in 150 acres against an abrupt mountain, and even a short ride can include trotting and cantering across meadows and through woods. From May through October, 2- to 5-day English trail-riding vacations are offered (ride 2 to 3½ hours per day. A weekend, including Saturday dinner and breakfasts is $300; $130 for each additional day). A 6-day camp for girls (ages 12–15) is also offered. Riding groups are kept small, no more than four riders with one or two guides. The bright, uncluttered farmhouse has three guest rooms, 2½ baths. Inquire about carriage rides, sleigh rides, driving lessons, and cross-country skiing. Board is provided if you wish to bring your own horse.

Deepwood Farm (824-2595), a family-oriented business, offers regular riding programs April through November: lessons, sleigh rides, and 3- and 5-day summer camps for youngsters ages 6–10.

LLAMA TREKKING

Telemark Inn (836-2703), 10 miles west of Bethel. Treks offered April through October. Primarily for guests of the Telemark Inn, but treks ranging from 1 to 4 days into the surrounding wilderness are available to nonguests as well. Steve Crone offered the first llama treks in New England, and we took one of the first that he offered. The llamas carry your gear but you walk beside them. Rates: from $85 per adult, $65 per child for a day to $575 per adult, $425 per child for 4 days.

MOUNTAIN BIKING

Sunday River Mountain Bike Park (824-3000; 1-800-543-2SKI), White Cap Base Area, Sunday River Ski Area, Newry. Two chairlifts access 60 miles of bike trails. Lift and trail passes are sold at South Ridge Base Lodge. Lodging, lift, and meal packages are available. Rental bikes are available.

Bethel Outdoor Adventures (836-3607) offers scheduled, guided mountain bike tours as well as custom tours; rentals.

Mahoosuc Mountain Sports (824-3786), Route 26, Locke Mills, also rents mountain bikes.

ROCKHOUNDING

This corner of Oxford County is recognized as one of the world's richest sources of some minerals and semiprecious gems. More than a third of the world's mineral varieties can be found here. Gems include amethyst, aquamarine, tourmaline, and topaz. Mining has gone on around here since tourmaline was discovered at Mount Mica in 1821. Jim Mann's **Mt. Mann** (824-3030) on Main Street, Bethel, includes a mineral museum. In the cellar, kids (of all ages) can explore "Crystal Caves": a dimly lit "mine" in which rockhounds can fill their cardboard buckets (for a nominal fee) and then identify them back in the museum. **Perham's of West Paris** (674-2341; 1-800-371-GEMS), open 9–5 daily, offers maps to five local quarries. (Also see *Rockhounding* in "Oxford Hills and Lewiston/Auburn.") The **Annual Gem, Mineral, and Jewelry Show** (second weekend in July at Telstar High School) is a mega-mineral event with guided field trips to local quarries.

SWIMMING

There are numerous lakes and river swimming holes in the area. It is best to ask the chamber of commerce (see *Guidance*) about where access is currently possible. Reliable spots include:

Artist's Covered Bridge. Follow Sunday River signs north from Bethel, but continue on Sunday River Road instead of turning onto the ski-area access road. Look for the covered bridge on your left. Space for parking, bushes for changing.

Wild River in Evans Notch, Gilead, offers some obvious access spots off Route 113, as does the **Bear River,** which follows Route 26 through Grafton Notch.

WINTER SPORTS

DOGSLEDDING

Mahoosuc Mountain Adventures (824-2073), Bear River Road, Newry 04261. Polly Mahoney and Kevin Slater offer combination backcountry skiing and mushing trips. You can be as involved with the dogs as you want: an hour, a day, or a 3-day, 2-night trip.

Winter Journeys (928-2026) offers half-, full-, and multiday bed & breakfast dogsled trips.

Skijoring: Skiing behind dogs is a specialty at the **Telemark Inn** (see *Lodging*).

In the summer a chairlift takes mountain bikers to the top at Sunday River Resort.

CROSS-COUNTRY SKIING

Sunday River Ski Touring Center (824-2410), Bethel (based at Sunday River Inn, near the ski area). A total of 40 km of double-tracked trails loop through the woods, including a section to Artist's Covered Bridge. Thanks to the high elevation, careful trail prepping, and heavy-duty grooming equipment, snow tends to stick here when it's scarce in much of Maine. The center offers guided night skiing, rentals, instruction, and snacks.

Bethel Inn and Country Club (824-2175), Bethel. Trails meander out over the golf course and through the woods, offering beautiful mountain views, solitude, and challenges suitable for all levels. Skating and classic trails, rental equipment, and lessons available.

Carter's X-Country Ski Center (539-4848), Middle Intervale Road (off Route 26 south of the village), Bethel. Dave Carter, a member of one of Bethel's oldest families and a longtime cross-country pro, maintains some 65 km of wooded trails on 1,000 acres, meandering from 600 up to 1,800 feet in elevation; an easy loop connects two lodges and runs along the Androscoggin River. Reasonably priced equipment rentals and lessons.

Telemark Inn & Llama Farm (836-2703), West Bethel. These 20 km of high-elevation wooded trails and unlimited backcountry skiing terrain frequently represent the best cross-country skiing in the area—but Steve Crone issues a limited number of passes a day, preserving the wilderness feel of his resort for Telemark Inn guests. So call before coming and inquire about skijoring behind huskies!

Also see **Mahoosuc Mountain Adventures** under *Dogsledding*, and contact the **Bethel Ranger Station** for details about cross-country trails in the White Mountain National Forest (see *Hiking*).

DOWNHILL SKIING

✎ **Mount Abram Ski Resort** 9875-5003), Locke Mills. Sold once more in 1998, this remains a friendly, family-owned and -geared ski area: 35 trails and slopes, with some pleasant surprises, including two black diamond trails and a "cruiser" trail. The vertical drop is 1,030 feet. Facilities include 65–70 percent snowmaking; two double chairlifts and three T-bars; an expanded "barn red" lodge with lounge, snack shop, nursery, and ski rentals, PSIA ski school, special programs. Family-friendly rates: On weekends, a day pass is $31 adults, $18 juniors; weekdays it's $20 adults, $15 juniors. Night skiing Friday, Saturday, and Sunday.

✎♿ **Sunday River Ski Area** (824-3000; resort reservations, 1-800-543-2SKI), Newry 04217. Sunday River has become synonymous with snow. Powered by the incessant output of its snow guns and grooming fleet, it has shown substantial growth annually since the 1980s. Owner Les Otten now heads the American Ski Company, one of the world's largest ski resort–operating companies. It includes Killington, the mammoth Vermont ski resort for which the 23-year-old Otten first came to 12-trail Sunday River. That was in 1972, an era when environmentalists were calling the shots in Vermont, curtailing Killington's growth—so it happened that a big Vermont resort bought a little Maine ski area. Killington's Sherburne Corporation installed a chairlift and some snowmaking equipment, then got the green light to expand again on its own turf. In 1980 it sold Sunday River to Otten. It was from Killington that Otten imbibed an obsession with snowmaking and a sense of how trails can multiply along a range of mountains. What it lacks in altitude (the highest peak is just 3,140 feet) the resort makes up for in easy access to water, the essential ingredient in snowmaking.

At Sunday River, 126 trails and glades now lace eight interconnected mountain peaks, including the Jordan Bowl. Challenges include a 3-mile run from a summit and White Heat—"the steepest, longest, widest lift-served expert trail in the East." The trails are served by 18 lifts: 9 quad chairlifts (4 high-speed detachable), 4 triple chairlifts, 2 doubles, and 3 surface lifts. The vertical "descent" is 2,300 feet. Snowmaking is on 92 percent of the skiing terrain. Facilities include three base lodges and a Peak Lodge, ski shops, and several restaurants; a total of 6,000 beds are in condominium hotels with pools and Jacuzzis, town houses, slope-side **Summit** and **Jordan Grand** hotels, a **Snow Cap Inn** (really a lodge), and the **Snow Cap Ski Dorm** (geared to groups). The ski school offers Guaranteed Learn-to-Ski in One Day and Perfect Turn clinics, Munchkins for ages 4–6, Mogul Meisters for ages 7–12, a Junior Racing Program, and a Maine Handicapped Skiing Program. A half-pipe is lit for snowboarders at the White Cap Base Lodge. Lift tickets are $94 per adult and $58 per junior for 2 days on weekends; less midweek. Many lodging packages available.

ICE SKATING

In winter, a portion of Bethel's common is flooded, and ice skates can be rented from the cross-country center in the Bethel Inn. Skate rentals are also available at the public skating rink at Sunday River's White Cap Base Lodge.

SLEIGH RIDES

Telemark Inn, Sunday River Inn, and the **Bethel Inn and Country Club** (see *Lodging*) and **Speckled Mountain Ranch** (see *Horseback Riding*) all offer sleigh rides.

SNOWMOBILING

Local enthusiasts have developed a trail system in the area. Contact the chamber (see *Guidance*) for information on where to get maps. Maine and New Hampshire also maintain 60 miles of trails in the Evans Notch District. **Sun Valley Sports** (824-7553) on the Sunday River Road and **Bethel Outdoor Adventures** (836-3607) in Bethel rent snowmobiles.

LODGING

The **Bethel Chamber of Commerce** maintains a lodging reservations service: 824-3585 or 1-800-442-5826.

Sunday River Ski Area maintains its own toll-free reservation number: 1-800-543-2SKI, good nationwide and in Canada; the service is geared toward winter and condo information, but also serves local inns and B&Bs. Many other condos and rental homes are available in the Bethel area through **Maine Street Realty & Rentals** (824-2114; 1-800-824-6024) and **Rentals Unlimited** (824-4044; 1-800-535-2220). Also see Lake House and the Kedarburn Inn under *Lodging* in "Oxford Hills and Lewiston/Auburn."

INNS

🐾⚭ **Bethel Inn and Country Club** (824-2175; 1-800-654-0125), Bethel 04217. This rambling, yellow wooden inn and its annexes frame a corner of the town common. The lobby and parlor are large and formal, also comfortably dowdy, as is the downstairs **Mill Brook Tavern.** The formal dining room is truly elegant, with a Steinway, a fireplace, and windows overlooking the mountains (see *Dining Out*). The 60 rooms in the inn and guesthouses vary in size and view (request a larger room in back, overlooking the mountains), all with phones and private baths (adequate but 1950s-style). Families should opt for one of the 40 one- and two-bedroom town houses on the golf course. Facilities include a recreation center with a pool and hot tub, two saunas, exercise room, game room, and lounge. The pool is outdoors but heated to 91 degrees for winter use. The 18-hole golf course, with 7 holes dating from 1915 and 11 more added by Geoffrey Cornish, is a big draw, with golf-school sessions offered throughout the season. Facilities also include a tennis court, a boathouse with canoes and sailfish, and a sandy beach on Songo Pond, as well as an extensive cross-country ski network (see *Golf, Cross-Country Skiing,* and *Sleigh Rides*). From $138 in the inn; townhouses, $210–340. Many packages are available, especially off-season. Children ages 11 and under, free in room with parents. Please let us know how you found the service here: We love this old inn but have recently received several negative letters and hope it was just a glitch.

 Telemark Inn (836-2703), RFD 2, Box 800, Bethel 04217. It is a challenge to describe this unusual retreat, set among birch trees 2.5 miles off the nearest back road, surrounded by national forest. The feel is that of a north woods sporting camp—with a herd of llamas and team of huskies. Steve Crone is an avid naturalist who knows where to find beaver dams and peregrine falcon nests in the wilderness accessible from his own property. Hiking, canoeing, and mountain biking are also offered, and winter brings exceptional cross-country skiing and the opportunity to try "skijoring" (skiing behind huskies). Meals are served family-style at the round cherrywood table, supported by tree trunks. Built in classic "Maine rustic" style as a millionaire's retreat, the inn has five rooms sharing two baths and accommodates 12 to 17 guests, with plenty of common space including a large semi-enclosed porch and a living room with a magnificent mineral-studded fireplace. $95 per couple, $75 single with breakfast; $25 for additional person in room. Also see *To Do— Llama Trekking*.

 Philbrook Farm Inn (603-466-3831), 881 North Road, Shelburne, NH 03581. Open year-round. Twenty miles west of Bethel, just over the New Hampshire line, this family-geared place is on the fringe of the Bethel area. The long, meandering farmhouse, owned by the same family since 1861, sits above a floodplain of the Androscoggin River with the Mahoosuc Range at its back. Each of the 18 guest rooms in the house is different, all wallpapered and most furnished with the kind of hand-me-downs that most innkeepers scour the hills for; second-floor rooms have private baths and third-floor rooms share. Common rooms meander on and on (there's a working Estey organ in the parlor) and the dining room is large and paneled; the family-style meals are as old-fashioned as the rest of the place (fish on Friday, ham and beans on Saturday night; BYOB). There are also four seasonal efficiency cottages (each different), plus two without kitchens. Hiking is everywhere and in winter there are miles of cross-country trail (untracked) as well as snowshoeing possiblities. $125–145 per couple MAP.

 The Victoria (824-8060; 1-888-774-1235), 32 Main Street, Bethel 04217. Open year-round. Several of the 15 units in this grand old house were still works in progress when we stayed here and the restaurant was not yet a reality in the fall of 1998. The decor is high Victorian: lace, pillows, tasseled lamps. Each room has a phone along with a TV and a wet bar hidden away in a massive armoire. A full breakfast is included in the rates, which vary with the season, from $90 up; inquire about the suite with Jacuzzi.

Sudbury Inn (824-2174; 1-800-395-7837), Lower Main Street, Bethel

04217. A nicely restored village inn built in 1873 to serve train travelers (the depot was just down the street). The 10 guest rooms and seven suites are all different shapes and decors, but all have private baths. The dining room is open to the public and the basement-level **Suds Pub** (see *Eating Out*) is a year-round evening gathering spot. April through November, $65–95; ski season, $80–160 double, includes breakfast.

The Briar Lea (824-4717), Route 2/26, Bethel 04217. Gary Brearley has turned this handsome old farmhouse into an attractive six-room inn (all with private baths) serving breakfast and dinner to the public. The living room with its polished floors and deep blue wallpaper is particularly attractive, as is the neighboring breakfast room. $73–93; pets $10 extra.

BED & BREAKFASTS

Chapman Inn (824-2657), P.O. Box 1027, Bethel 04217. A find for both families and singles. New owners Fred and Sandra Kolm bring years in the hospitality business and new energy to this comfortable rambling white wooden inn on the common. Floors have been refinished and rooms refurnished (Fred's hobby is making furniture). Six units now have private baths and four share; options range from two apartments with full kitchens to a dorm in the attached barn. Common space includes an attractive living room and, in the barn, a game room with pool table and two saunas. Handy to cross-country trails at the Bethel Inn, also to village shops and restaurants. Summer: $59–79 per couple for a room or apartment, $10 less for singles, $25 per person for the dorm, breakfast included. Winter: $75–105.

Holidae House (824-3400; 1-800-882-3306), P.O. Box 851, Bethel 04217. A gracious Main Street house (the first in Bethel to be electrified), built in the 1890s by a local lumber baron. All guest rooms are furnished in comfortable antiques and have cable TV, phones, and private baths; there's also a studio and a three-bedroom apartment. Air-conditioning and whirlpool bath available. Common space includes a family room with a woodstove. $45–89 double, includes breakfast. Efficiencies $65 and up off-season to $150 in-season for four in the apartment that sleeps 8–10 (each extra person is $25).

Douglass Place (824-2229), Bethel 04217. A handsome, 20-room home that once took in summer boarders. Barbara Douglass, who raised four daughters here, graciously welcomes guests. There are four guest rooms—one with a queen-sized bed and three with twin beds—a game room (with piano, pool table, and Ping-Pong table), a Jacuzzi, and a big homey kitchen where breakfast is served. Attractive living and dining rooms, grounds, a gazebo, and a large barn. $50–60 includes continental breakfast with homemade muffins and fresh fruit; special rates for singles and children.

The Ames Place (824-3170), 46 Broad Street, Bethel 04217. Sally and Dick Taylor's pleasant 1850s home on the common has two spacious guest rooms, one with an extra-long double four-poster and a single bed in a corner ell and the other with an extra-long antique spool bed, a working fireplace, and a sitting area. Neither room is fussy but both have pleasing details like hooked rugs, fresh flowers, and well-chosen country antiques. The barn, accessible through the country kitchen, is filled with antiques—an array of furniture, furnishings, clothing, and jewelry, all gathered from the Bethel area. Common rooms include a comfortable living room and a sunny breakfast room in which a full breakfast is served. The grounds stretch back 6 acres with perennial gardens and an orchard.

❦ **L'Auberge** (824-2774; 1-800-760-2774), Mill Hill Road, Bethel 04217. A former barn (belonging to a long-vanished mansion), which especially lends itself to groups because of its splendid living room but also works well as a low-key inn. The five guest rooms and two suites are furnished with antiques, and all have private baths. Hidden away just off the common, it's literally around the corner from village shops and restaurants. $80–110 per night for a double (the high end is for the Theatre Suite) with breakfast. Dinner is also available to guests. Innkeeper Tom Readout, former owner of legendary Bosebuck Mountain Camps on Azicohos Lake, is a Registered Maine Guide whose services fishermen might like to employ.

♿ **Crocker Pond House** (836-2027), 917 New Bethel Road, Bethel 04217. Off by itself on the Shelburne-Bethel Road (5 miles from downtown Bethel), facing south toward Evans Notch, this is a long, shingled, one-room-deep house designed and built by the architect and builder Stuart Crocker. It's a beauty, filled with light and grace, and very quiet. Hiking and snowshoeing or just peace are what it offers (no in-room phones or TVs). There is also swimming in the 50-acre pond. $85 per room includes a full breakfast in-season.

🐾♿ **The Norseman** (824-2002), HCR 61, Box 50, Route 2, Bethel 04217. An old farmstead with 9 light, pleasant guest rooms and 22 more units in the old barn. Guests in the house have access to the big, comfortable living room, with its fireplace made from local stones, and the dining room, with a similar hearth where breakfast is served. The motel units are spacious and handicapped accessible; amenities include laundry room and game room, a deck and walking trails. $49–128 includes continental breakfast (seasonal).

SKI LODGES AND CONDOMINIUMS

🐾 **Sunday River Ski Area** (824-3000; resort reservations, 1-800-543-2SKI), P.O. Box 450, Bethel 04217. Now offers more than 6,000 "slope-side beds." There are condominium complexes, ranging from studios to three-bedroom units. Each complex has access to an indoor pool, Jacuzzi, sauna, laundry, recreation room, and game room; **Cascades** and **Sunrise** offer large common rooms with fireplaces, and **Fall Line** has a restaurant. **Merrill Brook Village Condominiums** have fireplaces, and many have whirlpool tubs. **South Ridge** also offers fireplaces in each unit, which range from studios to three-bedrooms. The 68-room

Snow Cap Inn has an atrium with fieldstone fireplaces, exercise room, and outdoor Jacuzzi, and the **Snow Cap Ski Dorm** offers reasonably priced bunks. The 230-room **Summit Hotel and Conference Center** has both standard and kitchen-equipped units and a health club with tennis courts, pool, and conference facilities; it offers rooms and studios as well as one- and two-bedroom efficiency units. The 195-room **Jordan Grand Hotel** is off by itself but linked by ski trails as well as road, circled by the mountains of the Jordan Bowl; facilities include a health club, swimming pool, and restaurants. Hotel prices: $95–787. Condo units are based in winter on ski packages from $99 per night or $370 per person for 5 days.

🚲♿ **Sunday River Inn** (824-2410), RFD 3, Bethel 04217. Just down the road from the big ski resort but its antithesis: a homey, very personal place. Steve and Peggy Wight have been welcoming guests since 1971, catering to cross-country skiers (see *Cross-Country Skiing* for details about its well-maintained trail system) and to Elderhostel groups in other seasons. A large fireplace, a selection of books, and quiet games are in the living room, and an adjacent room can be used for small conferences. A game room, sauna, and wood-heated hot tub just outside the back door are also available to guests. The 18 rooms (most with shared baths) range from dorms to private rooms in the inn or adjacent chalet. $44–80 per person includes two meals and cross-country ski passes; children's rates. Inquire about cluster house sites in the Red House Farm Village across the road.

Pine-Sider Lodge (665-2226), 481 Gore Road, Bryant Pond 04219-6113. Bill and Ernestine Riley designed and built Pine-Sider for families and groups. The lodge is divided into four efficiency units (the Rileys live in one), sleeping four to eight people. $250–325 per week in summer; $75–150 per night in ski season.

CAMPGROUNDS

🚲 **Littlefield Beaches** (875-3290), RFD 1, Box 4300, Bryant Pond 04219. Open Memorial Day to October. A clean, quiet family campground surrounded by three connecting lakes. Full hook-ups, laundry room, miniature golf, game rooms, swimming. Daily and seasonal rates are available, reduced rates in June and September.

Riverside Campground (824-4224; 1-800-533-3607). Route 2, Bethel. Jeff and Patty Parsons, owners of Bethel Outdoor Adventures (see *To Do—Canoeing and Kayaking*) operate a campground with RV and tent sites on the Androscoggin River, within walking distance of downtown shops and restaurants.

Also see **Papoose Pond** under "Oxford Hills and Lewiston/Auburn."

See *To Do—Camping* for noncommercial campgrounds in the White Mountain National Forest.

SPECIAL LODGING

The Maine House and the Maine FarmHouse (1-800-646-8737), Lake Road, Bryant Pond. An unusual lodging option, two self-service guesthouses geared to groups. The Maine House, sited on Lake Christopher, offers eight rooms (sleeping up to 29) sharing 6½ baths and features a large recreation room with a floor-to-ceiling hearth, a living room with Franklin stove, a fully equipped kitchen, cable TV and VCR, a steam room, washer and dryer, and a dock with canoes. The recently restored FarmHouse (75 feet from the Maine House), which can sleep 24, offers similar amenities (but no steam room); it can be rented as one- and two-bedroom suites.

🐾 **Nanny's Doggy Day Care** (824-4225), Route 2, West Bethel. Sunday River Ski Area does not permit pets in its condos or condo hotels and few local lodging places do; this unusually plush kennel fills a need.

WHERE TO EAT

DINING OUT

Bethel Inn and Country Club (824-2175), Bethel common. An elegant, formal dining room with a hearth and large windows overlooking the golf course and hills, with a year-round veranda. All three meals are open to the public. The menu offers a choice of a dozen entrées, including broiled marinated duck breast, rack of lamb, and maple-walnut-scented venison medallions; $15–21 including salad, starches, and vegetable. Leave room for dessert.

Briar Lea Inn (824-4717), Route 2/26 East, Bethel. The inn's pleasant dining room serves a full-course dinner. You might begin with a lobster roll ($4.95) and dine on crispy roast duck ($14.95); nightly specials are reasonably priced.

Sudbury Inn (824-2174), Main Street, Bethel. Breakfast, lunch, and dinner. A pleasant dining room and sunporch in a 19th-century village inn. The dinner menu includes chicken in pastry and baked Maine haddock filled with spinach and shiitake mushrooms. Entrées $12–23.

🏵 **The River Restaurant** (743-7816), on Route 26 at Snow Falls, Norway. Open daily except Monday for lunch and dinner. Known for its Sunday brunch buffet, a local favorite serving dinner entrées like salmon fettuccine chardonnay and crab cake sauté ($6.95–14.95).

Sunday River Resort operates several "fine dining" restaurants: **Legends** (824-5858) at the Grand Summit Resort Hotel, **Rosetto's Ristorante** (824-5094) at the White Cap Base Lodge, **Walsh & Hill** (824-5067) at Fall Line Condominiums, and **Grand Avenue Grille** (824-5000) at the Jordan Grand.

EATING OUT

Breau's (824-3192), just west of Bethel on Route 2. Will deliver, and the pizza is good. Homemade clam "chowdah," chili, burgers, subs, and salads are on the menu, too. Open from 7 AM for full breakfast. **Breau's 2** is in Locke Mills.

Bottle & Bag (824-3673), just the other side of the bridge, east of downtown Bethel on Route 2. A local favorite for all three meals: hearty omelets, soups, and salads as well as a grill and sandwiches, pasta dinners from $4.25, freshly made breads, desserts, beers.

Briar Lea Inn (824-4717), Route 2 east of Bethel. Open for breakfast except Tuesdays. Pancakes are the specialty, along with omelets, Belgian waffles, and Moose Biscuit Benedict.

Cafe di Cocoa (824-JAVA), 125 Main Street, Bethel. Open daily for breakfast, lunch, and takeout. Cathy di Cocoa's cheerful eatery specializes in crunchy and vegetarian dishes. Fresh juices, gourmet coffees.

Great Grizzly Bar and Steakhouse and **Matterhorn Wood-Fired Pizza and Fresh Pasta** (824-6271), Sunday River Road.

The Iron Horse (824-0961) at Bethel Station, Bethel. Open 5–midnight daily. Vintage rail cars feature steaks and seafood.

Jacqui's Restaurant (875-2250), Route 26, Locke Mills. Handy to Mount Abram, open for lunch and dinner weekdays, breakfast too on weekends but closed for dinner on Sunday. Road food with a consciously 1950s decor.

Skidder's Deli (824-3696), Main Street, Bethel. Good lunch bet: Create your own sandwich, or choose from standbys like a Reuben or a steak bomb. A few tables, better as a picnic source.

Suds Pub, downstairs at the Sudbury Inn, Main Street, Bethel. Entertainment Thursday through Saturday, otherwise a friendly pub with 5 draft and 25 bottled beers; a reasonably priced pub menu. Open year-round.

The Sunday River Brewing Co. (824-4ALE), junction of Sunday River Road and Route 2, North Bethel. Open from 11:30 daily. Dining areas surround brewing kettles and tanks. Patrons can choose from a variety of house brews to wash down soups and salads, burgers, and pizza. Often has live entertainment evenings.

ENTERTAINMENT

Casablanca Cinema (824-8248), a four-screen cinema in the new Bethel Station development (Cross Street), shows first-run films.
Also see "Oxford Hills and Lewiston/Auburn."

SELECTIVE SHOPPING

For more shops in this region, also see "Oxford Hills and Lewiston/Auburn."
ANTIQUES
Playhouse Antiques (see the Ames Place under *Bed & Breakfasts*) specializes in antiques from Bethel-area homes.
ARTISANS
Bonnema Potters (824-2821), Lower Main Street, Bethel. Open daily 8:30–5:30. Distinctive stoneware, noteworthy for both design and color: lamps, garden furniture, dinnerware, and the like produced and sold in Bonnema's big barn. Seconds are available.
Christian Ridge Pottery. See "Oxford Hills and Lewiston/Auburn."

GEM SHOPS

As noted in *To Do—Rockhounding,* this area is rich in semiprecious gems and minerals. Jim Mann at **Mt. Mann** (824-3030), Main Street, Bethel, mines, cuts, and sets his own minerals and gems. **Mt. Mica Rarities** (875-3060), Route 26 in Locke Mills, is also a source of reasonably priced Maine gemstones. Also see *Rockhounding* in "Oxford Hills and Lewiston/Auburn."

SPECIAL SHOPS

Books 'n' Things (824-0275; 1-800-851-3219), 162 Main Street, Bethel. A full-service bookstore.

Maine Line Products (824-2522), Main Street, Bethel. Made-in-Maine products and souvenirs, among which the standout is the Maine Woodsman's Weatherstick. We have one tacked to our back porch, and it's consistently one step ahead of the weatherman—pointing up to predict fair weather and down for foul. A second store, an expanded version of this old landmark, recently opened in Locke Mills: even more pine furniture, toys, wind chimes, buckets, birdhouses, etc.

Groan and McGurn's Tourist Trap and Craft Outlet (836-3645), Route 2, West Bethel. Begun as a greenhouse—to which the owners' specially silk-screened T-shirts were added. Now there is so much that an ever-changing catalog is available.

Mountain Side Country Crafts (824-2518), Sunday River Road, Newry. Made-in-Maine gifts.

Philbrook Place, 162 Main Street, Bethel, includes an interesting assortment of enterprises including **The Toy Shop, True North Adventure** (sleeping bags, maps, footwear, clothing), **Wild Rose** (eclectic clothing), **Bib & Tucker** (fleecewear), and **Vince & Cupboard** (gourmet and kitchenware).

Ruthie's Clothing (824-2989), Main Street, Bethel. Great selection of women's clothing.

For more shops in this region, also see "Oxford Hills."

SPECIAL EVENTS

All events take place in Bethel or Sunday River.

January: **Bethel Winter Festival**—free cross-country and alpine ski lessons, dogsled and sleigh rides, skijoring, contests.

February: **Androscoggin River Tour & Race** at Carter's X-Country Ski Center, Bethel. Special events every weekend at ski areas.

March: **Sunday River Langlauf Races** at the Sunday River Ski Touring Center *(first Saturday)*—for all ages and abilities.

April: **Pole, Paddle and Paw Race**—a combination ski and canoe event at the end of ski season *(always the first Saturday in April)*.

May: **Bethel Antiques Weekend.**

June: **Rotary Club Auction.**

July: **Bethel Historical Society Fourth of July Celebration. Bethel Open Air Art Fair** *(first Saturday).* **Strawberry Festival,** Locke Mills Union Church (date depends on when strawberries are ready; announced in local papers). The **Annual Gem, Mineral, and Jewelry Show** *(second weekend)* at Telstar High School)—exhibits, demonstrations, and guided field trips to local quarries. **Mollyockett Day** *(third Saturday)* festivities include a road race, parade, bicycle obstacle course, fiddler contest, fireworks, to honor an 18th-century medicine woman who helped the first settlers. **Annual Maine State Triathlon Classic,** Bethel *(last Saturday).*

August: **Andover Old Home Days** *(first weekend).* **Sudbury Canada Days,** Bethel—children's parade, historical exhibits, old-time crafts demonstrations, bean supper, and variety show *(second weekend).*

September: **Bethel Harvest Fest** *(third weekend).*

October: **Blue Mountain Arts & Crafts Festival** at Sunday River Ski Area *(Columbus Day weekend).*

December: A series of Christmas fairs and festivals climax with a **Living Nativity** on the Bethel common the Sunday before Christmas. **New Year's Eve** on the Bethel common—music, storytelling, fireworks.

Rangeley Lakes Region

Rangeley Lake itself is only 9 miles long, but the "Rangeley Lakes Region" includes 112 lakes and ponds, among them vast sheets of water with names like Mooselookmeguntic, Cupsuptic, and Aziscohos.

Be sure to approach the town of Rangeley via Route 17 and pull out at the Height o' Land. Below you, four of the five major Rangeley lakes glisten blue-black, ringed by high mountains. Patterned only by sun and clouds, uninterrupted by any village or even a building, this green-blue sea of fir and hardwoods flows north and west to far horizons.

A spate of 1863 magazine and newspaper stories first publicized this area as "home of the largest brook trout in America" and two local women ensured its fishing fame through ensuing decades. In the 1880s Phillips native Cornelia "Fly Rod" Crosby pioneered the use of the light fly-rod and artificial lure and in 1897 became the first Registered Maine Guide; in 1924 Carrie Stevens, a local milliner, fashioned a streamer fly from gray feathers and caught a 6-pound, 13-ounce brook trout at Upper Dam. Stevens took second prize in *Field & Stream*'s annual competition, and the Gray Ghost remains one of the most popular fishing flies sold.

The Rangeley Lakes Historical Society is papered with photographs and filled with mementos of the 1880s through the 1930s, an era in which trainloads of fishermen and visitors arrived in Rangeley every day throughout the summer. Some stayed right there in wooden summer hotels, but most boarded steamers bound for the smaller hotels and numerous sporting camps on islands and outlying lakes.

In the 1940s and 1950s hotels closed and burned, and in the 1980s many sporting camps were sold off as individual "condominiums," but the resort has continued to evolve as a magnificent, low-key destination.

Landlocked salmon now augments trout in both local lakes and streams, and fly-fishing equipment and guides are easy to come by. Moose-watching, kayaking, and canoeing, as well as hiking and golf, are big draws and there are more shops and restaurants, more events, and entertainment here than at any time since the 1930s.

Still, Rangeley is a town of 1,200 year-round residents and "downtown" is a short string of single-story frame buildings along the lake. The village of Oquossoc, 7 miles west, is just a scattering of shops and restaurants on a peninsula between Rangeley and Mooselookmeguntic

485

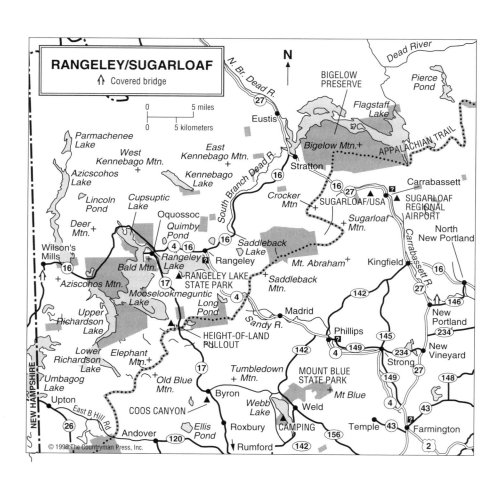

RANGELEY/SUGARLOAF

↟ Covered bridge

0 — 5 miles

0 — 5 kilometers

N

Dead River

N. Br. Dead R.

BIGELOW PRESERVE

Pierce Pond

27

Eustis

Flagstaff Lake

Parmachenee Lake

West Kennebago Mtn. +

East Kennebago Mtn. +

Bigelow Mtn.+

APPALACHIAN TRAIL

Azicscohos Lake

Kennebago Lake

16

Stratton

Carrabassett

Lincoln Pond

Cupsuptic Lake

Crocker Mtn

16

27

SUGARLOAF/USA

SUGARLOAF REGIONAL AIRPORT

South Branch Dead R.

Oquossoc

Quimby Pond

Sugarloaf Mtn.

North New Portland

Deer Mtn. +

4

16

16

Saddleback Lake

Carrabassett R.

Wilson's Mills

Bald Mtn.

Rangeley Lake

Rangeley

Mt. Abraham +

Kingfield

16

16

+ Aziscohos Mtn.

17

RANGELEY LAKE STATE PARK

Saddleback Mtn.

27

146

Mooselookmeguntic Lake

4

142

New Portland

Upper Richardson Lake

Long Pond

Madird

Sandy R.

Phillips

145

234

New Vineyard

Lower Richardson Lake

Elephant Mtn. +

HEIGHT-OF-LAND PULLOUT

142

4

149

Strong

234

27

148

Umbagog Lake

+ Old Blue Mtn.

17

Tumbledown + Mtn.

MOUNT BLUE STATE PARK

149

4

Upton

Byron

Webb Lake

Mt Blue

43

New Portland

26

East B Hill Rd.

COOS CANYON

Ellis Pond

Weld

Temple

43

Farmington

Andover

120

Roxbury

CAMPING

156

2

Rumford

142

43

© 1999 The Countryman Press, Inc.

NEW HAMPSHIRE

Lakes. Sure, the summer population zooms to 3,000, but both year-round homes and camps are hidden away by the water and much of that water is itself sequestered in woodland.

In recent years Rangeley has become much more of a year-round resort. Saddleback, Rangeley's 4,116-foot, 40-trail ski mountain, has attracted skiers for many decades and snowmobiling is now huge in Rangeley, taking advantage of one of Maine's most extensive and best-groomed trail networks along with the abundance of reasonably priced lodging in recently built second homes and all those old camps that, as "condos," have been winterized by their owners.

The most significant news about this western neck of the Maine woods is, however, that now it's being preserved. Within the past decade some 52 square miles have been protected through a cooperative venture involving state agencies and paper companies as well as the Rangeley Lakes Heritage Trust.

GUIDANCE

Rangeley Lakes Region Chamber of Commerce (864-5364; 1-800-MT-LAKES; www.rangeleymaine.com), P.O. Box 317, Rangeley 04970. Open year-round, Monday through Saturday 9–5. The chamber maintains a walk-in information center in the village, publishes a handy "Accommodations and Services" guide and an indispensable map, keeps track of vacancies, and makes reservations.

GETTING THERE

By air: **Mountain Air Service** (864-5307) will pick you up at the **Portland International Jetport** as well as at other New England airports; also serves remote ponds and camps.

By car: From points south, take the Maine Turnpike to exit 12 (Auburn), then take Route 4 to Rangeley. The slightly longer (roughly a half hour) but more scenic route is to turn off Route 4 onto Route 108 in Livermore, follow it to Rumford and then take Route 17 to Oquossoc (see *Scenic Drives*). From the Bethel area, take Route 17 to Rumford. From New Hampshire's White Mountains, take Route 16 East.

Note: In the introduction to "Western Mountains and Lakes Region" we suggest a driving tour of the region.

MEDICAL EMERGENCY

Rangeley Region Health Center (864-3303; after hours 1-800-398-6031), Dallas Hill Road, Rangeley.
Rangeley Ambulance (911).

TO SEE

MUSEUMS

In Rangeley

Rangeley Lakes Region Historical Society (864-3317), Main and Richardson Streets, Rangeley. Open late June through late September, Monday through Saturday 10–noon, until 2 on Monday, Wednesday, and Saturday. This is a great little museum occupying a former bank building in the middle of town, featuring photographs and local memorabilia from Rangeley's grand old hotels, sporting camps, trains, and lake steamers. Note the basement jail cell. Inquire about public programs on the third Wednesday in July and August, 7:30 PM.

✎ **Wilhelm Reich Museum** (864-3443), Dodge Pond Road, off Route 4/16 between Rangeley and Oquossoc. Open July and August, Tuesday through Sunday 1–5, Sundays in September 1–5; admission. The 175-acre property, Orgonon, is worth a visit for the view alone. Wilhelm Reich was a pioneer psychoanalyst (1897–1957) with controversial theories about sexual energy. A short documentary film profiles the man and his work. He is buried on a promontory overlooking a sweep of lake and mountains next to one of his many inventions, a "cloudbuster." The museum occupies a stone observatory that Reich helped design; it contains biographical exhibits, scientific equipment, paintings, and a library and study that remain as Reich left them. Inquire about summer Sunday workshops, natural-science programs for children, also Wednesday guided nature walks for all ages. The wooded trails on the property are open daily, 9–5.

✎ **Rangeley Lakes Region Logging Museum** (864-3939/5595), Route 16, one mile east of Rangeley Village. Open July and August weekends, 11–2 or by appointment. Founded by woodsman and sculptor Rodney Richard, featuring paintings about logging in the 1920s by local artist Alden Grant, also traditional wood carving and woods equipment. Inquire about Logging Museum Festival Days, usually the last weekend in July.

In Phillips

Also see *Scenic Drives*.

Phillips Historical Society (639-2881). Open August, Friday and Saturday 2–4, and by appointment June through October. The library and historical society are both in an 1820 house in the middle of the village. Exhibits include a significant Portland Glass collection and pictures of the town's own resort era (it had three hotels) and of the Sandy River Railroad (see *To Do—Railroad Excursion*).

Weld Historical Society (585-2586), Weld Village. Open July and August, Wednesday and Saturday 1–3, and by appointment. The 1842 house is filled with period furniture, clothing, and photographs. The original Town House (1845) houses farming, logging, and ice-cutting tools.

SCENIC DRIVES

Phillips/Weld/Byron/Oquossoc/Rangeley loop

Route 4 to Phillips and Route 142 to Weld. Follow Route 4 from Rangeley 12 miles south to Small's Falls (see *Green Space*) and on to Phillips, once the center of the Sandy River–Rangeley lakes "2-footer" line, now a quiet residential area. Plan to come the first or third Sunday of the month, or on foliage weekends, to ride the rails behind the steam train (see *To Do*). Stop at the Phillips Historical Society (see *To See*), and ask directions to **Daggett Rock**, a massive 50-foot-high boulder that the glaciers deposited several miles from town (off Route 142) having knocked it off Saddleback Mountain (the nearest place that matches it geologically). It's a pleasant mile's walk and has been the local sight-to-see in Phillips for more than a century. From Route 4 near Phillips, it's 12 miles on Route 142 to **Weld,** a quiet old lake village with several good hiking options, including **Tumbledown Mountain** and **Mount Blue.** You can also swim in **Lake Webb** at **Mount Blue State Park.**

Weld to Byron. From Weld, it's 12 miles to Byron. Drive 2 miles north on Route 142 to the State Beach sign; turn left, go 0.5 mile, and turn right on the first gravel road. This is Byron Road, well packed. Soon you follow the Swift River (stop and pan for gold) down into **Coos Canyon;** the picnic area and waterfalls are at the junction with Route 17 (see *To Do—Gold Panning* and *Swimming*). This is said to be the first place in America where gold was panned.

Route 17 to Oquossoc. From the picnic area, drive north on Route 17 for 10 miles to the **Height o' Land** (the pullout is on the other side of the road), from which the view is a spectacular spread of lakes and mountains; the view from the **Rangeley Lake Overlook** (northbound side of the road, a couple of miles farther) is the other direction.

From Oquossoc, it's a beautiful drive west along the lakes on Route 16 to Errol. Routhly 20 miles west of Rangeley, be sure to detour 0.3 mile to see the **Bennett Covered Bridge** (1898–99), spanning the Magalloway River in Wilsons Mills; follow signs to the Aziscohos Valley Camping Area.

Whether you are coming from Bethel or following the above loop, you pick up Route 17 in just beyond the **Mexico Chicken Coop Restaurant** (364-2710) on Route 2. Despite its exterior, this is a good way stop. The specialties are Italian, chicken, a huge salad bar, and fresh-baked pastries.

TO DO

AIRPLANE RIDES
Mountain Air Service (864-5307) offers 15-minute scenic flights, longer fire patrol flights, and flight instruction.

BIKING
Rangeley Mountain Bike Touring Co. (864-5799) offers a range of rental bikes and local touring maps. Inquire about the 12.5-mile Railroad Loop Trail.

BOAT RENTALS
Check with the chamber of commerce (see *Guidance*) about the more than a dozen places in town that rent motorboats, canoes, sailboats, and waverunners. **River's Edge Sports** (864-5582) in Oquossoc rents canoes and kayaks and offers shuttle service. **Oquossoc Marine** (864-5477) offers the largest choice of motorboats. Be sure to get out on a lake one way or another.

CAMPING
Wilderness camping is a part of what this area is about. The chamber of commerce (see *Guidance*) lists more than a dozen source of information about

KIM GRANT

Rangeley Lake

remote campsites. The Stephen Phillips Preserve (864-2003), Oquossoc, maintains 42 campsites with fireplaces, picnic tables, and toilet facilities; $10 per site per couple, $5 per teenager or extra person, $2 per child. Also see **Rangeley Lake State Park** under Green Space. **Aziscohos Valley Camping Area** (486-3271) in Wilsons Mills also offers easy boat access to Aziscohos Lake and the Magalloway River.

CANOEING

Rangeley is the departure point for an 8-mile paddle to Oquossoc. On Lake Mooselookmeguntic, a 12-mile paddle south to Upper Dam is popular, and many people portage around the dam and paddle another 8 miles down Upper Richardson Lake and through the Narrows to South Arm (also see *Camping*). Kayaks can be rented from **Rangeley Mountain Bike Touring** (see *Biking*) and **River's Edge Sports** (see *Fishing*); also see *Boat Rentals.*

If you don't know how to canoe, sign on with **Rich Gacki** (864-5136) for a guided early-morning paddle down the Kennebago River. Chances are you will see deer, ospreys, beavers, otters, and mink as well as moose (see *Moose-Watching*).

FISHING

As noted in the "Rangeley Lakes Region" introduction, it's fishing that put Rangeley on the map. Both brook trout and landlocked salmon remain plentiful, and while early spring and September remain the big fishing seasons, summer months now also lure many fishermen. With fish-finders and down-riggers those who use "spinning" rods and reels can now locate and catch both salmon and trout at the depths of 50 feet to which they drop in warm-weather months. Rangeley has, however, always been best known as a fly-fishing mecca, and both local sporting stores, **River's Edge Sports** (864-5582), Route 4 in Oquossoc, and the **Rangeley Region Sport Shop** (864-5615), Main Street, Rangeley, specialize in fly-tying equipment; they are also sources of advice on where to fish and with whom (a list of local guides is posted). Request a list of members of the **Rangeley Region Guides & Sportsmen's Association,** P.O. Box 244, Rangeley 04970. The group traces its origins to 1896. The current chamber of commerce guide also lists local Maine guides as well as camps that specialize in boats, equipment, and guides. Guiding service averages $150 per half day, $250 for a full day. Nonresident fishing licenses, available from sporting stores, are $10 per day, $35 for 7 days.

FEE FISHING

Dunham's Pure Water Hatchery & Fee Fishing Pond (639-2815), Mount Blue Road, off Route 4 in Avon, between Phillips and Strong. Open year-round, 7–7. A great spot for kids and nonfishermen to try their hand at catching a rainbow and brook trout or Atlantic salmon. You never miss. Equipment supplied. Fish are hatched in 23 pools housed in Bruce Dunham's barn and two haylofts. Dunham also sells seafood and a variety of fish.

GOLD PANNING

Coos Canyon, on Route 17, 23 miles south of Oquossoc (see *Scenic Drives*), is said to be the first place in America that gold was panned. The Swift River churns through a beautiful natural gorge and there are picnic tables as well as gold-panning lessons and equipment ($5) at the Coos Canyon Campground Store (364-3880).

GOLF

Mingo Springs Golf Course (864-5021), Proctor Road (off Route 4), Rangeley. A historic (since 1925), par-70, 18-hole course with lake views; instruction, carts, and club rentals.

Mini Golf Course (864-5799), 53 Main Street, Rangeley. Middle of the village: nine holes.

HIKING

The Rangeley regional map published by the chamber of commerce (see *Guidance*) outlines more than a dozen well-used hiking paths, including a portion of the Appalachian Trail that passes over **Saddleback Mountain.** The longest hike is up **Spotted Mountain** (4½ miles to the top), and the most popular is the trail to the summit of **Bald Mountain** (3 miles round-trip); both yield sweeping views of lakes, woods, and more mountains. Other favorites are Bemis Stream Trail up **Elephant Mountain** (6 hours round-trip) and the mile walk in to **Angels Falls**—which is roughly 4 miles off Route 17; be sure to use a current trail guide.

In Weld, the tried-and-true trails are **Mount Blue** (3¼ miles), and **Tumbledown Mountain** (a particularly varied climb with a high altitude).

HORSEBACK RIDING

✍ **Horseback Riding at Bald Mountain Camps** (864-3671). Trail rides are $40 per hour. Riding lessons and children's riding camp ($20 per day) also available.

MOOSE-WATCHING

✍ **Rich Gacki** (864-5136) in Oquossoc offers guided canoe trips departing the Rangeley Inn most days at 5 AM. This is a 3-hour expedition; reservations are required by 6 PM the previous day. We did see a moose, but that turned out to be just a small part of the experience on our early-morning paddle with Gacki. Breakfast at the Rangeley Inn is included in the price of the tour.

Route 16 north from Rangley to Stratton is a good bet for seeing moose at dusk; your chances improve if you drive all the way to dinner at the Porter House in Eustis (see *Dining Out* in "Sugarloaf and the Carrabassett Valley").

RAILROAD EXCURSION

✍ **Sandy River–Rangeley Lakes Railroad** (778-3621). Runs May through October on the first and third Sundays of each month, and continuously through Phillips Old Home Days in late August and Fall Foliage Days in late September and early October. $3 per adult, $2 per child ages 6–12. From 1873 until 1935, this narrow-gauge line spawned resort and lumbering communities along its 115-mile length. Begun as seven distinct lines, it was eventually acquired by the Maine Central, which built shops and a large roundhouse in Phillips. Over the past dozen years, volunteers have produced a replica of the old steam locomotive and the roundhouse, and others have helped lay a mile of track so that you can rattle along in an 1884 car just far enough to get a sense of getting around Franklin County "back when." A depot houses railroad memorabilia, and rolling stock now include five box cars and two cabooses.

SWIMMING

Rangeley Lake State Park offers a pleasant swimming area and scattered picnic sites (see *Green Space*). Day-use fee; free under age 12. There is also a town beach with lifeguards and a playground at Lakeside Park in the village of Rangeley. Almost all lodging places offer water access.

Mount Blue State Park also has a nice swimming area (see *Green Space*).

Birches Beach on Lake Mooselookmeguntic. Off Route 17 south from Oquossoc.

Coos Canyon, Route 17, Byron. See *Scenic Drives* and *Gold Panning*. It's terrifying to watch kids jump from the cliffs and bridge here, but there are several inviting pools among the smooth rocks and cascades.

WINTER SPORTS

SKIING

✍ **Saddleback Mountain** (864-5671; snow phone, 864-3380), Box 490, Rangeley 04970. This is a very big downhill ski area with a very small, fiercely loyal following. Saddleback itself, 4,116 feet high and webbed with 40 trails serviced by just two double chairs and three T-bars, forms the centerpiece in a semicircle of mountains rising above a small lake. Top-to-bottom snowmaking augments more than 200 inches of annual snowfall to keep the slopes open from November into April. Twelve thousand acres—comprising most of this natural bowl—are now under Saddleback ownership, and a major four-season resort is planned. Trails and slopes include glade skiing, a 2½-mile beginner trail, and an above-treeline snowfield in spring. The vertical drop is 2,000 feet. Most trails are a shade narrower and twistier than today's average, but most intermediate runs such as Haymaker and White Stallion are memorable cruising lanes. Experts will find plenty of challenge on Bronco Buster, Powderkeg, and the Nightmare Glades terrain, and there is plenty of backwoods skiing. Facilities include a cafeteria, lounge, ski school, shop, rentals, nursery, and mountain warming hut. $42 per adults weekends and holidays ($30 juniors), $28 midweek.

Nordic Touring Center at Saddleback (864-5671) claims to be the highest-altitude (2,400 feet) cross-country touring center in Maine. A 25 km network meanders around Saddleback Lake, but our favorite, higher, backcountry trails were damaged in an ice storm and are currently off-limits. A 26 km town-maintained trail network, tracked both for skating and touring, begins on Route 4 west of the village. More adventurous skiers will find no shortage of abandoned logging roads in the surrounding woods.

Mount Blue State Park (585-2347) also offers extensive cross-country skiing trails.

SNOWMOBILING

Rangeley's snowmobile club maintains 150 miles of well-marked trails connecting with systems throughout Maine and Canada. Snowmobile rentals are available from **Dockside Sports Center** (864-2424; 1-800-941-2424), **Oquossoc Marine** (864-5477), **Rev-It-Up Sport Shop** (864-2453), and **River's Edge Sports** (864-5582).

GREEN SPACE

Lakeside Park in the middle of the village of Rangeley is a great spot with picnic tables, grills, a playground, and a boat launch.

Rangeley Lake State Park (864-3858) covers 691 acres, including more than a mile of shoreline on the southern rim of Rangeley Lake between Routes 17 and 4. Open May 15 to early October. There are 40 scattered picnic sites, a pleasant swimming area, a boat launch, and a children's play area; $2 per person.

Mount Blue State Park (585-2347), Weld (off Route 156). Open May 30 to October 15. The 6,000-acre park includes Mount Blue itself, towering 3,187 feet above the valley floor, and a beachside tenting area (136 sites) on Lake Webb. The lake is 3 miles wide and 6 miles long, good for catching black bass, white perch, pickerel, trout, and salmon. Boats may be rented from the ranger, and there is a recreation hall complete with fireplace. The view from the Center Hill area looks like the opening of a Paramount picture. Despite its beauty and the outstanding hiking, this is one of the few state camping facilities that rarely fills up. $1.50 per person admission.

Small's Falls, Route 4 (12 miles south of Rangeley). The Sandy River drops abruptly through a small gorge, which you can climb behind railings. A popular picnic spot. You can follow the trail to the **Chandlers Mill Stream Falls,** equally spectacular.

Hunter Cove Wildlife Sanctuary, off Route 4/16, 2.5 miles west of Rangeley Village (across from Dodge Pond). A 95-acre Maine Audubon Society preserve with color-coded trails leading to the cove (boat launch), good for old and small legs, rich in bird life and bugs. Bring insect repellent, waterproof footwear, and a picnic (tables are near the parking lot and benches are scattered throughout).

Rangeley Lakes Heritage Trust (864-7311), Route 4/16, Oquossoc, open weekdays 9–4:30, Sunday 9–1. Since the trust's founding in 1991, over 10,000 acres have been preserved, including 20 miles of lake and river frontage, 10 islands, and a 2,443-foot mountain. Request the map/guide and inquire about the guided hikes and nature study programs offered.

The Stephen Phillips Memorial Preserve Trust (864-2003), part of the RLHT (see above) has preserved many miles of shore on Mooselookmeguntic and maintains a number of campsites (see *Camping*).

Also see *Lodging—Campgrounds*.

LODGING

INNS AND LODGES

Rangeley Inn and Motor Lodge (864-3341; 1-800-MOMENTS), Rangeley 04970. Open year-round. A blue-shingled, three-story landmark, partly an annex to a vanished grand hotel that stood across the road, overlooking the lake; the classic old hotel lobby dates from 1907. David and Rebecca Schinas are the new owners of this landmark, which marks the physical and social heart of the village. The 52 guest rooms are divided between the main building (12 with claw-foot tubs, some with water views, all crisply decorated and comfortably furnished) and 15 nicely decorated motel units, some with kitchenettes, whirlpool baths, and woodstoves, overlooking Haley Pond. Occasionally patronized by bus groups, so check if you want to avoid them. $60–119 double EP. All meals and special packages available.

Kawanhee Inn (585-2000), Weld 04285. (In winter contact Sturgis Butler and Marti Strunk, 778-3809 evenings; 7 High St., Farmington 04938.) Dining room open mid-June through Labor Day; lodging from May to October 15; cottages available from mid-May to mid-October. A traditional Maine lodge set atop a slope overlooking Lake Webb. The 11 guest rooms in the inn have recently been reduced to 9 larger, more comfortable rooms with added insulation (5 with private, 4 with shared baths). Request a lake view. The 12 one- and two-bedroom cabins are exceptional, each with a screened porch, fireplace, kitchen, and bath. All but Pine Lodge (really a house hidden away in the pines down the road from the inn) have lake views, and the latter compensates with its skylights, privacy, added amenities, and the fact that it is set up to accommodate pets. Meals are served in the large pine dining room and on the screened veranda overlooking the water (see *Dining Out*) and the open-beamed, pine-paneled living room has a massive central fireplace, a pool table, and numerous corners in which to read and talk. There is a private beach and dock; canoes are available, and the local hiking is outstanding. Be sure to get back in time to hear Sturgis play taps. Rooms $75–125 double; cabins $500–700 per week; less in shoulder seasons. Room rates include continental breakfast.

Bald Mountain Camps (864-3671; 1-888-392-0072), P.O. Box 332, Oquossoc 04964. Open mid-May to mid-September. This is the surviving part of a complex that dates from 1897. Nicely old-fashioned, with fireplaces in 15 cabins and a log-style dining room, a safe sand beach, tennis courts, horseback riding, and lawn games. Right on Mooselookmeguntic Lake and exuding the kind of hospitality found only under long-term ownership. Stephen Philbrick is your host. $110 per adult meals included; less for children and during May and June; some pets accepted.

Country Club Inn (864-3831), P.O. Box 680, Rangeley 04970. Open year-round except April and November. Surrounded by an 18-hole golf course and overlooking the lake, this is a golfer's dream. Built by a millionaire sportsman in the late 1920s, this place has the feel of a private club. Massive stone fireplaces face each other across a gracious living room walled in knotty pine and stocked with books and puzzles. You are drawn to the view of lakes and mountains from the deck, from the pub, and from tables in the dining room. Steve and Margie Jamison offer 20 rooms with picture windows and private baths. In winter you can cross-country ski from the door, and in summer there's an outdoor pool. $99 per couple B&B, $144 MAP; less in winter.

BED & BREAKFASTS

Lake Webb House (585-2479), P.O. Box 127, Route 142, Weld 04285. Open year-round. A pleasant, welcoming old farmhouse with a big porch, near the lake and village. Cheryl England makes the quilts that grace the beds in her three guest rooms (which share two baths) and also sells them. $45–55 double ($35 single!) includes a full breakfast. Cheryl also operates the Morning Glory Bake Shop (behind the house), good for breads, moose cookies, and whoopie pies.

Piper Brook Bed & Breakfast (864-3469), P.O. Box 139, Rangeley 04970. Just 3 miles from town, up and up a fairly rough road. Still under construction at this writing, but similar, we are told, to Martha Bekeny's previous B&B by this name. It's in almost exactly the same spot so we can vouch for the expansive view and country-elegant feel to the place, which offers large guest rooms, $85 for one with a king-sized bed, whirlpool, and view, from $65 for the other rooms. Don't be discouraged by the road up.

Oquossoc's Own (864-5584), P.O. Box 27, Oquossoc 04964. Open year-round. A homey B&B with on the snowmobile trail: 14 beds in five guest rooms sharing two baths. Guests attest to Joanne Koob's culinary skills (dinners are possible). $60 double or $30 per person includes a full breakfast.

SPORTING CAMPS

Geared to serious fishermen in May, June, and September, and to families in July and August, these are true destination resorts, but don't expect organized activities.

☀ **Bosebuck Mountain Camps** (446-2825; 474-5903 in winter), Wilsons Mills 03579. Open May through November. Accessible by boat or by a 14-mile private gravel road, the camps are sited at the remote end of Aziscohos Lake. We have not visited since ownership changed in 1998. The lodge houses a dining room overlooking the water and a sitting room filled with books; all heat is from woodstoves, and the nine cabins have electric lights, flush toilets, and showers, powered by a generator that runs 8 hours a day. Three full meals are included in the rate: $99 per person per night. Dogs welcome. Family rates in July and August ($56 per person) when fishing eases off. Fishing package rate available in July.

✎& **Grant's Kennebago Camps** (864-3608; 282-5264 in winter; 1-800-633-4815), P.O. Box 786, Rangeley 04970. Open after ice breaks up and through September. A serious fly-angler's haven located 9 miles up a private dirt road on Kennebago Lake. Large, excellent meals are served in the comfortable dining room with terrific lake views. Cabins are rustic, knotty pine with woodstoves and a screened-in front porch overlooking the water. Each has a dock and boat exclusively for your use during your stay. $105 per adult (3 days or more), $30 per child under 12, all meals included.

☀✎ **Lakewood Camps** (summer, 243-2959; winter, 392-1581), Middledam–Richardson Lake, Andover 04216. Open after ice breaks up through September. The specialty is landlocked salmon and trout; fly-fishing in 5 miles of the Rapid River. Twelve truly remote cabins; meals feature fresh-baked breads, cakes, and pies. Access is from Andover. This is very much the same place described in Louise Dickinson Rich's *We Took to the Woods*. $92 per person (2-day minimum), double occupancy includes three full meals; $40 per child under 12, $15 under age 5, pets $15. Tax and gratuity not included.

Also see Tim Pond Wilderness Camps in "Sugarloaf and the Carrabassett Valley."

COTTAGES AND CONDOS

✎ Rangeley still has an unusual number of traditional, family-geared "camps": cottages that were either originally built as part of a commercial complex and are now privately owned (hence "condos") or that have been built more recently as second homes. Many are now available year-round. Check with the chamber of commerce (see *Guidance*) for listings and local rental agents.

Clearwater Sporting Camps (864-5424), Oquossoc 04964. Open from ice-out through November. Five cottages, all different, are scattered on private waterfront ledges along Mooselookmeguntic Lake. Michael and Tina Warren also offer boat rentals, a boat launch, swimming, and guide service, specializing in fly-fishing. Camps $90 per day double; $580 per week.

Hunter Cove (864-3383), Mingo Loop Road, Rangeley 04970. Open year-round. Eight cottages on Rangeley Lake set on 6 wooded acres, each accommodating 2–6 people. Recently renovated; a half mile to golf, Saddleback, and the village. Daily $110–160, weekly $625–875.

Mooselookmeguntic House (864-2962), Haines Landing, Oquossoc 04964. The grand old hotel by this name is gone, but the eight log cabins are well maintained and occupy a great site with a beach and marina. Many of the one- and two-bedroom cabins are on the water and have fireplaces or woodstoves. $375–625 per week.

North Camps (864-2247), P.O. Box 341, Oquossoc 04964 (write to E. B. Gibson). Open spring through hunting season. Twelve cottages on Rangeley Lake among birches on a spacious lawn. Cottages have fireplaces or woodstoves, screened porches, and access to the beach, tennis, sailboats, fishing boats, and canoes. During July and August, rentals are available by the week only. Nightly rates and rates that include all three meals are available in spring and fall. $325–575 weekly.

The Terraces Housekeeping and Overnight Cottages (864-3771). Open ice-out through Columbus Day weekend. Comfortable cottages with large decks terraced on a step embankment on Rangeley Lake. $375–595 per week.

Saddleback Ski and Summer Lake Preserve (864-5671), Box 490, Rangeley 04970. There are two condo complexes at the ski resort—most units are exceptionally luxurious, with views over the lake. Some two dozen are usually available for rent. From three to five bedrooms, many with hot tubs, cable TV; all have access to the clubhouse with its game room. $285–495 in winter but inquire about 3-day ski/stay packages; much less in summer.

CAMPGROUNDS

For information and reservations in both the state parks described below, call 287-3821.

Rangeley Lake State Park (864-3858), between Routes 17 and 4, at the southern rim of Rangeley Lake. Some 50 campsites are well spaced among fir and spruce trees; facilities include a beach and boat launch, picnic sites, and a children's play area. $16 for nonresidents. There are also a number of private campgrounds and wilderness sites accessible only by boat; inquire at the chamber of commerce (see *Guidance*).

Mount Blue State Park (585-2347), Weld. Campsites tend to get filled up later than those in better-known parks (see *Green Space*).

WHERE TO EAT

DINING OUT

Also see restaurants described in "Sugarloaf and the Carrabassett Valley." **Porter House** in Eustis is a popular dining destination for Rangeley visitors.

The Gingerbread House (864-3602), Route 4/16 Oquossoc. Open for breakfast, lunch (except Sunday), and dinner. An ice cream parlor since the turn of the century, preserved and expanded by Ed Kfoury, a former IBM executive who helped found the Rangeley Lakes Heritage Trust. The old marble soda fountain is here, and the footprint of the old building has been preserved, but there's a hearth now and a wing and deck facing the pine trees in back. Lunch might be a crab cake sandwich and you can still just come for ice cream (try chocolate truffle) but at dinner time the tables are draped in linen and the menu ranges from spicy peanut noodles ($8.95) and pasta of the day ($13.95) to grilled duck breast ($19.95) and filet mignon with a béarnaise sauce ($23.95). Sunday-night specials range from steamers ($6.95) and BBQ ribs ($12.95) to black Angus sirloin ($19.95).

Rangeley Inn (864-3341), Main Street, Rangeley. Closed mid-April to late May; otherwise open for breakfast and dinner daily. An attractive, old-fashioned hotel dining room with a high, tin ceiling and a reputation for fine dining. You might want to inquire if chef co-owner Rebecca Schinas is in the kitchen (she was the night we dined) because the fare tends to be particularly good. Choices might range from pasta San Lorenzo ($12.95) to frenched rack of lamb ($21.95). All dinners include soup or salad.

Kawanhee Inn (585-2000), Weld. Open for dining nightly, mid-June to September. One of Maine's most picturesque, traditional-style lodges is the setting for candlelight meals in the open-beamed dining room or screened porch overlooking Lake Webb. Fresh flowers garnish the tables, and meals are thoughtfully prepared. The chef is recognized as one of the best around, making all baked goods from scratch; the menu might include baked chicken breast stuffed with onion, feta, and spinach, served with creamy Parmesan sauce ($13.95), a Caesar salad with grilled shrimp ($10.95), a selection of pastas (from $10.95), and poached salmon with a lobster Boursin sauce ($15.95). Entrées include salad, vegetables, and warm breads. Maine lobster available every night.

Country Club Inn (864-3831), Rangeley. Open every evening summer and fall, weekends in winter by reservation only. The inn sits on a rise above Rangeley Lake, and the dining room windows maximize the view. The menu might include veal sautéed with Swiss cheese, tomatoes, and parsley, or baked jumbo shrimp with crab stuffing. Entrées run $10.95–16.50.

Bald Mountain Camps (864-3671), Bald Mountain Road, Oquossoc. Dinner by reservation is available to nonguests in this classic sporting-camp dining room by the lake. The set menu varies with the night. Friday it's steamed lobster or baby back ribs or grilled chicken served with corn fries and "Maine Guide" desserts. BYOB.

EATING OUT

People's Choice Restaurant (864-5220), Main Street, Rangeley. Open daily 6 AM–9 PM. Lunch choices include fresh-dough pizza, and the dinner specialty is a barbecue platter with pork chops, a half chicken, and a slab of ribs. The lounge features weekend bands and the largest dance floor around (everyone comes).

Tavern Dining at the Rangeley Inn (864-3341), 51 Main Street. Every town should have a friendly heart like this, a pub with reasonably priced pub grub like steakburgers (with bacon and cheese.)

Our Place Cafe (864-5844), Main Street and Richardson Avenue, Rangeley. Open for breakfast and lunch; Sunday for breakfast only. Ownership changed in 1998 but this is still the favorite place in town for breakfast; great omelets.

Red Onion (864-5022), Main Street, Rangeley. Open daily for lunch and dinner. A friendly Italian-American dining place with a sunroom and *Biergarten;* fresh-dough pizzas and daily specials.

Frog Rock Cafe (864-3351), Main Street, Rangeley. Open for lunch and dinner. Alias Road Kill Cafe, still the same owners and menu with choices like the Skunk Breath Burger and Boggy Doggy; also a lake view from the back deck. We hope the food itself has improved since we tried it.

The Four Seasons Cafe (864-5291), Oquossoc. Don't be put off by the Budweiser sign. Inside there is a bar, along with a woodstove, tables with checked green cloths, and a big menu with Mexican dishes, salads, good soups, sandwiches, and vegetarian specials; a great place for a reasonably priced dinner of maybe mussels ($5.95) and prime rib (two dinners on Thursday for $18.95). Fresh-dough pizzas are also a specialty and Sunday brunch features omelet du jour with homefries ($4.25).

Fineally's (864-2955), Saddleback Mountain Road, Rangeley. Open Tuesday through Sunday year-round for dinner. Best in summer when a screened deck is the place to watch the sun set over the mountains. Mexican specialties and standard fare like veal Marsala and linguine with meatballs.

Pine Tree Frosty (864-5894), middle of Main Street. Try the lobster roll packed full of meat; all this and Gifford's ice cream.

Lakeside Convenience (864-5818), Main Street, Rangeley. Great fried chicken, usually in at 9 AM and sold out by 2 PM.

ENTERTAINMENT

✒ **Lakeside Youth Theater** (864-5000), Main Street, Rangeley. A recently renovated landmark that offers first-run films, matinees on rainy days when the flag is hung out, art films on Thursday nights. Off-season shows on weekends.

People's Choice Restaurant (864-5220), Main Street, Rangeley. The lounge section is separate from the dining part of this popular restaurant, and on weekends year-round its large dance floor, which is inlaid with carved fish, is jammed with couples dancing to live bands. This is the one place that summer people and locals, loggers, skiers, and snowmobilers really mix.

Rangeley Friends of the Performing Arts sponsors a July and August series of performances by top entertainers and musicians at local churches, lodges, and the high school. For the current schedule check with the chamber of commerce (see *Guidance*).

SELECTIVE SHOPPING

Alpine Shop (864-3741), Main Street, Rangeley. Open year-round, daily. The town's premier clothing store, name-brand sportswear, and Maine gifts. Check out its bargain basement across the street (down a ways).

Blueberry Hill Farm (864-5647), Dallas Hill Road, off Route 4 east of Rangeley. Stephanie and Don Palmer offer two large rooms of antiques, featuring fine quilts, baskets, furniture, and glass, also crafts and used books, a Wildlife Studio and antique fly-rods, reels, and Don Palmer's own hand-carved decoys.

Books, Lines, and Thinkers (864-4355), Route 4 (above the video store), Rangeley. Open year-round, hours vary off-season. Wess Conally offers a good selection of art as well as books and music, also antiques.

First Farm (864-5539), Gull Pond Road, Rangeley. Open seasonally, Monday, Tuesday, Friday, Saturday 10–5. Roughly a mile north of town, marked from Route 16. Kit and Linda Casper's farm and farm shop have become a Maine legend.

Frost Country (864-3309), Route 4 at South Shore Drive. Joan Frost's own painted furniture is worth a stop, and the quality of other crafted items—quilts, paintings, wooden loons, jewelry—is also high.

✒ **The Mad Whittler** (864-5595), Main Street, Rangeley. Rodney Richard sculpts animals and folk characters using a chain saw and jackknife, and his son Rodney Richards Jr. executes his own whimsical creations with similar tools; chances are one or the other will be there working away. Look for the "open" flag.

❧ **The Nature Store** (864-2771), Pond Street. In the middle of town but with windows on Haley Pond, an attractive store featuring ecological gifts, toys, and books.

Yarn Barn (864-5917), Bald Mountain Road, Oquossoc. Open Monday through Saturday 10–5. A wide selection of yarns, cross-stitch kits, canvas, floss, weaving supplies, fleece for spinning, books, classes.

(Also see River's Edge and Rangeley Region Sport Shop under *Fishing*.)

SPECIAL EVENTS

All events are in Rangeley unless otherwise noted.

January: **Rangeley Snodeo**—cross-country ski races.

March: **Annual Sled Dog Race. Bronco Buster Ski Challenge** at Saddleback.

July: **Independence Day** parade and fireworks; **Old-Time Fiddlers Contest;** and **Logging Museum Festival Days. Heritage Day Fair** in Weld Village (*final Saturday*).

August: **Sidewalk Art Festival; Annual Blueberry Festival;** and **Phillips Old Home Days** (*third week*).

October: **Apple Festival** (*first Saturday*).

November: **Holly Fair.**

December: **Christmas Fair,** at the Episcopal church; and **Walk to Bethlehem Pageant,** Main Street, Rangeley. **Giving Tree Celebration.**

Sugarloaf and the Carrabassett Valley

The second-highest mountain in the state, Sugarloaf/USA faces another 4,000-footer across the Carrabassett Valley—a narrow defile that accommodates a 17-mile-long town.

Carrabassett Valley is a most unusual town. In 1972, when it was created from Crockertown and Jerusalem townships, voters numbered 32. The school and post office are still down in Kingfield, south of the valley; the nearest drugstore, chain supermarket, and hospital are still in Farmington, 36 miles away. There are just around 325 full-time residents (males outnumber females and the average age is 34), but there are now more than 5,000 "beds." Instead of "uptown" and "downtown," people say "on-mountain" and "off-mountain."

On-mountain, at the top of Sugarloaf's access road, stands one of New England's largest self-contained ski villages: a dozen shops and more than a dozen restaurants, a seven-story brick hotel, and a church. A chairlift hoists skiers up to the base lodge from lower parking lots and from hundreds of condominiums clustered around the Sugarloaf Inn. More condominiums are scattered farther down the slope, all served by a chairlift. From all places you can also ski down to the Carrabassett Valley Ski Touring Center, Maine's largest cross-country trail network.

More than 800 condominiums are scattered among firs and birches. To fill them in summer, Sugarloaf has built an outstanding 18-hole golf course, maintains one of the country's top-rated golf schools, fosters a lively special events program, promotes rafting, mountain biking, and hiking, and even seriously attempts to eliminate blackflies.

Spring through fall the focus also shifts off-mountain to the backwoods hiking and fishing north of the valley. Just beyond the village of Stratton, Route 27 crosses a corner of Flagstaff Lake and continues through Cathedral Pines, an impressive sight and a good place to picnic. The 30,000-acre Bigelow Preserve, which embraces the lake and great swatches of this area, offers swimming, fishing, and camping. Eustis, a small outpost on the lake, caters to sportsmen and serves as a P.O. box for sporting camps squirreled away in the surrounding woodland.

Kingfield, at the southern entrance to the Carrabassett Valley, was founded in 1816. This stately town has long been a woodworking center

502

and produced the first bobbins for America's first knitting mill; for some time it also supplied most of the country's yo-yo blanks. It is, however, best known as the one-time home of the Stanley twins, inventors of the steamer automobile and the dry-plate coating machine for modern photography. The Stanley Museum includes fascinating photos of rural Maine in the 1890s by Chansonetta, sister of the two inventors. Kingfield continues to produce wood products and also offers some outstanding lodging and dining.

The Carrabassett River doesn't stop at Kingfield. Follow it south as it wanders west off Route 27 at New Portland, then a short way along Route 146, to see the striking, vintage 1841 Wire Bridge. Continue on Route 146 and then west on Route 16 if you are heading for The Forks and the North Woods; to reach the coast, take Route 27 south through Farmington, a gracious old college town with several good restaurants and an unsual opera museum.

GUIDANCE

Sugarloaf Area Chamber of Commerce (235-2100), RR 1, Box 2151, Carrabassett Valley 04947. The chamber is well stocked with brochures on the area as well as statewide information. It also offers an areawide, year-round reservation service (235-2500; 1-800-THE-AREA) for lodging places on and off the mountain. Sugarloaf's toll-free reservations and information number for the eastern seaboard is 1-800-THE-LOAF; you can also call 237-2000.

GETTING THERE

By air: **Portland International Jetport** (779-7301), 2½ hours away, offers connections to all points. **Rental cars** are available at the airport. *By car:* From Boston it theoretically takes 4 hours. Take the Maine Turnpike to exit 12 (Auburn), then Route 4, to Route 2, to Route 27; or take I-95 to Augusta, then Route 27 the rest of the way. (We swear by the latter route, but others swear by the former.)

GETTING AROUND

In ski season, the **Valley Ski Shuttle Bus** runs from the base lodge to the Carrabassett Valley Ski Touring Center and Route 27 lodges.

MEDICAL EMERGENCY

Franklin Memorial Hospital (778-6031), Farmington.

Sugarloaf/USA has its own emergency clinic, and the **Mount Abram Regional Health Center** (265-4555) has both a full-time nurse and a physician's assistant. Dr. Christopher Smith (265-5088), Kingfield's kindly country doctor, responds beyond business hours.

TO SEE

MUSEUMS

Stanley Museum (265-2729), School Street, Kingfield. Open year-round except April and November, Tuesday through Sunday 1–4. Suggested donation: $2 per adult, $1 per child. Housed in a stately wooden school

KIM GRANT

The Wire Bridge in New Portland

donated by the Stanley family in 1903, this is a varied collection of inventions by the Stanley twins, F. O. and F. E. (it was their invention of the airbrush in the 1870s that made their fortune). Exhibits range from violins to the steam car for which the Stanleys are best known. Three Stanley Steamers (made between 1905 and 1916) are on exhibit; also fascinating photos of rural Maine in the 1890s and elsewhere through the 1920s by Chansonetta Stanley Emmons, sister of the two inventors.

Nordica Homestead Museum (778-2042), Holley Road, off Route 4/27 north of Farmington. Open June through Labor Day, Tuesday through Sunday 10–noon and 1–5; also September and October by appointment. Admission $2. This 19th-century farmhouse is the unlikely repository for the costumes, personal mementos, and exotic gifts given the opera star Lillian Norton, who was born here (she later changed her name to Nordica).

Nowetah's American Indian Museum, Route 27, New Portland. Open daily 10–5. Don't dismiss this place as just another tourist trap. Nowetah Timmerman, a member of the Susquehanna and Cherokee tribes, displays Native American artifacts from the United States, Canada, and South America. A special room holds over 300 Maine baskets and bark containers, also quill embroidery, trade beads, and more.

HISTORIC SITES

Kingfield Historical Society (265-2729), Church Street, Kingfield. Open August and September, Sundays 1–4; also by appointment. Local memorabilia of the narrow-gauge railroad, the Stanley family, and Maine's first governor, William King; also 19th-century clothes, dolls, and a general store.

Dead River Historical Society (246-2271), Stratton. Open weekends in summer 11–3. Displays memorabilia from the "lost" towns of Flagstaff and Dead River, flooded in 1950 to create the present 22,000-acre, 24-

mile Flagstaff Lake. When the water is low you can still see foundations and cellar holes, including that of a round barn in the Dead River.

Wire Bridge, on Wire Bridge Road, off Route 146 (not far) off Route 27 in New Portland. Nowhere near anywhere, this amazing-looking suspension bridge across the Carrabassett River has two massive, shingled stanchions. The bridge is one of Maine's 19th-century engineering feats (it was built in 1841). There's a good swimming hole just downstream and a place to picnic across the bridge; take a right through the ball field and go 0.5 mile on the dirt road. Note the parking area and path to the river.

FOR FAMILIES

✒ **The Western Maine Children's Museum** (235-2211), Route 27, Carrabassett Valley. Open Saturday, Sunday, and Monday, 1–5. $2.50 per person. Plenty of hands-on exhibits include math and science tables, a dress-up corner, a big indoor sand pile, computers, and a cave with real crystals.

✒ **Sugarloaf Outdoor Adventure Camp** (237-6909) Riverside Park, Route 27, Carrabassett Valley. Runs weekdays mid-July through August. Begun as a town program and now operated by Sugarloaf. Open to visitors (reservations required); designed for ages 5–12: archery, swimming, biking, golf, climbing, camping, etc. Inquire about the teen adventure program.

The Deer Farm (628-5361), Millay Hill Road, North New Portland (posted from Wire Bridge Road; see *Historic Sites*). Open daily until sunset. $1 admission entitles visitors to grain with which to feed Scott Oliver's herd of varied deer.

Red School House Museum (778-4215), Route 2/4, Farmington. Open Tuesday through Friday, 9–4. A schoolhouse built in 1852, old desks, books, and memorabilia; also houses the Greater Farmington Chamber of Commerce.

SCENIC DRIVES

Route 142 from Kingfield to Phillips (11 miles) runs through farmland backed by Mount Abraham. Stop at the **Phillips Historical Society** and **Daggett Rock** (see *Scenic Drives* in "Rangeley Lakes Region") and continue to **Mount Blue State Park** (see *Green Space* in "Rangeley"); return to Kingfield via New Vineyard and New Portland, stopping to see the **Wire Bridge** (see *Historic Sites*).

Route 16 though North New Portland and Emden is the most scenic as well as the most direct route from Kingfield to the Upper Kennebec Valley and Moosehead Lake.

TO DO

BOATING

See *Fishing* for rental canoes, kayaks, and motorboats.

FISHING

Thayer Pond at the **Sugarloaf Outdoor Center,** Route 27, is a catch-and-release pond open to the public, with fly-fishing lessons, canoe rentals, and fee-fishing. The village of of Stratton, north of Sugarloaf/USA, serves as the gateway to serious fishing country. **The Dead River Sport Shop** (246-4868) rents canoes as well as offering a large selection of gear and locally tied flies; **Northland Cash Supply** (246-2376) is a genuine backwoods general store that also carries plenty of fishing gear; **T&L Enterprises** (246-4276) rents motorized boats and canoes; and the **White Wolf Inn** (246-2922) rents canoes and kayaks. In Eustis, both **Tim Pond** and **King & Bartlett Sporting Camps** (see *Lodging*) are traditional fishing enclaves. In Farmington, Red Oak Sports (778-5350) rents boats and **Aardvark Outfitters** (778-3380) offers a wide selection of fly-fishing gear. Inquire about fly-fishing schools at Sugarloaf.

GOLF

Sugarloaf/USA Golf Club (237-2000), Sugarloaf/USA. This spectacular, 18-hole, par-72 course, designed by Robert Trent Jones II, is ranked among the nation's best, as is its golf school (now allied with Mount Snow's long-established Original Golf School). Inquire about weekend and midweek golf programs and packages.

Junior Golf Camp (5 midweek days), designed for ages 12–18, is offered several times between mid-June and mid-August.

HIKING

There are a number of 4,000-footers in the vicinity and rewarding trails up **Mount Abraham** and **Bigelow Mountain.** The Appalachian Trail signs are easy to spot on Route 27 just south of Stratton; popular treks include the 2 hours to Cranberry Pond or 4 hours–plus (one way) to Cranberry Peak. The chamber of commerce (see *Guidance*) usually stocks copies of the Maine Bureau of Parks and Lands' detailed map to trails in the 35,000-acre **Bigelow Preserve,** encompassing the several above-treeline trails in the Bigelow Range (the trails are far older than the Preserve, which dates from 1976 when a proposal to turn these mountains into "the Aspen of the East" was defeated by a public referendum).

West Mountain Falls on the Sugarloaf Golf Course is an easy hike to a swimming and picnic spot on the South Branch of the Carrabassett River. Begin at the Sugarloaf Clubhouse.

Poplar Stream Falls is a 51-foot cascade with a swimming hole below. Turn off Route 27 at the Valley Crossing and follow this road to the abandoned road marked by a snowmobile sign. Follow this road 1.5 miles.

MOOSE-WATCHING

Moose Cruises (237-6830) depart from the Sugarloaf/USA Outdoor Center, July through September, Wednesday and Saturday evenings: View a video while sipping complimentary champagne and ride the "Moose Express" van to likely moose-watching spots.

MOUNTAIN BIKING

Sugarloaf/USA offers 50 miles of marked trails ranging from flat to vertical. Pick up maps, rentals, and information at the **Sugarloaf/USA Bike Shop** (237-6998) at the Village Center. A popular ride begins here at the bottom of the lifts and is a steady downhill all the way down the access road and along the old narrow-gauge railway bed to the Carrabassett Valley Town Park. On Friday, Saturday, and Sunday you even avoid the schlep back up by hopping the Bike Shuttle. **The Sugarloaf/USA Outdoor Center** (237-2000), Route 17, is also a source of maps, info, and rentals and is the hub of a trail system designed for cross-country skiers that also serves bikers well. More adventurous bikers can, of course, hit any number of abandoned logging roads. Inquire about guided tours.

Moose Cruises (237-6830), depart from the Sugarloaf/USA Outdoor Center, July-September, Wednesday and Saturday, evenings: view a video while sipping complimentary champagne and ride the "moose Express" to likely moose-watching spots.

SWIMMING

Cathedral Pines, Route 27, Stratton. Just north of town, turn right into the campground and follow signs to the public beach on Flagstaff Lake; changing rooms, playground. Free.

Among the **Carrabassett River**'s popular swimming holes: **Riverside Park,** Route 27, 0.5 mile south of Ayotte's Country Store, features a natural water slide and a very small beach, ideal for small children. Look for a deeper swimming hole off Route 27, 0.5 mile south of Riverside Park on the corner of the entrance to Spring Farm.)

Also see Wire Bridge in *To See.*

WHITE-WATER RAFTING

An easy day trip. See outfitters described in "The Upper Kennebec Valley and Moose River Valley" and reserve a ride: phone 1-800-RAFT-MEE.

WINTER SPORTS

CROSS-COUNTRY SKIING

Sugarloaf/USA Outdoor Center (237-6830), Route 27, Carrabassett Valley. Open in-season 9 AM–dusk. This is Maine's largest touring network, with 95 km of trail loops, including race loops (with snowmaking) for timed runs. Rentals and instruction are available. The center itself includes the Klister Kitchen, which serves soups and sandwiches; space to relax in front of the fire with a view of Sugarloaf; and a rental area.

Titcomb Mountain Ski Touring Center (778-9031), Morrison Hill Road (off Route 2/4), Farmington. A varied network of 25 km of groomed trails and unlimited ungroomed trails; used by the University of Maine at Farmington.

DOWNHILL SKIING

Sugarloaf/USA (general information, 237-2000; snow report is ext. 6808; on-mountain reservation number is 1-800-THE-LOAF). Sugarloaf Mountain Corporation was formed in 1955 by local skiers, and growth was steady but slow into the 1970s. Then a boom decade produced one of New England's largest self-contained resorts, including a base village complete with a seven-story brick hotel and a forest of condominiums.

SUGARLOAF NEWS BUREAU

Fly-fishing near Sugarloaf

Sugarloaf has been expanding and improving snowmaking and services ever since. Snowmaking now even covers its snowy cap. In 1996 Sugarloaf was absorbed by the Bethel-based American Skiing Company.

Trails number 126 and glades add up to 45 miles. The vertical drop is a whopping 2,820 feet. The 14 lifts include a gondola, a detachable quad, a triple chair, eight double chairs, and one T-bar. Facilities include a Perfect Turn Development Center, a Perfect Kids school, ski shop, rentals, base lodge, cafeteria, nursery (day and night), game room, and a total of 22 bars and restaurants. The nursery is first-rate; there are children's programs for 3-year-olds to teens; also mini-mountain tickets for beginners. Call for current 1-day lift rates (also multiday, early- and late- season, and packaged rates). Under age 6, lifts are free.

DOGSLED RIDES

T.A.D. Dog Sled Services (246-4461; 237-2000), P.O. Box 147, Stratton 04982. Tim Diehl offers rides by his team of Samoyeds, "The White Howling Express." The 1½-mile rides leave approximately every half hour throughout the day during ski season from his base on Route 27 just north of the Sugarloaf access road. Drop by just to see his friendly, frisky dogs, all of whom were unwanted pets until Diehl adopted and trained them.

ICE SKATING

Sugarloaf/USA Outdoor Center (237-6830) maintains a lighted rink and rents skates.

SNOWMOBILING

Snowmobile trails are outlined on many maps available locally; a favorite destination is **Flagstaff Lodge** (maintained as a warming hut) in the

Bigelow Preserve. **Flagstaff Rentals** (246-4276) and **T&L Enterprises** (246-2922), both in Stratton, rent snowmobiles. Inquire about guided tours.

LODGING

On-Mountain

Sugarloaf/USA Inn and Condominiums (1-800-THE-LOAF; 237-2000), Carrabassett Valley 04947. Some 330 ski-in, ski-out condominiums are in the rental pool. Built gradually over the last 20 years (they include the first condos in Maine), they represent a range of styles and sites; when making a reservation, you might want to ask about convenience to the base complex, the Sugarloaf /USA Sports and Fitness Club (to which all condo guests have access), or the golf club. The 42-room **Sugarloaf Inn** offers attractive standard rooms and fourth-floor family spaces with lofts; there's a comfortable living room with fireplace, a solarium restaurant (see *Dining Out*); the front desk is staffed around the clock; the inn is handy to the health club, also to the mountain. Packages from $79 per person in winter, from $99 in golf season.

    ♿ **Grand Summit Resort Hotel & Conference Center** (1-800-527-9879), RR 1, Box 2299, Carrabassett Valley 04947. So close to the base complex that it dwarfs the base lodge, this is a massive, seven-story, 120-room brick condominium hotel with a gabled roof and central tower. Rooms are large and well furnished, and most have small refrigerators and microwaves. There are also two 2-bedroom suites, each with a living room and kitchen, and two palatial tower penthouses, each with three bedrooms, three baths, and a hot tub. There's a library and a health club with a large hot tub and plunge pool, sauna, and steam room. $90–300 per night, multiday discounts, less in summer.

Off-Mountain

INNS AND BED & BREAKFASTS

    ✎ **The Herbert** (265-2000; 1-800-THE-HERB), P.O. Box 67, Kingfield 04947. Open year-round. This three-story hotel was billed as a "palace in the wilderness" when it opened in 1918 in the center of Kingfield. The "fumed oak" walls of the lobby gleam, and there's a fire in the hearth beneath the moose head. Soak up the warmth from richly upholstered chairs and enjoy music from the grand piano. The attractive dining room is frequently filled, and the fare is exceptional (see *Dining Out*). The 28 rooms and four suites are comfortably furnished with antiques, and many bathrooms feature Jacuzzis. $49–165.

Three Stanley Avenue (265-5541), Kingfield 04947. Designed by a younger brother of the Stanley twins, now an attractive bed & breakfast next to the more ornate One Stanley Avenue, also owned by Dan Davis (see *Dining Out*). There's a nice feel to this place, and each room is different. Number 2 has twin beds and a bath with claw-foot tub; number 1, an ornate sleigh bed with claw-foot tub. We also like number 6 (no bath), and number 4 is good for a family (one double, one twin bed). Although there's no common room, guests are welcome to use the elegant sitting room with flocked wallpaper and grandfather clock next door at One Stanley Avenue. In summer, the lawns and woods are good for walking. Breakfast is included. $50–60, less midweek and summer.

River Port Inn (265-2552), Route 27, Kingfield 04947. An 1840 roadside house on the edge of town (and on snowmobile I-84) with five guest rooms sharing two baths, a living room, and a big, friendly dining area in which guests tend to linger over home-baked breakfast fare. $45–55 per couple.

Tranquillity Bed & Breakfast (246-4280), P.O. Box 9, Stratton 04982. Open Memorial Day through November. Guy Grant has transformed an old barn into an informal lodge with an attractive living/dining room overlooking Flagstaff Lake. The boat ramp is just across Route 27. Private baths, full breakfast included, $55.

MOTEL

🐾 **Spillover Motel** (246-6571), P.O. Box 427, Stratton 04982. An attractive, two-story, 19-unit (11 nonsmoking) motel just south of Stratton Village. Spanking clean, with two double beds to a unit, color cable TV, phone. $58–74, $5 for each additional person; includes continental breakfast; $5 for pets.

SPORTING CAMPS

🐾 **Tim Pond Wilderness Camps** (243-2947), Eustis 04936. Open after the ice breaks up through November. In business since the 1860s and billed as "the oldest continuously operating sporting camp in America." The lure in spring and September is fly-fishing for native square-tailed trout. There are 10 log cabins, each with a fieldstone fireplace or woodstove; three meals are served in the lodge. Canoes and motorboats are available for use on this clear, remote lake, surrounded by 4,450 acres of woodland, also good for hiking. $98 single per night, includes three meals; half price for children under age 12; no charge under age 5. Closed in August.

🐾 **King & Bartlett Fish and Game Club** (243-2956), Eustis 04936. A century-old sporting camp catering to fishermen and hunters, set on its own 30,000 acres—including 14 ponds and lakes and four major streams. Each of the 14 log cabins can sleep two to six people; all have lake views, full baths, and daily maid service. Meals are served in the central lodge. Dogs welcome. $140 per person per night, $695 for 6 nights includes all meals. Inquire about family rates and Maine guide service.

CAMPGROUNDS

🐾 **Cathedral Pines Campground** (246-3491), Route 27, Eustis. Open mid-May through September. Three hundred town-owned acres on Flagstaff Lake, with 115 tent and RV sites set amid towering red pines and a rec hall, beach, and canoe and paddleboat rentals.

🐾 **Deer Farm Camps & Campground** (265-4599), Tufts Pond Road, Kingfield. Open mid-May to mid-October. Fifty wooded tent and RV sites near

Tufts Pond (good swimming); facilities include a store, playground, and hot showers.

For a list of rental units, ranging from classic old A-frames to classy condos, contact the Sugarloaf Area Chamber of Commerce (see *Guidance*).

WHERE TO EAT

DINING OUT

Porter House (246-7932), Route 27, Eustis. Dinner Wednesday through Sunday year-round. A country farmhouse located 12 miles north of Sugarloaf, drawing patrons from Rangeley and Kingfield and beyond. The four small dining rooms are lit by fire and candlelight. Sip a drink while you study the menu, which (of course) includes Porter House steak (market price). Entrées begin at $9.95 for a char-grilled boneless skinless chicken breast Dijon or a garden vegetable patty; children's menu available. All breads, soups, and desserts are homemade. Full bar and wine list. Your chef-hosts are Beth and Jeff Hinman.

One Stanley Avenue (265-5541), Kingfield. Closed May to December; otherwise open after 5 PM except Monday. Reservations are a must. Small, but generally considered one of the best restaurants in western Maine. Guests gather for a drink in the Victorian parlor, then proceed to one of the two intimate dining rooms. Specialties include veal and fiddlehead pie, sweetbreads with applejack and chives, maple cider chicken, and saged rabbit with raspberry sauce. We have seldom savored more tender meat or moister fish, and the herbs and combinations work well. Owner-chef Dan Davis describes his methods as classic, the results as distinctly regional. $15–30 includes fresh bread, salad, vegetables, starch, coffee, and teas, but it's difficult to pass on the wines and desserts.

The Herbert (265-2000), Main Street, Kingfield. Dinner is served after 5 PM, Wednesday to Monday. Sunday brunch 12–2:30. This elegant old hotel dining room gleams with cut glass; service is friendly; dress is casual; and the wine list is extensive. A recent summer menu included free-range chicken breast with a cranberry, walnut, and herb stuffing, topped with a tangy cranberry glaze; and shrimp Athens, sautéed with tomatoes, garlic, dill, and black olives, topped with feta cheese (both $16.95).

Hug's Italian Cuisine (237-2392), Route 27, Carrabassett Valley. Open Tuesday through Sunday, November through April. A small eatery featuring northern Italian–style delicacies such as shiitake mushroom ravioli with walnut pesto Alfredo ($15.95).

The Seasons (237-6834), Sugarloaf Inn, Carrabassett Valley. Breakfast daily, and dinner 6–9. Request a table in the glass-walled section of the dining room. The menu ranges from roasted vegetable cassoulet ($12.95) to filet mignon with a foie gras mousse and a puff pastry hat ($19.95).

EATING OUT

Longfellow Restaurant & Riverside Lounge (265-4394), Kingfield. Open year-round for lunch and dinner (from 5 PM). An attractive, informal dining place in a 19th-century building decorated with photos of 19th-century Kingfield. There's a pubby area around the bar, an open-beamed dining room, and an upstairs dining space with an outdoor deck overlooking the river. Great for lunch (homemade soups, quiche, crêpes, and a wide selection of sandwiches); a find for budget-conscious families at dinner. Children's plates are available.

The Shipyard Brewhaus at the Sugarloaf Inn (237-6837), Sugarloaf Access Road. Open 4:30–9:30. A grand old ornate bar with Shipyard brews on tap occupy a pleasant corner of the inn (the former library), an appealing setting for reasonably priced pub fare including pizzas and burgers, salad, and lobster bisque.

Mainely Yours (246-2999), Stratton Village. Open 5 AM–9 PM Monday through Friday, 6 AM–10 PM Saturday, 7–4 Sunday. Better known as "Cathy's Place" (owner Cathy Preda is a well-known local chef) and decorated with renditions of Elvis, this is the best road food around.

Tufulio's Restaurant & Bar (235-2010), Valley Crossing, Route 27, 6 miles south of Sugarloaf. Open from 5 PM, Sunday at 4. A pleasant dining room with large oak booths, specializing in every kind of pizza, a wide selection of pastas and microbrews, children's menu, game room.

The Wirebridge Diner (628-6229), Route 27, New Portland. Open 6 AM–2 PM, closed Mondays. A classic diner with wooden booths and stained glass, originally opened in Haverhill, Massachusetts, moved to Waterville, Maine, in the 1940s, here in the 1960s: great onion rings and sandwiches (a cheeseburger is $1.99). It's not on the menu, but order "the Bud": a BLT with tuna, cheese, and sweet onion. Ask directions to the Wire Bridge (see *To See*).

The Woodsman, Route 27, Kingfield, north end of town. Pine paneled, decorated with logging tools and pictures, a friendly, smoky barn of a place, good for stacks of pancakes, great omelets, endless refills on coffee, homemade soups and subs, local gossip.

Theo's Microbrewery & Pub (237-2211). Home of the Sugarloaf Brewing Company's pale ale. Burgers, steaks, salads, and pastas also served. Monday is two-for-one pizza night.

In Farmington

F. L. Butler Restaurant & Lounge (778-5223), Front Street. Open for lunch weekdays, dinner Monday through Saturday, Sunday 10–8. Steaks, a variety of fish dishes, and Italian dishes served in a brick-walled tavern. $6.95–16.95. A good way stop en route to Sugarloaf.

The Granary Brewpub (779-0710), 23 Pleasant Street. Open daily 11–11. Home of the Narrow Gauge Brewing Company, obviously popular with local college students and faculty, featuring a large menu of soups, sandwiches, and moderately priced entrées like chicken stir-fry and ribs.

The half-dozen house brews are all American-style ales; draft stout is also served.

The Homestead Bakery Restaurant (778-6162), 20 Broadway (Route 43), Farmington. Open for breakfast and lunch daily, also for dinner Tuesday through Saturday as Maria's Italian Restaurant. The best place in town for breakfast and lunch and a good dinner stop en route to Sugarloaf.

Gifford's Ice Cream (778-3617), Route 4/27, Farmington. Open seasonally from 11 AM. Nearby Skowhegan is home base for this exceptional ice cream that comes in 40 flavors. Foot-long hot dogs also served.

SELECTIVE SHOPPING

Ritzo & Royal Studio Gallery (265-4586), at the "Brick Castle," Route 27 on the northern fringe of Kingfield. Open Thursday through Sunday, 11–5:30. An exceptional selection of locally crafted jewelry, rugs, pottery, furniture and other woodwork, glass, and Patricia Ritzo's own paintings.

Kingfield Wood Products (265-2151), just off Depot Street, Kingfield. Open weekends 9–4. A trove of small and interesting wooden items made on the spot: wooden apples and other fruit, toys, and novelty items.

Sugarloaf Sports (265-2011), Kingfield. Open daily. Sports equipment and clothing carried with the season.

✐ **Devaney, Doak & Garret** (778-3454), 29 Broadway, Farmington. Open daily. A bookstore worthy of a college town, one with a good children's section. Music and comfortable seating invite lingering.

Books, Lines, and Thinkers (265-5584), Main Street, Kingfield. Wess Conall's full-service bookstore offers a good selection of titles, also music, art, and antiques.

Mainestone (778-6560), 11 Front Street, Farmington. Ron and Cindy Gelinas craft much of the jewelry—all made from Maine-mined gems—and carry the work of other local craftspeople.

SPECIAL EVENTS

January: **White White World Winter Carnival**—broom hockey, chili cookoff, bartenders' race, and discounts at Sugarloaf/USA.

March: **St. Patrick's Day Leprechaun Loppet**—a 15-km, citizens' cross-country race at Sugarloaf/USA Outdoor Center.

April: **Easter Festival** at Sugarloaf—costume parade, Easter egg hunt on slopes, and sunrise service on the summit; **Reggae Festival** weekend.

May: **Sugarloaf Marathon.**

August: **Kingfield Days Celebration**—4 days with parade, art exhibits, potluck supper; **Old Home Days** in Stratton, Eustis, and Flagstaff; **weekend jazz series,** Sugarloaf/USA.

September: **Kingfield 10K Foot Race and Sugarloaf Uphill Climb; Franklin County Fair,** Farmington.

October: **Skiers' Homecoming Weekend,** Sugarloaf Mountain.

December: **Yellow-Nosed Vole Day,** Sugarloaf Mountain. **Chester Greenwood Day,** Farmington, honors the local inventor of the ear-muff with a parade and variety show in Farmington.

VI. THE KENNEBEC VALLEY

Augusta and Mid Maine
The Upper Kennebec Valley and Moose River Valley,
Including The Forks and Jackman

Rafting the Kennebec River

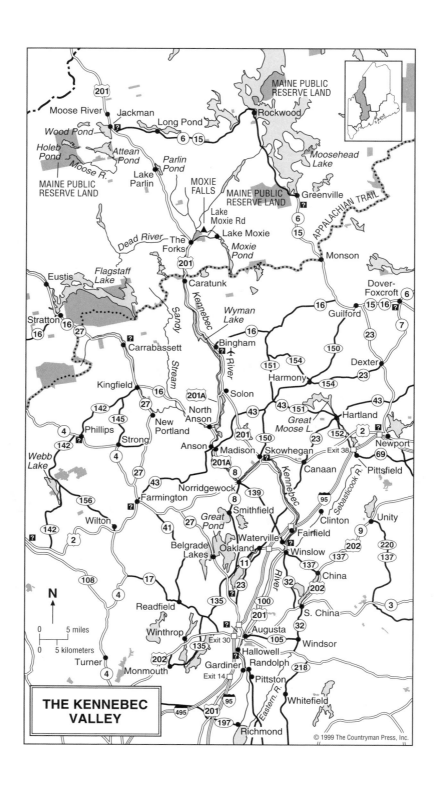

THE KENNEBEC
VALLEY

© 1999 The Countryman Press, Inc.

Augusta and Mid Maine

Augusta, the capital of Maine, rises in tiers above the Kennebec River at its head of shipping navigation. This position provided a good hunting and fishing ground for the area's earliest inhabitants, the Norridgewock and Kennebec tribes of the Algonquians. In 1625 the Pilgrims sailed to this spot and traded "seven hundred pounds of good beaver and some other furs" with the Native Americans for a "shallop's load of corn." They procured a grant to the Kennebec, from Gardiner to a waterfall halfway between Augusta and Waterville, with a strip of land 15 miles wide on either side of the bank. At the Native American village of Cushnoc (present-day Augusta), they built a storehouse and, with the proceeds of their beaver trade, were soon able to pay off their London creditors.

With the decline of the fur trade and rising hostilities with the Native Americans, these settlers sold the tract of land to four Boston merchants for just 400 pounds. The merchants had plans—farming, timber, and shipyards. War halted these plans, however, and the settlers fled, but they returned in 1754 when the British built Fort Western. The area was selected as the capital in 1827, and a statehouse, designed by Charles Bulfinch and built of granite from neighboring Hallowell, was completed in 1832. During the mid–19th century, this area boomed: Some 500 boats were built along the river between Winslow and Gardiner, and river traffic between Augusta and Boston thrived. The era is still reflected by the quaint commercial buildings lining the river downstream in Hallowell and Gardiner, both good places to shop and dine.

Today Augusta remains worth a visit, if only to see one of the most interesting state museums in the country; exhibits vividly depict many aspects of landscape, industry, and history.

This lower Kennebec Valley is rolling, open farmland, spotted with lakes. Just north of the city the seven lakes in the Belgrade Lakes region form an old resort area, blessed with cottage colonies that need not advertise and plenty of recreation, from mail-boat excursions and canoe rides to relaxation plain and simple. East of the city, the China Lakes form another low-profile haven. Good summer theater can be found in Waterville (upriver), Monmouth (another old resort area west

517

of town), and Skowhegan (also known for its art school). In the past few years, attractive old homes and family farms throughout this region have opened their doors to guests—who are discovering not only the beauty of the immediate area but also that "Mid Maine" is the only true hub in this sprawling state, handy to many parts of the coast, the Western Mountains and Lakes, and the North Woods.

GUIDANCE

Kennebec Valley Chamber of Commerce (623-4559), P.O. Box E, University Drive, Augusta 04332. The office is off I-95 (the exit for Route 27) in the civic center complex. This is a year-round source of information, primarily on the area from Augusta to Gardiner.

Belgrade Lakes Region, Inc., P.O. Box 72, Belgrade 04917, maintains a seasonal (late June to September) information booth on Route 27 and also publishes a pamphlet guide to the area.

China Area Chamber of Commerce (445-2890), Box 317, South China 04358. Year-round.

Mid-Maine Chamber of Commerce (873-3315), P.O. Box 142, Waterville 04903. Open year-round.

GETTING THERE

By air: **Colgan Air** (1-800-272-5488) connects Augusta with Boston. **Pine State Air** (1-800-353-6334) offers the only intrastate air travel in Maine, with scheduled service from Augusta to Presque Isle.

By bus: **Vermont Transit** serves Augusta and Waterville.

By car: You don't have to take the Maine Turnpike to reach the Augusta area; from points south, I-95 is both quicker and cheaper (I-95 and the turnpike merge just south of Augusta). If you are not in a hurry, the most scenic route to Augusta from points south is to follow the Kennebec River up Route 24 through Bowdoinham and Richmond.

MEDICAL EMERGENCY

Kennebec Valley Medical Center (626-1000), 6 East Chestnut Street, Augusta. **Mid-Maine Medical Center** (873-0621), North Street, Waterville. **Waterville Osteopathic Hospital** (873-0731), Waterville, also offers emergency service. **Redington-Fairview General Hospital** (474-5085), Fairview Avenue, Skowhegan.

VILLAGES

Richmond. If you follow the Kennebec River from Brunswick to Gardiner, you will be rewarded with views of Merrymeeting Bay and then of rolling farmland sloping to the river. Richmond, at first glance, seems to be just another small mill town, but its onion-domed churches recall its Russian population, which numbered as many as 500 in the 1950s and 1960s. Cross the bridge in the middle of the village to find the Pownalborough Court House, which we have described in "Wiscasset."

Hallowell. This village is much the same as it was over 100 years ago. The store names may be different, but the Water Street commercial blocks, with two- and three-story, vintage mid-19th-century buildings, are definitely worth a stroll; known throughout New England for its number of antiques shops. Also note the restaurants described under *Where to Eat.*

Gardiner. Located where the Kennebec and Cobbossee Rivers meet, this old industrial (shoe, textile, and paper) town has been nicely restored. Nineteenth-century Main Street remains a great place in which to stroll and eat; also see *Entertainment.*

TO SEE

State House (287-2301), State Street, Augusta. Open year-round, Monday through Friday 8:30–4:30. Much modified since the original design by Charles Bulfinch; its size has actually doubled. A 180-foot dome replaces the original cupola. There are markers that will lead you on a self-guided tour, but guided tours are available. In 1998, considerable interior renovation was taking place.

Blaine House (287-2301), State Street, Augusta. Open year-round, Monday through Friday 2–4, and by appointment. A 28-room mansion built in the 1830s by a Captain James Hall of Bath, later purchased by James Blaine, a Speaker of the US House of Representatives, a US senator, and twice secretary of state. Blaine was known as the plumed knight when he ran for the presidency in 1884, battling "Rum, Romanism, and Rebellion." His daughter gave the mansion to the state in 1919, and it has since served as home for Maine governors.

Colby College (872-3000), Waterville (2 miles from exit 33 off I-95; marked). Founded in 1813, Colby College is the 12th-oldest liberal arts college in the nation. It enrolls close to 1,700 students from almost every state and more than 25 countries. Its campus is set on more than 700 acres, with traditional brick and ivy-covered buildings, and there are several attractions worth noting, including the **Colby College Museum of Art** (see *Museums*); **Perkins Arboretum and Johnson Pond,** a 128-acre arboretum and bird sanctuary with nature trails and a picnic area; the **Portland String Quartet,** in residence here, with several concerts throughout the year as well as a summer string-quartet institute; the **Strider Theater,** a 274-seat theater offering a variety of programs and performances throughout the year; and the **Harold Alfond Athletic Center,** which has seen much expansion in recent years and now includes a track, four tennis courts, an Olympic-sized pool, an ice arena, a large gymnasium, and fitness rooms.

A well-organized booklet guides you through a walking tour of the campus; be sure to pick one up at the admissions office.

MUSEUMS

Maine State Museum (287-2301), State Capitol Complex, State Street (Route 201/27), Augusta. Open weekdays 9–5, Saturday (and most holidays) 10–4, and Sunday 1–4. Free. Turn into the parking lot just south of the capitol building. This outstanding museum isn't even marked from the street! You have to know that it's in the State Library in order to find it.

Without question, this is the best state museum in New England. Allow at least an hour. The exhibit "12,000 Years in Maine" traces the story of Maine's Native Americans with reproductions of petroglyphs and genuine ancient artifacts. This fascinating exhibit also dramatizes early European explorations and 19th-century attempts to explore the state's antiquities. Elsewhere, the museum re-creates a variety of Maine's landscapes and traditional industries: fishing, agriculture, granite quarrying, ice harvesting, shipbuilding, and lumbering. "Made in Maine" depicts more than a dozen 19th-century industrial scenes: textile mills and shops producing shoes, guns, fishing rods, and more. What makes these scenes most fascinating is their incredible, lifelike quality and the attention to detail. The 1846 narrow-gauge locomotive "Lion" stands like a mascot in the lobby. The fourth-floor addition houses an exhibit featuring highlights of 25 years at the museum.

Colby College Museum of Art (872-3228), Colby College, Waterville. Open 10 AM–4:30 PM Monday through Saturday; Sunday 2-4:30. Free admission. Founded in 1959, this wonderful museum has a permanent collection of 18th-, 19th-, and 20th-century art that is displayed in spacious, appealing galleries. In 1998 construction began on yet another wing, which will add 8,000 square feet to the display space. This 11-gallery addition will exclusively house some 150 works from the permanent collection which have to this point remained in storage. Three will exhibit 18th-century work, two will house 19th-century paintings and sculpture, another is for Impressionist paintings, two for primitive 19th-century work, and two galleries will be devoted to 54 works by John Marin, who spent most of his summers in Maine; much of his work in oils and watercolors reflects Maine subjects, from Mount Katahdin to seascapes. The Paul J. Schupf wing, opened in 1996, roatates over 400 paintings and sculptures by artist Alex Katz. The museum also offers special exhibits, gallery talks, lectures, and receptions throughout the year. The museum shop sells museum publications, gifts, jewelry, notecards, postcards, and posters.

✍ **Children's Discovery Museum** (622-2209), Water Street, Augusta. An excellent hands-on museum, with displays that include a life-sized board game that teaches about the Atlantic salmon, a stage where kids can videotape a performance and then watch themselves on TV, post office, diner, and supermarket play areas. Their newest exhibit is a construction site, complete with real equipment. Also a weather station and communications center with computers and ham radio. Days and hours of operation vary; call for information.

HISTORIC SITES

Fort Western Museum on the Kennebec (626-2385), City Center Plaza, 16 Cony Street, Augusta. Open Memorial Day to July 4, 1–4 daily; July 4 to Labor Day, 10–4 weekdays, 1–4 weekends; Labor Day through Columbus Day, 1–4 weekends only. Groups and school programs year-round. $4.50 adults, $2.50 children. The original 16-room garrison house has been restored to reflect its use as a fort, trading post, and lodge from 1754 to 1810. The blockhouse and stockade are reproductions. Costumed characters answer questions and demonstrate 18th-century domestic activities. Special events on summer Sundays, as well as many annual events.

Redington Museum and Apothecary (872-9439), 64 Silver Street, Waterville. Open mid-May through September, Tuesday through Saturday 2–6, and by appointment. $2 admission; $1 ages 18 and under. The local historical collection: furniture, Civil War and Native American relics, a children's room, period rooms, and a 19th-century apothecary.

Monmouth Museum (933-4444), Monmouth (at the intersection of Routes 132 and 135). Open Memorial Day through September, Tuesday through Sunday 1–4; year-round by appointment (933-2287 is the answering machine; or call Annie Smith, 933-2752). $3 per adult, $1 per child. A collection of buildings: 1787 Blossom House, stencil shop (1849), blacksmith shop, freight shed, and carriage house.

Waterville-Winslow Two Cent Bridge, Front Street, Waterville. One of the only known remaining toll footbridges in the country. Toll-taker's house on Waterville side. Free.

Fort Halifax, Route 201, Winslow (1 mile south of the Waterville-Winslow bridge at the junction of the Kennebec and Sebasticook Rivers). Just a blockhouse remains, but it is original, built in 1754—the oldest blockhouse in the United States. There is also a park with picnic tables here.

Cumston Hall, Main Street, Monmouth. Open year-round, weekdays during business hours. Vintage 1900, this ornate wooden building would look more at home in India than Mid Maine. Monmouth native Harry H. Cochrane not only designed but also decorated the building with murals, detailing, and stained glass. He also composed the music and conducted the orchestra at the building's dedication. It houses the town offices, library, and the Theater at Monmouth, a repertory company specializing in Shakespeare (see *Entertainment*).

Arnold Historical Society Museum (582-7080), off Route 17, Pittston. Open July and August, Saturday, Sunday, and holidays 10–4, and by appointment. $1.50 per adult, $.50 per child over age 6. An 18th-century house in which Benedict Arnold and Aaron Burr stayed for a couple of nights in the fall of 1775 on their way to attempt to capture Quebec. The army camped on Swan Island in Richmond (see *Green Space*), and about 600 men and supplies continued upriver in *bâteaux*—the flat-bottomed boats that are exhibited here in the barn. The house is furnished to period, and picture panels depict the Arnold expedition.

✎ **Norlands Living History Center** (897-4366), RD 2, Box 1740, Livermore 04254. Take Norlands Road off Route 108 between Livermore and Livermore Falls. Open July and August, daily 10–4, for general tours of

MAINE OFFICE OF TOURISM

Norlands Living History Center in Livermore

all buildings. $4.50 per adult, $2 per student. Also open by reservation for live-in weekends and weeklong programs, year-round. An incredible 450-acre living-history complex re-creates life in the late 19th century. The working farm with barn and farmer's cottage, church, stone library, and Victorian mansions of the Washburn family are open to visitors. This is the genuine 1870–90 rural experience; visitors become scholars in the one-room schoolhouse and hear the story of the famous Washburn sons. Those living-in assume the identity of a 19th-century character, carrying out chores (cooking, mending, working the farm) just as they would have if they had been living here then. Chris's husband and oldest son went for a weekend and have never been the same. Try it. Come for a special weekend like Heritage Days in June, the Autumn Celebration in late

September, or Christmas in early December. Three-day live-in week-ends are also offered in February, April, May, and November.

SCENIC DRIVES

See *Scenic Drives* in "Belfast, Searsport, and Stockton Springs."

TO DO

BALLOONING

Sails Aloft (623-1136), Augusta, offers sightseeing flights in central and mid coast Maine. Starts at $125 per person.

BOAT EXCURSIONS

Great Pond Marina (495-2213; 1-800-696-6329), Belgrade Lakes Village. Operates the mail boat on Great Pond (the inspiration for the book and movie *On Golden Pond*); the mail-boat ride costs $7 per adult, $5 per senior, $4 per child. Also moorings, boat rentals (canoes, sailboards, sailboats, fishing boats), and service.

FISHING

Belgrade Lakes are known as a source of smallmouth bass; **Day's Store** in Belgrade Lakes Village devotes an entire floor to fishing gear. Boat rentals are available (see *Boat Excursions*).

FOR FAMILIES

Inside Out Playground (877-8747), Sterns Cultural Center, 93 Main Street, Waterville. Indoor playground includes a toddler area, wooden pirate ship structure, toy cars and trucks. Open year-round; great for rainy days. Many special programs including story time, crafts, parenting workshops, playgroups, and creative movement.

GOLF AND TENNIS

Belgrade Lakes Golf Club (495-GOLF) is a a new 18-hole golf course, designed by renowned English golf architect Clive Clark. Just off Route 27 with views of both Great and Long Ponds. Fees vary with season. Call for current fees and tee time.

Natanis Golf Club (622-3561), Webber Pond, Vassalboro, offers a 27-hole course; tennis courts. **Waterville Country Club** (465-7773), Waterville (off I-95). Eighteen holes, clubhouse, carts, and caddies.

SWIMMING

Peacock Beach State Park, Richmond (just off Route 201, 10 miles south of Augusta). A small, beautiful sand beach on Pleasant Pond; lifeguards and picnic facilities. $1 per adult, free under age 12.

Public beaches include **Sunset Camps Beach** on North Pond in Smithfield, and **Willow Beach** (968-2421), China. Although public access is limited at the Belgrade and China Lakes, every cottage cluster and most rental "camps" there are on the water.

Lake St. George State Park (589-4255), Route 3, Liberty. A pleasant, clean, clear lake with a sandy beach and changing facilities, a perfect break if you are en route from Augusta and points south to the coast.

CROSS-COUNTRY SKIING

Natanis Golf Club (622-3561), Webber Pond, Vassalboro, has groomed trails and rental equipment. **Pine Tree State Arboretum** (see *Green Space*) also has lots of space for good skiing.

GREEN SPACE

Pine Tree State Arboretum (621-0031), 153 Hospital Street, Augusta. (At Cony Circle—the big rotary across the bridge from downtown Augusta—turn south along the river; it's a short way down on the left, across from the Augusta Mental Health Institute.) Open daily dawn to dusk. Visitors center open 8–4 weekdays. There are 224 acres, with trails through woods and fields. More than 600 trees and shrubs (including rhododendrons and lilacs), as well as hostas and a rock garden. Cross-country ski trails too.

Swan Island, Richmond. A state-owned wildlife management area. Day use and overnight camping; prior reservations (287-1150) necessary for both, since only 60 visitors are allowed on the island at any one time. $3 day visit, $5 overnight camping. The landing is in Richmond Village, where Department of Inland Fisheries and Wildlife employees transport visitors to the island. Tours are available in an open, slat-sided truck; plenty of area for walking. The southern portion is restricted, but staff will accompany you on a tour (also see *Campgrounds*).

Jamies Pond Wildlife Management Area (623-4021), Meadow Hill Road, Hallowell. These 550 acres of woodlands, managed by the Maine Department of Inland Fisheries and Wildlife, include trails good for walking and cross-country skiing, and a 107-acre pond.

Also see *Swimming*.

LODGING

BED & BREAKFASTS

&   **Maple Hill Farm** (622-2708; 1-800-622-2708; info@maplebb.com), RFD 1, Box 1145, Hallowell 04347. Little more than 4 miles from the turnpike and downtown Augusta, this pleasant old house with a new addition sits on 130 acres of fields and woods with trails and a spring-fed swimming hole by a quarry. Scott Cowger and Vincent Hannan offer seven rooms furnished in a pretty country style, some with bedspreads that were made in Hallowell. All have phones and air-conditioning, and one suite has a Jacuzzi tub. Although there were some shared baths when we stopped by, all were slated to have a private bath by the end of 1998. As you meander up the driveway by the big red barn, watch for chickens (which provide the morning eggs) happily pecking by the side of the road. Other animals on the farm include a goat, two sheep, a llama, two cows (one a dwarf), and a dog. The carriage house has been transformed into a roomy function space, and weddings and meetings are frequently held here.

Full breakfast served in the dining room/art gallery is included in the $65–125 double rates.

✍ **Home-Nest Farm** (897-4125), Baldwin Hill Road, Box 2350, Kents Hill 04349. Closed March and April. This is a wonderful old family estate, with three historic homes on the extensive property. The main house, built in 1784, offers a panoramic view of the White Mountains. Lilac Cottage (1800) and the Red Schoolhouse (1830) are available for rent as separate units. The property has been in host Arn Sturtevant's family for six generations; his grandchildren are the eighth generation to sleep there. Arn can relate some interesting family tales while showing you Civil War memorabilia. The sheep are a lot of fun to watch. $50 per room, $80–95 for houses with one to three bedrooms; breakfast included.

✍ **Independence Farm** (622-0284), RR 1, Box 6857, Webber Pond Road, Vassalboro 04989. This 1820s farmhouse overlooks Webber Pond. Now that their eight children are grown, Pat (a craftsperson with her own store in Hallowell) and Bob Riedman raise llamas on their 55-acre spread, as well as geese, chickens, and a dog. Two large guest rooms have private baths, and a third is frequently used for children, who are very welcome here. The country decor includes lovely stenciling. There's a canoe for summer use, and in winter cross-country ski rentals and trails are available at the nearby 27-hole golf course. $55 double includes a full farm breakfast.

Richmond Bed and Breakfast and Sauna (737-4752; 1-800-400-5751), off Route 197, Richmond 04357. Open year-round. A handsome Federal home with five guest rooms with shared bath, kitchen privileges, sauna, hot tub, and pool. There are actually six saunas, available by the hour. Visitors should be aware that clothing is optional here, and there are those who opt not to wear any. Use of all facilities for guests. $65–85 double includes continental breakfast.

HOTEL

Best Western Senator Inn and Spa (622-5804; 1-800-528-1234 reservations), Western Avenue, Augusta. A longtime local hot spot for political figures, this property, with 103 guest rooms and suites, extends farther back from the road than you'd expect. Back-wing rooms are quieter and more private. Walking and cross-country skiing trails, indoor and outdoor pools and hot tubs, fireplace rooms available. In-room amenities include clock radios, coffeemakers, irons, and telephones. The three-story spa is a wonderful addition to the place, with exercise machines, a nonchlorinated bromine pool, face and body salons, yoga, step- and water-aerobics classes, and spa luncheon packages. Seven conference rooms and a guest laundry are also part of the facility. $69–199 depending on room and season includes a cooked-to-order breakfast in the dining room.

CAMPS AND COTTAGES

& **Bear Spring Camps** (397-2341), Route 3, Box 9900, Oakland 04963. Open mid-May through September. A family resort and fishing spot with 75 percent repeat business. Serious anglers come in early May for trout and salmon, and in July there's still bass. Each of the 32 cottages has a

bathroom, hot and cold water, shower, and heat, as well as an open fireplace. They are right on the water; each has its own dock and motorboat (sailboat rentals are available). There's a tennis court and a variety of lawn games, and the swimming is great (the bottom is sandy). Meals are served in the main house. Weekly rates from $450 per couple in shoulder months to $1,640 for eight in high season, including all meals.

✍ **Castle Island Camps** (495-3312), Belgrade Lakes 04918. Open May through mid-September. In winter, contact Horatio Castle, 1800 Carambola Road, West Palm Beach, FL 33406 (407-641-8339). A dozen comfortable-looking cottages clustered on a small island (connected by bridges) in 12-mile Long Pond. This is the second generation of Castles to maintain the camps, geared to fishing (the pond is stocked; rental boats are available). Meals are served in the small central lodge. There is an open fireplace in the community building, and a rec room with pool tables, Ping-Pong, and darts. Weekly and children's rates are available, and include all meals.

🐾✍ **Alden Camps** (465-7703), RFD 2, Box 1140, Oakland 04963. Vesta (Alden) Putnam and her husband, George, have run these camps, founded by A. Fred Alden in 1910 with just one rental unit, since 1956. They now offer 18 rustic cottages scattered among the pines on the shores of East Lake. Recreational activities include fishing, golf nearby, swimming, water-skiing, boating, tennis, hiking, and several playing fields. Children are welcome and pets can be accommodated for an extra fee. $90–135 daily; $540–810 weekly in high season includes all three meals.

CAMPGROUNDS

Steve Powell Wildlife Management Area (Swan Island), in Merry-meeting Bay off Richmond. State-owned Swan Island is managed as a wildlife preservation area in Merrymeeting Bay, a vast tidal bay that's well known among birders. Limited camping in primitive Adirondack shelters is available, along with a motorboat shuttle from Richmond, through the Department of Inland Fisheries and Wildlife: 287-1150.

Lake St. George State Park (589-4255), Route 3, Liberty, offers 38 camp-sites and a boat launch ($13 for nonresidents).

WHERE TO EAT

DINING OUT

Slate's (622-9575), 167 Water Street, Hallowell. Breakfast, lunch, and dinner Tuesday through Friday, brunch and dinner Saturday, brunch-only on Sunday. Coffeehouse atmosphere in three adjoining storefronts with brick walls, tin ceilings, changing art, a great bar, and a patio in back. The brunch menu is huge and hugely popular. The dinner menu changes daily but might include scrod baked with Brie and fresh blue-berries, or cashew chicken on rice. Live music Friday and Saturday night, and during Sunday brunch. $8.95–14.95.

KIM GRANT

The A-1 Diner in Gardiner

Village Inn (495-3553), Route 27, Belgrade Lakes. Open April through December, 5–9 PM Monday through Saturday and Sunday 11:30 AM–8 PM. New owners Allen and Doris Danforth are continuing the traditions of this rambling old place with a lake view and early-bird specials. The specialty is duckling, roasted for up to 12 hours and served with a choice of sauces. Entrées $9.95–16.95.

Johann Sebastian B. (465-3223), 40 Fairfield Street, Oakland. Open Wednesday through Saturday for dinner in summer; Friday and Saturday the rest of the year. A Victorian house in the Belgrade Lakes area. Specialties include chicken cordon bleu and sauerbraten; homemade European pastries and dessert drinks. $11–21.50.

River Cafe (622-2190), 119 Water Street, Hallowell. Open for lunch and dinner Monday through Friday. Downstairs lounge open Saturday as well, 4 PM to whenever. Mediterranean-American specialties include shish kebab and shish Tawook (marinated chicken tips cooked over an open flame and rolled in Lebanese bread). Reservations required for dinner. $10.95–16.95.

Senator Restaurant (622-5804), 284 Western Avenue, Augusta. Open daily 6:30 AM to 10 PM. A big, all-American dining room (buses are welcome) within the Senator Inn complex. Seafood specialties include seafood medley (shrimp, haddock, crab cake, and scallops), filet and seafood béarnaise, and crab cakes; excellent salad bar. Entrées $11.95–18.95.

EATING OUT

The A-1 Diner (582-4804), 3 Bridge Street, Gardiner, is a popular spot for any meal. Open Monday through Saturday for all three meals, but just 8 AM–1 PM on Sunday (open 5 AM weekdays, 6 AM Saturday). A vintage

1946 Worcester diner with plenty of Formica, blue vinyl booths, blue and black tile, a 14-stool, marble-topped counter, and a neon blue and pink clock with the slogan TIME TO EAT. The waitress seems to know everyone in the place at breakfast, and everyone seems to know each other. You won't find just typical diner fare here, however. The breakfast menu includes banana-almond French toast and a wide variety of omelets, as well as eggs and hash; the meat loaf has a Cajun accent, the split-pea soup, an Italian, and the chili, a Latin. Greek lemon soup is a specialty. Beverages range from herbal tea to imported beers and wines. But you can always get tapioca pudding, and the route to the rest room is still outside and in through the kitchen door.

Burnsie's Homestyle Sandwiches (622-6425), State Street, Augusta, between the Capitol and the rotary. Open 8–4 weekdays only. This is the perfect place if you're visiting the Maine State Museum. Keep your car parked where it is and walk up past the Capitol to this out-of-place house, a source of famous lobster rolls, Reubens, and a variety of sandwiches, many named for local legislators. Although there is no real place to eat in the shop, if it's a nice day the picnic tables in the park just across the river, adjoining Fort Western, offer the best view in town.

✔ **Roseland,** Route 201/200 approximately 4 miles north of Augusta. A popular family-style restaurant for many years, with such favorites as turkey dinner or ham steak. Good for kids, casual comfortable atmosphere.

Augusta House of Pancakes, Western Avenue, Augusta. This place has grown from a pancake house to a restaurant serving full meals at reasonable prices. A favorite among locals.

Pedro's (582-5058), 161 Water Street, Gardiner. Open for lunch and dinner Tuesday through Saturday. A comfortable, casual place with a Mexican and southwestern menu.

Railway Cafe (737-2277), 64 Main Street, Richmond. Open Monday through Saturday 6:30 AM–8 PM, later Friday and Saturday, Sunday 7–4. Minutes off I-95, this pleasant restaurant makes a great road-food stop: A wide choice of morning omelets and lunchtime sandwiches, burgers, salads, and pizzas, and a huge, reasonably priced dinner menu including "Just for Kids." Allow a few minutes to walk around this historic Kennebec River town (see *Villages, Green Space,* and *Swimming*).

Third Rail Cafe (873-6526), adjacent to the Railroad Square Cinema, Waterville. Lunch and dinner. A good place to go before or after a show. Menu includes such unique choices as roasted vegetable tart and Mediterranean lamb stew.

COFFEE HOUSES

Jorgensen's Cafe (872-8711), Main Street, Waterville. A large, funky café with at least a dozen flavored coffees, as well as tea and espresso choices. The deli serves quiche, soups, salads, and sandwiches with several delicious bread options. Coffee and tea supplies, gourmet foods.

Java Joe's (622-1110), Water Street, Augusta. Cozy place with baked goods, an interesting lunch menu, and the usual coffee and espresso drinks.

Kennebec Coffee Co., Water Street, Hallowell. Soft golden walls and comfy couches and chairs. Plenty of coffee choices as well as terrific muffins, bagels, light lunch options.

ENTERTAINMENT

Theater at Monmouth (933-2952), P.O. Box 385, Monmouth. Performances Wednesday through Sunday in July, Tuesday through Sunday in August; matinees and children's shows vary. Housed in Cumston Hall, a striking turn-of-the-century building designed as a combination theater, library, and town hall. A resident company presents classics and contemporary shows.

Waterville Opera House (873-7000) has a number of shows throughout the year, including music performances and theater productions. It also offers ballet, jazz, tap, acting, and other classes.

Gaslight Theater (626-3698), 1 Winthrop Street, Hallowell, has several productions per season.

Johnson Hall (582-3730), Water Street, Gardiner. The second-floor 450-seat theater, dating from 1864, is presently under restoration, but a 100-seat studio performance space designed for workshops and small performances has already been restored. This is home for the **Institute for the Performing Arts** (classes in magic, juggling, etc.) offered by Benny and Denise Reehl, the powers behind the semiannual New England Vaudeville Festival. Check local calendars for periodic performances.

Railroad Square Cinema (873-6526), Main Street, Waterville. Heading north on Route 201 (College Avenue), turn left between Burger King and the railroad tracks. Art and foreign films in a very popular, casual atmosphere. Rebuilt after a fire, now in a separate building with a café (see *Eating Out*).

SELECTIVE SHOPPING

The mid-19th-century commercial buildings along **Water Street in Gardiner** have hatched some interesting shops.

The heart of Belgrade Village is **Day's Store** (495-2205). Open year-round, recently expanded to serve as general store; state liquor store; fishing license, gear, boot, and gift source; and rainy-day mecca. **Maine Made Shop,** open late May through Labor Day, stocks pottery, books, and Maine souvenirs.

ANTIQUES SHOPS

The picturesque riverside lineup of shops in Hallowell harbors fewer antiques dealers than it did a few years ago, but it is still a worthwhile browsing street. **Dealer's Choice,** 108 Water Street, is a 70-plus dealer mall with a wide range. **Hatties Antiques,** 148 Water Street, specializes in fine antique jewelry, antique lamps, clocks, and art glass.

ART GALLERIES

A dozen galleries in public buildings and private homes, within a short drive of each other, are listed in an art tour brochure promoting the area as the Kennebec Valley Art District. Pick up the brochure at the chamber (see *Guidance*).

BOOKSTORES

Children's Book Cellar (872-4543), 5 East Concourse, Waterville.

Leon H. Tebbets Bookstore, 164 Water Street, Hallowell, is a book lover's delight; 36,000 closely packed titles (closed Sunday in winter).

Barnes & Noble Booksellers (621-0038), the Marketplace at Augusta, directly across from the Augusta Civic Center. A new full-service bookstore with music and computer software sections, as well as a café.

FACTORY OUTLETS

Carleton Woolen Mills Factory Outlet (582-6003), Griffin Street, Gardiner. Fabrics, woolens, and notions.

Cascade Fabrics, Oakland. Open Monday through Saturday 8:30–4:30. A genuine mill store.

Dexter Shoe Factory Outlet (873-6739), Kennedy Memorial Drive, Waterville.

SPECIAL EVENTS

July: **The Whatever Family Festival**, in the week surrounding the Fourth of July, has recently moved its central focus to Capitol Park. Children's performances, soap box derby, Learn the River Day, entertainment, carnival, and more. **China Connection**—public supper, pageant, road race, pie-eating and greased pig contests in China. **Old Hallowell Days** *(third week)*. **Annual Scottish Games & Gathering of the Scottish Clans,** sponsored by the St. Andrew's Society of Maine, Thomas College, Waterville.

The Upper Kennebec Valley and Moose River Valley, Including The Forks and Jackman

Commercial rafting on the Kennebec began in 1976 when fishing guide Wayne Hockmeyer discovered the rush of riding the whitewater through dramatic, 12-mile-long Kennebec Gorge. On his first ride through the gorge, Hockmeyer had to contend with logs hurtling all around him, but, as luck would have it, 1976 also marked the year in which environmentalists managed to outlaw log runs on the Kennebec.

Eighteen rafting companies now vie for space to take advantage of up to 8,000 cubic feet of water per second released every morning from late spring through mid-October from Central Maine Power's Harris Hydroelectric Station. No more than 1,000 rafters are, however, allowed on the river at a time. In order to compete, outfitters based in and around The Forks have added their own lodging; several of these operations have evolved into year-round sports-based resorts, thanks in good part to the genuine winter appeal of this area, primarily to snowmobilers but also to cross-country skiers.

Empty as it seemed when rafting began, this stretch of the Upper Kennebec had been a 19th-century resort area. A now-vanished, 100-room, three-story Forks Hotel was built at the confluence of the Kennebec and Dead Rivers in the middle of The Forks in 1860 and was well known for its steady flow of liquor (Maine was legally dry at the time). Summer hotels were scattered along the rivers and nearby lakes, and guests hiked wilderness trails to sights such as Moxie Falls. A half-dozen remote sportsmen's camps on fishing ponds date from this period.

Route 201 North from Skowhegan is the traditional access to the Upper Kennebec Valley, but the river itself curves west to Norridgewock before heading north to Solon and Bingham. Solon, with its Greek Revival meeting house, old hotel, and general store, still seems a part of the long-settled valley but Bingham (just 8 miles north) has the feel of the woodland hub it is. A couple of miles north of Bingham is the 155-foot-high hydro dam, built in the 1930s by Central Maine Power, which walls back the river, raising it more than 120 feet, creating wide, shimmering Wyman Lake. The lake gradually narrows as Route 201 follows it north and is best viewed from the rest area at its northern end. Drive slowly and carefully along this twisty road. It's frequented by both speeding lumber trucks and lumbering moose.

North of The Forks, Route 201 traverses lonely but beautiful wilderness. Wildlife abounds: More than 100 species of birds have been seen in the region, and this section of the Kennebec is the only US river supporting five types of game fish. The route is known as the Arnold Trail because Benedict Arnold came this way in 1775 to Quebec City, which—it's worth noting—is just 86 miles north of Jackman.

Jackman and Moose River form a community (divided by a brief bridge) on Big Wood Lake. In warm weather you notice that something is missing here and don't realize what it is unless you revisit in winter (November through April). It's snow. Snow fills in the gaps of this shrunken old border community with its outsized French-Canadian Catholic Church and matching (defunct) convent, some good restaurants, motels, and reasonably priced camps. It's also the base for exceptional canoeing and kayaking. A former rail junction, it's now a major hub of Maine's snowmobiling network. From Route 201 we urge you to branch off on Route 15/6, the lonely, 31-mile road that follows the Moose River east to Moosehead Lake.

GUIDANCE

Skowhegan Chamber of Commerce (474-3621), P.O. Box 326, Skowhegan 04976, maintains a year-round information center on Russel Street, just off Route 201.

Jackman–Moose River Chamber of Commerce (668-4171) maintains a seasonal information center (with rest rooms) in Lakeside Town Park and a year-round office in downtown Jackman.

GETTING THERE

By car: Rail service is long gone from this obvious transport corridor, now traversed only by Route 201. Take I-95 to exit 36, then Route 201 North all the way to The Forks. The approach from the Rangeley and Sugarloaf areas, Route 16, is a beautiful drive.

MEDICAL EMERGENCY

Bingham Area Health Center (672-4187); regional ambulance service (672-4410).

Jackman Region Health Center (268-6691) is on Route 201, Jackman.

Redington-Fairview General Hospital (474-5085) offers 24-hour emergency care (for ambulance service dial 911).

TO SEE

NATURAL BEAUTY SPOTS

Moxie Falls (90 feet high) is said to be the highest falls in New England. The view is striking, and well worth the detour from The Forks (see *Hiking*).

Attean View. Heading north toward Jackman from The Forks, only one rest area is clearly marked. Stop. The view is splendid: Attean Lake and the whole string of other ponds linked by the Moose River, with the western mountains as a backdrop. There are picnic tables.

MUSEUMS AND HISTORIC SIGHTS

Skowhegan History House (474-2415), Norridgewock Avenue, Skowhegan. Open mid-June to mid-September, Tuesday through Friday 1–6. A Greek Revival brick house exhibiting 19th-century furnishings, artifacts, and local maps. Admission by donation.

Margaret Chase Smith Library Center (474-7133), Skowhegan. Open year-round, Monday through Friday 10–4. Set above the Kennebec, an expanded version of Senator Smith's home is a research and conference center housing records, scrapbooks, news releases, tape recordings, and memorabilia from over three decades in public life.

Skowhegan Indian and Norridgewock Monument. Billed as "the world's largest sculptured wooden Indian," this 62-foot-high statue is dedicated to the memory of the Maine Abenakis. It's just off Route 201 near the Kennebec. Abenaki heritage is particularly strong in this area. In the early 18th century, the French Jesuit Sebastian Rasle established a mission in nearby Norridgewock, insisting that Native American lands "were given them of God, to them and their children forever." Rasle and his mission were wiped out by the English in 1724. The site of the village is marked by a pleasant riverside picnic area in a pine grove. (Take Route 201A from Norridgewock toward Madison across the bridge and up a steep hill. Turn left 3 miles from the top of the hill on Father Rasle Monument Road; it's 3 more miles to the cemetery and picnic site.) Note that Route 201A rather than 201 follows the Kennebec here. In the middle of Norridgewock, you might also want to stop by Oosoola Park to see the totem pole topped by a frog (this is also a good picnic spot and boat-launch site). Ancient Native American petroglyphs have been found in Emden.

L. C. Bates Museum (453-4894), Route 201, Hinckley. Open Wednesday through Saturday 10–4:30, Sunday 1–4:30. $2.50 per adult, $1 per child. Right on the road but part of the campus of the Good-Will Hinckley School (founded in 1889 for "disadvantaged chidden"), this ponderous Romanesque building houses a large and wonderfully dated collection including stuffed birds and Native American artifacts.

South Solon Meeting House, just off Route 210, Solon. Open year-round. An 1842 Greek Revival building with murals and frescoes by WPA and Skowhegan School artists.

TO DO

CANOEING AND KAYAKING

The Moose River Bow Trip is a Maine classic: A series of pristine ponds form a 42-mile meandering route that winds back to the point of origin, eliminating the need for a shuttle. The fishing is fine, remote campsites are scattered along the way, and the put-in place is accessible. One major portage is required. Canoe rentals are available from a variety of local sources. Several rafting companies rent canoes and offer guided trips, but the specialists here are Registered Maine Guides Amy and Leslie McKennedy at **Cry of the Loon Outdoor Adventures** (668-7808) in Jackman. Canoe rentals are also plentiful in Jackman.

FISHING

Fishing is what the **sporting camps** (see *Lodging*) are all about. The catch is landlocked salmon, trout, and togue. Rental boats and canoes are available.

GOLF

Moose River Golf Course (668-5331), Route 201, Moose River (just north of Jackman). Mid-May through mid-October; club rental, putting green, nine holes.

HIKING

Hiking possibilities abound in this area. The standout is Moxie Falls, an 89-foot waterfall considered the highest in New England, set in a dramatic gorge. It's an easy ⅔-mile walk from the trailhead (it can be very muddy and wet). Turn off Route 201 onto Moxie Road on the south side of the bridge across the Kennebec in The Forks. Park off the road at the trailhead sign on your left.

MOOSE-WATCHING

The best time to see a moose is dawn or dusk. Favorite local moose crossings include Moxie Road from The Forks to Moxie Pond; the Central Maine Power Company road from Moxie Pond to Indian Pond; the 25 miles north from The Forks to Jackman on Route 201; and the 30 miles from Jackman to Rockwood on Route 6/15. Drive these stretches carefully; residents all know someone who has died in a car-moose collision.

MOUNTAIN BIKING

Local terrain varies from old logging roads to tote paths. Rentals are available from **Sky Lodge Resort** (1-800-416-6181) and **Northern Outdoors** (1-800-765-RAFT).

WHITE-WATER RAFTING

See the introduction to this chapter. Timid novice rafters have no reason to fear the 12-mile run down the **East Branch of the Kennebec River** from Harris Dam. The only scary Class IV and V whitewater is at Magic

Moxie Falls, Upper Kennebec River

Falls, which comes early in the trip, and after that it's all fun. On our second day we tried the slightly more challenging run on the **Dead River,** available less often (releases are less frequent), also offered by most outfitters. The safety records for all outfitters are excellent, or they wouldn't be in this rigorously monitored business. April through October all offer the basics: a river ride with a hearty steak cookout at its end and a chance to view (and buy) slides of the day's adventures. Standard charges are around $80 weekdays, $100 weekends. If you don't like getting your feet wet (especially early and late in the season when the water is frigid), you might ask about self-bailing rafts, but the big variant among outfitters is the nature of the lodging. It ranges from tent sites to inns and cabins to condo-style units—which they package into rates. To save phoning around for availability, you might call **Raft Maine** (1-800-723-8633); they have a web site: www.raftmaine.com.

✐ *Note:* Although white-water rafting began as a big singles sport, it is becoming more and more popular with families, who frequently combine it with a visit to Quebec City. Minimum age requirements vary but weight is also a consideration (usually no less than 90 pounds). We identify the outfitters who cater to kids and/or offer "Lower Kennebec" trips geared to children as young as 6 with our ✐ sign.

✐ **Northern Outdoors, Inc.** (663-2244; 1-800-765-7238), P.O. Box 100, The Forks 04985. Suzie Hockmeyer now heads up Northern Outdoors, the Kennebec's first and still its biggest outfitter. Its "Outdoor Adventure Center" includes an attractive open-timbered lodge with high ceilings, a huge hearth, comfortable seating, a cheerful dining room (see *Dining Out*), a bar, a pool, a private lake, platform tennis, volleyball and basketball, a sauna, and giant hot tub. Fishing and mountain biking, rock climbing and kayak tours are also available. Accommodations vary from riverside camping to lakeside cabins, from lodge rooms to "logdominiums" (condo-style units with lofts and a kitchen/dining area). In addition to rafting, they offer sportyak and guide-your-own raft adventures, fishing trips, rock climbing, a ropes course, canoe and kayak clinics. In winter the lodge caters to snowmobilers and cross-country skiers.

✍ **Adventure Bound** (888-606-7238), P.O. Box 88, Caratunk 04925, an offshoot of Northern Outdoors, specializes in youth groups and has its own base lodge and cabin tent village.

New England Outdoor Center (723-5438; 1-800-766-7238), 240 Katahdin Avenue, Millinocket 04462. Matt Polstein's is also one of the oldest, largest and classiest rafting operations. Lodging accommodations include the 17-room **Sterling Inn** in Caratunk, a 19th-century stage stop that dates from 1816 and offers attractive country inn–style guest rooms and delightful common rooms. Across the river on quiet Silver Cove (where Wyman Lake turns back into the Kennebec River and there's a good swimming beach), by the Osprey Center Base Lodge (housing a shop, changing rooms and showers, common area), are cabin tents and "guesthouses" (sleeping up to 10 people) with a full kitchen. Amenities include an outdoor Jacuzzi, sand volleyball, a dining pavilion, and kayak rentals.

Wilderness Expeditions (534-2242; 1-800-825-WILD), P.O. Box 41, Rockwood 04478. Wilderness maintains a base camp in The Forks with a pleasant central lodge, campsites, riverside cabin tents, and cottages. Facilities include swimming pool, hot tub, and volleyball court. Meal packages are available. This is an offshoot of the Birches Resort in Rockwood, a beautifully sited, full-service resort (see "Moosehead Lake"); some packages combine Kennebec and Dead River rafting with stays at the Birches.

✍ **Crab Apple White Water** (663-4491; 1-800-553-RAFT), The Forks 04985. A family-owned operation that won't stop growing! Crab Apple Acres began with an 1830s Cape with a fanlight over the door and flowery wallpaper in the seven guest rooms. The original Cape is still there as an option, but Crab Apple long ago added a neighboring annex with luxury motel-style units (with wet bars, fridges, Jacuzzis, and decks). A major new base camp is promised for the 1999 season. "Funyaks" (inflatable kayaks) and half-day "float trips" are also offered.

Maine Whitewater (672-4814; 1-800-345-MAIN), Gadabout Gaddis Airport, P.O. Box 633, Bingham 04920. Jim Ernst operates the second oldest rafting company on the river. His Bingham base complex includes a restaurant and lounge, game room, hot tub, private airport, and campground. The llamas that share the premises are fun to watch. Bike rentals. Inquire about Jim's 12-foot airboat, which may or may not be offering tours on the Kennebec this season.

Downeast Whitewater (603-447-3002; 1-800-677-7238), P.O. Box 119, Center Conway, NH 03813, maintains the seasonal Dew Drop Inn bed & breakfast on Pleasant Pond in Caratunk, as well as the Kelley Brook Resort with a restaurant, lounge, log cabins, cabin tents, and camping on Route 201.

✎ **Unicorn Rafting Expeditions** (668-07629; 1-800-UNICORN), Route 201, Lake Parlin 04945, has many packages for families at its Lake Parlin Resort, which offers lakefront cabins sleeping 4 to 10; also campsites and cabin tents. Facilities include a main lodge with fieldstone fireplace, lounge, pool table, hot tub, and heated swimming pool. Packages combining mountain biking, canoe trips, and/or "funyaking" are offered. Guided fishing expeditions, too. Lower Kennebec River trips are offered for families with children as young as age 6. Inquire about 4-day "family adventures" that include canoeing, camping, and mountain biking.

Magic Falls Rafting (800-207-7238), P.O. Box 9, The Forks 04985, has a base camp with a bed & breakfast (12 rooms), cabin tents, rooms in the Marshall Hotel and campsites on the banks of the Dead River in The Forks. Also offers "funyaks" (an inflatable cross between a canoe and a kayak) and rock climbing.

Moxie Outdoor Adventures (663-2231; 1-800-866-6943), SR 63, Box 60, The Forks 04985, operates out of Lake Moxie Camps, one of the oldest sporting camps around. Jock-geared, great lakeside spot, mountain biking, fishing, canoes and kayaks, hiking, and family-style meals. The reasonable price reflects the somewhat rougher comfort level.

Professional River Runners of Maine, Inc. (663-2229; 1-800-325-3911), P.O. Box 92, West Forks 04985, is a smaller company specializing in extended trips from 1–6 days. It operates a campground at a base camp near the Kennebec.

Windfall Rafting (668-4818; 1-800-683-2009), P.O. Box 505, Moose River 04945. Based in a classic, 1890s schoolhouse in Moose River (just north of downtown Jackman), Windfall has been in business one way or another since 1982. The Blake brothers run smaller-than-average groups and book you into the gamut of what's available in Jackman, from motel rooms through camps and campsites to splendid Sky Lodge (now available only to groups of 12 or more). It also offers inflatable kayak trips on Kennebec East Outlet.

WINTER SPORTS

CROSS-COUNTRY SKIING
Crab Apple Acres (663-4491; 1-800-553-RAFT) offers a dedicated network of cross-country trails in The Forks.

SNOWMOBILING
Snowmobiling is big in this region, with more than 100 miles of trails over mountains, rivers, and lakes and through woods with connections to Sugarloaf, the Moosehead area, and Canada. Rentals are available from

many of the rafting companies and other sources. Check with the Jackman Chamber of Commerce. For information about the region's rentals and lodging phone **Sledmaine**: 877-2SLED-ME.

LODGING

SPORTING CAMPS

While these camps were originally geared exclusively to fishermen, they now also welcome families and hikers.

Harrison's Pierce Pond Sporting Camps (524-0560, radiophone—let it ring and try again if it doesn't work; Columbus Day to May 15, or when unable to get through, call 603-524-0560), Box 315, Bingham 04920. Open May through Columbus Day. Sited on the Appalachian Trail, 20 miles from Bingham, 15 of it a dirt road. Fran and Tim Harrison have brought new life to this classic old log camp set on a hillside and over-looking a stream with a waterfall in the distance. Nine-mile-long Pierce Pond is a short walk across the stream and through the woods. Five of the nine log cabins have a half-bath, and there are three full-facility bathhouses on the premises. Rates include three abundant meals per day. Word has gotten out about Fran's cooking, and some people actu-ally drive the bumpy road for Sunday turkey or Friday lobster. $63–69 per person per day or $390–400 per week, includes all meals (based on double occupancy and 2-night minimum); half price for children; spe-cial summer rates July 12 through August 11 (3-night minimum). Group rates $53–59 per person per day, $350–390 per person per week for eight or more people.

Cobb's Pierce Pond Camps (628-2819 in summer; 628-3612 in winter), North New Portland 04961. There are 12 guest cabins, accommodating from two to eight people; each has a screened porch, woodstove, bath-room, and electricity. Home-cooked meals and between-meal snacks are served in the main lodge. This traditional sporting camp dates from 1902, and the Cobb family has been running it for more than four de-cades; 90 percent of the guests are repeats. It's the kind of place that doesn't advertise. It has a loyal following among serious fishermen; sand beaches nearby. Guiding services available. $65–75 per person per day includes three meals; children's rates.

Attean Lake Resort (668-3792; 668-7726 in winter), Jackman 04945. Open Memorial Day weekend through September. Sited on Birch Is-land in Attean Lake, surrounded by mountains. This resort has been in the Holden family since 1900; 14 seasonal cabins, luxurious by sports-lodge standards, with full baths, Franklin fireplaces, kerosene lamps, and maid service daily with a relatively new central lodge (the old one burned) in which meals are served. Fishing boats, kayaks, and canoes are available. A great place for canoeing, kayaking, sailing, and hiking. The resort is easily accessible from Jackman; you phone from the shore, and a boat fetches you. $225 per couple includes meals; weekly rates.

OTHER LODGING

Inn by the River (663-2181), Route 201, HCR 63, Box 24, West Forks 04985. Open year-round. Bill and Cori Cost, longtime teachers and rafting guides, have rebuilt—from scratch when it proved impossible to save the old building—a traditional inn on a bluff above the Kennebec. It's well done. The Great Room with its fireplace and piano opens onto a porch and gardens and the dining room has the same expansive view. Guest rooms have private baths and are all nicely furnished. Trails out the back door lead up into the woods and in winter connect with much of Maine. You might want to reserve dinner: $8.95 (for chicken cordon bleu) to $17.95 (for haddock stuffed with shrimp). There's also a pub for guests. $90–110 includes breakfast during rafting and snowmobiling season, otherwise $60–90.

Mrs. G's Bed & Breakfast (672-4034; 1-888-267-4833, PIN #2460), Box 389, Meadow Street, Bingham 04920. A tidy house on a side street in the middle of town. Frances Gibson (Mrs. G) delights in orienting guests to the full range of local hiking, biking, rafting, and cross-country skiing possibilities. There are four cheerful guest rooms, also a delightful loft dorm room with nine beds, perfect for groups; shared baths. $30 per person includes a fabulous full breakfast and state tax. A canoe is available.

Also see the **Sterling Inn,** run by New England Outdoor Center, under *White-Water Rafting*. Most lodging described for the outfitters in *White-Water Rafting* is available to nonrafters.

WHERE TO EAT

DINING OUT

Moose Point Tavern (668-4012), Jackman. Open daily in summer 5–9, otherwise Friday, Saturday, and Sunday, but check. Built on the shore of Big Wood Lake in the 1890s as the main lodge for Henderson's Sporting Camps, now destination dining for much of this neck of the woods, operated by former rafting guide Carolann Ouellette. Starters range from Poutine (if you don't know what it is, you don't want to) to shrimp cocktail; entrées run from Gorgonzola linguine with toasted walnuts ($9.75) to apricot mustard duck ($13.95). Wine is served.

Harrison's Pierce Pond Camps (672-3625), Bingham. We don't want to understate the taxing trip into Harrison's (see *Sporting Camps*), but if you happen to be spending a few days in this area and want a very special meal, it's worth the ride for the turkey dinner on Sunday, baked stuffed pork on Monday, steak teriyaki "Juline" on Tuesday, and so on. Lobster is served on Friday night. Breakfast served to Appalachian Trail hikers daily 7:30 with advance reservation; dinner is served promptly at 5:30, with reservations required at least 1 day in advance. $9.95 to market price for seafood.

Northern Outdoors (663-4466; 1-800-765-RAFT), Route 201, The Forks. The pine-sided dining room in the lodge is open daily year-round for all three meals. Informal, with great photos of The Forks in its big-time logging and old resort days adorning the walls. There's a brew pub and the food is good. Entrées $6–14.

✍ **Loon's Look-Out Restaurant** at Tuckaway Shores Cabins (668-3351) on Big Wood Lake, Jackman. Take Spruce Street off Route 201, bear right onto Forest Street, and it's at the end on the right-hand side. Open year-round, Friday through Sunday 5–9; they will open other days and times for groups of 10 or more. Takeout available. A great little Italian place with specialties like mozzarella bread nibblers, lasagna, and *bistecca a la pazzarella* (steak chunks with bell peppers, onions, mushrooms, sauce, and spices). Reservations recommended. $5.95–15.95. Children's menu $3–5.

EATING OUT

Heritage House Restaurant (474-5100), Madison Avenue, Skowhegan. Open Tuesday through Friday for lunch and daily for dinner. Locally rated as the best place to eat.

Old Mill Pub (474-6627), 41-R Water Street, Skowhegan. Open Monday through Saturday for lunch and dinner; also open Sunday in summer. A picturesque old mill building set back from the main drag with a seasonal deck overlooking the Kennebec. A friendly bar and scattered tables; sandwiches (a good Reuben), quiche, and specials for lunch; spinach lasagna or stir-fry shrimp for dinner.

Bloomfield's Cafe & Bar (474-8844), 40 Water Street, Skowhegan. Open daily for lunch and dinner. Stained glass, ferns, tile floors, and an exquisite copper moose head create a pleasant atmosphere in this corner store eatery. Pete's Wicked Ale and Moosehead are available, and the selection of sandwiches is wide; try Bloomie's Bomber.

🏵 **Thompson's Restaurant** (672-3245), Main Street, Bingham. Open daily for all three meals year-round. This inviting eatery has been in business since 1939 and still has an old-fashioned look, with deep booths. The menu includes homemade doughnuts, fresh fish, and often favorites like pea soup, baked beans, and custard pie; pizza, wine, and beer also served.

The New Marshall Hotel (663-4455), The Forks. Open for dinner most nights, live bands on weekends. A genuine old hotel with rooms still upstairs but a better place to eat than to sleep—the only real eatery, in fact, in the Forks.

Appleton's (663-2114), Route 201, The Forks. Open 6:30 AM–9 PM during rafting season. Pizzas, subs, and "breakfast burgers," Gifford's ice cream.

Four Seasons Restaurant (668-7728), Jackman. Open 5 AM–9 PM. One big room, booths, good road food, blackboard specials.

ENTERTAINMENT

✎ **Lakewood Theater** at Skowhegan, the Cornville Players (474-7176), RFD 1, Box 1780. Late May through mid-September. A community group performs in Maine's oldest summer theater. Broadway plays most evenings and occasional matinees; inquire about Saturday morning children's performances.

Skowhegan Drive-in (474-9277), Route 201 South. A genuine 1950s drive-in with nightly double features "under the stars" in July and August, weekends in June.

The Skowhegan Cinema (474-3451), 7 Court Street, is another period piece, dating from the 1920s, films nightly.

SPECIAL EVENTS

June and July: During its 9-week sessions the prestigious **Skowhegan School of Painting and Sculpture** sponsors a lecture series on weekday evenings that's free and open to the public; phone 474-9345.

August: **Skowhegan State Fair,** one of the oldest and biggest fairs in New England—harness racing, a midway, agricultural exhibits, big-name entertainment, tractor and oxen pulls.

September: **Oosoola Fun Day,** Norridgewock, includes the state's oldest frog-jumping contest (up to 300 contestants) around a frog-topped totem pole; also canoe races, crafts fair, flower and pet contests, live music, barbecue. **Fly-in,** Gadabout Gaddis Airport, Bingham.

VII. NORTHERN MAINE

Moosehead Lake Area
Katahdin Region Including Lower Piscataquis
Bangor Area
Aroostook County

Driving the logging roads of Aroostook County

JOSEPH DENNEHY

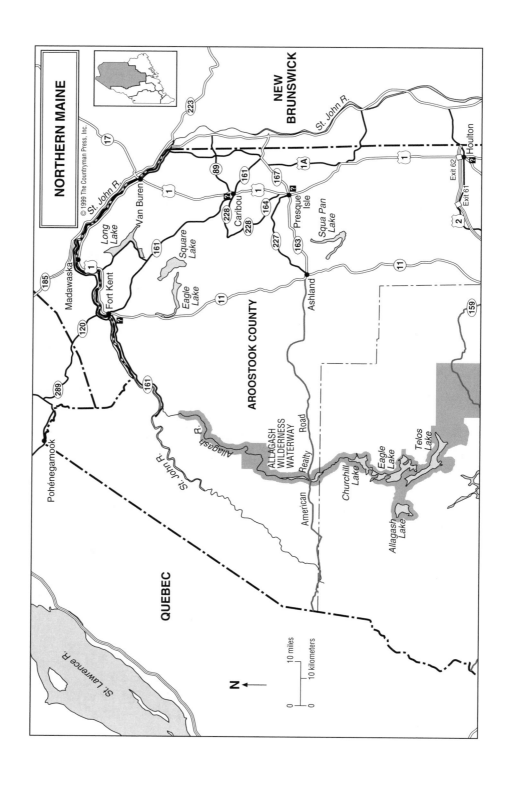

NORTHERN MAINE

© 1999 The Countryman Press, Inc.

NEW BRUNSWICK

QUEBEC

AROOSTOOK COUNTY

St. Lawrence R.

St. John R.

Pohénegamook

Madawaska

Fort Kent

Van Buren

Long Lake

Square Lake

Eagle Lake

Caribou

Presque Isle

Squa Pan Lake

Ashland

Houlton

Exit 62
Exit 61

Allagash R.

St. John R.

American Realty Road

ALLAGASH WILDERNESS WATERWAY

Churchill Lake

Eagle Lake

Telos Lake

Allagash Lake

N

10 miles
10 kilometers
0
0

185
120
289
161
1
2
161
11
17
223
89
161
228
228
164
1
167
1A
163
227
11
1
2
159
2

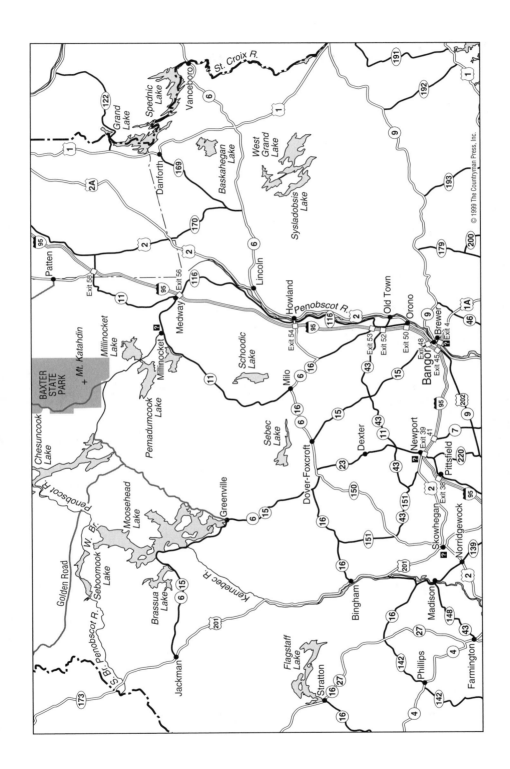

© 1999 The Countryman Press, Inc.

The North Woods

Like "Down East," Maine's "North Woods" may seem a bit of a mirage, always over the next hill. In fact, 17.6 of Maine's 22 million acres are forested, and much of that woodland lies in what we've described in this book as the "Western Mountains and Lakes Region."

Still, one particular tract of forest tends to be equated—mostly by out-of-staters—with the North Woods. That section is the 6½ million acres bordered to the north and west by Canada, which on highway maps shows no roads. This is the largest stretch of unpeopled woodland in the East, but wilderness it's not.

Private ownership of this sector, technically part of Maine's 10½ million acres known as the unorganized townships, dates from the 1820s when Maine was securing independence from Massachusetts. The mother state, her coffers at their usual low, stipulated that an even division of all previously undeeded wilderness be part of the separation agreement. The woods were quickly sold by the legislature for 12½ to 38 cents per acre, bought cooperatively by groups to cut individual losses.

The vast inland tracts, mostly softwood, increased in value in the 1840s when the process of making paper from wood fibers was rediscovered. It seems that the method first used in A.D. 105 had been forgotten, and New England paper mills were using rags at the time.

By the turn of the century, pulp and paper mills had moved to their softwood source and assumed management responsibility and taxes for most of the unorganized townships. Mergers have since increased the size (decreased the number) of these companies, and ownership of some of the largest is now based in Britain and South Africa. North Maine Woods, Inc., a consortium of more than 20 landowners, now pays the lion's share of the area's land tax and the cost of maintaining thousands of miles of private gravel roads, the ones not shown on the state highway maps but open to visitors who pay a fee and promise to abide by the rules (rule number one: Drive slowly and pull over to permit logging trucks to pass).

The private roads have multiplied since the end of log drives in the 1970s and have changed the look and nature of the North Woods. Many remote sporting camps, for a century accessible only by water, and more recently by air, are now a bumpy ride from the nearest town.

Many of the sporting camps themselves haven't changed since the turn of the century. Some have hardly altered since the 1860s, the era when wealthy "sports" first began arriving in Greenville by train from New York and Boston, to be met by Native American guides. The genuine old camps are Maine's inland windjammers: unique holdovers from another era. Many simply cater to descendants of their original patrons.

For the general public, two North Woods preserves have been set aside to provide a wilderness experience. These are 200,000-acre Baxter State Park and the 92-mile ribbon of lakes, ponds, rivers, and streams designated as the Allagash Wilderness Waterway.

There are three major approaches to this "North Woods." The longest, most scenic route is up the Kennebec River, stopping to raft in The Forks (see "The Upper Kennebec Valley and Moose River Valley"), and along the Moose River to the village of Rockwood at the dramatic narrows of Moosehead Lake, then down along the lake to Greenville, New England's largest seaplane base. (You can, of course, also drive directly to Greenville, exiting from I-95 at Newport.)

From Greenville you can hop a floatplane to a sporting camp or set off up the eastern shore of Moosehead to the woodland outpost of Kokadjo and on to the Golden Road, a 98-mile, private logging road running east from Quebec through uninterrupted forest to Millinocket. As Thoreau did in the 1850s, you can canoe up magnificent Chesuncook Lake, camping or staying in the tiny old outpost of Chesuncook Village. With increased interest in rafting down the West Branch of the Penobscot River through Ripogenus Gorge and the Crib Works, this stretch of the Golden Road has become known as the West Branch Region.

For those who come this distance simply to climb Mount Katahdin and to camp in Baxter State Park, the quickest route is up I-95 to Medway and in through Millinocket; it's 18 miles to the Togue Pond Gatehouse and Baxter State Park.

Northern reaches of Baxter State Park and the lakes beyond are best accessed from the park's northern entrance via Patten. Both Ashland and Portage are also points of entry, and Shin Pond serves as the seaplane base for this northernmost reach of the North Woods.

GUIDANCE

North Maine Woods (435-6213), Box 421, Ashland 04732, is a consortium of more than 20 major landowners that manages the recreational use of 2.8 million acres of commercial forest in northwestern Maine. It publishes map/guides that show logging roads and campsites, as well as a canoer's guide to the St. John River, a pamphlet about the organization that tells a bit of history and details the regulations and fees, and a list of outfitters and camps that are licensed and insured to operate on the property.

Maine Sporting Camp Association, P.O. Box 89, Jay 04239, publishes a booklet guide to its members. See *Sporting Camps* in "What's Where."

Moosehead Lake Area

As Route 15 crests Indian Hill, you see for a moment what Henry David Thoreau described so well from this spot in 1858: "A suitably wild looking sheet of water, sprinkled with low islands . . . covered with shaggy spruce and other wild wood."

Moosehead is Maine's largest lake, 40 miles long with more than 400 miles of shoreline, most of it owned by lumber companies. Greenville is the sole "organized" town.

Around the turn of the century, you could board a Pullman car in New York City and ride straight through to Greenville, there to board a steamer for Mount Kineo, a palatial summer hotel on an island halfway up the lake. Greenville began as a farm town, but it soon discovered its best crops to be winter lumbering and summer tourists—a group that, since train service and grand hotels have vanished, now consists largely of fishermen, canoeists, white-water rafters, and hunters, augmented in winter by snowmobilers, cross-country skiers, ice fishermen—and moose-watchers.

Unlike 1890s "sports" (the game hunters and trophy fishermen who put Moosehead Lake on the world's resort map), many current outdoorsmen want to watch—not kill—wildlife and to experience "wilderness" completely but quickly; that is, by plunging through white water in a rubber raft, pedaling a mountain bike over woods trails, or paddling an hour or two in Thoreau's trail or in search of a moose.

Moosehead has become Maine's moose mecca. Experts debate whether the name of the lake stems from its shape or from the number of moose you can see there. In 1992 the Moosehead Lake Region Chamber of Commerce launched MooseMainea, an off-season (mid-May to mid-June) festival that courts Moosemaniacs with a series of special events. Moose sightings during that month now average 3,500.

Immense and backed by mountains, Moosehead Lake possesses unusual beauty and offers a family a wide choice of rustic, old-fashioned "camps" at reasonable prices and an increasing number of attractive, even "romantic" rooms in inns and B&Bs. The town remains a lumbermen's depot with a salting of upscale, off-beat shops. It's also New England's largest seaplane base, with three competing flying services ready to ferry visitors to remote camps and campsites in the working woodland to the north and east.

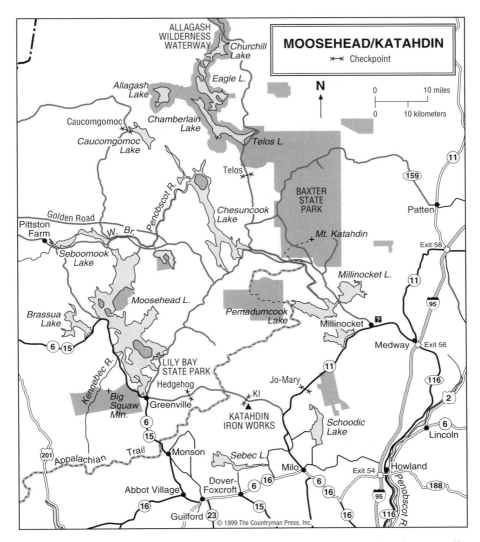

ALLAGASH
WILDERNESS
WATERWAY

Churchill
Lake

MOOSEHEAD/KATAHDIN

×—× Checkpoint

N

0   10 miles

0   10 kilometers

Eagle L.

Allagash
Lake

Caucomgomoc

Chamberlain
Lake

Caucomgomoc
Lake

Telos L.

11

159

Telos

BAXTER
STATE
PARK

Patten

Golden Road

Pittston
Farm

W. Br.

Penobscot R.

Chesuncook
Lake

Mt. Katahdin

Exit 58

Seboomook
Lake

Millinocket L.

11

95

Moosehead L.

Brassua
Lake

Pemadumcook
Lake

Millinocket

Medway   Exit 56

6 15

Kennebec R.

LILY BAY
STATE PARK

Hedgehog

Jo-Mary

11

116

2

Big
Squaw
Mtn.

Greenville

KI

KATAHDIN
IRON WORKS

Schoodic
Lake

6

Lincoln

6

15

201

Appalachian   Trail

Monson

Sebec L.

Milo

Exit 54

Howland

188

Abbot Village

Dover-
Foxcroft

6 16

6

16

95

Penobscot R.

Guilford 23

© 1999 The Countryman Press, Inc.

15

16

116

The community of Rockwood, a half-hour drive north of Greenville on the lake's west shore, is even more of an outpost: a cluster of sporting camps and stores between the lake and the Moose River. Hidden away here on the lake, overlooking Kineo, is the lake's leading resort, the Birches. An authentic old sporting camp with traditional lakeside cottages, it's set in 11,000 acres stretching back to Lake Brassua.

Rockwood sits at the lake's narrows, across from its most dramatic landmark: the sheer cliff face of Mount Kineo, a place revered by Native Americans. According to local legend, the mountain is the petrified remains of a monster moose sent to Earth by the Great Spirit as a punishment for sins. It was also the Native Americans' source of a flintlike stone used for arrowheads. The Kineo House once stood at the foot of this outcropping. First opened as a tavern in 1847, it evolved by 1884 into one of the largest hotels in America, accommodating 500 guests and maintaining its own farm as well as a golf course, yacht club, and stables.

Then came World War I, followed by the Great Depression. The hotel burned in 1938. Its annex has also recently vanished, leaving just a ghostly staff building, a huge elm tree, and a row of shingled Victorian-style summer homes, one now the Kineo House, a pleasant bed & breakfast serving lunch and dinner to outside guests.

Kineo is an islandlike peninsula, most of it now owned by the state, and the climb to the abrupt summit is one of the most rewarding hikes in all of New England.

Most Greenville visitors explore Moosehead's eastern shore at least as far as Lily Bay State Park, and many continue to the outpost village of Kokadjo (population: 5), prime moose-watching country. It's another 40 miles northeast over paper company roads to Chesuncook Lake and to Ripogenus Dam, from which logging roads lead north into the Allagash and east to Baxter State Park and Millinocket. We also strongly suggest driving or flying up to Pittston Farm to sample the fare and feel of a genuine lumber camp and driving—better yet skiing or dogsledding—to Little Lyford Camps and on into Gulf Hagas, a gorgeous stretch of the Appalachian Trail.

GUIDANCE

Moosehead Lake Region Chamber of Commerce (695-2702 or 695-2026; www.moosehead.net/moose/chamber.html), P.O. Box 581, Greenville 04441. A four-season resource. The walk-in information center up on Indian Hill (Route 15 south of town) is open daily in summer; 6 days a week from October through May.

Moosehead Vacation and Sportsmen's Association (534-7300), P.O. Box 366, Rockwood 04478, a source of year-round information about the Rockwood area.

GETTING THERE

By air: **Folsom's Air Service** (see *Getting Around*) offers charter service to Bangor, Augusta, and Portland.

By car: From points south, take the Maine Turnpike to exit 39 (Newport). Proceed up Route 7 to Dexter, then continue north on Route 23 to Sangerville (Guilford), then up Route 15 to Greenville. Note the longer, more scenic route up through The Forks and Jackman to Rockwood described in the introduction to "The Upper Kennebec Valley and Moose River Valley."

GETTING AROUND

By air: **Folsom's Air Service** (695-2821), Greenville. Billed as "Maine's largest seaplane operator," founded by Dick Folsom in 1946, now headed by his son Max. Until recently, Folsom's radiophone was the only link with the outside world for many camps. Inquire about "Floatplane Adventures," ranging from 15-minute flights ($20 per person) to hour-long

moose watches ($60 per person), and "Fly 'n' Dine" packages at remote
Pittston Farm ($55 per person including meal) and Northern Pride Lodge
($65 including meal). Folsom's will also taxi you to a wilderness lake for a
day of fishing, canoeing, or hiking ($50–85 per person).

Currier's Flying Service (695-2778), Greenville Junction. Offers day
trips, scenic flights including Allagash, Mount Katahdin, Mount Kineo,
and others, service to camps; will book camps and guides or set up
guided backcountry, cross-country ski trips.

Jack's Flying Service (695-3020) caters to Allagash canoe trips and
also offers fly-in to housekeeping cottages.

By boat: Shuttle Service to Mount Kineo from Rockwood is offered in
summer (every hour, 8 AM–5 PM) via the **Kineo House Shuttle** (534-
8812). **Rockwood Cottages** (534-7725) also runs a shuttle, especially
useful after 5 PM.

By car: If you plan to venture out on the network of private roads maintained by the lumber companies, be forewarned that it may be expensive,
in terms of both gate fees and damage to your car's suspension. You need
a high car, and preferably four-wheel drive.

MEDICAL EMERGENCY

Charles A. Dean Memorial Hospital and ambulance service (695-
2223), Greenville. Emergency aid is also available from **Maine State
Police Headquarters** (1-800-452-4664).

TO SEE

Moosehead Marine Museum (695-2716 in-season; for year-round information write P.O. Box 1151, Greenville 04441). Home for the S/S
Katahdin, a restored, vintage 1914 steamboat that cruises daily July
through Labor Day with 3-hour cruises three times a week and a 6-
hour Thursday trip to Mount Kineo, with time to walk around the island. Three-hour cruises also offered weekends, Memorial Day through
late September, more frequently during foliage weeks. Private charters
available. One of 50 steamboats on the lake at its height as a resort
destination, the *Katahdin* was the last to survive, converted to diesel in
1922 and in the 1930s modified to haul booms of logs, something we
can remember her doing in 1976, the year of the nation's last log drive.
This graceful, 115-foot, 150-passenger boat was restored through volunteer effort and relaunched in 1985. The museum's displays depict
the lake's resort history from 1836.

Eveleth-Crafts-Sheridan House (695-2909), Main Street, Greenville.
Guided tours offered in July and August, Wednesday through Friday,
1–4. Donation requested. Home of the Moosehead Historical Society,
a genuinely interesting 19th-century home, with displays on the region's
history, including early hotels and steamboats, a lumbering exhibit, and
changing exhibits on the "sunporch."

SCENIC DRIVES
Along the Western Shore

Follow Route 6/15 north through Greenville Junction. If **Squaw Mountain's** chairlifts are running (see *To Do*), the ride is well worth taking for the views. Continue to **Rockwood** and take the shuttle (see *Getting Around*) to **Mount Kineo;** allow the better part of a day for exploring this dramatic spot (see *Hiking* and *Dining Out*). From Rockwood you can continue north for 20 miles to the Northern/Bowater checkpoint (gate fee for out-of-staters). **Pittston Farm,** a short distance beyond, was once the hub of Great Northern operations for this entire western swath of North Woods. It's now a lodge known for lumber camp–style cooking (see *Eating Out*). Note that from Rockwood you can also continue on to Quebec City (via Jackman).

Along the Eastern Shore

Lily Bay State Park (695-2700), 8 miles north of Greenville, offers a sandy beach, a grassy picnicking area, and camping.

Kokadjo, 18 miles north of Greenville, is a 100-acre island of independently owned land on First Roach Pond, in the center of lumber company–owned forest. Most of the buildings here were once part of a lumbering station and are now camps attached to the **Kokadjo Trading Post** (see *Eating Out*); **Northern Pride Lodge** (see *Inns*) rents canoes and boats. If you continue north a few miles, you will hit a paper company checkpoint (fee for out-of-state vehicles). The road surface improves here and is fairly smooth (but you must now pull over to let lumber trucks pass); it improves even more in a dozen miles when you hit the **Golden Road** (see "The North Woods"). Turn right (east).

Cushing's Landing, at the foot of Chesuncook Lake, is worth a stop. The woodsman's memorial here was created from a post in the doorway of a Bangor tavern; it is decorated with tools of the trade and an iron bean pot. This is also the logical boat launch for visiting **Chesuncook Village,** one of the few surviving examples of a 19th-century North Woods lumbermen's village, now on the National Register of Historic Places. In summer, access is by charter aircraft from Greenville or by boat from Chesuncook Dam. In winter, you can come by snowmobile. Writing about the village in 1853, Henry David Thoreau noted, "Here immigration is a tide which may ebb when it has swept away the pines." Today a church, a graveyard (relocated from the shore to a hollow in the woods when Great Northern raised the level of the lake a few years ago), an inn, and a huddle of houses are all that remain of the village. (See Chesuncook Lake House under *Inns* for lodging and boat shuttle.)

Ripogenus Dam, just east of Chesuncook Lake, is the departure point for a number of white-water-rafting expeditions (see *White-Water Rafting/Kayaking*). This is one of the two major centers for white-water rafting in Maine—the other is The Forks (see "The Upper Kennebec Valley and Moose River Valley"). Beginning at the dam, the West Branch of the Penobscot drops more than 70 feet per mile—seething and roiling through Ripogenus Gorge—and continues another 12 miles with stretches of relatively calm water punctuated by steep drops. You can get a view of the gorge by driving across the dam. **Pray's Store** (723-8880), open year-round, sells most things you might need.

The Telos Road leads to the **Allagash Wilderness Waterway,** a 92-mile-long chain of lakes, ponds, rivers, and streams that snakes through the heart of the North Woods. The traditional canoe trip through the Allagash takes 10 days, but 2- and 3-day trips can be worked out. Brook trout, togue, and lake whitefish are plentiful. For details see *Canoeing the Allagash* in "What's Where," and *Canoe Rentals and Trips*, below.

TO DO

AIRPLANE RIDES
See descriptions of scenic flights offered by flying services under *Getting Around*.

BOAT EXCURSIONS
See **S/S *Katahdin*** at the Moosehead Marine Museum under *To See*.

Both the **Birches Resort** and **Evergreen Lodge** offer pontoon boat cruises (see *Moose-Watching*).

Also see *Canoe and Kayak Rentals and Trips* for guided excursions, and *Fishing* for guided fishing trips.

CANOE AND KAYAK TRIPS
Allagash Canoe Trips (695-3668), Greenville. A family business since 1953, offering professional guides and top equipment. Weeklong expeditions into the Allagash Wilderness Waterway (also special teen trips); a 4-day trip on the Penobscot River and on Chesuncook Lake.

Wilderness Expeditions (534-2242 or 534-7305; 1-800-825-WILD), P.O. Box 41, Rockwood 04478. Based at the Birches Resort, offering a variety of guided kayak trips including a 3-day/2-night tour up Moosehead Lake that retraces Thoreau's exact canoe route north from Greenville to Northeast Carry (35 miles); a 3-day tour on Lake Brassau; a day-trip to and around Mount Kineo; and a moose watch from Moosehead up into Baker Brook or Socatean Stream.

Moosehead Adventures (695-4434), Greenville. Licensed Maine guides Edie and Darrell Miles and Eric Sherman offer guided kayak tours (novices welcome) on Moosehead, ranging from 3 hours ($35) to overnight ($160 per adult, meals included).

CANOE AND KAYAK RENTALS
North Woods Outfitters (695-3288), Main Street, Greenville, rents Old Town canoes and Hydra kayaks; guide service available.

Moose River Landing (534-2897) and **Rockwood Cottages** (534-7725) rent canoes, kayaks, and motorboats.

Note: Most sporting camps also rent canoes or kayaks, and all the flying services will ferry canoes into remote backcountry (see *Getting Around*).

CHAIRLIFT RIDES

Chair Lift Ride at Squaw Mountain (695-1000), Route 6/15 between Greenville and Rockwood; generally weekends in summer and fall, but call ahead. Spectacular view of lake and mountains.

FISHING

Troll for landlocked salmon and brook trout in Moosehead Lake and fly-fish in the many rivers and ponds—rental boats and boat launches are so plentiful that they defy listing.

There are two prime sources of fishing information: the **Inland Fisheries and Wildlife** office (695-3756) in Greenville and the **Maine Guide Fly Shop and Guide Service** (695-2266), Main Street, Greenville. At the Fly Shop, Dan Legere sells 314 different flies and a wide assortment of gear; he also works with local guides to outfit you with a boat and guide or to set up a river float trip or a fly-in expedition. The resurgence of fly-fishing as a popular sport is reflected in the variety of gear and guides available in this shop. Deep lake trolling is, however, also popular, and Chris DiPala of **Mt. Kineo Guide Service** (534-7743), with a 25-foot Sea Ray equipped with numerous rods, reels, sonar, and digital down-riggers, can guarantee a catch, even midday in mid-August. For a list of local boat rentals as well as a list of local guides, check with the **Moosehead Lake Area Chamber of Commerce** (see *Guidance*). Also see listings in *Rustic Resorts,* all of which are on water and cater to fishermen.

Ice fishing begins January 1 and ends March 30. Ice-house rentals are available locally. Inquire at the chamber.

GOLF

Mount Kineo Golf Course (354-8812/2221). A spectacularly sited, nine-hole course at Kineo, accessible by frequent boat service from Rockwood; carts and club rentals.

Squaw Mountain Village Resort on Moosehead Lake (695-3609). A nine-hole course with lounge and restaurant.

HIKING

The two stellar, not-to-be-missed hikes in this area are:

Mount Kineo, an islandlike peninsula, has trails to the back side of the famous cliff that rises 763 feet above the water and the apron of land once occupied by the Kineo House resort (see *Lodging—Inns*). Most of the island (8,000 acres) is now state-owned and trails along its circumference and up the back of the cliff are maintained. Take the Indian Trail, which heads straight up over ledges that are a distinct green: This is one of the world's largest masses of rhyolite, a flintlike volcanic rock. This trail is shaded by red pines, oaks, and a surprising variety of hardwoods. The view down the lake from the fire tower is spectacular and there is an easy descent: the Bridle Trail. A carriage trail also circles the island, which is accessible from Rockwood by frequent water shuttle (see *Getting Around*). Bring a picnic or lunch at the Kineo House.

TIMOTHY ELLIS, JR.

Gulf Hagas

Gulf Hagas, billed as the Grand Canyon of Maine, is just 15 miles east of Greenville via the airport road (see "Katahdin Region" for details). In winter this is the far more accessible approach and a fabulous adventure (see *Dogsledding* and Little Lyford Camps under *Lodging—Rustic Resorts*).

Borestone Mountain Sanctuary, 10 miles out the Eliotsville Road from Route 6/15 at Monson, offers an information center (June 1 through October 1, 8 AM–dusk) maintained by the National Audubon Society; it's at Sunrise Pond, halfway up the 3-mile trail leading to a summit with a 360-degree view.

Check local sources for details about hiking **Big Spencer, Elephant Mountain,** and walking into **Little Wilson Falls,** a majestic, 57-foot cascade in a forested setting.

HORSEBACK RIDING AND WAGON RIDES

   ♿ **Northern Maine Riding Adventures** (564-3451/2965), P.O. Box 16, Dover-Foxcroft. Judy Cross, a Registered Maine Guide and skilled equestrian, offers 1-hour trail rides, centered-riding clinics, and day trips from her four-season facility; also overnight treks based at her camp in the backwoods around Katahdin Ironworks. Special-needs riders are welcome.

Rockies Golden Acres (695-3229), Greenville. Trail rides: 1½- to 2-hour rides through the woods to Sawyer Pond; mountain views. Call after 7 PM, or leave a message.

MOOSE-WATCHING

"Moosemainea," sponsored by the Moosehead Lake Chamber of Commerce mid-May through mid-June, is the largest, most colorful moose-watching event in New England; but chances are you can spot the lake's mascot any dawn or dusk, especially if you go on a guided moose-watching tour.

Greenville's three flying services offer moose-watching both strictly from the air and by flying into prime spots (see *Getting Around*).

Moose Cruises aboard pontoon boats are offered mornings and evenings both by the **Birches Resort** (534-7305) and by **Evergreen Lodge** (695-3241; 1-888-624-3993).

Bullwinkle's Guide Service (695-4338) and **Moose Safaris/Dogsled trips** (876-4907) offer 5-hour early-morning and evening moose cruises using vehicles and canoes.

MOUNTAIN BIKING

North Woods Outfitters (695-3288), Main Street, Greenville. Rents bikes and has trail information available.

The Birches (534-7305; 1-800-825-WILD), Rockwood, offers mountain bike rentals for use on its extensive cross-country ski network.

Northern Pride Lodge (695-2890) in Kokadjo also rents mountain bikes by the half day and day.

SWIMMING

See Lily Bay State Park under *To See*.

WHITE-WATER RAFTING AND KAYAKING

Moosehead Lake is equidistant from Maine's two most popular rafting routes—Kennebec Gorge and Ripogenus Gorge. **Wilderness Expeditions** (534-2242; 1-800-825-WILD), P.O. Box 41, Rockwood 04478, based at the Birches in Rockwood (see *Lodging—Rustic Resorts*), is a family-run business specializing in half-day white-water rafting trips on the Kennebec at East Outlet (minimum age is 7); also longer expeditions on the Kennebec from a base camp in The Forks and on the Penobscot from another base near Baxter State Park.

WINTER SPORTS

DOGSLEDDING

Song of the Woods (876-4736), Abbot 04406. Stephen Medera and his team of huskies not only offer sled rides but also short (from $15 for a half hour) to full-day trips on which you actually do the driving. After the first tangle around a tree, we were amazed at how smoothly the dogs responded to our commands on the 10-mile woods road (it's much smoother in winter than summer) into Little Lyford Camps (see *Lodging—Rustic Resorts*).

Moose Country Safaris and Dogsled Trips (876-4907) is the musher for the Lodge at Moosehead Lake (see *Lodging—Inns*).

CROSS-COUNTRY SKIING

Formal touring centers aside, this region's vast network of snowmobile trails and frozen lakes constitutes splendid opportunities for backcountry skiing. We've skied from the cabins at Chesuncook Lake House and Northern Pride Lodge in Kokadjo (see *Lodging—Inns*), which are all open in winter for cross-country skiers as well as snowmobilers.

Birches Ski Touring Center (534-7305), Rockwood. The resort maintains an extensive network of trails, recently expanded to take advantage of an 11,000-acre forested spread across the neck between Brassua and Moosehead Lakes. You can ski to Tomhegan, 10 miles up the lake, or out past the ice-fishing shanties to Kineo. Rentals and instruction; snowshoes, too.

Little Lyford Pond Camps (see *Lodging—Rustic Resorts*) offers a network of groomed trails connecting with backcountry trails including the Appalachian Trail and leading into Gulf Hagas. Chesuncook Lake House and Medawisla also cater to cross-country skiers (see *Lodging*).

DOWNHILL SKIING

Big Squaw Mountain Resort (695-1000). A ski resort since 1963, with one of New England's first base-area hotels, owned by Scott Paper (1970–1974) and then sold to the state, under whose ownership it languished for 11 years. It has had its ups and downs under private ownership since. Even in summer you are struck by the small number of trails streaking such a big mountain: just 22 trails but with a 1,750-foot drop. Skiers have terrific views of Moosehead Lake and Mount Katahdin. Lifts include a double chair, a triple chair, a T-bar, and a pony lift. Other facilities include a base lodge and cafeteria, ski school, ski shop, and lodging in 54 rooms. Lift tickets: $20 adult weekends, $15 senior, junior, and everyone midweek. On-mountain motel-style rooms begin at $39 per couple midweek ($5 per extra person).

SNOWMOBILING

Snowmobiling is huge in this area. The chamber publishes and sells a map of area snowmobile trails, which also offers information on area businesses catering to snowmobilers. **Moosehead Riders Snowmobile Club** proudly proclaims the area the "hub" of snowmobiling and offers a 24-hour trail condition report (695-4561). Its clubhouse is open Saturday and Sunday in winter. The club also sponsors guided tours. Interconnecting Trail System (ITS) routes 85, 86, and 87 run directly through the area, and there are many locally groomed trails as well. The Moosehead trail goes around the lake, avoiding formerly dangerous ice-out situations. Snowmobile rentals are available from **Bullwinkle's Guide Service** (695-3681) and **Evergreen Lodge B&B** (695-3241) in Greenville, **Kokadjo Trading Post** (695-3993) in Kokadjo, **Greenwood Motel** (695-3321) in Greenville Junction, and from the **Birches Resort** in Rockwood (534-7305). Inquire about guided tours.

LODGING

INNS

Greenville Inn (695-2206; 1-888-695-6000), Norris Street, Box 1194, Greenville 04441. Open all year (B&B November through May). A true lumber baron's mansion set atop a hill just off Main Street, with a sweeping view of Moosehead Lake. Rich cherry, mahogany, and oak paneling, embossed walls, working fireplaces, and an immense, leaded-glass window depicting a single spruce tree—all contribute to the sense of elegance. There are four second-floor rooms and one suite with a fireplace, also a more rustic suite in the carriage house (ideal for families). Two pine-paneled cottages were moved back to make way for four new cottages, all with views. The dining room, open to the public, is considered the best in northwestern Maine (see *Dining Out*). Your hosts are Elfi, Susie, and Michael Schnetzer. $95–165 in-season (includes European breakfast buffet), less mid-October to late May; $20 for extra person in room.

&   **The Lodge at Moosehead Lake** (695-4400), Box 1175, Lily Bay Road, Greenville 04441. Jennifer and Roger Cauchi have transformed a vintage 1916 hunting lodge into a phenomenon. Each of the 11 guest rooms (four with lake views) has been designed with immense care around a theme. In the "trout" room, for instance, brightly painted leaping trout have been sculpted into the bed's four-posters and matching mirrors; the fabric-covered walls are patterned with hooks and flies. Each room features equally spectacular carved four-poster beds depicting its theme (moose, bear, loon, totem). All rooms have cable TVs, gas fireplaces, and baths with Jacuzzi tubs. A carriage house holds three more luxurious suites. Roger delights in playing concierge, arranging fishing, hiking, rafting, or whatever else guests may desire. Common areas are comfortable and vast, including a downstairs billiards room, where there is always a puzzle in progress. A full breakfast is served in the glass-walled dining room, and dinner is also available to guests. Double-occupancy rates, including breakfast, are $175–395 May through October 31; in winter $175–395 includes dinner as well as breakfast.

Kineo House (534-8812), P.O. Box 397, Rockwood 04478. Open Memorial Day weekend through Columbus Day. The only place to stay on Kineo (see *Hiking*). The six guest rooms (most with private baths) are in one of the cottages once clustered around a mammoth—now all but vanished—grand hotel. Each room offers at least a glimpse of a water view. At night this is the quietest place around. Chip and Laurie Foster serve lunch to the public, dinner by reservation, and operate the Kineo shuttle (see *Getting Around*). Shuttle and breakfast are included in $80 double, $15 per extra person.

Northern Pride Lodge (695-2890), HCR 76, Box 588, Kokadjo 04441. Open year-round. Built as a hunting lodge for lumber baron Sir Harry Oaks, now run by Barb and Jeff Lucas as a friendly lodge with five guest rooms, each with enough beds for a family or group; shared baths. The living room has a hearth, stained-glass windows, and a sense of opulence; the dining room, on a glassed-in porch overlooking First Roach Pond, is open to guests daily and to the public Thursday through Sunday. There are also 24 campsites, rental canoes, motorboats, and mountain bikes. In winter the lodge caters to snowmobilers and cross-country skiers. $80 per couple May through November; $70 per couple December through

A camp on Moosehead Lake

April (includes breakfast). $59 per night for single; rates with all three meals are also offered.

Chesuncook Lake House (745-5330; or c/o Folsom's, 695-2821), Box 656, Route 76, Greenville 04441. Open year-round. An unpretentious, 1864 farmhouse built on the site of an older log cabin that served as the center for the lumbering camp (see Chesuncook Village under *To See— Scenic Drives*). There are 12 guest rooms and three housekeeping cabins. Maggie McBurnie, a native Parisian, serves three meals a day in summer. Guests are shuttled in from the Allagash Gateway Campsite on the Golden Road (723-9215) or can canoe in from Lobster Lake or other put-ins. Otherwise you can fly in from Greenville. This is a peaceful, magical spot. Registered Maine Guides and boats are available. $95–100 per person includes three meals in the inn (which closes in winter) or in the cabins (open year-round). Guests in the cabins can choose to do their own cooking, thus reducing the rate.

BED & BREAKFASTS

The Blair House Inn (1-888-918-8880), Lily Bay Road, P.O. Box 1288, Greenville 04441. Set high above Moosehead Lake at the top of Blair Hill, this is an expansive Victorian mansion (vintage 1891) that's been furnished with flair by Dan and Ruth McLaughlin, who have brought along their collection of Oak Park mission furniture from Chicago. The eight rooms all have private baths and four have wood-burning fireplaces. Our favorite is a less expensive room on the third floor with three lake-filled windows. There's wicker and a hot tub on the porch (also overlooking the lake), wine in the cellar, and a feel of unstuffy luxury throughout. $175–350, $150–235 off-season, includes a full breakfast and afternoon tea and hors d'oeuvres.

Devlin House (695-2229), P.O. Box 1102, Greenville 04441. A modern home high on the hill west of town with splendid views over meadows to the lake; a ground-level suite with a sitting room, and two rooms with king-sized beds, private baths, air-conditioning, and TV. Ruth Devlin is a longtime local resident who enjoys sharing her knowledge of the area. $75–125.

RUSTIC RESORTS (TRADITIONAL SPORTING CAMPS)

✔ **The Birches Resort** (534-7305/2241; 1-800-825-WILD), P.O. Box 41, Rockwood 04478. Open year-round. The Willards have turned this 1930s sporting camp into one of the most comfortable and satisfying family-geared resorts in Maine. It's sited in a birch grove overlooking Mount Kineo. Sixteen hand-hewn log cabins are strung along the lake, each with a porch, a Franklin stove or fireplace in a sitting room, and one to three bedrooms. All of the cabins have kitchens (some don't have ovens), but three meals are available in summer. The main lodge includes a cheerful, open-timbered dining room, an inviting lobby with a trout pool, and a living room with hearth room. Upstairs are four guest rooms with decks overlooking the lake (shared bath); there are also "cabin tents" near the lodge and several yurts scattered through the resort's 11,000 acres. Facilities include an outside hot tub and sauna; windsurfers, sailboats, kayaks, canoes, fishing boats, and mountain bikes are available. Cross-country skiing rentals and expeditions are also offered. From $40 double in the lodge. Housekeeping cottages are $90–180 per night, $695–995 per week in summer (less off-season) without meals. Cabin tents begin at $22 single per day. A variety of rafting, canoeing, and other packages are also available. The dining room is open to the public (see *Dining Out*).

🐾✔ **Little Lyford Pond Camps** (280-0016), Box 340, Greenville 04441. Open year-round. Reservations are required. Sited in a sheltered, alpine-looking valley, these camps were built in the 1870s as a logging company station on a tote road. The seven shake-roofed log cabins (without plumbing or electricity) sleep from one to four. Each has a private outhouse. Arlene and Bob LeRoy offer three meals and plenty of hospitality in the main lodge; facilities also include a cedar sauna, and hot showers. Gulf Hagas is a short hike and cross-country ski trails are maintained. In winter you can ski, fly, or dogsled in. The camps are 3.5 miles off the Appalachian Trail, 12 miles via a gated logging road from Greenville. $85 per person includes all meals (with an emphasis on vegetarian) and use of canoes. Two neighboring ponds offer an abundance of native brook trout and fly-fishing lessons are offered. We came in March via dogsled and enjoyed exceptional cross-country skiing into Gulf Hagas and around the camps.

🐾✔ **Nugent's Chamberlain Lake Camps** (695-2821), HCR 76, Box 632, Greenville 04441. Open year-round. The original camps on this site were built in the 1930s by Al and Patty Nugent. In 1987 the state awarded the lease of these camps to John Richardson and Regina Webster, who have rebuilt many of the old cabins, and built a couple of new ones, while retaining the old-fashioned feel. This is one of the most remote camps, nicely sited on the Allagash Wilderness Waterway, 50 miles north of Millinocket between Baxter State Park and Allagash Mountain. They are best reached via float plane (see *Getting Around*); otherwise it's a 4-mile boat or snowmobile ride up Chamberlain Lake. The eight housekeeping cabins have the traditional front overhang and outhouses; they sleep 2 to 16. Boats are available. AP, MAP, or housekeeping plans available. $22–60 per person.

Medawisla (radiophone year-round: 695-2690), HCR 76, Box 592, Greenville 04441. Open year-round. In this remote corner of the woods, the LeRoys offer six fully equipped cabins with woodstoves, flush toilets, and hot showers. Each can sleep from 2 to 10 people. These camps cater to a quiet clientele, and there is plenty of open space for peaceful relaxation. The "reading room" is a spot outside overlooking a dam that was once the only road in. Popular for fishing in spring, hunting in fall, cross-country skiing in winter, and as a getaway in summer. Meals available October through March. Boats and canoes are available. The loons of the sound track from the movie *On Golden Pond* were taped here. $60–90 double, housekeeping; weekly rates.

☞ **West Branch Ponds Camps** (695-2561), P.O. Box 1153, Greenville 04441. A 10-mile drive from the main road at Kokadjo. Open after the ice breaks up and through September; inquire about winter season. First opened as a moose-hunting lodge in the 1880s; the newest log cottage was built in 1938. Directly across the pond is the majestic bulk of Whitecap Mountain. Be warned: Not everyone likes the rusticity of these cabins (worn bedding on log beds), which all have heat, electricity, bath; three have Franklin stoves. Andy and Carol Stirling are third-generation owners, and Carol is well known for her cooking. Motorboats and canoes are available. The square central lodge (with a bell on top) has plenty of books and comfortable corners. $58 per person per day includes three meals and use of a canoe; children are half price.

❦ **Maynard's in Maine** (534-7703), Rockwood 04478. Open May through hunting season. "The only thing we change around here is the linen," says Gail Maynard, who helps run the sportsmen's camp founded by her husband's grandfather in 1919. Overlooking the Moose River, a short walk from Moosehead Lake, Maynard's includes a dozen tidy, moss-green frame buildings with dark Edwardian furniture, much of it from the grand old Mount Kineo Hotel. The lodge is filled with stuffed fish, moose heads, and Maynard family memorabilia, and furnished with stiff-backed leather chairs. A sign cautions DO NOT WEAR HIP BOOTS OR WADERS INTO THE DINING ROOM. Two meals a day are served and one "packed." $50 per person with three meals, $336 per week (single occupancy) for cabins.

CAMPS

Tomhegan Wilderness Resort (534-7712), P.O. Box 308, Rockwood 04478. Open year-round. A 10-mile ride up a dirt road from Rockwood Village;

1.5 miles of frontage on Moosehead Lake. Nine hand-hewn cottages along a wooden boardwalk with kitchens and living rooms, rocking chairs on the porches, full baths, and woodstoves; also efficiency units in the lodge. Very remote and peaceful; deer are frequently seen at close range. Boats and canoes are available; cross-country skiing and snowmobiling in winter. $654 weekly for four people in most camps, $565 off-season; efficiency units $99 per day, 2-day minimum.

☙✍ **Rockwood Cottages** (534-7725), Box 176, Rockwood 04478. Open year-round. Ron and Bonnie Searles maintain clean, comfortable housekeeping cottages with screened-in porches overlooking the lake and Mount Kineo just across the narrows. They are happy to advise about exploring Kineo and this less developed end of the lake. Boats, motors, and fishing licenses are available, and guests have free docking. There's also a sauna, a barbecue, and an impressive moose head. $65 per couple, $15 per additional person; $425 per couple per week, $75 per additional person.

✍ **Beaver Cove Camps** (695-3717; 1-800-577-3717), Greenville 04441. Open year-round. Eight miles north of Greenville on the eastern shore of Moosehead Lake are six fully equipped housekeeping cabins, each with full kitchen and bath. Owner Jim Glavine is a Registered Maine Guide specializing in fly-fishing. Guided hunting and snowmobile or ski touring also offered. $70 per night or $420 double per week.

🏅 **Spencer Pond Camps** (radio service, 695-2821), Star Route 76, Box 580, Greenville 04441. Open May to mid-November. Bob Croce and Jill Martel are continuing the traditions of this long-established cluster of six housekeeping camps (sleeping 2 to 10) in an unusually beautiful spot, accessible by logging road from Lily Bay Road. The hosts are warm and helpful, with plenty of suggestions for enjoying the wilderness. Guests are welcome to fresh vegetables from the garden. Gas and kerosene lights and hand-pumped water; each cottage is stocked with cooking utensils and dishes and has a private shower room (sunshower) and outhouse. A terrific base for birding, hiking, and mountain climbing. Canoes and motorboats (under 10 hp only) available. One- to 3-day canoe trips offered. $60–100 per couple, weekly rates available.

CAMPGROUNDS

Lily Bay State Park (695-2700), 8 miles north of Greenville. Ninety-three sites, many spaced along the shore; boat launch and beach.

Seeboomok Wilderness Campground (534-8824), HC 85, Box 560, Rockwood 04478-9712. Accessed by logging roads (some 28 miles from Rockwood), a peaceful, special place. Sites for both RVs and tents, Adirondack shelters on the water and six comfortable cabins with flush toilets, gas lights, basic utensils (no linens). Photos in the camp store (where there's a lunch counter) document this as the site of a World War II POW camp. Dick Sylvester and Janet Murphy are accommodating hosts who direct you to hiking, canoeing, fishing, and wildlife haunts. $8–12 per night, $10 for Adirondack shelters, $30–60 for cabins, weekly rates.

Maine State Bureau of Forestry (695-3721) maintains free (first-come, first-served) "authorized sites" (no fire permit required) and "permit sites" (permit required), scattered on both public and private land along Moosehead Lake and on several of its islands.

OTHER LODGING

On the way to Greenville

    Brewster Inn (924-3130), 37 Zion's Hill, Dexter 04930. Open year-round. Dexter is a proud old Maine town and this is its proudest house—fit for the governor who built it. Michael and Ivy Brooks have furnished the seven guest rooms and two suites with antiques and bright fabrics; request one overlooking the formal garden, the one with a whirlpool for two. Breakfast might be Swiss and broccoli quiche or apples stuffed with raisins and ham. $59–89 per couple.

The Guilford Bed & Breakfast (876-3477), P.O. Box 88, Elm Street, Guilford 04443. Harry and Lynn Anderson offer wonderful hospitality in their lovely post-Victorian home, a little off the beaten path. A good spot to stop if you are traveling Route 11 en route to the Moosehead or Katahdin regions. Common areas are inviting, especially the bright living room with fireplace and the wraparound porch. Rooms are light and airy, tastefully decorated. $50–75 per room depending on bath and season.

Shaw's Boarding House (997-3597), Pleasant Street, Monson. Open year-round. A short walk from the Appalachian Trail and patronized 99 percent by hikers, (snowmobilers in winter), Shaw's is a phenomenon in its own right, famed for the size of its breakfasts ($4.50) and dinners ($8). Beds are in a mix of private ($20 per person) and bunk rooms ($15 per person) in several adjoining buildings, with and without kitchen facilities.

WHERE TO EAT

DINING OUT

Greenville Inn (695-2206; 1-888-695-6000), Norris Street, Greenville. Dinner served nightly by reservation from 6 PM. Elfi Schnetzer has turned over the kitchen to her daughter Susie, who continues to delight diners with appetizers like smoked bluefish pâté and basil zucchini soup, and an ever-changing selection of entrées, which might include salmon with sauce verte and mashed potatoes or sirloin steak with green peppercorn sauce and roasted red potato. Leave room for dessert, maybe chocolate truffle tart with pecan crust or strawberries Romanoff. $17–28 (for full rack of lamb).

The Birches (534-2242), Rockwood. Open year-round: daily in summer, sporadically after that (call for times). This popular resort (see *Lodging— Rustic Resorts*) has one of the area's most attractive dining rooms—logsided with a massive stone hearth, a war canoe turned upside down in the open rafters, and hurricane lamps on the highly polished tables. The menu has undergone a transformation, offering healthier grilled or baked options. Specialties include prime rib and pork tenderloin with chutney. $11–16.95. Reservations suggested. There's also an inviting pub.

Kineo House (534-8812), Kineo. Open Memorial Day to Columbus Day. Reservations required for dinner. Catering to hikers at lunch (see Mount Kineo under *Hiking*), served daily, everything from burgers and lobster rolls to fish and chips. Dinner entrées might range from chicken pasta ($12.95) to lobster pie ($16.95). Getting here is half the fun: The regular water shuttle from Rockwood runs until 5 PM; inquire about return transport when you reserve. The ride back at sunset or after dark is, of course, the other half.

Northern Pride Lodge (695-2890), Kokadjo. The dining room in this classic lumber baron's hunting lodge (see *Lodging—Inns*) is a modified sunporch overlooking First Roach Pond. Dinner is served to the public Thursday through Sunday and might begin with smoked trout pâté, include roast duckling or beef stroganoff; entrées $14.95–18.95. Reservations suggested.

EATING OUT

Pittston Farm (call Folsom's Air Service: 695-2821). Open year-round except for the last 2 weeks in April. "Authentic" only begins to describe this classic outpost, a wilderness farm built around 1910 as a major hub of Great Northern's logging operations. Sited at the confluence of the North and South Branches of the Penobscot River a little more than 20 miles north of Rockwood, the white-clapboard lodge and its outlying barns and fields are now owned by Ken Twitchel (a veteran lumber-camp cook) and his wife, Sonja. Visitors are welcome for all-you-can-eat meals, which include thick, tasty soups and at least two kinds of meat, several vegetables (some grown outside), a salad bar, and freshly baked rolls, bread, and pastries. Reasonably priced buffet suppers are served at 5 and 6 PM; reservations are appreciated. Folsom's will fly you in and back from Greenville for $50–60 per person including the meal. Lunch is also a buffet, or it might be short-order. Upstairs lodging is available, with a number of quilt-covered beds, shared baths, very reasonably priced.

Kokadjo Trading Post (695-3993), Kokadjo. Open 6 AM–11 PM, earlier in hunting season. Fred and Marie Candeloro offer a cozy dining room/pub room with a large fieldstone fireplace and a view of First Roach Pond.

Maynard's Dining Room (534-7703). Dine (6–8) much as your grandparents would have here in the traditional old lodge dining room overlooking the Moose River. Choices vary with the night; Thursday it's either roast leg of lamb or meat loaf; $9.95 includes juice or soup, salad, choice of potato or veggie, bread, dessert, and beverage; BYOB.

In Greenville

Flatlander's Pub (695-3373), Pritham Avenue, Greenville. Open except Tuesday, 11 AM " 'til close." Hamburgers, chicken wings, deep-fried mushrooms, deli sandwiches; beer on tap and house wines; homemade chili, a good pea soup, and pies. Nice atmosphere; in the middle of town.

The Boom Chain (695-2602), Pritham Avenue. Open 6 AM–2 PM. A good bet for breakfast; a local gathering spot.

Kelly's Landing (695-4438), Greenville Junction. Open 7 AM–9 PM. A breakfast bar and large salad bar, fried seafood platter, roast chicken, sandwiches. A big, cheerful place with tables on the deck by the lake. Inquire about motel rooms with lakeside decks upstairs.

✍ **Auntie M's Restaurant** (695-2238), Main Street, Greenville. Open for all three meals but best for breakfast; homemade soups and specials. We love this place. Everything always tastes good.

ENTERTAINMENT

East Sangerville Grange Coffeehouse. Call Mr. Paperback (564-3646) in Dover-Foxcroft for schedule information and tickets. A major stop on New England's folk-music circuit. The first Saturday of every month, 7 PM; adult tickets $8, students $6.

SELECTIVE SHOPPING

Indian Hill Trading Post (695-3376), Greenville. Open daily year-round, Friday until 10 PM. Huge—a combination sports store, supermarket, and general store, stocking everything you might need for a week or two in the woods.

Moosehead Traders (695-3806), Moosehead Center Mall, Route 15 in downtown Greenville. The most upscale shop in the North Woods: furs, moose antlers, and moose antler furnishings (like chandeliers), antiques, books, and many tempting gifts. The ear is not for sale.

Great Eastern Clothing Store, a trendy emporium, has replaced the old landmark Indian Store in the Shaw Block and **Northwoods Outfitters**, selling sporting gear and wear (see *Canoe and Kayak Rentals*) now occupies the space vacated by the town's other old commercial landmark, Sanders Store.

Maine Mountain Soap and Candle Co. (695-3926), Route 15, downtown Greenville. The real thing. Good soap.

The Corner Shop (695-2142), corner of Main and Pritham (across from Great Eastern Clothing), Greenville; gifts, books, magazines.

Sunbower Pottery (695-2870), Scammon Road, Greenville, home of the "moose mug"; locally made gifts, artwork.

SPECIAL EVENTS

February: **Winter Festival,** Greenville—snowmobile events and poker runs.
Mid-May through mid-June: **Moosemainea** month, sponsored by the chamber of commerce, takes place throughout the area. It's big; see "What's Where."
July: The **Fourth of July** is big in Greenville.
August: **Forest Heritage Days,** Greenville.
September: **The International Seaplane Fly-In Weekend,** Greenville.

Katahdin Region Including Lower Piscataquis

Mile-high Mount Katahdin is the centerpiece not only for Baxter State Park but also for a surprisingly large area from which it is clearly visible. Like a huge ocean liner in a relatively flat sea of woodland, the massive mountain looms above the open countryside to the east, the direction from which it's most easily accessible.

Though the mountain and park are unquestionably its biggest drawing card, the Katahdin region offers its share of wooded lake country and represents one of the most reasonably priced destinations in Maine for families who want to get away together to hike and fish. White-water rafting on the West Branch of the Penobscot is another popular activity, with companies based near the Togue Pond gatehouse to Baxter State Park offering easy access to the river and the park. Winter recreation, especially snowmobiling, is becoming another large draw to the area.

Like Acadia National Park, Baxter State Park's acreage was amassed privately and given to the public as a gift. In this case, it was one individual—Governor Percival Baxter—who bought all the land himself, after unsuccessfully attempting to convince the state to do so during his political term. At the time (1931), no one seemed able to conceive why Maine, with all its forest, needed officially to preserve a swatch of woods as wilderness.

Decades of subsequent logging and present concerns for the future of this woodland have heightened the value of Governor Baxter's legacy and his mandate—the reason camping and even day-use admission to the park are strictly limited—to preserve at least these 201,018 acres of Maine's North Woods as wilderness.

The restaurants and beds nearest to Baxter State Park are in Millinocket, a lumbering outpost built by the Great Northern Paper Company around the turn of the century. The town is still centered on the big paper mills and the logging industry that feeds it. Route 11 from Millinocket into Lower Piscataquis county is a nice drive, and some of the towns along the way make good resting places for those heading to Katahdin Iron Works, Gulf Hagas, or to the Moosehead region.

GUIDANCE

The **Baxter State Park** information phone is 723-5140, or you can write to park headquarters, 64 Balsam Drive, Millinocket 04462. For details about making reservations, see *Green Space*. The attractive visitors center, which offers picnic tables, rest rooms, and a selection of published as well as free guides to the park, is 1 mile east of Millinocket on Route 11/157.

Katahdin Area Chamber of Commerce (723-4443; kacc@agate.net), 1029 Central Street, Millinocket 04462. The chamber maintains a seasonal information center on Route 11/157 east of Millinocket; it serves as a year-round source of information about the motels and restaurants that are chamber members.

Northern Katahdin Valley Regional Chamber of Commerce, P.O. Box 14D, Patten 04765, publishes a brochure focusing on the Patten area and points north and east.

Bowater/Great Northern Paper (723-2227), One Katahdin Avenue, Millinocket 04462, the largest landowner in this area, maintains thousands of miles of roads and hundreds of campsites. The company's map/guide to its lands is available at checkpoints on its roads and by writing to the office, attention "Public Relations."

GETTING THERE

The most direct route is I-95 to exit 56 at Medway (50 miles northeast of Bangor), and 10 miles into Millinocket. From here, it's about 10 miles to Millinocket Lake, and from there another few miles to the Togue Pond entrance to Baxter State Park.

GETTING AROUND

Katahdin Air Service Inc. (723-8378), P.O. Box 171, Millinocket. Available May through November to fly in to remote camps and shuttle in canoes and campers; will also drop hikers at points along the Appalachian Trail. **Scotty's Flying Service** (528-2626) at Shin Pond also serves wilderness camps.

MEDICAL EMERGENCY

Millinocket Regional Hospital (723-5161), 200 Somerset Street, Millinocket.

TO SEE

The Katahdin Iron Works. Open May through mid-October, 6 AM–8 PM. Turn at the small sign on Route 11, 5 miles north of Brownville Junction, and go another 6 miles up the gravel road. This state historic site is really not worth the effort unless you plan to continue on down the gravel road to hike in Gulf Hagas or to camp (see *Hiking* and *Campgrounds*). The spot was a sacred place for Native Americans, who found their yellow ocher paint here. From the 1840s until 1890, an ironworks

Katahdin Iron Works

prospered in this remote spot, spawning a village to house its 200 work-ers and producing 2,000 tons of raw iron annually. Guests of the Silver Lake Hotel (1880s–1913) here came on the same narrow-gauge rail-road that carried away the iron. All that remains is a big old blast fur-nace and iron kiln. Tours and books on the ironworks are offered by local author and backwoods guide Bill Sawtell (965-3971).

Patten Lumberman's Museum (528-2650), Shin Pond Road (Route 159), Patten. Open Memorial Day through September Friday through Sun-day and holidays 10–4; July and August, Tuesday through Sunday. $2.50 per adult, $1 per child. The museum, which encompasses more than 4,000 displays housed in 10 buildings, was founded in 1962 by bacteriologist Lore Rogers and log driver Caleb Scribner. Exhibits range from giant log haulers to "gum books," the lumberman's scrimshaw: intricately carved boxes in which to keep spruce gum, a popular gift for a sweetheart. There are replicas of logging camps from different periods, dioramas, machinery, and photos, all adding up to a fascinating picture of a vanished way of life. This road leads to the Matagamon Gate, the northern, less trafficked corner of Baxter State Park.

A. J. Allee scenic overlook, some 15 miles beyond the Medway exit. The view is of Mount Katahdin rising massively from woods and water.

The Golden Road, a 96-mile logging road owned by Great Northern Paper company runs from Millinocket to Quebec; 35 miles are paved, the rest gravel, but it is better maintained than most of the logging roads found in the North Woods. The best way to get from Millinocket to Greenville, with plenty of woods and river views. The chances of spotting a moose on this road are high (we haven't driven it yet without seeing one). Great Northern's outdoor classroom and hiking trail is along this road (see *Hiking*). Day use is free to Maine registered vehicles, $4 for out of state vehicles. Overnight camping is $5 per night per person.

The Ambajejus Boom House, Ambajejus Lake. Open year-round. Accessible from Spencer Cove on the Golden Road or via Katahdin View Pontoon Rides (723-5211; see *To Do*). Riverman Chuck Harris has single-handedly restored this old boom house, former quarters for log drivers, as a museum of the life during the river drives.

TO DO

BOAT EXCURSION
Katahdin View Pontoon Boat Rides (723-5211/9712), 210 Morgan Lane, Millinocket. Seasonal sightseeing cruises on a 24-foot pontoon boat along Millinocket Lake and into Mud Brook. Approximately 2 hours; the sunset cruise is a little longer and very popular (reservations suggested). Departs from Big Moose Cabins, Millinocket.

CANOEING AND KAYAKING
This area is often used as a starting point for trips on the Allagash (see *Canoeing* in "Aroostook County") and St. John Rivers. Good canoeing on the East and West (not for beginners). Branches of the Penobscot as well.

New England Outdoor Center (723-5438; 1-800-766-7238; canoekayak @neoc.com) offers a canoe and kayak school, guided tours, and rentals.

Moosehead Adventures (564-3452), 178 East Main Street, Dover-Foxcroft 04426. Offers guided kayak tours on Moosehead and Sebec Lakes, as well as on the Piscataquis River. Also guided canoe trips and hikes.

Penobscot River Outfitters (746-9349 in Maine; 1-800-794-5267 outside the state), Route 157, Medway 04460. Old Town rentals; specializes in 1- to 7-day canoe trips on the East and West Branches of the Penobscot.

Katahdin Outfitters (723-5700), in Millinocket, offers rentals, planning, transport, and shuttle for trips on the Allagash, St. John, and Penobscot.

Canoe rentals are also available in Peaks-Kenny State Park (see *Camp-grounds*).

For a more complete list of guide services, contact the **North Maine Woods office** (435-6213) in Ashland.

FISHING

We've been told that Dolby Flowage is good for bass fishing, and the West Branch of the Penobscot offers good salmon and trout fishing. **New England Outdoor Center** (723-5438) offers guided fishing trips.

SCENIC FLIGHT

Katahdin Air Service, Inc. (723-8378) offers several scenic flights daily, ranging from a 15-minute flight along the base of Mount Katahdin ($20 per person) to a day exploring Henderson Pond and Delosconeag Lake ($70 per person). Inquire about fly-and-dine packages.

HIKING

Baxter State Park. Ever since the 1860s—when Henry David Thoreau's account of his 1846 ascent of "Ktaadn" began to circulate—the demanding trails to Maine's highest summit (5,267 feet) have been among the most popular in the state. Climbing Katahdin itself is considered a rite of passage in Maine and much of the rest of New England. The result is a steady stream of humanity up and down the Katahdin trails, while other peaks, such as 3,488-foot Doubletop, offer excellent, little-trafficked hiking trails and views of Katahdin to boot. Many hikers base themselves at **Chimney Pond Campground** and tackle Katahdin from there on one of several trails. *50 Hikes in the Maine Mountains* by Cloe Chunn details many of Baxter's trails far better than we can here.

We did the **Sentinel Mountain Trail,** which we were told was the easiest climb up a mountain peak in the park. It was approximately 6½ miles round-trip, a moderate climb with lots of rocks and roots on the path. The trail can be wet and muddy, but the trees were so thick that even in a light rain, we didn't get soaked. At one point on the trail, you have to cross a brook on a wooden log bridge about 2 or 3 feet above the water. It's sturdy, but not great for people who aren't crazy about heights. The last bit of this trail is steeper, leading to the peak, where there is a loop trail. We were there on a foggy day so our view wasn't great, but we assume it is better when the weather is clear. From the same starting point (Kidney Pond Camps) you can choose the **Daicey Pond Trail,** a flat loop around the pond that we hear is a good spot to see moose. Just before Kidney Pond Camps is the **Doubletop Mountain Trail.** We were also told that the **South Turner Mountain Trail** from Roaring Brook via Sandy Stream Pond is a good wildlife-watching trail. In all, there are 46 mountain peaks and 175 miles of well-marked trails in Baxter. Allow 3 to 5 days at a campground like Trout Brook Farm Campground in the northern wilderness area of the park, or base yourself at Russell Pond (a 7- or 9-mile hike in from the road) and hike to the Grand Falls and Lookout Ledges. A free "Day Use Hiking Guide" is available from the park headquarters (see *Green Space*).

The Chimney Pond Trail is a popular approach to Mount Katahdin.

Gulf Hagas is most easily accessible (3.1 miles) from the Katahdin Iron Works (see *To See*). Billed as the "Grand Canyon of Maine," this 2½-mile canyon with walls up to 40 feet high was carved by the West Branch of the Pleasant River. The approach is through a 35-acre stand of virgin white pine, some more than 130 feet tall, a landmark in its own right (known as the Hermitage) and preserved by The Nature Conservancy of Maine. The trail then follows the river, along the Appalachian Trail for a ways, but turns off along the rim of the canyon toward dramatic Screw Auger Falls and on through the Jaws to Buttermilk Falls, Stair Falls, and Billings Falls. Allow 6 to 8 hours for the hike and plan to camp at one of the waterside campsites within the KI–Jo Mary preserve (see *Campgrounds*).

Great Northern's River Pond Outdoor Classroom and Hiking Trail is a 5.8-mile loop through both harvested and unharvested forest. Eleven sites along the way help visitors understand the multiple uses of this forest, as well as offering a chance to observe wildlife in its natural habitat. A handy brochure (available at Great Northern headquarters) outlines the sites in detail. For those not wishing to hike, most sites can be reached by car from the Golden Road (see *To See*).

MILL TOUR

Great Northern Paper offers tours of its East Millinocket Mill and Recycle Plant, late June through August, Monday, Tuesday, Thursday, and Friday 10:30–noon and 1:30–3. The tour takes you through each step of the process, giving visitors a better understanding of how paper is produced.

RAILROAD EXCURSIONS

Bangor & Aroostook Railroad Company (1-800-847-1505), Northern Maine Junction Park, RR 2, Box 45, Bangor 04401. This historic system offers scheduled weekend trips departing from a number of locations along its track in northern Maine. Trips average from 2 to 4 hours. Tickets start at $12 adults, $8 for children, and vary depending on destination.

SWIMMING

Peaks-Kenny State Park in Dover-Foxcroft is a great family beach, with lawns, playground equipment, and a roped-in swimming area. Hiking trails and camping.

WHITE-WATER RAFTING

Rafting on the West Branch of the Penobscot has gained increasing popularity in recent years. It has been deemed the ultimate challenge in Maine rafting, best for experienced rafters (to run the whole river you must be at least 15). Class V rapids include Exterminator, Nesowadnehunk Falls, and the Cribworks. Several white-water rafting companies maintain bases near the Togue Pond entrance to Baxter State Park; there are mid-May to mid-September departure points for day trips.

New England Outdoor Center (723-5438; 1-800-766-7238; rafting@neoc.com) built its beautiful Rice Farm facility a year ago and offers a range of options to rafters. The campground offers tent and cabin-tent sites, fire rings, and a showerhouse. Nearby Twin Pine Camps, on Millinocket Lake, are traditional sporting camps set in the woods, with an indoor pool and hot tub among the facilities. The lodge at Rice Farm has a popular restaurant, wraparound deck with water views, hot tub, changing room and showers, and a complete outfitters shop.

Northern Outdoors (1-800-765-RAFT) and **Wilderness Expeditions** (1-800-825-WILD; wwld@aol.com) share the **Penobscot Outdoor Center** on Pockwockamus Pond, where facilities include a bar, restaurant, hot tub, sauna, canoes, kayaks, and windsurfers; lodging is at campsites and in cabin tents.

Unicorn Rafting (1-800-UNICORN) has a new base in Millinocket; they also offer a 6-day Penobscot expedition tracing Thoreau's journey in the Maine woods.

WINTER SPORTS

CROSS-COUNTRY SKIING AND SNOWSHOEING

Katahdin Country Skis and Sports (723-5839), One Colony Place, Millinocket, offers rental skis. Trail maps to close to 60 miles of free groomed and backcountry trails are available here and from the local chamber.

Katahdin Lake Wilderness Camps (see *Lodging*) caters exclusively to cross-country skiers.

SNOWMOBILING

Snowmobiling is huge in this region. There are over 350 miles of groomed trails in the region, and more than 10 snowmobile clubs in the area to consult. A snowmobile map is available at the chamber (see *Guidance*), showing the ITS trails, as well as containing advertisements for many snowmobiling-geared businesses.

New England Outdoor Center has a fleet of 50 snowmobiles for rent, and lodging at their Rice Farm base. They offer half-day, full-day, and overnight guided snowmobile excursions, from tours through Baxter State Park, a maple sugar farm, and throughout Piscataquis, Penobscot, and Aroostook Counties, among other places.

GREEN SPACE

BAXTER STATE PARK

This 201,018-acre park surrounds Mount Katahdin, the highest peak in the state (5,267 feet). There are only two entry points: **Togue Pond Gate** near Millinocket, by far the most popular, is open 6 AM–9 PM, May 15 through October 15. **Matagamon Gate,** in the northeast corner of the park, is open 6 AM–9 PM. Nonresident vehicles pay an $8 day-use fee at the gate ($25 for the season). Vehicles with Maine plates are admitted free. Day-trippers should be aware that the number of vehicles allowed in the park is restricted, because of limited parking; arrive early to avoid being turned away.

The list of rules governing the park is long and detailed. No motorcycles, motorized trail bikes, or ATVs are allowed in the park. Bicycles can be used on maintained roads only. Snowmobiles are allowed in particular areas of the park only. Pets are not allowed in the park. The list goes on and on; be sure to pick up a copy at park headquarters or the chamber and read it through before heading in.

The park is open daily, but note the restricted camping periods and the special-use permits required from December 1 through March. Orchids, ferns, alpine flowers, and dozens of other interesting plants here delight botanists. Geologists are intrigued by Baxter's rhyolite, Katahdin granite, and many fossils. Birds and wildlife, of course, also abound. Rental canoes are available at several locations in the park.

Camping is only permitted May 15 to October 15 and December to April 1. As a rule, campsites are booked solid before the season begins; don't come without a reservation. In all there are 10 widely scattered campgrounds. Daicey Pond and Kidney Pond each offer traditional cabins with beds, gas lanterns, firewood, and table and chairs ($17 per person per night minimum; $30 for a two-bed cabin, $40 for a three-bed cabin, and $50 for a four-bed; children ages 1–6 are free, 7–16 are $10 per person). Six more campgrounds, accessible by road, offer a mix of bunkhouses, lean-tos, and tent sites (bunkhouses $7 per person per night; lean-tos and tenting space $6 per person per night; minimum $12 for both). There are two more backcountry, hike-in campgrounds, at Chimney Pond and Russell Pond, which are among the most popular. Beyond that there are several backcountry sites, available by reservation for backpackers. Some of these sites have restrictions, so be sure to contact the park before planning your trip.

Summer-season reservations (only accepted for the period between

May 15 and October 15; dates vary a little according to campground opening and closing dates; request information from park headquarters) must be made in person or by mail with the fee enclosed (check or cash), posted no earlier than December 26 of the year before you are coming (Baxter State Park, 46 Balsam Drive, Millinocket 04462). Send a stamped, self-addressed envelope if you want to receive a confirmation. No refunds.

Also see KI-JO Mary Multiple Use Forest under *Campgrounds*.

LODGING

Note: For details about a choice of motels handy to I-95, check with the Katahdin Area Chamber of Commerce (723-4443).

INNS AND BED & BREAKFASTS

The Sweet Lillian B&B (723-4894), corner of Katahdin and Pine Streets (88 Pine Street), Millinocket 04462. This hospitable way station is named after innkeeper Patty Vaznis' grandmother. Six clean, comfortable guest rooms with shared bath (third floor can be rented as a three-bedroom suite with private bath). Common living room on the first floor. Patty will cook dinners upon request at an additional cost. $40–50 includes full breakfast

Katahdin Area B&B (723-5220; 1-800-725-5220), 94–96 Oxford Street, Millinocket. Five clean, comfortable rooms with private baths and cable TV. Also a two-bedroom suite (sleeps five) with private bath and sitting area. Washer/dryer available for guest use, off-street parking. $40–55 includes full breakfast.

Carousel B&B (965-7741), Brownville 04414. Open mid-May through November. Three rooms in this pretty home in a quiet town. Exquisite murals adorn the walls throughout the house. One room has a private bath and a double bed. The other two, one with twins, one with a queen, share a bath. This is the most convenient lodging to Gulf Hagas. Betty Friend is warm and welcoming. $45 for private bath, $40 shared, includes a full breakfast.

Big Moose Inn (723-8391), Millinocket Lake, Millinocket 04462. Open June through October, but will open the lodge in winter for groups. A classic old summer inn has been a family-run business since 1976, offering 11 simple guest rooms with double or twin beds, 11 cabins, and a 40-site campground. Plenty of comfortable common areas in the lodge, as well as green rockers on the porch. Beautifully situated on the water, and not far from the Togue Pond entrance to Baxter State Park. Also a base for white-water rafting. The dining room is open to the public (see *Where to Eat*).

REMOTE RUSTIC CAMPS

Katahdin Lake Wilderness Camps, (723-9867) Box 398, Millinocket 04462. Open all year, and located at the end of a private, 3½-mile tote trail from Roaring Brook Road in Baxter State Park; it's an hour's walk. Al Cooper will meet you in summer with packhorses, or you can fly in from Millinocket Lake (723-8373). But most prefer the 16½-mile trip on skis beginning at the Abol Falls Store on the Penobscot River just outside Millinocket. Ten log cabins (with one to eight people per cabin) and a main lodge built on a bluff overlooking the lake; firewood, linens, kerosene lamps, and shower houses go with each cabin; several also have gas stoves for housekeeping. Sandy beaches, Registered Maine Guide available for fly-fishing lessons; hiking tours. $100 per day includes all three meals. Catering exclusively to cross-country skiers in winter.

Bradford Camps (746-7777), Box 729, Ashland 04732. Open following ice-out through November. Sited at the Aroostook River's headwaters, Munsungan Lake. Virtually inaccessible by land (unless you want to weather 47 miles on logging roads), this unusually tidy lodge has well-tended lawns and eight hand-hewn log cabins on the waterfront, all with full private baths. $100 per person per night includes meals, but boat and motor are extra. Family rates in July and August.

Shin Pond Village (528-2900), RR 1, Box 280, Patten. Ten miles down Route 159 from Patten. Open year-round. Craig and Terry Hill run this recreational facility, which offers 30 campsites, some nicely situated in woods off the road, six housekeeping cottages and five guest rooms. Set on a hill above Shin Pond, and there are nice views of Mount Chase. There is a snack bar and a nice little craft shop, and recreational opportunities abound. The north entrance to Baxter State Park isn't far. Cottages accommodate three to eight people, and have full bath, linens, towels, and cookware. Camping is $14.95 per night; cottages are $62–112 depending on number of people. American plan available.

Frost Pond Camps (radiophone: 695-2821), Box 620, Star Route 76, Greenville, ME 04441. Off the Golden Road near Ripogenous Dam, Rick and Judy Givens have operated these camps for over 25 years. Eight well-maintained housekeeping cottages (six on the waterfront) and 10 campsites on the shore of Frost Pond. Cabins have gas lights, refrigerators and stoves, and are heated by woodstoves in the spring and fall. One has plumbing, the others each have a pit toilet. Cabins accommodate two to eight people. A great base for exploring the wilderness, fishing, boating, and Allagash canoe trips (rentals and transportation available). $23.50–26 per person per night for cabins; discounts for longer stays. $13 per night for campsites.

CAMPGROUNDS

KI–Jo Mary Multiple Use Forest (695-8135). Open May through October, a 200,000-plus-acre tract of commercial forest stretching almost from Greenville on the west to the Katahdin Iron Works on the east and north to Millinocket. Seasonal checkpoints are open 6 AM–8 PM (Thursday through Saturday until 10 PM in May, June, and August, 10:30 PM in July). Primitive sites. Good fishing, hunting, and plenty of solitude. The **Jo Mary Lake Campground** (723-8117) is located within the forest, but offers modern facilities with flush toilets, hot showers.

Gulf Hagas (see *Hiking*), with 50 miles of the Appalachian Trail, 96 lakes, and 125 miles of brooks, streams, and rivers within its boundaries, along with 150 miles of roads over which lumber trucks have rights-of-way. There are over 60 authorized campsites, some on rivers and lakes. The day-use fee (for those between ages 15 and 70) is $4 for residents, $7 for nonresidents; the camping fee is a flat $4 per person. For reservations (valid only at least a month in advance), write North Maine Woods, Box 382, Ashland 04732.

Peaks-Kenny State Park (564-2003), Route 153, 6 miles from Dover-Foxcroft. Open mid-May through September for camping and for swimming in Sebec Lake.

Mattawamkeag Wilderness Park (746-4881), Mattawamkeag (off Route 2; a half-hour drive from the I-95 Medway exit). Fifty campsites, 11 Adirondack shelters, bathrooms, hot showers, small store, recreation building, picnic facilities, 15 miles of hiking trails, 60 miles of canoeing on the Mattawamkeag River with patches of white water, bass, salmon and trout fishing. An 8-mile gravel road leads into the park.

Scraggly Lake Public Lands Management Unit (contact the Bureau of Public Lands, Presque Isle: 764-2033), a 10,014-acre forested preserve laced with ponds and brooks. It has 12 "authorized" campsites (no fire permit needed). Scraggly Lake is good for salmon and brook trout; a half-mile hiking trail loops up Owls Head.

✒ **Katahdin Shadows Campground** (746-9349; 1-800-794-5267), Route 157, Medway. This is a full-service, family-geared four-seasons campground with a central lodge with a game room and board games, swimming pool, hot tub, dock, weekend hayrides, a big playground, athletic fields, free morning coffee, "community kitchen," tent and hook-up sites, hutniks, and well-designed cabins with kitchen facilities. Rick LeVasseur also offers canoe and boat rentals, hiking, cross-country skiing, and snowmobiling information. He also owns the motel across the road. $17–45 campground; $34–49 motel.

For camping in Baxter State Park, see *Green Space*.

WHERE TO EAT

Big Moose Inn and Restaurant (723-8391), Millinocket Lake, 8 miles west of Millinocket on the Baxter Park road, across from the lake. Open for dinner Wednesday through Saturday, June through early October. A popular place; reservations suggested. A pleasant Maine woods atmosphere with choices like seafood casserole, grilled or blackened swordfish, and pineapple-glazed baked ham. $9.95–15.95.

Angie's Restaurant (943-7432), Milo. Just in case you happen to be cutting over to the Katahdin Iron Works and Gulf Hagas from I-95 (take the Howland exit and the unnumbered woods road through Medford to Milo)—or for whatever other reason you happen to be in Milo—Angie's (across from the cemetery) is open for all three meals. Great road food, homemade sandwich bread, wooden booths, blue frilly curtains, dinner specials ranging from liver and onions to salmon steak.

River's Edge Restaurant (965-2881), Brownville Junction. Open Tuesday through Saturday 4–9. Johanna and James McGuinness have created an attractive dining room featuring seafood and pasta dinners. You can also get liver and onions or prime rib.

✍ **Schootic In/Penobscot Room** (723-4566), Penobscot Avenue, Millinocket. Open for lunch and dinner. George and Bea Simon are third-generation owners. Menu choices include pizza, calzones, seafood, and prime rib. New banquet facility seats up to 40 people. Children's menu. $4.95-14.95.

SPECIAL EVENTS

July: **Fourth of July celebration** in Millinocket features a weekend full of activities and a fireworks display.

September: **End of the Trail Festival**, a celebration at the end of the Appalacian trail, includes outdoor displays, Native American trail blessing, entertainment, demonstrations, outdoor skills contest, and more. **Annual Art Festival,** Millinocket.

October: For 3 weeks before Halloween, the scariest, most elaborate **haunted trolley ride** in Maine, sponsored by Jandreau's Greenhouse, Millinocket.

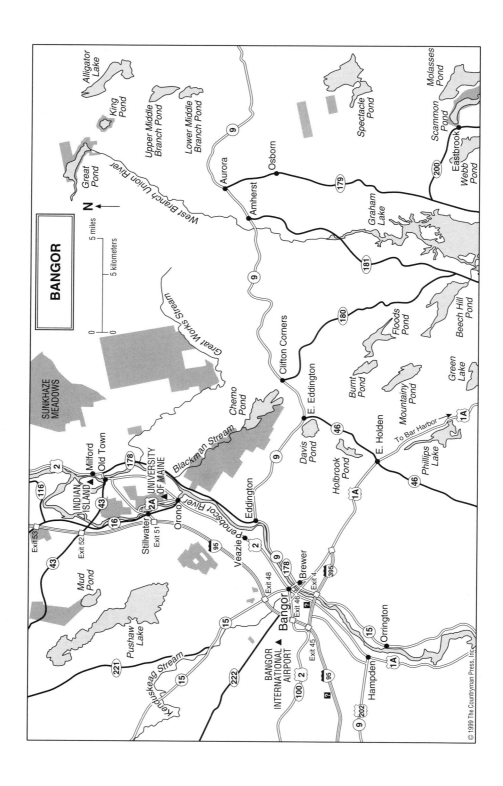

BANGOR

5 miles

5 kilometers

N

© 1999 The Countryman Press, Inc.

Bangor Area

It is no coincidence that the year 1820—when big-city merchants began buying timberland along the upper reaches of the Penobscot River—was also the year in which the Massachusetts District of Maine became a state and planted a white pine in the center of its official seal.

By the 1830s the Penobscot River was filled with pine logs, all of which were processed in the sawmills just above Bangor, where they were loaded aboard ships. By 1834–1836 land broker offices were springing up as land speculation reached its peak. Townships and lots were sold sight unseen several times over. In 1835 it was reported that two paupers who had escaped from Bangor's almshouse had each cleared $1800 by speculating in timberland (the land offices worked around the clock) by the time they were caught the next morning.

By the 1850s, Bangor was the world's leading lumber port, handling over $3 million worth of lumber in its peak year. During this boom, a section of the city came to be known as the Devil's Half Acre, where loggers flooded in after a long winter's work (and with a long winter's pay) to frequent the numerous taverns and brothels.

The Bangor of today is substantially different. The only Paul Bunyan around now is the 31-foot-high statue next to the chamber of commerce office. A 1911 fire wiped out the business district, and the end of the logging boom combined with urban renewal to leave the Devil's Half Acre a distant memory. Still, Bangor is Maine's second-largest city, and Bangor International Airport is the departure point for craft (admittedly air instead of sailing) bound for faraway points on the globe. The Bangor area also makes for a good resting spot for those venturing into the northern part of the state, to either the Baxter State Park region or the vast expanse of Aroostook County.

Two neighborhoods actually hint at the city's past grandeur. One is the West Market Square Historic District, a mid-19th-century block of shops. The other is the Broadway area, studded with the Federal-style homes of early prominent citizens and lumber barons' mansions. Across town, West Broadway holds a number of even more ornate homes, including the turreted Victorian home of author Stephen King (look for the bat-and-cobweb fence).

GUIDANCE

Bangor Region Chamber of Commerce (947-0307; www.bangor region.com), 519 Main Street, P.O. Box 1443, Bangor 04402-1443 (just off I-95 exit 45 to 495 East/exit 3B; across from the Holiday Inn), maintains a seasonal visitors information office in Paul Bunyan Park on lower Main Street (Route 1A). **The Bangor Convention and Visitors Bureau** (947-5205) shares the building, and is also a helpful source of information.

The **Maine Tourism Association** maintains two rest area/information centers on I-95 in Hamden between exits 43 and 44: northbound (862-6628) and southbound (862-6638).

GETTING THERE

By air: **Bangor International Airport** (942-0384) is served by Delta Air Lines, Northwest Airlink, and USAir Express. **Rental cars** are available at the airport.

By bus: **Greyhound** (942-1700) offers daily service to the downtown terminal. **Concord Trailways** (945-5000; 1-800-639-5150) has express trips, complete with movies and music, daily from Portland and Boston. **Cyr Bus Line** offers daily scheduled service all the way to Caribou, with stops in between.

By car: I-95 from Augusta.

GETTING AROUND

The Bus (947-0536) runs Monday through Saturday to Brewer, Bangor, Hampden, Veazie, Orono, and Old Town.

MEDICAL EMERGENCY

Eastern Maine Medical Center (973-7000), Bangor. **St. Joseph Hospital** (262-1000), Bangor.

VILLAGES

Hampden. Adjacent to Bangor, but offering a more rural setting. The academically excellent Hampden Academy and a well-known truck stop are found here.

Orono. A college town, housing the University of Maine, but still a small town, where most everyone knows everyone else. Downtown there are some nice shops and local dining landmarks, and on campus a multitude of cultural activities are available.

Old Town. Definitely a mill town, also the home of the famous Old Town Canoe factory. There's a great little museum worth visiting.

Indian Island. In 1786 the Penobscot tribe deeded most of Maine to Massachusetts in exchange for 140 small islands in the Penobscot River; they continue to live on Indian Island, which is connected by a bridge to Old Town. The 1970s discovery of an 18th-century agreement that details the land belonging to the tribe (much of it now valuable) brought the island a new school and a large community center, which attracts crowds to play high-stakes bingo (call 1-800-255-1293 for the sched-

KIM GRANT

Carving of legendary lumberman Paul Bunyan

ule). A general store in the center sells locally made crafts, as does the Moccasin Shop at Ernest Goslin's house on Bridge Street. A **Penobscot Nation Museum** (827-4153), 6 River Road, has posted hours, but we have yet to catch it open, so call before driving over. The island is accessible from Route 2, marked from I-95, exit 51.

Winterport. An old river town, once home of many sea captains, now a quiet little area with a historic district. Walking tour brochure available from area businesses.

TO SEE AND DO

MUSEUMS

Cole Land Transportation Museum (990-3600), 405 Perry Road (junction I-95 and I-395), Bangor. Open May 1 to October 30, daily 9–5. $3 per adult, senior citizens $2, under 18 free. A collection of 200 antique Maine vehicles going back to the 19th century: snowplows, wagons, trucks, sleds, rail equipment, and more.

Hose 5 Fire Museum (945-3229) 247 State Street, Bangor. Open by appointment. A working fire station until 1993, now a museum with firefighting artifacts from the area. Three fully restored fire engines, wooden water mains, and plenty of historical pictures. Free, but donations gladly accepted.

University of Maine museums, Route 2A, Orono. **Hudson Museum** (581-1901), 5746 Maine Center for the Arts (open Tuesday through Friday 9–4, Saturday and Sunday 11–4) is an exceptional anthropological collection including a special section on Maine Native Americans and Maine history. General tours for the public are offered in July and August on Tuesday and Thursday at 1 PM. **University of Maine Museum of Art** (581-3255), 109 Carnegie Hall (open weekdays 9–5, Saturday 1–4), shows a fraction of its 4,500-work collection, which includes an extensive selection of 19th- and 20th-century European and American prints by Goya, Picasso, Homer, and Whistler and Modern American paintings by George Inness, John Marin, Andrew Wyeth, and others. Tours are available by prior arrangement, and tours on tape are also available. **Page Farm & Home Museum** (open daily May 15 to September 15, 9–4; closed Sunday and Monday off-season). Free. Historical farm implements and household items from 1865 to 1940.

Old Town Museum (827-7256), North Fourth Street Extension, Old Town. Open early June through the end of August, Wednesday to Sunday 1–5. A former waterworks building houses a great little museum with exhibits on the Penobscot tribe and on local logging; early area photos; an original birch-bark canoe; well-informed guides.

Maine Forest and Logging Museum (581-2871), Leonard's Mills, off Route 178 in Bradley (take Route 9 north from Brewer; turn left on 178 and watch for signs). Open during daylight hours. "Living History Days" on two weekends, one in mid-July and another in October, with people in period attire yarding logs with horses or oxen and performing various duties using 18th-century tools. The museum is located on the site of a 1790s logging and milling community, and includes a covered bridge, water-powered sawmill, millpond, saw pit, stone dam, barn, and trapper's line camp. Special events throughout the season include Children's Day and Woodsmen's Day.

HISTORIC HOMES AND SITES

Bangor Historical Society Thomas A. Hill House (942-5766), 159 Union Street (at High Street), Bangor. Open April to mid-December, Tuesday through Friday 12–4 (also Saturdays, June through September). Admission is $5 per adult, children and members free. Downstairs has been restored to its 19th-century grandeur with Victorian furnishings and an elegant double parlor, while changing exhibits of city memorabilia are housed upstairs in this Greek Revival house. Architecture buffs might also want to check out the neighboring **Isaac Farrar Mansion** (941-2808), 166 Union Street, open weekdays 9–4 ($1 admission). A restored English Regency lumber baron's mansion with marble fireplaces, mahogany paneling, and stained-glass windows.

Mount Hope Cemetery in Bangor is one of the nation's oldest garden cemeteries, designed by noted Maine architect Charles G. Bryant. Hannibal Hamlin's grave is here.

BUS TOURS

Best of Bangor Bus Tours (942-5766), sponsored by the Bangor Historical Society, are offered every Thursday and the first Saturday of the month, July through September, departing from the chamber of commerce at 519 Main Street (see *Guidance*) at 10:30 AM; $5 per adult, children under 12 free.

FISHING

Bangor Salmon Pool. A gathering spot for salmon traveling upstream in the Penobscot River to spawn; located 2 miles south of Bangor, Route 9, Brewer.

GOLF

Bangor Municipal Golf Course (945-9226), Webster Avenue; 27 holes. **Penobscot Valley Country Club** (866-2423), Bangor Road, Orono; 18 holes. **Hermon Meadow Golf Club** (848-3741), Hermon; nine holes.

RAILROAD EXCURSION

See **Bangor & Aroostook Railroad Company** in "Katahdin Region."

SWIMMING

Jenkins' Beach. Popular beach on Green Lake for families with children. Store and snack bar.

Violette's Public Beach and Boat Landing (843-6876), East Holden (between Ellsworth and Bangor). $2 admission. Also on Green Lake, a popular spot for college students and young adults. Swim float with slide, boat launch, and picnic tables.

DOWNHILL AND CROSS-COUNTRY SKIING

Mt. Hermon Ski Area (848-5192), Newburg Road, Hermon (3 miles off I-95 from exit 43, Carmel, or off Route 2 from Bangor). Popular local ski area, with two T-bars and 17 runs (the longest is 3,500 feet); rentals available; base lodge, night skiing, snowboarding.

Hermon Meadow Ski Touring Center (848-3471). Approximately 6 miles of groomed trails on a golf course.

GREEN SPACE

Sunkhaze Meadows (827-6138), Milford. Just north of Bangor, this 9,337-acre refuge includes nearly 5 miles of Sunkhaze Stream and 12 miles of tributary streams. Truly a wild area, there are no visitor facilities on the property, though development of such is planned as funding becomes available. Recreation activities include canoeing, walking logging trails, hunting and fishing in accordance with Maine laws. Also excellent bird-watching and cross-country skiing opportunities.

A brochure titled **"Trails in the Bangor Region,"** available at the chamber visitors center, lists close to a dozen trails suitable for biking, walking, picnicking, running, hiking, cross-country skiing, and other nature activities.

LODGING

  ♧ **The Phenix Inn** (947-0411), 20 Broad Street, Bangor 04401. A historic inn located in the heart of downtown Bangor. The 32 rooms are each decorated a bit differently, some with mahogany beds. All have antique brass water faucets, private bath, air-conditioning, and TVs. There are two suites, one with a Jacuzzi bath, and an extended residency apartment. Innkeeper Paul Johnson is helpful and friendly. Expansions to the property include a TCBY next door, and plans for a fitness center are in the works. Continental breakfast is served in the pretty breakfast room. $75–90 in-season.

  ♧ **Highlawn Bed and Breakfast** (866-2272; 1-800-297-2272), 193 Main Street, Orono 04773. Betty Lee and Arthur Comstock have hosted guests in their majestic white house with front columns for 13 years. Six of the 17 rooms in this 1803 house are pretty guest rooms, but only 3 are rented at a time, which means each has a private bath. Five minutes from the University of Maine. Full breakfast (maybe pancakes or omelets) is included in their $55–70 year-round rates.

The Lucerne Inn (843-5123; 1-800-325-5123; info@lucerneinn.com), RR 3, Box 540, Holden 04429. A 19th-century mansion on Route 1A, overlooking Phillips Lake in East Holden. Best known as a restaurant (see *Dining Out*), it also has 25 rooms with private baths, working fireplaces, heated towel bars, whirlpool baths, phones, and TVs. $99–159 in-season includes continental breakfast. Lower rates off-season.

Hamstead Farm (848-3749), RFD 3, Box 703, Bangor 04401. Open year-round. Barns and outbuildings trail picturesquely behind a snug 1840s farmhouse. There are three pleasant guest rooms (one with private bath) with cozy, country-style decor. Resident animals include 175 turkeys, 40 cows, two brood sows, 20 feeder pigs, two barn cats, and two dogs. The farm is set on 150 acres, with a deck overlooking the backyard; a path leads into the village of Hermon. $45–50 double, $35–40 single includes a farm breakfast.

Note: Bangor also has many hotels and motels, mainly located by the mall and near the airport.

WHERE TO EAT

DINING OUT

The Lemon Tree (94-LEMON), 167 Center Street, Bangor. Open for lunch Monday through Saturday, dinner Tuesday through Sunday, and Sunday brunch. A small place with plenty of atmosphere, as well as delectable menu choices. "Great Beginnings" include fried dill pickles (try them!), and entrées feature plenty of pasta choices, salads, sandwiches, and several house specialties. $4.95–13.95.

Lucerne Inn (843-5123, 1-800-325-5123), Route 1A, East Holden (11 miles out of Bangor, heading toward Ellsworth). Open for dinner daily, as well as a popular Sunday brunch. A grand old mansion with a view of Phillips Lake. Specialties include shrimp Niçoise and veal Normandy. $11.95–19.95.

Pilot's Grill (942-6325), 1528 Hammond Street (Route 2, 1.5 miles west of exit 45B off I-95), Bangor. Open daily 11:30–9:30 (until 8 on Sunday). A large, long-established place with 1950s decor and a huge, all-American menu. $7–15.

EATING OUT

City Limits (941-9888), 735 Main Street, Bangor. Open for lunch and dinner daily. A large, casual place serving Italian specialties and seafood. Great breadsticks.

Captain Nick's (942-6444), 1165 Union Street, Bangor. Open daily for lunch and dinner. A large, locally popular place with good seafood, steaks.

Bagel Shop (947-1654), 1 Main Street, Bangor. Open Monday to Thursday 6–6, Friday 6–5, Sunday 6–2. A genuine, reasonably priced kosher restaurant, delicatessen, and bakery that features egg dishes, bagels, and chocolate cheesecake.

Governor's Take Out and Eat In (947-7704), 643 Broadway in Bangor; and Stillwater Avenue in Stillwater (827-4277). Open from early breakfast to late dinner. This is the original in a statewide chain. Popular at all meals, large breakfast menu, hamburgers to steaks, specials like German potato soup, fresh strawberry pie, ice cream.

Momma Baldacci's (945-5813), 12 Alden Street, Bangor. A longtime family-owned and -operated restaurant open for lunch and dinner, and serving Italian specialties at reasonable prices.

Dysart's (942-4878), Coldbrook Road, Hermon (I-95, exit 44). Open 24 hours. Billed as "the biggest truck stop in Maine"—one room for the general public and another for drivers. Known for great road food and reasonable prices. Homemade bread and seafood are specialties.

Pat's Pizza (866-2111), Mill Street, Orono. A local landmark, especially popular with high school and university students and families. Now franchised throughout the state, but this is the original with booths and

A sculpture on Market Square in Bangor

a jukebox, back dining room and downstairs tap room, plus Pat and his family still running the place. Pizza, sandwiches, full dinners.

BREW PUB

Bear Brew Pub (866-BREW), 36 Main Street, Orono. An upscale brew pub with a cozy atmosphere and a creative menu that includes Parmesan pesto scallops over pasta, and crabmeat primavera. Also offers sandwiches, pizza, and burgers. The beer is all brewed on the premises, along with root beer, cream soda, and ginger ale.

COFFEEHOUSES

New Moon Café (990-2233), 21 Main Street, Bangor. Spacious and open with a tile floor and interesting art on the walls, offering a wide variety of coffee and espresso drinks, smoothies, Italian sodas, sandwiches, wraps, and desserts. Live music many nights.

Intown Internet Café (942-0999; café@ime.net), 56 Main Street, Bangor. Several flavored coffees, breakfast and lunch, but the real focus here is the Internet access. Seven computers available for e-mail access, Internet access, word processing, and more.

ENTERTAINMENT

✎ **Maine Center for the Arts** (581-1755), at the University of Maine in Orono, has become the cultural center for the area. Hosts a wide variety of concerts and events, from classical to country-and-western, children's theater, and dance. Many performances are held in Hutchins Concert Hall, Maine's first concert hall.

✐ **Penobscot Theater Company** (942-3333; penthtr@agate.net), 183 Main
Street, Bangor. This company has been putting on quality shows for
more than 20 years. They recently purchased and renovated the Bangor
Opera House (Main Street, Bangor), and now offer performances in
both facilities throughout their nine-month season. In the summer the
company sponsors the Maine Shakespeare Festival and the Creative Arts
Program for young people.

Maine Masque Theater (581-1963), Hauck Auditorium, University of
Maine. Classic and contemporary plays presented October through
May by University of Maine theater students.

✐ **Theatre of the Enchanted Forest** (945-0800), 9 Central Street, Bangor.
Children's theater.

Bass Park (942-9000), 100 Dutton Street, Bangor. Complex includes
Bangor Auditorium, Civic Center, State Fair, and **Raceway** (featuring harness racing, Thursday through Sunday, May through July).
Band concerts in the park by the Paul Bunyan statue on Tuesdays in
summer.

Bangor Symphony Orchestra (942-5555). The symphony began in 1895
and is still going strong, with performances at the Bangor Opera House
from October through May.

Blue Ox (941-2337) is the independent professional baseball team in town.
They play at Mahaney Diamond at the University of Maine.

SELECTIVE SHOPPING

BOOKSTORES

Betts' Bookstore (947-7052), 26 Main Street, Bangor, is a full-service
bookstore specializing in Maine and Stephen King titles.

Mr. Paperback. Bangor is home base for this eastern Maine chain, with
stores here at Main Square (942-6494) and Airport Mall (942-9191). All
are fully stocked stores with Maine sections.

BookMarc's (942-3206), 10 Harlow Street, Bangor. A great little full-service
bookstore, with a cozy café.

✐ **The Booksource,** Crossroads Plaza, Bangor. A superstore with special
emphasis on multimedia and children's books.

Borders (990-3300), off Hogan Road at Bangor Mall. Part of a large chain,
but a great place to find what you are looking for, and grab an espresso
at the same time.

CANOES

Old Town Canoe & Kayak Factory Outlet Store (827-1530), 130 North
Main Street, Old Town. Varieties sold include fiberglass, wood, Kevlar,
Crosslink, and Royalex. Factory tour video shows how canoes are made.

SPECIAL SHOPS

Winterport Boot Shop, Twin City Plaza, Brewer. Largest selection of Red-
wing workboots in the Northeast. Proper fit for sizes 4–16, all widths.

✎ **The Briar Patch** (941-0255), 27 State Street, Bangor. A large and exceptional children's book and toy store.

Snow & Neally, 15 State Street, Bangor. An attractive showroom for the high-quality gardening tools that this family business has been producing since 1864.

The Grasshopper Shop (945-3132), West Market Square, Bangor. So many items, they now have two stores across the street from each other. Trendy women's clothing, toys, jewelry, gifts, housewares.

The Bangor Mall, Hogan Road (just west of the I-95 exit 49 interchange). The centerpiece of a whole range of satellite malls and stores. Since this is precisely the kind of strip most visitors come to Maine to escape, we won't elaborate, but it certainly has its uses.

SPECIAL EVENTS

April: **Kenduskeag Stream Canoe Race.**

July: **Bangor State Fair,** Bass Park—agricultural fair with harness racing. **Maine Shakespeare Festival** *(late July to early August)*—three shows performed in rotation outside on the bank of the Penobscot River; food vendors, bleachers, plenty of lawn space.

August: **WLBZ Downtown Arts Sidewalk Festival.**

September: **Paul Bunyan Festival Days**, at Paul Bunyan Park, featuring crafts, food, entertainment.

Aroostook County

Almost the size of Massachusetts, Aroostook is Maine's largest and least populated county. It's referred to simply as The County in Maine, and, contrary to its image as one big potato field, it's as varied as it is vast. Four million of Aroostook's 5 million acres are wooded—land that includes many major mountains, most of the Allagash Wilderness Waterway, and more than 1,000 lakes.

The Upper St. John Valley at the top of The County, a broad ribbon of river land backed by woodland in the west and by a high, open plateau in the east, has its own distinctly Acadian look, language, and taste. Central Aroostook—the rolling farmland around Fort Fairfield, Presque Isle, and Caribou—is generally equated with the entire county. It, too, has its appeal, especially around Washburn and New Sweden, sites of two of New England's more interesting museums. Houlton, the northern terminus of I-95 and the county seat, is in southern Aroostook, a mix of farmland, lonely woods, and lakes.

"Aroostook" is said to mean "bright," actually the best word we can think of to describe the entire county since the luminosity of its sky—broader than elsewhere in New England—is The County's single most striking characteristic, along with its location. Bounded by Canada on two sides and the North Woods on the third, Aroostook is so far off any tourist route that many New England maps omit it entirely. Maine pundits are fond of noting that Portland is as far from Fort Kent, the northern terminus of Route 1, as it is from New York City.

The conventional loop tour around The County is I-95 to its terminus at Houlton, then Route 1 north to Fort Kent and back down Route 11. We suggest doing it in reverse.

Many visitors actually enter The County in canoes, paddling up the Allagash River, which flows north and empties into the St. John River at Allagash, a minuscule hamlet that's become widely known as Mattagash to readers of novels (*The Funeral Makers, Once upon a Time on the Banks,* and *The Weight of Winter*) by Allagash native Cathie Pelletier. Local residents will tell you that the names of Pelletier's characters have been changed only as slightly as that of her town and that the interplay between Catholics and Protestants (descendants of Acadian and Scottish settlers, respectively) chronicled in her books remains very real. From

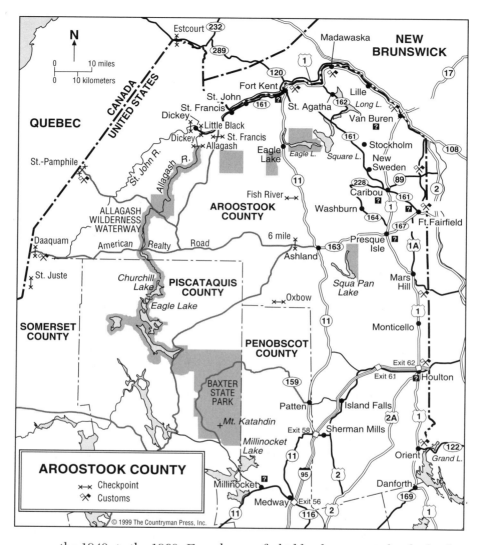

the 1940s to the 1960s French was a forbidden language in local schools, and students were punished for speaking it anywhere on school grounds.

Acadians trace their lineage to French settlers who came to farm and fish in Nova Scotia in the early 1600s and who, in 1755, were forcibly deported by an English governor. This *grand dérangement,* dispersing a population of some 10,000 Acadians, brutally divided families (a tale told by Longfellow in "Evangeline"). Many were returned to France, only to make their way back to a warmer New World (Louisiana), and many were resettled in New Brunswick, from which they were once more dislodged after the American Revolution when the British government gave their land to Loyalists from the former colonies.

In a meadow overlooking the St. John River behind Madawaska's Tante Blanche Museum, a large marble cross and an outsized wooden sculpture of a *voyageur* in his canoe mark the spot on which several hundred of these displaced Acadians landed in 1785. They settled both sides of the St. John River, an area known as Mattawaska ("land of the porcupine"). Not until 1842 did the St. John become the formal boundary dividing Canada and Maine.

The 1842 Webster-Ashburton Treaty settled the Aroostook War, a footnote in American history recalled in the 1830s wooden blockhouses at Fort Kent and Fort Fairfeld. Until relatively recently this bloodless "war" was the area's chief historic claim, but the valley's distinct Acadian heritage is gaining increasing recognition.

In 1976 a "Village Acadien" consisting of a dozen buildings was assembled just west of Van Buren. It's an interesting enough little museum village, but it only begins to tell the story evinced in the very shape of the St. John Valley towns—the houses strung out like arms from cathedral-sized Catholic churches at their centers.

Aroostook County still produces 1½ million tons of potatoes a year, but the family farms—once the staple of The County's landscape and social fabric—are fading, replaced by consolidated spreads that grow other crops, notably broccoli, barley, and sugar beets. The family potato farm is already the stuff of museum exhibits. Our favorites are in the New Sweden Museum, which commemorates not only family farms but also one of the most interesting immigration stories in American history.

The County is as far removed in time as it is in distance from Maine's more commercialized "Vacationland." You shop in craftspeople's and farmers' homes, ask locally for directions to the best places to walk, ski, and fish, feast on fiddleheads and *ployes* (buckwheat crêpes) rather than lobster. Most visitors, moreover, come in winter—to snowmobile or dogsled. Winter driving, we're told, is less daunting here than elsewhere in the Northeast because, thanks to the region's lowest temperatures, the snow is drier (no ice) as well as more plentiful. Summer temperatures also tend to be cooler than elsewhere, and in early July the potato fields are a spread of pink and white blossoms. Fall colors, which usually peak in the last weeks of September at the end of potato harvest, include reddening barley fields as well as maples.

GUIDANCE

As noted in the introduction, The County comprises three distinct regions. For details about northern Aroostook (the Upper St. John Valley), contact the **Greater Fort Kent Chamber of Commerce** (834-5354), P.O. Box 430, Fort Kent 04743. A walk-in information center at the blockhouse, staffed by the Boy Scouts, is open seasonally. For central Aroostook, contact the **Presque Isle Chamber of Commerce** (764-6561), P.O. Box 672, Presque Isle 04769; and for southern Aroostook, the **Houlton Chamber of Commerce** (532-4216),

109-B Main Street, Houlton 04730. The county has recently been trying to market itself as a tourist destination, with color brochures inviting people to "discover the other Maine." This campaign is headed by
the **Northern Maine Development Commission** (1-800-427-
8736), which will send you fact sheets that list lodging, dining, and
recreational options for all three regions.

The big walk-in information center in The County is maintained by the
Maine Tourism Association, just off I-95 in Houlton (532-6346).

Note the **North Maine Woods** information office on Route 1 in
Ashland described in "The North Woods."

GETTING THERE

By car: I-95 to Benedicta or Sherman Mills, then Route 11 up through
Patten, Ashland, and Eagle Lake to Fort Kent, from which you can
explore west to Allagash and east along the Upper St. John Valley to St.
Agatha and/or Van Buren. Stop at the New Sweden Museum, for a
meal in Caribou, and for a final overnight in the Houlton area.

By plane: Regularly scheduled service to **Presque Isle/Northern
Maine Regional Airport** is limited to **USAir Express** (1-800-428-
4322) and **Business Express** (1-800-345-3400). **Aroostook Aviations**
(543-6334), formerly Pine State Air, no longer offers regularly scheduled service but is available for charters. **Scotty's Flying Service** (528-
2626), Shin Pond, is a commercial seaplane operation geared to shut-
tling canoeists, hunters, and anglers in to remote lakes and put-in places
along the St. John, Allagash, and Aroostook Rivers.

By bus: **Cyr Bus Lines** (532-6868), Houlton, runs daily between the
Greyhound terminal in Bangor and Caribou, with stops in between.

MEDICAL EMERGENCY

Northern Maine Medical Center (834-3155), 143 East Maine Street,
Fort Kent.

Houlton Regional Hospital (532-9471), 20 Hartford Street, Houlton.

TO SEE

MUSEUMS

A brochure detailing the county's historical museums and attractions is avail-
    able from most chambers. Following are those we found of particular
    interest (in order of suggested routing).

See *To See* in the "Katahdin Region" chapter for details about the
    Lumberman's Museum in Patten.

Fort Kent Historical Society Museum (834-5121), Main and Market
    Streets. Open weekends mid-May through Labor Day. The former
    Bangor & Aroostook Railroad depot is filled with local memorabilia and
    exhibits on the economic and social history of the area, focusing on
    lumbering and agriculture.

Fort Kent Blockhouse Museum, off Route 1. Open Memorial Day
    through Labor Day, usually 9–dusk, maintained by the town and the

local Boy Scout troop. This symbol of the northern terminus of Route 1 is a convincingly ancient, if much restored, two-story 1830s blockhouse with documents and mementos from the Aroostook War. Be sure to wander down to the Fish River behind the blockhouse, a pleasant walk to picnic and tenting sites.

Madouesk Historic Center and Acadian Cross Shrine (728-4518), Route 1, Madawaska. Open early June through Labor Day, weekdays 9:30–4:30, Sunday 1:30–4:30. The complex includes the **Tante Blanche Museum** (local memorabilia) and, if you follow the dirt road behind the museum to the river, the 18th-century **Albert Homestead,** plus the *Voyageur* statue and stone cross described in the introduction to this chapter.

Acadian Village (566-2691 or 866-3972), Route 1, Van Buren. Open mid-June through mid-September, noon–5 daily, and by appointment. The 16 buildings include a school and store, a barbershop, a train station, old homesteads with period furnishings, and a reconstructed, 18th-century log church. $3 per adult, $1.50 per child.

Ste. Agathe Historical Society Museum (543-6364/6911), St. Agatha. The oldest house in this unusually pleasant village on Long Lake, the Pelletier-Marquis home dates just from 1854; it's filled with a sense of the town's unusually rich ethnic and social history.

New Sweden Historical Society Museum (896-3018; off-season, call Mabel Todd at 896-5843). Just east of Route 161, New Sweden. Open Memorial Day through mid-September, Tuesday through Saturday 1–4 and by appointment. Entering the community's reconstructed Kapitileum (meetinghouse), you are faced with the imposing bust of William Widgery Thomas, the Portland man sent by President Lincoln to Sweden in 1863 to halt the sale of iron to the Confederacy. Thomas quickly learned Swedish, married two countesses (the second after her sister died), and eventually devoted his sizable energies to establishing a colony of Swedish farmers in Maine. In 1870 the House of Representatives authorized the project, granting 100 acres of woodland to each Swedish family. A pink granite memorial in a pine grove behind the museum complex commemorates the arrival and hardships of those who settled here between 1870 and 1875. Despite the severe climate and thin soil (Thomas had been struck by the similarities between Sweden and northern Maine), New Sweden prospered, with 1,400 immigrants in 1895 and 689 buildings, including three churches, seven general stores, and two railroad stations. New Sweden's annual festivals draw thousands of local descendants. The museum remains a cultural touchstone for Swedes living throughout the Northeast, and the town continues to attract visitors from Sweden, even an occasional immigrant. Also check out nearby Thomas Park, with a picnic area, the monument and cemetery behind the museum, and the other historic buildings in New Sweden, including the Larsson Ostlund Log Home, Lars Noak Blacksmith and Woodworking Shop, and the one-room Capitol Schoolhouse.

The Salmon Brook Historical Society (455-4339), Route 164, Washburn. Open weekends mid-June to Labor Day 1–4, and by appointment. The pleasant 1852 **Benjamin C. Wilder Farmstead** (13 rooms of 1850–1900 period furnishings) and the **Aroostook Agricultural Museum** (potato-harvesting tools and trivia housed in the neighboring barn) offer a sense of life and potato farming in the late 19th century. Washburn's Taterstate Frozen Foods claims to have invented the frozen french fry.

Nylander Museum (493-4209), 393 Main Street, Caribou. Open Memorial Day through Labor Day, Wednesday through Sunday 1–5. A small but intriguing museum displaying permanent collections of fossils, minerals and rocks, shells and other marine life, butterflies and moths, birds, and early-man artifacts, most collected by Swedish-born Olof Nylander; also changing exhibits, and a medicinal herb garden in the back with over 80 specimens.

Caribou Historical Center (498-3095), Route 1, Caribou. Open June through early September, Tuesday through Saturday 9–5, or by appointment. A log building filled with local memorabilia from the mid–19th century to the 1930s, including antiques, historical papers, photographs, home furnishings, and tools. Also a replica of an 1860s one-room school with a bell in the cupola.

Northern Maine Museum of Science, University of Maine at Presque Isle. A new facility with many interesting exhibits, including a herbarium (library of plant species), a coral-reef environment, an extensive display of plant and shell specimens collected by Leroy Norton, who was a well-known local amateur naturalist, topographic maps, and Aroostook potato varieties, among much more. Be sure to pick up a copy of the museum guide.

Aroostook County Historical and Art Museum (532-4216), 109 Main Street, Houlton. Open by appointment. Same building as the Houlton Area Chamber of Commerce, and if there is enough staff, someone from the chamber will take you up. A large, well-organized, labeled, and well-maintained collection of local memorabilia.

Oakfield Railroad Museum (757-8575), Station Street, Oakfield. This 1910 Bangor & Aroostook railroad station is one of three remaining wood-frame railroad stations between Searsport and Fort Kent. Exhibits include photographs from the early days of the railroad, vintage signs and advertising pieces, maps, newspapers, a rail motor car, and a C-66 caboose.

Webb Museum of Vintage Fashion (862-3797 or 463-2404), Route 2, Island Falls. Open June through early October, Monday through Thursday 10–4. $3 adults, $2 seniors, $1 children under 12. Fourteen of the 17 rooms in this Victorian-era house are filled with some 6,000 articles of clothing amassed by Frances Stratton—hats, jewelry, combs, and mannequins dressed to represent the specific people to whom their outfits once belonged. It's a spooky, fascinating place, chronicling life in a small town as well as what its inhabitants wore from the 1890s to the

1950s. Each room has its own theme, and the collection rotates each year. *Note:* This museum can be accessed either from Route 11 (it's 9 miles east of Patten) or from I-95.

CHURCHES

As noted in the introduction to this chapter, tall, elaborate, French Canadian–style Catholic churches form the heart of most Upper St. John Valley villages: **St. Leonard** in Madawaska, **St. Louis** in Fort Kent (with distinctive open filigree steeples and a fine carillon), **St. David's** in the village of St. David, and **St. Luce** in Frenchville. When the twin-spired wooden church dominating the village of Lille was condemned, it was purchased by local resident Don Cyr (895-3339), who is converting it into **Le Musee et Centre du Mont-Carmel,** an Acadian cultural center and a setting for concerts and workshops. On Labor Day weekend the center sponsors the **Lille Classical Impressionist Music Festival.**

OTHER ATTRACTIONS

A. E. Howell Wildlife Conservation Center and Spruce Acres Refuge (532-6880/0676), Lycette Road off Route 1, North Amity (14 miles south of Houlton). Open May through November, 9–sunset; $3 adults, free under age 18. Art Howell, one of the best-known and -respected of Maine's more than 90 wild-animal "rehabilitators," nurtures bald eagles, bears, foxes, otters, and many more creatures that have been wounded and are being readied, if possible, for return to the wild. The center has 64 acres of woods with a picnic area and a pond stocked with fish for children; also a camping area for environmental groups. No dogs, please.

New Brunswick Botanical Garden (506-735-3074), Route 2, St.-Jacques, New Brunswick. Open June through mid-October, daily 9–dusk. More than 50,000 varieties are represented in this spread of both annuals and perennials.

SCENIC DRIVES

Flat Mountain. The single most memorable landscape that we found in all of Aroostook is easily accessible if you know where to turn. The high plateau is well named Flat Mountain and is just above but invisible from Route 1 east of Fort Kent. Ask locally about the road through the back settlements from Frenchville to St. Agatha, a lake resort with several good restaurants.

Watson Settlement Covered Bridge. Follow Main Street through Houlton's Market Square Historic District (a "Walking Tour Guide" to this area is available from the chamber of commerce) until it turns into Military Street (dating from the Aroostook War). Turn north on Foxcroft Road; in 2 miles note your first view of Mars Hill Mountain (the area's only mountain at 1,660 feet). The mountain's ownership was disputed in the Aroostook War; it is now a ski area. At roughly 3½ miles, note the road on your left descending to a small iron bridge across the Meduxnekeag River; the covered bridge, built in 1902, is midway down this hill. The road rejoins Route 1 ten minutes north of Houlton.

TO DO

CANOEING

Allagash Wilderness Waterway. This is considered *the* canoe trip in Maine, and after a 3-day expedition we agree. Since 3 days is not long enough for the whole trip (92 miles of lake and river canoeing), we put in at Round Pond and paddled the shorter 32-mile trip to Allagash. The first step in any Allagash trip is the planning, and though we pulled our trip together in 2 weeks, we recommend a longer time frame, to be sure of transportation arrangements, equipment planning, and the like. One of the first considerations is how to get into the waterway and where to leave your cars. Though it is possible to shuttle your own vehicles, leaving one at the beginning and one at the end, we recommend using a transportation service, which will bring you, your gear, and your canoes into your put-in spot and retrieve you at take-out. This simplifies the parking issue, you won't have to go back into the woods to retrieve your car at the end of the trip, and the transportation companies are experienced in negotiating the bumpy dirt roads which can lead to blown tires and rocks thrown at the windshield. **Norman L'Italien** (398-3187), P.O. Box 67, St. Francis, ME 04774 was well-informed, helpful, and friendly. After we checked in at the gate (road-use fee of $4 per person; overnight camping fee $4 per person per night), his driver Roy dropped us off at the bridge just above Round Pond and told us to call Norman when we were off the river. Norman also operates **Pelletier's Campground** in St. Francis, a good spot to stay the night before your departure. Keep in mind that the trip to the area from Sherman Mills, where you leave I-95, is at least 3 hours, so you will probably want to head up the night before your trip. Plan to arrive in daylight if you need to set up tents.

We found the river itself to be serene, unspoiled, and spectacular. Paddling and floating with the current, sunlight twinkling off the water, you'll feel you're truly in a wilderness paradise. One thing that surprised us was that even when the sun hid behind the clouds, it wasn't the least bit gloomy or less beautiful. We were there on Labor Day weekend, and the temperature was perfect. Bugs were light that time of year, which isn't always so in other seasons. Blackflies, mosquitoes, and no-see-ums can be brutal, so bring plenty of bug repellent, maybe even protective netting. On our trip, however, bugs were not a problem, and we slept out underneath the stars two of the three nights. Planning is essential for this trip. Remember that there are no stores around the next corner; if you leave it at home, you do without. Pack light, but bring enough spare clothing so that if some gets wet, you will still be comfortable. Pack in waterproof backpacks, or seal items in plastic bags to prevent soaking should your canoe tip. Bring extra garbage bags to wrap around sleeping bags and pillows. Don't forget a camera and extra film. Allagash Falls are par-

Allagash Wilderness Waterway

ticularly nice, and the portage around them is an easy ½-mile hike. The trail is very well kept, as is the picnic area at the beginning. This is actually a good place to cook a solid meal, using up your heaviest supplies before carrying your stuff around the falls. The trip after the falls is just one more overnight, and if you plan remaining meals accordingly you can lighten your load around the portage.

Campsites on the waterway were clean and well-maintained, with plenty of space for a group to spread out. Sites are available on a first-come, first-served basis, so the earlier in the day you begin paddling, the better choice you have. The river was far from crowded, even on a holiday weekend. We saw less than 15 people outside our group on our 3-day journey. The rangers, however, are quite attentive, keeping track of who is on the river, so there is no need to be nervous that you will be too isolated should something happen. If you are not an experienced canoeist, don't worry. A 3-day trip is easily manageable, without putting too much strain on infrequently used muscles. The whole waterway takes 7 to 10 days, and it is best to be flexible, especially on your end date, in case wind or rain delays your trip. If you are not comfortable venturing out on your own, several area guides can take you down the river. Following are a few suggestions. Contact North Maine Woods (see "The North Woods") for other guides available.

Allagash Guide Service (398-3418), Allagash, rents paddles and canoes, also offers transport and car pickup.

Allagash Canoe Trips (695-3668). Warren Cochrane and his father founded this company in 1953. He, his son, and other guides continue to lead trips, providing all equipment and meals. Trips vary in length.

Maine Canoe Adventures/Cross Rock Inn (398-3191), Route 162, Allagash. Gorman Chamberlain offers 5- to 7-day trips on the St. John and Allagash, also guided trips into the nearby Debouille area departing from his lodge; also offers three guest rooms, tenting area, canoe rentals.

Canoes-R-Us (834-6793), 2 Church Street, Soldier Pond (off Route 11 on the Fish River south of Fort Kent). Canoe rentals and help planning trips from Eagle Lake to Soldier Pond, from Soldier Pond to Fort Kent, and 1- to 3-day camping trips along the Fish River chain.

Eagle Valley Adventures (506-992-2827), Clair, New Brunswick, offers river trips on the Madawaska and St. John Rivers.

Note: The map/guide to the Allagash and the St. John Rivers (DeLorme Publishing, $4.95) is useful.

FARM TOUR

Knott-II-Bragg Farm (455-8386), Route 1, Box 150, Wade 04786. Open June through October, Tuesday through Saturday 9:30 AM–6 PM. $5 adults, $3.50 children; family rates available. Natalia Bragg gives a fantastic tour of the farm, including the herb gardens and flower gardens. Old-time skills are a way of life at the farm, and Natalia will describe such things as making butter, soap, and maple syrup, as well as give detailed explanations of the uses for the oils she makes from her herbs. Fee-fishing is available in Copper Penny Pond, and the gift shop sells items made on the farm, from soaps and oils to cedar "twig" handcrafted furniture. Natalia is warm, friendly, and fascinating. Ask for a copy of the tourist guide to Washburn that she put together, detailing all businesses in the northern Maine community.

FISHING

The catch is so rich and varied that it is recognized throughout the country. Salmon grow to unusual size, and trout are also large and numerous. The 80-mile Fish River chain of rivers and lakes (Eagle, Long, and Square Lakes) is legendary in fishing circles. Fish strike longer in the season than they do farther south, and fall fishing begins earlier. Contact the Maine Department of Inland Fisheries and Wildlife in Ashland (435-3231; in-state, 1-800-353-6334).

GOLF

The County's topography lends itself to golf, and the sport is so popular that most towns maintain at least a nine-hole course. The most famous course is 18 holes at **Aroostook Valley Country Club,** Fort Fairfield (476-8083), with its tees split between Canada and Maine. The 18-hole **Jo-Wa Golf Course** (463-2128) in Island Falls and the **Presque Isle Country Club** (764-0439) are also considered above par.

HIKING

See the Debouille preserve and Aroostook State Park under *Green Space.*

Fish River Falls. Ask locally for directions to the trail that leads from the former Fort Kent airport down along the river, an unusually beautiful trail through pines. Note the swimming holes below the falls. **The Dyke in Fort Kent** is also worth finding: a half-mile walk along the Fish River. The trail up **Mount Carmel** (views up and down the river valley) begins on Route 1 at the state rest area near the Madawaska–Grand Isle town line.

WINTER SPORTS

CROSS-COUNTRY SKIING

The same reliable snow that serves out-of-state snowmobilers allows residents to take advantage of hundreds of miles of trails maintained exclusively for cross-country skiing by local towns and clubs. Any town office or chamber of commerce (see *Guidance*) will steer you to local trails. Kate McCartney at the Old Iron Inn in Caribou compiled a brochure of northern Maine cross-country trails, which lists nine centers dedicated to the sport, including phone numbers, rates and locations.

SNOWMOBILING

Snowmobiling is the single biggest reason that visitors come to The County (update, 728-7228). It is the easiest ways to see some of the more remote sporting camps and wilderness areas, since riding over well-maintained trails is often smoother than bumping down logging roads in the summer. Trails lead from one end of the county to the other and are far too numerous for us to detail here. Call any Aroostook County chamber of commerce (see *Guidance*) for a "Trail Map to Northern Maine" detailing 1,600 miles of trails maintained by The County's 40-plus snowmobile clubs, including locations of clubhouses, warming huts, and service areas. On the back of the map are ads for several companies that cater to snowmobilers, from rentals and service to lodging and dining.

GREEN SPACE

Debouille Management Unit, including Debouille Mountain and several ponds, is a 23,461-acre preserve managed jointly by the state and North Maine Woods (charging gate and camping fees), accessible by gated logging roads from St. Francis and Portage. Campsites are clustered around ponds (good for trout) and near hiking trails leading to the distinctive summit of Debouille Mountain. For details, contact the Bureau of Public Lands in Presque Isle (764-2033).

Aroostook State Park (768-8341), marked from Route 1, just 4 miles south of Presque Isle. Open May 15 through October 15. A 600-acre park with swimming and picnicking at Echo Lake; also 30 campsites (June 15 through Labor Day only) at 1,213-foot Quaggy Joe Mountain— which offers hiking trails with views from the north peak across a sea of woodland to Mount Katahdin. Note the monument in the small **Maxie Anderson Memorial Park** next door; a tin replica of the *Double Eagle II* commemorates the 1978 liftoff of the first hot-air balloon to successfully cross the Atlantic.

Aroostook Valley Trail and **Bangor and Aroostook Trail** (493-4224). A 7½-mile recreational trail system connecting Caribou, Woodland, New Sweden, Washburn, Perham, Stockholm, and Van Buren. Many bogs, marshes,

wetlands, and streams are along these trails, which are owned by the Maine Bureau of Parks and Lands. Several parking lots and rest areas on the trails. Good for biking, walks, cross-country skiing, and snowmobiling.
Also see Allagash Wilderness Waterway under *Canoeing*, above.

LODGING

Given the unusual warmth and hospitality of Aroostook residents, we look forward to the day when more homes and farms will welcome visitors.

BED & BREAKFASTS

&. **Daigle's Bed & Breakfast** (834-5803), 96 East Main Street, Fort Kent 04743. This cheery modern house features a sunny, glass-walled, flower-filled dining room in which guests tend to linger over Doris Daigle's generous breakfast. The five guest rooms range from small with shared bath, to a spacious double with twin beds, to a room decorated in red and black with a refrigerator, TV, and phone. Guests are also welcome to join Elmer and Doris in the evening for drinks and snacks by the living room fireplace. $50–80 double.

Auberge du Lac (728-6047), Birch Point Road, St. David 04773. Open year-round. This small place is very quiet and private. From the road, you can hardly tell it is a B&B, but inside Grace Ouellette's attention to detail is obvious. The Ouellettes live downstairs, leaving visitors in the three guest rooms (one with private bath) to share a large, comfortable living room with a fireplace and a picture window overlooking Long Lake. Across the street is a stretch of land on the water with Adirondack chairs. $55–65 double includes a full breakfast.

Rum Rapids Inn (455-8096), Route 164, Crouseville 04738. Not far from Presque Isle, one of the oldest houses in The County (vintage 1839) is set in 15 acres on the Aroostook River. Innkeeper Clifton (Bud) Boudman offers candlelight dinners as well as two rooms (private baths) with all the comforts of home, including robes, TV/VCR with movie selections, and an honor-system snack bar. Common areas include a new solarium and spa, and a screened porch. Bud is happy to help with travel plans in Maine and the Maritimes. Dinners are by reservation only, and they only book one party per night. It's a multicourse event, and there are 17 entrée choices (each party must choose only 2) including Tuscan Primavera (a delicious pasta dish), steamed Maine lobster, and roast beef with Yorkshire pudding. Entrées $23–36. Overnight guests are offered the "chef's table" option if they would like to have dinner at the inn. Room rates are $78 double including a full "Scottish breakfast."

The Yellow House Bed & Breakfast (757-8797), 1040 Ridge Road, Oakfield 04763. Located 1½ miles off I-95 (exit 60) between Island Falls and Houlton, this vintage 1862 homestead has been in host Gina Clark's family since then. Clark, who has worked as an international tour guide, enjoys helping guests explore The County. The library features a collection of over 3,000 travel books. $25 per person with a shared bath, $35 for private. $100 for a family—three rooms and a bath. No alcohol, smoking, or pets.

Old Iron Inn (492-4766), 155 High Street, Caribou. Kate and Kevin McCartney offer four rooms (two with private bath, the other two sharing a bath and a half) decorated with antiques they have painstakingly chosen themselves. The collection of old irons throughout is impressive. The hosts are well-informed and happy to help plan a vacation in The County, and evening conversation in the common area is stimulating and interesting. Specialized libraries of Lincoln, aviation history, and mysteries, as well as subscriptions to 40 magazines, offer plenty of reading material to guests. Once a month the McCartneys host a music night, free and open to all. $39–49 includes a full breakfast.

SPORTING CAMPS

Allagash Gardners Sporting Camps (398-3168), Box 127, Allagash 04774. Open May through December. Five tidy camps along a ridge overlooking the confluence of the St. John and Allagash Rivers across the road from Roy and Mande Gardner's welcoming old farmhouse. Bed & breakfast and hiking, hunting, camping, and fishing guide service also offered. $30 double, $100 per week.

✍& **Moose Point Camps** (435-6156), Portage 04768. Open May 10 to early December. Ten log camps on the east shore of Fish Lake (5 miles long and connecting with other lakes linked by the Fish River). The central lodge features a library, a large stone fireplace, and a dining room overlooking the lake where meals are served (BYOB). The camps are 17 miles from Portage up a paper company road. $330 per person per week or $65 per person per day in spring and summer; ask about children's rates and hunters' packages. Boats and canoes available.

Libby Sporting Camps (435-8274), Drawer V, Ashland 04732. Open ice-out through November. One of the original sporting camps, family-operated for 100 years. Features hearty meals in the lodge and guides to take you to 40 lakes and ponds from the eight cabins. Also 10 outpost cabins on remote ponds and streams. Sited at the headwaters of the Aroostook and Allagash Rivers. Boat, motor and canoes available. $115 per person per night includes meals, boats, motor, and canoes.

MOTEL

Long Lake Motor Inn (543-5006), Route 162, St. Agatha 04772. Ken and Arlene Lermon pride themselves on the cleanliness and friendliness of this motel overlooking Long Lake. There is a lounge, and continental breakfast is included in $45 for standard room ($39 single), $65 for the suite, which has a Jacuzzi.

WHERE TO EAT

DINING OUT

✍ **Sirois' Restaurant** (834-6548), 84 West Main Street, Fort Kent. Henry Sirois operates this hospitable, homey restaurant with an extensive menu. Choices range from chicken to seafood, steaks, and Italian specialties. $6.95–18.95. Children's menu $2.95–3.95.

Long Lake Sporting Club (543-7584; 1-800-431-7584), Sinclair. Open daily July and August; the rest of the year closed on Monday. Sit down in the lounge with a drink, order, and then go to your table when it's ready. Specialties include steaks, seafood, jumbo lobsters (3–4 pounds). Right on Long Lake, with terrific views, dance floor, full-service marina. $8.95–16.95.

Lakeview Restaurant (543-6331), St. Agatha. Open daily for lunch and dinner. Set on a hilltop with a view across the lake and valley. Steak and seafood are the specialties. Live entertainment on summer weekends. Most entrées are around $10.

Daniel's (868-5591), 52 Main Street, Van Buren. A large restaurant and lounge open for lunch and dinner. At lunch, choose from sandwiches and light entrées like chicken stir-fry. The dinner menu includes linguine with white clam sauce, ribeye steak, and filet mignon. Also serves pressure-fried chicken dinners (party boxes available to go). Dinner entrées $8.75–13.95.

✎ **Joe Hackett's Steak & Seafood Restaurant & Butcher's Market** (496-2501), Route 1 south of Caribou. Open for dinner daily, lunch and dinner on Sunday. One of the best places to eat in central Aroostook—a modern, family-style restaurant specializing in prime beef and fresh fish. Dinner entrées range from Down East midgets (fried or broiled shrimp) to Broncobuster's Splurge (a 22-ounce Porterhouse steak); the "junior executive" menu includes a "buckaroo's wallet with a cow's blanket" (a cheeseburger). $7.50–13.95 (children's menu $2.25–3.75).

EATING OUT

Lil's (435-6471), Route 1, Ashland. Open 6 AM–8 PM. A counter and orange vinyl booths, homemade bread, pizza, outstanding sandwiches and pies, daily specials.

Ma & Pa's Sunrise Cafe (543-6177), Cleveland Road, St. Agatha. Open daily year-round, 5:30 AM–8 PM. Our favorite kind of eatery: a counter, tables, and a view. Features local items as specials, like chicken stew and *ployes* (buckwheat crêpes).

Doris's Cafe, Fort Kent Mills, open for breakfast and lunch; everything prepared from scratch.

Pierrette's Kitchen (834-6888), 57 East Main Street, Fort Kent. Pizza and sandwiches, plus specials like "road-kill chili" in a bright, friendly atmosphere. Ice cream, too.

The Dicky Trading Post, Allagash. Open 5 AM–7 PM. A combination general store (with stuffed bobcat and lynx), sporting-goods shop, and Formica-topped coffee shop.

Stan's Grocery, Route 161 north of Jemtland. Home of Stan's 10-cent cup of coffee, to be savored in a back booth of this indescribable store, the center for the surrounding summer community on Madawaska Lake. The pay phone next to the piano is roto-dial.

Frederick's Southside Restaurant (498-3464), 217 South Main Street, Caribou. Good home-style cooking, generous portions, reasonable prices.

The Courtyard Café (532-0787), 59 Main Street, Houlton. A great little place that has a more cosmopolitan feel than you might expect in Houlton. Great sandwiches, daily specials, coffee, and sweets.

Elm Tree Diner (532-3181), Bangor Road, Houlton. Open early and late, an outstanding classic diner that just celebrated its 50th year. Everything is made from scratch, daily specials.

SELECTIVE SHOPPING

Main Street Emporium, Main Street, Houlton. A nicely renovated old building with several small gift shops and a nice little café (see *Eating Out*).

Bradbury Barrel Co. (429-8188; 1-800-332-6021) P.O. Box A, 100 Main Street, Bridgewater 04735. Showroom of white-cedar barrels of all sizes as well as other wood products. Mail-order catalog. Tours of the company are available by prior arrangement.

Fish River Brand Tackle (834-3951), call for directions. Tackle made by Don Baker—one of his big metal flashers secured the $10,000 grand prize in the Lake Champlain Fishing Derby in 1994.

Bouchard Family Farm (834-3237), Route 161, Fort Kent. Stop by the family kitchen and buy a bag of *ploye* mix. *Ployes* are crêpelike pancakes made with buckwheat flour (no eggs, no milk, no sugar, no oil, no cholesterol, no fat—*c'est magnifique*).

✐ **Goughan Farms** (496-1731), Route 161, Fort Fairfield. Open weekdays 10–5, Sundays 12–5. Pick-your-own strawberries, also a farm stand, animal barn.

SPECIAL EVENTS

✐ *February:* **Mardi-Gras** in Fort Kent—the 5 days before Ash Wednesday bring a parade, ice sculptures, kids' day, Franco-American music, and exhibitions.

Early March: **The Can Am Sled Dog Race,** Triple Crown 60- and 250-mile races, starting and ending at Fort Kent.

June: **Acadian Festival** in Madawaska, with parade, traditional Acadian supper, and talent revue. **"Midsommar"** (*the weekend nearest June 21*), is celebrated at Thomas Park in New Sweden and at the New Sweden Historical Society Museum with Swedish music, dancing, and food.

604   NORTHERN MAINE

July: **Maine Potato Blossom Festival,** Fort Fairfield, features a week of activities including mashed-potato wrestling, Potato Blossom Queen pageant, parade, entertainment, dancing, industry dinner, and fireworks.

August: **Northern Maine Fair,** Presque Isle. **Potato Feast Days** in Houlton has arts and crafts, potato barrel–rolling contest, potato games, carnival, and more.

Index